Communications
in Computer and Information Science 2628

Series Editors

Gang Li❶, *School of Information Technology, Deakin University, Burwood, VIC,
Australia*
Joaquim Filipe❶, *Polytechnic Institute of Setúbal, Setúbal, Portugal*
Zhiwei Xu, *Chinese Academy of Sciences, Beijing, China*

Rationale
The CCIS series is devoted to the publication of proceedings of computer science conferences. Its aim is to efficiently disseminate original research results in informatics in printed and electronic form. While the focus is on publication of peer-reviewed full papers presenting mature work, inclusion of reviewed short papers reporting on work in progress is welcome, too. Besides globally relevant meetings with internationally representative program committees guaranteeing a strict peer-reviewing and paper selection process, conferences run by societies or of high regional or national relevance are also considered for publication.

Topics
The topical scope of CCIS spans the entire spectrum of informatics ranging from foundational topics in the theory of computing to information and communications science and technology and a broad variety of interdisciplinary application fields.

Information for Volume Editors and Authors
Publication in CCIS is free of charge. No royalties are paid, however, we offer registered conference participants temporary free access to the online version of the conference proceedings on SpringerLink (http://link.springer.com) by means of an http referrer from the conference website and/or a number of complimentary printed copies, as specified in the official acceptance email of the event.

CCIS proceedings can be published in time for distribution at conferences or as post-proceedings, and delivered in the form of printed books and/or electronically as USBs and/or e-content licenses for accessing proceedings at SpringerLink. Furthermore, CCIS proceedings are included in the CCIS electronic book series hosted in the SpringerLink digital library at http://link.springer.com/bookseries/7899. Conferences publishing in CCIS are allowed to use our online conference service (Meteor) for managing the whole proceedings lifecycle (from submission and reviewing to preparing for publication) free of charge.

Publication process
The language of publication is exclusively English. Authors publishing in CCIS have to sign the Springer CCIS copyright transfer form, however, they are free to use their material published in CCIS for substantially changed, more elaborate subsequent publications elsewhere. For the preparation of the camera-ready papers/files, authors have to strictly adhere to the Springer CCIS Authors' Instructions and are strongly encouraged to use the CCIS LaTeX style files or templates.

Abstracting/Indexing
CCIS is abstracted/indexed in DBLP, Google Scholar, EI-Compendex, Mathematical Reviews, SCImago, Scopus. CCIS volumes are also submitted for the inclusion in ISI Proceedings.

How to start
To start the evaluation of your proposal for inclusion in the CCIS series, please send an e-mail to ccis@springer.com

Cosimo Distante · Sebastiano Battiato
Editors

Image Processing and Vision Engineering

5th International Conference, IMPROVE 2025
Porto, Portugal, April 7–8, 2025
Proceedings

Editors
Cosimo Distante
CNR and University of Salento
Lecce, Italy

Sebastiano Battiato
University of Catania
Catania, Italy

ISSN 1865-0929 ISSN 1865-0937 (electronic)
Communications in Computer and Information Science
ISBN 978-3-032-01168-8 ISBN 978-3-032-01169-5 (eBook)
https://doi.org/10.1007/978-3-032-01169-5

© The Editor(s) (if applicable) and The Author(s), under exclusive license to Springer Nature Switzerland AG 2026

This work is subject to copyright. All rights are solely and exclusively licensed by the Publisher, whether the whole or part of the material is concerned, specifically the rights of translation, reprinting, reuse of illustrations, recitation, broadcasting, reproduction on microfilms or in any other physical way, and transmission or information storage and retrieval, electronic adaptation, computer software, or by similar or dissimilar methodology now known or hereafter developed.
The use of general descriptive names, registered names, trademarks, service marks, etc. in this publication does not imply, even in the absence of a specific statement, that such names are exempt from the relevant protective laws and regulations and therefore free for general use.
The publisher, the authors and the editors are safe to assume that the advice and information in this book are believed to be true and accurate at the date of publication. Neither the publisher nor the authors or the editors give a warranty, expressed or implied, with respect to the material contained herein or for any errors or omissions that may have been made. The publisher remains neutral with regard to jurisdictional claims in published maps and institutional affiliations.

This Springer imprint is published by the registered company Springer Nature Switzerland AG
The registered company address is: Gewerbestrasse 11, 6330 Cham, Switzerland

If disposing of this product, please recycle the paper.

Preface

This book contains the proceedings of the 5th International Conference on Image Processing and Vision Engineering. This year, IMPROVE is held in Porto, Portugal, on April 7–8, 2025. It was sponsored by the Institute was Systems and Technologies of Information, Control and Communication (INSTICC).

IMPROVE is a comprehensive conference of academic and technical nature, focused on image processing and computer vision scientific advances and practical applications. It brings together researchers, engineers and practitioners working in fundamental areas of image processing, developing new methods and techniques, including innovative machine learning approaches, as well as multimedia communications technology and applications of image processing and artificial vision in diverse areas.

IMPROVE 2025 received 33 paper submissions from 21 countries, of which nine 27% were accepted and published as full papers. A double-blind paper review was performed for each submission by at least 2, but usually 3 or more, members of the International Program Committee, which was composed of established researchers and domain experts.

The high quality of the IMPROVE 2025 program was enhanced by the keynote lectures delivered by distinguished speakers who are renowned experts in their fields: Alain Tremeau (Université Jean Monnet in Saint Etienne, France), João Ascenso (Instituto Superior Técnico, Portugal) and Valerio Giuffrida (University of Nottingham, UK).

All presented papers will be submitted for indexation by DBLP, Google Scholar, EI-Compendex, INSPEC, Japanese Science and Technology Agency (JST), Norwegian Register for Scientific Journals and Series, Mathematical Reviews, SCImago, Scopus, zbMATH and Web of Science / Conference Proceedings Citation Index.

Several awards, based on the combined marks of paper reviewing, as assessed by the Program Committee, and the quality of the presentation, as assessed by session chairs at the conference venue, were conferred at the conference's closing session as recognition for the best contributions.

The program for this conference required the dedicated effort of many people. Firstly, we must thank the authors, whose research efforts are reported here. Next, we thank the members of the Program Committee and the auxiliary reviewers for their diligent and professional reviewing. We would also like to deeply thank the invited speakers for their invaluable contribution and for taking the time to prepare their talks. Finally, a word of appreciation for the hard work of the INSTICC team; organizing a conference of this level is a task that can only be achieved by the collaborative effort of a dedicated and highly competent team.

We hope you all had an exciting and inspiring conference. We hope to have contributed to the development of our research community, and we look forward to having additional research results presented at the next edition of IMPROVE, details of which are available at https://improve.scitevents.org.

April 2025
Cosimo Distante
Sebastiano Battiato

Organization

Conference Chair

Sebastiano Battiato — University of Catania, Italy

Program Chair

Cosimo Distante — CNR and University of Salento, Italy

Program Committee

Alireza Alaei	Southern Cross University, Australia
Danilo Avola	Sapienza University, Italy
Tudor Barbu	University of Rome - Iasi Branch, Romania
Edurne Barrenechea	Public University of Navarre, Spain
Abdessamad Ben Hamza	Concordia University, Canada
Vittorio Bianco	National Research Council, Italy
Francesco Bianconi	University of Perugia, Italy
Darius Burschka	Technical University of Munich, Germany
Laurent Cohen	Université Paris Dauphine, France
Gábor Cseh	Centre for Energy Research, Hungary
Pedro de Rezende	University of Campinas, Brazil
Anastasios Doulamis	National Technical University of Athens, Greece
Zoran Duric	George Mason University, USA
Yakup Genc	Gebze Technical University, Turkey
Andrea Giachetti	Università di Verona, Italy
Bart Goossens	imec - Ghent University, Belgium
Yanhui Guo	University of Illinois Springfield, USA
Mahmoud Hassaballah	South Valley University, Egypt
Marcin Iwanowski	Warsaw University of Technology, Poland
Stefanos Kollias	National Technical University of Athens, Greece
Andrzej Materka	Lodz University of Technology, Poland
Mohsen Moghaddam	Shahid Beheshti University, Iran
George Papakostas	Democritus University of Thrace, Greece
Helio Pedrini	University of Campinas, Brazil
Alessandro Piva	Università degli Studi di Firenze, Italy

Volodymyr Ponomaryov Instituto Politecnico Nacional, Mexico
Saeed Shiry Ghidary Staffordshire University, UK
Carlos Silva University of Minho, Portugal
Jon Sporring University of Copenhagen, Denmark
Bernard Tiddeman Aberystwyth University, UK
Masahiro Yamaguchi Tokyo Institute of Technology, Japan
Jang-Hee Yoo ETRI, South Korea, Republic of
W. Mimi Diyana Zaki Universiti Kebangsaan Malaysia, Malaysia
Liming Zhang University of Macau, China
Djemel Ziou Université de Sherbrooke, Canada

Invited Speakers

Alain Tremeau Université Jean Monnet in Saint Etienne, France
João Ascenso Instituto Superior Técnico, Portugal
Valerio Giuffrida University of Nottingham, UK

Invited Speakers

JPEG AI: The First International Standard for Image Coding Based on an End-to-End Learning-Based Approach

João Ascenso

Departamento de Engenharia Electrotécnica e de Computadores, Instituto Superior Técnico, Lisboa, Portugal

Abstract. The JPEG Standardization Committee has recently standardized the JPEG AI standard, marking the introduction of the first image coding specification that utilizes an end-to-end learning-based method. By harnessing cutting-edge deep learning techniques, JPEG AI is designed with future practical applications in mind. The standard has undergone multiple refinements to ensure it is both mature and viable for image encoding and decoding, particularly on mobile devices. When compared to traditional coding systems, JPEG AI offers several distinct advantages: 1) improved rate-distortion performance that enhances perceptual visual quality; 2) considerably faster encoding speeds; and 3) the ability to support diverse optimization goals, such as coding for both human and machine use cases. Built on a learning-based image coding algorithm, JPEG AI generates a compact, single-stream compressed representation that boosts compression efficiency for human visualization, while also delivering strong performance for image processing and computer vision tasks. The goal is to provide a royalty-free baseline for the technology. This talk delves into the core technical principles behind the design of JPEG AI version 1 and presents an outlook on future advancements and extensions of the standard.

João Ascenso is a professor in the Department of Electrical and Computer Engineering at Instituto Superior Técnico and a member of the Multimedia Signal Processing Group at Instituto de Telecomunicações in Lisbon, Portugal. He earned his E.E., M.Sc., and Ph.D. degrees in Electrical and Computer Engineering from Instituto Superior Técnico in 1999, 2003, and 2010, respectively. He currently serves as the chair of the JPEG CPM (Coding and Performance for Machines) subgroup and the JPEG AI ad-hoc group, where he leads efforts focused on evaluating and developing event-based and learning-based image solutions. With over 150 publications in international journals and conferences, he has accumulated more than 5,000 citations and an h-index of 33. João Ascenso has served as an associate editor for IEEE Transactions on Image Processing, IEEE Signal Processing Letters, and IEEE Transactions on Multimedia. He was the Technical Program Chair for PCS2022 and EUVIP2022 and has contributed to the organizing committees of prominent international conferences, including IEEE ICIP 2023, IEEE ICME 2020, IEEE MMSP 2020, and IEEE ISM 2020. He has received three Best Paper Awards. His research interests include visual coding, quality assessment, 3D visual representation processing, machine coding, super-resolution, and denoising, among others.

A Deep Dive Into Regression

Valerio Giuffrida

School of Computer Science, University of Nottingham, UK

Abstract. Regression is an important task in machine learning and deep learning, driving a wide range of applications across several real-world applications. From surveillance and agriculture to remote sensing, medical imaging, manufacturing, and transportation, regression is essential for extracting insights and making predictions from data. This keynote will explore the fundamental importance of regression in these fields, with a particular focus on plant phenotyping and medical imaging. I will demonstrate how regression enables precise plant phenotyping, specifically in leaf counting— a key task for monitoring crop health and yield estimation. Through deep learning models trained for regression, we can accurately estimate of the number of leaves in rosette plants, supporting downstream applications in plant science. Transitioning to the medical domain, I will discuss the role of regression in predicting future MRI scans of patients with neurodegenerative conditions. In this context, diffusion models leverage regression to forecast disease progression, offering insights for early diagnosis and treatment planning. Through these real-world applications, this talk will highlight the importance and versatility of regression in modern AI-driven applications and the impact on advancing cross-disciplinary scientific research.}

Valerio Giuffrida is an Assistant Professor in Computer Vision at the School of Computer Science, University of Nottingham, and a member of the Computer Vision Lab (CVL). His research focuses on deep learning applied to biological problems, including plant and medical imaging analysis. As a Co-Investigator in the PhenomUK scoping project, Dr. Giuffrida contributes to advancing phenotyping technologies in the UK. He has also organized international workshops on computer vision in plant phenotyping at leading international conferences, fostering collaboration and knowledge exchange in this field.

Contents

Invited Speakers

Relevance of Human Body Pose Estimation Methods for Complex Dance
Movements Analysis 3
  *Philippe Colantoni, Rafique Ahmed, Prashant Ghimire,
  Damien Muselet, and Alain Trémeau*

Papers

SuperCrossViT: Integrating Superpixel Segmentation in Vision
Transformers for Advanced Medical Image Analysis 23
  Ahmed Lotfi Alqnatri and Wanda Benesova

A Multi-modal Approach for Face Anti-spoofing in Non-calibrated
Systems Using Disparity Maps 39
  Ariel Larey, Eyal Rond, and Omer Achrack

MsResNet: Multi-scale Edge-Enhanced ResNet for RGB-T Image
Segmentation 59
  Bikram Adhikari, Siyu Lei, Zoran Durić, and Duminda Wijesekera

Addressing Class Imbalance in Renal Amyloidosis Classification:
A Comparative Study of Few-Shot Learning and Conventional Machine
Learning Techniques 76
  *Alexsandro Silva Santos, Luciano Rebouças de Oliveira,
  Washington Luis Conrado dos Santos, and Angelo Amancio Duarte*

CerberusDet: Unified Multi-dataset Object Detection 95
  Irina Tolstykh, Mikhail Chernyshov, and Maksim Kuprashevich

MVIP - A Dataset and Methods for Application Oriented Multi-View
and Multi-Modal Industrial Part Recognition 111
  Paul Koch, Marian Schlüter, and Jörg Krüger

Assessment of Uncertainty and Variability in Simulation Tools Under
Foggy Conditions 131
  *Pierre Duthon, Mohamed Boudali, Amine Ben-Daoued, Rémi Regnier,
  Charlotte Segonne, and Frédéric Bernardin*

Automated and Explainable Detection of Multiple Diseases from Retinal
Fundus Images 143
    Shubha Masti, Tarunya Prasad, and Gowri Srinivasa

Rotation Invariance in Floor Plan Digitization Using Zernike Moments 162
    Marius Graumann, Jan Marius Stürmer, and Tobias Koch

Use of Orthogonal Encryption Functions in Commutative
Watermarking-Encryption 178
    Roland Schmitz and Christos Grecos

Gender Bias Mitigation in Advertisement Videos 201
    Thao My Tran Dinh, Thuy T. Nguyen, and Andrew M. Colarik

Superclass-Guided Hierarchical Learning for Action Anticipation 211
    Shin Suzuki, Naoshi Kaneko, and Kazuhiko Sumi

Cricket Bowling Action Recognition with Transformer-Based Models 227
    *Bigyan Subedi, Bishwambhar Dahal, Sirjana Bhatta, Sonish Maharjan,
    and Sushmita Poudel*

Deep Learning in Satellite and Aerial-Based Image Processing 244
    Alessia Sbriglio and Giovanni B. Palmerini

FoodLens: Fine-Grained and Multi-label Classification of Indian Food
Images 262
    *Jatin Alla, Yashas Samaga, Ashwin Vaswani, Praneeth Netrapalli,
    Shivani Kapania, Pradeep Kumar, and Narayan Hegde*

Automated Detection of Student Emotions for Engagement Verification
in Virtual Learning Environments 285
    Quoc Minh Quan Nguyen and Sonit Singh

Cross-Modality Learning in Ophthalmology: Is There a Need
for Increasing Variety in Data? 297
    Imen Chakroun and Julien Verplanken

Active Learning and the Various Flavors of Supervision for Object
Detection 309
    Nils Bischoff and Sven Tomforde

Smartphone-Based Detection of Cataract and Pterygium Using MobileNet:
A Unified Approach for Anterior Segment Photographed Images 330
   Wan Mimi Diyana Wan Zaki, Laily Azyan Ramlan,
   Nurul Syahira Mohamad Zamani, Marizuana Mat Daud,
   and Haliza Abdul Mutalib

Adaptive Resilience Framework Using Dynamic Feature Fusion for Robust
Fingerprint Biometrics Against Adversarial Perturbations 343
   Arslan Manzoor, Alessandro Ortis, and Sebastiano Battiato

Author Index 343

Invited Speakers

Relevance of Human Body Pose Estimation Methods for Complex Dance Movements Analysis

Philippe Colantoni, Rafique Ahmed, Prashant Ghimire, Damien Muselet, and Alain Trémeau(✉)

Laboratoire Hubert Curien - UMR 5516, Saint-Étienne, France
{philippe.colantoni,rafique.ahmed,prashant.ghimire,
damien.muselet,alain.tremeau}@univ-st-etienne.fr

Abstract. The relevance and robustness of pose estimation methods is of primary importance in dance movements analysis. The main objective of this keynote paper is to qualitatively compare the most recent pose estimation models for dance movements analysis and discuss their strengths and weaknesses. For this purpose, we developed a specific methodology and tools. The second objective of this paper is to discuss the interest of human body pose estimation for dance movements analyse and to show that the accuracy of body pose estimation is, in the context of dance movements analyse, important but less important than the accuracy of the dance movements modelling. Beyond these objectives, we also discuss the lack of efficient models to describe the kinematics of dance movements.

Keywords: Body pose estimation · Dance movements Analysis · Skeleton models

1 Introduction

The aim of this keynote paper is to discuss the relevance and efficiency of the most recent pose estimation methods in the field of dance movements analyse.

Motion Capture (MoCap) systems have been used in various fields such as sport or dance, as well as AR and VR. Marker-based MoCap systems utilizing multi-view cameras and marker suits provide accurate human pose in 3D but are less accessible than monocular camera systems. On the other hand, Human Mesh Recovery (HMR) from monocular models struggle with occlusion situations, complex and unusual human poses, low or non-uniform lighting conditions, loose or non-distinctives clothes.

3D human body reconstruction and shape estimation is a hot topic in computer vision. It is worth noting that estimating 3D parameters from one 2D view image or multi 2D views is an ill posed inverse problem, as different 3D points may be projected onto the same 2D point. This brings significant challenges to the 3D reconstruction problem. In recent year, many methods have been proposed to solve these problems.

Since the development of parametric human body models, such as SMPL [21], converting the human body reconstruction problem into a parametric regression problem, many progresses have been done, especially in the few last months. However, the improvement in 2D alignment comes at the cost of reduced 3D accuracy, as illustrated in [10]. This technical issue occurs when human body estimation model lacks camera intrinsic parameters.

Among these progresses, we can report:

- A more accurate estimation of camera intrinsics using a full perspective camera model like in [10, 26].
- A more accurate estimation of human pose using a cross-attention model like [13] which proposed a deformable attention transformer model to learn meaningful spatial relations from spatial features.
- A more accurate estimation of hands even if the image size processed by the models is still too low to well estimation fingers pose.
- A more accurate estimation of positioning human 3D meshes in the scene by regressing depth and option to add camera intrinsic information if available during model training [5].

The evaluation of a Human Mesh Recovery (HMR) method can be done from a single-frame (2D) model fitting, from a multi view reconstruction (3D) model fitting, or from a video sequence reconstruction (2D+T) model fitting. Most of human mesh model comparisons have focused on the accuracy of 3D pose estimation ignoring silhouette information of body shape. This information is nevertheless essential to well analyze the accuracy of a human shape recovery method. In order to improve the overall accuracy of human body model estimation, [36] introduced in July 2024 a silhouette loss function and a model vertex loss function into a human body model estimation loss function.

Since the survey paper on 3D human mesh recovery from monocular images published in January 2024 [39] and the survey paper on 3D Human Pose Estimation (HPE) and mesh recovery from deep learning published in July 2024 [20], many progresses have been done. Though remarkable progress has been achieved in the last months, this task is still challenging especially in the domain of performing arts, due to unusual body pose, complex body motions, heavy occlusions and self-overlapping, ubiquitous pose estimation related to intertwining between human bodies.

The kinematics of dance movements is an important feature which has been little investigated till recently. The kinematics of movements is not related straightforwardly to the change of pose between two consecutive frames of a video, it described the changes in dynamics of the various parts of the body from position, velocity and/or acceleration of points in the space. [3] proposed in May 2024 a computational kinematics method based on 17 macroscopic features such as the expandedness of the human body and the frequency of sharp movements. This paper focused on hip hop dance genres. Four categories of features has been used: - movement of the sacrum; - movement of the extremities; - global angular momentum around the sacrum; - expansion of the body from the sacrum. [12] proposed an automatic human motion classification and analysis method based on Laban Movement Analysis (LMA). The main limitation of this pilot work is that the extracted keypoints were defined by a 2D model ignoring the depth dimension. Laban Movement Analysis is defined by four dimensions:

effort, space, shape and body. Effort quality is defined by eight elements: light, strong, free, bound, sustained, quick, indirect and direct. The majority of these elements are related to motion features such as velocity and acceleration. Space quality is defined by six elements: side-open, side-across, up, down, forward and backward. These elements are related to the trajectory of human motions. Shape quality is defined by six elements: opening, enclosing, rising, sinking, advancing and retreating. Body quality is defined by three elements: impulsive, swing and impactive. [38] proposed a classification method based on three LMA components (body, shape and space) for the recognition of dance movements, especially for classic dance. A strong issue with manual annotation and feature extraction in dance videos is the low efficiency and strong subjectivity of expert's scoring and difficulty in handling complex movements [29].

The majority of computational model calculate Laban elements from skeleton features computed from a single-frame or a frames interval of a video sequence. The relevance of the automatic Laban Movement Analysis depends more on how the dynamic changes of different body parts (related to the position, distance, velocity and acceleration of skeleton points in the space) are characterized, than on the accuracy of the body pose estimation. It depends also of the duration of the frames interval and of the complexity of the dance genre. [29] proposed a feature extraction network based on 3D spatio-temporal description operators and a multi-scale aggregated network to extract spatial features of single-frame images and combine features (including keypoint coordinates, joint angles, time series, etc.) from consecutive frames in a video sequence. The main finding of this study are the following: - using keypoint coordinate information alone can capture static posture features, but may not fully describe the dynamic process of actions; - the joint angle information supplements the keypoint coordinate information and provides geometric relationships between skeletons, which helps to better identify complex poses and actions; - adding time series information help to better identify continuous actions and to capture the dynamic changes of actions; - the combination of keypoint coordinates, joint angles, and time series information improves the ability to recognize complex actions.

To be best of our knowledge, no method has yet defined a methodology to describe the full body movement of dancers and the differences of movement across diverse genres. Kinematics methods can be divided in two main categories: - handcrafted approaches and machine learning approaches. Handcrafted approaches have the advantage of having lower computational costs and being easily interpretable. Low-level features can capture local motion at the scale of specific keypoints. A combination of low-level features resulting in long feature vectors (typically several tens of values per frame) can be used to characterize a human body movement into many local measurements. Machine learning approaches often outperforms handcrafted methods but need deeper network and big dataset to learn relevant features and to train the network. The most effective approaches are those that go beyond examining each frame, using relationships between frames to derive temporal characteristics.

In order to eliminate the impact of: - incorrect estimation of camera intrinsics and extrinsics; - inaccurate estimation of human pose, shape and size; incoherencies of human pose estimation versus different viewpoints, on the action similarity evaluation, Zhang et al. proposed in [46] a human motion similarity evaluation method based on deep metric learning and a loss function consisting of three components: reconstruction loss, cross-reconstruction loss, and triplet loss.

Despite recent progresses in the field of computer vision, reported in [31], there is still a need to automatically identify the gesture (dance poses), poses and stance (pose recognition), recognize the dance forms, dance movement classification, etc. In some dance genres, hand gestures are more prominent among others as it is a flexible part of the human body that can convey meaningful context. Another essential part of dancing is the movement of the torso and the feet which have various meanings in different dance styles [31].

In the Sect. 2 of the paper we survey the most relevant pose estimation models for dance movements analysis and discuss their strengths and weaknesses. Next, in Sect. 3, we introduce the tools and the methodology implemented to perform a qualitative comparison of these models based on data features comparison from 3 frames of a video sequence. In Sect. 4, we present results obtained from 15 dance archives and discuss the robustness of the four models compared. Lastly, in Sect. 5, open issues and future directions are discussed.

2 Short Survey of Human Body Pose Estimation Models

Since the introduction of the SMPL model in 2015 [21], next of the SMPL-X model in 2019 [28], many progresses have been done in the domain. The main progresses are reported below. The information provided by body pose estimation models allows not only analysing body poses in individual frames, but also pose changes in consecutive frame sequences.

2.1 Body Pose Estimation Models

An abstract representation of the human body can be achieved simply by marking the body, hands, and face with key points and connecting them with lines. However, realistic modeling requires an accurate meshing of the body shape as well as facial expressions. This requires additional modeling of the pose and shape of the human body. Early works in 3D body surface modeling began with the use of primitive geometric shapes such as rectangles [16], cylinders [22]. However these body models tend to be unrealistic. Unlike these models, full body 3D scans provide accurate measurements of 3D body surface. Being able to learn a statistical body model using a large collection of 3D body scans refers to statistical body modeling. To convert a 3D scan into an animated 3D human body, three steps are required. First, a template mesh must be fitted to the pointcloud obtained from the scan. Second, the number of joints, their location, and their axis of rotation must be determined. Finally, all the vertices of the mesh surface must be linked to the skeleton for generating the animation. Some of the most popular methods for generating a statistical body model are discussed in the next section.

The Models:
1. **SMPL** [21]. The SMPL [21] model is one of the most widely used vertex-based parametric linear model. It learns the 3D human body representation using two primary parameters: shape and pose. The pose parameters define a standard skeleton rig with 23 joints, each associated with a rotation component. These joints are predicted using a joint regressor. Then, the shape parameters are coefficients derived from principal component analysis (PCA) performed on shape registrations from a multi-shape database with 1786 high-resolution 3D scans of people in diverse poses. Overall, SMPL represents a mapping function that transforms pose and shape parameters into a triangulated mesh.
2. **SMPL-H (SMPL + MANO)** [32]. SMPL [21], is only a body model which does not incorporate accurate 3D estimation of hands. This is because hands are often described by low resolution areas, especially in dance archives, and are partially or fully occluded. Encompassing hands movement along with the body is important to have a complete overall picture of human actions, expressions and emotions. Therefore, a new model called MANO (hand Model with Articulated and Non-rigid deformations) [32] was developed. This model was learned from around 1000 high resolution 3D scans of hands from 31 subjects. [32] attached MANO [32] with SMPL [21] resulting in a fully expressed body hand model (SMPL-H).
3. **SMPL-X (SMPL-H + FLAME)** [28]. After the introduction of FLAME model [17], where realistic 3D face and facial expression could be generated from corresponding 2D image of face, SMPL-X was introduced. SMPL-X combines SMPL with the FLAME head model [17] and the MANO hand model [32] to capture the expressive 3D body, hands and face features together from single RGB image. SMPL-X [28] is based on 75 rotational parameters for the global rotation and body, eyes, jaw poses; 24 low-dimensional PCA coefficients or 90 rotational parameters for hand poses; 10 parameters for the body shape and 10 parameters for the facial expressions. SMPL-X [28] efficiently predicts pose and shape parameters if the spatial resolution of the image is sufficient high to perceive subtle details such as fingers and pose hinges.
4. **STAR** [24]. Since its introduction, SMPL [21] has grown in popularity due to its features such as compact and straightforward parametrization. Regardless of its widespread use, it has several drawbacks, and a novel method called "STAR (Sparse Trained Articulated Regressor)" [24] was developed to overcome these limitations. The use of "global blend shapes" in SMPL leads to an enormous number of parameters. To reduce the number of parameters, a sparse formulation is developed which involves learning a subset of mesh vertices that are affected by each joint movement and defining per-joint pose correctives. Furthermore, because different forms deform differently in the real world, STAR learns shape-dependent pose-corrective blend shapes, in contrast to SMPL, which factors pose-dependent deformations. Finally, more male and female scans have been used to train STAR to enhance the form space of SMPL. Such improvements led to the observation that STAR outperforms SMPL by achieving superior model generalization even with fewer parameters.
5. **SUPR** [25]. A more recent learning-based technique known as "SUPR (Sparse Unified Part-Based Representation)" was introduced in [25] to overcome the shortcomings of prior methods such as the FLAME head model [17] and the MANO hand

model [32]. Techniques like FLAME [17] and MANO [32] are unable to capture the relative motion of various body parts because they are intended to estimate the poses of parts, such as the head or the hand, respectively. However, SUPR is trained jointly on both entire body and individual part models, allowing each joint to contribute to the sparse vertices of the model. SUPR can be divided into SUPR-Head, SUPR-Hand, and SUPR-Foot since it employs factorized representation. For feet, a non-linear deformation function is utilized for predicting the deformation that occurs when feet touch the ground, in addition to using 4D scans to record the motion of the toes. The accuracy of feet positions relative to the ground is of primary importance in dance pose estimation analysis. Although SUPR has more joints than the current models, particularly in the foot, it still uses the SMPL-X kinematic tree.

Models Mainly Used for Pose Estimation. Despite the emergence of new models for defining 3D body poses, such as STAR and SPUR. SMPL and SMPL-X are still the only models currently used for pose estimation in the literature. That's why we decided to use SMPL-X for our body modeling support.

Recent Pose Estimation Methods. HMR refers to reconstruction of a full 3D mesh of a human body from single monocular images. Thanks to the release of statistical body pose models as discussed in the previous section, human mesh recovery from single monocular images has gained significant attention. The human mesh recovery models use these statistical body pose models as foundation. We classify the human mesh recovery based on body pose models like SMPL and SMPL-X and discuss them in the next section. We discuss the latest models released since 2023.

1 - SMPL Based Methods

a. **HMR2.0 [11].** HMR2.0 is in particular able to encode and decode unusual human pose, i.e. to better capture difficult spatial relations, than previous methods. An effective system, 4DHumans, has been designed for reconstruction and tracking humans throughout time which uses HMR2.0 and PHALP [30]. The human mesh is recovered in the first stage using HMR2.0, and the humans are tracked in the second step using PHALP, a 3D tracking technique. For human reconstruction, the HMR2.0 technique employs ViT-H/16 [9], a "Huge" variant of ViT with 16×16 input and a standard transformer decoder [42]. The use of ViT makes HMR2.0 an entirely "transformerized" approach for human mesh recovery. Furthermore, the ability of the 4DHumans system to jointly recover the human mesh and track it makes the system efficient for real-time applications. Even though the proposed method is very efficient but the estimated bodies are limited to only either being image-aligned or only having precise 3D pose [10]. The model uses image size of 256×256 which is very low to model hands and fingers.

b. **ScoreHMR [37].** ScoreHMR is a novel "score-guided human mesh recovery" approach leveraging the diffusion models for solving the inversion problems for 3D pose reconstruction i.e. fitting the body to image. Particularly, first the estimates are obtained using existing models like HMR2.0 [11] and then these estimates are iteratively refined to obtain good alignment of body with the image. For refining the estimates, first they are inverted to latent space using DDIM [35] inversion technique and then guided sampling is used in loop to obtain the better alignment. The model uses input of 224 × 224.

c. **TokenHMR** [10]. Since the introduction of the HMR model based on a simplified weak perspective camera model, new models have been introduced based on more complex full perspective camera model. [10] shown that an incorrect uses of camera intrinsics can lead to misalignment between 2D features and 3D features. To reduce such misalignments, a new model was introduced in [10], it has two main components: a novel loss known as "Threshold-Adaptive Loss Scaling (TALS)" and TokenHMR. TALS is used to penalize 2D and 3D pseudo-ground-truth errors whereas TokenHMR uses classification to generate discrete tokens. Specifically, by tokenizing human poses, the continuous pose regression issue is transformed into a token prediction problem. By pre-training on large motion capture datasets, Vector Quantized-VAE (VQ-VAE) [41] is utilized to discretize continuous human pose. Despite this improvement, aligning 3D features with 2D pose estimates remains challenging. It is worth noting that the regressing method used to regress camera intrinsics struggles with images of dance performance without any vanishing points. To face this issue, Patel et al. proposed in November 2024 the CameraHMR model which estimates camera intrinsics from a field-of-view prediction model (Human-FoV) trained on a dataset of images containing people [26].

2 - SMPL-H/X Based Methods

a. **OSX** [18]. OSX introduced first one-stage pipeline to recover full body mesh without different networks for each body part. Previous methods relied on multi-stage pipeline [33,44], where hands and faces where enlarged and processed separately before fusing the results. This resulted in unnatural mesh articulation. OSX's high-resolution feature pyramid makes it more efficient than SMPL-X to predict pose and shape parameters for low-resolution images.

The one-stage pipeline includes a Component-aware Transformer (CAT) that consists of a global body encoder and a local component-specific decoder. The encoder captures the global body relationships, predicts body parameters, and provides a quality hierarchial featuremap for the decoder. The decoder then extracts high-resolution features specific to body parts. Finally, a keypoint-guided attention technique is used to accurately locate and estimate the hands and face parameters. The input image spatial size used during training is 256×192. The OSX has also contributed to the development of a large-scale Upper Body dataset (UBody) [18] with 2D and 3D annotations, considering the lack of scenes for downstream tasks like sign, emotion, and gesture recognition.

b. **SMPLer-X** [7]. In contrast to OSX, SMPLer-X adopts the one-stage approach without relying on a hierarchical feature extractor. SMPLer-X uses a Vision Transformer (ViT) backbone [9] to extract image features, a neck to predict the bounding boxes and cropping regions (hands, face), and regression heads for part-specific parameter estimation. It does not depend on third-party detectors or a heavy decoder. The image size used by the model is 512 × 384. While OSX uses limited datasets with less diversity and does not explore broader data combinations, limiting its generalizability, SMPLer-X investigates details of the Expressive human pose and shape estimation (EHPS) dataset [18,27,28,43,45], making it scalable and efficient for large datasets. SMPLer-X excels as a general foundation model, with its benchmarking and fine-tuning strategies showing the value of multi-dataset training and low-cost adaptation for diverse EHPS scenarios.

c. **Multi-HMR** [5]. The key feature of Multi-HMR is its extensive approach for recovering the 3D human mesh by addressing four critical aspects. First, by including detailed hand gestures and facial expression, it captures expressive body poses. Second, it processes frames with multiple people efficiently that ensures crowded scenes scalability. Third, it determines each person's location in 3D space and lastly, the model is adaptive as it can encompass camera intrinsic information if it is available. All of these is done in single-shot. The model introduces synthetic rendering dataset that includes humans close to the camera with hand poses variation that makes the training effective for expressive body poses, unlike other single-shot approaches which rely on high resolution multicrops of faces and hands. Opposite to HMR2.0 [11] that requires separate human detector for detection and single person mesh estimation on these detections, Multi-HMR does these two tasks in a single shot by using a Human Perception Head (HPH) block built using cross-attention blocks [15]. Additionally, Multi-HMR regresses and predicts depth, allowing to estimate individual locations in 3D space more accurately. The image resolution used is 448 × 448, which is quite low for accurate hands pose estimation when people are in the background of the scene. This model performs well when trained solely on synthetic datasets [4,6,27], however, when synthetic and real data [2,14,19] are combined the performance deteriorates [5].

d. **NLF** [34]. Oppositely to other models summarized above, Neural Rendering method (NLF) introduces a novel approach in December 2024 to 3D human mesh recovery, addressing challenges associated with large-scale, multi-dataset training. Unlike traditional methods that require reannotation to unify heterogeneous data formats, NLF leverages a common mapping between the human body space and the observation camera space. By employing a volumetric heatmap estimation and soft-argmax decoding, it localizes arbitrary points on the human body, enabling supervision from diverse data sources such as 2D/3D skeletons, dense poses, and meshes without reannotation. NLF trains a continuous field of point localizers, making it a universal detector for any point on the body. This flexibility allows for seamless mixed-dataset training and outputs detailed 3D predictions for any point set, eliminating the need for interpolation or manual conversion.

The method includes a Point Localizer Network (PLN) for feature extraction and heatmap generation, a Neural Localizer Field to generalize point localization, and a parametric body model fitting step for compact pose and shape representations. Unlike Multi-HMR, which struggles with performance when combining real and synthetic data, NLF achieves state-of-the-art by integrating both real and synthetic datasets effectively. However, limitations include frame-by-frame predictions without temporal cues and challenges with highly overlapping individuals or depth ambiguity. Despite these, NLF sets a new standard for generalist human pose and shape estimation.

2.2 Selected Methods

In a preliminary study [23], we conducted a comprehensive study, using dance videos from the AIST++ dataset [40], to compare the accuracy of 2D key points and the stability of 3D pose estimation methods under changing lighting conditions. We demonstrated that HMR2.0 provided better results than OSX and SMPLer-X.

Based on the discussion done in the previous section and this preliminary study, we selected for our new comparison framework the following methods: HMR2.0, TokenHMR, Multi-HMR and NLF. Since this preliminary study, we have extended our study to Multi-HMR, ScoreHMR, TokenHMR and NLF for comparison of 3D pose estimation methods.

Although ScoreHMR and TokenHMR are based on 2 different methodologies, they remain built on HMR2.0. Nevertheless, the use of tokens in TokenHMR seems to be a promising method for improving HMR2.0 results. Considering that Multi-HMR and NLF models are based on completely different architectures than the one used in our previous analyse, we thought it would be interesting to also use them in our comparison.

3 Data Used for Qualitative Comparison

In this section, we specify the data features that have been extracted from video sequences and the methods that have been use to extract them. We will then present the first video sequences we have chosen from dance archives provided by the EU PREMIERE project [8] and the reasons why we have chosen them.

3.1 Data Extracted

First, we have selected from this dataset a set of video sequences that we will use to challenge pose estimation methods. The selected sequences corresponds to short videos consisting of tens or hundreds of frames. Then, for each of these videos, we have estimated the 3D poses of each dancer/actor using the 4 methods selected above.

To ensure coherent data, the SMPL poses estimated by HMR 2.0 and TokenHMR were converted to SMPL-X. Obviously, this conversion does not provide an estimate of hand positions, and the results can only be used for poses comparison based on bodies without hands.

For each frame of each video, the following data were extracted: - **The 3D skeleton**: Composed of 127 3D key points; - **The 2D skeleton**: Composed of 127 2D key points; - **SMPL-X parameters** Composed as:

- Gender: Remains neutral.
- Shape Parameters: 10 values which control the body shape by representing variations in height, weight, and muscle mass.
- Pose Parameters: Define the 3D rotations of the body joints, including the global orientation of the body with 21 joints for the body pose, 15 joints for each hand, 1 joint for left eye, 1 joint for the right eye, 2 joints for the jaw pose.
- Global Orientation: Defines the overall orientation of the body in the 3D world, represented as a 3D rotation vector.

- Translation: Specifies the global position of the body in the 3D world.

For each video sequence, we have therefore access to:

- A video file made of N consecutive frames extracted from this sequence.
- A Python dictionary with, for each dancer/actor, N skeletons with SMPL-X parameters saved as a binary file (a pickle file).

3.2 Software Framework

To generate our dataset, we have set up a unique Python environment based on Python 3.11 and PyTorch 2.3.1 with CUDA 12.1. All the codes used for pose estimation have been adapted to work in this Python environment. Data generation has been automated as much as possible with a collection of Python scripts that were executed sequentially as part of our processing pipeline. However, we still rely on a manual phase for the extraction of small video sequences. For this we have chosen to use Lossless-Cut[1], an open source, multi-platform video extraction tool based on FFMPEG.

We complemented this processing framework with 2 web visualization tools based on the Three.js JavaScript library. A Python tool using the Flask library to display the contents of the binary files with the estimated poses, as well as a purely web-based tool, used in this keynote paper to display the generated data on a static web server. These two viewing tools share the same GUI (see Fig. 1). They can be used to display a human body as a mesh, as a skeleton, or as a combination of both (see Fig. 2).

3.3 Selected Video Sequences

To illustrate this keynote paper, we have selected 3 frames for each video sequence selected, with different samplings. These video sequences come from dance archives provided by the PREMIERE project [8]. To illustrate this keynote paper, we have selected frames with only one dancer per frame but the comparison study can be extended to more dancers.

The PREMIERE dataset includes 25 videos (19 dance performances and 6 theater performances). These video archives present various challenges that sometimes make it difficult or even impossible to recognize the 3D poses of the dancers/actors. These challenges result from:

1. Videos with low resolution.
2. Videos with compression artifacts.
3. Videos with interlacing.
4. Videos with motion blur (coming from low frame rates).
5. Videos with too low or too high illumination conditions, spot lights, very colored lights.
6. Dancers/actors with non-standard body poses.
7. Dancers/actors with Loose-fitting clothing.

---

[1] Lossless-Cut is available here: https://github.com/mifi/lossless-cut.

Fig. 1. Screenshot of the web-based visualization tool.

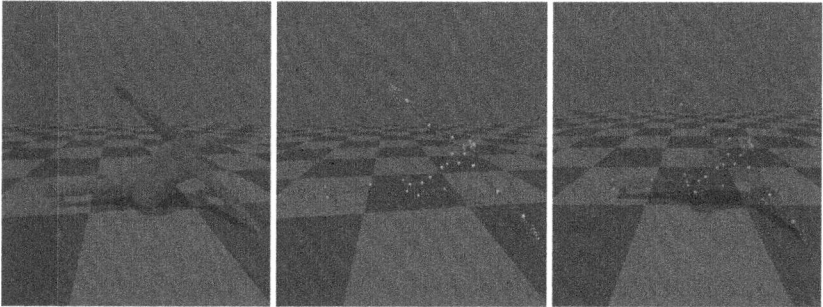

Fig. 2. Human body visualization as a mesh, as a skeleton, or as a combination of both.

For a fair comparison of pose estimation methods, we decided to exclude the following challenging study cases:

- Video frames where even an human cannot estimate the body pose of a dancer or an actor.
- Video frames with strong human occlusions or body contacts (see Fig. 3).
- Video frames where we cannot see the full body: zooms or where only the upper part of the body is visible (see Fig. 4).

Fig. 3. The front dancer occludes the dancer in the background. Image from *Extra Dry* video archive [8].

Fig. 4. The lower part of the dancer is not visible. Image from *Guintche by Marlene Monteiro Freitas* video archive [8].

Sub-set of Video Frames Selected for Comparison of Body Poses. Among these 25 archives we only select the most challenging video sequences for a qualitative comparison of pose estimation models. The dataset used for this comparison consists of 15 short video sequences of 3 frames each. The comparison that has been done could be easily extended to more video sequences, to a higher number of frames, or to any sampling of a video sequence. However, we would still be dependent on the frames selection phase from short video sequences, which can only be done manually.

These 15 sequences cover all together the various challenges listed above, some of them cover multiple of these challenges, as shown in Table 1.

4 Results and Discussion

4.1 Results

All data features extracted for each frame of each sequence of 3-frames selected for this paper are available on this website: https://www.couleur.org/articles/IMPROVE-2025/.

For each of these sequences of 3-frames, the visualization tools implemented enable to compare the results obtained by the 4 pose estimation models implemented, as illustration see example shown in Table 2. In order to have a common reference frame for displaying all these 3D poses, we estimated the 3D keypoints and mesh vertices by positioning the camera frames of these estimates at the same coordinate (0,0,0). As a

Table 1. Sequences and the corresponding challenges: (1) Videos with low resolution; (2) Videos with compression artifacts; (3) Videos with interlacing; (4) Videos with motion blur; (5) Videos with too low or too high illumination conditions, spotlights, very colored lights; (6) Dancers/actors with non-standard body poses; (7) Dancers/actors with loose-fitting clothing.

Sequence	Resolution	1	2	3	4	5	6	7
B5-seg1	1920 × 1080						×	
B5-seg2	1920 × 1080						×	
D1-seg4	640 × 474	×		×	×	×	×	
D4-seg3	640 × 474	×	×				×	
D4-seg4	640 × 474	×	×				×	
D5-seg2	710 × 540	×					×	
D7-seg1	1920 × 1080				×		×	
D7-seg2	1920 × 1080				×	×		
D7-seg3	1920 × 1080					×	×	
D8-seg2	1280 × 720				×	×	×	
D10-seg2	640 × 360	×	×			×	×	×
D10-seg3	640 × 360	×	×					×
D11-seg2	1920 × 1080				×			
D11-seg3	1920 × 1080						×	
D12-seg3	1280 × 720						×	×

result, when displaying successive poses in a sequence, the keypoint 15 (associated to the head of the displayed body) remains fixed.

4.2 Discussion

In Table 3 a qualitative assessment of the results is provided for the 4 pose estimation methods compared and for the 15 sequences selected. Best results are highlighted in bold. Values from 0 to 5 indicate the robustness of the results obtained. A result equal to 0 indicates that at least one pose was not detected in the sequence, while values between 1 and 5 indicate the quality of the estimates (1: poor estimate, 5: very good estimate relatively to visual assessment).

Results obtained with these 3D pose estimation models are consistent with the computational properties of these methods. NLF is, for most of the tests reported in this paper, the best model as it is able of estimating non-standard poses (very common poses in the dance sequences selected for this comparison study). HMR2 and TokenHMR are good for complex lighting conditions but TokenHMR allows better estimation of body shape. Multi-HMR, on the other hand, never achieves better results than the three other models.

Table 2. Results for one sequence of 3 frames: For each frame, we display the 3D skeleton of the dancer according to the corresponding estimation model.

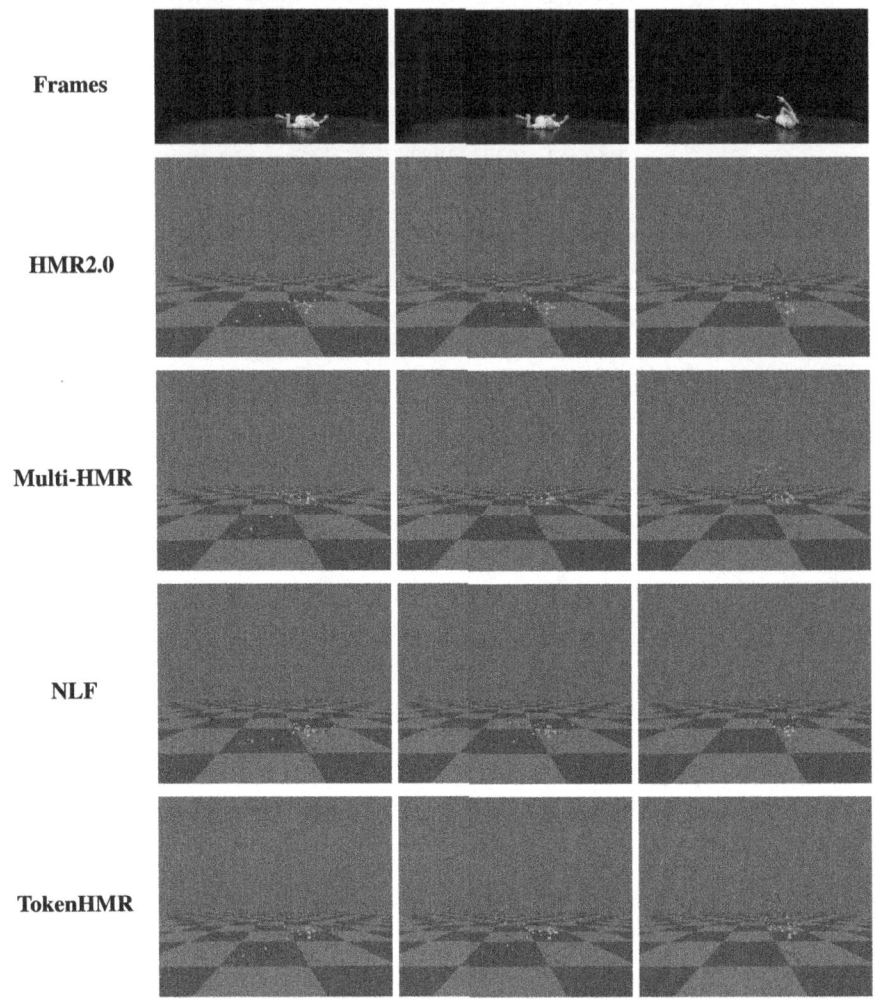

Table 3. Qualitative assessment of the robustness of pose estimation methods.

Sequences	HMR2.0	TokenHMR	Multi-HMR	NLF
B5-seg1	3	3	2	4
B5-seg2	3	3	2	4
D1-seg4	3	4	3	3
D4-seg3	3	3	2	4
D4-seg4	3	4	3	3
D5-seg2	3	4	0 (2 missing)	4
D7-seg1	3	4	3	4
D7-seg2	0 (2 missing)	0 (2 missing)	4	4
D7-seg3	3	4	2	3
D8-seg2	4	3	1	3
D10-seg2	3	3	3	5
D10-seg3	3	4	0 (1 missing)	5
D11-seg2	3	3	2	5
D11-seg3	3	3	0 (1 missing)	4
D12-seg3	3	4	3	5

5 Conclusion/Perspective

Human Mesh Recovery (HMR) can be use in dance to capture details such as body shape and gesture, position in the 3D space, thus offering direct insights of kinematics of dance performers and nuanced information on dancers pose. However, there are many real-time challenges due to which obtaining accurate HMR for dancers becomes very difficult such as complex lighting, ambiguous poses, nature of the motion, camera movement and occlusion.

Even though the occlusion problem has been extensively studied for year, robustness and stability are still need to be improved [39]. Even if motion jitters, i.e. irregular movement and variation across frames due to heavy occlusions have been smoothed thanks to regression-based temporal-based methods, there is still a need for improvement. Even if implicit representations approaches, as well as rendering techniques such as NeRF and Gaussian Splatting are capable of capturing fine details, these approaches lack sufficient robustness in pose estimation [20]. Bridging the gap between robust pose estimation and human body appearance details is still a challenging problem.

In this keynote paper we discuss the relevance and efficiency of the most recent pose estimation methods and made comparisons relatively to a specific application field. We demonstrate that NLF is the best model to estimate non-standard poses in dance and the most robust method in regards to challenging issues that human body movements analyse may face. We also discuss the interest of pose estimation for dance movements analyse and shown that the accuracy of pose estimation is, in the context of dance movements analyse, important but less important than the accuracy of the dance movements modeling.

The qualitative comparisons made were performed from short video sequences of 3 frames. These comparisons could be extended to more frames. In a future work, we will investigate a solution to automatically select the frames that characterizes any specific dance movement sequence. The first frame considered will characterize the movement initiate, the next ones will be selected based on body parts movement, velocity and acceleration, and the last frame will characterize the movement end.

Funding Information. This study was funded by HORIZON-CL2-2021-HERITAGE-000201-04 (grant number 101061303 - PREMIERE) [1].

References

1. Premiere - Performing arts in a new era (2024). https://premiere-project.eu/
2. Andriluka, M., Pishchulin, L., Gehler, P., Schiele, B.: 2D human pose estimation: New benchmark and state of the art analysis. In: Proceedings of the IEEE Conference on computer Vision and Pattern Recognition, pp. 3686–3693 (2014)
3. Baker, B., et al.: Computational kinematics of dance: distinguishing hip hop genres. Front. Robot. AI **11** (2024). https://doi.org/10.3389/frobt.2024.1295308
4. Baradel*, F., Armando, M., Galaaoui, S., Brégier, R., Weinzaepfel, P., Rogez, G., Lucas*, T.: Multi-HMR: multi-person whole-body human mesh recovery in a single shot. In: ECCV (2024)
5. Baradel, F., Armando, M., Galaaoui, S., Brégier, R., Weinzaepfel, P., Rogez, G., Lucas, T.: Multi-hmr: Multi-person whole-body human mesh recovery in a single shot. In: Leonardis, A., Ricci, E., Roth, S., Russakovsky, O., Sattler, T., Varol, G. (eds.) European Conference on Computer Vision, pp. 202–218. Springer, Cham (2025). https://doi.org/10.1007/978-3-031-73337-6_12
6. Black, M.J., Patel, P., Tesch, J., Yang, J.: BEDLAM: a synthetic dataset of bodies exhibiting detailed lifelike animated motion. In: Proceedings of the IEEE/CVF Conference on Computer Vision and Pattern Recognition, pp. 8726–8737 (2023)
7. Cai, Z., et al.: SMPLer-X: scaling up expressive human pose and shape estimation. In: Advances in Neural Information Processing Systems, vol. 36 (2024)
8. Colantoni, P., Muselet, D., Trémeau, A.: PRMR-d2.4-specifications for archived content. https://premiere-project.eu/resources/ (2023). [PREMIERE 2023]
9. Dosovitskiy, A.: An image is worth 16x16 words: transformers for image recognition at scale. arXiv preprint arXiv:2010.11929 (2020)
10. Dwivedi, S.K., Sun, Y., Patel, P., Feng, Y., Black, M.J.: TokenHMR: advancing human mesh recovery with a tokenized pose representation. In: Proceedings of the IEEE/CVF Conference on Computer Vision and Pattern Recognition, pp. 1323–1333 (2024)
11. Goel, S., Pavlakos, G., Rajasegaran, J., Kanazawa, A., Malik, J.: Humans in 4D: reconstructing and tracking humans with transformers. In: Proceedings of the IEEE/CVF International Conference on Computer Vision, pp. 14783–14794 (2023)
12. Guo, W., Craig, O., Difato, T., Oliverio, J., Santoso, M., Sonke, J., Barmpoutis, A.: Ai-driven human motion classification and analysis using laban movement system. In: Duffy, V.G. (eds.) International Conference on Human-Computer Interaction, pp. 201–210. Springer, Cham (2022). https://doi.org/10.1007/978-3-031-05890-5_16
13. Heo, J., Hu, G., Wang, Z., Yeung-Levy, S.: DeforHMR: Vision transformer with deformable cross-attention for 3D human mesh recovery arXiv:2411.11214 (2024)

14. Ionescu, C., Papava, D., Olaru, V., Sminchisescu, C.: Human3. 6M: large scale datasets and predictive methods for 3D human sensing in natural environments. IEEE Trans. Pattern Anal. Mach. Intell. **36**(7), 1325–1339 (2013)
15. Jaegle, A., Gimeno, F., Brock, A., Vinyals, O., Zisserman, A., Carreira, J.: Perceiver: general perception with iterative attention. In: International Conference on Machine Learning, pp. 4651–4664. PMLR (2021)
16. Ju, S.X., Black, M.J., Yacoob, Y.: Cardboard people: a parameterized model of articulated image motion. In: Proceedings of the Second International Conference on Automatic Face and Gesture Recognition, pp. 38–44. IEEE (1996)
17. Li, T., Bolkart, T., Black, M.J., Li, H., Romero, J.: Learning a model of facial shape and expression from 4D scans. ACM Trans. Graph. **36**(6), 194 (2017)
18. Lin, J., Zeng, A., Wang, H., Zhang, L., Li, Y.: One-stage 3D whole-body mesh recovery with component aware transformer. In: Proceedings of the IEEE/CVF Conference on Computer Vision and Pattern Recognition, pp. 21159–21168 (2023)
19. Lin, T.-Y., et al.: Microsoft COCO: common objects in context. In: Fleet, D., Pajdla, T., Schiele, B., Tuytelaars, T. (eds.) ECCV 2014. LNCS, vol. 8693, pp. 740–755. Springer, Cham (2014). https://doi.org/10.1007/978-3-319-10602-1_48
20. Liu, Y., Qiu, C., Zhang, Z.: Deep learning for 3D human pose estimation and mesh recovery: a survey. Neurocomputing **596**, 128049 (2024). https://doi.org/10.1016/j.neucom.2024.128049
21. Loper, M., Mahmood, N., Romero, J., Pons-Moll, G., Black, M.J.: SMPL: A skinned multi-person linear model. ACM Trans. Graphics (Proc. SIGGRAPH Asia) **34**(6), 248:1–248:16 (2015)
22. Nevatia, R., Binford, T.O.: Description and recognition of curved objects. Artif. Intell. **8**(1), 77–98 (1977)
23. Ojeleye, J.O., Bisht, P.S., Colantoni, P., Muselet, D., Tremeau, A.: ChromaPose: Robustness of 2D pose estimation under different color illuminations. In: Computational Color Imaging Workshop. LNCS, vol. 15193, pp. 193–206. Springer Nature Switzerland, Milan (Italie), Italy (2024). https://doi.org/10.1007/978-3-031-72845-7_14, https://hal.science/hal-04860651
24. Osman, A.A.A., Bolkart, T., Black, M.J.: STAR: sparse trained articulated human body regressor. In: Vedaldi, A., Bischof, H., Brox, T., Frahm, J.-M. (eds.) ECCV 2020. LNCS, vol. 12351, pp. 598–613. Springer, Cham (2020). https://doi.org/10.1007/978-3-030-58539-6_36
25. Osman, A.A., Bolkart, T., Tzionas, D., Black, M.J.: Supr: A sparse unified part-based human representation. In: Avidan, S., Brostow, G., Cissé, M., Farinella, G.M., Hassner, T. (eds.) European Conference on Computer Vision, pp. 568–585. Springer, Cham (2022). https://doi.org/10.1007/978-3-031-20086-1_33
26. Patel, P., Black, M.J.: CameraHMR: aligning people with perspective. arXiv:2411.08128 (2024)
27. Patel, P., Huang, C.H.P., Tesch, J., Hoffmann, D.T., Tripathi, S., Black, M.J.: Agora: avatars in geography optimized for regression analysis. In: Proceedings of the IEEE/CVF Conference on Computer Vision and Pattern Recognition, pp. 13468–13478 (2021)
28. Pavlakos, G., et al.: Expressive body capture: 3D hands, face, and body from a single image. In: Proceedings of the IEEE/CVF Conference on Computer Vision and Pattern Recognition, pp. 10975–10985 (2019)
29. Qin, W., Meng, J.: The research on dance motion quality evaluation based on spatiotemporal convolutional neural networks. Alexandria Eng. J. **114**, 46–54 (2025). https://doi.org/10.1016/j.aej.2024.11.025, https://www.sciencedirect.com/science/article/pii/S1110016824014509

30. Rajasegaran, J., Pavlakos, G., Kanazawa, A., Malik, J.: Tracking people by predicting 3D appearance, location and pose. In: Proceedings of the IEEE/CVF Conference on Computer Vision and Pattern Recognition, pp. 2740–2749 (2022)
31. Reshma, M., Kannan, B., Jagathy Raj, V., Shailesh, S.: Cultural heritage preservation through dance digitization: a review. Digit. Appli. Archaeol. Cult. Heritage **28**, e00257 (2023). https://doi.org/10.1016/j.daach.2023.e00257, https://www.sciencedirect.com/science/article/pii/S2212054823000024
32. Romero, J., Tzionas, D., Black, M.J.: Embodied hands: modeling and capturing hands and bodies together. ACM Trans. Graph. **36**(6), 245 (2017)
33. Rong, Y., Shiratori, T., Joo, H.: FrankMocap: a monocular 3D whole-body pose estimation system via regression and integration. In: Proceedings of the IEEE/CVF International Conference on Computer Vision, pp. 1749–1759 (2021)
34. Sárándi, I., Pons-Moll, G.: Neural localizer fields for continuous 3D human pose and shape estimation. arXiv preprint arXiv:2407.07532 (2024)
35. Song, J., Meng, C., Ermon, S.: Denoising diffusion implicit models. arXiv preprint arXiv:2010.02502 (2020)
36. Song, Y., Zhou, H.: 3D human mesh recovery with learned gradient (2024)
37. Stathopoulos, A., Han, L., Metaxas, D.: Score-guided diffusion for 3d human recovery. In: Proceedings of the IEEE/CVF Conference on Computer Vision and Pattern Recognition, pp. 906–915 (2024)
38. Sutopo, J., Abd Ghani, M.K., Burhanuddin, M., Tundo, T.: Dance gesture recognition using LABAN movement analysis with J48 classification. Indonesian J. Electr. Eng. Inf. (IJEEI) **11** (2023). https://doi.org/10.52549/ijeei.v11i2.4314
39. Tian, Y., Zhang, H., Liu, Y., Wang, L.: Recovering 3D human mesh from monocular images: a survey. IEEE Trans. Pattern Anal. Mach. Intell. **45**(12), 15406–15425 (2023). https://doi.org/10.1109/TPAMI.2023.3298850
40. Tsuchida, S., Fukayama, S., Hamasaki, M., Goto, M.: AIST dance video database: Multi-genre, multi-dancer, and multi-camera database for dance information processing. In: Proceedings of the 20th International Society for Music Information Retrieval Conference, ISMIR 2019. Delft, Netherlands (2019)
41. Van Den Oord, A., Vinyals, O., et al.: Neural discrete representation learning. In: Advances in Neural Information Processing Systems, vol. 30 (2017)
42. Vaswani, A.: Attention is all you need. In: Advances in Neural Information Processing Systems (2017)
43. Von Marcard, T., Henschel, R., Black, M.J., Rosenhahn, B., Pons-Moll, G.: Recovering accurate 3d human pose in the wild using IMUs and a moving camera. In: Proceedings of the European Conference on Computer Vision (ECCV), pp. 601–617 (2018)
44. Zhang, H., et al.: PyMAF-X: towards well-aligned full-body model regression from monocular images. IEEE Trans. Pattern Anal. Mach. Intell. **45**(10), 12287–12303 (2023)
45. Zhang, S., Ma, Q., Zhang, Y., Qian, Z., Kwon, T., Pollefeys, M., Bogo, F., Tang, S.: Egobody: Human body shape and motion of interacting people from head-mounted devices. In: Avidan, S., Brostow, G., Cissé, M., Farinella, G.M., Hassner, T. (eds) European conference on computer vision, pp. 180–200. Springer, Cham (2022). https://doi.org/10.1007/978-3-031-20068-7_11
46. Zhang, Y., Nie, L.: Human motion similarity evaluation based on deep metric learning. Sci. Rep. **14**(1), 30908 (2024)

Papers

SuperCrossViT: Integrating Superpixel Segmentation in Vision Transformers for Advanced Medical Image Analysis

Ahmed Lotfi Alqnatri(✉) and Wanda Benesova

Faculty of Informatics and Information Technologies, Slovak Technical University, Ilkovičova 2, 842 16 Bratislava, Slovakia
{ahmed.alqnatri,vanda_benesova}@stuba.sk

Abstract. Vision Transformers (ViTs) have revolutionized medical image analysis, yet they face challenges in simultaneously capturing global context and local anatomical details crucial for accurate diagnosis.

We present SuperCrossViT, an architecture that enhances the standard CrossViT framework by integrating superpixel segmentation for improved analysis of histopathological images. Our approach leverages superpixels to group pixels into meaningful tissue regions, preserving structural information while maintaining computational efficiency.

We evaluate our method on the task of metastatic cancer detection in lymph node Whole Slide Images (WSIs), performing binary classification of tumor versus normal tissue patches. Experimental results demonstrate that SuperCrossViT consistently outperforms baseline ViT and standard CrossViT architectures, achieving superior accuracy in distinguishing cancerous from normal tissues. Our findings suggest that the integration of superpixel segmentation with transformer based architectures offers a promising direction for enhancing the precision of computer aided diagnosis in histopathology.

Keywords: Computer vision · Vision transformers · Superpixel segmentation · Binary classification · Tumor detection · Lymph node analysis · Cross attention · Histopathology · Camelyon dataset · Medical image analysis · Whole Slide Images (WSI)

1 Introduction

The integration of advanced computational methodologies has become instrumental in modern medical diagnostics. Vision Transformers have emerged as a powerful paradigm for medical image analysis, leveraging their self-attention mechanism to model complex spatial relationships and capture long range dependencies in clinical imaging data [1]. However, balancing the capture of global contextual information while preserving fine grained anatomical details remains a significant challenge in medical image interpretation. To address this limitation, we propose SuperCrossViT, an enhanced CrossViT architecture that incorporates superpixel segmentation to effectively capture tissue-specific structures in histopathological images. We evaluate our approach on the challenging task of metastatic cancer detection in lymph node Whole Slide Images (WSIs), performing binary classification of tumor versus normal tissue patches. By grouping pixels into semantically meaningful regions, superpixels preserve structural information while optimizing computational efficiency. This integration proves particularly valuable in medical image analysis, where precise representation of anatomical features directly impacts diagnostic accuracy.

Our contributions are as follows:

1. **Superpixel Enhanced CrossViT Architecture for Histological Medical Data.** We propose an approach that integrates superpixel segmentation into a modified CrossViT architecture for histopathological image analysis. The method leverages a dual branch architecture where one branch incorporates superpixel based region analysis, enhancing the model's ability to capture meaningful tissue structures. We evaluate our approach on the challenging task of metastatic cancer detection in lymph node Whole Slide Images (WSIs), performing binary classification of tumor versus normal tissue patches.
2. **Comprehensive Evaluation on Histopathological Datasets.** We conduct experimental validation on histopathological image datasets of breast lymph node metastasis, demonstrating that our SuperCrossViT architecture achieves prominent performance compared to baseline Vision Transformers (ViT) and standard CrossViT models.

2 Related Work

In this section, we review relevant approaches for histopathological cancer detection, categorized by their methodological foundations.

2.1 Traditional Machine Learning Methods

Traditional machine learning approaches have laid the groundwork for automated cancer detection.

(Valkonen et al., 2017) [16] employed Support Vector Machines (SVM) with hand crafted features for circulating tumor cell detection. Their method utilized a combination of morphological features and intensity based descriptors, achieving a detection accuracy of 82%. However, these methods often require extensive feature engineering and may not capture complex patterns effectively.

(Li et al., 2022) [17] conducted a comprehensive review of traditional methods, highlighting that successful approaches often combined multiple feature types: color features (using RGB, HSV, and LAB color spaces), texture features (using LBP, GLCM, and Haralick descriptors), and shape features. Their analysis showed that while SVM and Random Forest classifiers dominated traditional approaches, these methods were limited by their reliance on hand crafted features and struggled with the complex patterns present in whole slide images. (Sun et al., 2022) [22] compared traditional machine learning (SVM) and deep learning methods for breast cancer metastasis detection in the CAMELYON17 challenge. The study examined various feature selection methods (SIFT, LBP, GLCM) and morphological features for SVM, and evaluated deep learning architectures (GoogLeNet, ResNet, VGG16, AlexNet), with GoogLeNet achieving the best results (FROC: 0.8074, AUC: 0.9935). While deep learning demonstrated superior accuracy and automated feature learning but required more resources, SVM offered better interpretability and efficiency with limited data. The authors concluded that both approaches complement each other - traditional ML excels with small datasets while deep learning performs better at scale.

2.2 Convolutional Neural Network Approaches

The advent of deep learning, particularly CNNs, marked a significant advancement in cancer detection.

(Ge et al., 2024) [18] proposed a Convolutional Ensemble Neural Network that combines multiple CNN architectures to leverage their complementary strengths. Their ensemble approach achieved 94.3% accuracy on the Camelyon16 dataset, demonstrating the effectiveness of model fusion.

(Fan et al., 2019) [2] further advanced CNN based approaches by introducing an improved pipeline combining the Otsu algorithm with morphological operations for preprocessing and hard negative mining for reducing false positives. Using Inception V3 and slide level SVM, their system achieved impressive results on the Camelyon16 dataset.

(Veeling et al., 2018) [21] introduced a rotation equivariant CNN architecture for digital pathology that leverages the inherent rotational and reflectional symmetries in histopathology images through group equivariant CNNs (G-CNNs). Their architecture, P4M DenseNet, modifies the standard DenseNet by incorporating group equivariant convolutions, adapted batch normalization, and group pooling layers to maintain equivariance under 90° rotations (p4) and reflections (p4m). The model demonstrated significant improvements over baselines across multiple datasets. These comprehensive results validate that explicitly encoding rotational symmetry through G-CNNs is more effective than traditional data augmentation approaches, particularly when training data is limited, while requiring fewer parameters due to improved parameter sharing.

2.3 Vision Transformer Approaches

Most recently, Vision Transformers (ViT) have emerged as a promising direction for histopathological image analysis.

(Xu et al., 2023) [19] introduced a hierarchical Vision Transformer architecture specifically designed for whole slide image analysis. Their method leverages self attention mechanisms to capture long range dependencies in histopathological images, achieving state of the art performance histopathological dataset. The transformer based approach showed particular strength in handling variable sized regions of interest and maintaining consistent performance across different magnification levels.

(Chen et al., 2023) [20] introduced dMIL Transformer, a novel two stage framework specifically designed for lymph node metastasis classification in whole slide images.

Their method leverages a double Max-Min multiple instance learning strategy combined with a Transformer based aggregator to integrate both morphological and spatial information. The framework achieved state of the art performance across multiple datasets, showing 7.50% AUC improvement on CAMELYON16 and 1.79% on CAMELYON17. The dMIL-Transformer showed particular strength in distinguishing challenging cases between ITC and Normal categories, while effectively handling spatial correlations between tumor regions through its novel position encoding scheme for discrete spatial information.

(Gul et al., 2022) [23] proposed Self-ViT-MIL, a novel approach combining self supervised Vision Transformers (ViT) with Multiple Instance Learning (MIL) for weakly supervised classification of whole slide images (WSIs). Their two-stage architecture first pretrains a ViT model in a self supervised manner using DINO [24] to learn rich feature representations without labels, followed by a MIL aggregator that uses global attention to localize cancerous regions. The model processes WSIs by dividing them into 224×224 non overlapping patches at $20\times$ magnification. Evaluated on the Camelyon16 dataset, Self-ViT-MIL achieved state of the art performance among MIL based approaches with an accuracy of 0.9147 and AUC of 0.9426, matching fully supervised baselines despite using only slide level labels. Their qualitative analysis showed that while the model had fewer false positives compared to previous methods like DSMIL, it exhibited lower coverage of cancerous regions in the localization task.

While these approaches have demonstrated significant progress, they still rely on fixed size patch tokenization, which may not optimally capture the inherent tissue structures in histopathological images. dMIL-Transformer addresses spatial relationships through position encoding but doesn't adapt to tissue boundaries, while Self-ViT-MIL's self supervised learning improves feature representation but maintains rigid patch divisions. Our proposed SuperCrossViT differentiates itself by introducing adaptive, content aware tokenization through superpixel segmentation, complementing the traditional patch based approach. This dual representation allows our model to better preserve fine grained anatomical details while maintaining the computational efficiency and global context benefits of standard ViT architectures.

3 Proposed Method

Vision Transformers (ViTs) have demonstrated success in image classification but their fixed size patch processing may not optimally capture natural structures in medical images. While using only superpixel based segmentation could better preserve anatomical structures, the computational overhead of superpixel generation makes it impractical for processing entire high resolution medical images. We propose SuperCrossViT, a dual branch architecture that strategically combines content aware superpixel segments with traditional square patches to balance accuracy and efficiency. The superpixel branch captures fine grained anatomical details and tissue boundaries, while the computationally efficient square patch branch maintains global context. By fusing these complementary representations through cross attention mechanisms, our model achieves higher accuracy than pure superpixel based approaches while maintaining reasonable computational latency. We evaluate this approach on the Camelyon16 dataset for lymph node metastasis detection, demonstrating improved detection performance compared to single branch architectures while keeping inference times practical for clinical deployment.

3.1 Overview of SuperCrossViT Architecture

Our proposed SuperCrossViT architecture, illustrated in Fig. 1, enhances the traditional CrossViT model by incorporating superpixel segmentation into one of its processing branches. This architecture consists of two complementary pathways:

- **Superpixel Branch.** Processes superpixel segments as patches to capture fine grained structural details. These content aware segments naturally adapt to tissue boundaries and intensity variations within the image, preserving crucial anatomical information. Unlike fixed patches that might split important structures, superpixels cluster similar pixels together, ensuring that distinct tissue regions remain intact. This preservation is particularly important for detecting subtle variations in cellular structures and tissue organization that are characteristic of metastatic regions.
- **Square Patch Branch.** Processes fixed size square patches to capture global context and maintain a broad understanding of the overall image composition. This traditional approach ensures the model retains the ability to recognize larger scale patterns and spatial relationships. While superpixels excel at preserving local details, fixed patches provide a consistent, grid based representation that helps maintain spatial coherence and capture long range dependencies across the image.

The combination of these two branches addresses the fundamental challenge of maintaining both local and global context. While the superpixel branch preserves fine grained anatomical details by respecting tissue boundaries and maintaining structural integrity within each segment, the square patch branch provides the necessary global context through its regular grid based processing. The cross attention mechanism between these branches allows the model to effectively integrate these complementary perspectives, enabling more accurate detection of metastatic regions that require both detailed cellular analysis and broader contextual understanding.

3.2 Superpixel Segmentation and Embedding

To generate meaningful content aware image segments, we utilize the Simple Linear Iterative Clustering (SLIC) algorithm, which creates superpixels based on both color similarity and spatial proximity in a 5D space (CIELAB color values and pixel coordinates). These generated superpixels are then embedded into a high dimensional space through a learnable linear transformation, converting their color and spatial information into a format suitable for transformer processing.

Superpixel Generation and Size Selection. We employ the Simple Linear Iterative Clustering (SLIC) algorithm [9] to generate superpixels. SLIC generates superpixels by clustering pixels based on their color similarity and proximity in the image plane.

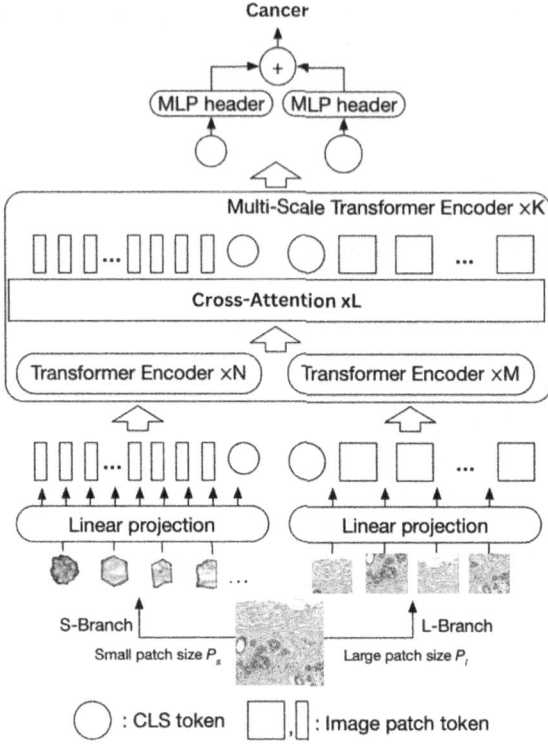

Fig. 1. SuperCrossViT Architecture.

The algorithm operates in a 5D space, using CIELAB color values (l, a, b) and pixel coordinates (x, y).

The selection of superpixel size is crucial for balancing the trade off between fine grained detail preservation and computational efficiency. Through extensive experimentation, we determined that an average superpixel size of $S \times S$ pixels (where $S = 16$) provides optimal performance for our task. This size selection ensures that superpixels are large enough to capture meaningful tissue structures while remaining small enough to preserve fine grained anatomical details. Larger superpixels ($S > 48$) tend to merge distinct tissue regions, potentially losing important diagnostic details, while smaller superpixels ($S < 16$) increase computational overhead without providing significant improvements in feature representation.

Given an input image and the chosen superpixel size parameter, we initialize K cluster centers $C_k = [l_k, a_k, b_k, x_k, y_k]$ at regular grid intervals S. These centers serve as seeds for the superpixel generation process.

To reduce computational complexity, each pixel is only compared to cluster centers within a $2S \times 2S$ region, where S^2 represents the approximate area of a superpixel. The distance measure D_s combines both color proximity and spatial proximity:

$$D_s = d_{lab} + \frac{m}{S} \cdot d_{xy} \tag{1}$$

where the color distance d_{lab} and spatial distance d_{xy} are defined as:

$$d_{lab} = \sqrt{(l_k - l_i)^2 + (a_k - a_i)^2 + (b_k - b_i)^2} \tag{2}$$

$$d_{xy} = \sqrt{(x_k - x_i)^2 + (y_k - y_i)^2} \tag{3}$$

The parameter m controls the compactness of the superpixels, with values typically ranging from 1 to 20. A larger value of m places more emphasis on spatial proximity, resulting in more compact superpixels, while a smaller value allows more flexible boundaries based on color similarity (Fig. 2).

Superpixel Embedding. Each superpixel (Superpixel$_k$) is represented as a feature vector containing both color and spatial information:

$$\text{Superpixel}_k = [l_k, a_k, b_k, x_k, y_k, w_k, h_k] \tag{4}$$

where (l_k, a_k, b_k) are the mean CIELAB color values of all pixels within the superpixel, (x_k, y_k) represent the centroid coordinates of the superpixel, and (w_k, h_k) denote its width and height. This 7 dimensional feature vector captures both the appearance and geometric properties of each superpixel.

We project these representations into a high dimensional embedding space using a learnable linear transformation:

$$\mathbf{e}_k = \mathbf{W}_e \cdot \text{Superpixel\_}k + \mathbf{b}_e \tag{5}$$

where:

- $\mathbf{e}_k \in \mathbb{R}^d$ is the output embedding vector of dimension d
- $\mathbf{W}_e \in \mathbb{R}^{d \times 7}$ is the learnable weight matrix
- $\text{Superpixel}_k \in \mathbb{R}^7$ is the input feature vector described above
- $\mathbf{b}_e \in \mathbb{R}^d$ is the learnable bias vector

This transformation maps the compact superpixel representation to the same dimensional space as the square patch embeddings, enabling subsequent cross attention operations between the two branches.

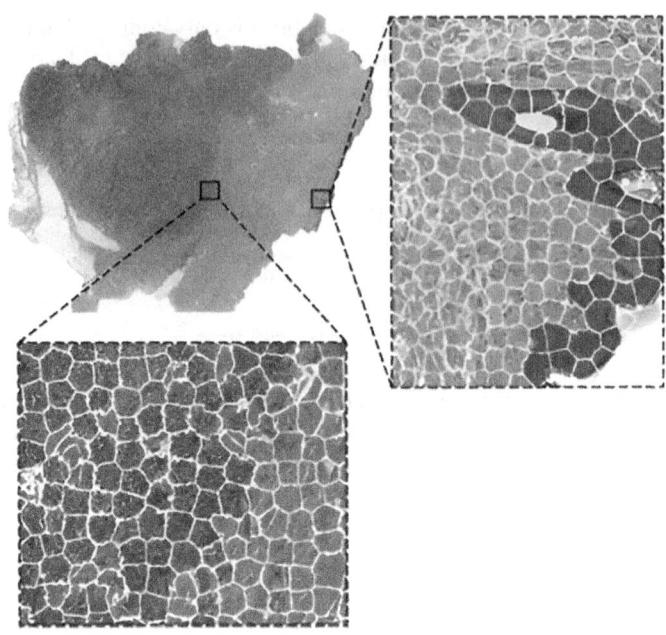

Fig. 2. WSI image segmentation using the SLIC superpixels algorithm [25].

3.3 Integration with CrossViT

We leverage CrossViT's inherent capability to combine multiple processing streams through cross attention. The superpixel and standard patch branches are processed separately through transformer encoders, then fused via cross attention mechanisms. This fusion enables rich interactions between content aware superpixel features and global contextual information, allowing each branch to benefit from the other's complementary representation:

$$\text{CrossAttention}(\mathbf{T}_1, \mathbf{T}_2) = \text{Attention}(\mathbf{Q}_1, \mathbf{K}_2, \mathbf{V}_2) + \text{Attention}(\mathbf{Q}_2, \mathbf{K}_1, \mathbf{V}_1) \quad (6)$$

where $\mathbf{T}_1$ and $\mathbf{T}_2$ are the token sequences from the superpixel and standard branches, respectively.

3.4 Classification Head

After the cross attention fusion combines information from both branches, the resulting representation undergoes further processing through additional transformer layers to refine the integrated features. The final sequence of tokens is represented as $\mathbf{Z} \in \mathbb{R}^{N \times D}$, where N is the number of tokens and D is the hidden dimension. These tokens are aggregated using mean pooling to obtain a single feature vector:

$$\text{Pool}(\mathbf{Z}) = \frac{1}{N} \sum_{i=1}^{N} \mathbf{Z}_i \quad (7)$$

The final classification is performed using a linear layer followed by softmax activation, which maps the pooled features to class probabilities:

$$\text{Prediction} = \text{Softmax}(\mathbf{W}_{cls} \cdot \text{Pool}(\mathbf{Z}) + \mathbf{b}_{cls}) \tag{8}$$

where:

- $\mathbf{W}_{cls} \in \mathbb{R}^{C \times D}$ is the learnable classification weight matrix, with C being the number of classes
- $\text{Pool}(\mathbf{Z}) \in \mathbb{R}^D$ is the pooled feature vector
- $\mathbf{b}_{cls} \in \mathbb{R}^C$ is the learnable classification bias vector

3.5 Dataset

We evaluate our model on the Camelyon16 dataset [5], which consists of high-resolution whole-slide images (WSIs) of lymph node sections stained with hematoxylin and eosin (H&E). The dataset includes 399 WSIs, with 270 training slides and 129 test slides, annotated for metastasis detection.

3.6 Data Preprocessing

The dataset underwent a comprehensive preprocessing pipeline to ensure optimal model training. First, we extracted non overlapping tiles from the whole slide images. To address stain variations across different samples, particularly those from two different medical centers, we applied color deconvolution to separate the hematoxylin and eosin (H&E) channels, followed by Optical Density (OD) transformation for normalization of each channel independently. This stain normalization approach specifically tackles the real world challenge of inter center staining protocol variations.

The data was then augmented using domain informed transformations. Geometric transformations (rotation and flipping) simulate the arbitrary orientation of tissue sections during slide preparation. Color jittering was specifically calibrated to match the observed H&E staining variations between the two medical centers in our dataset, focusing on independently adjusting the hematoxylin and eosin color channels within ranges observed in real clinical samples. Gaussian noise injection mimics the variation in image quality from different slide scanner systems. By anchoring these augmentation parameters to actual variations observed in our multicenter dataset, we ensure that the augmentations reflect realistic tissue appearance variations rather than arbitrary perturbations.

Tile Extraction. For tile extraction we used the following the parameters:

- **Tile Size.** 256 × 256 pixels.
- **Stride.** 256 pixels (non-overlapping tiles).
- **Normalization.** Optical Density (OD) transformation [10] to normalize stain variations.

In the Optical Density (OD) transformation, we aim to standardize the color intensity of the histopathological images to reduce variability caused by different staining protocols. For an image pixel value I, the OD value OD is computed as:

$$OD = -\log\left(\frac{I}{I_0}\right) \quad (9)$$

where I_0 is the maximum intensity value (typically 255 for an 8-bit image). This transformation emphasizes the stain components by converting the RGB values to OD space, allowing for more consistent color representation across images.

Data Augmentation. We implemented the following the data augmentation techniques:

- **Geometric Transformations.** A composition of rotations, flips, scaling, and shearing to enhance spatial invariance.
- **Rotation.** Each image tile I undergoes rotation transformation $R_\theta(I)$ with angle $\theta \sim \mathcal{U}(-5°, 5°)$, where $\mathcal{U}$ denotes uniform distribution, to increase robustness against orientation variations.
- **Scaling.** Anisotropic scaling transformation $S_\alpha(I)$ is applied with scaling factor $\alpha \sim \mathcal{U}(0.8, 1.2)$ to account for tissue size variations. The transformation can be expressed as:

$$S_\alpha(I)(x, y) = I(\alpha x, \alpha y) \quad (10)$$

- **Color Jittering.** Sequential adjustments to simulate staining variations:
  - Brightness: $b \sim \mathcal{U}(-0.2, 0.2)$
  - Contrast: $c \sim \mathcal{U}(0.8, 1.2)$
  - Saturation: $s \sim \mathcal{U}(0.8, 1.2)$
  - Hue: $h \sim \mathcal{U}(-0.1, 0.1)$
- **Noise Injection.** Gaussian noise addition to improve model robustness.
- **Gaussian Noise.** For an input image I, the noisy image I' is generated by adding noise sampled from a Gaussian distribution:

$$I'(x, y) = I(x, y) + \epsilon, \quad \text{where} \quad \epsilon \sim \mathcal{N}(0, \sigma^2) \quad (11)$$

where $\sigma = 0.01$ represents the noise standard deviation, and $\mathcal{N}(0, \sigma^2)$ denotes the normal distribution. This augmentation simulates acquisition noise and helps prevent overfitting.

3.7 Experimental Setup

We conducted a comprehensive evaluation of our proposed SuperCrossViT model against baseline architectures (ResNeT50, ViT and CrossViT) using a rigorous experimental framework. The models were trained using the Adam optimizer with carefully tuned hyperparameters, with early stopping to prevent over fitting. Performance was assessed using standard classification metrics (accuracy, precision, recall, F1 score, and ROC-AUC) through 5-fold cross validation to ensure robust evaluation. This setup enables fair comparison between the traditional CNN, patch based transformer approaches and our superpixel integrated method.

Model Configurations. We evaluate our proposed approach against established classical CNN and vision transformer architectures while maintaining consistent experimental conditions across all models.

- **Baseline Models.** ViT [1] and CrossViT [11].
- **Proposed Model.** SuperCrossViT as described in Sect. 3.1.

The baseline models were trained using standard image patches, while the proposed SuperCrossViT used both standard patches and superpixel patches. The CrossViT architecture served as the foundation for integrating superpixel information, leveraging cross-attention between the superpixel and standard branches.

Training Parameters. Key hyperparameters and optimization settings used during the model training process:

- **Optimizer.** Adam optimizer with a learning rate of 1×10^{-4}.
- **Batch Size.** 128.
- **Epochs.** 100 with early stopping based on validation loss.
- **Loss Function.** Cross-entropy loss.

The Adam optimizer is used to update the weights of the network. The learning rate of 1×10^{-4} was chosen to balance convergence speed and training stability. Early stopping was applied to prevent overfitting by monitoring the validation loss, and the model training was halted if there was no improvement for a set number of epochs.

Evaluation Metrics. We evaluated our model using standard classification metrics:

- **Accuracy.** Ratio of correctly classified samples to total samples.
- **Precision.** Measures positive predictive value:

$$\text{Precision} = \frac{TP}{TP + FP} \tag{12}$$

- **Recall.** Measures sensitivity to positive samples:

$$\text{Recall} = \frac{TP}{TP + FN} \tag{13}$$

- **F1 Score.** Harmonic mean of precision and recall:

$$F1 = 2 \times \frac{\text{Precision} \times \text{Recall}}{\text{Precision} + \text{Recall}} \tag{14}$$

- **ROC-AUC.** Area Under the Receiver Operating Characteristic Curve, measuring model discrimination ability.

3.8 Cross-Validation

We employed 5-fold cross-validation to ensure robust evaluation. The dataset was split into five subsets, with each subset used once as the validation data while the remaining subsets formed the training data. The final performance metrics were obtained by averaging the results from all five folds, providing a more generalized understanding of model performance.

4 Results

4.1 Quantitative Results

We conducted extensive experiments to validate the performance of our proposed SuperCrossViT model against baseline models, including ResNet50, ViT and CrossViT. The evaluation metrics include Accuracy, Precision, Recall, Specificity, F1 Score, and ROC-AUC.

Table 1. Performance Comparison of Models on the Camelyon16 Dataset.

Metric	ResNet50	ViT	CrossViT	SuperCrossViT
Accuracy	85.4	80.5	89.6	92.7
Precision	83.5	78.1	87.5	90.4
Recall	84.1	79.4	88.3	91.5
Specificity	85.6	82.3	90.2	93.8
F1 Score	83.8	78.7	87.9	90.9
ROC-AUC	87.3	85.2	91.1	95.6

Note: All values are percentages (%)

As seen in Table 1 and Table 2, the proposed SuperCrossViT model outperformed the baseline models across all evaluation metrics. Specifically, it achieved an improvement of 3.1% in accuracy over CrossViT and a significant increase of 12.2% over the standard ViT architecture. The improvement in the ROC-AUC score indicates a strong discriminative ability of SuperCrossViT, showcasing its robustness in distinguishing between cancerous and non cancerous tissues.

4.2 Ablation Studies

To better understand the contribution of different components of SuperCrossViT, we conducted ablation studies by removing the superpixel integration.

The results in Table 3 show that removing the superpixel integration leads to a drop in performance, highlighting the importance of using superpixels for capturing fine grained details. Similarly, however in dual branch superpixels integration the model could not outperform the single branch integration, we think it is due the ability that the larger square patches have in including more context to the batch, as demonstrated by the drop in F1 Score and ROC-AUC when this component is removed.

Table 2. Complete Performance Metrics For Average Values Across Folds.

Model	Metric	Average
ViT	ROC AUC	0.8071
	F1 score	0.7888
	Precision	0.7924
	Recall	0.7854
	Sensitivity	0.7854
	Specificity	0.7929
	Train acc	0.7894
	Train loss	0.1044
	Val acc	0.7891
	Val loss	0.1016
SuperpixelViT	ROC AUC	0.9891 ↑
	F1 score	0.9488 ↑
	Precision	0.9524 ↑
	Recall	0.9454 ↑
	Sensitivity	0.9454 ↑
	Specificity	0.9229 ↑
	Train acc	0.9594 ↑
	Train loss	0.0804 ↓
	Val acc	0.9447 ↑
	Val loss	0.1316 ↓
CrossViT	ROC AUC	0.9665 ↑
	F1 score	0.9447 ↑
	Precision	0.9489 ↑
	Recall	0.9405 ↑
	Sensitivity	0.9405 ↑
	Specificity	0.9495 ↑
	Train acc	0.9454 ↑
	Train loss	0.0752 ↓
	Val acc	0.9450 ↑
	Val loss	0.0838 ↓
SuperCrossViT	ROC AUC	0.9964 ↑
	F1 score	0.9739 ↑
	Precision	0.9782 ↑
	Recall	0.9696 ↑
	Sensitivity	0.9696 ↑
	Specificity	0.9789 ↑
	Train acc	0.9746 ↑
	Train loss	0.0672 ↓
	Val acc	0.9742 ↑
	Val loss	0.0760 ↓

Note: ↑ indicates improvement over ViT, ↓ indicates lower loss.

Table 3. Ablation Study Results.

Model Configuration	Accuracy	F1	ROC-AUC
One Branch Superpixel	97.4	97.9	99.6
Two Branches Superpixel	95.1	95.2	98.4
Baseline CrossViT	94.4	94.0	96.6

All values are percentages (%)

4.3 Cross-Validation Results

To further validate the robustness of SuperCrossViT, we employed 5-fold cross validation. The average metrics across all folds are summarized below:

Table 4. Cross-Validation Metrics for SuperCrossViT

Metric	Fold 1	Fold 2	Fold 3	Fold 4	Fold 5	Avg ± SD
Accuracy	97.3	97.4	97.5	97.3	97.4	97.4 ±0.01
Precision	97.7	97.7	97.8	97.7	97.8	97.7 ±0.01
Recall	96.8	96.9	97.0	96.9	96.9	96.9 ±0.01
F1 Score	97.3	97.3	97.5	97.4	97.3	97.5 ±0.01
ROC-AUC	99.6	99.6	99.6	99.6	99.6	99.6 ±0.03

All values are percentages (%). SD: Standard Deviation.

The cross validation results in Table 4 indicate that SuperCrossViT maintains consistent performance across different splits, demonstrating its robustness and generalizability for medical image analysis.

5 Conclusions

The experimental results clearly demonstrate the advantages of integrating superpixel segmentation into the CrossViT framework. The proposed SuperCrossViT model achieves superior accuracy by leveraging superpixels' inherent ability to preserve tissue boundaries and structural edges, which is particularly crucial in histopathological analysis. While the integration of superpixel segmentation introduces some preprocessing overhead, this is outweighed by the significant improvements in diagnostic performance, as model inference time remains comparable to traditional approaches.

The fundamental principle of our approach combining content aware superpixel representations with traditional patch processing is readily adaptable to various medical imaging domains. For instance, in dermatological imaging, superpixels could better capture lesion boundaries, while in radiological scans, they could enhance organ delineation. The architecture can be easily modified for different imaging modalities by adjusting superpixel parameters to match the characteristic scales and patterns of each domain, making SuperCrossViT a versatile framework for medical image analysis tasks where structural preservation is crucial.

5.1 Future Work

Several promising directions for future research include:

- **Alternative Superpixel Methods.** Investigating different superpixel generation techniques like Compact Watershed [12] or Neuro Activated Superpixels [13] to potentially improve structural feature capture.
- **Advanced Superpixel Embeddings.** Exploring sophisticated embedding techniques such as graph-based approaches [14] or positional embeddings [15] to enhance structural representation.
- **Regional Cross Attention.** Modifying the cross attention mechanism to process multiple superpixels simultaneously, potentially improving the capture of local spatial relationships.

These directions aim to further improve SuperCrossViT's effectiveness in medical image analysis.

References

1. Dosovitskiy, A.: An image is worth 16x16 words: transformers for image recognition at scale. arXiv preprint arXiv:2010.11929 (2020)
2. Fan, K., Wen, S., Deng, Z.: Deep learning for detecting breast cancer metastases on WSI. In: Chen, Y.-W., Zimmermann, A., Howlett, R.J., Jain, L.C. (eds.) Innovation in Medicine and Healthcare Systems, and Multimedia. SIST, vol. 145, pp. 137–145. Springer, Singapore (2019). https://doi.org/10.1007/978-981-13-8566-7_13
3. Yousefi, J.: Image binarization using Otsu thresholding algorithm. Ontario, Canada: University of Guelph **10** (2011)
4. Xia, X., Xu, C., Nan, B.: Inception-V3 for flower classification. In: 2017 2nd International Conference on Image, Vision and Computing (ICIVC), pp. 783–787. IEEE (2017)
5. Bejnordi, B.E., et al.: Diagnostic assessment of deep learning algorithms for detection of lymph node metastases in women with breast cancer. JAMA **318**(22), 2199–2210 (2017)
6. Tourniaire, P., Ilie, M., Hofman, P., Ayache, N., Delingette, H.: Attention-based multiple instance learning with mixed supervision on the camelyon16 dataset. In: MICCAI Workshop on Computational Pathology, pp. 216–226. PMLR (2021)
7. Lu, M.Y., Williamson, D.F.K., Chen, T.Y., Chen, R.J., Barbieri, M., Mahmood, F.: Data-efficient and weakly supervised computational pathology on whole-slide images. Nat. Biomed. Eng. **5**(6), 555–570 (2021)
8. He, K., Zhang, X., Ren, S., Sun, J.: Deep residual learning for image recognition. In: Proceedings of the IEEE Conference on Computer Vision and Pattern Recognition, pp. 770–778 (2016)
9. Achanta, R., Shaji, A., Smith, K., Lucchi, A., Fua, P., Süsstrunk, S.: SLIC superpixels compared to state-of-the-art superpixel methods. IEEE Trans. Pattern Anal. Mach. Intell. **34**(11), 2274–2282 (2012)
10. Alsubaie, N., Trahearn, N., Raza, S.E.A., Snead, D., Rajpoot, N.M.: Stain deconvolution using statistical analysis of multi-resolution stain colour representation. PLoS ONE **12**(1), e0169875 (2017)
11. Chen, C.F.R., Fan, Q., Panda, R.: CrossViT: cross-attention multi-scale vision transformer for image classification. In: Proceedings of the IEEE/CVF International Conference on Computer Vision, pp. 357–366 (2021)

12. Vincent, L., Soille, P.: Watersheds in digital spaces: an efficient algorithm based on immersion simulations. IEEE Trans. Pattern Anal. Mach. Intell. **13**(06), 583–598 (1991)
13. Boubekki, A., Fadel, S.G., Mair, S.: Leveraging activations for superpixel explanations. arXiv preprint arXiv:2406.04933 (2024)
14. Long, J., et al.: A graph neural network for superpixel image classification. J. Phys. Conf. Ser. **1871**, 012071 (2021)
15. Su, J., Ahmed, M., Lu, Y., Pan, S., Bo, W., Liu, Y.: RoFormer: enhanced transformer with rotary position embedding. Neurocomputing **568**, 127063 (2024)
16. Valkonen, M., Kartasalo, K., Liimatainen, K., Nykter, M., Latonen, L., Ruusuvuori, P.: Metastasis detection from whole slide images using local features and random forests. Cytometry A **91**(6), 555–565 (2017)
17. Li, X., et al.: A comprehensive review of computer-aided whole-slide image analysis: from datasets to feature extraction, segmentation, classification and detection approaches. Artif. Intell. Rev. **55**(6), 4809–4878 (2022)
18. Ge, R., Chen, G., Saruta, K., Terata, Y.: Detection of presence or absence of metastasis in WSI patches of breast cancer using the dual-enhanced convolutional ensemble neural network. Mach. Learn. Appl. **17**, 100579 (2024)
19. Xu, H., et al.: Vision transformers for computational histopathology. IEEE Rev. Biomed. Eng. **17**, 63–79 (2023)
20. Chen, Y., et al.: DMIL-transformer: multiple instance learning via integrating morphological and spatial information for lymph node metastasis classification. IEEE J. Biomed. Health Inform. **27**(9), 4433–4443 (2023)
21. Veeling, B.S., Linmans, J., Winkens, J., Cohen, T., Welling, M.: Rotation equivariant CNNs for digital pathology. In: Frangi, A.F., Schnabel, J.A., Davatzikos, C., Alberola-López, C., Fichtinger, G. (eds.) MICCAI 2018. LNCS, vol. 11071, pp. 210–218. Springer, Cham (2018). https://doi.org/10.1007/978-3-030-00934-2_24
22. Sun, T., Meng, T., Liu, Y.: CAMELYON 17 challenge: a comparison of traditional machine learning (SVM) with the deep learning method. Wirel. Commun. Mob. Comput. **2022**(1), 9910471 (2022)
23. Gul, A.G., Cetin, O., Reich, C., Flinner, N., Prangemeier, T., Koeppl, H.: Histopathological image classification based on self-supervised vision transformer and weak labels. In: Medical Imaging 2022: Digital and Computational Pathology, vol. 12039, pp. 366–373. SPIE (2022)
24. Caron, M., et al.: Emerging properties in self-supervised vision transformers. In: Proceedings of the IEEE/CVF International Conference on Computer Vision, pp. 9650–9660 (2021)
25. Petríková, D., Cimrák, I.: Survey of recent deep neural networks with strong annotated supervision in histopathology. Computation **11**(4), 81 (2023)

A Multi-modal Approach for Face Anti-spoofing in Non-calibrated Systems Using Disparity Maps

Ariel Larey, Eyal Rond, and Omer Achrack[✉]

Intel RealSense, Santa Clara, USA
{ariel.lahrey,eyal.rond,omer.achrack}@intel.com

Abstract. Face recognition technologies are increasingly used in various applications, yet they are vulnerable to face spoofing attacks. These spoofing attacks often involve unique 3D structures, such as printed papers or mobile device screens. Although stereo-depth cameras can detect such attacks effectively, their high-cost limits their widespread adoption. Conversely, two-sensor systems without extrinsic calibration offer a cost-effective alternative but are unable to calculate depth using stereo techniques. In this work, we propose a method to overcome this challenge by leveraging facial attributes to derive disparity information and estimate relative depth for anti-spoofing purposes, using non-calibrated systems. We introduce a multi-modal anti-spoofing model, coined Disparity Model, that incorporates created disparity maps as a third modality alongside the two original sensor modalities. We demonstrate the effectiveness of the Disparity Model in countering various spoof attacks using a comprehensive dataset collected from the Intel® RealSense™ ID Solution F455. Our method outperformed existing methods in the literature, achieving an Equal Error Rate (EER) of 1.71% and a False Negative Rate (FNR) of 2.77% at a False Positive Rate (FPR) of 1%. These errors are lower by 2.45% and 7.94% than the errors of the best comparison method, respectively. Additionally, we introduce a model ensemble that addresses 3D spoof attacks as well, achieving an EER of 2.04% and an FNR of 3.83% at an FPR of 1%. Overall, our work provides a state-of-the-art solution for the challenging task of anti-spoofing in non-calibrated systems that lack depth information.

Keywords: Face recognition · Anti-spoofing · Non-calibrated systems · Disparity maps

1 Introduction

In recent years, face recognition technologies have seen a significant increase in popularity across a wide line of products, including access control systems, phone unlocking mechanisms, digital payment platforms, and attendance tracking systems. Despite their widespread adoption, these systems remain susceptible to substantial security risks, such as Face-Spoofing (FS) or Face Presentation

Attacks (FPA). Consequently, detecting spoof attempts in modern face recognition systems has become an active area of research in both academia and industry. As a result, numerous papers and datasets have been introduced in this field [19,26], and anti-spoofing modules are increasingly being integrated into modern products prior to the face recognition phase (See Appendix A for more details).

The domain of spoof attacks can be categorized into two primary types: 2D attacks (e.g., printed papers, different types of screens) and 3D attacks (e.g., 3D masks made from rigid materials, silicone masks, fabric masks). For 2D attacks, stereo-depth cameras have demonstrated promising results [27]. However, stereo-depth cameras could be expensive and less feasible for widespread adoption in most real-life scenarios. On the other hand, Near-IR (NIR) sensors are less-expensive than stereo-depth cameras, and are used as a preferable option for lower-budget use cases and for large-scale distributed edge computing systems. Additionally, NIR sensors have also demonstrated high performance in detecting 3D FAS (e.g., masks) as reported in [8]. Another approach to address the FAS problem is the development of multi-modality systems. In this type of system, decisions are based on several modalities (e.g., visual information, NIR information, depth information or even temporal information from videos), which model different aspects of the physical environment. Utilizing multiple modalities can enhance robustness against various types of spoof attacks in real-world scenarios [13].

Our research is based on a relatively new and promising product in the market: Intel® RealSense™ ID Solution F455. This product features two NIR sensors coincides with the multi-modality approach, since the sensors utilize different color schemes, thereby enriching the texture information compared to a single color scheme system[1].

Moreover, the systems' sensors lack extrinsic calibration, which makes the product more affordable and suitable for lower-cost and scalable security systems. However, the absence of rectification information prevents the calculation of depth using stereo techniques. In this work, we introduce a unique method to overcome the lack of camera parameters knowledge, by leveraging facial attributes to derive disparity information and estimate relative depth for the anti-spoofing task. We train an anti-spoofing model using a multi-modal approach, where the model incorporates disparity information as an effective third modality, in addition to the two physical NIR sensor modalities.

An additional critical consideration for face recognition systems is data privacy. Various solutions in cloud computing address this concern, but our model is designed to operate in an edge-compatible manner. This approach effectively prevents the leakage of sensitive data, as the entire face recognition process is conducted on the edge device itself. Furthermore, this method offers the advantage of functioning independently of network connectivity, thereby making it suitable for a broader range of use cases. To meet the requirements for edge

---

[1] For further information about the exact sensor technical specifications, please visit the official website of the product: https://store.intelrealsense.com/intel-realsense-id-solution-f455-peripheral-version-with-software.html.

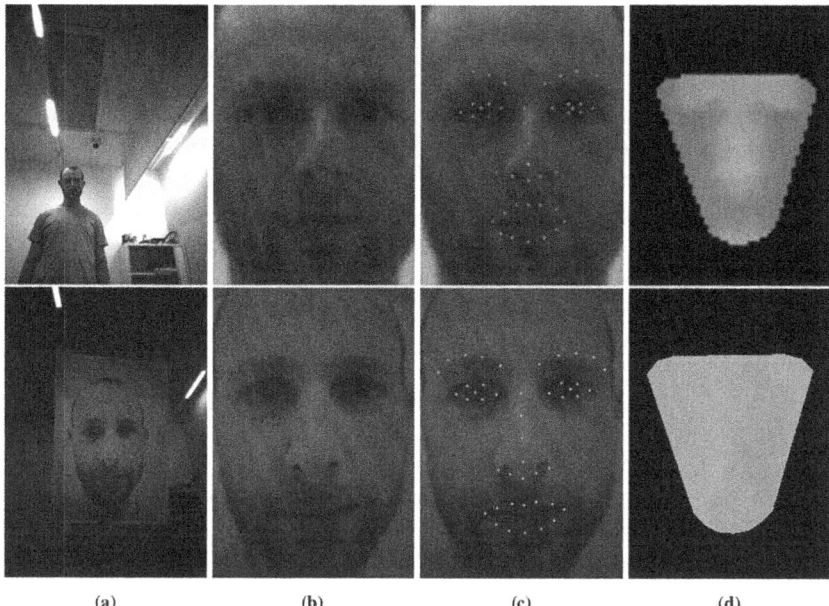

Fig. 1. Demonstration of disparity maps creation pipeline for live (top) and spoof (bottom) examples. First, image acquisition is performed by the device (a). Next, Face Detection is applied (b) followed by Facial landmarks extraction and sparse disparity calculation (c). Finally, disparity maps are produced by linear interpolation (d). Green represents higher disparity than the red. (Color figure online)

computing, our model is small in terms of memory footprint and with the ability to operate with lower precision.

To summarize, our contributions are as follows:

- Develop a novel method for extracting disparity information as a new virtual depth sensor data.
- Design and implement an anti-spoofing model that integrates three different modalities to achieve superior performance in detecting spoofing attacks, particularly with non-calibrated sensor inputs.
- Create multi modality solution for FAS system suitable for edge devices.

2 Related Work

FAS is an active research area in both industry and academia, where various sensors are examined and utilized to counter different spoofing attacks.

Multi-Modality FAS. Multi-modality is a robust mechanism that enables FAS systems to integrate various physical attributes from different sensors. In [8], the authors utilized visible light and NIR sensors with three levels of data fusion. In the Data Level Fusion, data from both modalities are concatenated across the channels and are used as input to a Convolutional Neural Network (CNN). In the Feature Maps Level Fusion, feature maps are computed separately for each modality via a CNN, then they are concatenated across the channels and are used as input to a sub-network classification module. In the Fully Connected Level Fusion, fusion is applied only to the final layers of the network. The final prediction probability is a weighted average of the probabilities from all three fusion sub-models. In [26], the authors utilized active stereo depth input, comprising RGB and NIR data. They integrated these inputs into a single decision at the CNN level using the Squeeze and Excitation (SE) mechanism [7]. In [13], the authors used Visual Transformer (ViT) blocks as a backbone for each modality (RGB and NIR). They also introduced a decision mechanism based on uncertainty estimation, with the authors adaptation of Monte Carlo sampling to evaluate the feature unreliability in each modality [9]. Based on the uncertainty score, they weighted the prediction in cross-modal attention fusion. In [24], the authors proposed using Central Difference Convolution (CDC) [25] to enhance the model's ability to capture intrinsic live or spoof features from each modality separately. Subsequently, the features are concatenated and processed by a single sub-model that produces a binary mask, where the final score is determined by averaging the values of the mask.

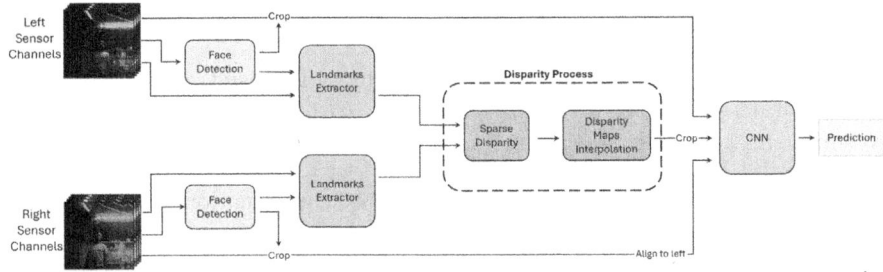

Fig. 2. Disparity Model full pipeline. Initially, faces are detected, and facial landmarks are extracted from the data of both sensors. These landmarks serve as key points for sparse disparity calculation along both the horizontal and vertical axes. This is followed by spatial interpolation, resulting in two disparity maps. Finally, the aligned right sensor crop, the left crop, and the disparity maps are concatenated and processed by a CNN to predict whether the input is a spoof or live.

Depth-Based FAS. The primary motivation for employing depth sensing in FAS systems is its robustness against 2D spoof attacks, which are the most common attacks in real-life scenarios. In [4], the authors utilized two streams during the process. The first stream employs a trained depth estimator using images extracted from a single source, while the second stream processes patches cropped from the RGB input. Finally, a unified decision is determined via a classification sub-model that employs a weighting mechanism between the scores from both streams. In [21], depth images captured using a Kinect device were utilized. The authors employed a CNN architecture, followed by a linear Support Vector Machine (SVM), to classify the extracted features into live or spoof categories. In [26], a PSPNet architecture [28] was trained to generate segmented depth maps. A decision rule was then applied to these predicted depth maps to determine whether the input was live or a spoof attack.

Temporal-Based FAS. Video-based FAS systems can capture liveness by analyzing motion patterns across the video, a capability that single-image FAS systems lack. In [23] the authors designed a Spatio-Temporal Anti-Spoofing Network (STASN), which comprises distinct sub-networks for spatial and temporal components. The authors augmented the spoof data by applying various noise patterns and transformations to their collected live samples, making them resemble spoof samples. In [11], the authors generated temporal feature vectors from cropped face regions of interest (ROIs) across the video. These vectors were calculated using temporal filtering and Fast Fourier Transform (FFT) and subsequently were classified by a Support Vector Machine (SVM). In [5] the authors employed a CNN combined with Long Short-Term Memory LSTM, [6] for anti-spoofing predictions from videos. They utilized Eulerian motion magnification [22] as part of the network's input process, to enhance subtle motions of live faces. In [3], the authors developed a dataset that enables the extraction of live or spoof information from motion. They captured videos for each sample at two known distances. Similar to our approach, they calculated distances between facial features extracted from two images. A feature vector for each sample was then created from these computed distances, and was classified using various deep learning and classical machine learning methods. In our work, we demonstrate that this approach is insufficient for the challenging task of anti-spoofing using non-calibrated sensors. To address this domain challenges, we introduce a method that leverages the raw distances of the facial features, into spatial proxy-depth information as an additional input to the anti-spoofing model.

3 Method

3.1 Camera Sensors Process

Standard RGB cameras are designed to produce visually appealing images based on human visual perception. Thus, various Digital Signal Processors (DSPs) are employed to process raw images and enhance their visual appeal. However, in Facial Anti-Spoofing (FAS) systems, the objective is fundamentally different. The primary goal is to extract features pertinent to distinguish between live and spoof images, rather than generating visually appealing images. Therefore, in our pipeline, the demosaicing algorithm [12] is not performed, and instead the raw Bayer pattern from the sensor, reshaped into four channels, is used. Specifically, two four-channel images are produced: one from the left sensor (s_l) and one from the right sensor (s_r). Further details are provided in Appendix B.

3.2 Disparity Maps

Certain forms of Spoof attacks are characterized by a unique facial structure. For instance, two-dimensional spoof attacks are composed of a plane within a sphere, whereas alternative attacks might be performed via other geometric structures, such as a cylinder. Occasionally, the information provided by texture alone is insufficient for the precise operation of anti-spoofing systems, necessitating the incorporation of three-dimensional geometric knowledge. In response to the absence of depth data in the system's ASIC, and the lack of intrinsic and extrinsic information from the sensors, we acquire three-dimensional knowledge through a specialized methodology.

Two images are under consideration, the initial one being derived from the left sensor (s_l), and the subsequent one from the right sensor (s_r). Both images are applied to a Face Detector (FD) model followed by a Facial landmarks extractor (LE). The latter yields 45 facial landmarks distributed across the face. Both the FD and LE models are specifically trained to process data from the Intel® RealSense™ ID Solution F455 and are dedicated to this domain. For additional details, please refer to Appendix C. Formally, this can be expressed as:

$$rect_k = FD(s_k) \quad (1)$$

$$lms_k = LE(rect_k, s_k) \quad (2)$$

where $k \in \{l, r\}$ refers to the sensor, $rect_k$ is the rectangle circumscribing the face captured by sensor k, and lms_k represents 45 facial landmarks extracted from sensor k image, while each facial landmark is a two-dimensional point within the image.

To estimate relative depth, we utilize pairs of landmarks from two sensors, each projected from the same 3D point on the sphere. For a given point on the face, denoted as P_i, and its corresponding facial landmarks from each sensor, $lms_{l,i}$ and $lms_{r,i}$ we can determine the disparity in each dimension by subtracting the former from the latter:

$$disp_{i,x} = lms_{r,i,x} - lms_{l,i,x} \quad (3)$$

$$disp_{i,y} = lms_{r,i,y} - lms_{l,i,y} \quad (4)$$

where $i \in \{1, 45\}$ is the facial landmark index, x and y represent the horizontal and vertical dimension within the image respectively, and $disp_{i,d}$ is the disparity of facial landmark i over dimension d.

Understanding disparity, the difference in image location of an object seen along two different lines of sight, can provide valuable insights into the depth relationships between facial features. For instance, in a capture of live instance in frontal pose, the tip of the nose should exhibit greater disparity than the pupil of the eye, given that the nose is closer to the camera system, unlike in some 2D spoof attacks. Another significant advantage of understanding disparity is the capability to estimate the depth of the entire head in relation to its size. This becomes particularly crucial when attempting to detect spoof attacks that are often carried out using smaller images. In calibrated stereo systems, disparity is typically computed using predefined system information. However, in our approach, we have calculated it utilizing the knowledge of facial attributes.

Finally, to complete the spatial disparity information of the face, we perform a linear interpolation (LI) across the pixels of the left sensor. This process is guided by the sparse disparity values derived from the facial landmarks.

$$dispmap_x = LI(lms_{l,x}, disp_x) \tag{5}$$

$$dispmap_y = LI(lms_{l,y}, disp_y) \tag{6}$$

where x and y represent the horizontal and vertical dimensions of the image respectively. $dispmap_d$ is the disparity-map calculated using the sparse disparity ($disp_d$) over dimension d. The linear interpolation is implemented using the SciPy[2] library [20]. Figure 1 presents live and spoof examples of disparity maps and their process steps.

3.3 Disparity Model

Data-Process. A dedicated deep learning model to predict 2D spoof attacks is developed by utilizing relative disparity knowledge. Given that the disparity map contains spatial pixel-wise data, it can be processed by convolutional neural network (CNN) kernels along with their corresponding texture maps on a pixel-wise basis. Specifically, the model's input comprises ten channels from three modalities: four channels from the left sensor, four channels from the right sensor, and two channels are the disparity maps both for horizontal and vertical dimensions. The complete multi-modal data process is illustrated in Fig. 2. The four-channel images from both sensors are first applied to a face-detection model and cropped around the detected face with extension of 15% per dimension. The image from the right sensor is then aligned to the left crop with four degrees of freedom in terms of scale and translation. Subsequently, the disparity maps, created based on the spatial structure of the left sensor, are cropped and concatenated with the two sensors crops. Finally, the 10-channels input is resized to 128 × 128 pixels and is fed into the disparity model.

---

[2] For further information about the exact Scipy interpolation implementation: https://docs.scipy.org/doc/scipy/reference/generated/scipy.interpolate.griddata.html.

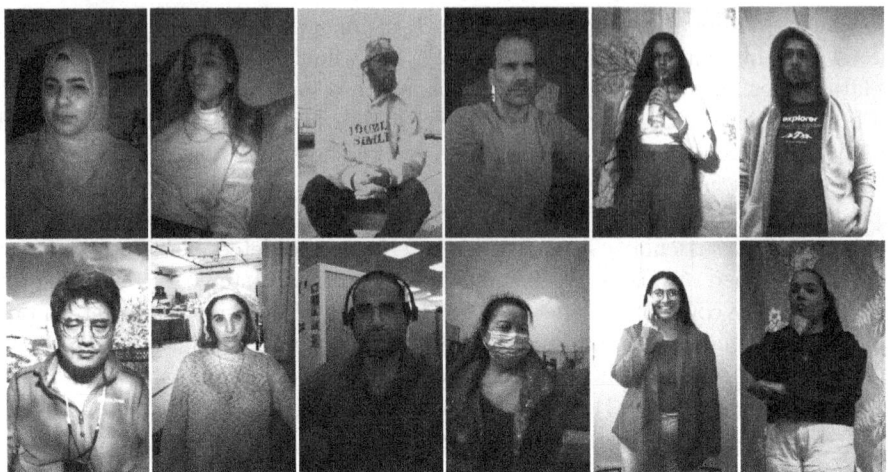

Fig. 3. Examples for live samples in the collected data.

Model Details. To achieve optimal product efficiency and the ability to operate on an edge device, the disparity model is based on a modified version of MobileNetV2 architecture [17]. The Disparity model comprises 27 convolution layers, each followed by a batch normalization layer and a ReLU activation function. This model contains approximately 1 million trainable parameters.

In security systems it is essential to obtain reliable predictive probabilities. This is particularly crucial when integrating multiple models, each with distinct probability decision thresholds. However, the conventional SoftMax loss function

Fig. 4. Examples for spoof samples in the collected data.

tends to exhibit overconfidence, which subsequently results in outputs that are unreliable as probability distributions [2,14,18]. To address this issue, a high Evidential Deep Learning loss is employed during the training of the model, thereby ensuring the generation of stable and well-calibrated outputs [18].

Data Augmentations. The disparity model employs a multi-modal approach, which results in a unique methodology for data augmentations during training. This technique comprises three levels of augmentation:

- Landmarks Augmentations. Augmentations are performed on facial landmarks to enhance stability against landmark extractor errors, which could lead to errors in the disparity maps. These augmentations include noising random number of landmarks, with random translation values per landmark. Another type of facial landmark augmentation simulates landmark extractor bias for an entire facial organ region (e.g., a shift in nose landmarks coordinates). For this augmentation, a facial organ is uniformly sampled, and all landmarks in that region are translated by the same magnitude. In both augmentations, the magnitude of translation is determined by a uniform sampling method, with a maximum limit set to 6% of the respective facial dimension. Additionally, we introduce the outlier augmentation, where the magnitude of the translation is uniformly sampled between 6% to 14% of the face size per dimension. In this scenario, up to four facial landmarks are translated with a larger magnitude to simulate outliers.
- Sensor Intensity Augmentations. To enhance robustness against a range of variables that influence the intensity of sensor outputs, a series of standard augmentations are applied directly to the output channels of these sensors. These augmentations include color jittering and mean-variance adjustments, which modify the brightness and contrast within the image. Additionally, noise is introduced to alter the intensity of individual pixels across the image, and motion blur is applied to mimic the blurring effect caused by head movements. It is important to note that these augmentations are exclusively applied to the direct outputs of the sensors, and not to the disparity maps.
- Spatial Augmentations. These augmentations, which include horizontal flipping, rotation, and shearing, are designed to effectively expand the training dataset. Furthermore, a cut-out augmentation technique is employed, wherein a specific region of the input is masked to minimize the model's dependency on particular regions during training. The ratio between the face and the background size is also augmented, and is being uniformly sampled between 40% to 80% during the cropping process. Additionally, the bounding box of the face undergoes a random translation, up to 20% of its size, prior to the cropping process. This is done to enhance the model's robustness against the face detector's errors. The same set of spatial augmentations is applied across all modalities including the disparity maps.

3.4 Model Ensemble Setup

The disparity model is designed to counteract unique structures of spoof attacks, particularly 2D attacks, by using additional proxy-depth knowledge. However, the disparity maps can mislead the model in 3D attacks scenarios where face geometry closely mimics reality. To address this, two additional models are trained to address 3D attacks.

The first additional model, referred to as the Left Model, processes inputs from the left sensor's four channels. The second model, coined as the Right Model, is designed to process data from the right sensor's four channels. Both these models share the same architectural design as the Disparity Model, with the exception of the input layer size. They also employ the same data augmentation techniques, barring the landmarks augmentations. Eventually, these three models are integrated into a 3-model-ensemble. The final decision is determined by an 'OR' operation applied to the spoof predictions. I.e. if any one of the models predicts a spoof attack for a given system input, the ensemble prediction is classified as a spoof attack.

Each model's decision threshold is determined using a dedicated software that seeks an optimal threshold combination among the models. This search is conducted in two stages: initially at high level with high granularity iterations, followed by a more detailed search with smaller granularities, centered around the results from the high-level search. This approach ensures a comprehensive and precise threshold determination.

4 Experiments

4.1 Data

In this study, we demonstrate our multi-modal approach, using data collected from the Intel® RealSense™ID Solution F455 NIR sensors, which comprises two non-calibrated sensors. The data was captured using 20 distinct systems, to avoid over-fitting to a single device. The collected live samples contained 10.7K different identities in various conditions, with total amount of approximately 1.7M images. These conditions included diverse background lighting, distances from the device (up to 2 m), head poses (up to 40 °C for yaw, pitch, and roll), locations (both indoors and outdoors), occluding accessories (such as hats, sunglasses, and face COVID-19 masks), and facial expressions (Fig. 3).

Moreover, variety of spoof attacks were collected. The 2D attacks involved printed papers of different sizes (A3, A4), television screens, and mobile phone screens as well as curved screens. In each 2D spoof attack, a face that fulfilled the real footage criteria was displayed. The 3D attacks incorporated cut papers placed over a live instance's face that revealed its nose, papers rolled into a cylinder, and latex masks worn by live individuals. In total, 2M various spoof data were collected (Fig. 4).

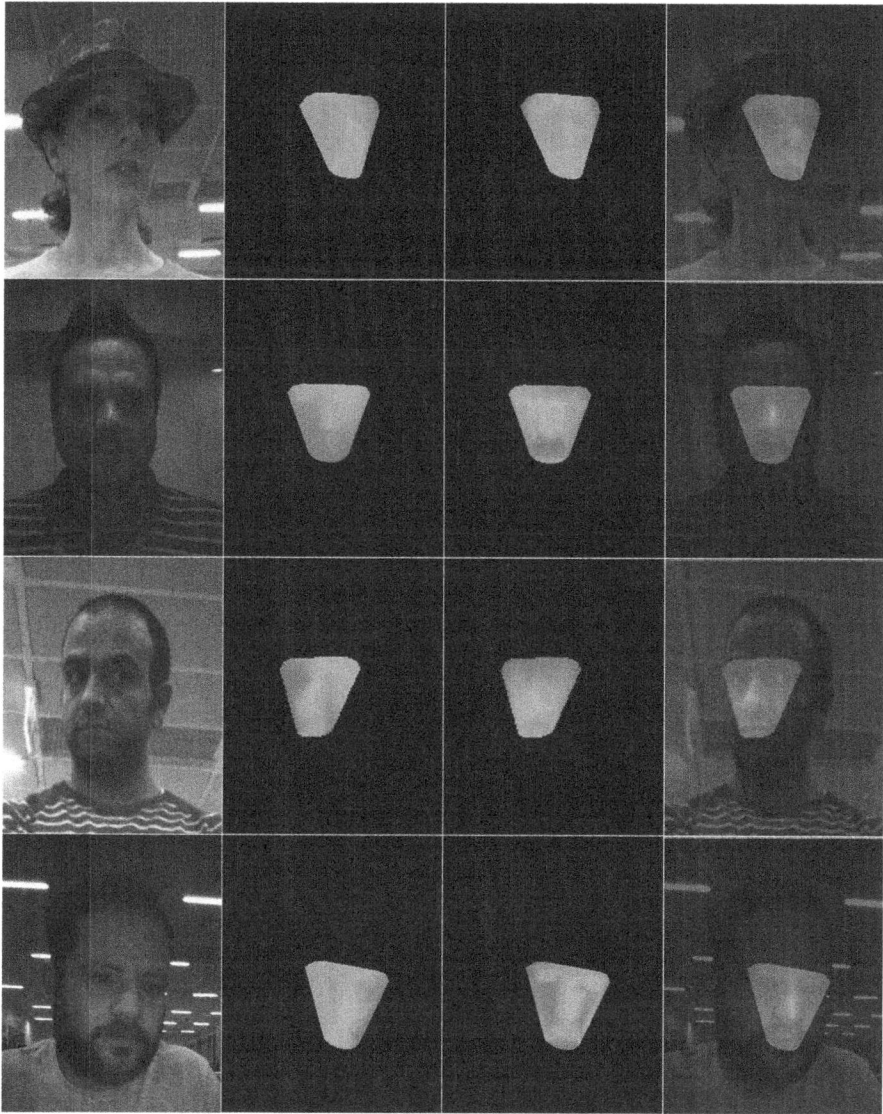

Fig. 5. Examples for disparity maps produced from live samples. The leftmost column shows the original image, while the next two columns display color-coded $dispmap_x$ and $dispmap_y$, with green indicating high disparity. The rightmost column overlays both maps on the original image. (Color figure online)

The dataset was divided such that 85% was allocated for training and 15% for validation. Additionally, an external test set comprising approximately 100,000 samples of both live and spoof attacks was collected separately to enhance the generalization of the evaluation. It is important to note that each dataset con-

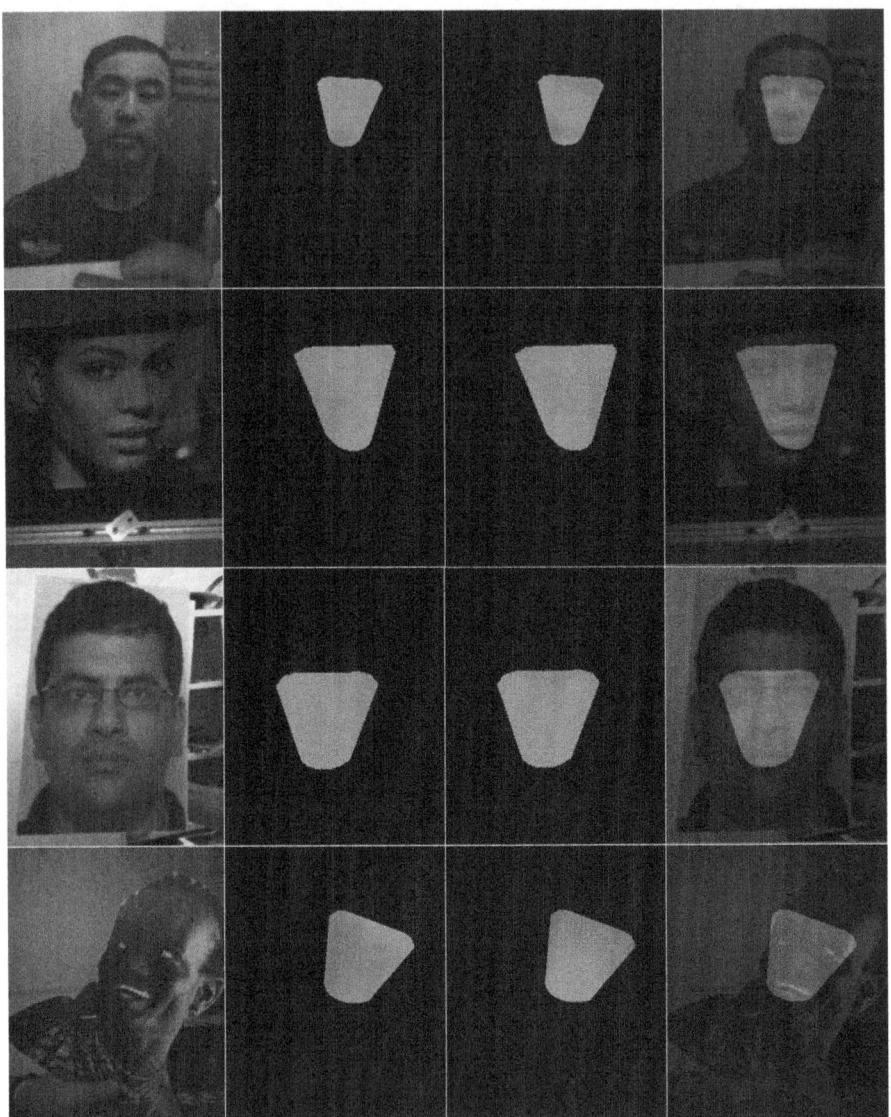

Fig. 6. Examples for Disparity maps produced from 2D spoof attacks samples. The leftmost column shows the original image, while the next two columns display color-coded $dispmap_x$ and $dispmap_y$, with green indicating high disparity. The rightmost column overlays both maps on the original image. (Color figure online)

tained different individual subjects. In the test and validation datasets, the proportion of 2D attacks within the total spoof data is larger than that of 3D attacks. This is based on the belief that 2D attacks more accurately reflect real-life scenarios, as they are easier to produce using simple means.

Table 1. Methods comparison for live and 2D attacks

	EER	FNR FPR = 0.05	FNR FPR = 0.03	FNR FPR = 0.01
Facial Features Pairs	34.45%	73.17%	78.93%	85.69%
CNN	6.47%	7.79%	10.83%	18.89%
Patch-CNN	5.87%	6.84%	9.89%	16.31%
Multilevel fusion	4.16%	3.99%	4.39%	10.71%
Disparity Model	**1.71%**	**0.64%**	**1.12%**	**2.77%**

Lower values indicate better performance.

4.2 Metrics

In our convention, live samples are classified as positive instances, while samples of spoof attacks are classified as negative instances. Consequently, the False Negative Rate (FNR) represents the proportion of failures among all live instances. On the other hand, the False Positive Rate (FPR) signifies the proportion of False predictions among all spoof attack instances.

The primary metric for assessing the models is the Equal Error Rate (EER), which is the error rate at which both FNR and FPR are equal. This approach ensures a balanced evaluation of the model's performance in identifying both positive and negative instances.

For product-oriented evaluation of the models, additional metrics are employed. In these cases, the decision thresholds are calibrated to ensure the model predicts a predefined FPR on the test benchmark. Once the FPR is fixed, the model's performance is assessed based on its FNR at the corresponding threshold. This evaluation is conducted for FPR values of 5% ($\frac{5}{100}$ miss acceptance rate), 3% ($\frac{3}{100}$ miss acceptance rate), and 1% ($\frac{1}{100}$ miss acceptance rate).

4.3 Experimental Setup

The disparity model is specifically designed to counter 2D attacks by leveraging additional proxy-depth knowledge. Consequently, we train and evaluate it using only live and 2D attacks samples. As baselines, we implemented four other anti-spoofing approaches inspired by the literature.

The first approach, termed Facial Features Pairs, involves calculating the Euclidean distance between all pairs of facial landmarks [3], resulting in a 2025-feature vector derived from 45 facial landmarks of each sensor source. Several multi-layer perceptrons (MLPs) were examined using the feature vectors as inputs, and we report the results for the MLP with the best performance.

Additionally, we trained a CNN model that processes data from both sensors as an 8-channel input. This model shares the same architecture as the disparity model, except for the first input layer. Another approach examined is the Patch-CNN, where patches of the concatenated data are processed by a shared CNN, and the final prediction is averaged among all patch outputs, as described in [4].

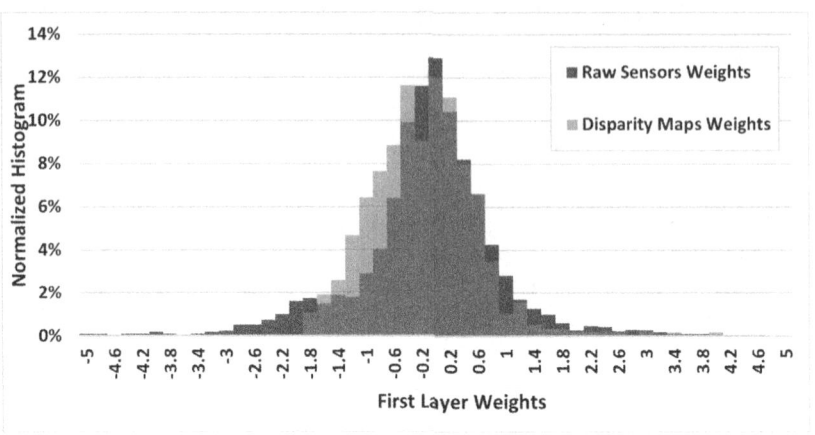

Fig. 7. First Layer's weights distribution.

Furthermore, we implemented the Multilevel Fusion model architecture from [8], adjusting the model size to approximately 1 million trainable parameters, similar to the size of the disparity model. In the original paper, the authors integrated data from Visual and NIR sensors at three steps of the deep learning pipeline [8]. Here, we perform the same integration, but by using data from the two NIR sensors of the Intel® RealSense™ ID Solution F455 device.

All models were trained on the same dataset using the TensorFlow framework [1] and two GeForce GTX 1080 Ti GPUs. We employed the ADAM optimizer [10] with a momentum of 0.9 and a learning rate of 1e-4. The training process involved a batch size of 32 over 20 epochs, where the checkpoint with the highest accuracy on the validation set was reported.

Finally, we trained the Left and Right models as complementary components of the model ensemble, specifically designed to address 3D attacks. These models share the same architecture and training procedure as the Disparity Model, with the addition of incorporating instances of 3D attacks into the dataset.

5 Results

5.1 Disparity Maps Examples

Figure 5 and Fig. 6 illustrate additional examples of live and spoof disparity maps, respectively. In these figures, each row corresponds to a different subject. The leftmost column displays the original image. Moving from left to right, the subsequent columns show the disparity maps generated along the horizontal axis ($dispmap_x$) and the vertical axis ($dispmap_y$). For ease of visualization, each disparity map is color-coded, with green indicating higher disparity values than red. Finally, to highlight the three-dimensional structure of the disparity spatially, both disparity maps are overlayed on the original image in the rightmost column. As observed, the live disparity maps replicate the three-dimensional structure of

Table 2. Disparity Model Ablation Study.

Components			Metric		
Left Sensor	Right Sensor	Disparity Maps	EER	FNR sFPR = 0.05	FNR FPR = 0.01
+		+	6.82%	9.01%	24.33%
	+	+	2.23%	1.02%	4.46%
+	+		6.47%	7.79%	18.89%
+	+	+	1.71%	0.64%	2.77%

Lower values indicate better performance.

the subject, whereas the disparity in two-dimensional spoof attacks exhibits a planar structure with linear spatial variations.

5.2 2D Attacks Comparison

In Table 1, we present our experimental results for the Disparity Model on the test benchmark, which includes both live and 2D attacks. Additionally, we provide results for other anti-spoofing methods across various metrics. The best result in each metric is highlighted in bold. We observe that our method achieves better results than other previous approaches in all metrics.

The Facial Features Pairs approach, which utilizes distances between facial landmarks including their sparse disparity information, performs poorly in our challenging domain. This can be attributed to its lack of texture information and the absence of spatial disparity information, which our method includes. Texture-based approaches that directly use the sensors data show better performance, with the Multilevel Fusion model outperforming the others with an EER of 4.16%.

However, our multi-modal method, which incorporates disparity maps in addition to raw sensors data as texture, demonstrates superior performance compared to the Multilevel Fusion model. Specifically, our method improves the EER by 2.45% and the FNR by 3.35%, 3.27%, and 7.94% at spoof acceptance rates of $\frac{5}{100}$, $\frac{3}{100}$, and $\frac{1}{100}$, respectively.

Furthermore, the ablation study presented in Table 2 highlights the significance of disparity maps in the disparity model. The results indicate that integrating disparity maps with the raw data from the right sensor (that includes an IR channel) outperforms the integration with the data from the left sensor. However, the combination of all components results in the highest performance.

Moreover, we analyzed the weights from the first convolutional layer of the Disparity model to assess the impact of each input type on the model's output. The disparity maps reached a maximum of value of 480, while the raw sensor data values could attain up to 1024. To ensure a fair comparison, the kernel weights of the disparity maps were scaled by a factor of ($\frac{480}{1024}$). The normalized histogram of the first layer's weights, as shown in Fig. 7, indicates that the weight values corresponding to the disparity maps are distributed similarly to those of the raw sensor data. This suggests that both input types contribute equally to the model's decision making.

Table 3. Model Ensemble results.

Spoof Attacks Means	EER	FNR FPR = 0.05	FNR FPR = 0.01	Test Set Size
Paper A4	2.10%	0.8%	6%	43132
Paper A3	1.48%	0.63%	1.82%	45242
TV screen	1.39%	0.32%	1.8%	41447
Desktop screen	0.86%	0.18%	0.65%	26696
Laptop screen	2.67%	1.35%	7.58%	35531
Tablet screen	0.74%	0.11%	0.52%	37332
Mobile Phone screen	0.75%	0.1%	0.57%	26745
Paper on Face	2.56%	1.34%	3.65%	26015
Latex Masks	3.57%	3.05%	6.11%	26119
All	2.04%	0.79%	3.83%	113403

Lower values indicate better performance.

5.3 Model Ensemble

Our ensemble comprises three models: the Left Model, the Right Model, and the Disparity Model. This ensemble was evaluated on the complete test set, which includes both 2D and 3D attacks. As presented in Table 3, the overall benchmark, encompassing all types of spoof attacks, yielded an Equal Error Rate (EER) of 2.04%, while for a false acceptance rate of $\frac{1}{100}$, FNR is 3.83%. Among the various spoof attack means, the tablet screen, mobile phone screen, and desktop screen exhibited the lowest EER of 0.74%, 0.75%, and 0.86%, respectively. In contrast, the challenging 3D Latex Masks, had the highest EER of 3.57%.

6 Conclusion

A crucial component in anti-spoofing systems is depth information, which is essential for addressing 2D attacks that exhibit unique 3D structures. However, systems that provide depth information are typically expensive and challenging to scale across large, distributed edge device networks. Conversely, non-calibrated systems are more cost-effective but lack depth information.

In this work, we introduce a novel method that overcomes this trade-off by leveraging facial feature knowledge to create proxy-depth maps from pairs of sensors. Our pipeline involves acquiring and processing images from both sensors, detecting faces, and extracting facial landmarks from each image. Using these pairs of facial landmarks, we calculate disparity in each dimension and interpolate all disparity points to produce a disparity map containing relative depth information.

We demonstrate the effectiveness of our method by incorporating the disparity maps as an additional input to a FAS system for edge devices. Our multi-modality anti-spoofing model provides a robust solution for FAS systems in real-life scenarios, outperforming other methods. Specifically, our method was tested on a large benchmark with approximately 100,000 samples, achieving an Equal Error Rate (EER) of 1.75%, which is 2.45% lower than the best compared method results. The Importance of the Disparity maps, is reflected in the conducted ablation study and in the CNN weights analysis as well. Furthermore, we show the effectiveness of a three-model ensemble over a larger benchmark that includes 3D attacks, achieving an EER of 2.04% and an FNR of 3.83% at a $\frac{1}{100}$ miss acceptance rate.

Future research could focus on enhancing the architecture of the Disparity Model by integrating attention mechanisms to better counter 3D spoof attacks. Additionally, exploring the use of advanced neural network architectures and transfer learning techniques may further improve the model's robustness and accuracy in diverse spoofing scenarios.

Overall, our work provides state-of-the-art (SOTA) results for non-calibrated sensor systems in the anti-spoofing task. The study was performed with data collected from the Intel® RealSense™ ID Solution F455 device, but our methodology can be performed on other types of non-calibrated sensors as well.

Acknowledgments. The authors would like to thank Nelkenbaum Ilya for developing sensor-specific Face-Detection module. At the same time the authors would like to thank Rubinstein Ron for developing the sensor-specific facial landmarks extraction model.

Disclosure of Interests. The authors have no competing interests to declare that are relevant to the content of this article.

Appendix

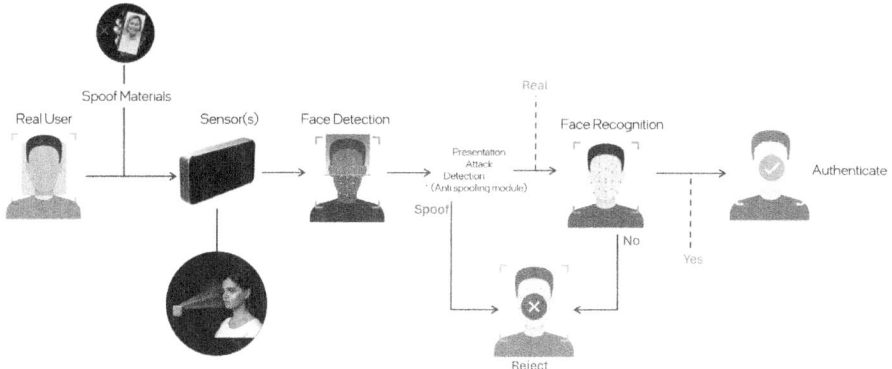

Fig. 8. Schematic view of typical Face Recognition pipeline.

A Face Authentication Pipeline

A typical pipeline for Face Authentication (FA) begins with image acquisition. The face within the image is detected using a dedicated face detector model, which predicts the bounding box around the face. Once the face is detected, by utilizing a dedicated anti-spoof model, it undergoes discrimination based on various features to determine whether it is a live face or a spoof attack. If the anti-spoofing step identifies the processed image as a spoof, the pipeline is terminated. Otherwise, representative features are extracted from the image in the final step. These image features are then compared to other features representing a specific identity to ascertain whether the captured image corresponds to that specific identity. Figure 8 illustrates the FA pipeline.

B Raw Bayer Pattern Process

In our pipeline the raw Bayer pattern of the sensor is processed directly (without demosaicing). The Bayer pattern of each sensor consists of 2×2 pixels, where each pixel within this pattern is considered as a single channel, resulting in a four-channel input for each sensor. Additionally, the right sensor includes an infrared (IR) channel with its own dedicated pixels. An example for left sensor pattern is presented in Fig. 9.

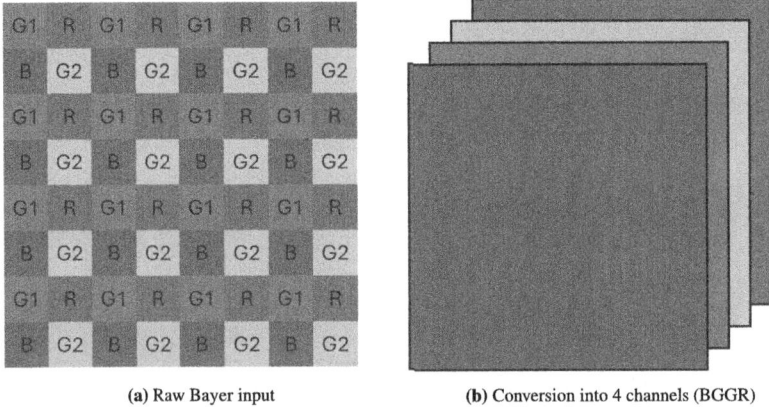

(a) Raw Bayer input   (b) Conversion into 4 channels (BGGR)

Fig. 9. Conversion process of Bayer pattern into four Channels BGGR image. The spatial resolution is reduced by a factor of two in each dimension to create four channels image instead of one.

C Supplementary Models

As part of the pipeline, each sensor's data is cropped around the face using a dedicated face detector (FD) model. This FD model processes a single channel from the sensor (green) and predicts the coordinates of a bounding box around the face, along with a confidence score. The architecture of the FD model is based on YOLO, and it refines its initial anchors during the detection process [15]. The model is trained on grayscale images from approximately 200,000 subjects and is subsequently fine-tuned with around 5,000 annotated samples collected from the Intel® RealSense™ ID Solution F455. Another integral component of our pipeline is the Facial Landmarks Extractor (LE). Similar to the Face Detector (FD), the LE processes a single channel and predicts the coordinates of 45 facial landmarks: 5 for each eyebrow, 7 for each eye, 9 for the nose, and 12 for the lips. The architecture of the LE is a variation of U-Net [16], followed by a CNN regressor to predict the 45 2D coordinates. It is trained using approximately 240,000 images rendered from 3D scans under various environmental conditions, head poses, and lighting scenarios. Additionally, around 160,000 samples containing RGB images and images captured with the Intel® RealSense™ ID Solution F455 were labeled and incorporated into the training process.

References

1. Abadi, M.: Tensorflow: learning functions at scale. In: Proceedings of the 21st ACM SIGPLAN International Conference on Functional Programming, pp. 1–1 (2016)
2. Achrack, O., Kellerman, R., Barzilay, O.: Multi-loss sub-ensembles for accurate classification with uncertainty estimation. arXiv preprint arXiv:2010.01917 (2020)
3. Anthony, P., Ay, B.: Active face spoof detection using image distortion analysis. Turkish J. Sci. Technol. **17**(2), 435–450 (2022)
4. Atoum, Y., Liu, Y., Jourabloo, A., Liu, X.: Face anti-spoofing using patch and depth-based CNNs. In: 2017 IEEE International Joint Conference on Biometrics (IJCB), pp. 319–328. IEEE (2017)
5. Ge, H., Tu, X., Ai, W., Luo, Y., Ma, Z., Xie, M.: Face anti-spoofing by the enhancement of temporal motion. In: 2020 2nd International Conference on Advances in Computer Technology, Information Science and Communications (CTISC), pp. 106–111. IEEE (2020)
6. Greff, K., Srivastava, R.K., Koutník, J., Steunebrink, B.R., Schmidhuber, J.: LSTM: a search space odyssey. IEEE Trans. Neural Netw. Learn. Syst. **28**(10), 2222–2232 (2016)
7. Hu, J., Shen, L., Sun, G.: Squeeze-and-excitation networks. In: Proceedings of the IEEE Conference on Computer Vision and Pattern Recognition, pp. 7132–7141 (2018)
8. Jiang, F., Liu, P., Zhou, X.: Multilevel fusing paired visible light and near-infrared spectral images for face anti-spoofing. Pattern Recogn. Lett. **128**, 30–37 (2019)
9. Kendall, A., Badrinarayanan, V., Cipolla, R.: Bayesian SegNet: model uncertainty in deep convolutional encoder-decoder architectures for scene understanding. arXiv preprint arXiv:1511.02680 (2015)
10. Kingma, D.P.: Adam: A method for stochastic optimization. arXiv preprint arXiv:1412.6980 (2014)
11. Li, X., Komulainen, J., Zhao, G., Yuen, P.C., Pietikäinen, M.: Generalized face anti-spoofing by detecting pulse from face videos. In: 2016 23rd International Conference on Pattern Recognition (ICPR), pp. 4244–4249. IEEE (2016)

12. Li, X., Gunturk, B., Zhang, L.: Image demosaicing: a systematic survey. In: Visual Communications and Image Processing 2008, vol. 6822, pp. 489–503. SPIE (2008)
13. Lin, X., et al.: Suppress and rebalance: Towards generalized multi-modal face anti-spoofing. In: Proceedings of the IEEE/CVF Conference on Computer Vision and Pattern Recognition, pp. 211–221 (2024)
14. Neumann, L., Zisserman, A., Vedaldi, A.: Relaxed softmax: efficient confidence auto-calibration for safe pedestrian detection (2018)
15. Redmon, J.: You only look once: Unified, real-time object detection. In: Proceedings of the IEEE Conference on Computer Vision and Pattern Recognition (2016)
16. Ronneberger, O., Fischer, P., Brox, T.: U-Net: Convolutional Networks for Biomedical Image Segmentation. In: Navab, N., Hornegger, J., Wells, W.M., Frangi, A.F. (eds.) MICCAI 2015. LNCS, vol. 9351, pp. 234–241. Springer, Cham (2015). https://doi.org/10.1007/978-3-319-24574-4_28
17. Sandler, M., Howard, A., Zhu, M., Zhmoginov, A., Chen, L.C.: MobilenetV2: inverted residuals and linear bottlenecks. In: Proceedings of the IEEE Conference on Computer Vision and Pattern Recognition, pp. 4510–4520 (2018)
18. Sensoy, M., Kaplan, L., Kandemir, M.: Evidential deep learning to quantify classification uncertainty. In: Advances in Neural Information Processing Systems, vol. 31 (2018)
19. Steiner, H., Kolb, A., Jung, N.: Reliable face anti-spoofing using multispectral SWIR imaging. In: 2016 International Conference on Biometrics (ICB), pp. 1–8. IEEE (2016)
20. Virtanen, P., et al.: SciPy 1.0 Contributors: SciPy 1.0: fundamental algorithms for scientific computing in Python. Nat. Methods **17**, 261–272 (2020). https://doi.org/10.1038/s41592-019-0686-2
21. Wang, Y., Nian, F., Li, T., Meng, Z., Wang, K.: Robust face anti-spoofing with depth information. J. Vis. Commun. Image Represent. **49**, 332–337 (2017)
22. Wu, H.Y., Rubinstein, M., Shih, E., Guttag, J., Durand, F., Freeman, W.: Eulerian video magnification for revealing subtle changes in the world. ACM Trans. Graphics (TOG) **31**(4), 1–8 (2012)
23. Yang, X., et al.: Face anti-spoofing: Model matters, so does data. In: Proceedings of the IEEE/CVF Conference on Computer Vision and Pattern Recognition, pp. 3507–3516 (2019)
24. Yu, Z., et al: Multi-modal face anti-spoofing based on central difference networks. In: Proceedings of the IEEE/CVF Conference on Computer Vision and Pattern Recognition Workshops, pp. 650–651 (2020)
25. Yu, Z., et al: Searching central difference convolutional networks for face anti-spoofing. In: Proceedings of the IEEE/CVF Conference on Computer Vision and Pattern Recognition, pp. 5295–5305 (2020)
26. Zhang, L., Sun, N., Wu, X., Luo, D.: Advanced face anti-spoofing with depth segmentation. In: 2022 International Joint Conference on Neural Networks (IJCNN), pp. 1–6 (2022). https://doi.org/10.1109/IJCNN55064.2022.9892826
27. Zhang, S., et al.: A dataset and benchmark for large-scale multi-modal face anti-spoofing. In: Proceedings of the IEEE/CVF Conference on Computer Vision and Pattern Recognition, pp. 919–928 (2019)
28. Zhao, H., Shi, J., Qi, X., Wang, X., Jia, J.: Pyramid scene parsing network. In: Proceedings of the IEEE Conference on Computer Vision and Pattern Recognition, pp. 2881–2890 (2017)

MsResNet: Multi-scale Edge-Enhanced ResNet for RGB-T Image Segmentation

Bikram Adhikari[(⊠)], Siyu Lei, Zoran Durić, and Duminda Wijesekera

Department of Computer Science, George Mason University, Fairfax, VA, USA
{badhika5,slei4,zduric,dwijesek}@gmu.edu

Abstract. Intelligent transportation systems rely heavily on robust scene understanding under varying environmental conditions for decision-making and driver assistance. In this paper, we introduce a novel MsResNet: Multi-scale Edge-Enhanced ResNet for RGB-thermal image segmentation, combining RGB and thermal images to address challenges introduced by varying lighting conditions in scene understanding. MsResNet incorporates multi-scale guided filtering to enhance edge definitions and contrast, and it uses attention-based cross-fusion to dynamically integrate features from RGB and thermal modalities across their spatial dimensions. In addition, a weighted compound loss function refines the predictions at the region, boundary, and pixel levels. Experimental results in the MF and KAIST datasets suggest that MsResNet performs on par with current state-of-the-art models, with reduced parameters and inference time, achieving IoU scores of **59.8** and **50.24**, respectively. These results demonstrate the suitability of the model for real-time ADAS applications and scene understanding.

Keywords: Coordinate Cross Attention (CCA) · Contrast Limited Adaptive Histogram Equalization (CLAHE) · Atrous Spatial Pyramid Pooling (ASPP) · Feature fusion

1 Introduction

Scene understanding and accurate inference of the driving environment help intelligent transportation system in efficient navigation and decision-making. Recent advances in sensor technologies and pattern recognition techniques have enhanced modern vehicles' understanding of their operating context with respect to their surroundings, improving scene inference capabilities and providing drivers with more accurate and pertinent information for advanced driver assistance systems (ADAS). A key feature of modern ADAS is region- or segment-based inference, allowing vehicles and humans to distinguish between distinct regions of interest or obstacles during navigation [17]. One of the most commonly used techniques for segmentation involves capturing an RGB image of the scene and passing it through deep learning-based segmentation models to obtain region segmentation. While economical and easy to implement, RGB-based models are best suited for stationary indoor conditions with proper lighting, as the data can suffer from various noise and disturbances caused by changing lighting, motion, and weather conditions.

Fig. 1. Multi-step guided image enhancement for RGB and thermal images. (a) on the left represents original RGB and thermal image pair, while (b) on the right represents enhanced RGB and thermal image pair.

Fig. 2. Cases depicting issues in segmentation when relying solely on the RGB channel. The top row (a) and (b) represents daytime scenarios, while the bottom row (c) and (d) illustrates nighttime conditions. Case (a): Oversaturation during daytime caused by natural light reflecting off shiny surfaces, thereby occluding objects behind them. Case (b): Challenges in object detection due to blending, either because the object and its surroundings share similar colors or due to lighting conditions. Case (c): Oversaturation during nighttime caused by lights emitted from objects, such as vehicles, which obscure objects behind them. Case (d): A combination of over- and under-saturation during nighttime conditions, caused by low illuminance and external light sources.

To overcome these limitations, researchers have integrated data from multiple sensors to improve unified segmentation models for human and vehicle interaction [31]. RGB-Thermal fusion is one such method, combining thermal images with RGB data to enhance traditional RGB segmentation models. Because thermal images are unaffected by variation in illumination, they can reveal features obscured in RGB images due to overexposure or underexposure [13].

Existing approaches to RGB-T-based semantic segmentation models often treat the thermal image as a fourth input channel, which are then processed through recent advancements in deep segmentation networks [27,31].While effective depending on the chosen network, these approaches can become overly reliant on RGB channels for accurate predictions. As a result, they are prone to lighting inconsistencies, where RGB images may experience over- or under-saturation, as shown in Fig. 2. RGB images are highly susceptible to sudden changes in lighting conditions caused by natural or external light sources.

Although thermal images are also affected by sunlight—particularly when the environment consists of materials with similar thermal conductivity that have been exposed to the sun for prolonged periods—thermal images tend to be more robust than RGB images in cases involving dynamic objects or when the camera itself is in motion, such as in dash cameras. Thermal images are much more feature-rich than RGB images in scenarios of over- and under-saturation, as detailed in the four cases shown in Fig. 2. Furthermore, although large inference models achieve high segmentation accuracy, they may be impractical for deployment in vehicular systems.

To address these challenges, we propose the MsResNet: Multi-scale Edge-Enhanced ResNet model, built on the ResNet101 architecture, for RGB-T-based semantic segmentation in driving scenes. The major contributions of our work are:

- We explore edge features in thermal and RGB images using multi-scale guided filtering. This approach improves contrast and brightness in RGB images, making previously occluded features more visible, while refining edges and enhancing boundary separation in thermal images as seen in Fig. 1. Additionally, we prioritize areas of interest in the environment for feature enhancement by applying weight maps to salient regions in the detail layers extracted through multi-scale filtering. This enhancement has significantly improved segmentation of weak and small regions that are often overlooked in standard inference.
- We also introduce a Coordinate Attention-based Cross-Fusion for feature fusion after inference, which pools input features along spatial dimensions (height and width) to capture long-range dependencies, particularly along edges where RGB and thermal information vary in relevance. This cross-attention fusion mechanism selectively emphasizes features in the RGB and thermal domains based on the strengths of each modality, dynamically weighting regions where each modality excels.
- We use a weighted compound loss at the region, boundary, and pixel levels for parameter optimization of our MsResNet. Experimental results on two urban driving scene datasets demonstrate that our model performs on par with state-of-the-art (SOTA) methods **(achieving an IoU of 59.8 on the MF Dataset [10] and 50.24 on the KAIST Dataset [15])** while requiring significantly fewer training parameters and shorter inference times, making it well-suited for practical applications.

The rest of the paper is organized as follows. Section 2, Related Works, discusses current research on sensor fusion-based semantic segmentation, with a focus on RGB-T. Section 3, Methodology, elaborates on our approach to fusion for efficient semantic segmentation. In Sect. 4, Experimentation and Results, we present the results and findings of our approach on publicly available datasets. Section 5, Discussion, provides insights into our research and outlines future directions. Additionally, Sect. 4.6, Ablation Studies, provides a detailed explanation of our choices in model parameters, an analysis of the approach, and a thorough review of the issues with the existing dataset for RGB-T segmentation.

2 Related Works

Semantic segmentation is an important task in scene understanding. To maintain spatial relationships in the image, the convolution structure is explored widely. With transformer emergence, the attention structure is largely exploited in semantic segmentation models. Attention modules embedded in model structure could improve the adaptive performance of models, enabling them to focus on regions with higher importance, and improve the contextual features extraction. Because of integration of attention with convolution structure, the overall performance of semantic segmentation improves.

2.1 Semantic Segmentation in RGB and Multi Modalities

Long et al. [21] proposed the pioneering model FCN, consisting of fully convolutional layers to address semantic segmentation problems. DeepLab [18] proposed leveraging the convolutional layers and Conditional Random Fields. Based on the FCN, Badrinarayanan et al. [3] employed an encoder and decoder structure, SegNet, with a refined upsample method to perform nonlinear upsampling to recover from low-resolution feature maps. In the medical segmentation field, Ronneberger et al. [25] proposed the U-Net, to combine multi-scale feature information. In DeeplabV2 [4], Chen et al. introduced the atrous spatial pyramid pooling module based on the DeepLab foundation. Zhao et al. [34] proposed PSPNet, pyramid scene parsing network, which combines different-region-based context aggregation through the pyramid pooling module together with the proposed pyramid scene parsing network. Influenced by the self-attention module's success in computer vision tasks [9], researchers also incorporated self-attention modules in semantic segmentation. Strudel et al. [26] proposed Segmenter by fine-tuning pre-trained ViT from image classification. Researchers now focus on multi-modalities, fusing complementary features, including depth, RGB, LiDAR, and multiple views. Yang et al. [30] proposed the CMX model, which fuses RGB and modal-agnostic data sources. To exploit the structure further, Zhang [32] proposed a model, CMNeXt, to fuse RGB data with other types of data sources, whereas RGB works as a pivotal part.

2.2 Semantic Segmentation in RGB-T Modal

While previous works achieved high performance in RGB image semantic segmentation, there is still need for the RGB-T semantic segmentation because the quality of RGB images decreases drastically under low light conditions and therefore feature extraction become problematic. The complementary qualities of RGB and thermal image will make the model more robust under adverse environmental conditions. The RGB sensors also have failures when meeting circumstances such as flares, straight light, and darkness and light switching cases. Fusing the data from RGB and thermal sensors would make the system more safe and robust. The advantages of the specific model could also be transferred to multi-modal structure design. Ha et al. [10] proposed a symmetric structure model, named MFNet. The model design employed two encoders corresponding to RGB and thermal modal, and one decoder for the fused features from two encoders. The features are concatenated together from two encoding modules. The MFNet dataset introduced with the model is exploited in many successive models. Using the similar structure, Sun et al. [27] proposed RTFNet consisting of two encoders one each of RGB modality and thermal modality. By adding the two features element-wise, one decoder works for upsampling and restoring the resolution of the output for both modalities. Based on the RTFNet structure, Deng et al. proposed a FEANet [7] that further exploits the structure by adding a Feature Enhancement Attention Module after each convolution block of ResNet. The attention module is used to further exploit cross-channel and spatial relationships. Different from these designs, Zhang et al. [33] employ a different model, ABMDRNet, including three modules aiming at removing the difference between the two modalities. The modules combine, process and enhance the features from two modalities, then generate a resulting feature to decode. As the encoders extract features, they are trained by comparing the output with the image of the other modality. Another structure design proposed by Zhou et al. [35], GMNet, uses deep and shallow feature fusion modules to fuse and differentiate multiple levels of features. Through interconnecting different levels of features, the decoders generate corresponding segmentation outputs at three kinds of labels. In SGFNet [29], Wang et al. used two special modules in extracting and fusing features of two modalities. After extracting semantic information from thermal images, the features are fused with RGB features at each level.

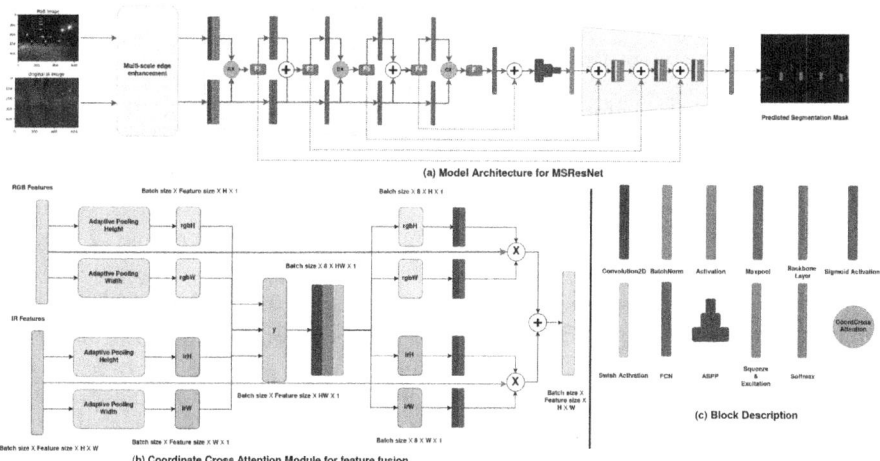

Fig. 3. Architectural description of MsResNet. (a) Overall model architecture of MsResNet. (b) Detail model architecture of Coordinate Cross Attention module involved in feature fusion. (c) Labels for the unnamed blocks used in the model architecture design.

3 Methodology

3.1 Base Model Overview

The base model utilizes an encoder-decoder architecture with a cross-attention-based feature fusion mechanism, as shown in Fig. 3. Inspired by the RTFNet architecture [27], we process the RGB and thermal channels of an image using separate base models. Prior to passing the RGB and thermal images through the inference module, we enhance the thermal image using a weighted importance map generated through our multi-scale edge detection pipeline. The RGB base encoder employs a pre-trained ResNet-101 backbone (DeepLabV3) model [5], which has been pretrained on ImageNet [8] for feature extraction. The thermal encoder mirrors this setup; however, it replaces the first convolution layer to accommodate single-channel thermal inputs. Let F_i^{RGB} and F_i^T denote features obtained by passing the input through $i \in (1, 4)$ blocks of the ResNet model. The intermediate features are then passed into the novel *Coordinate Cross-Attention* (CCA) for fusion. The output from the final encoder and fusion layer goes through an *Atrous Spatial Pyramid Pooling* (ASPP) block, which captures features at multiple scales before feeding them into a *Feature Pyramid Network (FPN)*. The FPN enhances the resolution of feature maps, supplying the decoder model with high-level features while maintaining spatial detail for precise localization.

We introduce a skip connection before the successive decoder block by merging the input to the decoder with intermediate fused outputs from the corresponding encoder blocks. This skip connection from the encoder helps preserve fine details that may be lost during downsampling. The output from the final decoder block serves as the segmentation results. We utilize the weights from the final batch normalization in our loss function to improve weighted loss propagation.

3.2 Edge Enhancement Pre-processing

As shown in Fig. 3 (b), before being passed to the main model, the RGB and thermal images undergo a multi-scale edge enhancement process, which includes a series of filtering, sharpening, and enhancement steps. An edge in color image is defined by discontinuity in three-dimensional color space typically described as a boundary within an image with significant change in intensity compared to neighboring pixels [1]. Initially, the images are decomposed into base and detail layers using a multi-scale guided filtering technique. These decomposed images are then processed through CLAHE (Contrast Limited Adaptive Histogram Equalization) [24] to enhance contrast while preserving details, optimizing the input for the segmentation task.

The multi-scale guided weighted filtering [28] acts as an efficient edge-preserving operator. Starting with single channel thermal image, for various window sizes $r \in \{3, 5, 7\}$, the input image I and guidance image G (which may be the same as the input image) are passed through a guided filter. This filter outputs O by modeling the local relationship between the input and guidance images using linear coefficients a and b, as defined in Eq. 1:

$$O = a \cdot I + b \tag{1}$$

The values of a and b are computed within a local window of size $(2r + 1) \times (2r + 1)$, where:

$$a = \frac{\text{cov}(I, G)}{\sigma_I^2 + \epsilon}, b = \mu_G - a \cdot \mu_I \tag{2}$$

Here, μ_I and μ_G represent the mean values of the input image I and the guidance image G within the window of size r, σ_I^2 is the variance of I, and $\epsilon = 0.01$ is a regularization term that controls the smoothness. From the guided filter, we get the base and detail feature layers across all the scales of r.

For each scale's detail layer, we compute a saliency map using frequency-tuned filtering [2]. The saliency maps from adjacent scales $i, i+1$ are compared to create binary weight maps, assigning a value of 1 to pixels where the saliency at the lower scale i is greater than that at the higher scale $i+1$. These binary weight maps are then refined through guided filtering to ensure spatial smoothness and continuity.

For the RGB image, each channel is processed individually through the same multi-scale guided filtering and weight map computation. The detail layers are then combined with the CLAHE-enhanced base layer. Figure 1 illustrates the improvement in edge definitions for the RGB and thermal images after processing through the multi-scale edge enhancement module.

3.3 Coordinate Cross-Attention (CCA) for Feature Fusion

Building on fusion techniques used in feature fusion for image processing [11,12], [22], we propose a variant of coordinate attention to fuse the RGB and thermal features in our work. As shown in Fig. 3, the CCA module integrates attention mechanisms over RGB and thermal features by splitting the input tensors along the spatial dimensions of height and width. The features across these dimensions are pooled independently, allowing the network to capture long-range dependencies more effectively than traditional attention mechanisms.

The pooled RGB and thermal features are concatenated and passed through a series of convolutional and batch normalization layers, followed by the final Swish activation function [23], defined as:

$$Swish(x) = x \cdot (1 + exp(-x))^{-1} \quad (3)$$

As illustrated in Fig. 3(b), the concatenated features are then reassigned and processed through a convolutional layer to generate attention maps along the spatial dimensions. These learned attention maps are applied to reweight the original input features, enhancing key areas across the height and width dimensions as described by the following equation:

$$fusedFeature = identityFeature \times a_h^{feature} \times a_w^{feature} \quad (4)$$

where, $fusedFeature$ represents the attention map-fused RGB/thermal features, and a_h and a_w represent the spatial attention maps along the height and width for these features. Finally, the thermal and RGB features are summed and passed through SE block [14], computed as:

$$y = \sigma(W_2 \cdot ReLU(W_1 \cdot (z))) \quad (5)$$

where $z = AvgPool(fusedFeature)$ represents the global average pooling of the fused features, W_1 and W_2 are learned weights in the fully connected layers, and σ is the sigmoid activation. The SE block recalibrates the features by learning channel-wise dependencies, ensuring that the channels most relevant to the segmentation task are given higher emphasis.

3.4 Composite Loss Function

To optimize the performance of our model, we design a composite loss function that integrates Dice loss with focal regularization, cross-entropy loss, and multiclass root mean squared error (MSE). This combination aims to address class imbalances, penalize incorrect predictions, and focus on difficult examples. The multiclass MSE loss is defined as:

$$MSE(y_{true}, y_{pred}) = (y_{true} - y_{pred})^2 \qquad (6)$$

The Root Mean Squared Error is thus given as:

$$Loss_{RMSE} = \sqrt{mean(MSE + \epsilon)}, \qquad (7)$$

where y_{pred} is predicted segmentation mask, y_{true} is true segmentation mask and ϵ is a regularization constant.

Dice loss measures the overlap between the predicted and ground truth distributions, while focal loss addresses class imbalance by focusing on hard-to-classify examples. We combine Dice loss with focal regularization, as defined by:

$$Loss_{DF} = loss_{Dice} + loss_{focal}, \qquad (8)$$

where,

$$loss_{Dice} = 1 - \frac{2\sum(y_{pred} \cdot y_{true})}{\sum y_{pred} + \sum y_{true} + \epsilon} \qquad (9)$$

where, y_{pred} is predicted segmentation mask, y_{true} is true segmentation mask and ϵ is a regularization constant set to 10^{-6} to avoid division by 0. The formula for focal loss is given as:

$$loss_{focal} = -\alpha \cdot (1 - p_t)^\gamma \cdot log(p_t), \qquad (10)$$

where α is balancing parameter set to 1.2, p_t is the predicted probability for the true class deduced by using the softmax function applied to the model's output logits and γ is set to 2 to focus and improve model inferences on hard classes.

Finally, we integrate $Loss_{RMSE}$ and $Loss_{DF}$ in a weighted fashion with cross entropy loss $Loss_{ce}$ given as:

$$Loss_{ce} = -\frac{1}{N} \sum_{n=1}^{N} \sum_{i=1}^{C} y_{n,i} \log(p_{n,i}), \qquad (11)$$

where N is the batch size, C is the number of classes, $y_{n,i}$ is the one-hot encoded ground truth label for the ith class of the nth sample and $p_{n,i}$ similar to p_t is the predicted probability for the ith of the nth sample obtained by passing output logits through a softmax function. The final composite loss function is given as:

$$Loss_{total} = w_{df} \cdot Loss_{DF} + w_{ce} \cdot Loss_{ce} + w_{MSE} \cdot Loss_{MSE}, \qquad (12)$$

The values for w_{df}, w_{cross}, w_{MSE}, λ_F were determined through extensive experimentation, which is detailed in the ablation study subsection.

4 Experimentation and Results

4.1 Dataset Introduction

MF Dataset. The MF dataset, introduced at the 2017 IROS as part of the MFNet model implementation [10], contains RGB and thermal images captured at a resolution of 480×640 pixels. It consists of 1,569 images of urban driving scenes, with 820 daytime images and 749 nighttime images. The dataset is designed to segment images into eight commonly encountered classes in driving scenarios: car, person, bike, curve, car stop, guardrail, color cone, and bump.

KAIST Dataset. Originally introduced as a dataset for pedestrian detection [15], the KAIST dataset was later adapted for evaluating datasets and models in RGB-T-based segmentation tasks [16]. This modified version contains 950 RGB and thermal images with a resolution of 640×512 pixels. This dataset is more detailed and is designed to segment images into 19 classes following the Cityscapes [6] annotation format: road, sidewalk, building, wall, fence, pole, traffic light, traffic sign, vegetation, terrain, sky, person, rider, car, truck, bus, train, motorcycle, and bicycle.

4.2 Training

For model training, we used an Intel Core i9 processor with an NVIDIA RTX 3060Ti graphics card. For the MF Dataset, we followed the data splits and preparation from RTFNet [27], which allocated approximately 16% of the data for both testing and validation, with the remaining 68% reserved for training. For the KAIST Dataset, we utilized the data splits from CMX [31] to train and test the model. We set the batch size to two and employed a progressively decaying learning rate. The model was trained for 200 epochs or until convergence.

4.3 Evaluation on MF Dataset

Table 1 compares our proposed MsResNet model with well-established models on the MF Dataset. The results are based on data reported in their respective papers and the findings presented in CMX [31]. The MsResNet model, utilizing the ResNet-101 backbone, outperforms or matches existing models with a mean accuracy (mAcc) of 73.8 and a mean intersection over union (mIoU) of 59.5 across all classes in the MF Dataset. We further evaluated the model's performance on the Daytime and Nighttime RGB-T splits, as shown in Table 2. Figure 4 shows the performance of MsResNet in segmentation tasks at night and day, comparing it to current SOTA models, RTFNet and FEANet. In this figure, we observe that MsResNet performs better in segmenting minority classes, such as curves and bumps, which are not clearly visible in either the RGB or thermal images. We attribute this improvement to the image edge-filtering enhancement. However, this enhancement also leads to some minor erroneous detections, which we discuss in our ablation study. However, as shown in Table 1, MsResNet consistently outperformed other models on both larger classes, such as Cars and Pedestrians, while also maintaining performance on par with state-of-the-art models for more challenging smaller classes, such as guardrails, curves, and bumps. We attribute this improvement to the combination of pre-processing enhancements, efficient feature fusion, and the careful selection and fine-tuning of loss functions.

Based on comparisons with existing research, our model performs best in semantic segmentation of nighttime scenes with underexposed areas, achieving an mIoU of 59.8 and an mAcc of 74.5. It also matches the best model for daytime scenes with overexposed areas, with an mIoU of 47.2 and an mAcc of 65.3. However, performing segmentation across only 9 classes introduces vagueness in the segmentation mask, with a significant portion of the regions remaining unlabelled.

4.4 Evaluation on KAIST Dataset

In contrast to the limited segmentation in the MF Dataset, the KAIST Dataset provides 20 distinct classes for segmentation, allowing for more diverse and detailed segmentation masks. However, this also makes it more challenging for the model to distinguish between subclasses of a general parent class (e.g., differentiating between a rider and a person). As shown in Table 3, our model excels at segmenting hard-to-detect classes while maintaining accuracy in segmenting easier ones, achieving an mIoU of 50.2 and an accuracy of 55.4. Furthermore, it achieves results comparable to state-of-the-art (SOTA) models, even in more complex and finer segmentation tasks, and has specifically outperformed other models in segmenting obstacles crucial for vehicular perception, such as motorcycles and bikes.

Table 1. Results on the MF Dataset. Highlighted values in each column indicate the highest value in that category while the underlined values indicate the second highest.

Model	Unlabeled	Car	Pedestrian	Bike	Curve	Car Stop	Guardrail	Cone	Bump	Class Average	mIoU
MFNet [10]	96.8	82.9	85.2	74.2	29.2	27.3	0	25.2	43.3	59.1	51.6
SegNet [3]	96.9	83.3	72.1	76.8	58.3	31.9	0	0	63.9	53.7	58.3
RTFNet [27]	98.5	87.4	70.3	62.7	45.3	29.8	0	29.1	55.7	63.7	53.2
CMX [31]	98.3	90.1	75.2	64.5	50.2	35.3	8.5	54.2	60.6	-	59.7
ABMDRNet [33]	97.8	84.8	69.6	60.3	45.1	33.1	5.1	47.4	50	69.5	54.8
FEANet [7]	-	87.8	71.1	61.1	46.5	22.1	6.6	55.3	48.9	73.2	55.3
SegMiF [20]	98.5	91.1	75.2	68	50.8	43	9.7	57.6	57.9	-	61.3
VPFNet [19]	-	87.1	73.9	62.6	48.2	31.7	9.4	52.3	55.3	70.9	57.6
MsResNet (Ours)	98.3	89.3	74.1	64.5	48.7	42.2	8.9	54.7	59.2	74.5	59.8

4.5 General Evaluation of Performance

Based on the analysis of the MsResNet across two datasets, we observed that the models performed exceptionally well in scene segmentation for nighttime images while achieving comparable results for daytime segmentation.

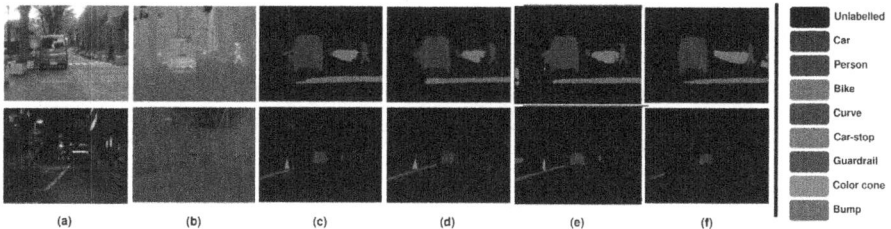

Fig. 4. Performance comparison for segmentation for input (a) RGB image and (b) thermal image; (c) represents model output for FEANet, (d) represents ground truth, (e) model output from Our MsResNet and (f) from RTFNet.

Table 2. Comparative tables of model performance on Nighttime and Daytime images from MF-Dataset. Highlighted values in each column indicate the highest value in that category while the underlined values indicate the second highest.

Model	Daytime mIoU(%)	Nighttime mIoU(%)
MFNet	31.6	36.8
RTFNet	45.8	54.8
ABMDRNet	46.7	55.5
GMNet	<u>49</u>	57.7
FEANet	39.85	50.1
CMX	**52.5**	<u>59.4</u>
MsResNet	47.2 (65.3 mAcc)	**59.8 (74.5 mAcc)**

Although the overall IoU scores of 59.8 and 50.24 may not seem high, it is important to consider the classes included in the segmentation task. For instance, when focusing on the segmentation of large dynamic obstacles such as cars, the IoU scores are significantly higher, at 89.3 and 84.0, respectively.

The drop in overall IoU is primarily due to the segmentation of smaller objects with sharp and fine segmentation masks. These objects often blend into their surroundings because of similar color or thermal depth, such as guardrails (8.9 IoU) in the first dataset and traffic lights (14.2 IoU) in the second dataset. The most challenging class for segmentation has been guardrails due to two primary reasons: first, the nature of the obstacle, which involves narrow segmentation areas and is not completely solid; and second, the improper labeling of guardrails in some images, as observed in Fig. 5. These and other labeling issues may have impacted the overall model's performance and generalization. We have also discussed this issue further in the discussion and future work sections.

4.6 Performance Evaluation

One of the primary objectives of this research was to explore how the model could be effectively utilized in a practical setting for inference. Based on the configuration

Table 3. Results on the KAIST Dataset. Highlighted values in each column indicate the highest value in that category while the underlined values indicate the second highest.

Model	Road	Sidewalk	Building	Fence	Pole	Traffice light	Traffic sign	Sky	Person	Car	Bus	Motorcycle	Bicycle	mIoU
CMX	**97.7**	<u>53.8</u>	**90.2**	**47.1**	**46.2**	<u>10.9</u>	**45.1**	**93.5**	**74.5**	**91.6**	<u>59.7</u>	**46.1**	0.2	<u>46.2</u>
RTFNet	94.6	39.4	86.6	0.6	0	0	0	<u>92.8</u>	58.4	<u>87.7</u>	0	0	0.5	28.7
MFNet	93.5	23.6	75.1	0.1	9.1	0	0	90.4	24	69.6	0.3	0	0.6	24
MsResNet	<u>96.2</u>	**57.4**	81.5	<u>46.8</u>	<u>36.4</u>	**14.2**	<u>35.7</u>	90.7	<u>61.2</u>	84.0	**74.1**	<u>43.0</u>	**23.9**	**50.2**

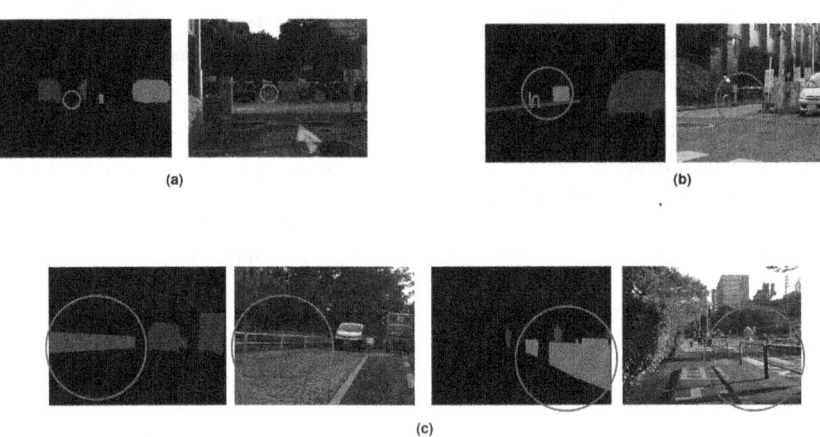

Fig. 5. Discrepancies in the manual annotation of segmentation masks, especially in minority classes, are evident. Instances in this example are taken from the MF Dataset as ground truth label and RGB image pair: Case (a) The guardrails visible between the vehicle and the human are not annotated in the provided labels. Case(b) In some instances, the entire area of the obstacles is segmented, while in others, the segmentation mask closely follows the original shape of the obstacle. Case(c) For certain instances, the metallic railings separating the sidewalks from the vehicle roadway are segmented as guardrails, while in others, they are labeled as car stops.

outlined in Subsection B (Training) of Section IV (Experimentation and Results), we observed during training that pre-processing enhancements did not significantly impact the baseline model's performance but improved the model's predictions by more than 5%.

The model achieved an inference speed of 10–11 images per second during training. In the testing or prediction phase, with a batch size of 1, the average time cost per frame was 24.06 milliseconds, corresponding to an inference speed of 45.82 frames per second (fps). With the model capable of real-time inference, we aim to use it for efficient sensor fusion and segmentation tasks in real-world driving experiments in our future research.

4.7 Ablation Study

While we introduced multi-scale guided weighted filtering, it was crucial to select an appropriate clip size and window size for CLAHE to maintain image details while ensuring color consistency.

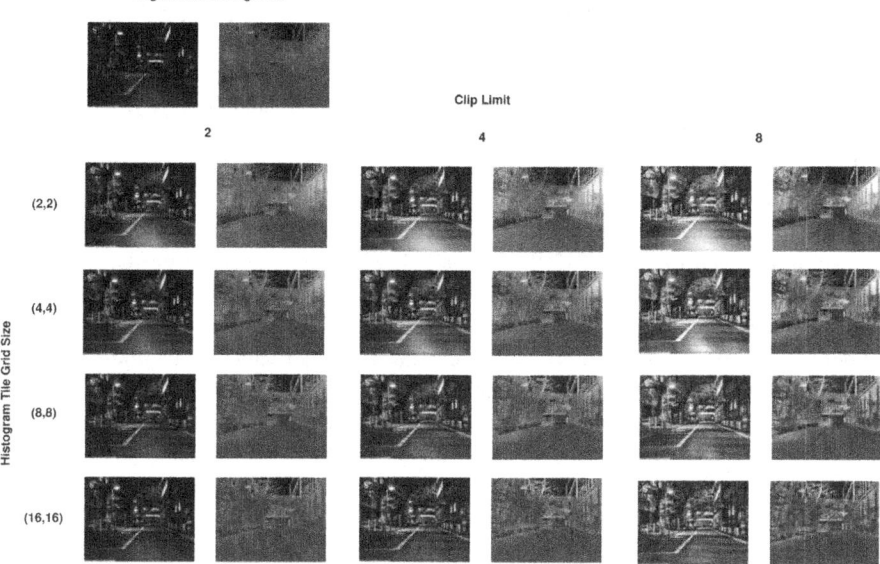

Fig. 6. Effect of Histogram Tile Grid and Clip Limit on Image Contrast and Sharpness in RGB-T Image Pairs: The horizontal axis represents the clip limit for enhancement, and the vertical axis represents the histogram tile size.

To achieve this, we experimented with multiple clip sizes, as shown in Fig. 6. The clip limit specifies the contrast threshold for local histogram equalization, preventing over-amplification of noise by clipping the histogram at a defined value. The tile grid size defines the dimensions of the grid into which the image is divided for local contrast enhancement. Based on our experiments, we found that a clip limit of 4.0 and a tile size of (8,8) worked best for low-light nighttime conditions. However, this still introduced significant noise in the RGB image space during daytime conditions.

As shown in Tables 1 and 3, RTFNet without any block enhancements exhibited a significantly lower mIoU compared to current state-of-the-art (SoTA) models. Pre-processing with edge enhancement and the use of coordinate cross-attention to merge RGB and thermal features resulted in improved performance across all classes in both the MF Dataset and the KP Dataset.

Regarding the specific enhancement blocks used in our experiments, the ASPP block with Squeeze and Excitation contributed to a 3% improvement in overall performance on the MF Dataset, while the CCA block combined with pre-processing accounted for a 4% performance gain over the baseline RTFNet model. However, during parameter tuning of the CCA-based feature merging, we observed that although CCA blocks enhanced model performance, they also introduced additional computational costs, which increased with the number of CCA blocks. To balance accuracy and efficiency, alternating CCA blocks with traditional summative feature merging yielded the best results.

For the choice of loss function, we experimented with various region-based and pixel-value-based loss functions before finalizing a combined loss function. This function consists of batch dice loss, focal loss, and RMSE loss, weighted according to factors that were empirically determined to maximize mIoU and accuracy. For the MF Dataset, the optimal weighting factors were found to be $w_{DF} = 1$, $\alpha = 1.2$, $w_{ce} = 0.5$ and $w_{MSE} = 2$. For the KAIST Dataset, the best results were achieved with $w_{DF} = 2$, $\alpha = 1$, $w_{ce} = 1$ and $w_{MSE} = 2$.

To evaluate how well the model generalizes to new data, we tested it on the FMB-Dataset introduced in SegMif [20]. The model achieved an average mIoU of 61–63% on test inferences across the 8 major classes, and over 55% mIoU across all 15 segmentation classes. These results are comparable to current state-of-the-art models. The model's strong performance across diverse datasets further validates its inference capability for RGB-T based scene segmentation. Finally, upon further analysis of the available dataset, we identified biases introduced by manual annotation. Examples of such annotations are shown in Fig. 5. In case (a), we observe missing annotations in finer segmentation regions. In case (b), discrepancies are evident in the choice of annotation regions, where some annotations consider the overall bounding area as the region of interest, while others follow the shape of the object. In case (c), issues arise due to inconsistent labeling by annotators, where the same object is assigned different labels in different instances, leading to poor model adaptation in those cases.

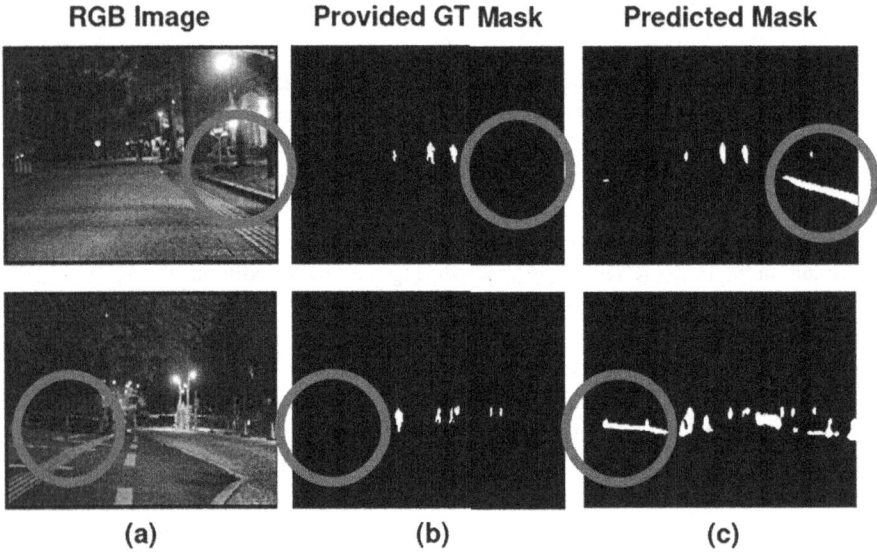

Fig. 7. Examples illustrating problems with manual annotations, sample taken from MF Dataset: (a) on the left: original RGB image, (b) in the center: provided ground truth (GT) mask, which appears incomplete, and (c) on the right: predicted segmentation mask with correct features missing from the ground truth annotation. The major region of discrepancy is highlighted with a red circle in each of the images. (Color figure online)

As shown in Fig. 7, incomplete annotations (middle column) negatively impacted the model's performance. While our segmentation correctly identified the regions (right column), the model's accuracy and training suffered due to these incomplete annotations. This could explain why some state-of-the-art (SoTA) models performed better when pixelation or noise was introduced into the training dataset. Similar to the Cityscapes dataset, there is a clear need for accurately annotated, peer-reviewed datasets to better evaluate model performance and accuracy. We are actively working to address this gap in our ongoing research.

5 Discussion and Future Works

This research presents a novel MsResNet: Multi-scale Edge-Enhanced ResNet as an image enhancement technique for RGB-T image segmentation, which utilizes a filtering-based approach to improve RGB and thermal data for better segmentation performance. By integrating Coordinate Cross-Attention-based feature fusion, and optimizing model features and parameters through extensive experimentation, our approach improves upon small-scale CNN-based networks, performing on par with newer transformer-based models. Our experiments on publicly available datasets MF and KAIST, validate the effectiveness of our method, and the inference time of the model highlights its capability for real-world segmentation tasks.

However, while investigating the existing dataset, we identified a major issue with the segmentation masks generated using single-module sensors or manual annotations. As discussed in the ablation study, these inconsistencies forced the model to overfit to specific datasets rather than generalize across scenes. Addressing this limitation is crucial for the broader applicability of RGB-T segmentation models.

To address this challenge and advance RGB-T-based scene inference, we propose capturing multi-perspective segmentation masks using a sensor suite and presenting unified segmentation masks. These refined masks would provide a robust foundation for training and benchmarking future models, minimizing reliance on manually annotated, error-prone data.

In the future, we also plan to explore the model's adaptability to diverse environmental conditions and further enhance the robustness of RGB-T segmentation. This will include developing newer, lightweight models and incorporating advanced mathematical techniques for image enhancement.

References

1. A color edge detector and its use in scene segmentation. IEEE Trans. Syst. Man Cybern. **7**(11), 820–826 (1977). https://doi.org/10.1109/TSMC.1977.4309631
2. Achanta, R., Hemami, S., Estrada, F., Susstrunk, S.: Frequency-tuned salient region detection. In: 2009 IEEE Conference on Computer Vision and Pattern Recognition, pp. 1597–1604 (2009). https://doi.org/10.1109/CVPR.2009.5206596
3. Badrinarayanan, V., Kendall, A., Cipolla, R.: SegNet: a deep convolutional encoder-decoder architecture for image segmentation. IEEE Trans. Pattern Anal. Mach. Intell. **39**(12), 2481–2495 (2017). https://doi.org/10.1109/TPAMI.2016.2644615

4. Chen, L.C., Papandreou, G., Kokkinos, I., Murphy, K., Yuille, A.L.: DeepLab: semantic image segmentation with deep convolutional nets, Atrous convolution, and fully connected CRFS. IEEE Trans. Pattern Anal. Mach. Intell. **40**(4), 834–848 (2018). https://doi.org/10.1109/TPAMI.2017.2699184
5. Chen, L.C., Papandreou, G., Schroff, F., Adam, H.: Rethinking Atrous convolution for semantic image segmentation. ArXiv abs/1706.05587 (2017). https://api.semanticscholar.org/CorpusID:22655199
6. Cordts, M., et al.: The cityscapes dataset. In: CVPR Workshop on the Future of Datasets in Vision, vol. 2, p. 1 (2015)
7. Deng, F., et al.: FeaNet: feature-enhanced attention network for RGB-thermal real-time semantic segmentation. In: 2021 IEEE/RSJ International Conference on Intelligent Robots and Systems (IROS), pp. 4467–4473 (2021). https://doi.org/10.1109/IROS51168.2021.9636084
8. Deng, J., Dong, W., Socher, R., Li, L.J., Li, K., Fei-Fei, L.: ImageNet: a large-scale hierarchical image database. In: 2009 IEEE Conference on Computer Vision and Pattern Recognition, pp. 248–255. IEEE (2009)
9. Dosovitskiy, A., et al.: An image is worth 16x16 words: transformers for image recognition at scale. In: International Conference on Learning Representations (2021). https://openreview.net/forum?id=YicbFdNTTy
10. Ha, Q., Watanabe, K., Karasawa, T., Ushiku, Y., Harada, T.: MFNET: towards real-time semantic segmentation for autonomous vehicles with multi-spectral scenes. In: 2017 IEEE/RSJ International Conference on Intelligent Robots and Systems (IROS), pp. 5108–5115 (2017). https://doi.org/10.1109/IROS.2017.8206396
11. Hou, Q., Zhang, L., Cheng, M.M., Feng, J.: Strip pooling: Rethinking spatial pooling for scene parsing. In: Proceedings of the IEEE/CVF Conference on Computer Vision and Pattern Recognition, pp. 4003–4012 (2020)
12. Hou, Q., Zhou, D., Feng, J.: Coordinate attention for efficient mobile network design. In: Proceedings of the IEEE/CVF Conference on Computer Vision and Pattern Recognition (CVPR), pp. 13713–13722 (2021)
13. Hou, Y.L., Song, Y., Hao, X., Shen, Y., Qian, M., Chen, H.: Multispectral pedestrian detection based on deep convolutional neural networks. Infrared Phys. Technol. **94**, 69–77 (2018)
14. Hu, J., Shen, L., Sun, G.: Squeeze-and-excitation networks. In: Proceedings of the IEEE Conference on Computer Vision and Pattern Recognition, pp. 7132–7141 (2018)
15. Hwang, S., Park, J., Kim, N., Choi, Y., So Kweon, I.: Multispectral pedestrian detection: Benchmark dataset and baseline. In: Proceedings of the IEEE Conference on Computer Vision and Pattern Recognition, pp. 1037–1045 (2015)
16. Kim, Y.H., Shin, U., Park, J., Kweon, I.S.: MS-UDA: multi-spectral unsupervised domain adaptation for thermal image semantic segmentation. IEEE Robot. Autom. Lett. **6**(4), 6497–6504 (2021). https://doi.org/10.1109/LRA.2021.3093652
17. Lai, C.Y., Wu, B.X., Shivanna, V.M., Guo, J.I.: MTSAN: multi-task semantic attention network for ADAS applications. IEEE Access **9**, 50700–50714 (2021). https://doi.org/10.1109/ACCESS.2021.3068991
18. Liang-Chieh, C., Papandreou, G., Kokkinos, I., Murphy, K., Yuille, A.: Semantic image segmentation with deep convolutional nets and fully connected CRFS. In: International conference on learning representations arXiv:1412.7062 (2015)
19. Lin, B., Lin, Z., Guo, Y., Zhang, Y., Zou, J., Fan, S.: Variational probabilistic fusion network for RGB-T semantic segmentation. arXiv preprint arXiv:2307.08536 (2023)
20. Liu, J., et al.: Multi-interactive feature learning and a full-time multi-modality benchmark for image fusion and segmentation. In: Proceedings of the IEEE/CVF International Conference on Computer Vision, pp. 8115–8124 (2023)

21. Long, J., Shelhamer, E., Darrell, T.: Fully convolutional networks for semantic segmentation. In: Proceedings of the IEEE Conference on Computer Vision and Pattern Recognition, pp. 3431–3440 (2015)
22. Misra, D., Nalamada, T., Arasanipalai, A.U., Hou, Q.: Rotate to attend: Convolutional triplet attention module. In: Proceedings of the IEEE/CVF Winter Conference on Applications of Computer Vision. pp. 3139–3148 (2021)
23. Ramachandran, P., Zoph, B., Le, Q.: Swish: a self-gated activation function (2017). https://doi.org/10.48550/arXiv.1710.05941
24. Reza, A.M.: Realization of the contrast limited adaptive histogram equalization (CLAHE) for real-time image enhancement. J. VLSI Sig. Process. Syst. Signal Image Video Technol. **38**, 35–44 (2004)
25. Ronneberger, O., Fischer, P., Brox, T.: U-Net: convolutional networks for biomedical image segmentation. In: Navab, N., Hornegger, J., Wells, W.M., Frangi, A.F. (eds.) MICCAI 2015. LNCS, vol. 9351, pp. 234–241. Springer, Cham (2015). https://doi.org/10.1007/978-3-319-24574-4_28
26. Strudel, R., Garcia, R., Laptev, I., Schmid, C.: SegMenter: transformer for semantic segmentation. In: Proceedings of the IEEE/CVF International Conference on Computer Vision, pp. 7262–7272 (2021)
27. Sun, Y., Zuo, W., Liu, M.: RTFNET: RGB-thermal fusion network for semantic segmentation of urban scenes. IEEE Robot. Autom. Lett. **4**(3), 2576–2583 (2019). https://doi.org/10.1109/LRA.2019.2904733
28. Toet, A., Hogervorst, M.A.: Multiscale image fusion through guided filtering. In: Target and Background Signatures II, vol. 9997, pp. 170–182. SPIE (2016)
29. Wang, Y., Li, G., Liu, Z.G.: SGFNet: semantic-guided fusion network for RGB-thermal semantic segmentation. IEEE Trans. Circ. Syst. Video Technol. **33**, 7737–7748 (2023). https://api.semanticscholar.org/CorpusID:259578116
30. Yang, Y., Shan, C., Zhao, F., Liang, W., Han, J.: On exploring shape and semantic enhancements for RGB-X semantic segmentation. IEEE Trans. Intell. Veh. **9**, 2223–2235 (2024). https://api.semanticscholar.org/CorpusID:259965120
31. Zhang, J., Liu, H., Yang, K., Hu, X., Liu, R., Stiefelhagen, R.: CMX: cross-modal fusion for RGB-X semantic segmentation with transformers. IEEE Trans. Intell. Transp. Syst. **24**(12), 14679–14694 (2023). https://doi.org/10.1109/TITS.2023.3300537
32. Zhang, J., et al.: Delivering arbitrary-modal semantic segmentation. In: Proceedings of the IEEE/CVF Conference on Computer Vision and Pattern Recognition, pp. 1136–1147 (2023)
33. Zhang, Q., Zhao, S., Luo, Y., Zhang, D., Huang, N., Han, J.: AbmdrNet: adaptive-weighted bi-directional modality difference reduction network for RGB-T semantic segmentation. In: Proceedings of the IEEE/CVF Conference on Computer Vision and Pattern Recognition (CVPR), pp. 2633–2642 (2021)
34. Zhao, H., Shi, J., Qi, X., Wang, X., Jia, J.: Pyramid scene parsing network. In: Proceedings of the IEEE Conference on Computer Vision and Pattern Recognition, pp. 2881–2890 (2017)
35. Zhou, W., Liu, J., Lei, J., Yu, L., Hwang, J.N.: GMNET: Graded-feature multilabel-learning network for RGB-thermal urban scene semantic segmentation. IEEE Trans. Image Process. **30**, 7790–7802 (2021). https://doi.org/10.1109/TIP.2021.3109518

Addressing Class Imbalance in Renal Amyloidosis Classification: A Comparative Study of Few-Shot Learning and Conventional Machine Learning Techniques

Alexsandro Silva Santos[1], Luciano Rebouças de Oliveira[2], Washington Luis Conrado dos Santos[3], and Angelo Amancio Duarte[4]($\boxtimes$)

[1] Graduate Program in Computer Science, State University of Feira de Santana, Av. Transnordestina, s/n, Feira de Santana 44036-900, Brazil
[2] Intelligent Vision Research Lab, Computer Science Department, Federal University of Bahia, Rua Prof. Aristides Novis, 2, Salvador 40210-630, Brazil
lrebouca@ufba.br
[3] Structural and Molecular Pathology Lab, Gonçalo Moniz Institute, Fundação Oswaldo Cruz, Rua Waldemar Falcão, 121, Salvador 40296-710, Brazil
washington.santos@fiocruz.br
[4] High-Performance Computing Lab, Department of Technology, State University of Feira de Santana, Av. Transnordestina, s/n, Feira de Santana 44036-900, Brazil
angeloduarte@uefs.br

Abstract. Class imbalance presents a significant challenge in Computational Pathology, particularly in classifying rare diseases such as renal amyloidosis. This paper investigates the effectiveness of Few-Shot Learning (FSL), specifically through prototypical networks, alongside conventional methods to enhance the automatic classification of renal glomeruli from biopsy images. A novel multi-stain dataset is introduced, comprising 11,674 annotated images across nine glomerular lesion classes, including amyloidosis, stained with four different dyes. The study compared baseline CNN models with FSL approaches, both with and without Cost-Sensitive Learning (CSL). The FSL-CSL-Ensemble achieved the highest F1-Score of 93.8%, surpassing the performance of related studies that addressed datasets with less severe imbalance ratios. This study underscores the potential of FSL in classifying renal amyloidosis, especially when combined with CSL, and suggests the possibility of eliminating the need for Congo red staining, the current gold standard for diagnosis. The findings highlight the necessity of developing innovative approaches like FSL to improve outcomes in medical image analysis, where data scarcity is prevalent.

Keywords: Class imbalance · Few-shot learning · Computational pathology · Glomeruli classification

1 Introduction

Computational Pathology (CPATH) has emerged as a powerful tool in the diagnosis and classification of various diseases, particularly in the field of nephrology. Among the myriad of renal pathologies, the ones caused by glomerular lesions present a unique challenge due to the diverse morphological characteristics and clinical implications. Accurate classification of glomerular lesions is crucial for proper diagnosis, prognosis, and treatment planning. However, the complexity and variability of glomerular lesions, coupled with the scarcity of certain pathologies, that often yield imbalanced classes, pose significant challenges for traditional machine learning approaches in CPATH.

Class imbalance is a pervasive issue in CPATH, particularly in the context of disease classification. This imbalance occurs when one or more classes in a dataset are significantly underrepresented compared to others. In the context of glomerular lesions, this issue is especially pronounced due to factors inherent to medical data and disease prevalence, such as the rarity of certain diseases or conditions, difficulty and cost of data acquisition, ethical and privacy concerns, variability in disease progression, and bias in data collection.

A prime example of this class imbalance challenge is evident in the classification of renal amyloidosis, a rare but severe condition affecting the kidneys. Amyloidosis is characterized by the abnormal deposition of misfolded proteins, called amyloid fibrils, in various organs, including the kidneys. In renal amyloidosis, these deposits accumulate in the *glomeruli*, the kidney's filtration units, leading to progressive organ dysfunction and potentially fatal outcomes [15].

The classification of renal amyloidosis presents several unique challenges: a) Rarity- Amyloidosis is a relatively uncommon condition, resulting in limited available data for training machine learning models; b) Morphological Similarity- Amyloid deposits can sometimes resemble other glomerular lesions, making differentiation challenging even for experienced pathologists; c) Staining Variability- The gold standard for amyloidosis diagnosis, Congo red staining [24], can be inconsistent and requires specialized expertise to interpret correctly; and d) Heterogeneity- Amyloidosis can present with various patterns and distributions of amyloid deposits, further complicating classification efforts.

These challenges contribute significantly to the under-representation of amyloidosis in datasets with images of glomeruli. Consequently, in the context of computational pathology, samples of renal amyloidosis are vastly outnumbered by those of more common renal conditions or healthy tissue. This pronounced imbalance poses a substantial challenge for traditional machine learning approaches, which tend to be biased towards the majority class, potentially leading to missed diagnoses of this critical condition.

Classical approaches to tackle class imbalance typically fall into three categories: data-level methods, algorithm-level methods, and hybrid methods [7]. Data-level techniques, such as oversampling and undersampling, aim to balance the dataset by adjusting the number of samples in each class. Algorithm-level methods, including cost-sensitive learning and ensemble techniques like bagging and boosting, modify the learning process to compensate for class imbalance.

Hybrid methods combine both, data and algorithm-level approaches. While these techniques have shown success in many applications, they often struggle with extreme imbalances or when dealing with limited data availability, as is common in rare diseases like renal amyloidosis.

Few-Shot Learning (FSL) approaches [5] have emerged as a promising solution to address data sparsity scenarios and mitigate the operational costs associated with dataset annotation, particularly in contexts where data is limited [23]. FSL is designed to learn effectively from a small number of labeled examples, making it especially suitable for rare disease classification tasks in computational pathology.

While initially developed to tackle data scarcity, FSL has increasingly found application in addressing class imbalance problems [2]. This expansion of FSL's utility has given rise to a new research direction known as Class Imbalance Few-Shot Learning (CIFSL) [13]. CIFSL leverages the inherent ability of FSL to learn effectively from a small number of labeled examples, making it especially suitable for rare disease classification tasks, offering the potential to overcome the limitations of traditional class imbalance techniques, especially when dealing with rare conditions in computational pathology. However, the application of CIFSL to the specific challenge of glomerular lesion classification, particularly renal amyloidosis, remains largely unexplored.

In this study, we present a comparative analysis between conventional techniques and Few-Shot Learning (FSL) as strategies for addressing class imbalance in glomerular disease diagnostics, with a specific focus on amyloidosis. Our approach begins with the development of a baseline model using established methods to combat class imbalance, namely resampling [21] and cost-sensitive learning (CSL) [12], which serves as a benchmark for subsequent comparisons. We then construct a series of FSL classifiers utilizing prototypical networks, employing the same architectural foundations as our baseline models for the embedding functions. To further enhance performance, we integrate standard N-way-K-shot episodic training with CSL. Finally, we create an ensemble-based model using the top-performing individual models. Throughout our analysis, we employ the F1-Score as our primary metric for model comparison. This choice is deliberate, as the F1-Score provides a balanced measure of precision and recall, avoiding the potential bias towards the majority class that can occur with other metrics such as accuracy [11]. This comprehensive approach allowed us to rigorously evaluate the efficacy of FSL in managing class imbalance within the context of rare glomerular disease classification.

This study aimed to address critical gaps in computational pathology for renal disease classification through several key objectives. We introduce a novel, large-scale dataset of 11,674 annotated glomeruli images across nine lesion classes and four staining techniques, addressing the scarcity of comprehensive, multi-stain datasets in renal pathology (dataset available under request). Our research compares the performance of conventional machine learning techniques with Few-Shot Learning (FSL) approaches in classifying renal amyloidosis, focusing particularly on addressing extreme class imbalance. We explore an innovative combination of FSL with Cost-Sensitive Learning to further improve classification performance in the context of severe class imbalance. Of particular interest is our investigation into the use of non-specific stains for amyloidosis classification, which could potentially eliminate the need for specialized Congo red staining in the diagnostic process. This aspect is especially significant as the current method of diagnosing amyloidosis requires biopsy slides to be processed using Congo red, a specific staining technique. Our proposed method aims to accurately diagnose amyloidosis from glomeruli images stained with common dyes like Periodic Acid-Schiff (PAS) and Hematoxylin and Eosin (H&E). Our results showed that this approach could significantly simplify the diagnostic process, leading to faster and more cost-effective diagnoses of this disease.

By addressing these objectives, our study seeks to advance the field of computational pathology in renal disease classification, potentially improving diagnostic accuracy and efficiency in clinical practice. Furthermore, our findings may serve as a basis for the development of methods for the classification of other rare diseases characterized by significant class imbalance in medical imaging datasets.

2 Related Works

In addressing the class imbalance in medical imaging, researchers have employed various innovative approaches. Mahbub *et al.* proposed an algorithmic method using a novel cost function, Center-Focused Affinity Loss (CFAL), for histological dataset imbalance. They achieved an F1-Score of up to 83% on a substantial dataset of 277,524 samples with an imbalance ratio (IR) of approximately 1:3 [9]. Walsh and Tardy focused on mammography image classification, comparing traditional imbalance techniques with generative adversarial networks (GAN). Their proposed method, "Artifacting", achieved an AUCROC of 76.8% on a highly imbalanced dataset (IR 1:19) containing 20.000 images [22]. Raj *et al.* introduced a data augmentation technique called the "Crossover-based Technique", which generates new samples by combining existing images. Applied to CNN training on three medical datasets, this method achieved an impressive Macro F1-Score of 98% in a multi-class brain tumor detection task [14]. These studies demonstrate the potential of diverse approaches in addressing class imbalance across various medical imaging domains, from histopathology to mammography and brain tumor detection, highlighting the ongoing challenge and the need for innovative solutions in this field.

Few-shot learning (FSL) has gained attention not only for addressing data scarcity but also for tackling class imbalance, sometimes referred to as Class Imbalance Few-shot Learning (CIFSL). Deng and Li combined Transfer Learning (TL), FSL, resampling techniques, and image masking methods for white blood cell classification and counting in blood samples with an imbalance ratio of 1:6 [3], achieving an AUCROC of up to 88%. Medela et al. applied an FSL approach with Siamese Neural Networks to transfer knowledge from a multiclass colon dataset to healthy and cancerous tissues of the colon, breast, and lung [10].

Using only 60 samples per class in the support set, they achieved up to 90% Balanced Accuracy (BAC) on balanced datasets. Abbas proposed the Intelligence Medical Imaging Recognition (IMR-FSL) model for image retrieval, testing it on the TCIA (Clark et al., 2013) and KVASIR (Pogorelov et al., 2017) datasets [1]. Their model demonstrated impressive performance with 95% sensitivity, 96.5% specificity, 0.96 AUC, and 97.5% accuracy. Titoriya and Singh utilized Prototypical Networks (PN) and Model Agnostic Meta-Learning (MAML) across four datasets for cancer diagnosis, two of which were imbalanced [20]. Their study reported accuracy up to 84.56% for a 2-way-2-shot configuration on the query set.

These studies showcase the versatility of FSL in addressing both data scarcity and class imbalance across various medical imaging applications, from blood cell analysis to cancer diagnosis.

3 Methods

Our methodology aimed at comparing baseline classifier models trained on the entire dataset of images against models trained solely on images stained with the Periodic Acid-Schiff (PAS) dye. This comparison allowed us to assess the impact of stain selection on model performance. Additionally, we investigated the potential benefits of incorporating Cost-Sensitive Learning (CSL) to address the inherent class imbalance within the dataset, evaluating whether this approach can enhance the classifiers' performance. Furthermore, we aimed to explore the efficacy of Few-Shot Learning (FSL) techniques to determine if they can further improve model accuracy when dealing with limited data, as is often the case in medical imaging. Through these evaluations, our goal was to identify optimal strategies for enhancing the automatic classification of renal amyloidosis.

Throughout our analysis, we employ the F1-Score as our primary metric for model comparison. This choice is deliberate, as the F1-Score provides a balanced measure of precision and recall, making it particularly suitable for evaluating classifiers on imbalanced datasets [4].

In the context of our highly imbalanced dataset, where amyloidosis cases are significantly outnumbered by other glomerular lesions, accuracy alone can be misleading. A model that simply predicts the majority class for all instances could achieve high accuracy without actually identifying any amyloidosis cases. The F1-Score, being the harmonic mean of precision and recall, penalizes such behavior and provides a more nuanced evaluation of model performance.

Moreover, in clinical applications like renal pathology, both false positives and false negatives can have significant consequences. False positives may lead to unnecessary treatments or anxiety for patients, while false negatives could result in delayed or missed diagnoses. The F1-Score, by considering both precision and recall, helps us balance these concerns and identify models that perform well in both aspects.

Additionally, the F1-Score is particularly useful when dealing with rare conditions like amyloidosis. It gives equal weight to precision and recall, ensuring that models are evaluated not just on their ability to avoid false positives (precision), but also on their capacity to identify true positive cases (recall) in a sparse dataset.

By consistently using the F1-Score across our different experimental setups - from baseline models to Few-Shot Learning approaches - we maintain a standardized basis for comparison. This allows us to effectively assess the relative strengths of different methodologies in addressing the class imbalance challenge in glomerular lesion classification.

3.1 Dataset

We developed a comprehensive dataset comprising 11,674 glomeruli images, meticulously extracted from whole slide images (WSI) of renal biopsies. These high-quality images were stored in JPEG format to balance detail preservation and storage efficiency. Our dataset encompasses a wide spectrum of pathological conditions, reflecting the complexity of renal pathology: normal glomeruli (without lesions), amyloidosis lesions, pure sclerosis without crescent, hypercellularity-type lesions, pure hypercellularity-type lesions without crescent, crescentic glomerulonephritis, membranous nephropathy, sclerosis, and podocytopathy.

To ensure a robust representation of each condition, we employed four distinct histological staining techniques, each offering unique insights into glomerular structure and pathology: AZAN trichrome (AZAN), hematoxylin and eosin (HE), periodic acid-methenamine silver (PAMS), and periodic acid-Schiff (PAS).

The images in the dataset exhibit dimensional variability, ranging from 607 × 751 pixels to 1024 × 768 pixels, reflecting the natural variation in glomerular size and shape. All images maintain a consistent high resolution of 300 × 300 dpi, ensuring detailed visualization of glomerular structures.

Table 1 provides a detailed distribution of samples across pathological conditions and staining techniques, offering a quantitative overview of the dataset's composition. Figure 1 presents representative images of glomeruli stained with each technique, visually demonstrating the morphological diversity captured in our dataset. This comprehensive approach to dataset construction ensures a rich, varied foundation for training and evaluating our machine-learning models in glomerular lesion classification.

Table 1. Original dataset distribution, by lesion and staining. (0) Amyloidosis, (1) Normal, (2) Pure Sclerosis, (3) Hypercellularity, (4) Pure Hypercellularity, (5) Crescent Glomerulonephritis, (6) Membranous Nephropathy, (7) Sclerosis, (8) Podocytopathy.

	Class	AZAN	HE	PAMS	PAS	Total
pos	0	31	145	96	102	**374**
neg	1	223	1,585	345	542	**2,695**
	2	234	672	104	472	**1,482**
	3	257	1.890	0	987	**3,134**
	4	60	0	0	164	**224**
	5	121	467	157	359	**1,104**
	6	136	712	324	367	**1,539**
	7	0	276	122	219	**617**
	8	90	65	106	244	**505**
	Total	**1,152**	**5,812**	**1,254**	**3,456**	**11,674**

3.2 Data Pre-processing

The amyloidosis lesion was designated as the positive class, with all other glomerular lesions grouped into a single negative class. This resulted in a highly imbalanced dataset with an imbalance ratio of approximately 1:30, reflecting the rarity of amyloidosis in clinical settings.

For a complete model evaluation, we employed a 75:25 train-test split. The 75% training portion underwent K-fold cross-validation, so we could take a robust performance estimation by detecting variance in the model performance across different samples. This approach facilitated fair comparisons between different models. We partitioned the source set into $K = 5$ folds, where $(K-1)/K$ of the images were used for training and $1/K$ reserved for validation. The decision to use five folds instead of the more commonly recommended ten folds in cross-validation literature was driven by the limited number of samples in some classes, particularly the rare lesions such as amyloidosis. With five folds, we ensured a sufficient number of minority class samples in each fold for meaningful evaluation, while still maintaining the benefits of cross-validation. This strategy struck a balance between robust performance estimation and the practical constraints imposed by our dataset's class imbalance, allowing for more reliable model assessment in the context of rare disease classification.

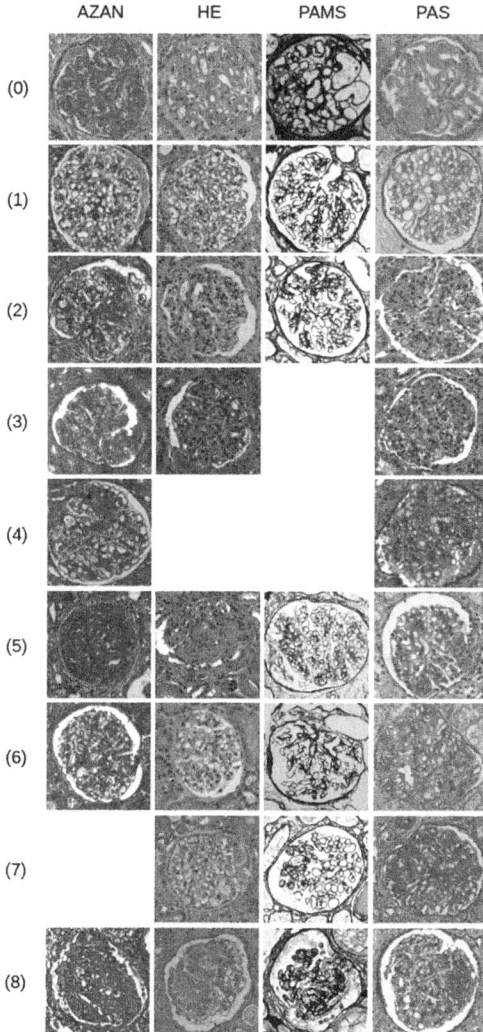

Fig. 1. Samples of images in the dataset according to the class of lesion and type of stain. Blank squares indicate no sample of a lesion in the stain. (0) Amyloidosis, (1) Normal, (2) Pure Sclerosis, (3) Hypercellularity, (4) Pure Hypercellularity, (5) Crescent Glomerulonephritis, (6) Membranous Nephropathy, (7) Sclerosis, (8) Podocytopathy

Our study encompassed two distinct experimental paradigms: a comprehensive multi-stain analysis utilizing the entire dataset of 11,674 images across all four staining techniques, and a single-stain-focused analysis employing a subset of 3,456 images exclusively stained with Periodic Acid-Schiff (PAS). Both experimental sets underwent identical preprocessing and partitioning procedures to ensure consistency and comparability of the results. The selection of PAS for our focused analysis was based on several key factors. Firstly, PAS uniquely captured all types of lesions present in the original dataset. Secondly, PAS is ubiquitous in nephropathology and general pathology practices worldwide. Its pervasiveness is due to its ability to highlight important structural elements such as basement membranes, glycogen, and neutral mucopolysaccharides, making it an indispensable tool in the diagnosis of various renal pathologies. This widespread use enhances the translational potential and clinical relevance of our findings. Lastly, focusing on PAS offered the potential to streamline diagnostic workflows. This experiment was designed to evaluate whether PAS-only models could accurately classify the full spectrum of glomerular lesions, compare their performance to multi-stain models, and explore the potential for optimizing biopsy analysis. By assessing the efficacy of this single, commonly used stain for comprehensive lesion classification, we aimed to investigate opportunities to reduce procedural complexity, improve diagnostic efficiency, and enhance cost-effectiveness in pathological examinations. This approach not only addresses the technical aspects of machine learning in pathology but also considers the practical implications for clinical workflow and resource allocation in diagnostic nephropathology, potentially paving the way for more standardized and efficient diagnostic processes.

To establish a robust comparison, we implemented multiple strategies to address the inherent class imbalance in our dataset. Initially, we established a baseline training the models with a dataset using classical random oversampling to achieve a balanced 1:1 ratio of positive (amyloidosis) to negative (other lesions) samples across all folds, providing a standard benchmark in imbalanced learning scenarios. Then, we took the unbalanced dataset and developed models incorporating cost-sensitive learning, assigning higher weights to the minority class during training to mitigate bias towards the majority class without altering the underlying data distribution. For the Few-Shot Learning (FSL) experiments utilizing prototypical networks, we deliberately avoided resampling techniques. This decision was based on the fundamental principle of prototypical networks, which leverage the average of sample embeddings to calculate class prototypes. We hypothesized that introducing duplicate samples through oversampling might introduce noise and potentially degrade the quality of the learned prototypes, leading to suboptimal model performance.

To ensure the validity and generalizability of our results, we conducted final model validation on the initially reserved 25% test set, which crucially maintained the original dataset's imbalanced proportions, reflecting real-world class distributions and providing a more realistic assessment of model performance in clinical scenarios. This comprehensive methodological approach enables a rigorous and statistically sound evaluation of each model's predictive capabilities across diverse data subsets, allows for a fair comparison between traditional machine learning approaches and FSL techniques in the context of extreme class imbalance, mitigates potential biases, reduces the risk of overfitting, and provides insights into the effectiveness of different strategies for handling class imbalance in the specific context of glomerular lesion classification.

3.3 CNN Models

We employed six pre-trained convolutional neural network (CNN) architectures: EfficientNet-B0, EfficientNet-B4, Inception-v3, ResNet-18, ResNet-50, and VGG-16. These architectures were chosen based on their proven performance in various image classification tasks and their distinct architectural features.

EfficientNet models, developed by Tan and Le [19], are known for their ability to balance network depth, width, and resolution. They achieve state-of-the-art accuracy on ImageNet while being up to 10 times smaller and faster than previous models. The B0 and B4 variants were selected to compare the performance of a smaller, more efficient model (B0) against a larger, potentially more powerful one (B4) in the context of our glomerular lesion classification task.

Inception-v3, introduced by Szegedy et al. [18], is designed to be computationally efficient while maintaining high accuracy. Its use of factorized convolutions and aggressive regularization makes it particularly suitable for tasks where computational resources may be limited, as is often the case in medical image analysis settings.

Residual Networks (ResNet), developed by He et al. [6], address the vanishing gradient problem in deep networks through the use of skip connections. This allows for the training of much deeper networks, potentially capturing more complex features in the images. We included both ResNet-18 and ResNet-50 to evaluate whether the increased depth of ResNet-50 provides significant benefits in our specific classification task.

Despite being an older architecture, VGG-16 [8] remains relevant due to its simplicity and effectiveness. Its uniform architecture makes it easier to interpret and modify, which can be advantageous when fine-tuning for specific medical imaging tasks.

The models were trained using a learning rate of 0.001, batch size of 32, and Stochastic Gradient Descent optimizer. Training proceeded for a maximum of 100 epochs, with an early stopping mechanism implemented with patience of 10 epochs to prevent overfitting. These diverse architectures were selected to provide a comprehensive baseline for our study. By comparing their performance, we aim to identify which architectural features are most beneficial for glomerular lesion classification, particularly in the context of the class imbalance present in our dataset. This comparison also allows us to assess whether more complex, modern architectures offer significant advantages over simpler, more established models in this specific medical imaging context. Furthermore, these pre-trained models allow us to leverage transfer learning, potentially mitigating the impact of our limited dataset size.

Furthermore, these pre-trained models allow us to leverage transfer learning, potentially mitigating the impact of our limited dataset size. While these models were initially trained on natural images (ImageNet), previous studies have shown that the low-level features learned by CNNs can be effectively transferred to medical imaging tasks, providing a strong starting point for our fine-tuning process.

3.4 Classical Approach for Class Imbalance

To establish a comprehensive baseline for our study, we implemented two distinct strategies to address the inherent class imbalance in our dataset. First, we trained models using a dataset balanced through classical random oversampling. This technique achieved a 1:1 ratio of positive (amyloidosis) to negative (other lesions) samples across all folds, providing a standard benchmark in imbalanced learning scenarios. Second, we developed models using the original unbalanced dataset, incorporating cost-sensitive learning (CSL). This approach assigned weights to the loss function inversely proportional to each class's sample count, thereby prioritizing the minority class during training. This method mitigates bias towards the majority class without altering the underlying data distribution.

To rigorously assess the impact of CSL, we trained each architecture both with and without its implementation. The models were subsequently ranked in descending order based on their F1 scores across the 5-fold cross-validation, with the F1 score chosen due to its balanced consideration of precision and recall, crucial in imbalanced classification tasks.

Following this initial evaluation, we identified the three top-performing architectures based on their aggregate scores. These selected models underwent full training using the entire training set (75% of the original dataset), with the remaining 25% reserved as a hold-out set for final validation. This approach maximized data diversity during training, enhancing the generalizability of our classifiers.

To leverage the collective strengths of these top-performing models, we developed an ensemble-based classifier, referred to as *Baseline-ensemble*. This ensemble method combines the predictions of individual models, potentially improving overall accuracy and robustness.

This systematic approach to model selection, training, and ensemble construction ensured a robust baseline for comparison with our Few-Shot Learning models. It provides a comprehensive evaluation of different architectural and training strategies in the context of glomerular lesion classification, particularly for the rare condition of renal amyloidosis.

3.5 Few-Shot Learning for Class Imbalance

Few-Shot Learning (FSL) leverages prior knowledge gained from training on a large, labeled dataset, to perform efficiently on small classification tasks within a specific domain of interest. FSL employs a unique training paradigm known as episodic training, which mimics the few-shot scenario during the learning process. In the FSL framework, the core concept is the N-way-K-shot task. Here, N represents the number of classes to be distinguished, while K denotes the number of examples provided for each class. These examples form the *support set*, a small, labeled dataset used for learning. The model's performance is then evaluated on a separate *query set*, which contains new, unseen examples from the same classes. This approach allows the model to adapt quickly to new tasks with minimal data [25].

Among FSL methodologies, metric-based approaches, particularly prototypical networks, have gained prominence. In these networks, the support set samples are used to generate class prototypes. This is achieved through an embedding function, typically a Convolutional Neural Network (CNN), denoted as f_ϕ, where ϕ represents the network parameters [16]. The function f_ϕ transforms input samples into a feature space where similar samples cluster together. Class prototypes are then computed as the mean of the embedded support samples for each class.

Classification of a new sample in prototypical networks involves comparing its embedding to these class prototypes. This comparison is performed using a distance function d, commonly either cosine similarity or Euclidean distance. The new sample is assigned to the class whose prototype is nearest in the embedding space, effectively leveraging the model's ability to learn meaningful representations from limited data [17].

For training the FSL models we used a metric-based approach with prototypical networks. Each model was trained using the same folds used in the baseline experiment, with each fold comprising a support set for prototype generation and a query set for validation. We implemented episodic training following the standard N-way-K-shot FSL paradigm, with $N = 2$ (binary classification) and $K = 30$ for the training stage's support set, and $K = 15$ for the validation stage's query set. The values for K were selected based on the number of samples in the minority class. Specifically, for each fold, the training set included 60 samples, and the validation set contained 16 minority samples, which facilitated testing on a final imbalanced set with 25 minority samples. The models were trained over 100 epochs, with 200 episodes per epoch, and included an early stopping mechanism that was triggered after 10 epochs without performance improvement.

During each fold's episodes, we stored the optimal parameter and prototype states for each model. We hypothesized that cross-validation would enhance prototype construction by leveraging the entire training set. Post-training, each model was evaluated against the reserved 25% imbalanced test set using its best fold-specific state.

We explored two distance functions for classification: Euclidean distance and cosine similarity. Experimental results demonstrated a significant performance advantage for cosine similarity.

Following a methodology analogous to the baseline classifier, we selected the top three performing models based on the F1 score to construct two ensemble-based models: *FSL-Ensemble* (without CSL) and *FSL-CSL-Ensemble* (with CSL applied). This approach aimed to leverage the collective predictive power of the most effective prototypical network models while mitigating class imbalance challenges.

4 Results and Discussion

Here we present the results of the experiments outlined in Sect. 3, which focused on comparing the effectiveness of conventional machine learning techniques with Few-Shot Learning (FSL) for classifying amyloidosis in renal glomeruli. The experiments investigated the performance of pre-trained convolutional neural network (CNN) architectures as baseline models, both with and without cost-sensitive learning (CSL), and compared these to FSL models using prototypical networks. We explore the impact of stain selection on model performance, comparing models trained on the entire dataset (with all stains) to those trained exclusively on Periodic Acid-Schiff (PAS) stained images. Additionally, we discuss the effectiveness of combining conventional approaches like CSL with FSL techniques to enhance classification accuracy.

4.1 Results Using Classical Approach

Figure 2 presents a comparative analysis of F1-scores achieved by various convolutional neural network (CNN) architectures in the classification of renal amyloidosis, with a particular emphasis on the impact of stain selection. The results demonstrate a consistent performance advantage for models trained on the complete dataset, which incorporates all four staining techniques, over those trained exclusively on Periodic Acid-Schiff (PAS) stained images. This performance disparity suggests that the diverse visual information provided by multiple staining methods contributes significantly to enhanced model accuracy.

Within each stain selection group, certain architectures exhibit superior performance. For the full dataset, VGG-16, ResNet-18, and EfficientNet-B0 achieve the highest F1 scores. In contrast, when trained solely on PAS-stained images, EfficientNet-B0, ResNet-50, and ResNet-18 emerge as the top performers. This variation in architectural efficacy across staining subsets indicates that the optimal choice of CNN architecture for amyloidosis classification may be contingent on the specific staining technique employed in the training data. These findings underscore the importance of considering both architectural design and staining methodology in developing robust classification models for renal pathology.

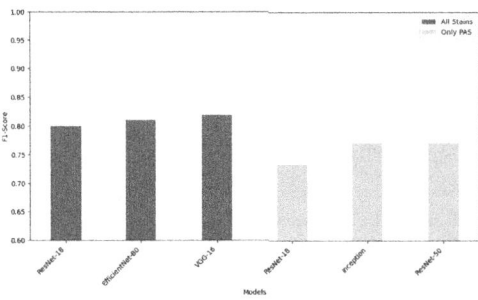

Fig. 2. Comparison of F1-Scores between models trained on samples from all stains (blue) and those trained solely on PAS-stained samples (red). (Color figure online)

Based on the superior performance of models trained on samples from all stains, we selected these models for further optimization using cost-sensitive learning (CSL). Figure 3 illustrates the impact of the CSL application, which, as hypothesized, resulted in significant performance enhancements across all architectures. Notably, the ensemble classifier, integrating VGG-16, ResNet-18, and

EfficientNet-B0, achieved the highest F1-Score among all models. This marked improvement can be attributed to the ensemble method's capacity to synergistically leverage the unique strengths of each constituent architecture, thereby enhancing overall classification accuracy and model robustness. The combination of diverse staining information, cost-sensitive learning, and ensemble techniques demonstrates a powerful approach to addressing the challenges of renal amyloidosis classification in imbalanced datasets.

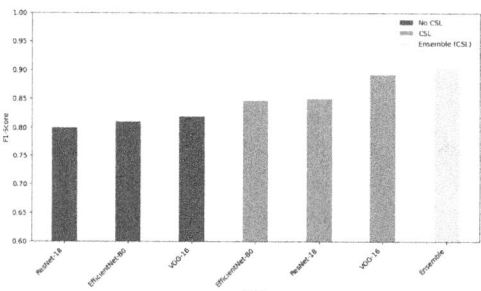

Fig. 3. Comparison of F1-scores for baseline models trained on multi-stain samples, without (blue) and with (red) cost-sensitive learning (CSL). The ensemble-based model (green) demonstrates superior performance. (Color figure online)

4.2 Results Using Few-Shot Learning

Figure 4 reveals a significant divergence in performance trends between baseline models and Few-Shot Learning (FSL) models. While baseline models trained on the complete multi-stain dataset consistently outperformed those trained exclusively on PAS-stained images (as shown in Fig. 2), FSL models exhibit the opposite behavior. FSL models trained solely on PAS-stained images achieve superior results compared to their counterparts trained on the full multi-stain dataset.

This performance disparity can be attributed to the unique learning mechanism of prototypical networks employed in our FSL models. Prototypical networks generate class prototypes by averaging the embeddings of samples in the support set. When the training dataset encompasses images with diverse staining characteristics, as in the full dataset, the resulting embedding space can be heterogeneous. This heterogeneity potentially introduces outliers that negatively impact the representativeness of the prototypes.

Conversely, utilizing a dataset with a single stain, such as PAS, produces a more homogeneous embedding space, leading to more robust and representative prototypes. This homogeneity enables the FSL model to generalize more effectively from limited data, a crucial aspect of FSL where models are trained on a small number of samples.

Therefore, while a diverse dataset proves beneficial for traditional machine learning models, as evidenced by the baseline model performance, the unique characteristics of FSL and its reliance on prototype-based learning render a homogeneous dataset, even if limited to a single stain, more advantageous for achieving optimal performance. This finding underscores the importance of considering the specific learning paradigm when selecting and preparing datasets for different machine-learning approaches in medical image analysis.

The application of Cost-Sensitive Learning (CSL) to models trained on PAS-stained images yielded a significant performance improvement, as illustrated in Fig. 5. Following the methodology employed for the baseline classifier, we constructed an ensemble using the three top-performing models. This ensemble achieved a remarkable F1-Score of 93.8%, surpassing all individual models. This outstanding result underscores the ensemble classifier's ability to effectively leverage the strengths of multiple architectures, particularly when combined with CSL in the context of Few-Shot Learning. The superior performance of this approach demonstrates its potential for addressing the challenges of class imbalance and limited data in renal amyloidosis classification.

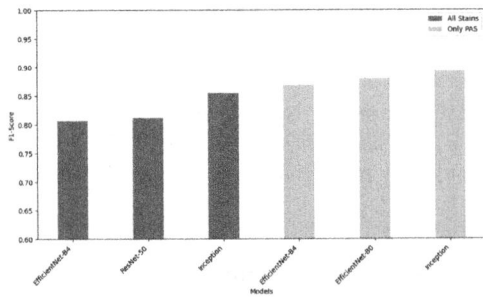

Fig. 4. Comparison of F1-scores for Few-shot Learning (FSL) models trained with images in all stains (blue) and models only trained with images in PAS stain (red). Models for PAS stain demonstrate superior performance. (Color figure online)

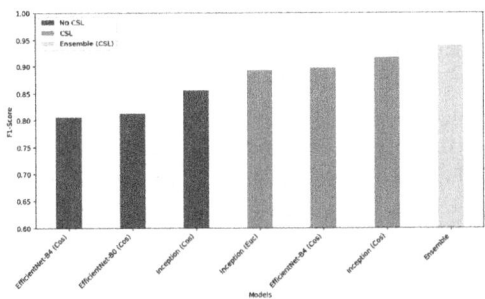

Fig. 5. Comparison of F1-scores for Few-Shot Learning (FSL) models trained on PAS-stained images, without (blue), and with (red) Cost-Sensitive Learning (CSL), and the ensemble model. Only one model yielded the best result using Euclidean distance (Euc). The vast majority achieve the best performance using cosine similarity (Cos) as distance metrics in the prototypical networks. The ensemble-based model (green) demonstrates superior performance. (Color figure online)

Table 2 presents the F1 scores of the five best-performing classifiers. Few-shot learning (FSL) demonstrates significant potential for renal amyloidosis classification, particularly when combined with Cost-Sensitive Learning (CSL). However, several limitations warrant further investigation.

The generalizability of this approach to other glomerular lesions requires careful examination, as our study focused specifically on amyloidosis. Future research should evaluate FSL's efficacy in classifying lesions with diverse visual characteristics and varying levels of data availability. The reliance on PAS staining for optimal performance raises concerns about applicability in settings where this technique is not standard practice. Our findings highlight the potential impact of specific staining methods on FSL model performance, emphasizing the need for comprehensive validation across various staining protocols.

While stratification helps mitigate bias in prototype construction, the risk of biased prototypes persists if the limited samples available do not fully capture the lesion's true diversity. Additionally, the computational demands and complexity of FSL, especially with sophisticated architectures like prototypical networks, may present implementation challenges in resource-constrained environments.

Our results indicate that conventional CNNs require substantially more data for effective generalization, as evidenced by the baseline performance disparity between models trained on the entire dataset versus those trained solely on PAS samples. In contrast, FSL classifiers, particularly prototypical networks, demonstrate superior performance with limited data. This phenomenon can be attributed to the fact that large volumes of data may introduce outliers, potentially compromising the accuracy of generated prototypes.

These findings underscore the potential of FSL in addressing the challenges of limited data and class imbalance in medical image classification, while also highlighting areas requiring further research and optimization.

Table 2. Rank of the 5 best classifiers. The term CSL indicates using of cost-sensitive learning while *Cos* and *Euc* indicate the type of distance metric for few-shot-learning (FSL) models.

Architecture	Dataset	F1-Score
FSL-CSL-Ensemble + CSL	PAS	0.938
Inception + CSL (Cos)	PAS	0.916
Baseline-Ensemble	ALL	0.905
EfficientNet-B4 + CSL (Cos)	PAS	0.897
Inception + CSL (Euc)	PAS	0.893

5 Conclusions

This study investigated the integration of conventional Machine Learning (ML) techniques with Few-Shot Learning (FSL) to improve the automatic classification of renal amyloidosis. The inherent imbalance in the dataset, with amyloidosis being a rare condition, posed significant challenges for traditional ML methods. The results indicate that while standard ML approaches, even those designed to address class imbalance, may not independently achieve robust performance, their combination with FSL shows considerable promise.

Our ensemble-based model achieved an impressive F1-score of 93.8%, surpassing related studies that dealt with datasets featuring less severe imbalance ratios. Incorporating established methods like Cost-Sensitive Learning (CSL) with FSL techniques significantly enhanced overall classification performance. The superior outcomes observed with FSL models, particularly when applied to PAS-stained samples, highlight FSL's ability to leverage limited data for improved generalization, which is crucial in medical datasets often lacking data abundance.

A significant contribution of this research is the development of a novel multi-stain dataset consisting of 11,674 images of renal glomeruli (available under request), annotated across nine classes with four different stains. This dataset addresses a crucial gap in computational pathology, given the challenges associated with gathering and annotating such a large volume of glomerular images.

The study also highlights the potential for classifying amyloidosis without relying on Congo red staining, the current diagnostic gold standard. If successful, this innovative approach could significantly streamline the diagnostic process. The findings encourage further exploration of this methodology for other glomerular lesions, potentially leading to a computer-aided diagnosis tool that would greatly aid pathologists in diagnosing glomerular diseases.

Additionally, the research underscores the limitations of conventional CNN approaches when faced with limited data, as evidenced by lower performance with stratified data in baseline models. This emphasizes the need for innovative approaches like FSL to improve outcomes when dealing with scarce data, a common challenge in medical image analysis.

Future work should focus on expanding the dataset to include a wider variety of amyloidosis presentations and exploring advanced techniques to further reduce prototype bias. This will enhance the robustness and accuracy of FSL models in classifying renal amyloidosis and ensure better generalization across different manifestations of the disease.

Acknowledgements. All authors belong to the Pathospotter project, which is partially sponsored by Fundação de Apoio à Pesquisa do Estado da Bahia (FAPESB), grant TO P0008/15 and Inova Fiocruz – Innovative ideas. Angelo Duarte is also sponsored by Universidade Estadual de Feira de Santana (UEFS), grant FINAPESQ TO 115/2024. Washington LC dos-Santos and Luciano Oliveira have research scholarships from Conselho Nacional de Desenvolvimento Científico e Tecnológico (CNPq), grants 306779/2017 and 308580/2021-4, respectively. This work was also partially supported by CAPES-PROAP 2023/2024 grants.

References

1. Abbas, Q.: An intelligent medical image classification system using few-shot learning. Concurr. Comput.: Pract. Exp. **35**(2), e7451 (2023). https://doi.org/10.1002/cpe.7451
2. Billion Polak, P., Prusa, J.D., Khoshgoftaar, T.M.: Low-shot learning and class imbalance: a survey. J. Big Data **11**(1) (2024)
3. Deng, Y., Li, H.: Deep learning for few-shot white blood cell image classification and feature learning. Comput. Methods Biomech. Biomed. Eng.: Imaging Vis. **11**(6), 2081–2091 (2023). https://doi.org/10.1080/21681163.2023.2219341
4. Diallo, R., Edalo, C., Awe, O.O., A. Vance, E.: Machine learning evaluation of imbalanced health data: a comparative analysis of balanced accuracy, MCC, and F1 score. In: Awe, O.O., A. Vance, E. (eds.) STEAM-H: Science, Technology, Engineering, Agriculture, Mathematics & Health, pp. 283–312. Springer, Cham (2025). https://doi.org/10.1007/978-3-031-72215-8_12
5. Fei-Fei, L., Fergus, R., Perona, P.: One-shot learning of object categories. IEEE Trans. Pattern Anal. Mach. Intell. **28**(4), 594–611 (2006). https://doi.org/10.1109/TPAMI.2006.79
6. He, K., Zhang, X., Ren, S., Sun, J.: Deep residual learning for image recognition. In: 2016 IEEE Conference on Computer Vision and Pattern Recognition (CVPR), pp. 770–778 (2015). https://api.semanticscholar.org/CorpusID:206594692
7. Johnson, J.M., Khoshgoftaar, T.M.: Survey on deep learning with class imbalance. J. Big Data **6**(1), 1–54 (2019). https://doi.org/10.1186/s40537-019-0192-5
8. Liu, S., Deng, W.: Very deep convolutional neural network based image classification using small training sample size. In: 2015 3rd IAPR Asian Conference on Pattern Recognition (ACPR), pp. 730–734 (2015). https://doi.org/10.1109/ACPR.2015.7486599
9. Mahbub, T., Obeid, A., Javed, S., Dias, J., Hassan, T., Werghi, N.: Center-focused affinity loss for class imbalance histology image classification. IEEE J. Biomed. Health Inform. **28**(2), 952–963 (2024). https://doi.org/10.1109/JBHI.2023.3336372
10. Medela, A., et al.: Few shot learning in histopathological images: reducing the need of labeled data on biological datasets. In: 2019 IEEE 16th International Symposium on Biomedical Imaging (ISBI 2019), pp. 1860–1864 (2019). https://doi.org/10.1109/ISBI.2019.8759182
11. Megahed, F.M., Chen, Y.J., Megahed, A., Ong, Y., Altman, N., Krzywinski, M.: The class imbalance problem. Nat. Methods **18**(11), 1270–1272 (2021)
12. Mienye, I.D., Sun, Y.: Performance analysis of cost-sensitive learning methods with application to imbalanced medical data. Inform. Med. Unlock. **25**, 100690 (2021). https://doi.org/10.1016/j.imu.2021.100690, https://www.sciencedirect.com/science/article/pii/S235291482100174X
13. Ochal, M., Patacchiola, M., Vazquez, J., Storkey, A., Wang, S.: Few-shot learning with class imbalance. IEEE Trans. Artif. Intell. **4**(5), 1348–1358 (2023). https://doi.org/10.1109/TAI.2023.3298303
14. Raj, R., Mathew, J., Kannath, S.K., Rajan, J.: Crossover based technique for data augmentation. Comput. Methods Program. Biomed. **218**, 106716 (2022). https://doi.org/10.1016/j.cmpb.2022.106716, https://www.sciencedirect.com/science/article/pii/S016926072200102X
15. Said, S.M., et al.: Renal amyloidosis: origin and clinicopathologic correlations of 474 recent cases. Clin. J. Am. Soc. Nephrol. **8**(9), 1515–1523 (2013)

16. Snell, J., Swersky, K., Zemel, R.: Prototypical networks for few-shot learning. In: Proceedings of the 31st International Conference on Neural Information Processing Systems, NIPS 2017, pp. 4080–4090. Curran Associates Inc., Red Hook (2017)
17. Sümer, Ö., Hellmann, F., Hustinx, A., Hsieh, T.C., André, E., Krawitz, P.: Few-shot meta-learning for recognizing facial phenotypes of genetic disorders. Stud. Health Technol. Inform. **302**, 932–936 (2023)
18. Szegedy, C., et al.: Going deeper with convolutions. In: 2015 IEEE Conference on Computer Vision and Pattern Recognition (CVPR), pp. 1–9 (2015). https://doi.org/10.1109/CVPR.2015.7298594
19. Tan, M., Le, Q.: EfficientNet: rethinking model scaling for convolutional neural networks. In: Chaudhuri, K., Salakhutdinov, R. (eds.) Proceedings of the 36th International Conference on Machine Learning. Proceedings of Machine Learning Research, vol. 97, pp. 6105–6114. PMLR (2019). https://proceedings.mlr.press/v97/tan19a.html
20. Titoriya, A.K., Singh, M.P.: Few-shot learning on histopathology image classification. In: 2022 International Conference on Computational Science and Computational Intelligence (CSCI), pp. 251–256 (2022). https://doi.org/10.1109/CSCI58124.2022.00048
21. Tyagi, S., Mittal, S.: Sampling approaches for imbalanced data classification problem in machine learning. In: Singh, P.K., Kar, A.K., Singh, Y., Kolekar, M.H., Tanwar, S. (eds.) Proceedings of ICRIC 2019. LNEE, vol. 597, pp. 209–221. Springer, Cham (2020). https://doi.org/10.1007/978-3-030-29407-6_17
22. Walsh, R., Tardy, M.: A comparison of techniques for class imbalance in deep learning classification of breast cancer. Diagnostics **13**(1) (2023). https://doi.org/10.3390/diagnostics13010067
23. Wang, Y., Yao, Q., Kwok, J.T., Ni, L.M.: Generalizing from a few examples: a survey on few-shot learning. ACM Comput. Surv. **53**(3) (2020). https://doi.org/10.1145/3386252
24. Yakupova, E., Bobyleva, L., Vikhlyantsev, I., Bobylev, A.: Congo red and amyloids: history and relationship. Biosci. Rep. **39**(1) (2019). https://doi.org/10.1042/BSR20181415, https://www.sciencedirect.com/science/article/pii/S1573493519002832
25. Zhang, R., Liu, Q.: Learning with few samples in deep learning for image classification, a mini-review. Front. Comput. Neurosci. **16**, 1075294 (2022)

CerberusDet: Unified Multi-dataset Object Detection

Irina Tolstykh, Mikhail Chernyshov, and Maksim Kuprashevich(✉)

Layer Team, R&D Department, SALUTEDEV, Tashkent, Uzbekistan
mvkuprashevich@gmail.com

Abstract. Conventional object detection models are usually limited by the data on which they were trained and by the category logic they define. With the recent rise of Language-Visual Models, new methods have emerged that are not restricted to these fixed categories. Despite their flexibility, such Open Vocabulary detection models still fall short in accuracy compared to traditional models with fixed classes. At the same time, more accurate data-specific models face challenges when there is a need to extend classes or merge different datasets for training. The latter often cannot be combined due to different logics or conflicting class definitions, making it difficult to improve a model without compromising its performance. In this paper, we introduce CerberusDet, a framework with a multi-headed model designed for handling multiple object detection tasks. The proposed model is built on the YOLO architecture and efficiently shares visual features from both the backbone and neck components, while maintaining separate task heads. This approach allows CerberusDet to perform very efficiently while still delivering optimal results. We evaluated the model on the PASCAL VOC dataset and Objects365 dataset to demonstrate its abilities. CerberusDet achieved state-of-the-art results with a 36% reduction in inference time. The more tasks are trained together, the more efficient the proposed model becomes compared to running individual models sequentially. The training and inference code, as well as the model, are available as open-source (https://github.com/ai-forever/CerberusDet).

Keywords: Object detection · Parameter sharing · Representation similarity analysis · Multi-dataset detection · Open vocabulary detection

1 Introduction

Adding new categories to an existing real-time application that uses Object Detection (OD) involves several significant challenges. A key issue is that object categories annotated in one dataset might be unannotated in another, even if the objects themselves appear in images from the latter. Additionally, merging different datasets may often be impossible because of differing annotation logic and incomplete class overlaps. At the same time, such applications require efficient pipelines, which limits the usage of separate data-specific models. These challenges highlight the need for a unified model that

Fig. 1. Illustration of the work of the CerberusDet trained on three datasets with different labels. We trained a model using the PASCAL VOC dataset and two subsets from the Objects365 dataset with animals and tableware categories. See training details in Sect. 4.

can efficiently handle multiple datasets and object categories without sacrificing accuracy or increasing computational complexity. In this work, we aim to address these limitations by presenting CerberusDet, a framework designed for multi-task object detection that optimizes performance and resource utilization (Fig. 1).

The goal of this work is *to build a unified model trained on multiple datasets* that does not degrade in accuracy compared to individually trained models, while using a smaller computational budget. CerberusDet is designed to train a single detection neural network on multiple datasets simultaneously. We also demonstrate an approach to identify the optimal model architecture, as not all tasks can be trained together. A notable challenge lies in determining which parameters to share across which tasks. Suboptimal grouping of tasks may cause negative transfer [41], the problem of sharing information between unrelated tasks. Additionally, with computational resource constraints, the proposed approach allows for selecting an architecture that meets the requirements. To evaluate the proposed CerberusDet model, we conduct experiments with open data and obtain results comparable to separated data-specific state-of-the-art models, but with one unified neural network. We base the presented architecture on YOLO [44], leveraging its efficiency and scalability. Although our task shares similarities with continual learning, particularly Task-Incremental Learning, it differs in that the model trains on multiple datasets and tasks at the same time, rather than sequentially, thereby minimizing the risk of catastrophic forgetting and negative transfer.

An alternative approach to extending the detector model with new categories is the use of Open-Vocabulary Object Detectors (OVDs) [20], which have recently gained popularity. However, OVDs often lack the accuracy of data-specific detectors, require a lot of training data, and are prone to overfitting to base classes [5,47]. We prioritize high accuracy over the flexibility of OVDs. The proposed architecture allows us to add new classes as needed while preserving the accuracy of previously learned ones, making our approach more suitable for the required needs. Notably, this approach has been deployed and validated in our production environment, demonstrating its robustness and reliability in practical applications.

The key contributions of our paper are as follows:

- We propose a method for multi-dataset and multi-task object detection, utilizing an efficient parameter-sharing strategy and training procedure.
- We introduce a flexible framework for multi-dataset object detection, named CerberusDet, which can be tailored to various computational requirements and tasks. We publicly release the code, along with pre-trained models, to support further research and development.
- We demonstrate the effectiveness of CerberusDet through experiments on both large-scale and smaller datasets, achieving state-of-the-art performance with reduced computational cost.

2 Related Works

Object Detection. There are many different detection models. Two-stage detectors, such as Faster R-CNN [36] and Cascade R-CNN [4] first generate region proposals, which are then refined and classified. Single-shot convolutional detectors like YOLO [35], SSD [28] or EfficientDet [43] skip the region proposal stage and produce final localization and labels prediction at once. Recently popularized detection transformers like DAB-DETR [27] or CO-DETR [54] use a transformer encoder-decoder architecture to predict all objects at once.

We built CerberusDet model based on the implementation of the YOLO architecture by Ultralytics [44], as YOLOv5/YOLOv8 models are fast and achieve SOTA results on various tasks. YOLOv5 uses anchors for the detection head which is composed of convolutional layers for multi-scale features. YOLOv8 is an anchor-free model with a decoupled head to process separately objectness, classification, and bounding box regression tasks based on multi-scale features.

Multi-Task Learning: (MTL) aims to improve both efficiency and prediction accuracy for individual tasks over separately trained models. The two most commonly used ways to perform MTL are hard or soft parameter sharing of hidden layers [37]. Authors of [10,12,16,25,26,29,33] apply the first one to share most of the parameters between all tasks and to find a representation that captures all of the tasks. Soft parameter sharing is utilized in works [13,13,32,49,49], where individual tasks possess their own parameter sets interconnected either through information sharing or by requiring parameter similarity.

Most multi-task models in the computer vision domain focus on addressing different CV tasks, such as classification and semantic segmentation [26]; segmentation, depth and surface normals [16]. UberNet [22] learns 7 computer vision problems under a single architecture. GrokNet [1] learns unified representation to solve several image retrieval and a large number of classification tasks. In this paper, we apply MTL to address multiple detection tasks, where each task uses its own dataset with a unique set of labels.

To design optimal multi-task network architectures, the authors of [41,42,45] [3,19,51] apply various strategies that rely on understanding task relationships. In this work, we use the Representation Similarity Analysis (RSA) method [14,15] [23] to estimate task affinity, following a similar approach to that described in [45].

Different optimization techniques were proposed in [7,11,38,50] for MTL systems, which aim to reduce conflicts between tasks by adjusting the direction of task gradients. In this paper, we employ a gradient averaging method, but any other optimization method can be utilized as well for training the proposed CerberusDet model.

Multi-dataset Object Detection: aims to leverage multiple datasets to train one visual recognition model to detect objects from different label spaces. Some works [46,48] build specific modules to adapt feature representations related to different domains. Others [52,53] train one model with unified multi-dataset label spaces. To create a detector with an unified label space across all datasets, the authors of [53] automatically learn mappings between the common label space and dataset-specific labels during training. The current paper focuses on a model with shared parameters but dataset-specific outputs. The authors of [52] train a detection model with pseudo ground truth for each dataset generated by task-specific models to merge label spaces, while our framework does not require annotations from different datasets to be combined. ScaleDet [6] also unifies label space from multiple datasets by utilizing text CLIP [34] embeddings.

Open-Vocabulary Object Detection: (OVD) models aim to recognize objects of categories not present at training time. Novel categories are described by text inputs and the detectors are try to establish a semantic connection between object regions and object labels chosen from a possibly very large vocabulary [2,18,20]. The association of objects and labels typically is done through large pre-trained vision-language matching methods like CLIP [8,18,20,24].

OVD models may be used for expanding the label set of a detector model if pre-trained models have knowledge of the target data domain, aligning textual embedding space with visual features during training [8,18,24,30,31]. The authors of [20] train an open-vocabulary detector based on CLIP text and image embeddings to detect 1,203 categories from the LVIS dataset. They initially train the detector on base categories and then expand it to cover all rare categories in the dataset.

3 Model

3.1 Method

In this paper, we propose the CerberusDet model that allows multiple detection tasks to be learned in a shared model. Each detection task is a separate task, which employs its own dataset with the unique set of labels.

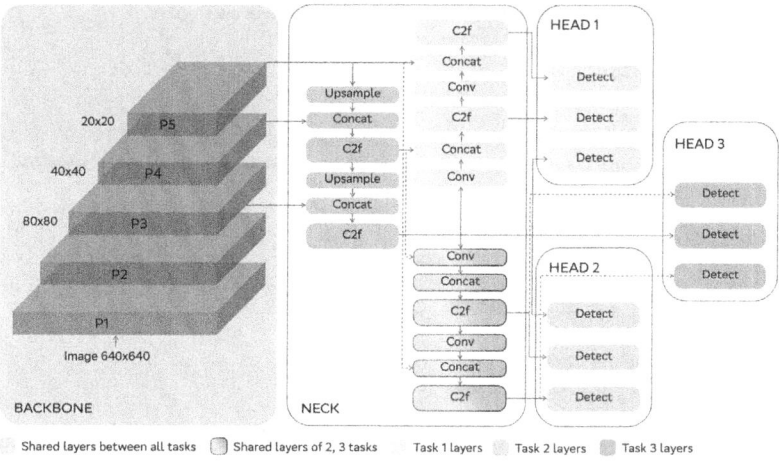

Fig. 2. Diagram of an example of the CerberusDet architecture based on YOLOv8, illustrated with three tasks. Each neck module can be shared between tasks or be task-specific. The CerberusDet model optimizes computational resources by sharing all backbone parameters across tasks, while each task retains its own unique set of parameters for the head.

The CerberusDet model is built upon the YOLO [44] architecture. It optimizes computational resources by sharing all backbone parameters across tasks, while each task retains its own unique set of parameters for the head. The neck layers can either be shared or be specific to the task. One of the possible variants of YOLOv8-based CerberusDet architecture for three tasks is illustrated in Fig. 2. With the standard YOLOv8x architecture and 640 input image resolution, the model backbone consists of 184 layers and 30M parameters. The neck has 6 shareable modules with 134 layers and 28M parameters. Each head consists of 54 layers and 8M parameters.

By sharing the backbone across multiple tasks, our training approach achieves significant computational budget economy compared to the sequential inference of separate models for each task. Figure 3 illustrates the inference speed of CerberusDet, which is based on the YOLOv8x architecture. The figure compares the inference times for two scenarios: one where all neck parameters are task-dependent, and another where these parameters are shared across tasks. The results highlight the computational efficiency gained through parameter sharing.

3.2 Parameters Sharing

We decided to employ the hard parameter sharing technique for multi-task learning, given its demonstrated efficiency and its ability to enhance per-task prediction quality by leveraging information across tasks during training [37]. Hard parameters sharing allows us to have sets of parameters that are shared across tasks, and sets of parameters that are task-specific. Based on YOLO architecture we have sets of sharable parameters at the module level. E.g. YOLOv8x has 6 parameterized neck modules, so each task may share each of them with another task.

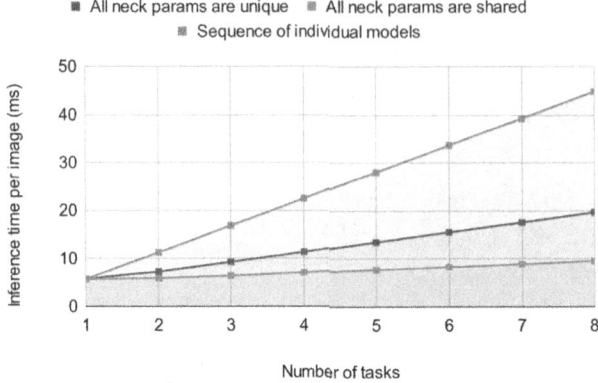

Fig. 3. Comparison of inference time of YOLOv8x-based CerberusDet models and the sequence of individual models. Measurements were made with FP16 precision on a V100 GPU with a batch size of 32.

To decide what modules to share across which tasks we employ the Representation Similarity Analysis [14, 15, 45] method to estimate task similarity at each neck module that can be shared or task-specific. Then for each possible architecture variant we calculate an RSA-based similarity score (*rsa score*) and *computational score*. The first one shows the potential performance of an architecture and the second one evaluates its computational efficiency. Within the available computational budget, we select the architecture with the best *rsa score*. Let the architecture contain l shareable modules and we have N tasks, the algorithm for selecting the architecture looks as follows:

- Select a small representative subset of images from the test set of each task.
- Using task-specific models, extract features for the selected images from each module.
- Based on the extracted features, calculate Duality Diagram Similarity [14] (DDS) - computing pairwise (dis)similarity for each pair of selected images. Each element of the matrix is the value of (1 - Pearson's correlation).
- Using the Centered Kernel Alignment (CKA) [23] method on the DDS matrices, compute representation dissimilarity matrices (RDMs) - an NxN matrix for each module. Each element of the matrix indicates the similarity coefficient between two tasks.
- For each possible architecture, using values from the RDM matrices, compute the *rsa score*. It is calculated as the sum of the task dissimilarity scores at every location in the shareable model layers. It is defined as $rsa\ score = \sum_{m=1}^{l} S_m$, where S_m (Eq. 1) is found by averaging the maximum distance between the dissimilarity scores of the shared tasks in the module l.
- For each possible architecture calculate *computational score* using Eq. 2.
- We select the architecture with the best combination of rsa score and computational score (the lower is the better), or we choose the architecture with the lowest rsa score within the set constraint on computational score.

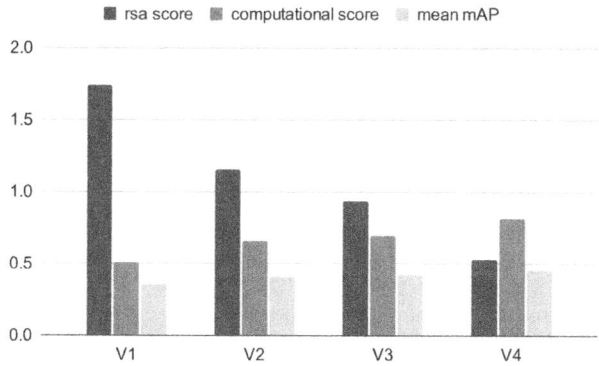

Fig. 4. *rsa score*, *computational score* and average mAP of 4 different models trained for 3 tasks.

$$S_m = \frac{1}{|\{\mathcal{T}_i, \ldots, \mathcal{T}_k\}|} \times \sum_{j=i}^{k} \max\{RDM(j,i), \ldots, RDM(j,k)\} \quad (1)$$

where $\{\mathcal{T}_i, \ldots, \mathcal{T}_k\}$ - shared tasks at module l.

$$computational\ score = \frac{inference\_time}{(N * single\_inference\_time)} \quad (2)$$

To evaluate the chosen approach, we selected 4 architectures with different RSA scores and computational scores, trained models and compared the average metric values. Figure 4 demonstrates that model accuracy increases while the RSA score decreases and computational complexity increases. To calculate the computational score, the V100 GPU was used and the batch size was equal to 1.

3.3 Training Procedure

Let's consider a set of tasks $\{\mathcal{T}_1, \ldots, \mathcal{T}_n\}$. Different combinations of these tasks may share a set of model parameters. Let $\theta_{shared} = \{\theta_{i..k}, \ldots \theta_{j..m}\}$ be the sets of shared parameters between different groups of tasks $\{i, \ldots, k\}, \ldots, \{j, \ldots, m\}$. Algorithm 1 represents the end-to-end learning process of the proposed CerberusDet model. During training, we iterate through tasks, sample mini-batches from the corresponding dataset and calculate the loss and gradients for the parameters related to the current task. Next, we average the gradients for the shared parameters across task groups and update their values according to Eq. 3.

Algorithm 1. CerberusDet training process.
___
Require:
N – total number for tasks,
$\{D_1,\ldots,D_n\}$ – datasets for tasks $\{\mathcal{T}_1,\ldots,\mathcal{T}_n\}$,
$\{\theta_1,\ldots,\theta_n,\theta_{shared}\}$ – task-specific and shared parameters,
$\{L_1,\ldots,L_n\}$ – task-specific loss functions

1: **while** training not converged **do**
2:      $g_{shared} \leftarrow 0$
3:      **for** $i = 1$ to N **do**
4:          $g_i \leftarrow 0$
5:          $X_i \leftarrow$ a mini batch from D_i for task $\mathcal{T}_i$
6:          // Compute task-specific model output
7:          $Y \leftarrow M(X_i, \mathcal{T}_i)$
8:          // Calculate gradients for task-specific parameters
9:          $g_i \leftarrow \frac{\partial L_i}{\partial \theta_i}(Y, Y^*)$
10:          // Accumulate gradients for shared parameters
11:          $g_{shared} \leftarrow g_{shared} + \frac{\partial L_i}{\partial \theta_{shared}}(Y, Y^*)$
12:      **end for**
13:      // Update parameters
14:      **for** $i = 1$ to N **do**
15:          $\theta_i \leftarrow \theta_i - \alpha * g_i$
16:      **end for**
17:      $\theta_{shared} \leftarrow \theta_{shared} -$ learning rate $\cdot$ avg(g_{shared}, M) ▷ Eq. 3
18: **end while**
___

$$\theta_{\{i,\ldots,k\}} = \theta_{\{i,\ldots,k\}} - (\alpha * \frac{1}{|\{i,\ldots,k\}|} * \sum_{j \in \{i,\ldots,k\}} \frac{\partial L_j}{\partial \theta_{\{i,\ldots,k\}}}) \quad (3)$$

where $\{i,\ldots,k\}$ represents the group of tasks with shared parameters $\theta_{\{i,\ldots,k\}}$, α is the learning rate, L_j is the loss for task j.

The speed and effectiveness of joint training are strongly influenced by the loss functions of individual tasks. Since these loss functions can have different natures and scales, it is essential to weigh them correctly. To find the optimal weights for the loss functions, as well as other training hyperparameters, we employ the hyperparameter evolution method.

During the training process, we discovered that the model's performance significantly suffers if the samples within each batch are not balanced carefully and thoroughly. To address this, we implemented a strategy to ensure that all classes are adequately represented in each iteration according to their frequency in the dataset.

3.4 The Impact of Training Settings

The techniques described in the previous two sections were used in a series of experiments with our proprietary data. Table 1 presents the results of the impact of each technique. We use proprietary data in these experiments, as they exhibit a sufficient level

Table 1. The impact of sequentially applying various techniques in YOLOv5x-based CerberusDet training for 3 tasks. The baseline model shares all parameters between tasks, except for the heads. It was trained without balanced sampling and without hyperparameters tuning.

Methods applied during training	Δ mAP@0.5:0.95
w/o balanced sampling, w/o arch search, w/o hypersearch	+0%
with balanced sampling	+5%
with balanced sampling, all neck+head layers are task specific	+11%
with balanced sampling, with arch search	+1%
with balanced sampling, with arch search, with hypersearch	+1.2%

of inter-task consistency to ensure the clarity of the experiments. Models were trained for 3 tasks, where the baseline being an architecture where all parameters of the model, except for the heads, were shared among tasks. The first task's dataset comprises 22 categories with 27,146 images in the training set and 3,017 images in the validation set. The dataset of the second task consists of 18 categories with 22,365 images in the training set and 681 images in the validation set. The dataset of the third task comprises 16 categories with 17,012 images in the training set and 3,830 images in the validation set. To compare the influence of architecture search method on the result, we also trained the model, where all neck parameters are task-specific. Then, we compare the accuracy improvement of the discovered architecture relative to it.

Mentioned models were built on top of YOLOv5x with an input image resolution of 640 × 640, measurements were made with FP16 precision on the V100 GPU.

4 Open-Source Datasets Experiments

In this section, we outline the CerberusDet's experimental setup, results, and training configuration. Additionally, we conducted a comparative analysis between CerberusDet and standalone YOLOv8 models using public datasets.

Notably, our comparison also incorporates the Open Vocabulary Detector YOLO-Worldv2-X [9], which was trained on a comprehensive set of base classes from the Objects365 [39], GoldG [21], and CC3M [40] datasets at a resolution of 640. This inclusion enables an evaluation of a model that employs a zero-shot approach for class expansion, allowing comparison with traditional detection models.

Our analysis includes the presentation of metrics such as mean average precision (mAP): mAP@0.5 and mAP@0.5:0.95, alongside measurements of the models inference speed with FP16 precision on a V100 GPU.

4.1 Datasets

We conducted experiments on datasets of varying sizes and characteristics to evaluate the performance of the CerberusDet model compared to YOLOv8. The datasets used include both large-scale and smaller, more focused sets:

- **PASCAL VOC** [17]. A smaller, widely-used benchmark dataset with 20 object classes. The combined training set (VOC 2007 + VOC 2012) consists of 16,551 images, with 4,952 images in the test set. This dataset is designed to evaluate models on general object detection tasks with limited data.
- **Objects365** [39]. A large-scale dataset with 365 object classes and over 1.7 million training images, along with 79,578 images in the validation set. It provides a diverse and extensive set of categories, making it suitable for large-scale, real-world object detection tasks.
- **Objects365 Subsets.** To simulate multi-dataset detection with several smaller datasets, we created two subsets of Objects365:
    - **Objects365 Animals.** Contains 19 animal classes with 14,295 training images and 5,413 validation images.
    - **Objects365 Tableware.** Contains 12 tableware-related classes with 269,675 training images and 24,645 validation images.

To create an Objects365 subset, all non-empty images containing annotations for at least one object of a target class were selected. Images without annotations or those containing only objects from unrelated classes were filtered out. A detailed list of classes and the filtering code are available in the project repository.

By using both large (Objects365) and small (PASCAL VOC, Objects365 subsets) datasets, we ensure that the experimental comparison evaluates the model's performance across different data scales and domain complexities.

4.2 Models Training

Initially, we trained four individual YOLOv8x models on each of the datasets mentioned in Sect. 4.1. These models were trained with input resolution of 640×640, a batch size of 32, and mixed precision, serving as a baseline.

Next, we trained the CerberusDet model on two datasets, Objects365 and PASCAL VOC, whose sizes differ by a factor of 100. Due to this significant imbalance, we adjusted the sampling strategy described in Sect. 3.3 to ensure proportional data exposure. In each iteration, the model was consistently fed samples from the Objects365 dataset, while VOC samples appeared every 104th iteration. Despite this imbalance, the model was trained over multiple epochs, fully revisiting both datasets. It was trained with a batch size of 40 and converged in 38 epochs.

We also trained the CerberusDet model on three datasets: Objects365 tableware, Objects365 animals, and PASCAL VOC. As in the previous experiment, there was a significant imbalance in data size between the Objects365 tableware dataset and the other two. To address this, we again adjusted the sampling strategy to balance data exposure. In each iteration, the model was fed 40 samples from Objects365 tableware

Table 2. Comparison of the performance of CerberusDet models trained on two or three datasets, the OVD detector, and YOLOv8 dataset-specific models. Inference time measurements were conducted on a V100 GPU with a batch size of 32 and FP16 precision. [†] indicates that the Ultralytics version of the model was used. **Bold** text indicates the best result for a given dataset, while underlined text indicates the second-best result.

Model	Train Set	Test Set	mAP 0.5	mAP 0.5:0.95	Speed(ms)
YOLOv8	VOC 2007/2012	VOC 2007	0.92	0.76	5.6
YOLOv8	O365	O365	0.38	0.29	5.6
YOLOv8	O365 animals	O365 animals	0.55	**0.43**	5.6
YOLOv8	O365 tableware	O365 tableware	**0.68**	**0.56**	5.6
YOLO-Worldv2-X[†]	O365 + GoldG + CC3M-Lite	VOC 2007	0.83	0.69	7.7
		O365	0.31	0.24	
		O365 animals	0.37	0.3	
		O365 tableware	0.50	0.40	
CerberusDet	VOC 2007/2012 + O365	VOC 2007	**0.93**	**0.77**	7.2
		O365	**0.46**	**0.36**	
CerberusDet	VOC 2007/2012 + O365 animals	VOC 2007	0.92	0.75	7.2
		O365 animals	**0.57**	**0.43**	
CerberusDet	VOC 2007/2012 + O365 animals + O365 tableware	VOC 2007	**0.93**	0.76	10
		O365 animals	0.54	0.42	
		O365 tableware	**0.68**	**0.56**	

and 4 samples each from Objects365 animals and PASCAL VOC. The model converged in 29 epochs.

Additionally, we trained the CerberusDet model on two datasets: PASCAL VOC and Objects365 animals to assess how the metrics change when a new dataset is added. This model was trained using a standard procedure with a batch size of 32 on a single V100 GPU.

All training procedures used the same set of hyperparameters inherited from the single-task YOLOv8x models. CerberusDet models leverage the YOLOv8x architecture as their backbone. Each detection task uses the vanilla YOLOv8 head, with all neck parameters being dataset-specific. For initialization, we utilized transfer learning by loading pre-trained weights on COCO for the backbone and neck, provided by the YOLOv8 authors, while the head parameters were initialized randomly.

CerberusDet models were trained with mixed precision, the SGD optimizer and synchronized batch normalization using 8 H100 GPUs. The input resolution was set to 640×640 pixels.

4.3 Experimental Results

The experimental results are presented in Table 2.

We can observe that all three CerberusDet models either achieve the same accuracy as the individual YOLOv8 models or outperform them. When comparing CerberusDet trained on two datasets (VOC, O365 animals) to one trained on three (VOC, O365 animals, O365 tableware), we can see that adding another dataset to the training has minimal impact on the accuracy for the first two datasets.

In comparison with YOLO-Worldv2-X, a specialized CerberusDet models demonstrate a significant advantages. This comparison confirms the hypothesis that OVD detectors, while flexible and capable of rapidly adapting to new classes, generally fall short of the accuracy achieved by specialized detectors like CerberusDet.

When evaluating model inference speed, CerberusDet remains efficient, performing inference for two datasets in 7.2 milliseconds on a single NVIDIA V100 GPU with FP16 precision, faster than separate YOLOv8 models (11.2 ms). Extending CerberusDet to three datasets increases inference time to 10 milliseconds, which is still one-third faster than using three separate models. For two tasks, CerberusDet also shows a slight advantage over YOLO-Worldv2-X, with 7.2 ms compared to 7.7 ms.

While we did not explicitly measure training time for comparison, it can be inferred that CerberusDet demonstrates efficiency advantages due to its multi-task learning structure. Since CerberusDet processes multiple datasets in a single training cycle, the theoretical training time could potentially approach that of training N separate models, where N is the number of datasets. However, by sharing visual features across tasks and benefiting from knowledge transfer during joint training, CerberusDet can optimize parameter updates, often resulting in faster overall training compared to sequential training of individual models.

The results demonstrate effectiveness of the CerberusDet across diverse datasets, even when a significant imbalance in the amount of data is present. Results also highlight an advantage over the zero-shot approach while maintaining flexibility in class expansion.

5 Limitations

The outlined training process is highly sensitive to optimization hyperparameters such as learning rate, loss weights, momentum, and weight decay. Therefore, we recommend conducting a hyperparameter search to achieve the best training results. The necessary scripts for this process are provided with the code.

In some cases, different multi-gradient descent algorithms may be more beneficial instead of gradient averaging. Notable examples include MGDA [11] and Aligned-MTL [38].

When training a model on multiple tasks, it is important to identify which tasks can share more parameters and which require fewer shared parameters. To address this, we use the RSA algorithm, which, while requiring models trained for individual tasks, is still faster than iteratively testing all possible architecture variations with different parameter-sharing schemes. However, if training such models is not feasible, our approach can still be applied using a parameter-sharing scheme where all neck layers are task-dependent. While this may not be the most optimal solution, it remains more efficient than sequentially inferring single models.

Our method is built upon the YOLO architecture, and we have not conducted experiments with other architectures, such as alternative convolutional models or transformer-based detectors. However, the core idea of our approach is architecture-agnostic and could be adapted to other model types. Exploring these adaptations and their effectiveness will be a focus of future work.

6 Conclusions

In this work, we introduced CerberusDet, a scalable and adaptive framework for multi-task object detection. The proposed method achieves results comparable to separated data-specific state-of-the-art models while utilizing approximately 36% less computational budget in case of training for two tasks. The more tasks are trained together, the more efficient the proposed model becomes compared to running individual models sequentially.

The challenge of handling separate and conflicting datasets without requiring unified annotation was addressed, offering significant value for future research and real-world applications.

The proposed approach, based on YOLO, efficiently shares visual features across different tasks. Hard parameter sharing and Representation Similarity Analysis (RSA) were employed to optimize task-specific performance while maintaining high computational efficiency.

Extensive experiments were conducted on both proprietary production-scale data and open-source datasets (PASCAL VOC and Objects365). The findings highlighted the model's superior performance and versatility.

Experiments with the zero-shot approach showed that using OVD in a similar scenario across multiple datasets (>2) does not provide an advantage. In key metrics, especially those important in real-world applications such as speed and, most importantly, accuracy, OVD performs worse. This gap is explained by the need for a large amount of data for training, including target data, and the tendency to overfit on base classes. The only real advantage of the zero-shot approach in the current scenario is its speed and flexibility in adding potentially new and infinite categories, which can be useful in developing and testing class schemes. In practice, CerberusDet can be viewed as an intermediate solution between traditional detectors and OVD, taking the best of both.

Furthermore, CerberusDet is designed to be easily expandable, supporting additional tasks beyond object detection, such as attribute recognition and embedding calculation.

To support the research community and practitioners, the framework - including algorithms' implementation, all necessary code, and the model trained on open-source data—has been made publicly available. These resources aim to facilitate further research and practical applications, providing a foundation for significant improvements and innovations in the future.

Disclosure of Interests. The author conducted this research as part of their work at SALUT-EDEV and has no other competing interests that could influence the content of this article.

References

1. Bell, S., et al.: GrokNet: unified computer vision model trunk and embeddings for commerce. In: Proceedings of the 26th ACM SIGKDD International Conference on Knowledge Discovery & Data Mining, pp. 2608–2616 (2020)
2. Bianchi, L., Carrara, F., Messina, N., Gennaro, C., Falchi, F.: The devil is in the fine-grained details: evaluating open-vocabulary object detectors for fine-grained understanding. arXiv preprint arXiv:2311.17518 (2023)
3. Bruggemann, D., Kanakis, M., Georgoulis, S., Van Gool, L.: Automated search for resource-efficient branched multi-task networks. arXiv preprint arXiv:2008.10292 (2020)
4. Cai, Z., Vasconcelos, N.: Cascade R-CNN: delving into high quality object detection. In: Proceedings of the IEEE Conference on Computer Vision and Pattern Recognition, pp. 6154–6162 (2018)
5. Chaoyang Zhu, L.C.: A survey on open-vocabulary detection and segmentation: past, present, and future. arXiv preprint arXiv:2307.09220 (2024)
6. Chen, Y., et al.: ScaleDet: a scalable multi-dataset object detector. In: Proceedings of the IEEE/CVF Conference on Computer Vision and Pattern Recognition, pp. 7288–7297 (2023)
7. Chen, Z., Badrinarayanan, V., Lee, C.Y., Rabinovich, A.: GradNorm: gradient normalization for adaptive loss balancing in deep multitask networks. In: International Conference on Machine Learning, pp. 794–803. PMLR (2018)
8. Cheng, T., Song, L., Ge, Y., Liu, W., Wang, X., Shan, Y.: Yolo-world: real-time open-vocabulary object detection. arxiv 2024. arXiv preprint arXiv:2401.17270
9. Cheng, T., Song, L., Ge, Y., Liu, W., Wang, X., Shan, Y.: Yolo-world: real-time open-vocabulary object detection. In: Proceedings of the IEEE Conference on Computer Vision and Pattern Recognition (CVPR) (2024)
10. Chennupati, S., Sistu, G., Yogamani, S., A Rawashdeh, S.: MultiNet++: multi-stream feature aggregation and geometric loss strategy for multi-task learning. In: Proceedings of the IEEE/CVF Conference on Computer Vision and Pattern Recognition Workshops (2019)
11. Désidéri, J.A.: Mutiple-gradient descent algorithm for multiobjective optimization. In: European Congress on Computational Methods in Applied Sciences and Engineering (ECCOMAS 2012) (2012)
12. Doersch, C., Zisserman, A.: Multi-task self-supervised visual learning. In: Proceedings of the IEEE International Conference on Computer Vision, pp. 2051–2060 (2017)
13. Duong, L., Cohn, T., Bird, S., Cook, P.: Low resource dependency parsing: cross-lingual parameter sharing in a neural network parser. In: Proceedings of the 53rd Annual Meeting of the Association for Computational Linguistics and the 7th International Joint Conference on Natural Language Processing (volume 2: Short Papers), pp. 845–850 (2015)
14. Dwivedi, K., Huang, J., Cichy, R.M., Roig, G.: Duality diagram similarity: a generic framework for initialization selection in task transfer learning. In: Vedaldi, A., Bischof, H., Brox, T., Frahm, J.-M. (eds) ECCV 2020. LNCS, vol. 12371, pp. 497–513. Springer, Cham (2020). https://doi.org/10.1007/978-3-030-58574-7_30
15. Dwivedi, K., Roig, G.: Representation similarity analysis for efficient task taxonomy & transfer learning. In: Proceedings of the IEEE/CVF Conference on Computer Vision and Pattern Recognition, pp. 12387–12396 (2019)
16. Eigen, D., Fergus, R.: Predicting depth, surface normals and semantic labels with a common multi-scale convolutional architecture. In: Proceedings of the IEEE International Conference on Computer Vision, pp. 2650–2658 (2015)
17. Everingham, M., Van Gool, L., Williams, C.K.I., Winn, J., Zisserman, A.: The PASCAL visual object classes challenge 2012 (VOC2012) results. http://www.pascal-network.org/challenges/VOC/voc2012/workshop/index.html

18. Feng, C., et al: PromptDet: towards open-vocabulary detection using uncurated images. In: Avidan, S., Brostow, G., Cissé, M., Farinella, G.M., Hassner, T. (eds) ECCV 2022. LNCS, vol. 13669, pp. 701–717. Springer, Cham (2022)
19. Fifty, C., Amid, E., Zhao, Z., Yu, T., Anil, R., Finn, C.: Efficiently identifying task groupings for multi-task learning. Adv. Neural. Inf. Process. Syst. **34**, 27503–27516 (2021)
20. Gu, X., Lin, T.Y., Kuo, W., Cui, Y.: Open-vocabulary object detection via vision and language knowledge distillation. arXiv preprint arXiv:2104.13921 (2021)
21. Kamath, A., Singh, M., LeCun, Y., Misra, I., Synnaeve, G., Carion, N.: MDETR–modulated detection for end-to-end multi-modal understanding. arXiv preprint arXiv:2104.12763 (2021)
22. Kokkinos, I.: UberNet: training a universal convolutional neural network for low-, mid-, and high-level vision using diverse datasets and limited memory. In: Proceedings of the IEEE Conference on Computer Vision and Pattern Recognition, pp. 6129–6138 (2017)
23. Kornblith, S., Norouzi, M., Lee, H., Hinton, G.: Similarity of neural network representations revisited. In: International Conference on Machine Learning, pp. 3519–3529. PMLR (2019)
24. Kuo, W., Cui, Y., Gu, X., Piergiovanni, A., Angelova, A.: F-VLM: open-vocabulary object detection upon frozen vision and language models. arXiv preprint arXiv:2209.15639 (2022)
25. Leang, I., Sistu, G., Bürger, F., Bursuc, A., Yogamani, S.: Dynamic task weighting methods for multi-task networks in autonomous driving systems. In: 2020 IEEE 23rd International Conference on Intelligent Transportation Systems (ITSC), pp. 1–8. IEEE (2020)
26. Liao, Y., Kodagoda, S., Wang, Y., Shi, L., Liu, Y.: Understand scene categories by objects: a semantic regularized scene classifier using convolutional neural networks. In: 2016 IEEE international conference on robotics and automation (ICRA), pp. 2318–2325. IEEE (2016)
27. Liu, S., et al.: Dab-DETR: dynamic anchor boxes are better queries for DETR. arXiv preprint arXiv:2201.12329 (2022)
28. Liu, W., et al.: SSD: single shot multibox detector. In: Leibe, B., Matas, J., Sebe, N., Welling, M. (eds.) ECCV 2016, Part I. LNCS, vol. 9905, pp. 21–37. Springer, Cham (2016). https://doi.org/10.1007/978-3-319-46448-0_2
29. Long, M., Cao, Z., Wang, J., Yu, P.S.: Learning multiple tasks with multilinear relationship networks. Adv. Neural Inf. Process. Syst. **30** (2017)
30. Ma, Z., Yang, Y., Wang, G., Xu, X., Shen, H.T., Zhang, M.: Rethinking open-world object detection in autonomous driving scenarios. In: Proceedings of the 30th ACM International Conference on Multimedia, pp. 1279–1288 (2022)
31. Minderer, M., et al.: Simple open-vocabulary object detection. In: Avidan, S., Brostow, G., Cissé, M., Farinella, G.M., Hassner, T. (eds) ECCV 2022. LNCS, vol. 13670, pp. 728–755. Springer, Cham (2022). https://doi.org/10.1007/978-3-031-20080-9_42
32. Misra, I., Shrivastava, A., Gupta, A., Hebert, M.: Cross-stitch networks for multi-task learning. In: Proceedings of the IEEE Conference on Computer Vision and Pattern Recognition, pp. 3994–4003 (2016)
33. Nekrasov, V., Dharmasiri, T., Spek, A., Drummond, T., Shen, C., Reid, I.: Real-time joint semantic segmentation and depth estimation using asymmetric annotations. In: 2019 International Conference on Robotics and Automation (ICRA), pp. 7101–7107. IEEE (2019)
34. Radford, A., et al.: Learning transferable visual models from natural language supervision. In: Meila, M., Zhang, T. (eds.) Proceedings of the 38th International Conference on Machine Learning. Proceedings of Machine Learning Research, vol. 139, pp. 8748–8763. PMLR (2021). https://proceedings.mlr.press/v139/radford21a.html
35. Redmon, J., Divvala, S., Girshick, R., Farhadi, A.: You only look once: unified, real-time object detection. In: Proceedings of the IEEE Conference on Computer Vision and Pattern Recognition, pp. 779–788 (2016)
36. Ren, S., He, K., Girshick, R., Sun, J.: Faster R-CNN: Towards real-time object detection with region proposal networks. Adv. Neural Inf. Process. Syst. **28** (2015)

37. Ruder, S.: An overview of multi-task learning in deep neural networks. arXiv preprint arXiv:1706.05098 (2017)
38. Senushkin, D., Patakin, N., Kuznetsov, A., Konushin, A.: Independent component alignment for multi-task learning. In: Proceedings of the IEEE/CVF Conference on Computer Vision and Pattern Recognition, pp. 20083–20093 (2023)
39. Shao, S., et al.: Objects365: a large-scale, high-quality dataset for object detection. In: 2019 IEEE/CVF International Conference on Computer Vision (ICCV), pp. 8429–8438 (2019). https://doi.org/10.1109/ICCV.2019.00852
40. Sharma, P., Ding, N., Goodman, S., Soricut, R.: Conceptual captions: a cleaned, hypernymed, image alt-text dataset for automatic image captioning. In: Proceedings of ACL (2018)
41. Standley, T., Zamir, A., Chen, D., Guibas, L., Malik, J., Savarese, S.: Which tasks should be learned together in multi-task learning? In: International Conference on Machine Learning, pp. 9120–9132. PMLR (2020)
42. Sun, X., Panda, R., Feris, R., Saenko, K.: AdaShare: learning what to share for efficient deep multi-task learning. Adv. Neural. Inf. Process. Syst. **33**, 8728–8740 (2020)
43. Tan, M., Pang, R., Le, Q.V.: EfficientDet: scalable and efficient object detection. In: Proceedings of the IEEE/CVF Conference on Computer Vision and Pattern Recognition, pp. 10781–10790 (2020)
44. Ultralytics: docs.ultralytics.com (2023). https://docs.ultralytics.com/. Accessed 22 Apr 2024
45. Vandenhende, S., Georgoulis, S., De Brabandere, B., Van Gool, L.: Branched multi-task networks: deciding what layers to share. arXiv preprint arXiv:1904.02920 (2019)
46. Wang, X., Cai, Z., Gao, D., Vasconcelos, N.: Towards universal object detection by domain attention. In: Proceedings of the IEEE/CVF Conference on Computer Vision and Pattern Recognition, pp. 7289–7298 (2019)
47. Wu, J., et al.: Towards open vocabulary learning: a survey. arXiv preprint arXiv:2306.15880v4 (2024)
48. Xu, H., Fang, L., Liang, X., Kang, W., Li, Z.: Universal-RCNN: universal object detector via transferable graph R-CNN. In: Proceedings of the AAAI Conference on Artificial Intelligence, vol. 34, pp. 12492–12499 (2020)
49. Yang, Y., Hospedales, T.M.: Trace norm regularised deep multi-task learning. arXiv preprint arXiv:1606.04038 (2016)
50. Yu, T., Kumar, S., Gupta, A., Levine, S., Hausman, K., Finn, C.: Gradient surgery for multi-task learning. Adv. Neural. Inf. Process. Syst. **33**, 5824–5836 (2020)
51. Zamir, A.R., Sax, A., Shen, W., Guibas, L.J., Malik, J., Savarese, S.: Taskonomy: disentangling task transfer learning. In: Proceedings of the IEEE Conference on Computer Vision and Pattern Recognition, pp. 3712–3722 (2018)
52. Zhao, X., Schulter, S., Sharma, G., Tsai, Y.-H., Chandraker, M., Wu, Y.: Object detection with a unified label space from multiple datasets. In: Vedaldi, A., Bischof, H., Brox, T., Frahm, J.-M. (eds.) ECCV 2020, Part XIV. LNCS, vol. 12359, pp. 178–193. Springer, Cham (2020). https://doi.org/10.1007/978-3-030-58568-6_11
53. Zhou, X., Koltun, V., Krähenbühl, P.: Simple multi-dataset detection. In: Proceedings of the IEEE/CVF Conference on Computer Vision and Pattern Recognition, pp. 7571–7580 (2022)
54. Zong, Z., Song, G., Liu, Y.: DETRs with collaborative hybrid assignments training. In: Proceedings of the IEEE/CVF International Conference on Computer Vision, pp. 6748–6758 (2023)

MVIP - A Dataset and Methods for Application Oriented Multi-View and Multi-Modal Industrial Part Recognition

Paul Koch[1(✉)], Marian Schlüter[1], and Jörg Krüger[1,2]

[1] Fraunhofer IPK, Pascalstraße 8-9, 10587 Berlin, Germany
paul.koch@ipk.fraunhofer.de
[2] Technische Universität Berlin, Pascalstraße 8-9, 10587 Berlin, Germany

Abstract. We present MVIP, a novel dataset for multi-modal and multi-view application-oriented industrial part recognition. Here we are the first to combine a calibrated RGBD multi-view dataset with additional object context such as physical properties, natural language, and super-classes. The current portfolio of available datasets offers a wide range of representations to design and benchmark related methods. In contrast to existing classification challenges, industrial recognition applications offer controlled multi-modal environments but at the same time have different problems than traditional 2D/3D classification challenges. Frequently, industrial applications must deal with a small amount or increased number of training data, visually similar parts, and varying object sizes, while requiring a robust near 100% top 5 accuracy under cost and time constraints. Current methods tackle such challenges individually, but direct adoption of these methods within industrial applications is complex and requires further research. Our main goal with MVIP is to study and push transferability of various state-of-the-art methods within related downstream tasks towards an efficient deployment of industrial classifiers. Additionally, we intend to push with MVIP research regarding several modality fusion topics, (automated) synthetic data generation, and complex data sampling – combined in a single application-oriented benchmark.

Keywords: Multi-View · Multi-Modal · Industrial Part Recognition · Artificial Intelligence · Dataset

1 Introduction

Vision-based classification systems have a broad range of industrial applications, e.g., 1) the intensification and sorting of incoming components into a warehouse; 2) the quality inspection and automated documentation of kitting and packaging processes; 3) key component identification of a broken machine to rapidly locate a fitting replacement within the warehouse. In reverse logistic, vision-based classification systems are used to identify old car components and classify them for remanufacturing, helping to reduce their relative carbon footprint [56]. Ever since the success of AlexNet [38] in 2012 related work for Vision-based classification has been developed with the ImageNet [10] classification benchmark [13,23,28,33,41,42,69]. Due to these milestones, data-driven image processing heuristics have found their way into industrial applications, increasingly replacing traditional image processing approaches [47,54,55,60]. Especially, it is noticeable that small problems with limited resources can thrive from transfer learning via publicly available pre-trained weight. A survey by Mazzei&Ramjattan [45] (2022) report a general increase in Vison-AI related publications since 2016. Here, they identify most work to be grounded on CNN based AI-architectures (e.g. ResNet) and encourage research towards the accessibility of state-of-the-art (SOTA) AI methods for easier adoption. However, a survey by Bertolini et al. [4] (2021) finds that AI methods are limited to small groups of large international companies. Hence, small businesses thrive from accessible and adoptable AI-methods, while large companies can afford to push the SOTA towards their needs. Regarding vision-based classification, most public research focuses on single-view image classification. Although due to the nature of larger industrial objects (e.g., see Fig. 1) and the high similarity within objects, it is occasionally impossible to derive the correct object class from a single view. Therefore, we investigate within this work the SOTA for multi-view classification systems in order to identify their transferability towards our application oriented industrial part recognition benchmark (MVIP).

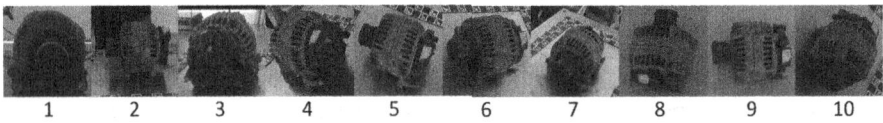

Fig. 1. An indexed ROI cropped MVIP image set featuring ten simultaneously captured Views.

With MVIP we contribute a novel multi-view (MV) and multi-modal (MM) dataset. For data acquisition, we designed a digitization and recognition station (see Fig. 2) as one could expect to be found on site in an industrial application for part recognition. The station is equipped with a vast set of task-relevant sensors (ten calibrated RGBD cameras and a scale) in order to investigate; A) which data benefits the industrial part recognition, and B) how to design and efficiently train a robust MV and MM model for industrial part recognition. In addition to the color, depth, and weight modalities, other modalities such as package-size (width, height, length), natural language tags (descriptions), and super-classes (general class spanning a common subset of classes, e.g. tool, car-component, etc.) are available in the dataset. This allows further research regarding modality-fusion and training or sampling methods. The calibrated MV-dataset allows 3D reconstruction of scenery and objects, which enables research regarding (automated) synthetic data generation and 3D based object recognition.

Our contributions with MVIP are manifold: 1) a novel multi-view (MV) and multi-modal (MM) dataset for application-oriented industrial part recognition; 2) a set of baseline investigations for MV and MM industrial object recognition; 3) a novel auxiliary loss for MV classification tasks; 4) Transformer-based MV-fusion; and 5) a novel approach for conditional MV-decoding for part recognition. With MVIP, we want to narrow the gap between related basic research and real industrial ML applications.

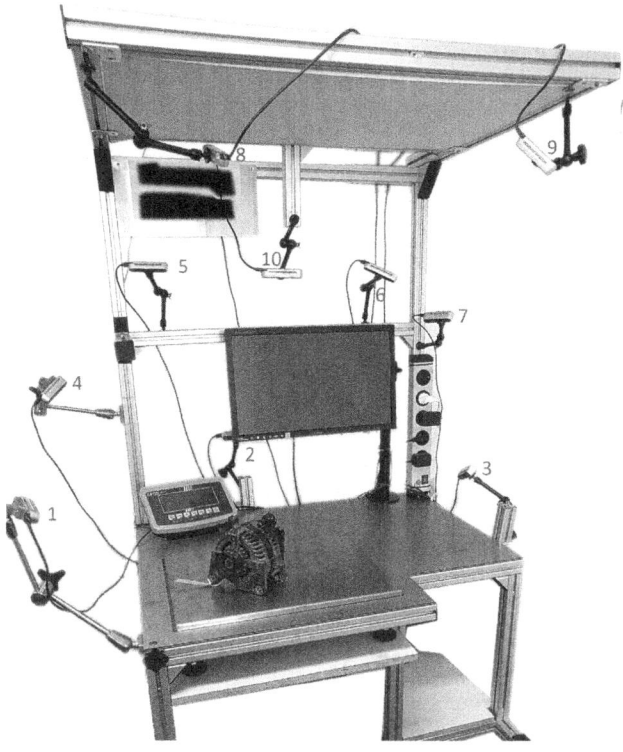

Fig. 2. Digitisation station used for MVIP.

2 Related Works

Multi-View: A recent (2021) survey on image fusion techniques [34] identifies MV-fusion among other fusion techniques as an ongoing research topic, which is increasingly attracting more attention. Fusion can happen at different stages in a model architecture. Related works on MV-fusion employ a single image encoder to transform a set of images into vector-space (view tokens) and apply late fusion techniques [2,3,12,17,19,22,29,30,32,58,59,66,74]. The zoo of related SOTA late fusion techniques can be grouped into non-trainable, node-wise view-weighting ($\odot$), intra-view aware ($\leftrightarrow$), and inter-view aware ($\updownarrow$) methods. Consider tokenized view embeddings $\chi \in \mathbb{R}^{I \times J}$, where I is the number of views and J the number of hidden nodes, then $\odot = \forall_{j=1}^{J} \Sigma_{i=1}^{I} \chi_{ij} \nu_{ij}$, $\updownarrow = \Sigma_{j=1}^{J} F(\chi_j)$, and $\leftrightarrow = \Sigma_{j=1}^{J} \forall_{I=1}^{I} F(\chi_i)$. F is a trainable function and ν is a scalar found by some implementation of $F (\subset \chi)$. E.g. pooling methods [66] are non-learn-able node-wise view-weighting methods for view aggregation. Likewise, convolution and fully-connected layers can be used to train a inter-view aware node-wise view-weighting policy. Otherwise, methods such as Squeeze-and-Excitation [27] (S.&E.) use the individual embedding to determine a node-wise weighting, allowing an intra-view aware view aggregation. Methods based on concatenation of view embeddings [12,30,74] are inter-view and intra-view aware. Recent

SOTA methods for View-Fusion have success with trainable [74] and non-trainable [22] view aggregation methods.

RGBD: Unlike MV-fusion, SOTA methods for RGBD-related downstream tasks also employ hybrid fusion, where color and depth signals are gradually fused downstream. The work related to hybrid fusion can be grouped into methods that gradually fuse depth information with color information ($d \rightarrow c$) [31] and a bi-directional fusion $c \leftrightarrow d$ [40,67]. Depth directed fusion ($c \rightarrow d$) appears to be unnoticed in related work. Other work for RGBD-fusion-based downstream tasks employ late-fusion-based methods [15, 29,48,72,73].

Transformers: Ever since the introduction of Transformers [71] into vision problems [13] they push the SOTA within vision-based downstream tasks [5,6,41,42,78, 81]. Due to their universal capabilities, transformers are found to be well suited to fuse information from different modalities [20,40,51,53,64,65,73]. Here, Omnivore [20] and Omnivec [64,65] use token-based modality fusion to reach state-of-the-art results on RGBD-based scene classification on SUN-RGBD [63]. Therefore, we investigate the usage of Transformer-based methods for MV-fusion within industrial applications for part recognition.

MM and MV DataSets: Datasets for 6D-object-pose-estimation [16,25,26,77], RGBD-segmentation [9,18,61,63] and RGBD-instance-detection [16,18,25,77] drive RGBD based research within their related downstream tasks. Within MV and classification problems it is a common method within the field of 3D-part-recognition to render a set of 2D views from 3D parts and use image encoders to adopt MV-fusion for a combined classification [2,17,22,29,30,32,66,74]. This research results in a vast set of synthetic [7,36,37,46,75] and real world [1,14,24,35,52,57,70,76] RGB(D) datasets for MV-fusion and classification investigations. Real-world MV datasets frequently use video-based capturing methods. Thus, MV can be sampled from the video. MV-RGBD [35] uses a turn table to capture objects from multiple fixed view points, while FewSOL [50] and GraspNet [16] use a robot to capture object(s) from multiple view points. Albeit the use of synthetic industrial components [36,37] and fixed view points, none of the available datasets addresses a realistic industrial application for part recognition. Moreover, recent work within machine vision leverages the combination of images with other modalities such as natural language (NL) [51,53]. With MVIP, we are the first to our knowledge to bring the physical properties of objects, natural language, and MV-RGBD images into a single benchmark for application-oriented industrial part recognition.

3 Methods

The MVIP Dataset is captured on a digitization station as illustrated in Fig. 2. Ten RGBD cameras are mounted on the table construction, all facing a common point on the integrated scale. An ArUco-Board is surrounding the scale (see Fig. 3), thereby a 6D-Pose can be determined for each camera at any given time, given the camera's intrinsic parameters. Thus, the cameras are calibrated to each other within each captured image set (see Fig. 1). Due to the arrangement of camera perspectives and calibration, one set of images covers most of the object surface and allows 3D construction of the objects (Fig. 3).

Fig. 3. Simple 3D-Object-Reconstruction given a single image set from MVIP.

The front of the table is not equipped with cameras to provide space for a worker.

Each object class featured in the dataset is rotated during digitization 12 times (approximately 30° steps), given a subjective "natural laying" position (see Fig. 2 for illustration). Since some objects have multiple "natural laying" positions, 12 rotations are repeated according to the subjective assessment of the worker. For test (5) and validation (5) purposes, ten additional image sets are captured, where the worker randomly moves the object on the scale according to a natural laying position.

Fig. 4. Subset of industrial parts featured in the MVIP dataset.

Figure 4 illustrates a subset of objects featured in the dataset. In addition to image data, the dataset features meta-data for all objects; weight, package size (length, width, height), object class, super-classes (general class spanning a common subset of classes), natural language (NL) tags, and generated view-wise object segmentation masks (thus, also ROI Bounding Boxes). For the segmentation masks, we annotated a small subset of 5% and finetuned a segmentation model [49] to generate the remaining masks. This works well since the segmentation task is rather easy. The calibrated MV RGBD design of the dataset enables anyone to employ methods for 3D-Object-Point-Cloud and 3D-Scene-Reconstruction, 6D-Object-Pose Estimation, and Synthetic-Data generation. In total, MVIP features 308 classes of industrial components (e.g. hammer, generator, camera adapter), which are grouped into 18 super-classes (e.g. tools, car components, metal part). From eight categories (shapes, colors, materials, textures, conditions, size, weight, and density), MVIP uses 77 NL-Tags to describe the classes. These tags describe in natural language the objects' conduction (diry, rusty, clean, etc.), shapes (round, sharp, edgy, pointy, etc.), and other visual attributes. MVIP has a total of ≈ 570 k images (all with resolution of 1280×720), while 71.276 are RGB images. Each RGB image has the corresponding counterpart images: depth, HHA (following [21]), mean-RGB (mean images are averaged temporally over $1\ sec$ for more stable data), mean depth, and segmentation (mask of the industrial part). Additionally, each image set is associated to a specific background set (scene without the industrial part). The ≈ 282 k images are available for training, while the ≈ 108 k images are used for validation and the other ≈ 108 k images for test. The industrial components featured in MVIP are set to be at least the approximate size of a fist (in a subjective assessment of the worker) and the maximum 350 mm $\times$ 450 mm $\times$ 300 mm with weight of <15 kg.

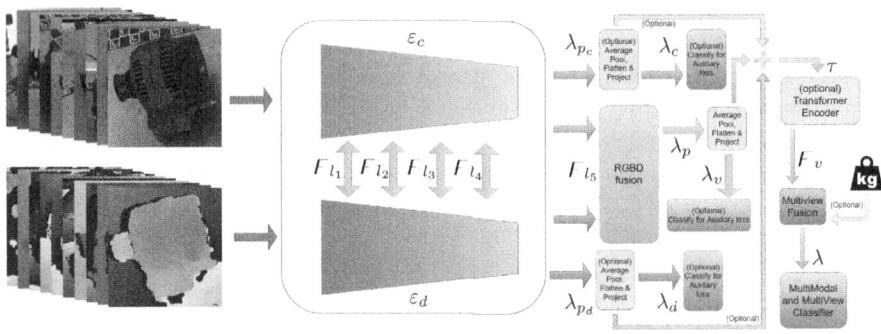

Fig. 5. Multi-view architecture used to train and evaluate our experiments, please find further description within our methods.

Architecture: Inspired by related work, we created a modular training architecture (see Fig. 5) in order to study ML-based industrial part recognition with MVIP. Our architecture uses a pre-trained CNN backbone [23,69]. Given the views V, the color and depth encoders $\epsilon_{c|d}$ project their inputs $\forall_{v=1}^{V} c_v|d_v \in \mathbb{R}^{Ch_{c|d},H,W} \rightarrow \forall_{v=1}^{V} \forall_{i=1}^{I} l_{c|d,v,i} \in \mathbb{R}^{Ch_{emb_i} \times H/2^i \times W/2^i}$.

In our implementation, we use the ResNet50 [23] encoding architecture $\epsilon_{c|d}$ where $I = 5$. At every embedding stage $l_{c|d,v,i} = \epsilon_{c|d,i}(\hat{l}_{c|d,v,i-1})$ a RGBD-fusion F_{l_i} combines the embeddings $l_{c\wedge d,v,i} \rightarrow \hat{l}_{c|d,v,i}$, where $\hat{l}_{c|d,v,0} = c_v|d_v$ and F_{l_i} is either a one-directional fusion $x = c|d$; $\hat{l}_{x,v,i}$, $\hat{l}_{\neg x,v,i} = F_{l_i}(l_{c \wedge d,v,i})$, $l_{\neg x,v,i}$ or bi-directional fusion $\hat{l}_{c,v,i}$, $\hat{l}_{d,v,i} = F_{l_i}(l_{c \wedge d,v,i})$.

The final fused embedding $\hat{l}_{v,I} = F_I(l_{c \wedge d,v,I}) \in \mathbb{R}^{Ch_{emb_I} \times H/2^I \times W/2^I}$ is passed through an average pooling layer followed by a flattening before being projected via the fully connected layer λ_p into the view embeddings $\chi_v \in \mathbb{R}^{1 \times Ch_V}$. Optionally, the non-fused embeddings $l_{c|d,v,I}$ are also passed through an average pooling layer followed by a flattening and projected via a fully connected layer $\lambda_{c|d}$ into the auxiliary output $O_{v,c|d} \in \mathbb{R}^{1 \times N}$, where N is the number of classes. Likewise, χ_v is projected by λ_v into $O_v \in \mathbb{R}^{1 \times N}$. The view embeddings χ_v are stacked for a combination of embeddings $\chi = cat(\forall_{v=1}^{V} \chi_v)$. An optional transformer encoder τ [71] can be applied in χ to employ self-attention between all χ_v.

Eventually, we use MV-fusion F_v to reduce the dimension of $\chi \in \mathbb{R}^{V \times Ch_v} \to \in \mathbb{R}^{1 \times Ch_v}$ before a final fully connected layer λ projects $\chi \to 0 \in \mathbb{R}^{1 \times N}$. Optionally, our transformer-based implementations for F_v additionally take the object weight in kg as input, which is used as an anchor (conditional decoding [53]). Likewise to Positional Encoding [71] we encode the object weight into a sequence of cosine and sine frequencies and add the vector to the decoding signal of our transformer-based MV-fusion implementations. For RGB-MV classification, the modules ϵ_d and $\forall_{i=1}^{I-1} F_{l_i}$ are removed, while F_{L_I} is an identity function and $\forall_{i=1}^{I} \hat{l}_{c,v,i} = l_{c,v,i}$.

MV-Fusion Implementations: In our experiments, we study different MV-fusion types within MVIP and effect of scaling the trainable parameters. We summarize the implementations in our investigations in Table 4. These methods (in addition to τ) are implementations of F_v and are used to reduce the tokenized embeddings of the views V. Following related work, we use the pooling aggregation introduced by [66] in 2015 and is still used recently [22]. Following Feng et al. [17] we implement a Conv.-based node-wise view aggregation which gradually fuses the views in sequential layers. However, most related work on view aggregation is designed for problems with 12 and 20 views for 3D object recognition [30,32,74]. E.g., Wei et al. [17] uses a graph-based view aggregation implementation which is only suitable for views V where $V/4 > 1$ & $V/4 \in \mathbb{N}$. Regarding Transformers (τ, Tr-En, Tr-EnDE) we are the first to our knowledge to bring the attention mechanism to tokenized view aggregation. Here τ is a simple Transformer encoder, introduced by Vaswani et al. [71]. The Transformer encoder-decoder (Tr-EnDe) [71] is used by Carion et al. [5] to extract information from encoded image information through a trainable decoding query and cross-attention. We adopt this approach for view aggregation by decoding class information with a single trainable query from the tokenized view embeddings. Dosovitskiy et al. [13] append a trainable decoding query to the tokenized embeddings before forwarding it through the Transformer encoder (Tr-En) [71]. Afterwards, a final classification is done only on the basis of the output at the index of the trainable query. Thus, the attention mechanism is applied while reducing the number of trainable parameters compared to the encoder-decoder approach. The transformer-based view aggregation methods are intra- and inter-view aware, since the attention mechanism can attend to every node. Furthermore, we adopt the Squeeze-and-Excitation Networks (S&E) introduced by Hu et al. [27] as a comparison for intra-view-aware view aggregation. Here, each tokenized view embedding is attending to every node within the view and used to determine a node-wise scalar, which is used for a simple sum view aggregation. In our shared-S&E (S.S&E) we use a single module to compute the scalars for every view, rather then having a individual S&E module for every view. An overview of the implemented fusion methods can be seen in Table 1.

Table 1. Implementation details concerning the MV-fusion methods used in this work. We denote the MV-fusion types with $\odot$ for node-wise view-weighting, $\updownarrow$ for intra-view aware, and $\leftrightarrow$ for inter-view aware methods.

MV-fusion	Types	Params.	Blocks/Layers
Max Pool [66]	$\odot$	–	–
Mean [66]	$\odot$	–	–
Conv. [17]	$\odot \updownarrow$	13	3 Layers
S&E [27]	$\odot \leftrightarrow$	0.4Mio	1 Block
S.S&E [27]	$\odot \leftrightarrow$	0.13Mio	1 Block
MLP	$\updownarrow \leftrightarrow$	13Mio	3 Layers
Tr-En [13]	$\updownarrow \leftrightarrow$	8.4mio	1 Block
Tr-EnDe [5]	$\updownarrow \leftrightarrow$	21mio	1 Block
τ [71]	$\updownarrow \leftrightarrow$	8.4mio	1 Block

Multi Head Auxiliary Loss: Inspired by related work [5,39,68] we introduce a novel auxiliary loss for MV classification which is defined as;

$$\zeta_v = \zeta_{cls}(o_v, y_v) \qquad (1)$$

$$\zeta_{v_{CD}} = \frac{1}{3}(\zeta_{cls}(o_v, y_v) + \zeta_{cls}(o_{v_c}, y_v) + \zeta_{cls}(o_{v_d}, y_v)) \qquad (2)$$

$$\zeta_{MH} = \frac{1}{V+1}(\zeta_{cls}(o, y_v) + \Sigma_{v=1}^{V}\zeta_v) \qquad (3)$$

$$\zeta_{MH_{RGBD}} = \frac{1}{V+1}(\zeta_{cls}(o, y) + \Sigma_{v=1}^{V}\zeta_{v_{CD}}) \qquad (4)$$

where ζ_{cls} denotes cross-entropy-loss, y is the MV target class, y_v is the view wise target class, V is the number of Views, and o, o_v, o_{v_c}, and o_{v_d} are the overall, full-view, color-view, and depth-view predictions, respectively. With our multi head auxilary loss (MH-loss) we embrace gradients view-wise within each encoding modality, thus forcing contributions from every view and modality, which hinders the classifier to specify/overfit on a certain view and modality. This is especially important if the pretrained encoder initially favors a certain modality or view.

Weight-Based Classification: The object weight ω $[kg] \in \mathbb{R}$ is a one-dimensional non-unique property. Thus, classifying objects purely based on weight is ambiguous, since the probability that the objects share a common $\omega \pm e$ is large, where e is the scale resolution. The scale use in MVIP has a constant weight error of only 0.002 kg, but is heavily affected by offsetting objects from the scale center. Thus, any weight-based classifier must be robust to disturbances in the weight measurement. Following positional encoding [71] (PE) we use a set of $d \in \mathbb{N}$ sine-cosine functions with varying frequencies to encode the weight ω into a vector of size $1 \times 2d$. We Train a 4-Layer MLP to upscale the weight $1 \times 2d \rightarrow 1 \times d_h$, where d_h is the number of hidden nodes. Eventually, a fully-connected layer (FC) is used for classification. During training, we apply randomly a constant or proportional weight error uniformly sampled from the distribution ± 0.01 kg or 0.01ω [kg], respectively. We train PropertyNet using cross-entropy loss and Adam Optimizer for 10k epochs with a scheduled cosine one-cycle learning rate between $10^{-7} \nearrow 10^{-6} \searrow 10^{-9}$ (max at 50% training) and a batch size of 512.

4 Experiments and Discussion

Experiment Design: All experiments are conducted on the same machine ($2 \times$Nvidia RTX 3090) with the same set of hyper-parameters for training. For fair comparison, the batch-size stays constant at 32, which means that the largest model utilizes the 48GB GPU-RAM at most, while smaller models theoretically could have used a larger batch size. For a baseline establishment, the ResNet-50 [23] architecture with pre-trained ImageNet [10] weights is used as an image encoder. We train our classifiers with our auxiliary loss and Adam optimization at an cosine one cycle [62] scheduled learning rate of $10^{-5} \nearrow 10^{-4} \searrow 10^{-6}$ (max at 50% training). If not stated otherwise, we report the maximum observed accuracy out of five runs on MVIP for 50 epochs with ROI crops, colorjitter, flip, rotation and random view order augmentations on three view RGB with a resolution of 224×224 pixels (ROI crops are up-sampled if needed). During testing, we fix the view order and also indexes if additional views are available during training.

Stability and Resolution: In Table 2 we investigate the stability of our proposed architecture w.r.t. 3-view-RGB and our MH-loss. Here we find our MH-loss to yield superior and more stable results compared to pure end-to-end training with cross-entropy-loss.

Table 2. Stability of our implementations w.r.t. three view RGB and trainable MV-fusion parameters (Params.).

MV-fusion	#	τ	Params.	%	$\%_{MH}$
Max Pool	0		0	73.7 ± 0.4	$\mathbf{94.6 \pm 0.2}$
Conv.	0		13	$\mathbf{89.6 \pm 2.0}$	94.3 ± 0.9
Conv.	1		8.4Mio	66.7 ± 4.9	91.2 ± 0.8

In Table 3 we inspect the effect of using a higher resolution, the usage of multi-scale inputs, and up-sampling of ROI crops. Despite our observations regarding the input resolution, we continue our experiments with an input size of 224×224 without multi-scale to keep a constant batch size in every experiment.

Table 3. ROI cropped 3 view RGB results concerning resolution. Multi-Scale varies the resolution ±10% while Up-Sampling scales the roi crop to the desired resolution instead of forcing a bigger ROI crop. 512 × 512 with multi-scale has a decreased batch size in order to fit in our GPU-RAM.

Resolution	Multi-Scale	Up-Sampling	BS	%
224 × 224	–	–	32	81.4
224 × 224	–	✓	32	82.7
224 × 224	✓	✓	32	88.8
512 × 512	–	–	32	88.2
512 × 512	–	✓	32	**92.9**
512 × 512	✓	✓	14	91.6

MV-Fusion: In Table 4 we report the results concerning view aggregation. We find that our MH-loss yields superior results across the board. Interestingly we observe max pooling to lose performance with view increase (especially without our MH-Loss). This phenomenon might be explained by an accumulated self-reinforcing view specific feature extraction, which is more likely to lead to overfitting and only present for the Max pooling implementation. Our MH-loss circumvents this overfitting phenomenon due to additional view-wise backpropagation. As we employ random view ordering during training to reduce overfitting (see Table 5), we observe the trainable node-wise weighing convolution to collapse towards average pooling. Moreover, we find that our classifiers tend to overfitting with increasing MV-fusion complexity and view numbers. Here we find that the lightweight intra-view weighing approach of S.S&E yields marginal gains compared to non-trainable view aggregation. Transformer-based implementations are notoriously hard to train with a tendency to overfit [5,13,71,79]. Related work found self-supervised (SSL) pre-training to be key to the success of transformer-based implementations [6,11,44], which opens for further SSL-based investigation for tokenized view aggregation with transformers. Likewise, we find from the training logs that the trainable but not pre-trained view aggregation to be less efficient w.r.t. training time. Thus, pre-training is crucial for efficient training of complex view aggregation methods. We conclude that trainable inter view aware methods for view aggregation are not adding compared to non-trainable alternatives as the view order is invariant. However, we see the potential for complex intra-view & inter-view aware methods, such as transformers, to yield better results if (pre)trained in larger datasets.

Saturation of Accuracy: In Fig. 6 we summarize our results regarding increasing the number of input views in our MV-architecture, available views within the training data, and the effect of reducing the number of training image sets. Here we observe the most significant performance gain already with two views, while reaching a saturation of accuracy at around five views. Further increasing the number of views does not significantly improve the performance w.r.t. MV nor the number of training samples. Similar to our MV-fusion related results (see Table 4), we observe a significant performance drop with three Views. It can further be observed that some training samples w.r.t view ID and rotation ID appear to corrupt the training and cause overfitting. We identify

Table 4. Results concerning 2&3 view fusion on MVIP. The number of τ indicates how many Transformer-Encoding blocks are used before MV-fusion (see Fig. 5). All experiments trained for 100 epochs. The $\%_{MH}$ denotes results concerning classifiers trained with our MH-loss. We denote the MV-fusion types with $\odot$ for node-wise view-weighting, $\updownarrow$ for intra-view aware, and $\leftrightarrow$ for inter-view aware methods.

MV-fusion	Fusion-Types	Trainable Parameters	Layers or Blocks	τ	%		$\%_{MH}$	
					2 Views	3 Views	2 Views	3 Views
Max Pool [66]	$\odot$	–	–	–	88.2	74.4	95.3	94.7
Mean [66]	$\odot$	–	–	–	**92.9**	87.9	95.3	**95.5**
Conv. [17]	$\odot$	13	3l	–	91.6	**92.1**	94.6	**95.5**
Conv. [17]	$\odot$	8.4mio	1B+3L	1	84.5	72.5	93.4	92.4
S&E [27]	$\odot \leftrightarrow$	Views×0.13mio	Views×1L	–	91.9	84.2	94.5	94.6
S.S&E [27]	$\odot \leftrightarrow$	0.13Mio	1L	–	91.2	83.7	**95.6**	94.5
MLP	$\updownarrow \leftrightarrow$	Views×4.3Mio	3L	–	86.2	80.5	93.7	93.6
Tr-En [13]	$\updownarrow \leftrightarrow$	8.4mio	1B	–	74.44	56.5	94.6	92.0
Tr-De [5]	$\updownarrow \leftrightarrow$	21Mio	1B	–	88.4	78.1	95.3	94.6

the view IDs two and seven as being especially affected by artifacts introduced by the worker. Moreover, we argue that certain view/rotation configurations emerge more overlapping and occurrences of artifacts which are affecting the statistical generalization.

Augmentations such as jittered ROI-crops, flips, and rotations are found to be default settings for training single-view image processing models in order to diversify the dataset and regularize the learning. However, it can be argued that using such methods for MV-approaches might hinder the model from "considering" the 3D nature of a given presented part. Investigations on the effect of keeping the 3D structure complete of any part during MV-training can be found in Table 5. Here we observe that our methods within MVIP have a general problem with overfitting, even after background elimination via ROI crops. We find random ordering of views to be most important in order to hinder the classifiers to overfit. We also investigate shuffling views regarding class and view index in hope of better results due to a more generalized image encoder ϵ and less overfitting on fixed but order-invariant view sets. For inter-class shuffling we switch to binary-cross-entropy-loss in a pre-training stage 1 (30%), and disable it in a stage 2 to train a classifier with cross-entropy-loss. Here we observe no further generalization; in fact, the performance decreases, which indicates that maintaining the image set structure is important for MV-classification. One could try to use single-view pre-training rather than view shuffling for a better pretrained image encoder ϵ, which we investigate further in Table 6. In our implementation, we find a pre-training stage to be unfavorable. This could be due to a catastrophic forgetting of generalized weights from Imagenet pre-training before reaching the end-to-end MV classification training.

RGBD Encoding has been found to be a modality that adds value to several downstream vision tasks such as classification [15,29], detection [48], and especially segmentation [31,40,73] where the depth signal is well suited to find and refine contours.

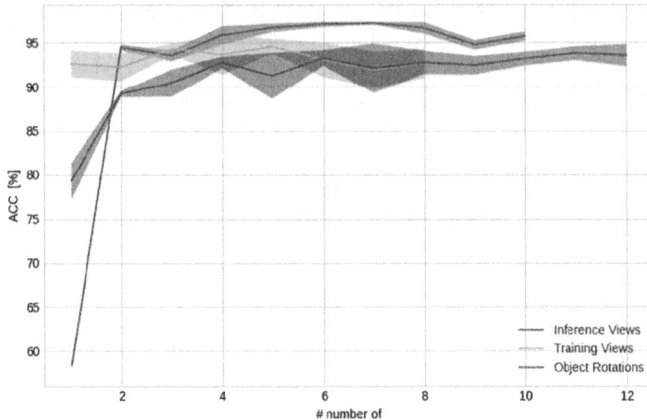

Fig. 6. Views: Results concerning increasing the number of input views included in the MV-architecture (Inference Views), number of views available during training of a 3 view RGB classifier, and the number of available training image sets (Object Rotations) for 3 view RGB classifier.

Table 5. Results concerning MV-augmentations and MV shuffling methods. View wise (VW) and class wise (CW) shuffling between MV image sets.

Crop	Flip	Rotate	Random View	Shuffle Views	%
✓	–	–	–	–	64.0
✓	✓	–	–	–	67.1
✓	–	✓	–	–	80.8
–	✓	✓	–	–	79.8
✓	✓	✓	–	–	82.7
✓	✓	✓	✓	–	**94.9**
✓	✓	✓	✓	VW & CW	90.26
✓	✓	✓	✓	¬VW & CW	92.0
✓	✓	✓	✓	$VW \& \neg CW$	84.3
✓	✓	✓	✓	¬ VW & ¬ CW	81.7

Depth information has the potential to extract features invariant to condition/instance-based color artifacts. Hence, yielding a better generalization towards unseen object instances. However, we find that both bi-directional ($c \leftrightarrow d$) [40,67] and towards color-directed $d \rightarrow c$ [31] fusion is corrupting the RGB encoding (see Table 7), with the caveat that our findings are on the basis of S.&E.-based [27] RGBD-fusion rather than the direct implementation used by [31,40,67] in order to yield more general and comparable results. Albeit the usage of further regularization with extra depth noise augmentation and image-wise normalization (removing absolute distances), we find our depth directed fusion ($c \rightarrow d$) implementation to reach at best near-on-par performance with

Table 6. Results concerning pre-trained-weights for the image encoder ϵ w.r.t. available views to sample from during training and the number of test views.

Tag	Train Views	Test Views	Pretrained on	%
A-SV	1	1	ImageNet	57.9
B-SV	3	1	ImageNet	85.5
C-SV	10	1	ImageNet	**88.4**
MV	3	3	ImageNet	**94.0**
MV	10	3	ImageNet	93.6
A-MV	3	3	A-SV	62.2
B-MV	3	3	B-SV	91.4
C-MV	10	3	C-SV	84.4

Table 7. Results concerning 3 view RGBD-fusion trained for 200 epochs with our RGBD MH-loss function and where $\%_{VCD}$ denotes the accuracy achieved when applying MV-fusion f_v on the concatenated embeddings from the RGBD view, color, and depth signals (see Fig. 5). Here, we use S.&E. [27] for efficient baseline RGBD-fusion. We mark a * where we use pre-trained depth encoding weights from [31].

Input	Norm.	Fusion	%	$\%_{VCD}$
3RGB (Base)	–	–	**94.6**	–
HHA [21]	–	–	44.2	–
D	–	–	51.6	–
D	✓	–	47.2	–
D* [31]	–	–	46.2	–
3RGBD	–	$c \leftarrow d$	84.0	–
3RGBD	–	$c \leftrightarrow d$	81.1	–
3RGBD	–	$c \rightarrow d$	93.6	93.8
3RGBD	✓	$c \rightarrow d$	–	**94.5**
3RGBHHA	–	$c \rightarrow HHA$	93.1	94.0
3RGBD	✓	–	94.0	–
3RGBD* [31]	✓	–	93.6	–

pure MV RGB. It appears that the depth information is at best an opening for overfitting. Related work uses HHA [21] (horizontal, height, angle) encoded depth rather than a simple one-dimensional standardized signal for better results [43], which we cannot report. However, with our findings regrading pre-trained depth encoding weights [31], we argue that the key reason for the RGBD failure is a quality mismatch between color and depth feature extraction. While sophisticated and suitable pre-trained encoders for color images are broadly available, we observe mainly pre-trained depth encoders for segmentation downstream tasks that are fundamentally different. Self-supervised RGBD pre-training methods such as [80] are promising for efficient training, but not broadly accessible yet, nor does it allow end-to-end training of an RGBD encoder with intermediate RGBD-fusion (Table 8).

Table 8. Results concerning multi modal fusion between MV RGB data and the object weight [kg]. PE denotes the usage of Positional-Encoding [71], while PN denotes a pre-trained network (PropertyNet) for upsampling the PE encodings (PN' is frozen during training).

Input	Weight Encoding	Weight Fusion	Top 1	Top 3	Top 5
W	PE + PN	–	64.0	88.3	97.4
2RGB	–	–	94.6	**99.0**	**99.5**
2RGBW	PE	Tr-De.	94.9	98.8	99.3
2RGBW	PE+PN	Tr-De.	94.7	98.8	99.3
2RGBW	PE+PN'	Tr-De.	**95.1**	98.6	99.3
3RGB	–	–	**94.6**	98.6	99.1
3RGBW	PE	Tr-De.	94.1	98.2	98.9
3RGBW	PE+PN	Tr-De.	93.5	**98.7**	**99.2**
3RGBW	PE+PN'	Tr-De.	93.6	98.3	98.8

Anchor-Based Decoding: Moreover, we investigate the effect of using weight encoding ($PE(\omega)$) as anchor for the MV-fusion Transformer-Decoder (F_v) such that the decoder query $Q = Q_{emb} + PE(\omega)$ or $Q = WN(PE(\omega))$, where Q_{emb} is a trainable parameter of size $1 \times d_d$. However, we can only report marginal gains within different metricise, which can be explained by the PropertyNet (PN) accuracy and general weight modality limitation within MVIP. However, anchor-based decoding becomes potentially beneficial when enriching the anchored information (add further property dimensions) or within problems that are not purely solvable by image information (e.g. occluded features/materials which are detectable by physical properties such as weight).

5 Conclusion

We present MVIP, a novel multi-view and multi-modal application oriented dataset for industrial part recognition. The intention of the dataset is to narrow the gap between basic research in ML-based computer vision regarding part recognition and real world industrial applications. MVIP enables researchers to investigate a wide range of open research questions combined in a single benchmark, spanning several domains. Within our experiments, we identify a general lack of strong multi-modal encoders and fusion mechanisms, which can leverage robust and efficient finetuning on industrial downstream tasks. Furthermore, we identify a general risk of overfitting within our end-to-end trained MV problem, which we hypothesize to be related to a statistical increase of MV artifacts and to a low batch size. However, we achieve a baseline Top 1 accuracy of >95% and Top 5 of 99.5% within MVIP using a MV-RGB classifier due to our novel MH-loss, which we find to yield more stable and better results across the board for MV-fusion.

Regarding future work, we aim to investigate the (automatic) generation of synthetic data via MVIP's options for object and scene 3D-reconstruction. Here, one can use MVIP's calibrated RGBD setup to generate textured CAD and point cloud data, which in turn simulations can laverage to create unlimited diverse data in a controlled setup. In addition to classification, these synthetic data generation can also be employed in combination with the NL-tags on object conditions and objects masks to generate data for defect/anomaly and condition detection/classification. Moreover, with MVIP new techniques for MV-augmentation, MV-sampling, and MV-regularization (similar to our MH-Loss) can be investigated that leverage knowledge regarding views, super-classes, and natural language tags. Methods for multi-modal pre-training and fusion between image-based data such as RGB, Depth, and physical properties (width, height, length, weight) as well as natural language tags should can be explored. Other future work can also use MVIP to investigate dataset curation with respect to the selected cameras and the number of images – aiming for more efficient training and adaptation. Following [8], we would also encourage researchers to investigate incremental learning on MVIP, since industrial use cases often have a rapidly changing range of objects.

Acknowledgments. We would like to thank everyone at the Fraunhofer IPK involved in the MVIP project. A special thanks to Vivek Chavan and Maulik Jagtap for their contributions to the dataset design and the digitization.

Source Code and Data. Please find all the source code related to our experiments, dataset handling, and a download link to MVIP here: Github: https://github.com/KochPJ/multi-view-part-recognition.

References

1. Ahmadyan, A., Zhang, L., Wei, J., Ablavatski, A., Grundmann, M.: Objectron: a large scale dataset of object-centric videos in the wild with pose annotations. CoRR abs/2012.09988 (2020). https://arxiv.org/abs/2012.09988
2. Bai, S., Bai, X., Zhou, Z., Zhang, Z., Latecki, L.J.: GIFT: a real-time and scalable 3D shape search engine. In: 2016 IEEE Conference on Computer Vision and Pattern Recognition (CVPR), pp. 5023–5032 (2016). https://doi.org/10.1109/CVPR.2016.543
3. Barbosa, A., Marinho, T., Martin, N., Hovakimyan, N.: Multi-stream CNN for spatial resource allocation: a crop management application. In: Proceedings - 2020 IEEE/CVF Conference on Computer Vision and Pattern Recognition Workshops, CVPRW 2020, pp. 258–266. IEEE Computer Society Conference on Computer Vision and Pattern Recognition Workshops, IEEE Computer Society (2020). https://doi.org/10.1109/CVPRW50498.2020.00037. Publisher Copyright: 2020 IEEE; 2020 IEEE/CVF Conference on Computer Vision and Pattern Recognition Workshops, CVPRW 2020; Conference date: 14-06-2020 Through 19-06-2020
4. Bertolini, M., Mezzogori, D., Neroni, M., Zammori, F.: Machine learning for industrial applications: a comprehensive literature review. Expert Syst. Appl. **175**, 114820 (2021). https://doi.org/10.1016/j.eswa.2021.114820, https://www.sciencedirect.com/science/article/pii/S095741742100261X

5. Carion, N., Massa, F., Synnaeve, G., Usunier, N., Kirillov, A., Zagoruyko, S.: End-to-end object detection with transformers. CoRR abs/2005.12872 (2020). https://arxiv.org/abs/2005.12872
6. Caron, M., et al.: Emerging properties in self-supervised vision transformers. CoRR abs/2104.14294 (2021). https://arxiv.org/abs/2104.14294
7. Chang, A.X., et al.: ShapeNet: an information-rich 3d model repository. CoRR abs/1512.03012 (2015). http://arxiv.org/abs/1512.03012
8. Chavan, V., Koch, P., Schlüter, M., Briese, C.: Towards realistic evaluation of industrial continual learning scenarios with an emphasis on energy consumption and computational footprint. In: 2023 IEEE/CVF International Conference on Computer Vision (ICCV), pp. 11472–11484 (2023). https://doi.org/10.1109/ICCV51070.2023.01057
9. Dai, A., Chang, A.X., Savva, M., Halber, M., Funkhouser, T.A., Nießner, M.: ScanNet: richly-annotated 3D reconstructions of indoor scenes. CoRR abs/1702.04405 (2017). http://arxiv.org/abs/1702.04405
10. Deng, J., Dong, W., Socher, R., Li, L.J., Li, K., Fei-Fei, L.: ImageNet: a large-scale hierarchical image database. In: 2009 IEEE Conference on Computer Vision and Pattern Recognition, pp. 248–255. IEEE (2009)
11. Devlin, J., Chang, M., Lee, K., Toutanova, K.: BERT: pre-training of deep bidirectional transformers for language understanding. CoRR abs/1810.04805 (2018). http://arxiv.org/abs/1810.04805
12. Dolata, P., Mrzygłód, M., Reiner, J.: Double-stream convolutional neural networks for machine vision inspection of natural products. Appl. Artif. Intell. 31(7–8), 643–659 (2017). https://doi.org/10.1080/08839514.2018.1428491
13. Dosovitskiy, A., et al.: An image is worth 16×16 words: transformers for image recognition at scale. CoRR abs/2010.11929 (2020). https://arxiv.org/abs/2010.11929
14. Downs, L., et al.: Google scanned objects: a high-quality dataset of 3D scanned household items (2022). https://doi.org/10.48550/ARXIV.2204.11918
15. Eitel, A., Springenberg, J.T., Spinello, L., Riedmiller, M., Burgard, W.: Multimodal deep learning for robust RGB-D object recognition. In: 2015 IEEE/RSJ International Conference on Intelligent Robots and Systems (IROS), pp. 681–687 (2015). https://doi.org/10.1109/IROS.2015.7353446
16. Fang, H.S., Wang, C., Gou, M., Lu, C.: GraspNet-1billion: a large-scale benchmark for general object grasping, pp. 11441–11450 (2020). https://doi.org/10.1109/CVPR42600.2020.01146
17. Feng, Y., Zhang, Z., Zhao, X., Ji, R., Gao, Y.: GVCNN: group-view convolutional neural networks for 3D shape recognition. In: 2018 IEEE/CVF Conference on Computer Vision and Pattern Recognition, pp. 264–272 (2018). https://doi.org/10.1109/CVPR.2018.00035
18. Geiger, A., Lenz, P., Urtasun, R.: Are we ready for autonomous driving? The KITTI vision benchmark suite. In: 2012 IEEE Conference on Computer Vision and Pattern Recognition, pp. 3354–3361 (2012). https://doi.org/10.1109/CVPR.2012.6248074
19. Geras, K.J., Wolfson, S., Kim, S.G., Moy, L., Cho, K.: High-resolution breast cancer screening with multi-view deep convolutional neural networks. CoRR abs/1703.07047 (2017). http://arxiv.org/abs/1703.07047
20. Girdhar, R., Singh, M., Ravi, N., van der Maaten, L., Joulin, A., Misra, I.: Omnivore: a single model for many visual modalities. In: CVPR (2022)
21. Gupta, S., Girshick, R.B., Arbelaez, P., Malik, J.: Learning rich features from RGB-D images for object detection and segmentation. CoRR abs/1407.5736 (2014). http://arxiv.org/abs/1407.5736
22. Hamdi, A., Giancola, S., Li, B., Thabet, A.K., Ghanem, B.: MVTN: multi-view transformation network for 3D shape recognition. CoRR abs/2011.13244 (2020). https://arxiv.org/abs/2011.13244

23. He, K., Zhang, X., Ren, S., Sun, J.: Deep residual learning for image recognition. CoRR abs/1512.03385 (2015). http://arxiv.org/abs/1512.03385
24. Henzler, P., et al.: Unsupervised learning of 3d object categories from videos in the wild. CoRR abs/2103.16552 (2021). https://arxiv.org/abs/2103.16552
25. Hinterstoisser, S., et al.: Model based training, detection and pose estimation of texture-less 3D objects in heavily cluttered scenes. In: Lee, K.M., Matsushita, Y., Rehg, J.M., Hu, Z. (eds.) ACCV 2012. LNCS, vol. 7724, pp. 548–562. Springer, Heidelberg (2013). https://doi.org/10.1007/978-3-642-37331-2_42
26. Hodan, T., Haluza, P., Obdržálek, S., Matas, J., Lourakis, M.I.A., Zabulis, X.: T-LESS: an RGB-D dataset for 6D pose estimation of texture-less objects. CoRR abs/1701.05498 (2017). http://arxiv.org/abs/1701.05498
27. Hu, J., Shen, L., Sun, G.: Squeeze-and-excitation networks. CoRR abs/1709.01507 (2017). http://arxiv.org/abs/1709.01507
28. Huang, G., Liu, Z., Weinberger, K.Q.: Densely connected convolutional networks. CoRR abs/1608.06993 (2016). http://arxiv.org/abs/1608.06993
29. Jia, K., Lin, J., Tan, M., Tao, D.: Deep multi-view learning using neuron-wise correlation-maximizing regularizers. CoRR abs/1904.11151 (2019). http://arxiv.org/abs/1904.11151
30. Jiang, J., Bao, D., Chen, Z., Zhao, X., Gao, Y.: MLVCNN: multi-loop-view convolutional neural network for 3D shape retrieval. In: Proceedings of the AAAI Conference on Artificial Intelligence, vol. 33, no. 01, pp. 8513–8520 (2019). https://doi.org/10.1609/aaai.v33i01.33018513, https://ojs.aaai.org/index.php/AAAI/article/view/4869
31. Jiang, J., Zheng, L., Luo, F., Zhang, Z.: RedNet: residual encoder-decoder network for indoor RGB-D semantic segmentation. CoRR abs/1806.01054 (2018). http://arxiv.org/abs/1806.01054
32. Kanezaki, A.: RotationNet: learning object classification using unsupervised viewpoint estimation. CoRR abs/1603.06208 (2016). http://arxiv.org/abs/1603.06208
33. Karen, S., Andrew, Z.: Very deep convolutional networks for large-scale image recognition. Computer Vision and Pattern Recognition (2014). https://arxiv.org/abs/1409.1556
34. Kaur, H., Koundal, D., Kadyan, V.: Image fusion techniques: a survey. Arch. Comput. Methods Eng. **28**(7), 4425–4447 (2021). https://doi.org/10.1007/s11831-021-09540-7
35. Lai, K., Bo, L., Ren, X., Fox, D.: A large-scale hierarchical multi-view RGB-D object dataset (2011)
36. Kim, S., Chi, H.G., Hu, X., Huang, Q., Ramani, K.: A large-scale annotated mechanical components benchmark for classification and retrieval tasks with deep neural networks. In: Proceedings of 16th European Conference on Computer Vision (ECCV) (2020)
37. Koch, S., et al.: ABC: a big cad model dataset for geometric deep learning. In: The IEEE Conference on Computer Vision and Pattern Recognition (CVPR) (2019)
38. Krizhevsky, A., Sutskever, I., Hinton, G.E.: ImageNet classification with deep convolutional neural networks. In: Pereira, F., Burges, C., Bottou, L., Weinberger, K. (eds.) Advances in Neural Information Processing Systems, vol. 25. Curran Associates, Inc. (2012). https://proceedings.neurips.cc/paper/2012/file/c399862d3b9d6b76c8436e924a68c45b-Paper.pdf
39. Lin, T., Dollár, P., Girshick, R.B., He, K., Hariharan, B., Belongie, S.J.: Feature pyramid networks for object detection. CoRR abs/1612.03144 (2016). http://arxiv.org/abs/1612.03144
40. Liu, H., Zhang, J., Yang, K., Hu, X., Stiefelhagen, R.: CMX: cross-modal fusion for RGB-X semantic segmentation with transformers. arXiv preprint arXiv:2203.04838 (2022)
41. Liu, Z., et al.: Swin transformer V2: scaling up capacity and resolution. CoRR abs/2111.09883 (2021). https://arxiv.org/abs/2111.09883
42. Liu, Z., et al.: Swin transformer: hierarchical vision transformer using shifted windows. CoRR abs/2103.14030 (2021). https://arxiv.org/abs/2103.14030

43. Long, J., Shelhamer, E., Darrell, T.: Fully convolutional networks for semantic segmentation. In: 2015 IEEE Conference on Computer Vision and Pattern Recognition (CVPR), pp. 3431–3440 (2015). https://doi.org/10.1109/CVPR.2015.7298965
44. Luo, H., et al.: Self-supervised pre-training for transformer-based person re-identification. arXiv preprint arXiv:2111.12084 (2021)
45. Mazzei, D., Ramjattan, R.: Machine learning for industry 4.0: a systematic review using deep learning-based topic modelling. Sensors **22**(22) (2022). https://www.mdpi.com/1424-8220/22/22/8641
46. Mo, K., et al.: PartNet: a large-scale benchmark for fine-grained and hierarchical part-level 3D object understanding. CoRR abs/1812.02713 (2018). http://arxiv.org/abs/1812.02713
47. Naranjo-Torres, J., Mora, M., Hernández-García, R., Barrientos, R.J., Fredes, C., Valenzuela, A.: A review of convolutional neural network applied to fruit image processing. Appl. Sci. **10**(10) (2020). https://doi.org/10.3390/app10103443
48. Ophoff, T., Van Beeck, K., Goedemé, T.: Exploring RGB+depth fusion for real-time object detection. Sensors **19**, 866 (2019). https://doi.org/10.3390/s19040866
49. Oquab, M., et al.: DINOv2: learning robust visual features without supervision (2023)
50. P.J, J., Chao, Y.W., Xiang, Y.: FewSOL: a dataset for few-shot object learning in robotic environments (2022). https://doi.org/10.48550/ARXIV.2207.03333
51. Radford, A., et al.: Learning transferable visual models from natural language supervision. CoRR abs/2103.00020 (2021). https://arxiv.org/abs/2103.00020
52. Reizenstein, J., Shapovalov, R., Henzler, P., Sbordone, L., Labatut, P., Novotný, D.: Common objects in 3D: large-scale learning and evaluation of real-life 3D category reconstruction. CoRR abs/2109.00512 (2021). https://arxiv.org/abs/2109.00512
53. Rombach, R., Blattmann, A., Lorenz, D., Esser, P., Ommer, B.: High-resolution image synthesis with latent diffusion models. CoRR abs/2112.10752 (2021). https://arxiv.org/abs/2112.10752
54. Schlüter, M., et al.: Ai-enhanced identification, inspection and sorting for reverse logistics in remanufacturing. Procedia CIRP **98**, 300–305 (2021). https://doi.org/10.1016/j.procir.2021.01.107, https://www.sciencedirect.com/science/article/pii/S2212827121001372. The 28th CIRP Conference on Life Cycle Engineering, 10–12 March 2021, Jaipur, India
55. Schlüter, M., Niebuhr, C., Lehr, J., Krüger, J.: Vision-based identification service for remanufacturing sorting. Procedia Manuf. **21**, 384–391 (2018). https://doi.org/10.1016/j.promfg.2018.02.135
56. Schlüter, M., et al.: Green incremental learning - energy efficient ramp-up for AI-enhanced part recognition in reverse logistics. Procedia CIRP **116**, 414–419 (2023). https://doi.org/10.1016/j.procir.2023.02.070, https://www.sciencedirect.com/science/article/pii/S2212827123000847. 30th CIRP Life Cycle Engineering Conference
57. Sedaghat, N., Brox, T.: Unsupervised generation of a viewpoint annotated car dataset from videos. In: IEEE International Conference on Computer Vision (ICCV) (2015). http://lmb.informatik.uni-freiburg.de//Publications/2015/SB15
58. Seeland, M., Mäder, P.: Multi-view classification with convolutional neural networks. PLOS ONE **16**, 1–17 (2021). https://doi.org/10.1371/journal.pone.0245230
59. Setio, A.A.A., et al.: Pulmonary nodule detection in CT images: false positive reduction using multi-view convolutional networks. IEEE Trans. Med. Imaging **35**(5), 1160–1169 (2016). https://doi.org/10.1109/TMI.2016.2536809
60. Shahrabadi, S., Castilla, Y., Guevara, M., Magalhães, L.G., Gonzalez, D., Adão, T.: Defect detection in the textile industry using image-based machine learning methods: a brief review. J. Phys.: Conf. Ser. **2224**(1), 012010 (2022). https://doi.org/10.1088/1742-6596/2224/1/012010

61. Silberman, N., Hoiem, D., Kohli, P., Fergus, R.: Indoor segmentation and support inference from RGBD images. In: Fitzgibbon, A., Lazebnik, S., Perona, P., Sato, Y., Schmid, C. (eds.) ECCV 2012. LNCS, vol. 7576, pp. 746–760. Springer, Heidelberg (2012). https://doi.org/10.1007/978-3-642-33715-4_54
62. Smith, L.N., Topin, N.: Super-convergence: very fast training of residual networks using large learning rates. CoRR abs/1708.07120 (2017). http://arxiv.org/abs/1708.07120
63. Song, S., Lichtenberg, S.P., Xiao, J.: Sun RGB-D: A RGB-D scene understanding benchmark suite. In: CVPR (2015)
64. Srivastava, S., Sharma, G.: OmniVec: learning robust representations with cross modal sharing (2023). https://arxiv.org/abs/2311.05709
65. Srivastava, S., Sharma, G.: OmniVec2 - a novel transformer based network for large scale multimodal and multitask learning. In: Proceedings of the IEEE/CVF Conference on Computer Vision and Pattern Recognition (CVPR), pp. 27412–27424 (2024)
66. Su, H., Maji, S., Kalogerakis, E., Learned-Miller, E.G.: Multi-view convolutional neural networks for 3D shape recognition. In: Proceedings of the ICCV (2015)
67. Su, Y., Yuan, Y., Jiang, Z.: Deep feature selection-and-fusion for RGB-D semantic segmentation. CoRR abs/2105.04102 (2021). https://arxiv.org/abs/2105.04102
68. Szegedy, C., et al.: Going deeper with convolutions. CoRR abs/1409.4842 (2014). http://arxiv.org/abs/1409.4842
69. Tan, M., Le, Q.V.: EfficientNet: rethinking model scaling for convolutional neural networks. CoRR abs/1905.11946 (2019). http://arxiv.org/abs/1905.11946
70. Uy, M.A., Pham, Q., Hua, B., Nguyen, D.T., Yeung, S.: Revisiting point cloud classification: a new benchmark dataset and classification model on real-world data. CoRR abs/1908.04616 (2019). http://arxiv.org/abs/1908.04616
71. Vaswani, A., et al.: Attention is all you need. CoRR abs/1706.03762 (2017). http://arxiv.org/abs/1706.03762
72. Wang, C., et al.: Densefusion: 6d object pose estimation by iterative dense fusion. CoRR abs/1901.04780 (2019). http://arxiv.org/abs/1901.04780
73. Wang, Y., Chen, X., Cao, L., Huang, W., Sun, F., Wang, Y.: Multimodal token fusion for vision transformers. In: Proceedings of the IEEE/CVF Conference on Computer Vision and Pattern Recognition (CVPR), pp. 12186–12195 (2022)
74. Wei, X., Yu, R., Sun, J.: View-GCN: view-based graph convolutional network for 3D shape analysis. In: IEEE/CVF Conference on Computer Vision and Pattern Recognition (CVPR) (2020)
75. Wu, Z., Song, S., Khosla, A., Tang, X., Xiao, J.: 3D shapenets for 2.5D object recognition and next-best-view prediction. CoRR abs/1406.5670 (2014). http://arxiv.org/abs/1406.5670
76. Xiang, Y., Mottaghi, R., Savarese, S.: Beyond pascal: a benchmark for 3D object detection in the wild. In: IEEE Winter Conference on Applications of Computer Vision, pp. 75–82 (2014). https://doi.org/10.1109/WACV.2014.6836101
77. Xiang, Y., Schmidt, T., Narayanan, V., Fox, D.: PoseCNN: a convolutional neural network for 6D object pose estimation in cluttered scenes. CoRR abs/1711.00199 (2017). http://arxiv.org/abs/1711.00199
78. Xie, E., Wang, W., Yu, Z., Anandkumar, A., Alvarez, J.M., Luo, P.: SegFormer: simple and efficient design for semantic segmentation with transformers. CoRR abs/2105.15203 (2021). https://arxiv.org/abs/2105.15203
79. Zhang, H., Duan, J., Xue, M., Song, J., Sun, L., Song, M.: Bootstrapping ViTs: towards liberating vision transformers from pre-training. CoRR abs/2112.03552 (2021). https://arxiv.org/abs/2112.03552

80. Zhao, X., Pang, Y., Zhang, L., Lu, H., Ruan, X.: Self-supervised representation learning for RGB-D salient object detection. CoRR abs/2101.12482 (2021). https://arxiv.org/abs/2101.12482
81. Zhu, X., Su, W., Lu, L., Li, B., Wang, X., Dai, J.: Deformable DETR: deformable transformers for end-to-end object detection. CoRR abs/2010.04159 (2020). https://arxiv.org/abs/2010.04159

Assessment of Uncertainty and Variability in Simulation Tools Under Foggy Conditions

Pierre Duthon[1]([✉]), Mohamed Boudali[2], Amine Ben-Daoued[1], Rémi Regnier[2], Charlotte Segonne[1], and Frédéric Bernardin[1]

[1] Cerema, Research Team "Intelligent Transport Systems", 8-10 Rue Bernard Palissy, CEDEX 2, 63017 Clermont-Ferrand, France
`pierre.duthon@cerema.fr`
[2] Laboratoire National de Métrologie et D'essais (LNE), 78197 Trappes, France

Abstract. Intelligent mobility systems are increasingly making use of AI for various functions, including navigation, sign recognition, road tracking, and obstacle detection. To achieve certification up to SAE Level 3 and more in the future, manufacturers must prove that their vehicles maintain adequate safety within their operational design domain through rigorous testing in diverse scenarios. Sensor simulation tools including degraded weather conditions (physical, numerical or hybrid) must be employed. In this study as part of the PRISSMA project, a proof of concept is proposed to characterize and evaluate the protocols and four different kind of simulation tools that enable AI algorithm certification under degraded weather conditions.

Keywords: Simulation tools · Degraded weather conditions · Autonommous vehicle · Artificial vision

1 Introduction

The increased use of AI in vehicle industries is a real turning point in the validation of these intelligent vehicles. Vehicles equipped with partially automated driving capabilities can now achieve certification up to SAE Level 3 [9]. To achieve this, manufacturers must prove that their vehicles maintain adequate safety within their operational design domain (ODD) through rigorous testing in diverse scenarios [15]. In particular, this task concerns the first braking-related advanced driver assistance system (ADAS) that has been implemented as an "Automatic Emergency Braking" (AEB) [6]. Qualifying these systems requires extensive verification across numerous scenarios, including those with degraded weather conditions. However, due to cost and safety concerns, these tests cannot always be performed in real-world conditions, especially when some tests pose risks or are too infrequent to yield sufficient data. For this reason, sensor simulation tools and degraded weather conditions (physical, numerical or hybrid) must be employed.

These simulation tools can be real, purely virtual or can combine the physical sensor with simulated inputs. For real simulation, test chambers are available to reproduce a variety of weather conditions, such as fog or rain [10]. The purely virtual simulators can be physically-based [3] or empirical [4]. The latter family of simulators is real-time but not the former. On the other hand, the former can be validated physically, unlike the latter, which can deviate from reality. The last family combines simulation with real tests [12]. In the language of certification, which is now being established, we speak about X in the Loop (XiL) testing, with X representing the Software (SiL), the Hardware (HiL) or the entire Vehicle (ViL). In the HiL and ViL cases, we can imagine that the vehicle's real sensor is fooled by a screen system that makes the vehicle believe it's seeing things that don't exist. The advantage of not only relying on software during simulation is that other disruptive elements can be considered during testing, such as sensor electronics, system response times, or vehicle dynamics in the case of ViL. These simulation tools need to be validated and qualified, as they may be used for certification. In particular, it is necessary to check these points:

- What scenarios should be considered to ensure the reliability of AI-based algorithms during certification? Specifically, what are the minimum scenario combinations required to guarantee a certain level of error and uncertainty during evaluation?
- The reproducibility of a test from one tool to another: what are the differences in results between the different simulation tools (real or numerical)?

This document is part of the PRISSMA project consisting in defining verification, evaluation, and validation methodologies and protocols allowing to calculate both the tools/models and system of systems levels of performance/quality/representativeness. Bringing together around twenty French partners, the PRISSMA project is particularly focused on the 'safety demonstration' of mobility systems using Artificial Intelligence (AI) techniques. This work is an extension of a previous one, with two major novelties [12]: addition of purely simulated and HiL data, addition of a low-level metric.

In the remainder of this paper, the methodology employed will be presented first, followed by a description of the experimental process, before concluding with an analysis of the results obtained.

2 Methodology

The present study aims to serve as a proof of concept (POC) to characterize and evaluate the protocols and simulation tools that enable AI algorithm certification under degraded weather conditions. We have chosen to study the case of fog which is the weather condition that has the greatest impact on an optical vision system while being difficult to control for tests on tracks or open roads. This study specifically focuses on evaluating the simulation tools rather than the AI algorithms themselves. Four simulation tools are evaluated and compared, ranging from physical simulations to purely numerical simulations. To achieve this, the simulation tools are used to create identical scenarios simulating adverse weather conditions, generating image datasets for comparative analysis. Two metrics are used for this evaluation: a "high-level" metric based on the AI detection algorithm and a "low-level" metric based on contrast measurement directly on the raw image pixel data.

2.1 Simulation Tools

Regarding the simulation tools, the first one is a physical simulation tool called the PAVIN fog and rain platform of the Cerema, which allows the production of various and reproducible fog and rain conditions [10]. Located in Clermont-Ferrand, France, the PAVIN platform measures 30 m in length, 5.5 m in width, and 2.20 m in height. These dimensions enable the reproduction of an urban scene, and with the addition of a removable greenhouse, it is also possible to simulate both day and night conditions on this platform [10]. The weather conditions on this platform are calibrated from a meteorological point of view, including the calibration of intensities, drop size, and velocity.

The second one is the K-HiL simulator which is based on the Koschmieder law. This simulator applies the visibility attenuation theory of Koschmieder, defined a century ago [7], to clear weather visible images. This theory makes it possible to determine the luminance of a black object on a sky background by an attenuation of the visibility due to the extinction of the medium between the object and the observer. According to the Koschmieder law, the Meteorological Optical Range (MOR), also called visibility V (in m) is related to the extinction coefficient b_{ext} (in m^{-1}), if we consider that the minimum contrast identifiable by an observer is 0.05 (i.e., 5%) [5,17].

$$V = \frac{-\ln(0.05)}{b_{ext}} \quad (1)$$

Based on the attenuation law of Beer–Lambert [7,8], the object luminance $L_{x,y}$ of a pixel (x, y) at a distance of $d_{x,y}$ with intrinsic luminance of $L_{0;x,y}$ and L_s, being the luminance of the air light, can be described by the following relation:

$$L_{x,y} = L_{0;x,y} \exp(-b_{ext} d_{x,y}) + L_s(1 - \exp(-b_{ext} d_{x,y})) \quad (2)$$

The equation requires three main parameters: the MOR value (V), the background luminance (Ls), and the depth of objects in the images $(d_{x,y})$. The depth can be extracted from the stereoscopic camera images. The visibility values depend on the artificial fog parameters from the tests [12]. Finally, the background luminance is considered as the mean luminance of 10% of the brightest pixels of the image.

The third simulation tool, known as LEIA Simulation, utilizes proprietary software purchased by LNE called 4D Virtualiz Sim (4DV Sim) [1], a 3D simulator designed for robotics and the automotive field. This digital twin software allows users to create scenarios from scratch using items from the software's library or by importing 3D models of buildings, vegetation, and more. In this study, a 3D model of the PAVIN platform, created by Cerema, is imported into the 4DV simulator. The simulator enables users to specify parameters such as the time of day (day or night), weather conditions (clear or foggy), human appearance and routes. It also supports various sensors including stereo cameras, Lidar, GPS, and more.

The final simulation tool, called LEIA Immersion, is a test bench developed by LNE. It consists of a physical camera, a screen, and a high-definition video projector. The camera is positioned in front of the screen, where images from various datasets are projected. To prevent light disturbances, tests using this simulation tool are conducted in a darkroom.

Fig. 1. Example of YOLO detections on two Clear Weather images with different pedestrians. Colors: Green is for $confidence > 0.9$, Yellow is for $0.9 > confidence > 0.7$, Orange is for $0.7 > confidence > 0.5$, Red is for $0.5 > confidence > 0.3$. (Color figure online)

2.2 Metrics

Metric Based on a Pedestrian Detection Algorithm. As previously stated, two metrics are employed to evaluate the four simulation tools. The first metric, called "high-level," evaluates the AI detection algorithm, focusing specifically on pedestrian detection as an illustrative example. Concerning the pedestrian detection algorithm, the third version of YOLO detection algorithm [11] was chosen in this study. It is indeed a very common algorithm in the literature on object detection. Moreover, it is very easy to handle. The library of objects available in this version contains 80 items. The algorithm requires two main parameters: the confidence threshold (a value between 0 and 1) of the labeling and the object to label in the images. Only the class "person" is labeled in this study and the confidence threshold chosen is explained in the following section. The YOLO algorithm takes the image datasets generated by the various simulation tools as input and outputs whether or not a pedestrian is detected, as well as the bonding box of the pedestrian in image. These outputs are then used to compute the widely used metric for evaluating the validity of a detection, which is the intersection over union (IOU) between the bounding box provided by YOLO and the ground truth bounding box given by the simulators. The intersection is calculated following the equation:

$$IOU(frame) = \frac{\text{Area of Overlap}}{\text{Area of Union}} \quad (3)$$

The precision-recall curve is then calculated based on the results of intersection over union values. The obtained curve shows the trade-off between precision and recall for different confidence threshold values from the YOLO algorithm. As an example, the different detections obtained by the YOLO algorithm, for different levels of confidence, from 0.3 to 1, on two images from the database are presented in the Fig. 1. The top image of the Fig. 1 shows the 9 YOLO labels with two labels far from the pedestrian present in the scene, yet for one of them a confidence value greater than 0.5. Then, the area under the curves (AUC) score is calculated. A large AUC value represents both high recall and high precision. A high precision value indicates a low false positive rate (good confidence value but no ground truth label), and a high recall value indicates a low false negative rate (low confidence value but ground truth has a label).

Metric Based on Contrast Evaluation. The first "high-level" metric was proposed in the previous section in order to evaluate the image datasets from a detection algorithm point of view. To complete our analysis, we propose here a "low-level" metric, at the opposite end of the processing chain. To do this, we are proposing a metric based on a contrast measurement directly on the raw image pixel data. This metric is directly inspired by the definition of the physical quantity describing fog density: the Meteorological Optical Range (MOR). In fact, fog density is characterized by a measure of contrast. To calculate the contrast ratio, we first need to define two zones in the image, one dark and one bright, which must be at an equal distance from the camera. It is important to take two zones at equal distances because the impact of fog is proportional to the distance between the target and the camera. Once the two zones have been defined, the pixel values in each zone are averaged to obtain the luminances L_{dark} and L_{bright}. The contrast is then calculated using the following expression:

$$Contrast = C = \frac{L_{bright} - L_{dark}}{L_{dark}} \quad (4)$$

Contrast therefore varies from 0 to 1. The denser the fog, the lower the contrast. This approach calculating contrast was applied to 9 pairs of zones (dark and light), from all the images in the various databases. The Fig. 2 shows the zones used. As shown in this figure, the choice was made to take pairs of zones at different distances to see if the variation in contrast is indeed similar for different depths.

3 Experiments

3.1 Evaluation Protocol

The objective of this study is to evaluate and compare the fog generation capabilities of four simulation tools. This evaluation involves testing scenarios where pedestrians walk in a road scene under various weather conditions (clear weather and two types of fog) and seasons, with clothing representative of summer or winter. To conduct this evaluation, a first database is created in clear weather and fog conditions on the PAVIN platform. This involves recording real pedestrians navigating a road scene using a camera. After these initial tests, a database with real images acquired in clear weather and

Fig. 2. Presentation of the 9 measurement zones for the contrast method.

fog conditions is available. Next, fog is added to the real data acquired in clear weather using the K-HiL model. Once the model has been applied, a second database with digitally simulated fog is available. Thanks to a digital twin of the platform (3D model), the same scenarios are reproduced independently in the LEIA Simulation. It enables the same data to be created in a virtual world (full 3D simulation). This makes it possible to obtain a third database with clear weather and fog conditions.

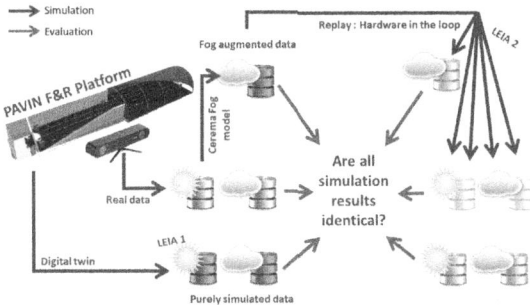

Fig. 3. Presentation of the protocol used to obtain the various databases to be compared as part of the study.

To better address HiL simulations, we use the LEIA Immersion. This simulator enables us to replay a database in front of a real camera to produce images as if the camera had captured the scene directly. This is important in the context of vehicle evaluation, as it enables the entire processing chain to be included in the evaluations (sensor, electronics, cables, central processing unit, etc.). Here we have chosen to use the LEIA Immersion to compare the PAVIN and LEIA Simulation databases, resulting in 2 new databases taking HiL into account. In the end, there are 5 databases from various simulation tools for comparison. An overview of this is provided in Fig. 3 Each of these five variants contains identical clear weather and fog conditions. These five variants are named and summarized in Table 1 with those replayed in LEIA Immersion specifically marked with an asterisk *.

Table 1. Nomenclature and description of the databases used in the study.

Variant name	Acquisition method	Type	Peds num.	Total number of videos
PAVIN	A real camera records pedestrian on the PAVIN platform. The platform can reproduce clear weather or fog	Real	100	3 weather conditions × 100 pedestrians × 2 sequences = 600
K-HiL	Camera data from the PAVIN database (clear weather) is reused. Using the K-HiL simulator, digital fog is added to the images	HiL	100	2 weather conditions × 100 pedestrians × 2 sequences = 400
LEIA	The platform's digital twin is used to recreate scenarios in an entirely virtual world, thanks to the LEIA Simulation	SiL	36	3 weather conditions × 36 pedestrians × 2 sequences = 216
PAVIN*	PAVIN database replay into LEIA Immersion	HiL	100	3 weather conditions × 100 pedestrians × 2 sequences = 600
LEIA*	LEIA database replay into LEIA Immersion	HiL	36	3 weather conditions × 36 pedestrians × 2 sequences = 216

3.2 Scenario Description

The scenario tests involve creating a realistic urban environment on the PAVIN Fog and Rain platform. This setup includes a Renault Megane vehicle, trees, a wooden picnic table, various traffic signs, ground marking strips, and orange traffic cones. A 3D model (digital twin) encompassing all these elements is also created.

For each trial, the pedestrians follow the same path through the platform and repeat it twice, consecutively, to ensure repeatability. In addition to walking at a moderate pace, the pedestrians also find themselves sitting on the bench at the picnic table. To represent a wide variety of pedestrians, various characteristics have been made variable:

– Clothing: 50% of the clothing is representative of summer weather and 50% of winter weather.
– Accessories: a selection of pedestrians carry accessories with different sizes.
– Gender: 60% of the pedestrians are male and 40% are female.

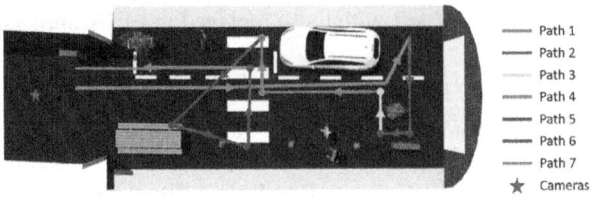

Fig. 4. Path of the pedestrians during the tests following the colored lines and arrow directions.

To capture the pedestrians walking through the PAVIN platform, two sensors were used:

- A stereoscopic camera (ZED 2I from StereoLabs [14]) to obtain visible images and depth information. The focal lens of the camera is 4 mm, the frame rate is 19 fps, and the image size is 1280 × 720 pixels.
- A thermal camera named Serval 640 GigE from Xenics [13], with a frame rate of 25 fps, and the image size is 640 × 480 pixels.

The stereoscopic camera is used for data acquisition and to obtain the depth information required for the K-HiL simulator. The thermal camera, after a preliminary geometrical calibration, is employed to label the stereoscopic camera's images in dense fog. This is necessary because the pedestrian is almost invisible to the ZED 2I camera in dense fog, making labeling extremely challenging. Both cameras are positioned at the beginning of the greenhouse as shown in Fig. 4. Regarding the LEIA Simulation, a digital model of the ZED 2I camera is available in 4DV Sim and will be used for data acquisition. Moreover, 4DV Sim provides a labeling process to label the camera's images. In LEIA Immersion, the same stereoscopic ZED 2I camera used on the PAVIN platform is employed to capture the projected images.

In meteorology, fog is characterized using the MOR noted as V [16]. MOR, measured in meters, denotes the distance at which the human eye can no longer perceive contrast on a calibrated white-and-black target. The smaller the MOR, the denser the fog. In meteorology, fog is considered present when the MOR is below 1000 m [16], and in a road context, when it is below 400 m [2]. The three types of weather conditions chosen are in this study:

- Clear weather (CW): it allows for a reference scene without disturbances due to the presence of fog.
- Medium fog (MF): with a MOR of 23 m, it allows modifying the general aspect of the objects of the scene by leaving all the elements of the visible scene detectable.
- Dense fog (DF): with a MOR of 10 m, it allows elements of the background to disappear for the stereo camera but not for the thermal camera.

4 Results

4.1 Qualitative Analysis of Different Simulation Variants

Before starting to analyze the results, it is important to take a visual look at the images obtained for the different databases. The Fig. 5 therefore shows the images obtained for

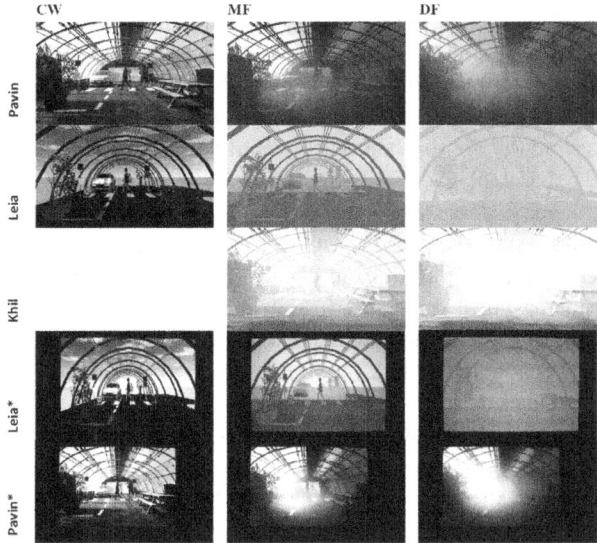

Fig. 5. Example of an image for different weather conditions and simulation modes.

a similar pedestrian, in the same location, under different weather conditions and for different simulation modalities.

In this figure, we can see that there are variations in rendering between the different simulation modalities. For example, clear-weather images from LEIA are more contrasted than those filmed in real life on PAVIN. The replay version * of the databases also significantly increases contrast. As far as fog is concerned, the models tend to make the fog visually too clear, compared with the real data from PAVIN. This phenomenon is well known in the literature for empirical fog models [3]. For heavy fog, the LEIA version also lacks contrast. In the case of PAVIN*, we can also see that the camera is overexposed in places, while other areas are underexposed. This means that the dynamic range of the video projection equipment used is not sufficient. Similarly, in the case of the two versions *, the framing is not ideal, resulting in black borders (and therefore under-resolution in the useful area). Further results will show whether these differences really matter: do artificial intelligence algorithms behave in the same way with the different modalities? Thanks to the proposed contrast method, the qualitative findings we've just made can be confirmed quantitatively with a metric.

4.2 High Level Metric

First, we propose to analyze the overall results obtained by the YOLO algorithm on all the databases. The Table 2 shows the AUC score obtained for each database variant, in the three weather conditions of clear weather, medium fog and dense fog. The AUC score varies from 0 to 1; the higher the AUC score, the better the algorithm. The first observation is that data from the PAVIN* database completely prevent the algorithm from detecting pedestrians. The AUC scores for this variant are extremely low. A check of the detections shows that the algorithm has great difficulty in detecting pedestrians on PAVIN* images, missing them on around three quarters of the images. This is because the PAVIN* images have very degraded dynamics. This is due to a change in equipment (different video protection for PAVIN* and LEIA*). Replaying an existing database is therefore not particularly appropriate. With regard to pure simulation tests, we can see that the LEIA database achieves fairly similar results to PAVIN, with a difference for dense fog, which appears less complicated for the algorithm in the LEIA database (AUC = 0.35) than in the PAVIN database (AUC = 0.29). The addition of the HiL aspect in the LEIA* base, with the replay in front of the real camera, lowers the score for clear weather, while increasing it for heavy fog. In the case of clear weather, this can no doubt be explained by the fact that the image dynamics are very specific. The camera is filming a bright screen in a very dark room. It therefore has difficulty in making a good exposure setting. This could be compensated for by taking care to fix the exposure settings of the cameras when testing in LEIA Immersion. The final variation is the K-HiL variant, in which fog is added to the initially fog-free real images. For this variant, the effect of the fog is stronger than for the PAVIN base with real fog. This suggests that the background luminance and fog density settings should be reviewed for this model. Beyond the results between databases, the table also shows that the choice of fog densities is not very well chosen for the evaluation of an algorithm. Medium fog seems too light (detection too easy), while dense fog is too dense (detection almost impossible). For evaluation purposes, therefore, much more variable fog ranges are required.

Table 2. AUC scores obtained for the Yolo algorithm on the different variants of the database, for an IOU of 0.5.

	CW	MF	DW
PAVIN	0.93	0.89	0.29
K-HiL		0.80	0.25
LEIA	0.92	0.86	0.35
PAVIN*	0.09	0.12	0.02
LEIA*	0.84	0.84	0.42

4.3 Low Level Metric

Following this analysis of the output of an AI-based algorithm, it is interesting to see what the contrast levels of the different databases are. As explained in the method, the contrast ratio was measured at 9 points in the image. In Table 3, we propose an average result for the 9 zones, to check whether some variants are indeed more contrasted than others. From the point of view of contrast, the databases * are close to reality. Although they appear to be far apart visually, they are actually quite close numerically. On the other hand, we can see that the LEIA and K-HiL simulations do not represent reality well in terms of contrast. It is interesting to note that the results obtained by the high-level and low-level metrics are not correlated at all. This shows that the contrast ratio of the images (although a very good representative of fog) is not sufficient to assess the quality of computer-generated images for the evaluation of AI algorithms. Other factors such as saturation, colorimetric and resolution should perhaps be taken into account.

Table 3. Contrast score obtained on different variants of the database.

	CW	MF	DW
PAVIN	0.76	0.30	0.12
K-HiL		0.11	0.02
LEIA	0.89	0.19	0.02
PAVIN*	0.66	0.25	0.13
LEIA*	0.77	0.29	0.04

5 Conclusion

The aim of the Cerema-LNE POC was to identify the key points to be considered for the approval of vehicles using AI, in test conditions requiring the use of digital or physical simulation. This POC was based on tools such as the PAVIN Fog and Rain platform and the Leia Simulation and Immersion simulators. The work focused on an example of a critical application for road safety: the detection of vulnerable road users (pedestrians) in foggy conditions. This POC demonstrated several key elements:

- The boundary conditions for the AI algorithms are not easy to find. In the example of fog, the pedestrian detection algorithms quickly go from very good detection to no detection. Finding the boundary test cases (scenario, pedestrian route, pedestrian environment, and weather conditions) is therefore not easy. This is due to the structure of the algorithms based on AI, in which numerous threshold effects come into play. This raises even more questions about the test scenarios to be put in place, especially as these scenarios will have to evolve over time as the detection capabilities of the algorithms evolve.
- The different simulation methods (HiL or not, pure digital simulation, etc.) do not produce the same results on AI based algorithms. There is therefore a lot of work to be done on improving and validating the systems put in place (simulators, HiL injection...). While the geometry of the scene appears to be good, lighting conditions, surface properties and sensor characteristics need to be considered to obtain images that are closer to reality.
- As mentioned above, our results show that the different simulation variants (pure numerical, HiL, etc.) do not lead to the same scores when evaluating AI algorithms. We have then compared the images using a low-level metric. It is surprising to see that the two types of comparison (high level i.e. close to the AI algorithms and low

level i.e. close to the raw images) do not give the same results. Some simulation modalities obtain very different scores on the AI algorithms, whereas the low-level metric shows that the images are similar. As AI algorithms are black boxes, it is therefore difficult to define metrics that can tell whether images from two simulation modalities are similar or not. A great effort of research needs to be done in this area, in search of reliable combined metrics.

Acknowledgement. The work in this paper was carried out as part of the French national PRISSMA project funded by BPI as part of the Grand Défi IA of the Innovation Council and the Ministry of Ecological and Solidarity Transition.

References

1. 4D Virtualiz: 4d virtualiz website (2024). https://www.4d-virtualiz.com/
2. AFNOR: NF p99-320 - recueil des données météorologoiques et routières (1989)
3. Ben-Daoued, A., Duthon, P., Bernardin, F.: Sweet: a realistic multiwavelength 3D simulator for automotive perceptive sensors in foggy conditions. J. Imaging **9**(2) (2023). https://doi.org/10.3390/jimaging9020054
4. Dosovitskiy, A., Ros, G., Codevilla, F., Lopez, A., Koltun, V.: Carla: An open urban driving simulator. In: Conference on Robot Learning, pp. 1–16. PMLR (2017)
5. Gordon, J.I.: Daytime visibility, a conceptual review (1979). sIO Ref. 80-1
6. ISO: ISO/DIS 22733-2(EN), road vehicles - test method to evaluate the performance of autonomous emergency braking systems - part 2: Car to pedestrian (2023)
7. Koschmieder, H.: Theorie der horizontalen sichtweite. Beiträge zurPhysik der freien Atmosphäre **12**, 33–55 (1924)
8. Lee, Z., Shang, S.: Visibility: how applicable is the century-old Koschmieder model? J. Atmos. Sci. (2016). https://doi.org/10.1175/JAS-D-16-0102.1
9. Li, Y., Duthon, P., Colomb, M., Ibanez-Guzman, J.: What happens for a ToF LiDAR in fog? Trans. Intell. Transp. Syst. (2020). https://arxiv.org/abs/2003.06660
10. Liandrat, S., Duthon, P., Bernardin, F., Ben Daoued, A., Bicard, J.L.: A review of Cerema PAVIN fog & rain platform: from past and back to the future. In: ITS World Congress, Los Angeles, United States (2022). https://hal.archives-ouvertes.fr/hal-03844483
11. Redmon, J., Farhadi, A.: YOLOv3: an incremental improvement. CoRR abs/1804.02767 (2018). http://arxiv.org/abs/1804.02767
12. Segonne, C., Duthon, P.: Qualification of the PAVIN fog and rain platform and its digital twin for the evaluation of a pedestrian detector in fog. J. Imaging **9**(10) (2023). https://doi.org/10.3390/jimaging9100211
13. STEMMER IMAGING: Serval-640-GigE thermal camera datasheet (2015). https://www.pei-france.com/uploads/txe_tim/STEMMER_28330.pdf. Accessed 07 June 2023
14. Stereolabs: ZED 2i Datasheet Feb2022 (2022). https://www.stereolabs.com/assets/datasheets/zed-2i-datasheet-feb2022.pdf. Accessed 05 June 2023
15. United Nations: Un regulation no 157 – uniform provisions concerning the approval of vehicles with regards to automated lane keeping systems [2021/389] (2021)
16. World Meteorological Organization: The guide to hydrological practices (WMO no. 168) (2009)
17. World Meteorological Organization: Guide to Meteorological Instruments and Methods of Observation (2014 edition updated in 2017; WMO-No. 8). World Meteorological Organization (2014)

Automated and Explainable Detection of Multiple Diseases from Retinal Fundus Images

Shubha Masti[✉], Tarunya Prasad, and Gowri Srinivasa

PES Centre for Pattern Recognition, Department of Computer Science and Engineering,
PES University, Bengaluru, India
ssmasti@gmail.com

Abstract. This study explores the explainable detection of three diseases—pathological myopia, glaucoma, and diabetic retinopathy—using retinal fundus images. Both deep learning and feature-based methods are examined for each condition. The deep learning approaches employ transfer learning, while UNet-based models are utilised for feature segmentation. Feature maps are created from segmented features and passed through simple CNNs to detect diseases. Data augmentation techniques are applied across methods to enhance performance, and Grad-CAM/Grad-CAM++ are used to interpret and validate the insights gained from the deep learning models. Our results include accuracy, precision, and recall of 98% for pathological myopia, 97% for glaucoma, and 92% for diabetic retinopathy presence. For diabetic retinopathy grading, Cohen's kappa scores of 0.83 (linear) and 0.90 (quadratic) were obtained.

Keywords: Fundus images · Image segmentation · Myopia · Glaucoma · Diabetic retinopathy · Transfer learning · Lesion segmentation · Interpretability

1 Introduction

Eye diseases pose a significant global health challenge that often leads to vision impairment or blindness if neglected [31]. Conditions such as pathological myopia, diabetic retinopathy, and glaucoma are among the most common, affecting millions of people around the world. Most diseases progress without early symptoms and, without an early diagnosis, can cause potential harm. The advancement in Imaging technologies and Machine Learning models that can automatically detect the presence of such diseases [4] offers timely intervention and can help mitigate vision loss.

Myopia [25] occurs when a person has difficulty seeing distant objects clearly because the eye cannot properly focus on light. Sometimes, it can become pathological [18], limiting vision to very close objects. This results in specific changes in the optic disc, such as abnormal tilting, obliqueness, and elongation. The macula and fovea regions are significantly affected by degenerative changes and cannot be observed clearly. Detecting the optic disc, lesions, areas of retinal atrophy, and thinning or degeneration of retinal tissue aids in its diagnosis.

Glaucoma [15] is a group of eye diseases that damage the optic nerve, causing vision loss and blindness. It usually results from high intraocular pressure caused by fluid buildup. The cup-to-disc ratio [17] is a diagnostic marker for glaucoma. As the cup enlarges relative to the disc, the ratio also increases and indicates disease progression.

Diabetic retinopathy [34] occurs when diabetes damages retinal blood vessels and nerve tissue. If left untreated, it could potentially lead to vision loss and blindness. The disease progresses through multiple stages, with different features indicating different stages [32]. Subtle changes in the optic disc or thinning of the Retinal Nerve Fiber Layer indicate early stages, and lesions like hard exudates or vitreous haemorrhage, indicate later stages.

2 Related Work

Both deep learning and feature-based learning approaches have been used to detect pathological myopia. A simple CNN achieved an impressive Area Under the Curve (AUC) [22]. Transfer learning using the backbone of Xception was used [8] to detect pathological myopia. Lesion segmentation was combined with detecting myopia using CNN [13] for explainable diagnosis. The model PAMELA [16] identified the parapapillary atrophy to detect pathological myopia automatically by segmenting the optic nerve head region and then using SVM classifier.

Multiple AI-based approaches have been explored for automatic detection of glaucoma [3]. Transfer learning leveraged pre-trained CNNs like ResNet [27], InceptionV3 [29] and DenseNet [19] to detect glaucoma automatically. For explainable diagnosis, the Cup-to-Disc Ratio has been extensively used by segmenting the optic cup and disc [11]. Other features like Retinal Nerve Fiber Layer (RNFL) thickness, Ganglion Cell with the Inner Plexiform Layer (GCIPL), and Ganglion Cell Complex (GCC) were also used [21].

CNNs have been extensively used to detect and grade diabetic retinopathy automatically using image-based and lesion-based methods [2]. Data augmentation is often used to enhance performance. The deep learning approach with a custom CNN outperformed other lesion-based methods for detecting DR [35]. Transfer learning was leveraged to create an ensemble method using three pre-trained models [14] to detect DR, and for multi-stage retinopathy grading [33]. A multi-task learning approach was used [7] to segment lesions and grade retinopathy by combining pre-trained VGG16 and UNet. Red lesions were segmented using various deep learning architectures [37], leading to improved grading performance due to the lesion information. Image enhancement techniques like CLAHE [24] and ESRGAN [1] were used to preprocess images before segmenting lesions using deep learning techniques.

3 Datasets

The PALM dataset was created for the Pathologic Myopia Challenge (PALM) [9], a Satellite Event of the ISBI 2019 conference. It consists of 1200 retinal fundus images annotated with labels indicating the presence or absence of pathological myopia, along with coordinates for fovea localization. It also contains segmentation masks for the optic disc in 1144 images, retinal atrophy in 870 images and detachment in 24 images as pictured in Fig. 1. IDRiD [20], though designed for diabetic retinopathy, contains 80 images with optic disc masks and thus was also used for testing.

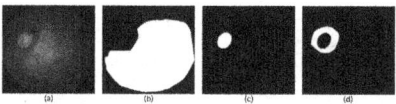

Fig. 1. Features for Pathological Myopia: (a) Original Fundus Image (b) Retinal Detachment (c) Optic Disc (d) Retinal Atrophy.

A Satellite Event of the MICCAI 2018 conference held the Retinal Fundus Glaucoma Challenge (REFUGE) [10]. The dataset was created for glaucoma detection and optic cup and disc analysis. It comprises 1200 retinal fundus images, each annotated with an optic disc and cup segmentation mask, marked by different grey levels as shown in Fig. 2. The publicly available dataset also contains labels indicating the absence or presence of glaucoma and the coordinates for fovea localization for 800 images (two-thirds). DRISHTI-GS [30] contains 100 images annotated with optic cup and disc. It also has annotations for the presence and absence of glaucoma. However, the orientation of images is different, with the optic disc positioned centrally rather than at the sides, and the dataset size is small. Origa [36] offered a more extensive collection with 650 images annotated for glaucoma presence or absence.

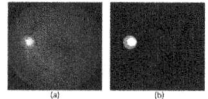

Fig. 2. Features for Glaucoma: (a) Original Fundus Image (b) Optic Cup (black) and Disc (grey).

The Diabetic Retinopathy Dataset (DDR)[1] is a comprehensive resource for diabetic retinopathy (DR) screening and lesion analysis, introduced in 2019. The dataset comprises 13,673 retinal fundus images collected from 9,598 patients, annotated with five levels of DR severity and a sixth for low image quality. Additionally, 757 images were meticulously annotated for four types of DR-related lesions: microaneurysms, haemorrhages, hard exudates, and soft exudates, pictured in Fig. 3. IDRiD was again used for testing, containing 80 images annotated with the same five levels of DR severity and four lesion types.

4 Approach

Our aim was to detect pathological myopia, glaucoma, and diabetic retinopathy in one fundus image. We explored both deep learning and feature-based machine learning for each disease. Deep learning models were validated using Grad-CAM and Grad-CAM++ for interpretability by comparing their generated heatmaps with segmentation masks to

---

[1] DDR Dataset available at: https://www.kaggle.com/datasets/tinnkanjananuwat/ddr-dataset.

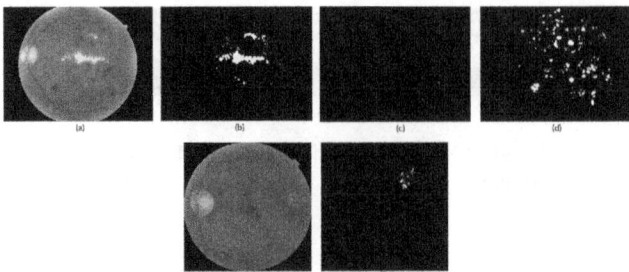

Fig. 3. Features for DR: (a) Fundus Image with (b) Hard Exudates, (c) Microaneurysm and (d) Haemorrage. (e) Fundus Image with (f) Soft Exudates.

confirm that they learned relevant information. Feature-based models were inherently explainable. The general approach is outlined in Fig. 4, from preprocessing to disease identification. Our implementation details can be accessed online.[2]

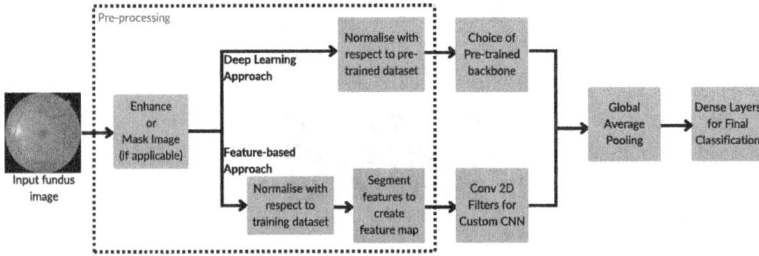

Fig. 4. Schematic Representation of our Architecture for Disease Detection.

4.1 Pathological Myopia

Deep Learning Approach. We leveraged state-of-the-art CNN architectures [12,28] pre-trained on the ImageNet dataset [6] as the backbone of our architecture. Fully connected layers were added after flattening to perform binary classification (Yes/No). Figure 5 depicts the overall architecture. The preprocessing steps were as per the pre-trained model chosen. All models were trained using a 70/10/20 train/validation/test split, with Adam optimizer, learning rate 0.001, and the categorical cross-entropy loss function over 20 epochs with batch size of 32. Data augmentation was applied, including a rotation range of 40, width and height shift ranges of 0.2, shear and zoom ranges of 0.2, and random horizontal flipping.

Feature-Based Approach. UNet [23] was used to segment all features from the PALM dataset. Data augmentation techniques were applied to address the imbalance in detachment masks, including random horizontal and vertical flips, 90-degree rotations,

---

[2] Implementation details available at: https://github.com/trunya/automated-detection-eye-disease.

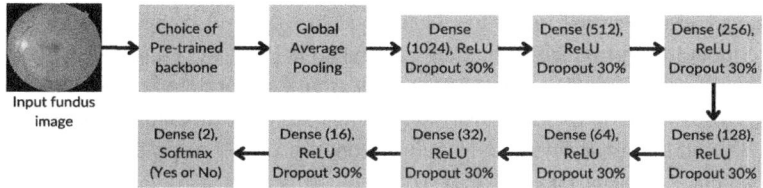

Fig. 5. Deep Learning Architecture Used for Detection of Pathological Myopia.

adjustments to brightness and contrast, elastic transformations, Gaussian blurring, and cropping. These segmentation models were trained using a 70/10/20 train/validation/test split, with Adam optimizer, learning rate 0.001, and the binary cross-entropy loss function over 50 epochs. We used a batch size of 32 for optic disc, 16 for retinal atrophy and 10 for retinal detachment.

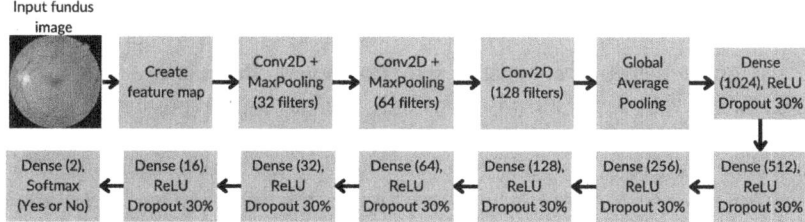

Fig. 6. CNN Architecture for Pathological Myopia Detection Using Features.

These features were then used for the classification of pathological myopia. The features were extracted and combined to make feature maps as inputs to a CNN, shown in Fig. 6. The model was trained using a 70/10/20 train/validation/test split, with Adam optimizer, learning rate 0.001, and the categorical cross-entropy loss function. Early stopping was implemented with a patience value of 20.

4.2 Glaucoma

Like myopia, we tried to use transfer learning backbones pre-trained on the ImageNet dataset, as pictured in Fig. 5, for binary classification. We also attempted deep learning from scratch with simple CNN architectures. However, most datasets were severely imbalanced and failed to learn any meaningful patterns. Even when sampled to have a more balanced distribution, both approaches failed to perform better than random guesses.

Thus, we focused on the feature-based approach, prioritizing the segmentation of the optic cup and disc. We simultaneously segmented the cup and disc, using two grey levels to indicate the different parts. Again, UNet was used for segmentation, and the REFUGE dataset was used to train the model. Data augmentation techniques, including random horizontal and vertical flips, 90-degree rotations, brightness and contrast adjustments, elastic transformations, Gaussian blurring, and cropping, were applied to enhance model performance. When tested on the DRISHTI-GS dataset, these augmentations significantly improved performance due to the different orientations. The model was trained using a 70/15/15 train/validation/test split, with Adam optimizer, learning rate 0.001, and the binary cross-entropy loss function. Early stopping was implemented with a patience value of 10 and batch size of 16.

For the detection of glaucoma, we extracted the optic cup and disc as a feature map and passed it into a custom CNN, similar to the architecture pictured in Fig. 6. An additional convolution layer with 256 filters was added before the global average pooling layer. Instead of calculating the cup-to-disc ratio, the mask was directly used as input to evaluate whether the model could learn effectively. Separate models were trained using the REFUGE and ORIGA datasets to examine the impact of dataset imbalance. The models were trained using a 70/10/20 train/validation/test split, with Adam optimizer, learning rate 0.001, and the categorical cross-entropy loss function. Early stopping was implemented with a patience value of 20 and batch size of 32.

4.3 Diabetic Retinopathy

Since we grade diabetic retinopathy into five levels, the models built are multi-classifiers. First, they detect the presence or absence, and only if present do they further grade the disease. Zero indicates the absence of retinopathy, and levels 1-4 correspond to the different progressive stages. Preprocessing techniques such as CLAHE (Contrast Limited Adaptive Histogram Equalization) and overlaying red masks were utilized to enhance some model's performance.

The preprocessing techniques are pictured in Fig. 7, where it is evident that certain features are more effectively highlighted with CLAHE, while others are better emphasized using red masks.

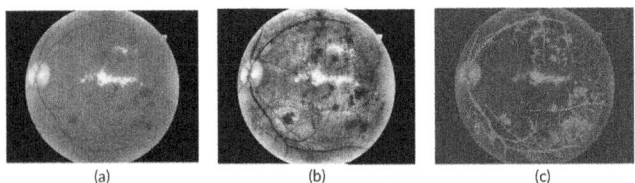

Fig. 7. Enhancement techniques used: (a) Original Fundus Image (b) CLAHE (c) Red Masked Image. (Color figure online)

CLAHE (Contrast Limited Adaptive Histogram Equalization) is an image processing technique designed to improve the contrast of images, particularly in scenarios where global histogram equalization fails. It improves details in small regions of the image while reducing noise. In our approach, we first applied median filtering with a 3×3 kernel. The image was then converted to LAB colour space (L: Luminosity, A: Green-to-magenta colour component, B: Blue-to-yellow colour component). CLAHE was applied to the Luminosity channel using 8×8 tiles and a clip limit 6.0 to control noise and prevent excessive contrast. Finally, the image was converted back to the RGB colour space.

Red masks were created by identifying pixels within specified ranges of red hues in the HSV colour space. Two separate masks were made from two ranges of red (0-12 and 170-180°). These masks were combined, converted back to RGB space and overlayed on the original image with a transparency of 0.3 for the mask.

Deep Learning Approach. Similar to the pathological myopia approach, we leveraged the ResNet50 as a transfer learning backbone. Figure 8 depicts the overall model architecture with a multi-classifier for presence and grading. We also used median filtering and CLAHE to enhance the image before normalizing. The models were trained using a 70/10/20 train/validation/test split, with Adam optimizer, learning rate 0.001, and a multi-loss function including categorical cross-entropy loss for grading and binary cross-entropy loss for presence. Early stopping was implemented with a patience value of 10 and batch size of 64. Models were trained on a balanced subset of 4000 images due to class imbalance.

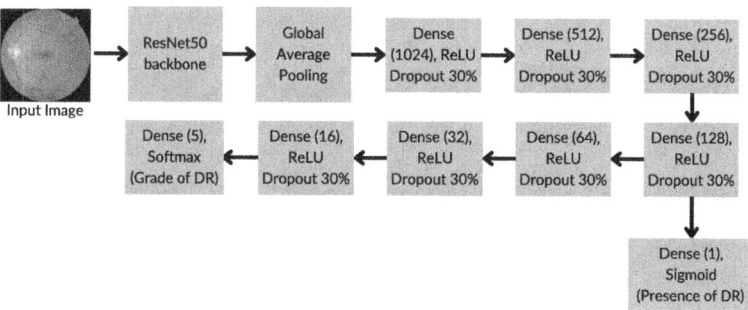

Fig. 8. Deep Learning Architecture Used for Detection and Grading of Diabetic Retinopathy.

Feature Based Approach. The important lesions for DR included haemorrages, microaneurysms, hard exudates, and soft exudates. UNet was once again used to segment these features. To address the challenge of incomplete annotated masks—some of the 757 marked images lacked annotations or contained minimal features (especially microaneurysms and haemorrages) akin to finding a needle in a haystack— preprocessing and data augmentation techniques were used. The loss function was also modified to combine binary crossentropy and dice loss.

Hard exudates were segmented by augmenting the training set to include only the positive samples, reducing the total set to 483 images.

Only 239 images had any soft exudates marked. Data augmentation was performed on these positive images, including random horizontal and vertical flips, 90-degree rotations, adjustments to brightness and contrast, elastic transformations, Gaussian blurring, and cropping to increase the set to 717 images. Additionally, 30 randomly selected negative images were also included.

Haemorrages were segmented by applying median filtering followed by CLAHE enhancement during preprocessing.

Microaneurysms were particularly difficult to segment due to the tiny nature of the masks. Most of the time, they were not even noticeable to the human eye. For preprocessing, we used red-masked images. Data augmentation was also performed on positive images, including random horizontal and vertical flips, 90-degree rotations, adjustments to brightness and contrast, elastic transformations, Gaussian blurring, and cropping, along with 25 random negative images to increase the set to 749 images.

All segmentation models were trained using a 70/10/20 train/validation/test split, Adam optimizer, learning rate 0.001, with the combined loss function (binary cross entropy and dice loss) across 75 epochs with a batch size of 16.

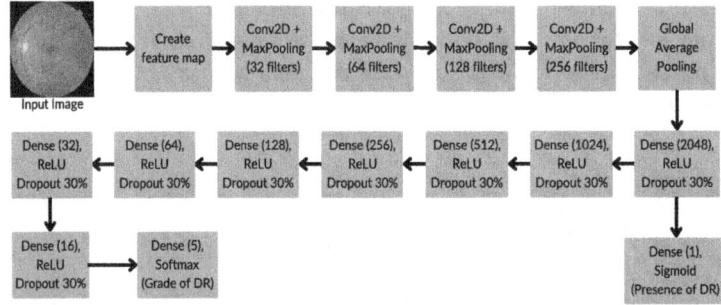

Fig. 9. Feature-based Approach for Detection and Grading of Diabetic Retinopathy.

A simple CNN-based multi-classifier was used to detect and grade retinopathy, depicted in Fig. 9, with the input being the feature map created from the four segmentation models. A balanced subset of 4000 images was chosen to train and test. This was particularly advantageous due to the computational overhead of segmenting features. The model was trained using a 70/10/20 train/validation/test split, with Adam optimizer, learning rate 0.001, and a multi-loss function including categorical cross-entropy loss for grading and binary cross-entropy loss for presence. Early stopping was implemented with a patience value of 10 and batch size of 32.

5 Results and Discussion

5.1 Pathological Myopia

The performance for feature segmentation are summarised in Table 1, and the results for the classification of pathological myopia are detailed in Table 2.

The overall performance of detachment is lower than that of other features, mainly due to a lack of samples during both training and testing. Although data augmentation was applied, it was still considerably lower than other features. On testing, we noticed that detachment masks would be segmented even when not present in the original eye. So, we did not use this feature to detect pathological myopia.

Table 1. Performance Metrics Across Datasets for PM Features.

Feature	Dataset	Accuracy (%)	AUC-ROC Score	IoU	Dice
Optic Disc	PALM	**99.55**	**0.9975**	**0.9955**	**0.9977**
	IDRiD	98.67	0.6463	0.9866	0.9933
Retinal Atrophy	PALM	94.48	0.9597	0.9364	0.9652
Detachment	PALM	79.48	0.8902	0.6486	0.7780

The AUC-ROC score of optic disc segmentation reduces on the IDRiD dataset, while the IoU and Dice scores remain high. IoU and Dice scores are calculated with a threshold of 0.5. This discrepancy suggests that the model's ability to rank positive pixels higher than negative ones is poor across different thresholds on the IDRiD dataset. This could be due to its lower contrast imaging, and since we did not train the model with augmentations, it cannot adapt effectively.

Retinal atrophy and detachment were only tested within the PALM dataset. The IoU for detachment is notably lower because it penalises all types of misclassification. In contrast, the Dice score performs better since the detachment model tends to predict a mask that spans most of the eye, and most ground truth masks also typically cover 1/2 to 3/4 of the eye. Although the prediction is inaccurate, it overlaps with much of the ground truth, boosting the Dice score. However, IoU strictly penalises all misclassifications, resulting in a lower score.

Table 2. Pathological Myopia Classification.

Approach	Model	Accuracy (%)	Precision (%)	Recall (%)
Deep Learning	ResNet50 backbone	**98.92**	**98.92**	**98.91**
	VGG16 backbone	97.58	97.62	97.58
Feature Based	Optic Disc	83.33	83.37	83.33
	Optic Disc & Retinal Atrophy	92.75	93.21	92.75

ResNet50 performs the best among the deep learning approaches. This is due to its deeper network architecture, improved gradient flow and more robust feature representations.

For the feature-based approach, using the optic disc alone yields good results, but the addition of retinal atrophy clearly enhances the performance of the model.

5.2 Glaucoma

The performance for feature segmentation is summarized in Table 3. As previously mentioned, deep learning models did not perform satisfactorily, so we do not present them. The feature-based results for glaucoma detection are presented in Table 4.

The model was evaluated for the optic cup (the inner, darker region) and the optic disc (the outer, lighter region), as distinguishing between these structures is important for glaucoma detection. For the optic cup, the evaluation focused on comparing threshold levels of 0 against 0.5 and 1, while for the optic disc, the comparison was between threshold levels of 1 and 0.5 against 0. Note that these pictured masks are inverted for easier visualisation.

Table 3. Performance Metrics Across Datasets for Glaucoma Features.

Feature	Dataset	Accuracy (%)	AUC-ROC Score	IoU	Dice
Optic Cup	REFUGE	**99.86**	0.9259	**0.9986**	**0.9993**
	DRISHTI-GS	**99.28**	0.7444	**0.9928**	**0.9964**
Optic Disc	REFUGE	99.79	**0.9740**	0.9979	0.9989
	DRISHTI-GS	98.68	**0.9208**	0.9866	0.9933
Optic Cup & Disc	REFUGE	99.83	0.950	0.9926	0.9963
	DRISHTI-GS	98.98	0.8324	0.9837	0.9918

The performance slightly reduces when tested on DRISHTI-GS. This is due to lower-contrast images and different orientations (cup and disk at the centre of the image instead of the side). Overall, optic disc segmentation (outer region) is better than optic cup (inner region). This distinction is crucial for glaucoma identification, making it reassuring that the performance degradation is minimal on the REFUGE dataset, as it is used to train the classification model.

Table 4. Performance Metrics Across Datasets for Glaucoma Classification.

Training Dataset	Testing Dataset	Accuracy (%)	Precision (%)	Recall (%)
REFUGE	REFUGE	**97.38**	**97.42**	**97.38**
	ORIGA	73.23	70.53	73.23
ORIGA	ORIGA	81.38	80.30	81.38
	REFUGE	**91.75**	**90.55**	**91.75**

Both ORIGA and REFUGE were used as training datasets to investigate the impact of dataset balance. ORIGA offers a slightly better class balance, resulting in superior performance across datasets. When trained on REFUGE, it seems to overfit, as evidenced by the degraded performance when tested on ORIGA.

5.3 Diabetic Retinopathy

The performance for feature segmentation is summarised in Table 5. Detection and grading of diabetic retinopathy are detailed in Table 6 & 7.

The accuracies remain consistently high, primarily because the lesions are tiny. Most are predicted as zero and correctly identified. While the AUC-ROC score is high, the Dice and IoU scores are low. This suggests that the model is able to detect the presence of lesions relatively well but struggles with identifying their exact locations. This is a common challenge for DR lesions, as they do not form distinct regions; the ground truth often consists of many small dots rather than a solid area. Note that the Dice score is also higher than the IoU since it is incorporated into the loss function

When visualised, most lesions seem to be adequately segmented in the DDR dataset, as shown in Fig. 10. However, IoU and Dice are absolute, and small changes in the segmentation are penalised. When tested on IDRiD, there is a noticeable performance degradation, likely due to the lower contrast in images. Additionally, enhancement techniques that improved performance on the DDR dataset may have been less effective for IDRiD, as the images in this dataset tend to be darker with a more pronounced red component. From accuracy and AUC-ROC scores, we infer that the presence of lesions is being detected correctly.

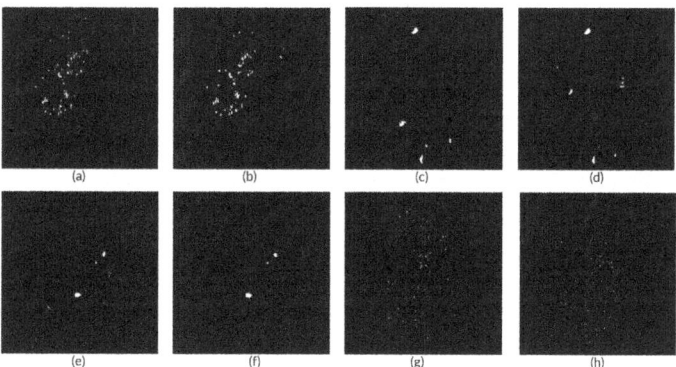

Fig. 10. Ground truth (left) and Predicted mask (right) for Hard Exudates (a) & (b), Soft Exudates (c) & (d), Haemorrages (e) & (f) and Microaneurysms (g) & (h).

Table 5. Performance Metrics Across Datasets for DR Features.

Feature	Dataset	Accuracy (%)	AUC-ROC Score	IoU	Dice
Hard Exudates	DDR	99.78	**0.970**	0.3444	**0.4779**
	IDRiD	99.38	**0.72**	**0.3121**	**0.453**
Soft Exudates	DDR	**99.89**	0.737	**0.3554**	0.4774
	IDRiD	99.54	0.662	0.2023	0.318
Haemorrages	DDR	99.74	0.954	0.3476	0.455
	IDRiD	99.02	0.599	0.1541	0.2529
Microaneurysms	DDR	99.19	0.8883	0.0495	0.0814
	IDRiD	**98.60**	0.6379	0.0152	0.0291

Table 6. Performance Metrics Across Datasets for DR Presence.

Model	Dataset	Accuracy (%)	Precision (%)	Recall (%)
ResNet50	DDR	92	88.71	**96.25**
	IDRiD	69.96	69.49	98.85
ResNet50 (Enhanced Input)	DDR	**93.4**	**92.34**	94.6
	IDRiD	74.41	73.176	97.98
Feature Based	DDR	78.73	83.89	71.1
	IDRiD	80.81	85.88	85.63

The models demonstrate consistent performance in detecting retinopathy across all phases. Among the ResNet approaches, enhancing images increases accuracy and precision scores across datasets but slightly decreases the recall score. Interestingly, the ResNet approaches outperform our CNN feature-based method for the DDR dataset, but the opposite is true for the IDRiD dataset. Again, this can be attributed to the different contrast levels of IDRiD images, as ResNet approaches are trained on higher contrast images.

Table 7. Performance Metrics Across Datasets for DR Grading.

Model	Dataset	Accuracy (%)	Precision (%)	Recall (%)	Cohen's (linear)	Cohen's (quadratic)
ResNet50	DDR	79.05	**80.6**	79.05	**0.8301**	**0.9096**
	IDRiD	30.6	**58.85**	30.62	**0.4241**	**0.6029**
ResNet50 (Enhanced Input)	DDR	**79.35**	79.15	**79.35**	0.8289	0.9067
	IDRiD	29.06	58.71	29.07	0.405	0.5929
Feature Based	DDR	59.25	45.425	59.25	0.5685	0.6838
	IDRiD	**40.69**	42.96	**40.69**	0.4078	0.5227

In addition to accuracy, we used Cohen's Kappa weighting to measure grading performance. The grading system includes five levels—0 for no retinopathy and grades 1-4 ranging from mild to proliferative—making a weighted score more representative, as misclassifying grades 1 and 2 is less severe than misclassifying grades 1 and 4. While we present both linear and quadratic weightings, quadratic weighting is more suitable given the exponential difference in severity between grades 0 and 4.

ResNet methods outperform our feature-based method. Enhancing input is not particularly advantageous as it yields similar results across datasets. Grading performance noticeably decreases for all methods on IDRiD, with accuracy alone improving when using our feature-based method. From confusion matrices pictured in Fig. 11, we can see that for a given grade, most misclassifications occur at adjacent levels. Grade 2, being in the middle, is the most frequently misclassified grade and is often mistaken for grade 1.

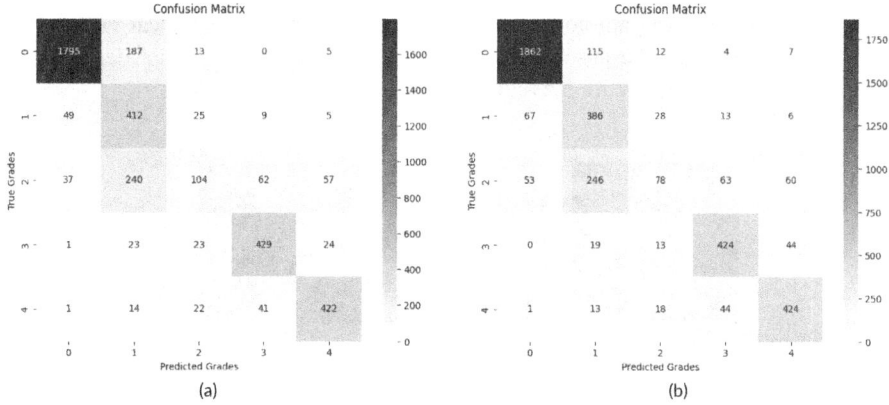

Fig. 11. Confusion matrices for DR grading using ResNet methods (a) Without enhancement and (b) with enhancement on DDR dataset.

6 Interpreting Results

Grad-CAM (Gradient-weighted Class Activation Mapping) [26] is a technique used to visualize and understand decisions made by CNNs. It generates a heatmap that highlights the regions of an input image most relevant to the network's prediction by using the gradients of the predicted. Grad-CAM++ [5] is an enhancement of Grad-CAM that addresses its limitations in handling overlapping object regions and weak signals by using second-order and first-order gradients. Both methods are helpful in medical imaging to explain deep learning models by identifying critical features, such as lesions or structural abnormalities, that influenced the model's diagnosis.

We used Grad-CAM and Grad-CAM++ to interpret the deep-learning methods used for pathological myopia and diabetic retinopathy. For glaucoma, we utilized our predicted feature masks to interpret the results.

6.1 Pathological Myopia

Fig. 12 illustrates a pathological myopic eye, along with the Gradcam and Gradcam++ heatmaps of the ResNet50 model overlayed on the original image. The red regions in the heatmap indicate regions of higher significance, as depicted in the scale. We also present two segmentation masks (optic disc and retinal atrophy). Figure 13 highlights the heatmaps for a non-pathological myopic eye.

For the positive samples, we infer from the heatmap that the regions of interest overlap with the optic disc and retinal atrophy masks. Gradcam++ shows us that the optic disc region has a stronger influence on the model's decision-making (at least for positive samples). This aligns with our feature-based results; using the optic disc alone achieves sufficiently high accuracy.

In negative examples, the regions of interest appear to be around the fovea and macula. Although we do not have masks of these features, structural changes in this region indicate the presence of pathological myopia, as discussed earlier. A clear view of this area may also suggest the absence of pathological myopia, as no other degenerative features are present to obscure the region, unlike in positive examples.

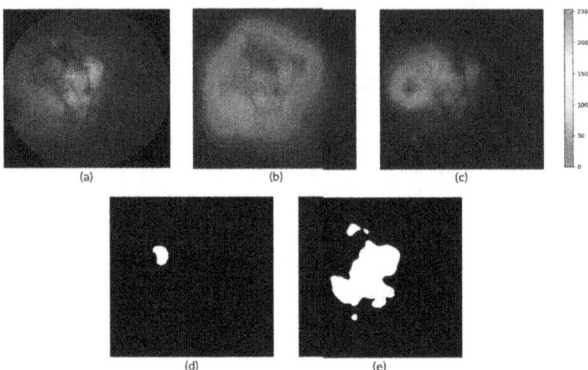

Fig. 12. (a) Pathological Myopic eye with (b) GradCam (c) GradCam++ (d) Optic Disc (e) Retinal Atrophy.

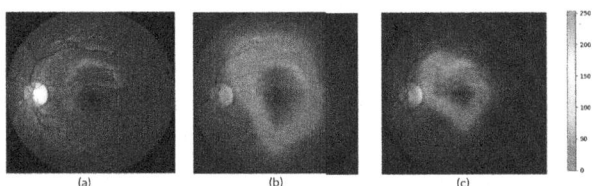

Fig. 13. (a) Non-pathological Myopic eye with (b) GradCam (c) GradCam++.

6.2 Glaucoma

Fig. 14 presents glaucoma-positive and glaucoma-negative images from both datasets with their corresponding segmentation masks.

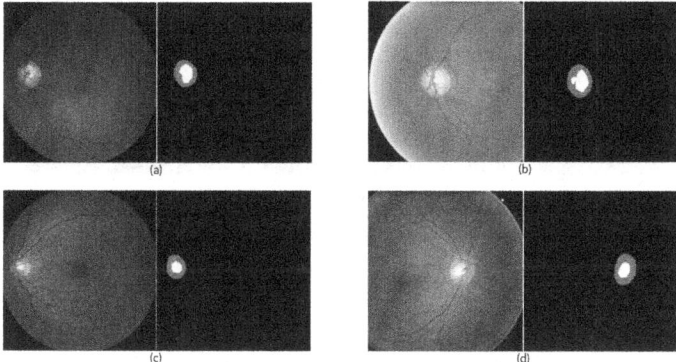

Fig. 14. Glaucomatous images from (a) REFUGE & (b) ORIGA and non-glaucomatous images from (c) REFUGE & (d) ORIGA with their corresponding masks.

In the glaucomatous image masks, the optic cup is distorted and larger, indicating glaucoma. We do not need to calculate the cup-to-disk ratio explicitly, as the mask visualises the change in the optic cup. On the other hand, the non-glaucomatous image masks look normal, with a noticeably larger distance between the cup and the disc.

6.3 Diabetic Retinopathy

Fig. 15 depicts the early stages (1 and 2) of diabetic retinopathy. The heatmap's regions of interest are focused around the optic disc and the surrounding vessels. Subtle changes in this area can indicate mild stages of diabetic retinopathy. The overlap of the regions of interest aligns with our findings, as grade 2 is the most frequently misclassified stage as grade 1.

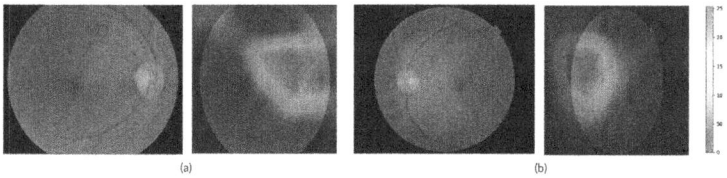

Fig. 15. Original image (left) and GradCam (right) (a) Stage 1 and (b) Stage 2.

Figure 16 depicts the later stage (stage 3). The heatmap region now includes lesions such as hard exudates, soft exudates, and hemorrages, as verified with the predicted masks.

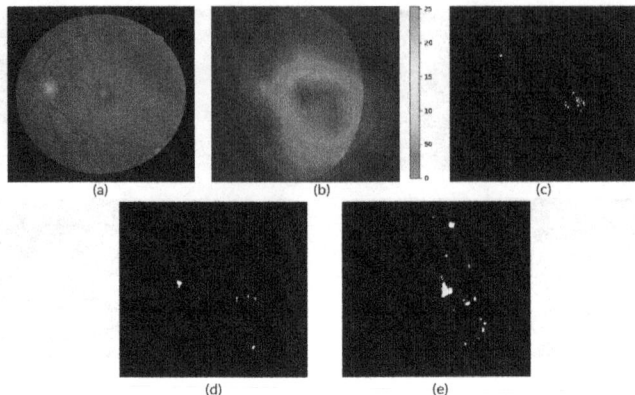

Fig. 16. Stage 3 (a) Original image, (b) GradCam and masks for (c) Hard Exudates, (d) Soft Exudates and (e) Haemmorages.

Figure 17 depicts the last stage (stage 4), the most severe. Although most of the lesions are present at this stage, the heatmap primarily overlaps with the area of vitreous hemorrage, which is noticeable in the blurry regions in the image. This is more clearly visualised in the enhanced image.

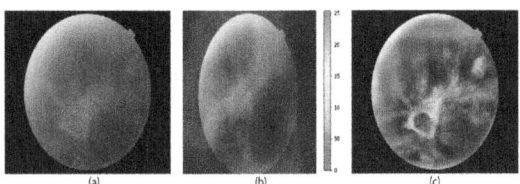

Fig. 17. Stage 4 (a) Original image, (b) GradCam and (c) Enhanced image.

7 Conclusion

Our study demonstrates the potential for explainable, multi-disease detection using retinal fundus images. By integrating deep learning and feature-based approaches, we achieved robust detection and grading of pathological myopia, glaucoma, and diabetic retinopathy.

For pathological myopia, transfer learning methods utilising a ResNet backbone achieved the best performance, with Grad-CAM visualisations validating their effectiveness. These models identified features beyond those captured by the dataset's segmentation masks. Feature-based models also performed well, and including retinal atrophy along with the optic disc significantly improved its performance.

In glaucoma detection, the imbalance of datasets was a barrier that transfer learning methods could not overcome. Feature-based methods utilising optic cup and disc segmentation proved the most reliable, aligning with the wide use of the cup-to-disc ratio for glaucoma diagnosis.

In the case of diabetic retinopathy, various enhancement and preprocessing techniques were employed to segment lesions effectively. However, the spotty distribution of lesions resulted in relatively low performance metrics. A balanced dataset significantly improved both performance and computational efficiency. Transfer learning with a ResNet backbone once again proved to be the most effective, with Grad-CAM visualisations highlighting regions of interest beyond the identified lesions.

Data augmentation techniques substantially enhanced performance, particularly across datasets. UNet models had adequate performance for feature segmentation. Challenges such as dataset imbalance, cross-dataset variability, and the segmentation of subtle features underscore opportunities for further research by expanding datasets, refining preprocessing techniques for diverse imaging conditions, and designing more robust architectures that generalise effectively across populations.

Our study emphasises the importance of interpretability in machine learning models for disease detection. Grad-CAM visualisations corroborate model predictions and provide clinicians a means to understand the decision-making.

We hope this study contributes to the transformative potential of automated and interpretable machine learning in advancing retinal disease diagnosis, paving the way for broader clinical adoption.

References

1. Alwakid, G., Gouda, W., Humayun, M., Jhanjhi, N.Z.: Deep learning-enhanced diabetic retinopathy image classification. DIGITAL HEALTH **9**, 20552076231194944 (2023). https://doi.org/10.1177/20552076231194942
2. Alyoubi, W.L., Shalash, W.M., Abulkhair, M.F.: Diabetic retinopathy detection through deep learning techniques: a review. Inf. Med. Unlocked **20**, 100377 (2020). https://doi.org/10.1016/j.imu.2020.100377
3. Ashtari-Majlan, M., Dehshibi, M.M., Masip, D.: Glaucoma diagnosis in the era of deep learning: a survey. Expert Syst. Appl. **256**, 124888 (2024). https://doi.org/10.1016/j.eswa.2024.124888
4. Balyen, L., Peto, T.: Promising artificial intelligence-machine learning-deep learning algorithms in ophthalmology. Asia-Pacific J. Ophthalmol. **8**(3) (2019), https://journals.lww.com/apjoo/fulltext/2019/05000/promising_artificial_intelligence_machine.13.aspx
5. Chattopadhay, A., Sarkar, A., Howlader, P., Balasubramanian, V.N.: Grad-cam++: generalized gradient-based visual explanations for deep convolutional networks. In: 2018 IEEE Winter Conference on Applications of Computer Vision (WACV). pp. 839–847 (2018). https://doi.org/10.1109/WACV.2018.00097
6. Deng, J., Dong, W., Socher, R., Li, L.J., Li, K., Fei-Fei, L.: Imagenet: a large-scale hierarchical image database. In: 2009 IEEE Conference on Computer Vision and Pattern Recognition. pp. 248–255 (2009). https://doi.org/10.1109/CVPR.2009.5206848
7. Foo, A., Hsu, W., Lee, M.L., Lim, G., Wong, T.Y.: Multi-task learning for diabetic retinopathy grading and lesion segmentation. In: Proceedings of the AAAI Conference on Artificial Intelligence, vol. 34, no. 08, pp. 13267–13272 (2020). https://doi.org/10.1609/aaai.v34i08.7035

8. Freire, C.R., da Costa Moura, J.C., da Silva Barros, D.M., de Medeiros Valentim, R.A.: Automatic lesion segmentation and pathological myopia classification in fundus images (2020). https://arxiv.org/abs/2002.06382
9. Fu, H., et al.: Palm: Pathologic myopia challenge (2019). https://doi.org/10.21227/55pk-8z03
10. Fu, H., et al.: Refuge: Retinal fundus glaucoma challenge (2019). https://doi.org/10.21227/tz6e-r977
11. Haleem, M.S., Han, L., Hemert, J., Li, B., Fleming, A., Pasquale, L.R., Song, B.J.: A novel adaptive deformable model for automated optic disc and cup segmentation to aid glaucoma diagnosis. J. Med. Syst. **42**(1), 1–18 (2017). https://doi.org/10.1007/s10916-017-0859-4
12. He, K., Zhang, X., Ren, S., Sun, J.: Deep residual learning for image recognition. In: 2016 IEEE Conference on Computer Vision and Pattern Recognition (CVPR). pp. 770–778 (2016). https://doi.org/10.1109/CVPR.2016.90
13. Hemelings, R., Elen, B., Blaschko, M.B., Jacob, J., Stalmans, I., De Boever, P.: Pathological myopia classification with simultaneous lesion segmentation using deep learning. Comput. Methods Programs Biomed. **199**, 105920 (2021). https://doi.org/10.1016/j.cmpb.2020.105920
14. Jiang, H., Yang, K., Gao, M., Zhang, D., Ma, H., Qian, W.: An interpretable ensemble deep learning model for diabetic retinopathy disease classification. In: 2019 41st Annual International Conference of the IEEE Engineering in Medicine and Biology Society (EMBC). pp. 2045–2048 (2019). https://doi.org/10.1109/EMBC.2019.8857160
15. Lee, D.A., Higginbotham, E.J.: Glaucoma and its treatment: a review. Am. J. Heal. Syst. Pharmacy **62**(7), 691–699 (2005). https://doi.org/10.1093/ajhp/62.7.691
16. Liu, J., et al.: Detection of pathological myopia by pamela with texture-based features through an svm approach. J. Healthc. Eng. **1**, 1–12 (2010). https://doi.org/10.1260/2040-2295.1.1.1
17. Muramatsu, C., Nakagawa, T., Sawada, A., Hatanaka, Y., Hara, T., Yamamoto, T., Fujita, H.: Determination of cup-to-disc ratio of optical nerve head for diagnosis of glaucoma on stereo retinal fundus image pairs. In: Karssemeijer, N., Giger, M.L. (eds.) Medical Imaging 2009: Computer-Aided Diagnosis. vol. 7260, p. 72603L. International Society for Optics and Photonics (2009). https://doi.org/10.1117/12.811461
18. Ohno-Matsui, K.: Pathologic myopia. Asia-Pacific. J. Ophthalmol. **5**(6), 415–423 (2016). https://doi.org/10.1097/APO.0000000000000230
19. Ovreiu, S., Paraschiv, E.A., Ovreiu, E.: Deep learning & digital fundus images: Glaucoma detection using densenet. In: 2021 13th International Conference on Electronics, Computers and Artificial Intelligence (ECAI). pp. 1–4 (2021). https://doi.org/10.1109/ECAI52376.2021.9515188
20. Porwal, P., Pachade, S., Kamble, R., Kokare, M., Deshmukh, G., Sahasrabuddhe, V., Meriaudeau, F.: Indian diabetic retinopathy image dataset (idrid) (2018). https://doi.org/10.21227/H25W98
21. Raja, H., Hassan, T., Akram, M.U., Werghi, N.: Clinically verified hybrid deep learning system for retinal ganglion cells aware grading of glaucomatous progression. IEEE Trans. Biomed. Eng. **68**(7), 2140–2151 (2021). https://doi.org/10.1109/TBME.2020.3030085
22. Rauf, N., Gilani, S.O., Waris, A.: Automatic detection of pathological myopia using machine learning. Sci. Rep. **11**(1), 16570 (2021). https://doi.org/10.1038/s41598-021-95205-1
23. Ronneberger, O., Fischer, P., Brox, T.: U-net: Convolutional networks for biomedical image segmentation (2015). https://arxiv.org/abs/1505.04597
24. Santos, C., Aguiar, M., Welfer, D., Belloni, B.: A new method based on deep learning to detect lesions in retinal images using yolov5. In: 2021 IEEE International Conference on Bioinformatics and Biomedicine (BIBM). pp. 3513–3520 (2021). https://doi.org/10.1109/BIBM52615.2021.9669581

25. Saw, S.M., Katz, J., Schein, O., Chew, S., Chan, T.: Epidemiology of myopia. Epidemiologic reviews **18**, 175–87 (1996). https://doi.org/10.1093/oxfordjournals.epirev.a017924
26. Selvaraju, R.R., Cogswell, M., Das, A., Vedantam, R., Parikh, D., Batra, D.: Grad-cam: Visual explanations from deep networks via gradient-based localization. In: 2017 IEEE International Conference on Computer Vision (ICCV). pp. 618–626 (2017). https://doi.org/10.1109/ICCV.2017.74
27. Serener, A., Serte, S.: Transfer learning for early and advanced glaucoma detection with convolutional neural networks. In: 2019 Medical Technologies Congress (TIPTEKNO). pp. 1–4 (2019). https://doi.org/10.1109/TIPTEKNO.2019.8894965
28. Simonyan, K., Zisserman, A.: Very deep convolutional networks for large-scale image recognition (2015). https://arxiv.org/abs/1409.1556
29. Singh, A., Sengupta, S., Lakshminarayanan, V.: Glaucoma diagnosis using transfer learning methods. In: Zelinski, M.E., Taha, T.M., Howe, J., Awwal, A.A.S., Iftekharuddin, K.M. (eds.) Applications of Machine Learning. vol. 11139, p. 111390U. International Society for Optics and Photonics (2019). https://doi.org/10.1117/12.2529429
30. Sivaswamy, J., Krishnadas, S.R., Datt Joshi, G., Jain, M., Syed Tabish, A.U.: Drishti-gs: Retinal image dataset for optic nerve head(onh) segmentation. In: 2014 IEEE 11th International Symposium on Biomedical Imaging (ISBI). pp. 53–56 (2014). https://doi.org/10.1109/ISBI.2014.6867807
31. Stevens, G.A., et al.: Global prevalence of vision impairment and blindness: magnitude and temporal trends, 1990–2010. Ophthalmology **120**(12), 2377–2384 (2013). https://doi.org/10.1016/j.ophtha.2013.05.025
32. Stitt, A.W., et al.: The progress in understanding and treatment of diabetic retinopathy. Prog. Retin. Eye Res. **51**, 156–186 (2016). https://doi.org/10.1016/j.preteyeres.2015.08.001
33. Tymchenko, B., Marchenko, P., Spodarets, D.: Deep learning approach to diabetic retinopathy detection (2020). https://arxiv.org/abs/2003.02261
34. Wang, W., Lo, A.C.Y.: Diabetic retinopathy: pathophysiology and treatments. Int. J. Molecular Sci. **19**(6) (2018). https://doi.org/10.3390/ijms19061816
35. Xu, K., Feng, D., Mi, H.: Deep convolutional neural network-based early automated detection of diabetic retinopathy using fundus image. Molecules **22**(12) (2017). https://doi.org/10.3390/molecules22122054
36. Zhang, Z., et al.: Origa-light: an online retinal fundus image database for glaucoma analysis and research. In: 2010 Annual International Conference of the IEEE Engineering in Medicine and Biology. pp. 3065–3068 (2010). https://doi.org/10.1109/IEMBS.2010.5626137
37. Zhou, Y., Wang, B., Huang, L., Cui, S., Shao, L.: A benchmark for studying diabetic retinopathy: Segmentation, grading, and transferability. IEEE Trans. Med. Imaging **40**(3), 818–828 (2021). https://doi.org/10.1109/TMI.2020.3037771

Rotation Invariance in Floor Plan Digitization Using Zernike Moments

Marius Graumann[✉][iD], Jan Marius Stürmer[iD], and Tobias Koch[iD]

German Aerospace Center (DLR), Institute for the Protection of Terrestrial Infrastructures, Sankt Augustin, Germany
{marius.graumann,jan.stuermer,tobias.koch}@dlr.de

Abstract. Nowadays, a lot of old floor plans exist in printed form or are stored as scanned raster images. Slight rotations or shifts may occur during scanning. Bringing floor plans of this form into a machine readable form to enable further use, still poses a problem. Therefore, we propose an end-to-end pipeline that pre-processes the image and leverages a novel approach to create a region adjacency graph (RAG) from the pre-processed image and predict its nodes. By incorporating normalization steps into the RAG feature extraction, we significantly improved the rotation invariance of the RAG feature calculation. Moreover, applying our method leads to an improved F1 score and IoU on rotated data. Furthermore, we proposed a wall splitting algorithm for partitioning walls into segments associated with the corresponding rooms.

Keywords: Graph neural network · Floor plan digitization · Computer Vision · Zernike moments · Vectorization · Indoor spatial data

1 Introduction

A floor plan is a drawing that shows the shape, size, and arrangement of rooms in a building as viewed from above. Floor plans consist of structural indoor elements, such as walls, windows, doors, stairs, and spatial elements, like rooms and corridors. Structural and spatial elements in floor plans play a crucial role while designing, understanding, or remodelling indoor spaces [12], when simulating pedestrians movements and when creating 3D models [3,6]. Floor plans are often generated using computer-aided design (CAD), but are frequently stored as raster images or in printed form [17]. During this conversion the images become blurred or rotated, which poses a problem for complex architectural drawings [11]. Moreover, the floor plans are no longer machine readable.

Floor plan classification is a difficult task, as there is no standard notation in architectural and engineering companies. Therefore, coloring, line width and used symbols differ [13]. Furthermore, the classification should suffice higher-level geometric and topological conditions, i.e., doors are embedded in walls and walls delimit rooms. Moreover, the room layout can depend on the use case, e.g., apartments or office rooms can have different room layouts [12]. Therefore, learning based approaches are most promising.

© The Author(s), under exclusive license to Springer Nature Switzerland AG 2026
C. Distante and S. Battiato (Eds.): IMPROVE 2025, CCIS 2628, pp. 162–177, 2026.
https://doi.org/10.1007/978-3-032-01169-5_10

Another challenge are complex building layouts. Office buildings, schools, exhibition buildings for example can have complex structures such that some walls are not vertical, horizontal or straight. Popular floor plan training data consists mostly of data depicting apartments with nicely behaved structures, e.g., walls are vertical or horizontal. To handle more complex structures that are not represented inside the training set, the classification analysis has to be rotation invariant. Moreover, rotation invariance is essential, as it enables scanned floor plans to be analyzed more reliably due to possible rotation from imprecise scanning.

In this paper, we present an enhanced method based on the work in [9] to classify floor plan components and further extract relations, such as room-door connections in a RCG. We explain how certain attributes (moments) are adjusted to achieve translation invariance.

The paper is structured as follows: First, we introduce current state-of-the-art approaches in Sect. 2. Second, we introduce our end-to-end-pipeline consisting of the enhanced feature extraction method (Sect. 3). In Sects. 4 and 5, we elaborate on the experimental setup and show the results. Next, we discuss the results and further benefits or drawbacks in Sect. 6, and draw our conclusion in Sect. 7.

2 Related Work

Several approaches towards the classification and analysis of floor plans exist. Therefore, we give an overview about these approaches and then concentrate on work that treats rotation invariant methods based on Zernike moments.

2.1 Floor Plan Classification

To achieve floor plan reconstruction, different methods might be applied. Machine learning based approaches are promising for handling the wide spectrum of different floor plans and perform better in comparison to rule based methods [1].

The task of converting 2D floor plans to semantic 3D models was addressed by [3]. Their approach utilized Faster-RCNN with a ResNet backbone for window and door detection, resulting in bounding boxes. For wall detection, they employed the FPN architecture paired with a ResNet backbone, which produced segmentation masks for walls. The obtained segmentations and bounding boxes underwent post-processing to vectorize walls, doors, and windows, which were then used to construct the 3D model. On the CubiCasa5K dataset, the IoU of these vectorized components reached 0.8. The method was neither trained nor tested on rotated floor plans.

One common approach for precise classification with deep learning-based methods is image segmentation. In [8] image segmentation and detection (YOLOX-based) were jointly trained using the attention based MuraNet to detect windows, walls and doors in floor plans. MuraNet performed better than YOLOv3 and U-Net on the CubiCasa5k dataset. Rotated floorplans were not considered in their research.

In [2], symbols such as doors were captured by SURF [4] yielding good results with respect to rotation and scale invariance. However, wall extraction relies on classical computer vision techniques, including erosion and dilation with a 3×3 kernel, which unfortunately lacks scale and rotation invariance.

Mingxiang Chen et al. introduced the Graph Neural Network (GNN)-based Line Segment Parser (GLSP) [14]. Their approach leveraged GNNs to predict the class of line segments, such as Door, Wall, or Window. The authors also proposed a novel embedding technique called Rotated Region of Interest (RRoI) Pooling. This method enables more effective feature extraction for rotated lines by considering their rotational variations in contrast to traditional Region of Interest (RoI) pooling. However, rotation invariance was not explicitly addressed.

Scanned documents are often slightly rotated, scaled and noisy. This issue was tackled by [10] by introducing a geometric feature-based approach for floor plan image retrieval that aims to be rotation and scale invariant. It achieved good results on floor plans from the ROBIN dataset that were rotated by ±5°.

2.2 Rotation Invariance Through Zernike Moments

[9] leveraged Graph Neural Networks (GNNs) for indoor element classification in floor plans. Their method involved constructing a Region Adjacency Graph (RAG) with Zernike moments as the node attributes. They experimented with various GNN architectures and found that GraphSAGE and their novel Distance-Weighted Graph Neural Network (DWGNN) performed best. Although they claimed rotation invariance, their experimental results were limited to 90° rotated floorplans. On a newly labeled subset of CubiCasa5k, [9]'s approach achieved promising F1 scores for indoor element classification. These findings demonstrate the potential of GNNsand Zernike moments for rotation invariant indoor classification. Zernike moments are rotation invariant and hence are well suited as features.

Zernike polynoms were introduced by F. Zernike in [7]. Using these polynoms, Zernike moments were defined in image analysis via the general theory of moments. In [15] various moments were examined and compared regarding their sensitivity to image noise, information redundancy and capability for image representation. Zernike and pseudo-Zernike moments outperformed the other moments in these important aspects of image recognition. This leads to Zernike moments now being used widely in image processing due to their many favourable qualities including rotation invariance.

In [16], Xiang et al. investigated the practical and theoretical rotation, scale and translation invariance of Zernike moments in image processing. To achieve this invariance, they proposed a normalization step to be applied prior to calculating Zernike moments. Experimental results demonstrated that this approach retained the invariance of the amplitude of Zernike moments when images were loosely rotated.

3 Methods

Our method builds upon Jaeyoung Song et al.'s [9] GNN framework, enhancing their work by modifying the feature extraction to improve rotation invariance and embedding it within an end-to-end workflow.

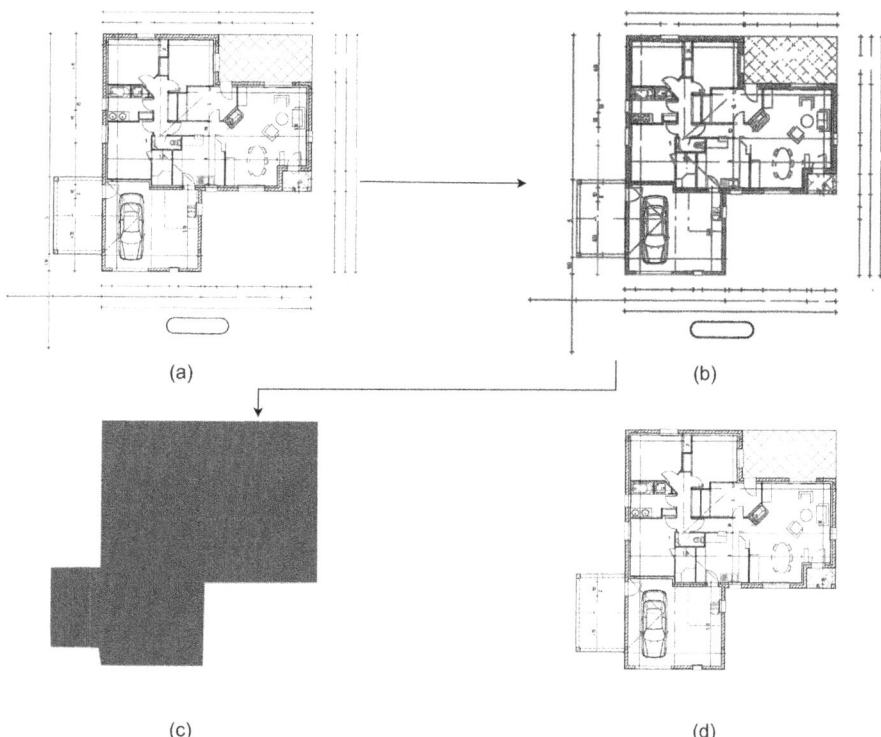

Fig. 1. Filter of building (a) Input image after text removal and dilation (b) red the detected contours and green the largest contour (c) refined polygon of largest contour (d) Filtered building. (Color figure online)

We begin with pre-processing, removing additional information from floor plan images. The pre-processed image is used to create the RAG. Next, a GNN is applied for the classification of the RAG nodes. During post-processing the detected indoor elements are converted into usable information for, e.g., room-door connectivity and 3D reconstruction.

3.1 Pre-processing

Floor plans often contain excessive information that can overwhelm the GNN, including text, measurement lines, and legends. To filter out the necessary information, we follow a series of steps.

First, the image is converted into a binary format using a threshold, making the image black and white where the white pixels are the background. Next, EasyOCR is applied to detect the text in the image with bounding boxes that are then coloured white.

To improve contour detection, we remove potential noise and holes by applying a 3×3 dilation kernel, which refines the contour edges. We utilize OpenCV's border-following algorithm to detect the contours in the image Fig. 1(a).

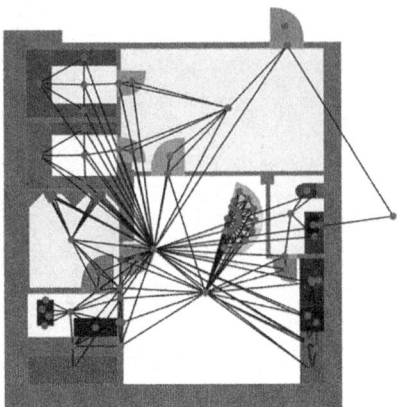

Fig. 2. RAG of Floorplan. Every polygon has a unique color and is represented by a blue node inside the graph. The node is at the center of mass of the polygon. Two nodes are connected if the corresponding polygons are adjacent. (Color figure online)

After detecting the contours, we select the largest one (see Fig. 1(b)) and interpret it as an exterior of a polygon. To refine this polygon, we first subtract a circle of radius 5 and than add the circle with radius 5 using the Minkowski sum (later referred to as debuff and buff). This process effectively removes small gaps and ensures that the building's outline is represented accurately as shown in 1(c).

Finally, we colour the complement of the polygon white and the resulting image contains only the filtered building Fig. 1(d).

3.2 RAG Generation and Normalization

The image is vectorized, where each vector (further referred to as polygon) becomes a node in the RAG. In accordance with [9], for every node and its corresponding polygon, we extract the connectivity of the node within the RAG (see Fig. 2) and determine the area of the corresponding polygon. Additionally, we extract the amplitude of Zernike moments up to order $n_{max} \in \mathbb{N}$ with non-negative repetition $m \geq 0$.

Furthermore, we apply the following normalization steps to the polygons to ensure invariance. For each polygon P from the vectorization, we centralize P such that the centroid of P is at the origin of the image to assure translation invariance as demonstrated in [16]. The method from [16] is applied to achieve scale invariance, i.e., each polygon P with area A_P is scaled with a factor $F_P = \sqrt{\frac{A}{A_P}}$, such that $P' = P \cdot F_P$. This scaling process maintains the centroids position at the origin of the image, while ensuring that every polygon P' has the same area $A \in \mathbb{R}^+$.

However, since we do not apply a uniform scaling factor to the entire image but use a unique scaling factor F_P for each polygon P, we must ensure that the Zernike moments of the scaled polygon P' are computed correctly. This requires that P' lies within the circle with radius r, on which the Zernike moment is calculated.

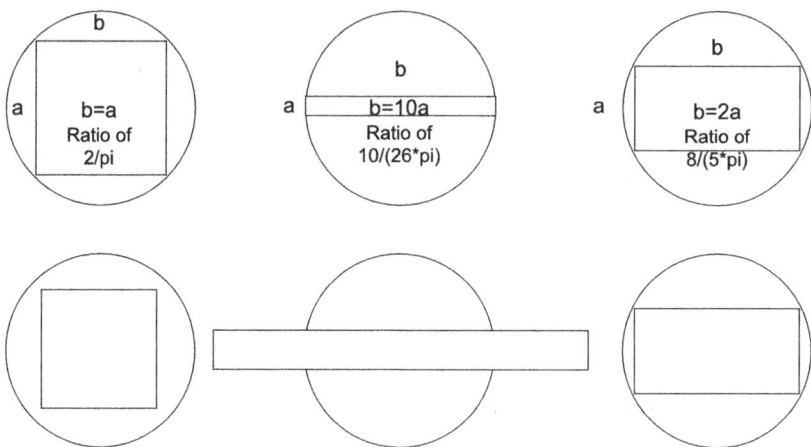

Fig. 3. Top: Rectangles with different sides a, b. Bottom: The Polygons are scaled with F_P. The polygons with invariant ratio greater than $c = 0.5$ are inside the circle with radius r after scaling.

Let $A = cr^2\pi$. By Lemma 2, P' lies within the circle with radius r if and only if $c \leq \frac{A_P}{R_P^2\pi}$, where R_P is the radius of the smallest circle centered at the origin containing P, as defined in Definition 1. The selection of c is a trade-off, as selecting c small weakens the requirement for the whole area to be captured by C_r, but also risks down scaling and information loss in practice.

In Fig. 3 there is an illustration of the invariant ratio in form of rectangular polygons with sides a, b with different ratios, left to right: a=b with invariant ratio $\frac{2}{\pi} \approx 0.64$, a=2b with invariant ratio $\frac{8}{5\pi} \approx 0.51$ and a=10b with invariant ratio $\frac{10}{26\pi} \approx 0.12$. The polygons are scaled with $F_P = \sqrt{\frac{cr^2 \cdot \pi}{A_P}}$, $c = 0.5$ where A_P is the area of the polygon to scale and r the radius of the circle. We can see that polygons with an invariant ratio greater than $c = 0.5$ are completely captured inside the circle with radius r, hence the Zernike moments of the whole polygon would be captured.

Definition 1. *Let $M \subset \mathbb{R}^n$ closed. We define the radius of the smallest circle centered at the origin that contains M as*

$$R_M := min\{r \in \mathbb{R} | \|v\| \leq r \ \forall v \in M\}.$$

Let $M \subset \mathbb{R}^n$ and $c \in \mathbb{R}$ with $c \cdot M = cM := \{cv| \ v \in M\}$.
λ is the Lebesgue measure.

Lemma 1. *Let $r, F \in \mathbb{R}^+$ and $M \subset \mathbb{R}^n$ closed, Lebesgue measurable with $\lambda(M) > 0$. It holds that*

$$F \cdot M \subset C_r \iff F \leq \frac{r}{R_M}.$$

Proof. Note that $\lambda(M) > 0 \Rightarrow R_M > 0$.

$$F \leq \frac{r}{R_M} \iff \frac{r}{F} \geq R_M$$
$$\stackrel{Definition\ 1}{\iff} \|v\| \leq \frac{r}{F} \quad \forall v \in M$$
$$\iff \|Fv\| = F\|v\| \leq r \quad \forall v \in M$$
$$\iff F \cdot v \in C_r \quad \forall v \in M \iff F \cdot M \subset C_R$$

□

Lemma 2. *Let $c \in \mathbb{R}^+$, $M \subset I \subset \mathbb{R}^2$ closed and Lebesgue measurable with $\lambda(M) > 0$. For $F = \sqrt{\frac{c \cdot r^2 \pi}{\lambda(M)}}$ it holds that*

$$F \cdot M \subset C_r \iff c \leq \frac{\lambda(M)}{R_M^2 \pi}.$$

$$F \cdot M \subset C_r \stackrel{Lemma\ 1}{\iff} \sqrt{\frac{c \cdot r^2 \pi}{\lambda(M)}} = F \leq \frac{r}{R_M}$$
$$\iff \frac{\pi c}{\lambda(M)} \leq \frac{1}{R_M^2} \iff c \leq \frac{\lambda(M)}{R_M^2 \pi}$$

□

Note: Choosing $c \cdot r^2 \pi = A$ we have

$$\lambda(F \cdot M) = \lambda(M) \cdot F^2 = \lambda(M) \frac{cr^2 \pi}{\lambda(M)} = A$$

according to Lebesgue measure properties in $\mathbb{R}^2$.

3.3 Node Classification

The RAG is fed into a GNN which predicts the labels of the nodes of the RAG. Details can be found in [9]. This results in a labeled graph consisting of the classes room, wall, door, window, stair, object, porch and outer space.

3.4 Post-processing

We apply several post-processing steps to refine the labeled RAG to be applicable for different use cases.

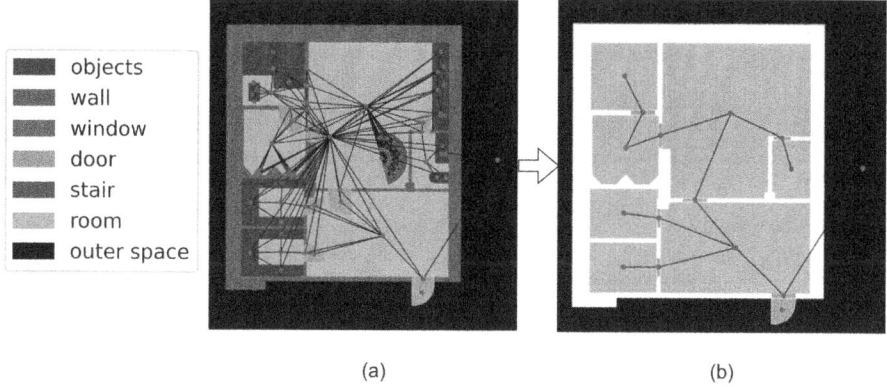

Fig. 4. (a) RAG with labels (b) Room connectivity Graph.

Door Splitting. For some applications, such as pedestrian flow simulations or floor plan recommendation systems, further knowledge of the relations between rooms is required. This information can be stored in a room connectivity graph, which contains the complete rooms, doors, and outer space polygons as its nodes. Rooms should be connected to doors if a room can be entered and exited through that door and the same holds for the outer space. In Fig. 4 the input RAG and the created room connectivity graph is shown.

First, we recreate the room from labeled polygons. As some objects, such as toilets, showers etc., are part of a room, we need to merge these objects with the room they are located in. The same applies to stairs and door swing areas (see Door Splitting).

Iterative objects, stairs, and door swings polygons are merged into room polygons, if they are connected in the RAG. We then update the new room boundaries and repeat these steps until no changes occur. Note that the object, stair and door swing nodes do not have to be deleted, they can be used as information associated with the room.

Next, we approximate the new room polygons using the Douglas-Peucker algorithm, which helps straighten diagonal lines that were pixel precise before. We also buff and debuff the room polygons to remove small holes inside them, which result from noise, imprecise vectorization or merging. The outer wall is created from the interior of the outer space polygon.

Usually, doors in floor plans are displayed with the door swing area. The door swing area is part of the room, while the other part is enclosed inside the wall. If two door polygons are neighboring in the RAG, we label the larger door polygon as the door swing area and the smaller part as the door part that is embedded within the wall.

Wall Splitting. First, we want to obtain the entire wall, including windows and doors embedded within it. Doors and windows are contained within a wall. As described in Room Connectivity, we follow the same procedure to merge the door and window nodes into the wall nodes. The resulting wall is then approximated using the Douglas-Peucker algorithm. A resulting wall polygon is shown in Fig. 5 (b).

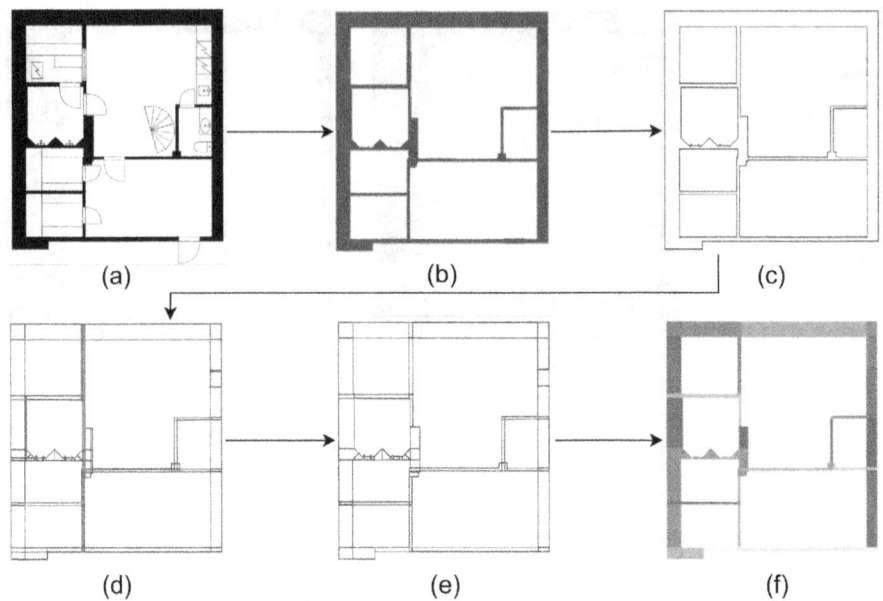

Fig. 5. Demonstration from input image to splitted walls (a) Input image (b) Wall polygon (c) Interior and exterior linear rings of polygon (d) Added separation lines (e) Crossing lines removed (f) polygon creation of remaining lines.

To be able to store information about different parts of the wall regarding materials or width, which are useful for several applications, such as the generation of 3D or even Building Information Models (BIM), the wall polygons have to be split in a reasonable manner. To achieve this, we must split the wall into parts associated with individual rooms and load-bearing walls. To accomplish this, polygons are detected by finding separation lines and constructing the polygon out of these, as implemented in the Algorithms 1 and 2 and illustrated in Fig. 5.

The wall polygons are merged into a multi-polygon P_{wall} (see Fig. 5 (b)). Each polygon can be defined by its exterior and interior linestrings as shown in Fig. 5 (c). For every point on each linestring in P_{wall} (Algorithm 1, lines 2–25), we search for lines where the polygon should be split. For every line contained in the interior or exterior of the polygon (lines 5-14), the shortest line between this line and point is determined and called *shortest_line* (line 7). If the *shortest_line* is inside the wall polygon and fulfills the *filter* criteria, the line is a potential separation line and gets appended to *candidates* (lines 8-12). The *filter* function can depend on the use case, we have chosen the *filter* function to return true if *shortest_line* is (almost) orthogonal to *line* or any of the two lines in *line_string* that contains *point*.

The candidates are sorted ascending according to the length of the lines (line 15) and the shortest line *best_candidate* becomes a separation line (line 17). Then, we search for the next longer line inside *candidates* that has an angle of at least 40° to *best_candidate*. If this line exists it also becomes a separation line (lines 18-23). After

Algorithm 1. Separation lines.

```
1: Let P_wall be the multi polygon of all wall polygons and linestrings be the set of line strings
   from the interior and exterior of the polygons in P_walls.
2: for line_string in linestrings do
3:     for point in line_string(points) do
4:         candidates ← list()
5:         for line_string2 in linestrings do
6:             for line in line_string2(lines) do
7:                 shortest_line ← shortestline(point, line)
8:                 if shortest_line ⊂ P_wall then
9:                     if filter(args) then
10:                        candidates append shortest_line
11:                    end if
12:                end if
13:            end for
14:        end for
15:        sort candidates ascending
16:        best_candidate ← candidates[0]
17:        separation_lines append ← best_candidate
18:        for candidate in candidates do
19:            if angle(candidate, best_candidate) > 40 then
20:                separation_lines append ← candidate
21:                break
22:            end if
23:        end for
24:    end for
25: end for
26: separation_lines ← remove_crossing_lines(separation_lines append)
27: return separation_lines
```

all the points have completed this procedure Fig. (see 5 (d)), we proceed with the last steps to remove the larger line from any two lines in *separation_lines* that cross and return the remaining *separation_lines* (lines 26, 27) (see Fig. 5 (e)).

The resulting wall parts can easily be associated with their corresponding rooms, using the RAG with updated neighbourhoods.

Polygon Construction. Furthermore, these new lines (see Fig. 5 (e)) have to be assigned correctly to the respective polygons. Therefore, according to Algorithm 2, we select a random point inside P_{wall} (line 4). We then iteratively add lines closest to this point, provided that the shortest line between the point P and the *line* does not intersect with any previously added line (lines 5-15).

For every *line* in *added_lines*, we check that the line between the point P and the midpoint mp of the *line* does not intersect with any other line in *added_lines*. If it does intersect, we remove this *line* from *added_lines* (lines 16-28). The convex hull of these lines constitutes the new polygon (line 29). This polygon is subtracted from P_{wall} (line 30), and the process is repeated until P_{wall} is empty (lines 2-31). An example of the resulting polygons is shown in Fig. 5 (f).

Algorithm 2. Polygon construction.

1: lines ← all lines from linestrings of P_{wall}
2: **while** $|P_{wall}| > 1$ **do**
3:    added_lines ← list()
4:    $P \in P_{wall} : dist(P, lines) > \epsilon$
5:    sort lines ascending according to distance to point
6:    **for** line in lines **do**
7:      is_crossing ← false
8:      **for** added_line in added_lines **do**
9:        **if** shortest_line(P, line) intersects added_line **then**
10:          is_crossing ← true
11:        **end if**
12:      **end for**
13:      **if** not is_crossing **then** added_lines append(line)
14:      **end if**
15:    **end for**
16:    **for** line in added_lines **do**
17:      is_crossing ← false
18:      **for** added_line in added_lines **do**
19:        mp ← middle point of line
20:        **if** shortest_line(P, mp) intersects added_line **then**
21:          **if** line $\neq$ added_line **then**
22:            is_crossing ← true
23:          **end if**
24:        **end if**
25:      **end for**
26:      **if** is_crossing **then** added_lines remove(line)
27:      **end if**
28:    **end for**
29:    new_poly ← convex_hull(added_lines)
30:    $P_{wall} \leftarrow P_{wall} - new\_poly$
31: **end while**

4 Experiments

To evaluate the performance of the modified features, we conducted a series of experiments on different datasets. We provide some details about the datasets used and the implementation of the experiments.

4.1 Dataset

For the experiments we used the CubiCasa and CVC datasets.

CubiCasa. We used the same dataset as in [9], i.e., 400 high-quality floor plans from the CubiCasa5K dataset, which contain different apartment floor plans. The dataset contains SVG formatted floor plan images with vectorized polygons, where a class is assigned to each polygon. These classes are structural elements (walls, windows, doors, and stairs), spatial elements (rooms, porches, and outer space), and objects. When comparing the CubiCasa dataset with the CVC dataset we relabel objects, stairs and porches as rooms because the CVC dataset does not contain these relabeled classes. To the best of our knowledge, this is the only dataset where the vectorized image is completely labeled.

We split the CubiCasa dataset into fixed training (280), test (80), and validation (40) sets. To create a rotated test dataset, we augmented the test set images with a rotation of $45°$. To fit the rotated image onto the canvas, the canvas had to be enhanced, leading to higher resolution images. The additional pixels were set to be white. The rotated images were vectorized, and the RAG features were calculated. The newly created polygons were labeled with the label that had the highest IoU value of the rotated labeled polygons.

CVC. We further used the CVC dataset, which contains 122 scanned floor plan documents divided in 4 different subsets regarding their origin and style. The labels are in SVG format and the classes are structural elements (rooms, walls, doors, windows, parking doors and room separations). We interpret parking doors as doors and ignore the room separation labels. Some areas on the floor plan are not labeled, e.g., stairs.

The floor plans contain additional information, e.g., rooftops, text, measure lines. The dataset was pre-processed using the pre-processing steps described in Sect.3.1. Due to poor vectorization into the correct indoor elements the data was not suitable for use as training data. The entire 122 floor plans were used as a test dataset.

4.2 Implementation

We used the DWGNN with an LSTM aggregator and six layers. We trained for 40 epochs with a learning rate of 0.01 and batch size of 1. We trained on the CubiCasa training dataset with different invariant ratios of 100, 8^{-1} and 80^{-1} and one without the proposed normalization. The features contained 16 Zernike moments (up to order 6). The evaluation occurred before the post-processing steps. Zernike moments were calculated with the functions provided in [5]. The hardware characteristics used for the experiments were an Intel Xeon Platinum 8260 CPU, an Nvidia Quadro RTX 8000 GPU and 192 GB of RAM.

5 Results

In Table 1 and 2 the average was taken over all classes except the outer space class. In Table 1 we see the comparison of classification with different invariant ratios for the normalization step on different datasets. The average F1 scores on the CubiCasa dataset range from 94.1% to 95.27% having very similar performance with different invariant ratios. The wall and window detection in the CubiCasa dataset with invariant ratio 300 outperformed the other invariant ratios with an excellent F1 score (97.96%, 98.32%) and IoU (95.99%, 96.7%). On the other hand, the class detection with an invariant ratio of 3^{-1} provided the most consistent F1 scores and IoU's across all classes, performing well on every class detection task and achieving the highest average F1 score (95.27%).

Table 1. Comparison of different invariant ratios on different testing data sets. The model was trained on the CubiCasa dataset.

		CubiCasa			CubiCasa rotated			CVC		
invariant ratio		300	3^{-1}	80^{-1}	300	3^{-1}	80^{-1}	300	3^{-1}	80^{-1}
F1	wall	**97.96**	95.06	94.6	82.62	90.11	**92.24**	33.98	**45.67**	43.08
	window	**98.32**	97.46	91.18	76.79	**79.41**	78.19	7.17	3.72	**12.69**
	door	93.24	94.95	**95.24**	79.71	**87.65**	83.61	2.14	1.87	3.04
	room	88.98	93.62	**95.37**	67.34	91.84	**96.53**	51.86	76.83	**78.51**
	outer space	87.58	93.98	**96.57**	87.08	98.33	**99.61**	81.18	94.01	**94.81**
IoU	wall	**95.99**	90.58	89.76	70.39	82.01	**86.6**	20.47	**29.59**	27.46
	window	**96.7**	95.05	83.78	62.32	**65.84**	64.2	3.72	1.90	**6.78**
	door	87.34	90.39	**90.9**	66.27	**78.01**	71.83	1.08	**9.40**	1.54
	room	80.14	88.01	**91.15**	50.76	84.91	**93.29**	35.01	62.38	**64.62**
	outer space	77.91	88.65	**93.37**	77.11	96.72	**99.22**	68.32	88.70	**90.14**
Average F1		94.62	**95.27**	94.1	76.61	87.25	**87.64**	23.79	32.02	**34.33**

Table 2. Comparison of indoor classification with and without the proposed normalization steps on the CubiCasa rotated dataset. The model was trained on the CubiCasa data set.

	80^{-1}		no normalization	
	F1	IoU	F1	IoU
objects	**61.10**	**43.98**	42.61	27.08
wall	**92.18**	**85.50**	88.72	79.78
window	**78.25**	**64.72**	24.82	14.17
door	**83.44**	**71.59**	36.81	22.56
stair	13.32	7.13	**34.43**	**20.80**
room	**94.54**	**89.64**	87.48	77.74
porch	**46.24**	**30.07**	40.02	25.02
outer space	**99.61**	**99.22**	99.15	98.32
Average	**67.01**	**56.09**	50.7	38.16

The differences between invariant ratios become more apparent in the rotated CubiCasa and CVC datasets. On both datasets, classification with an invariant ratio of 300 yielded the lowest average F1 scores and IoU values. For the rotated CubiCasa dataset, the results were not as good as those for the non-rotated CubiCasa dataset, but using an invariant ratio of 3^{-1} or 80^{-1} still showed promising performance as can be seen in the average F1 score (87.25%, 87.64%). The F1 score and IoU for the window and door classes were highest when using the invariant ratio of 3^{-1} (window: 79.41%, 65.84%, door: 87.65%, 78.01%). Otherwise, the invariant ratio of 80^{-1} performed best with an average F1 score of 87.64%.

The results on the CVC dataset were less impressive overall. Only the room and outer space classification exhibited reasonable performance when using an invariant ratio of 3^{-1} or 80^{-1}. The highest F1 score for wall detection was achieved with an invariant ratio of 3^{-1}, resulting in a value of 45.67%, while the highest IoU was 29.59%. In contrast, the window and door classification showed F1 scores and IoU values in the single digits. The classification with invariant ratio 80^{-1} had the best average F1 score of 34.33%.

In Table 2, we compare the adjusted calculation of Zernike moments as described in Sect. 3.2 with an invariant ratio of 80^{-1} versus without normalization steps. The average F1 score and average IoU when normalizing the polygons are significantly higher at 67.01% and 56.09%, respectively, compared to 50.7% and 38.16% when leaving out the normalization steps. The wall, door, room, and outer space classes exhibit high F1 scores and IoU values when using an invariant ratio of 80^{-1}. However, the object porch and stair detection show relatively low scores. When not normalizing only the stair class achieved a higher F1 score and IoU than when normalizing. In all other classes, our proposed method improved upon the original scores, particularly in window and door detection, where the scores more than double when normalizing.

6 Discussion

We added a normalization step in the feature extraction and established an invariant ratio to improve the Zernike moment calculation. The normalization steps clearly improved rotation invariance as seen in the results on the rotated CubiCasa dataset. Interestingly, stair nodes were not classified correctly after rotation, which may be due to similarity with object nodes. Overall, the method was capable of classifying most indoor elements correctly despite never seeing rotated floor plans. Furthermore, the performance on the rotated CubiCasa dataset improved clearly with smaller invariant ratios.

The generalization to an unseen dataset also improved with smaller invariant ratios but did not perform as well as on the CubiCasa dataset. Recall that a smaller invariant ratio corresponds to a smaller scaling factor, meaning more shape information is captured by Zernike moments. It's interesting to see that better generalization occurs with more visual information, as visuals differ between datasets. The overall poor generalization to the CVC dataset is likely due to the more complex RAG in the CVC dataset, caused by additional information such as rooftops, as they are depicted by schematic lines splitting room polygons. Also, some nodes in the RAG are represented by polygons containing areas of room and door, making labeling tasks ambiguous, e.g., doors with no enclosed area. This is due to the vectorization step only vectorizing connected areas. Text removal and possible symbol removal could be done with inpainting that reconstructs the covered spatial information for a preciser vectorization.

The vectorization process has its drawbacks, but it also offers advantages, including capturing the precision of floor plans with a level of detail that can surpass the provided ground truth. A notable benefit is that the vectorization can be used to divide the entire floor plan into meaningful segments, enabling the creation of a RAG that includes relevant neighborhoods for real life applications. This has proven particularly useful in post-processing and offers potential for further integration with 3D models.

For floor plans with few additional technical details, e.g., escape and rescue plans, the vectorization may be enhanced with additional object detection or splitting vectors into smaller parts. On more technical drawings like the CVC dataset, a segmentation approach seems more suitable.

Moreover the presented wall splitting algorithm has shown desired wall splitting results on the cubicasa dataset but has not been evaluated with a metric or tested on complex buildings with, e.g., round walls.

7 Conclusion

We presented an end-to-end pipeline from input image to a RCG and indoor element classification, ready for use with 3D models. Our pipeline consists of four stages: preprocessing the input image to remove text and some additional information, a RAG generation with feature extraction, prediction of indoor element classes of RAG nodes using a graph neural network (GNN), and post-processing steps to extract the RCG and apply a wall splitting algorithm. As part of our pipeline we introduced a novel rule based wall splitting algorithm that returns walls that can be associated with rooms and are convex.

Furthermore, we enhanced the feature extraction when generating the RAG by utilizing normalization steps and established an invariant ratio that provides a criterion to ensure that a polygon is fully captured when calculating Zernike moments. To evaluate the performance of the normalization and the influence of the invariant ratio, we performed experiments on the CubiCasa and CVC dataset, with different invariant ratios and an ablation study of the normalization method. The performance on the rotated Cubicasa data increased significantly using these normalization steps, and further improvements were achieved by choosing a small enough invariant ratio.

References

1. Automatic floor plan analysis and recognition, https://www.sciencedirect.com/science/article/pii/S0926580522002217
2. Ahmed, S., Liwicki, M., Weber, M., Dengel, A.: Improved automatic analysis of architectural floor plans. In: 2011 International Conference on Document Analysis and Recognition (ICDAR 2011). pp. 864–869. IEEE, Piscataway, NJ (2011). https://doi.org/10.1109/ICDAR.2011.177
3. Barreiro, A.C., Trzeciakiewicz, M., Hilsmann, A., Eisert, P.: Automatic reconstruction of semantic 3d models from 2d floor plans **28**, 1–5 (2023). https://doi.org/10.23919/MVA57639.2023.10215746, http://arxiv.org/pdf/2306.01642v1
4. Bay, H., Ess, A., Tuytelaars, T., van Gool, L.: Speeded-up robust features (surf). Comput. Vis. Image Underst. **110**(3), 346–359 (2008). https://doi.org/10.1016/j.cviu.2007.09.014
5. Coelho, L.P.: Mahotas: Open source software for scriptable computer vision. J. Open Res. Softw. **1** (2013). https://doi.org/10.5334/jors.ac
6. Deshmukh, P., Kulkarni, S., Samuel, D., Mishra, J., Sankpal, L.J., Kulkarni, C., Kulkarni, P.: 2d to 3d floor plan modeling using image processing and augmented reality. In: 2023 International Conference on Recent Advances in Electrical, Electronics & Digital Healthcare Technologies (REEDCON). pp. 682–687. IEEE, Piscataway, NJ (2023). https://doi.org/10.1109/REEDCON57544.2023.10151165

7. von F.Z.: Beugungstheorie des schneidenver-fahrens und seiner verbesserten form, der phasenkontrastmethode. Physica **1**(7), 689–704 (1934). https://doi.org/10.1016/S0031-8914(34)80259-5
8. Huang, L., Wu, J.H., Wei, C., Li, W.: Muranet: Multi-task floor plan recognition with relation attention **14193**(6), 135–150 (2023). https://doi.org/10.1007/978-3-031-41498-5_10, http://arxiv.org/pdf/2309.00348v1
9. Song, J.: Framework for indoor elements classification via inductive learning on floor plan graphs (2021). https://www.mdpi.com/2220-9964/10/2/97
10. Khade, R., Jariwala, K., Chattopadhyay, C., Pal, U.: A rotation and scale invariant approach for multi-oriented floor plan image retrieval. Pattern Recogn. Lett. **145**, 1–7 (2021). https://doi.org/10.1016/j.patrec.2021.01.020
11. Kim, S., Park, S., Kim, H., Yu, K.: Deep floor plan analysis for complicated drawings based on style transfer. J. Comput. Civil Eng. **35**(2) (2021). https://doi.org/10.1061/(ASCE)CP.1943-5487.0000942
12. Liu, C., Wu, J., Kohli, P., Furukawa, Y.: Raster-to-vector: Revisiting floorplan transformation. In: 2017 IEEE International Conference on Computer Vision. pp. 2214–2222. IEEE Xplore Digital Library, IEEE, Piscataway, NJ (2017). https://doi.org/10.1109/ICCV.2017.241
13. Macé, S., Locteau, H., Valveny, E., Tabbone, S.: A system to detect rooms in architectural floor plan images. In: Doermann, D. (ed.) Proceedings of the 9th IAPR International Workshop on Document Analysis Systems. pp. 167–174. ACM Other Conferences, ACM, New York, NY (2010). https://doi.org/10.1145/1815330.1815352
14. Mingxiang Chen, C.P.: Parsing line segments of floor plan images using graph neural networks: Mingxiang chen, cihui pan realsee beijing, china 100085 (2023). https://arxiv.org/abs/2303.03851.pdf
15. Teh, C.H., Chin, R.T.: On image analysis by the methods of moments. IEEE Trans. Pattern Anal. Mach. Intell. **10**(4), 496–513 (1988). https://doi.org/10.1109/34.3913
16. Xiang, S.: On invariance analysis of zernike moments in the presence of rotation with crop and loose modes. Multimedia Tools and Applications **57**(1), 29–48 (2012). https://doi.org/10.1007/s11042-010-0539-6
17. Yang, J., Jang, H., Kim, J., Kim, J.: Semantic segmentation in architectural floor plans for detecting walls and doors. In: Li, W., Li, Q., Wang, L. (eds.) CISP-BMEI 2018. pp. 1–9. IEEE, Piscataway, NJ (2018). https://doi.org/10.1109/CISP-BMEI.2018.8633243

Use of Orthogonal Encryption Functions in Commutative Watermarking-Encryption

Roland Schmitz[1(✉)] and Christos Grecos[2]

[1] Stuttgart Media University, Nobelstrasse 10, 70569 Stuttgart, Germany
schmitz@hdm-stuttgart.de
[2] Thessaloniki, Greece

Abstract. While commutativity of watermarking and encryption is a desirable feature in many application scenarios, it is hard to find robust watermarking schemes and secure ciphers which are able to commute with each other, because there are no visual features to use for embedding the mark in the encrypted domain.

In the present paper we investigate if orthogonal maps, which form a large subclass of norm-preserving maps, are suitable for image encryption within the framework of a commutative watermarking-encryption (CWE) scheme. Specifically, we show that these maps, if used properly, have a much larger key space and leave a smaller statistical residue in the ciphertext than other norm-preserving maps like sign-bit encryption and permutation ciphers currently being used in CWE.

Keywords: Watermarking · Encryption · Commutative watermarking-encryption

1 Introduction

For many years, digital watermarks have been used as security mechanism to ensure the authenticity of multimedia data. When multimedia data such as images or videos are stored at some cloud provider P, however, a combination of different security mechanisms such as watermarking and encryption can be advantageous. For example a client A might wish to keep her data confidential with respect to P and stores them in encrypted form. P on the other hand, feels the need to process the encrypted data, e.g. by invisibly inserting a logo or metadata with the help of a digital watermark. If the data are encrypted by a convential algorithm, however, any change of the encrypted data will make decryption impossible. What is needed here is a combination of watermarking and encryption algorithms so that watermarking can be applied in the encrypted domain.

In another scenario, A inserts the watermark herself into the plaintext image data and stores the image at P. For security reasons, P encrypts the data, but A still wants to have the option to detect the watermark without having to decrypt the data first. In this scenario, the watermark is inserted in the plaintext domain, but extracted in the ciphertext domain.

C. Grecos—Independent Researcher.

© The Author(s), under exclusive license to Springer Nature Switzerland AG 2026
C. Distante and S. Battiato (Eds.): IMPROVE 2025, CCIS 2628, pp. 178–200, 2026.
https://doi.org/10.1007/978-3-032-01169-5_11

These examples show that in cloud computing there arises a need for encryption and watermarking algorithms that are compatible, or *commutative*. But also in buyer-seller scenarios [12] as they appear in Digital Rights Management (DRM), commutativity of watermarking and encryption is beneficial. For example, a seller might sell individually watermarked copies of a work to his customers (also called *fingerprinting*). However, the copyright owner, in order to prevent the seller from distributing plaintext copies without her consent, does only provide encrypted versions of the work to the seller, and sends the encryption key to the customers after payment. Here it is beneficial if the seller can fingerprint the encrypted data without having to decrypt them first. Moreover, the fingerprint should be detectable after the customers have decrypted their individual copies.

Commutativity means it is possible to insert the watermark either into the plaintext or the ciphertext, and to detect it in the plaintext or ciphertext domain, irrespective of where it was embedded. More formally, the equation

$$\mathcal{M}_{W_K}(\mathcal{E}_K(I), m) = \mathcal{E}_K(\mathcal{M}_{W_K}(I, m)) \qquad (1)$$

should hold, where $\mathcal{E}$ is the encryption function, K is the encryption key, $\mathcal{M}$ is the marking function, W_K is the watermarking key, I is the plaintext media data and m is the mark to be embedded. The resulting commutative combination of watermarking and encryption is called a *CWE scheme*. However, it is hard to find robust watermarking schemes for CWE, because when embedding in the encrypted domain, there are no visual features for the watermark embedder to rely on [17]. On the other hand, most ciphers used in CWE schemes offer medium security only, because they either have to leave a certain feature space of the plaintext data invariant so that the watermarks can be embedded in this feature space or leave a part of the plaintext data unencrypted (see Sect. 2.4 for details). This means there is a fundamental tradeoff between security of the cipher and robustness of the watermark: The higher the security level of the cipher, the lower the robustness of the watermark, because less statistical or perceptual features are available for embedding.

In this contribution we propose to use *orthogonal maps* as the encryption part $\mathcal{E}$ in (1), in combination with a suitable watermarking scheme, in order to get a better trade-off between security of the cipher and robustness of the watermark. Orthogonal maps are linear maps that are characterized by the fact that in their matrix representation, column vectors and row vectors are orthogonal to each other.

The idea of using them for image encryption is motivated by one of the main properties of an orthogonal map M, namely that it leaves the vector norm of an input vector x invariant, i.e.

$$\|M(x)\| = \|M \cdot x\| = \|x\| \qquad (2)$$

Thus, the vector norm is an *invariant feature* of the cipher map M. If we can find a corresponding watermarking scheme that embeds the watermark by modifying the norm of a feature vector, we get a CWE scheme. Sphere Hardening Dither Modulation (SHDM) [2] provides such a watermarking scheme.

The contributions of the present paper are as follows:

- Orthogonal maps allow for the use of robust, norm-modifying watermarking algorithms in CWE schemes. We show how orthogonal maps can be used for image encryption within a CWE scheme in a secure way.
- We show that orthogonal maps offer a larger key space and leave a smaller statistical plaintext trace in the ciphertext than other norm-preserving maps used in CWE like permutation ciphers and or sign-bit encryption. More specifically, we show that the mean of the squared greyvalues is preserved in the ciphertext, whereas permutation ciphers preserve the complete histogram and sign bit encryption preserves the absolute values of the greyvalues.
- We show that an earlier approach described in [22] for using orthogonal maps as encryption functions in a CWE scheme is insecure.

The rest of the paper is organized as follows: In Sect. 2 we summarize some of the earlier work in CWE. Section 3 reviews essential properties of orthogonal maps. In Sect. 4 we describe how orthogonal maps can be used for image encryption within a CWE scheme, and in Sect. 5 we review SHDM as the watermarking part of the CWE scheme. In Sect. 6 we investigate the security properties of orthogonal maps, and in Sect. 7 we experimentally test the commutativity of orthogonal maps with SHDM-based watermarking in the spatial and wavelet-domain, respectively. Finally, Sect. 8 concludes the paper.

2 Related Work

There are currently four basic approaches to commutative watermarking-encryption for raw image data, which are characterized by their different encryption and watermarking approaches and their different working domains.

2.1 Partial Encryption Schemes

The first commutative watermarking-encryption schemes were based on partial encryption schemes. This means only a part of the image is encrypted, while the other part is used for watermarking. Usually, the perceptually more important parts are encrypted, leading to less robust watermarking. For example, in [20], the data undergo four-level discrete wavelet transformation first. Then, the low-level wavelet coefficients are fully encrypted, while for the medium- and high-level coefficients, only the signs are encrypted. while the absolute values of are watermarked. In [6], a secret parameter is used to construct a secret transform domain, the Tree-Structured-Haar (TSH) Transform, where encryption and watermarking takes place. Thus, the watermark embedder and encryptor need to know about the secret parameter generating the transform domain. For encryption and watermarking, the transform coefficients are quantized to generate B bitplanes. The N most significant bitplanes are encrypted, and $B - N - 1$ of the remaining bitplanes are watermarked. In another typical example [8], audio files undergo a discrete wavelet-transform (DWT) first. The DWT-coefficients of audio files to be encrypted are then selected depending on the application scenario (e.g. full encryption mode, preview mode, medium quality, etc.). The watermark is embedded into the remaining DWT-coefficients. Finally, in [14], the plaintext data are decomposed into two parts using an orthogonal map, where one part is encrypted and the other part is watermarked.

In partial encryption schemes, the tradeoff between security of encryption and robustness of watermarking mentioned in Sect. 1 becomes most obvious. The security of the cipher increases with the amount of perceptually important data which are encrypted, while on the other hand the robustness of watermarking decreases, if perceptually less important data are available for watermarking.

2.2 Homomorphic Encryption Schemes

In homomorphic encryption schemes it is possible to transfer basic algebraic operations like addition and multiplication on the plaintexts to the corresponding ciphertexts, i.e., they are transparent to encryption [12, Sec. 2.1]. More formally, the relation

$$E_K(T(m)) = T^*(E_K(m)) \qquad (3)$$

should hold, where E_K is the encryption function, T is a transformation and T^* is some variant of the transformation [13]. On comparison with Eq. (1), we see that if watermarking is based on the transformation T, one gets a CWE scheme. Possible homomorphic transformations are provided by exponentiation modulo n, multiplication modulo n and addition modulo n (including the bitwise XOR operation).

In contrast to partial encryption schemes, here all image data are fully encrypted. However, a homomorphic watermarking operation may seriously affect the fidelity, i.e. the visual difference between unmarked original and marked image. In [18], for example, addition modulo n is used for watermarking and encryption, where n is the number of greyvalues. However, modular addition operation causes overflow or underflow for certain pixels which need to be handled in a prepocessing step during the encryption operation, making the system only "quasi-commutative". In [13], another homomorphic CWE scheme is discussed that is based on homomorphic encryption and a standard watermarking function, namely the Paillier cryptosystem [21] and the Patchwork watermarking algorithm [4]. However, here encryption is computationally very costly as it is based on a probabilistic public-key encryption algorithm.

2.3 Compression-Oriented Schemes

The problem of robustness of the watermark against compression goes away if the watermark is embedded into the bitstream after encoding. The CWE schemes presented in this section might also be categorized as partial encryption schemes, as certain important parts of the bitstream are encrypted and others watermarked. However, they are bound to a certain compression standard. Moreover, the robustness issue is resolved only with regard to compression, but not with regard to other attacks like setting the watermarked parts of the bitstream to default values.

The CWE scheme presented in [5] encrypts the intra-prediction modes and the sign bits of the DCT coefficients within the H.264 bitstream. The watermarking part is based on Quantized Index Modulation (QIM) [7] applied on the absolute values of the DCT coeffients. In the method presented in [9] encryption and watermarking is based on syntax elements within the HEVC bitstream. One subset is selected for data hiding, and another for encryption. In [10] and [11], watermarking and encryption are integrated into forming a protected JPEG-LS bitstream for medical images.

2.4 Invariant Encryption Schemes

In contrast to partial encryption schemes, in an invariant encryption scheme the image data are fully encrypted. However, the encryption operation is weakened to leave a certain subspace of the data invariant. This subspace may in turn be used for watermarking. The larger this subspace, the more robust the watermarking scheme can be made.

In [19], the sign bits of DCT coefficients are encrypted by using a stream cipher. This leaves their absolute values invariant, and they are watermarked by means of dithered modulation. In [25], a permutation cipher is applied to the image, which has the histogram of greyvalues as invariant subspace. By exchanging selected histogram bins, a watermark can be embedded.

In [24], permutation ciphers or sign-bit encryption are applied on selected subsets of transform coefficients. As these ciphers do not change the norm of the plaintext vectors, a robust watermarking technique called Sphere-Hardening-Dither-Modulation (SHDM) (see [2,3]) can be applied. SHDM embeds the watermark by modulating the norm of selected feature vectors (see Sect. 5 for details). However, both permutation ciphers and sign-bit encryption can only provide low to medium-level security: If sign-bits are encrypted, e.g. by means of a stream cipher, roughly 50% of the visual information stays intact. For permutation ciphers, it is shown in [15] that for a permuted $H \times H$ square image with L grey levels $O(\log_L(H^2))$ known plaintexts are sufficient to recover half of the plaintext pixels. The present paper uses the same invariant subspace as in [24] and also builds on SHDM for watermarking, but uses a much larger class of norm preserving maps for encryption, namely *orthogonal maps* (see Sect. 3).

In a number of recent works, vector maps which are used in geographic information systems have been simultaneously encrypted and watermarked using the invariant encryption approach (see [16,22,23]). In a vector map, the image data are represented as ordered arrays of points, lines connecting points and polygons made up of lines. As there are no pixels and grey values, these works are not directly comparable to the scheme presented here. Still, we briefly describe these works here, because the encryption algorithms deployed there are norm-preserving. In [16], for example, the ordering of points in the vector map is permuted, leaving their coordinates unchanged. The coordinates are in turn watermarked. Finally, in [22], orthogonal maps are also used as encryption part in a CWE scheme, where the authors encrypt the matrix of plaintext data A by multiplying it by an orthogonal matrix, and use the singular values of A as invariant feature space for watermarking. However, as we show in Sect. 3, this simple encryption approach has serious security problems. In Sect. 4 we therefore describe a novel and better way to encrypt using orthogonal maps.

3 Orthogonal Maps

Let V be a real vector space and M be a linear map $M : V \to V$. M is called **orthogonal**, if its matrix representation has the property

$$M^t = M^{-1} \tag{4}$$

If $M = (v_1, v_2, \ldots, v_n)$, this property implies $v_i \cdot v_j = 0, i \neq j$ and $\|v_i\| = 1 \forall i$. The same is true for the row vectors of M. Note that because the column and row vectors of M are normalized to unit length, they really should be called *orthonormal maps*, but this term is very uncommon in the mathematical literature. Note further that permutation maps and sign-bit encrypting maps can be seen as simple examples of orthogonal maps: In a permutation map, each row vector consists of $(n-1)$ zeros and a single one, with the ones being located at different places. In sign-bit encryption, the matrix is diagonal matrix, where 1 and -1 are randomly distributed over the diagonal.

3.1 Invariance Properties

Vector Norm. Orthogonal maps preserve the **vector norm** defined by $\|v\|^2 = v^t \cdot v$, because they preserve the scalar product: Let u and v be two column vectors of the same dimension. Then we have for their scalar product:

$$u^t \cdot v = u^t \cdot (M^t M) \cdot v = (u^t \cdot M^t) \cdot (Mv) = (Mu)^t \cdot (Mv) \tag{5}$$

The preservation of vector norms is a consequence of the fact that orthogonal maps are a sequence of elementary rotations and reflections at coordinate axes, both of which do not change the length of a vector (cf. [1], p.47). In the context of the present paper, preservation of vector norms is vital because the watermarking algorithm described in Sect. 5 works by modifying the norm of feature vectors. Thus, the embedded marks are not disturbed by ciphering or deciphering.

Singular Values. The **singular values** of a matrix A are the eigenvalues of $A^t \cdot A$. An orthogonal map M may be used to encipher an image A by the naive approach

$$C = M \cdot A, \tag{6}$$

where C is the cipher image matrix.

In the naive approach, the singular values of A are preserved in C, because

$$C^t \cdot C = (M \cdot A)^t \cdot (M \cdot A) = (A^t \cdot M^t) \cdot (M \cdot A) = A^t \cdot A \tag{7}$$

For this reason, watermarking schemes which modify the singular values of an image matrix can in principle be combined with naive orthogonal map encryption as in Eq. (6) to form another instance of an invariant CWE scheme. This is proposed in [22].

However, an attacker observing C may use Eq. (7) to her advantage and compute $C^t \cdot C = A^t \cdot A$, thereby effectively canceling out the effect of the encryption matrix M on the plaintext A.

3.2 Generation

The (n, n) orthogonal matrices M in our implementation are generated by the following algorithm:

- Initialize a Pseudo-Random Number Generator (PRNG) by the encryption key K.
- Generate n random n-dimensional column vectors $u_1, \ldots, u_n$ by drawing their components uniformly from the interval $[-1, 1]$.
- orthogonalize $\{u_1, \ldots, u_n\}$ by the Gram-Schmidt-Algorithm. The result is the orthogonal set $\{v_1, \ldots, v_n\}$.
- Put $v_1, \ldots v_n$ as column vectors into a matrix M.

3.3 Statistical Properties

Despite having been generated by a uniform random distribution, the entries of the column and row vectors of on orthogonal matrix M follow a normal distribution. More specifically, they are $\mathcal{N}(0, 1/n)$-distributed. The underlying reason for this is that all these vectors are normalized to unit length, i.e. they are uniformly distributed directions on the unit n-sphere.

More formally, this can be seen as follows: Let $x = (x_1, \ldots, x_n)$ be a random vector, where all components x_i are uniformly drawn from $I = [-1, 1]$. Then the x_i have expectation value $E(x_i) = 0$ and variance $\text{Var}(x_i) = 1/3$.

Let $y = \frac{x}{\|x\|}$ be the normalized version of x. Then each component y_i also has expection value $E(y_i) = 0$. Their variance is given by given by

$$\text{Var}(y_i) = E(y_i^2) - (E(y_i))^2 = E(y_i^2) = \frac{1}{n}, \tag{8}$$

because

$$1 = E(\sum_{i=1}^{n} y_i^2) = \sum_{i=1}^{n} E(y_i^2).$$

Moreover, the y_i are normally distributed, because the distribution of the scalar product of y by some fixed unit vector u is a linear combination of the distributions of the y_i. More specifically, let S be the scalar product of y and u:

$$S = y^t \cdot u = \sum_{i=1}^{n} u_i \cdot y_i \tag{9}$$

Now S has expectation $E(S) = 0$, and its variance is given by

$$\text{Var}(S) = \sum_{i=1}^{n} \text{Var}(u_i y_i) = \sum_{i=1}^{n} u_i^2 \cdot \text{Var}(y_i) = \frac{1}{n}, \tag{10}$$

because u is a unit vector. Because y is also a unit vector, y represents a uniform random direction on the unit sphere. Therefore, the distribution of the angle between u and y should be independent of u. But this is only the case if the y_i are normally distributed, because only in this case the scalar product $S = y^t \cdot u$ has a distribution that is independent of u. In fact, we have $S \sim \mathcal{N}(0, 1/n)$.

4 Image Encryption by Orthogonal Maps

Orthogonal maps act on their input vectors as a series of rotations about different axes and reflections about different hyperplanes. They may be used to encipher greyvalues in the spatial domain or transform coefficients in the discrete wavelet or discrete cosine domain.

4.1 Spatial Domain

The most obvious approach to using an orthogonal map M for enciphering a plaintext image P would be to use matrix multiplication to compute the cipher image C as in Eq. (6):

$$C = M \cdot P.$$

This the approach proposed in [22]. However, apart from the problem pointed out in Sect. 3.1, in this approach the plaintext data do not get sufficiently decorrelated: Let C_{ij} be the greyvalue of the cipher image in row i and column j. Then

$$C_{ij} = \sum_{k=1}^{H} M_{ik} \cdot P_{kj}, \tag{11}$$

where H is the height of the plaintext image and M is a (H, H) orthogonal map.
Therefore, we have

$$C_{ij} - C_{i,j+1} = \sum_{k=1}^{H} M_{ik} \cdot (P_{kj} - P_{k,j+1}) \tag{12}$$

and

$$|C_{ij} - C_{i,j+1}| \leq \sum_{k=1}^{H} |M_{ik}| \cdot |P_{kj} - P_{k,j+1}| \tag{13}$$

This means an existing high horizontal correlation of grey values in the plaintext image is increased by the multiplication by M, because the row vector entries of M are clustered around zero (as we have seen in the last section, they have expectation 0 and a low variance). This becomes apparent in the horizontal stripes in cipher image in Fig. 1 and is confirmed by the two scatterplots in Fig. 2. The visual performance measure used here and in the rest of the paper is the *Mean Square Error* (MSE) between two images I_1 and I_2, defined as

$$MSE(I_1, I_2) = \frac{1}{W \cdot H} \sum_{i=1}^{H} \sum_{j=1}^{W} |I_1(i,j) - I_2(i,j)|^2 \tag{14}$$

where W is the width and H is the height of the images.

The horizontal correlation issue can be avoided by switching between different orthogonal matrices $M^{(i)}$ for encryption or by choosing the plaintext vectors randomly.

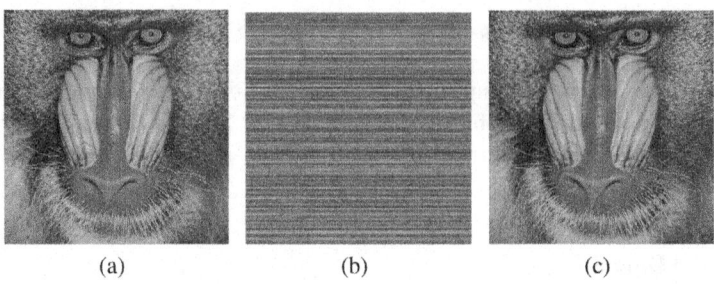

Fig. 1. Naive orthogonal map encryption approach $C = M \cdot P$ in the spatial domain (a) Plaintext Image P; (b) Cipher Image C ($MSE = 3.82 \times 10^4$); (c) Deciphered Image.

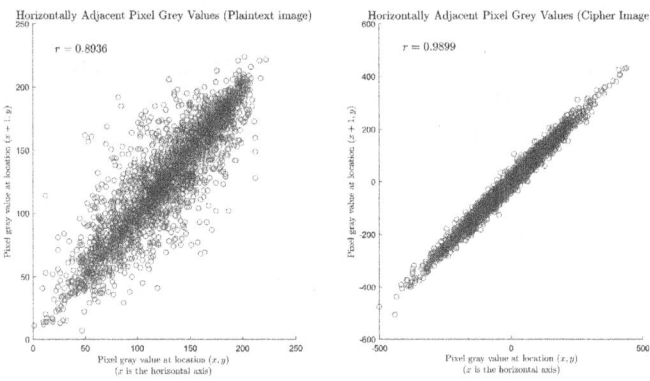

Fig. 2. Scatter Plot of Horizontally Adjacent Grayvalues in Plaintext Image (left) and Naive Cipher Image (right).

In the first approach, the plaintext image is represented as a collection of H-dimensional column vectors,

$$P = \left(v^{(1)} \cdots v^{(W)} \right), \tag{15}$$

where W is the width of the plaintext image. Then each plaintext vector $v^{(i)}$ is multiplied by a different matrix (H, H)-matrix $M^{(i)}$. The result is the cipher image matrix

$$C = \left(M^{(1)} v^{(1)} \cdots M^{(W)} v^{(W)} \right), \tag{16}$$

which is shown in Fig. 3 for the baboon image.

The horizontal correlation issue is effectively resolved (see Fig. 4).

Additionally, from Eq. (16) we get

$$C^t = \begin{pmatrix} (M^{(1)} v^{(1)})^t \\ \vdots \\ (M^{(W)} v^{(W)})^t \end{pmatrix} \tag{17}$$

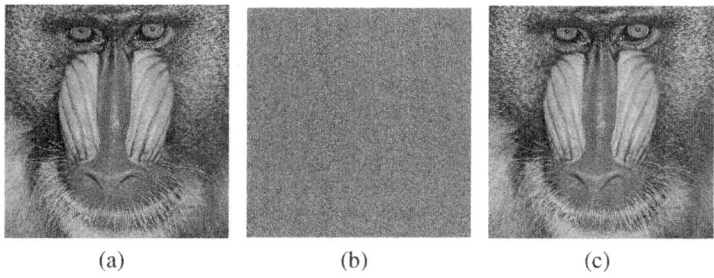

Fig. 3. Encrypting the baboon image columnwise in the spatial domain using different orthogonal maps. (a) Plaintext Image P; (b) Cipher Image C ($MSE = 3.85 \times 10^4$); (c) Deciphered Image.

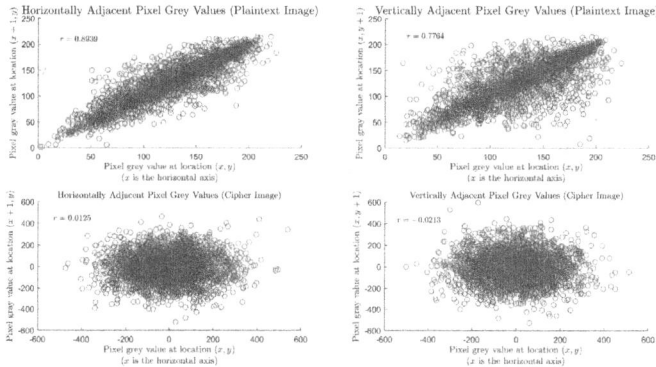

Fig. 4. Correlation of Neighbouring Pixels. The respective correlation coefficients are given in the upper left corner of each subfigure. Upper Row: Horizontal and Vertical Correlation of Plaintext Image. Lower Row: Horizontal and Vertical Correlation of Cipher Image.

and therefore

$$(C^t \cdot C)_{ij} = ((M^{(i)} v^{(i)})^t \cdot (M^{(j)} v^{(j)}) = (v^{(i)})^t \cdot ((M^{(i)})^t \cdot M^j) \cdot v^{(j)} \quad (18)$$

The diagonal elements can be further evaluated to

$$(C^t \cdot C)_{ii} = \|v^{(i)}\|^2 \quad (19)$$

Thus, the norm of the plaintext vectors $v^{(i)}$ is the only plaintext information leaking out of the matrix $C^t \cdot C$ if the encryption scheme from Eq. (16) instead of the one in Eq. (6) is used. This leakage cannot be avoided because of the norm-preserving property of the orthogonal matrix C.

Note that the resulting cipher map is still linear, which means it can be represented by a single (very large) matrix acting on the plaintext image represented as a column vector P of dimension $H \times W$. While it is possible to construct a non-linear norm-preserving map by switching between different maps in a way that depends on the norm of the input vector[1].

In order to be commutative with SHDM as watermarking part, but also for performance reasons, we chose the second encryption approach mentioned above in our experiments. This approach works by choosing the plaintext vectors $v^{(i)}$ randomly under control of a secret key WK_1. This key is a shared secret between the encryption part and the watermarking part. As is explained in Sect. 5, SHDM works by modifying the norm of feature vectors that are randomly selected from the input image. The feature vectors chosen by SHDM and chosen by the encryption part need to be the same, therefore they need to share WK_1. The complete encryption process is shown in Fig. 5.

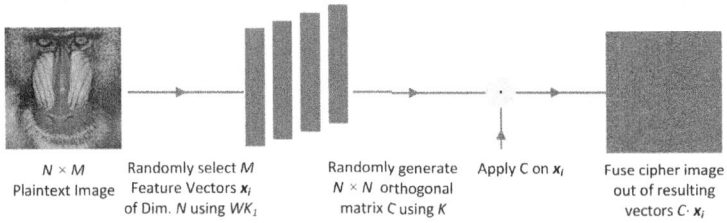

Fig. 5. Flow chart of the encryption process using a single orthogonal map. WK_1 is a secret shared between encrption and watermarking part.

In order to experimentally assess the visual effect of the resulting map, we applied it onto a set of 50 greyscale images of dimension 512×512 pixels. The resulting MSEs from this test are shown in Fig. 7. The average MSE is 2.7768×10^4.

4.2 DWT-Domain

For testing orthogonal encryption in the DWT-domain, we first performed a three-level DWT on the plaintext image and encrypted the resulting DWT-coefficients of the third approximation (the LL_3-coefficients), using the approach of Eq. (16). The results for the baboon image are shown in Fig. 6. Note that lower-level subband information is still visible in the cipher image. Of course it is possible to include more DWT-coefficients into the encryption process if a stronger visual effect is required.

As in the spatial doman, we also applied the cipher with the same settings on 50 testimages of dimension 512×512 pixels. The results for both domains are shown in Fig. 7. The average MSE in the DWT domain (Layer 3) is 7.3144×10^3. As to be expected, it is lower than the average MSE in the spatial domain by a factor of about four, because we only encrypted the LL_3 coefficients. As Fig. 7 shows, the layer n of the DWT does not have a strong influence on the MSE, as long as only LL_n coefficients encrypted, although for larger n more and more information from lower layer subbands are visible in the cipher image.

---

[1] See https://www.mathcounterexamples.net/non-linear-map-preserving-euclidean-norm/ for an example of a non-linear, norm-preserving map.

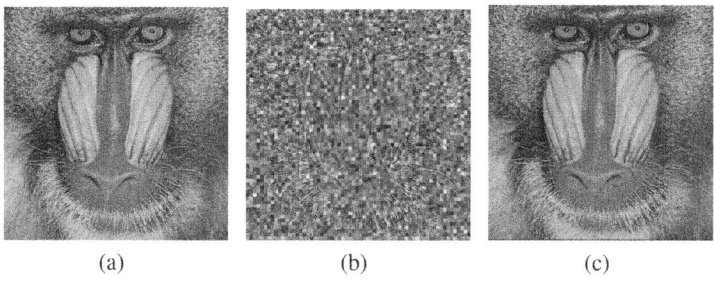

Fig. 6. Encrypting the baboon image columnwise in the DWT domain (LL_3-coefficients only) with different orthogonal maps. (a) Plaintext Image P; (b) Cipher Image C ($MSE = 2208.1$); (c) Deciphered Image.

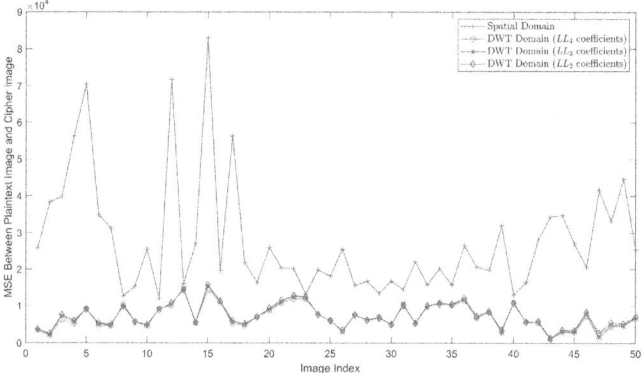

Fig. 7. Visual Effect of Encrypting 50 Images in the Spatial and in the DWT Domain (LL_2, LL_3 and LL_4-coefficients).

4.3 Encryption Time

The computationally most expensive part of the proposed encryption scheme is the generation of the orthogonal maps. We therefore measured the time needed to generate a random orthogonal map of a certain size $N \times N$, and compared with the time needed to generate a permutation of size N. To put these measured times into perspective, we also measured the time needed to perform a DWT with varying layers for a fixed image, which is naturally the first step for all encryption schemes working in the discrete wavelet-domain. The results are shown in Fig. 8.

While generating permutations is faster than generating orthogonal maps, Fig. 8 shows that the computing the DWT is clearly the most expensive step, with the exception of very large input images. In these cases we recommend to perform a DWT first and to apply the orthogonal maps on the higher-layer DWT coefficients. Otherwise, encrypting in the spatial domain is superior to encrypting in the DWT domain in terms of security and performance, because here all image data are encrypted (see also Figs. 3

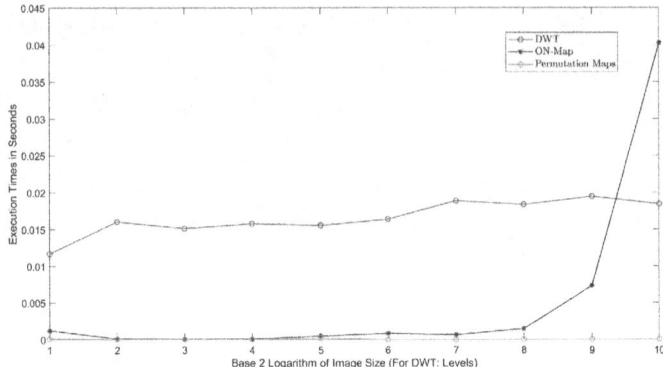

Fig. 8. Time needed to generate orthogonal maps of size $N \times N$, permutations of size N and to perform DWT in varying layers.

and 6.) Moreover, as Fig. 9 shows, the overall encryption speed in the spatial domain is largely comparable to that of sign-bit and permutation ciphers.

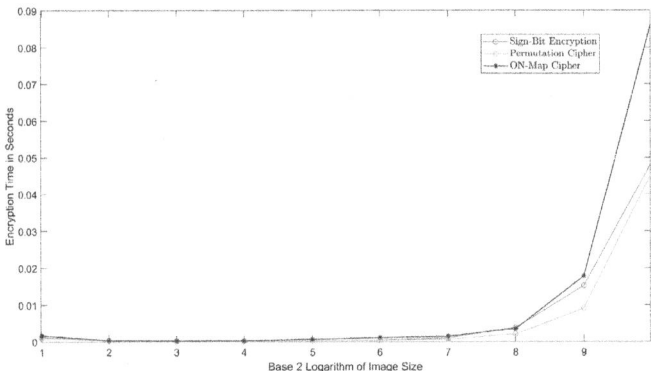

Fig. 9. Time needed to images of encrypt images of size $N \times N$ by sign-bit encryption, permutations and orthogonal maps.

5 Watermarking by SHDM

Sphere Hardening Dither Modulation, or SHDM for short, was proposed by Balado in [2] and [3] as an alternative to STDM (Spread-Transform Dither Modulation), which was proposed in [7]. Both SHDM and STDM have in common that in order to embed a single bit b, a multidimensional host vector x is extracted from the cover work C_0 and modified using some dithered quantization function Q_b, where different message bits lead to different dither values. Moreover, both schemes show a superior robustness against additive independent Gaussian distortions [2]. While in STDM the projection $x^t \cdot u$ of the host vector x onto some random vector u is quantized, in SHDM the norm $\|x\|$ is quantized. SHDM was chosen as the watermarking part in the proposed CWE scheme because of its high robustness against common signal-processing based attacks [3] and because it works in a clearly defined feature space, namely the norm of the host vectors selected from the cover works. As orthogonal maps leave this feature space invariant (see Sect. 3.1), we get a CWE scheme in the sense of Eq. 1.

More specifically, the embedding rule for a single bit $b \in \{0, 1\}$ is in SHDM given by

$$y = Q_{b,d}(\|x\|) \cdot \frac{x}{\|x\|}, \qquad (20)$$

where the quantization function is given by

$$Q_{b,d}(\|x\|) = \Delta \cdot \lfloor \frac{\|x\| - d - b\Delta/2}{\Delta} \rfloor + d + b \cdot \Delta/2 \qquad (21)$$

Here, Δ is the quantization constant and d is a dithering value that is determined pseudorandomly by the watermarking key. A larger value for Δ implies a higher robustness of the watermarking scheme, but also introduces larger visual distortions [2,3]. Note that the embedding rule (20) does not change the direction of the feature vector, which is advantageous in terms of visual distortions introduced by embedding. Figure 10 provides an embedding example, where a 128-bit watermark has been embedded in the spatial domain.

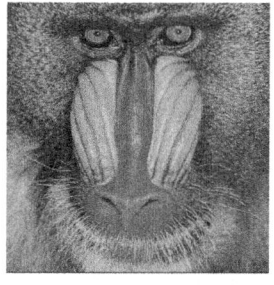
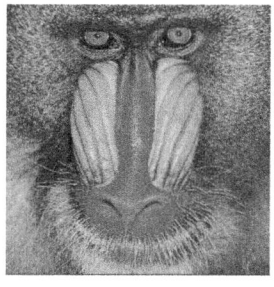

(a)   (b)

Fig. 10. Embedding 128 bit by the SHDM Method in the spatial domain ($\Delta = 50$). (a) Plaintext Image; (b) Marked Image ($MSE = 0.100$).

Extraction of the embedded bit is done via

$$b = \arg\min_{b \in \{0,1\}} |\|\tilde{y}\| - Q_{b,d}(\|\tilde{y}\|)|, \qquad (22)$$

where $\tilde{y}$ is the disturbed signal vector at the detector site.

Figure 11 shows the good robustness of SHDM in the wavelet domain against JPEG2000 compression for different Δ-values. Here, the DWT up to level 3 was performed and the level 3 coefficients were marked.

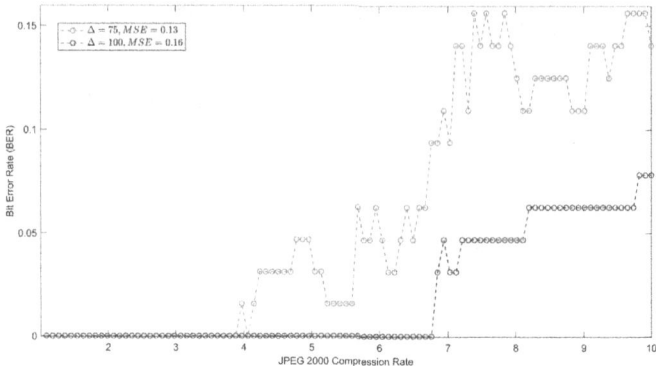

Fig. 11. Robustness of the SHDM Method in the wavelet domain against JPEG2000 compression.

In our earlier work [24], the watermarking key W_K used by SHDM is split into two parts:

$$W_K = (WK_1, WK_2), \qquad (23)$$

where the first part WK_1 controls how the host vectors x are chosen pseudo-randomly from the cover work. The second part WK_2 modifies the quantization function Q_b acting on $\|x\|$ by pseudorandomly choosing d. In order to be commutative with watermarking, the encryption function needs to be applied to the same input vector x as was selected by the marking function. While it is possible to simply select the column vectors of the cover work for marking and as input vectors for encryption, the pseudo-random selection offers greater security against malicious attackers.

6 Security Considerations

6.1 Key Space

The generation process described in Sect. 3.2 is governed by a pseudorandom number generator (PRNG) with an initial secret seed K, whose bitlength is larger than 128. However, there must also be sufficiently many orthogonal maps of a certain dimension.

Assuming the plaintext image has height H, we need to know how many (H, H) orthogonal maps exist. Following the process decribed in Sect. 3.2, we have $(H - 1)$ degrees of freedom for the first column vector v_1 (we are losing one degree of freedom because of the need to normalize v_1). The second column vector v_2 needs to be normalized as well, but it also must be orthogonal to v_1, so we get $H - 2$ degrees of freedom. Continuing in this line, we have $\sum_{i=1}^{H-1}(H - i) = H(H - 1)/2$ degrees of freedom for the complete matrix. Each degree of freedom is filled by a 64 bit double precision number. Therefore we can generate $2^{32H(H-1)}$ orthogonal maps of the required dimension. For example, if we have a square plaintext image with dimension 512×512 pixels, then the set of orthogonal matrices is sufficiently large to withstand a brute-force attack even if we encrypt only the DWT coefficients of the LL_n subband, as long as $n \leq 7$, because then the LL_7-subband has height $H = 4$. So there are $2^{128 \cdot 3}$ different orthogonal maps in this case.

On the other hand, sign-bit encryption of a square image of height H can be represented by a (H, H) diagonal matrix, where the diagonal entries are either -1 or 1. Accordingly, there are 2^H different matrices representing sign bit encryption. So here we need $H \geq 128$. Moreover, there are $(H^2)!$ different permutations for a (H, H) image. Using Stirling's formula and setting $H = 2^n$, we may approximate this number as $(H^2)! \approx \sqrt{2\pi} \cdot 2^{2n2^n + n}$. On the other hand, with $H = 2^n$, the number of orthogonal matrices becomes approximately $2^{32 \cdot 2^{2n}} = 2^{2^{2n+5}}$.

Comparing key lengths in bit, we get $2^{2n+5} > 2n2^n + n \; \forall n \geq 1$, so the keyspace for orthogonal matrices in general is much larger than for sign bit or permutation matrices. In order to get a key length ≥ 256 bits, we need $n \geq 2$ in the case of orthogonal matrices and $n \geq 5$ for permutations, where $H = 2^n$ is the height of the plaintext image.

6.2 Distance from Identity

A large distance from the identity map is a necessary, but not sufficient condition for having a secure cipher map M. One might ask whether it is possible that accidentally a map M is created that is very close to the identity matrix E. Intuitively, both E and M can be seen as points on a high-dimensional unit sphere, as both have matrix norm 1. Thus, if M is randomly generated, there is only a small probability that M is close to E, and the maximum distance between M and E is 2. This idea may be formalized.

Let the distance d between E and M be defined as $d = \|E - M\|$, where the matrix norm $\|A\|$ is the square root of the absolute value of the largest singular value of A. Then, for orthogonal maps M, we always have $\|E - M\| \leq 2$.

This is because the largest singular value of $E - M$ is the largest eigenvalue of

$$(E - M)^t \cdot (E - M) = 2E - M - M^t. \tag{24}$$

Now, let v be an eigenvector of M with eigenvalue λ. Then v is also an eigenvector for $(E - M)^t \cdot (E - M)$, with eigenvalue $2 - \lambda - \lambda^{-1}$. Because of $\|Mv\| = \|v\|$, all (possibly complex) eigenvalues $\lambda = a + ib \in \mathbb{C}$ of M must have modulus $a^2 + b^2 = 1$. Thus, $-1 \leq a \leq 1$ for all eigenvalues λ of M. If an eigenvalue of M is real, it is either equal to 1 or -1. Moreover, because of $a^2 + b^2 = 1$, we have

$$2 - \lambda - \lambda^{-1} = 2 - (\lambda + \lambda^{-1}) = 2 - 2a \in \mathbb{R}. \tag{25}$$

Thus, $\|E - M\| = \sqrt{2 - 2a_m}$, where a_m is the real part of the eigenvalue of M that yields the largest eigenvalue of $(E - M)^t \cdot (E - M)$, i.e. the real part of an eigenvalue that is closest to -1. Thus, $\|E - M\| \leq 2$. Because real eigenvalues are either 1 or -1, the following three cases may occur:

1. All eigenvalues of M are real and equal to 1. This means $M = E$ and $\|E - M\| = 0$.
2. Some eigenvalues of M are complex, with real part $-1 < a < 1$ and all real eigenvalues of M (if there are any) are equal to 1. This means $0 < \|E - M\| < 2$.
3. M has at least one real eigenvalue that is equal to -1. In this case, $\|E - M\| = 2$. This happens if M consists of some combination of rotations and a reflection at some hyperplane. These matrices are called **rotreflections**.

In order to estimate the probabilities for the three cases and to get an idea of how the distances are distributed, we conducted an experiment where we generated 1000 random $(512, 512)$ orthornormal matrices and computed their distance from the identity matrix. The result is shown in Fig. 12.

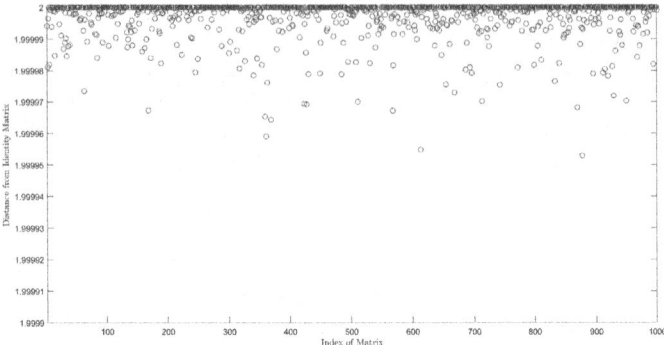

Fig. 12. Distance of 1000 randomy generated orthogonal matrices from identity. Note the scale of the vertical axis.

Case 2 was by far the most probable in this experiment (probability 0.916). The minimal distance from identity observed in this trial was 1.99995. The probability that the distance was larger than 1.999975 was 0.984. In our later experiments we enforced this criterion when generating the matrices for encryption.

6.3 Key Sensitivity

In this subsection we first ask how distant two orthogonal maps M_1, M_2 are which were generated by different keys. The distance is again defined as $d = \|M_1 - M_2\|$. In a similar vein as above one can show that the maximum distance of M_1 and M_2 is two, and our experiments show that in practice this maximum is always attained.

In another experiment, we computed the MSE between the plaintext image P and an image $P_1 = D_{K_2}(E_{K_1}(P))$ obtained from encrypting P in the spatial domain, first using key K_1 and then decrypting it using another key K_2 for 50 test images. The result is shown in Fig. 13.

The average MSE obtained in this test for the spatial domain was 2.6707×10^4 and is comparable to the average MSE computed from the values in Fig. 7, where we tested the impact of a single encryption operation in the spatial domain. In the DWT domain, we get similar results: The average MSE for the key sensitivity test is 6.7879×10^3, whereas the average MSE for a single encryption in the DWT domain was 7.3144×10^3 (see Sects. 4.1 and 4.2, respectively).

6.4 Cipher Statistics

Note the bell-shaped form of the cipher image histogram on the right in Fig. 14. The cipher pixel gray values are normally distributed because each cipher pixel $CP(i)$ is

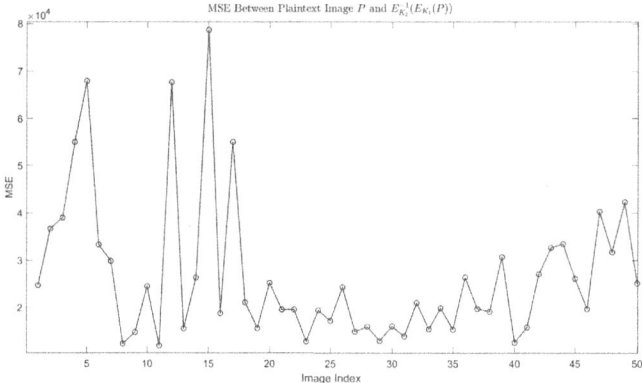

Fig. 13. Encrypting 50 Images with key K_1 and decrypting with different key K_2. Note the scale of the vertical axis.

the result of multiplying a row vector m_i of a random orthogonal matrix M by some randomly selected vector x:

$$CP(i) = \sum_{j=1}^{n} M_{ij} \cdot x_j \tag{26}$$

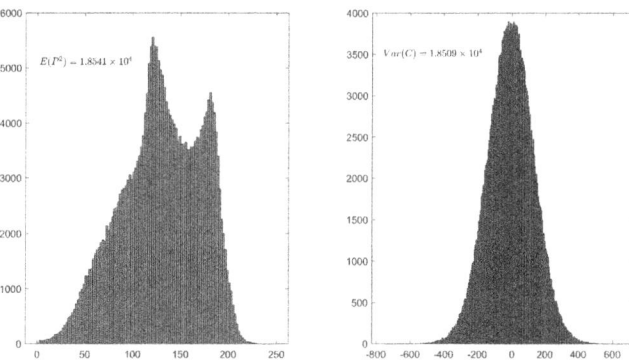

Fig. 14. Histograms of Baboon Plain and Cipher Image. The variance of the cipher image distribution approximately equals the expectation of the squared plaintext greyvalues.

As the $CP(i)$ are linear combinations of the normally distributed M_{ij}, they are normally distributed themselves. Their expectation value is 0, because $E(M_{ij}) = 0$ for fixed i. The variance of the $CP(i)$ is given by

$$\text{Var}(CP(i)) = \sum_{j=1}^{n} \text{Var}(M_{ij}x_j) = \sum_{j=1}^{n}(E(M_{ij}^2 x_j^2) - E(M_{ij})E(x_j))$$
$$= \sum_{j=1}^{n} E(M_{ij}^2)E(x_j^2)$$

But $E(M_{ij}^2) = 1/n$, because each m_i is a unit vector. Moreover, because x is randomly drawn from the distribution of plaintext pixels, each x_j^2 has the same distribution as P^2, where P is some randomly drawn plaintext pixel. Therefore we get

$$\text{Var}(CP(i)) \approx E(P^2) \tag{27}$$

(see also Fig. 14). This result can be interpreted as a residual statistical feature of the plaintext left in the ciphertext when using orthogonal maps for encryption. Other invariant encryption functions that are suitable for CWE leave larger traces: Permutation ciphers leave the complete plaintext histogram untouched, whereas sign bit encryption leaves the distribution of the squared plaintext pixel values invariant.

6.5 Linearity

Orthogonal maps can be represented by matrices and are therefore linear. In general, linearity is considered a weakness in cipher maps, because their matrix representation may be reconstructed by chosen plaintext attacks, where the plaintexts are the basis vectors of the underlying vector space. Here, if applied on an $H \times H$ pixel image in the spatial domain, the map acts on the $H \times H$-dimensional image vector formed by all grayvalues of the image. This means H^2 chosen plaintexts and corresponding ciphertexts would be enough to recover the orthogonal matrix. Linearity of the cipher also implies that similar plaintexts are mapped onto similar ciphertexts, and that the plaintext differences stay intact. This issue becomes relevant when encrypting subsequent frames in a video, for example. We therefore recommend to change the encryption key which governs the generation of the orthogonal matrices on a per image basis, especially in high-security environments. For video encryption, a possible solution could be to couple the initial seed K of the random number generator used to generate orthogonal maps with the video frame number, so that each frame will is encrypted by a different map.

6.6 Comparison with Other Norm-Preserving Maps

From a security point of view, the most important advantage of orthogonal maps in general compared to permutation maps or sign-bit encryption is their ability to disguise the image histogram (see Fig. 14). Permutations, on the other hand, preserve the complete histogram, whereas sign-bit encryption preserves the absolute values of the encrypted values, with a corresponding histogram shape that is similar to the plaintext histogram.

In Table 1 the different security properties of sign-bit encryption, permutation ciphers and orthogonal maps in general are summarized.

Table 1. Security Parameters of Orthogonal Maps, Sign Bit Encryption and Permutations.

	Orthogonal Maps	Permutations	Sign Bit Encryption
Linearity	✓	✓	✓
$\log_2$(Number of Maps)*	2^{2n+5}	$2n2^n + n$	2^n
Number of Plaintexts Needed **	$O(H^2)$	$O(H^2)$	$O(H)$
Statistical Trace	$E(P^2(i,j))$	Histogram, $E(P(i,j))$	$\|P(i,j)\|\forall i,j$

*: for encryption of $2^n \times 2^n$ pixel image
**: for successful chosen-plaintext attack on $H \times H$ encrypted (sub-)image

7 Commutativity of Watermarking and Encryption

As orthogonal maps preserve the norm of the input vectors, they are theoretically commutative with SHDM, which embeds the mark by modifiying the norm of selected vectors. In this section, we experimentally test if this property also holds in practice.

7.1 Comparing Marked Encrypted and Encrypted Marked Image

Although both orthogonal encryption maps and the watermarking function operate with floating-point numbers, our experiments have shown that encryption and decryption are fully commutative in practice. When the cipher process is combined with SHDM-based watermarking, either the selected vectors x are marked first (mark-then-encrypt) or the cipher vectors $y = M \cdot x$ are marked (encrypt-then-mark). Because of the norm-preserving property of M, the final result is the same in both cases. Here we showcase the result for the spatial case and the baboon image(see Fig. 15).

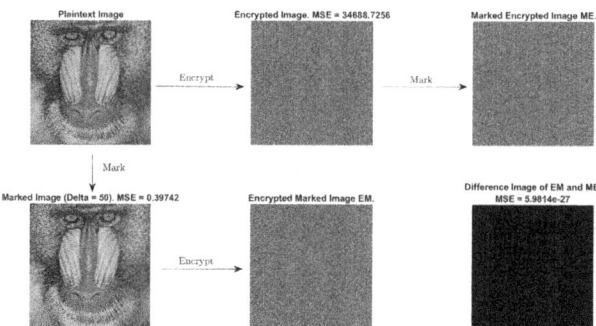

Fig. 15. Commutativity of Orthogonal Encryption with SHDM in the spatial domain.

Note the extremely small difference between marked encrypted image ME and encrypted marked image EM, which is true also for the wavelet domain. These small differences are caused by the use of floating point numbers in our scheme and have no further effects. This is confirmed by our experiments, where we tested the commutativity of watermarking and encryption for 50 test images of size 512×512 pixels in the spatial and the DWT-domain (see Fig. 16). In theory, the image size has no influence of the commutativity of watermarking and encryption, and further experiments with images of varying size have confirmed this.

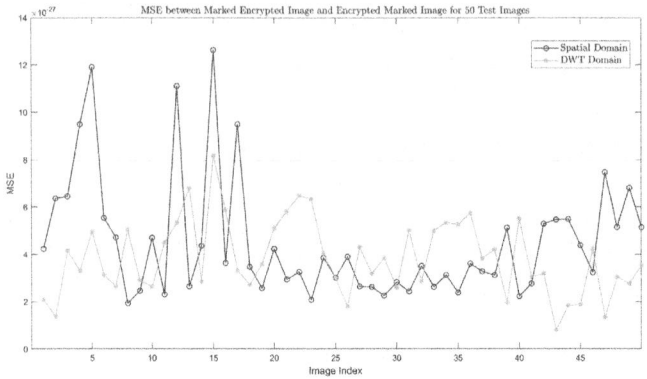

Fig. 16. Commutativity of Orthogonal Encryption with SHDM in the Spatial and DWT Domain for 50 Test Images. Note the scale of the vertical axis.

7.2 Embedding and Extracting the Watermark in Plaintext and Ciphertext Domain

It is an important property of CWE schemes that the watermark can be embedded in the plaintext domain or the cipher domain, and can be extracted from both domains irrespective of the embedding domain. We tested this by embedding a 128-bit watermark into 50 test images either into the plaintext image or after applying an orthogonal $\mathcal{E}$ for encryption.

In both the spatial and the DWT domain, and for all test images, the watermark could be extracted without errors either from the encrypted marked image

$$EM = \mathcal{E}_K(\mathcal{M}(I, m))$$

or from the marked encrypted image

$$ME = \mathcal{M}(\mathcal{E}_K(I), m)$$

We also tested the influence of the decryption operation, by decrypting either $ME = \mathcal{M}(\mathcal{E}_K(I), m)$ or $EM = \mathcal{E}_K(\mathcal{M}(I, m))$. In theory, this leads to the marked plaintext image $\mathcal{M}(I, m)$. In our experiments, we could extract the watermark successfully from the result of the decryption operation for all 50 test images.

8 Conclusion

We have proposed to use orthogonal maps for image encryption in connection with a watermarking algorithm that quantizes the norm of randomly selected feature vectors. As we have demonstrated theoretically and experimentally, the combination of the two algorithm yields a commutative watermarking-encryption (CWE) scheme based on the invariant encryption approach. Compared to other norm-preserving maps like sign-bit encryption and permutations, orthogonal maps offer an exponentially larger key space and a smaller statistical trace of the plaintext, which comes apparent when comparing the corresponding plaintext and ciphertext histograms. Therefore, the proposed CWE scheme allows to couple the good robustness properties of the SHDM watermarking algorithm with a strong encryption algorithm.

We have further shown that encryption by orthogonal maps may happen in either the spatial, or DWT-domain and that the commutativity property holds in both domains. Therefore, the encryption domain can be chosen according to the domain where the watermark is to be embedded. One drawback that orthogonal maps share with permutations and sign-bit encryption consists in the fact that they are linear, which means that similar plaintexts will be encrypted to similar ciphertexts, which is especially relevant in video encryption.

In our future work, we will investigate how the proposed CWE scheme can be expanded for video encryption and watermarking, in particular if is possible to include the time dimension of the video in the scheme, i.e. if it is possible to authenticate the temporal sequence of the video frames by means of the watermark.

References

1. Aggarwal, C.C.: Linear algebra and optimization for machine learning, vol. 156 (2020)
2. Balado, F.: New geometric analysis of spread-spectrum data hiding with repetition coding, with implications for side-informed schemes. In: Barni, M., Cox, I., Kalker, T., Kim, H.-J. (eds.) IWDW 2005. LNCS, vol. 3710, pp. 336–350. Springer, Heidelberg (2005). https://doi.org/10.1007/11551492_26
3. Balado, F., Hurley, N., Silvestre, G.: Sphere-hardening dither modulation. In: Security, Steganography, and Watermarking of Multimedia Contents VIII, vol. 6072, p. 60720V. International Society for Optics and Photonics (2006)
4. Bender, W.R., Gruhl, D., Morimoto, N.: Techniques for data hiding. In: Storage and Retrieval for Image and Video Databases III, vol. 2420, pp. 164–173. SPIE (1995)
5. Boho, A., et al.: End-to-end security for video distribution: the combination of encryption, watermarking, and video adaptation. IEEE Signal Process. Mag. **30**(2), 97–107 (2013)
6. Cancellaro, M., Battisti, F., Carli, M., Boato, G., De Natale, F.G., Neri, A.: A commutative digital image watermarking and encryption method in the tree structured HAAR transform domain. Signal Process. Image Commun. **26**(1), 1–12 (2011)
7. Chen, B., Wornell, G.W.: Quantization index modulation: a class of provably good methods for digital watermarking and information embedding. IEEE Trans. Inf. Theory **47**(4), 1423–1443 (2001)
8. Datta, K., Gupta, I.S.: Partial encryption and watermarking scheme for audio files with controlled degradation of quality. Multimedia Tools Appl. **64**, 649–669 (2013)

9. Guan, B., Xu, D., Li, Q.: An efficient commutative encryption and data hiding scheme for HEVC video. IEEE Access **8**, 60232–60245 (2020)
10. Haddad, S., Coatrieux, G., Cozic, M.: A new joint watermarking-encryption-JPEG-LS compression method for a priori a posteriori image protection. In: 2018 25th IEEE International Conference on Image Processing (ICIP), pp. 1688–1692 (2018)
11. Haddad, S., Coatrieux, G., Moreau-Gaudry, A., Cozic, M.: Joint watermarking-encryption-jpeg-ls for medical image reliability control in encrypted and compressed domains. IEEE Trans. Inf. Forensics Secur. **15**, 2556–2569 (2020)
12. Herrera-Joancomartí, J., et al.: ECRYPT European Network of Excellence in Cryptology, first summary report on hybrid systems, D.WVL.5 (2005). http://www.ecrypt.eu.org/ecrypt1/documents/D.WVL.5-1.0.pdf
13. Jiang, L.: The identical operands commutative encryption and watermarking based on homomorphism. Multimedia Tools Appl. **77**(23), 30575–30594 (2018). https://doi.org/10.1007/s11042-018-6142-y
14. Jiang, L., Xu, Z., Xu, Y.: Commutative encryption and watermarking based on orthogonal decomposition. Multimedia Tools Appl. **70**, 1617–1635 (2014)
15. Li, S., Li, C., Chen, G., Bourbakis, N.G., Lo, K.T.: A general quantitative cryptanalysis of permutation-only multimedia ciphers against plaintext attacks. Signal Process. Image Commun. **23**(3), 212–223 (2008)
16. Li, Y., Zhang, L., Wang, X., Zhang, X., Zhang, Q.: A novel invariant based commutative encryption and watermarking algorithm for vector maps. ISPRS Int. J. Geo Inf. **10**(11), 718 (2021)
17. Lian, S.: Multimedia Content Encryption (2009)
18. Lian, S.: Quasi-commutative watermarking and encryption for secure media content distribution. Multimedia Tools Appl. **43**(1), 91–107 (2009)
19. Lian, S., Liu, Z., Ren, Z., Wang, H.: Commutative encryption and watermarking in video compression. IEEE Trans. Circuits Syst. Video Technol. **17**(6), 774–778 (2007)
20. Lian, S., Liu, Z., Zhen, R., Wang, H.: Commutative watermarking and encryption for media data. Opt. Eng. **45**(8) (2006)
21. Paillier, P.: Public-key cryptosystems based on composite degree residuosity classes. In: Stern, J. (ed.) EUROCRYPT 1999. LNCS, vol. 1592, pp. 223–238. Springer, Heidelberg (1999). https://doi.org/10.1007/3-540-48910-X_16
22. Ren, N., Zhao, M., Zhu, C., Sun, X., Zhao, Y.: Commutative encryption and watermarking based on SVD for secure GIS vector data. Earth Sci. Inf. **14**, 2249–2263 (2021)
23. Ren, N., Zhu, C., Tong, D., Chen, W., Zhou, Q.: Commutative encryption and watermarking algorithm based on feature invariants for secure vector map. IEEE Access **8**, 221481–221493 (2020)
24. Schmitz, R.: Use of SHDM in commutative watermarking encryption. EURASIP J. Inf. Secur. **2021**(1), 1–12 (2021)
25. Schmitz, R., Li, S., Grecos, C., Zhang, X.: A new approach to commutative watermarking-encryption. In: De Decker, B., Chadwick, D.W. (eds.) CMS 2012. LNCS, vol. 7394, pp. 117–130. Springer, Heidelberg (2012). https://doi.org/10.1007/978-3-642-32805-3_10

Gender Bias Mitigation in Advertisement Videos

Thao My Tran Dinh(✉) , Thuy T. Nguyen , and Andrew M. Colarik

School of Science, Engineering and Technology, RMIT University, Ho Chi Minh City, Vietnam
{s3411684,thuy.nguyen43,andrew.colarik}@rmit.edu.vn

Abstract. Gender bias in Artificial Intelligence (AI) has been a concern as AI systems are increasingly employed in real-life applications. Despite efforts to mitigate bias, challenges remain in addressing gender bias embedded in machine learning systems, particularly in automated feature extraction processes. This paper examines the presence and impacts of gender bias in AI within the domain of automated feature extraction in computer vision, focusing on online video advertisements, which inherently reflect societal stereotypes. We highlight the limitations of existing mitigation techniques, emphasizing the need for transparency, comparability, and explainability in addressing bias. By systematically analyzing feature extraction methods and their normative harms, we propose a framework for evaluating gender bias by transforming video data into quantifiable features using pre-trained models and analyzing these features through various dimensions grounded in psychology and marketing research. We will employ a multistage approach including video annotation, automated feature extraction, unsupervised learning techniques, and supervised training models. This work provides actionable insights for reducing gender bias and enhancing fairness in AI systems.

Keywords: Gender bias · AI fairness · Feature extraction · Computer vision · machine learning · Advertisement videos

1 Introduction

Gender bias in Artificial Intelligence (AI) becomes increasingly concerning as AI integrates rapidly in government, business, and other organizations processes [1]. Although AI systems are designed to provide equitable assistance, unjustified distinctions in these systems can occur against certain gender groups [2]. These gender-discriminative influences are evident in high-stakes contexts such as hiring and justifying criminal suspects [3], alongside daily activities such as content curation [4], advertisement, entertainment recommendation [5] and other technologies [6]. Integrating these biased systems into real-life applications may amplify such biases, revealing potential counterproductivity of AI. For instance, male voices are more easily recognized than female voices in medical software [7] and women are shown more expensive STEM job advertisements than men [8]. Consequently, the research and practice communities have devoted substantial attention and efforts to mitigate these biases and their impacts, striving to ensure a future where technology serves every gender fairly.

As many AI systems are built from machine learning algorithms [3], the fundamental issue of gender bias stems from the training data these algorithms use, which captures existing societal prejudices [9]. Various strategies, often encompassing modifying algorithms and creating balanced training datasets, have been implemented to reduce algorithmic bias and enhance robustness in AI applications (Table 1).

Table 1. Gender bias mitigation technique examples.

System	Technique
Natural Language Processing (NLP)	Word embeddings [10–12] Crowd-sourcing dataset [13, 14] Coreference resolution balancing gender representation [15]
Computer Vision	Adversarial learning [16] Ensemble method [17] Balanced datasets [3] FairFace [18]
Decision-making system	Similar approaches along the AI development pipeline [1]

However, treatments for gender bias in AI often operate independently due to varying contexts and the specific normative harms they address, resulting in techniques that are difficult to compare and explain [1, 19]. This highlights the need to enhance explainability in selecting gender bias notions and their inherent harms, specifically what bias and what harm, as well as to improve comparability through appropriate metrics selection, enabling other studies to adopt these metrics effectively. Additionally, in Computer Vision, there is a significant gap in understanding how biased the automatic feature extraction can be. Since Computer vision systems typically transform image data to tabular features through these automated processes, these automations could introduce or even amplify gender bias in the preprocessing phase [20]. Establishing a clear and operational definition of gender bias and its normative harms, specifically within the domain of feature extraction, could be a significant advancement in mitigating gender bias in AI systems.

This paper addresses this gap by pointing out the limitations of existing mitigation techniques and proposing a framework to evaluate the presence and consequences of gender bias in feature extraction, applied to online video advertisements. Using pre-trained models, video data is transformed into quantifiable features, which are then analyzed according to established dimensions of gender bias from psychology and marketing research. The paper begins by outlining the foundation to such bias and then details the proposed framework and its methodology.

2 Foundation of Gender Bias

This section provides an overview of the foundational factors contributing to gender bias in AI. As observed from these factors, effective mitigation could involve possessing domain knowledge to apply suitable preprocessing methods, conducting thorough evaluations during feature extraction and selection, and ensuring that model performances are both comparable and transparent about potential harms. Additionally, leveraging AI fairness insights and fostering a diverse development team with rigorous standards are crucial steps.

2.1 Data Imbalance

Imbalanced representations of gender groups in training data, whether intentional or not, can lead to biased AI performance [1, 21]. Since AI algorithms rely heavily on personal data, addressing gender bias requires a strong focus on social inclusion and individual representation [22]. While these factors can be skewed due to systematic errors and inherent disadvantages [23], digital platforms also perpetuate such discrimination through predefined user segmentations and varying types of user engagement [22]. Therefore, it is crucial to implement strategies that ensure equitable social inclusion and representation for all genders.

Furthermore, data is often collected without labels, posing challenges such as manual labels selection for specific purposes [21]. For instance, classifying a "good" employee should be based on ranking rather than predefined categories [23]. This issue might arise when over-representation of one gender in training data can lead to biased probabilistic distributions, suggesting the need for alternative learning techniques like unsupervised or reinforcement learning.

Additionally, more open and updated benchmark datasets across various domains are needed [24]. Older datasets may not capture current trends and may not meet modern methods' requirements for large data volumes [24]. Methods such as Generative Adversarial Networks (GAN) can generate fair data from existing data [2], but complex models such as Deep Neural Networks are vulnerable to GAN attacks, reducing this method's effectiveness [1]. Therefore, understanding dataset characteristics and applying appropriate preprocessing methods are essential to reduce such bias in AI.

2.2 Challenges in Feature and Proxy Treatments

Gender bias in feature selection arises when chosen features fail to highlight genders' crucial differences [23]. If key differences are underrepresented, AI models may inaccurately predict information. While collecting additional features could address this issue, the cost efficiency might pose a significant barrier [23]. Constraints in time, finance and human resources may lead to a lack of appropriate features, presenting challenges in gender-fair distributions from AI models.

Proxy variables, which reflect the correlation between sensitive data and features, also perpetuate gender bias in AI systems [1, 21, 23]. Simply put, even if a gender feature is removed, its implication persists through relationships with other features. This happens even on diversified and gender bias-free training data due to encoded gender membership, called "redundant encodings" [25]. Thus, balancing the weight on each gender is more problematic than merely removing all the gender-related features.

Moreover, feature selection could amplify gender bias in AI Computer vision, as its labeling and feature extraction are often processed automatically [20]. One popular method to represent visual data is converting it to tabular versions, which mostly use automatic feature extraction tools to prevent introducing subjectivity. However, while this process itself can reflect gender bias, its impact on AI performance is often excluded from examination [20]. These challenges pose the need to evaluate gender bias during feature extraction and feature selection in visual data.

2.3 Diversified yet Incomparable Mitigating Techniques

Various techniques have been proposed to address gender bias in AI systems, however, many of which do not clearly specify their motivations or establish their normative concerns [19]. The lack of collaboration with other fields like social science, ethics, and law makes it difficult to define how harmful AI gender bias is, who it affects, and through which actions. For example, techniques to mitigate gender bias in NLP often conflate immediate representational harms with distant allocational harms and rely on imagined downstream effects [19]. These confusing targets and unclear consequences make it hard to effectively achieve their objectives.

Moreover, fairness and bias might not be fixed concepts and may need different approaches in different contexts [1, 21, 24]. This leads to different methods addressing different motivations, making them incomparable [1, 19]. Therefore, multidisciplinary incorporation is emphasized as a potential solution for creating analysis and evaluation standards [1, 9, 19]. For instance, the contrasting findings from multiple psychological scales in word embeddings experiments are uninterpretable [26]. These results might remain unexplainable until similar investigations using the same psychological scales are conducted.

The quest to generalize these techniques across various applications remains challenging, mainly because the inner workings of AI algorithms are not well understood [1, 21]. Dynamic real-world data may differ significantly from training data, making it difficult to modify AI algorithms given the limited ability to predict the impact of changes in model inputs or parameters. This reality highlights the critical importance of robust testing methods [27]. These challenges suggest the need for easy-to-understand evaluation methods that are comparable and clearly explain any potential harms, paving the way to ensure AI reliability, fairness and transparency.

2.4 Lack of Performance Evaluation Methods

After investigating performance evaluation metrics for gender bias in AI, there may be limited research in this area. To address this, we explore "Fair AI", a broader concept designed to measure bias and reduce discrimination across various subgroups [21]. While Fair AI may primarily focus on various aspects like race, gender and age, its following evaluation metrics can also be applied to gender bias (Table 2).

Table 2. Fairness evaluation metrics.

Metric	Description
Group calibration	Ensuring equal estimated probabilities match actual outcomes across groups [28]
Balance for positive and negative classes	Maintaining equal average scores for both positive and negative classes across groups [28]
Equalized odds	Ensuring equal true and false positive rates among groups, along with other score-related criteria [21]
Statistical parity	Also known as Count/Demographic Parity in Computer vision [20], this common fairness notion ensures equal likelihood of events for all groups [28]. However, it may hide sensitive subgroup information [25]
Earthmover distance	Measuring the effort needed to make the distribution of one group similar to another [25]

Achieving all fairness conditions simultaneously is mathematically impossible [28]. Therefore, practitioners should choose the most suitable fairness notion for their specific context. By leveraging the insights from Fair AI, robust evaluation metrics for gender bias can be developed to create fair and inclusive AI systems.

2.5 Unstandardized Development Process

Another factor may be the lack of balanced gender representations in AI development teams, leading to the lack of diverse mindsets [29]. Targets of gender stereotypes and their evaluators often restrict their behavior to avoid negative reactions [26, 30]. Barocas & Selbst [23] also highlight that biased practitioners can manipulate processes to hide discriminatory intentions, exacerbating the issue in gender-imbalanced teams. Despite sounding subjective, these opinions remain in literature as diversity problems in the AI workforce. For example, Buolamwini & Gebru [3] found that a lack of awareness to distinguish certain categories in the development teams leads to collection biases during the development processes.

Nevertheless, AI systems still require human oversight to prevent amplifying gender bias [21]. Therefore, institutional operations and regulatory frameworks are impactful factors to preserve awareness of gender bias. Expert groups like the IEEE Algorithmic Bias Working Group are working to develop better standards and practices for AI [31], alongside governmental efforts like the European Union's 2021 proposal, Title VII of the American anti-discrimination law, and ISO8000 for data quality. By embracing diversity and adhering to rigorous standards, fairer and more inclusive AI systems can be generated, ensuring that technology benefits everyone regardless of their gender.

3 Proposing a Mitigation Strategy

Our proposed framework evaluates the effectiveness of automated feature extraction in video data and its impact on gender bias, bridging the gap between biased representations and normative harms. Similar to [32], we will examine how stereotypical errors in machine learning systems affect individuals. [32] highlights that stereotype-reinforcing errors harm women, while certain violating errors harm men, prioritizing human judgment over predefined stereotype inventories. However, their selection criteria for online annotators lacks clarity, as there may be multiple domains, cultures and more attributes that differentiate the annotator groups. Thus, the surveyed result could be subjective to change due to varying demographics. Furthermore, while [32] focuses on the impact of these errors, we aim to identify where they originate within machine learning systems, fostering transparency and enabling the development of more responsible systems.

This study proposes an evaluation approach to gender bias in Computer vision's automated feature extraction and its potential consequences, using an online advertisement video dataset. The dataset "Automatic Understanding of Image and Video Advertisements" [33] is chosen due to its advertisement strategic design to persuade consumers, the availability of both qualitative and quantitative metrics, and its prior use in visual rhetoric research. The experiment includes four stages:

Stage 1 involves annotation of the videos by psychology and marketing experts to differentiate between gender bias and gender segmentation. For instance, an advertisement targeting only one gender may scientifically and non-biasedly depict much of that gender to appeal to the target segment. However, if the message delivered portrays gender bias, even when targeting a single gender, the advertisement should be annotated as having gender bias. To ensure consistency and integrity, the annotation process should establish clear guidelines and provide efficient training for experts, alongside collaborative domain knowledge-based analysis and stringent quality control measures.

Stage 2 focuses on feature extraction related to gender bias representations using auto feature extraction algorithms in visual and audio recognition. To identify the inherent harms from gender bias in video commercials, it is crucial to extract and group features related to gender bias representations and then evaluate their impact on consumer opinions and actions. These features encompass communication purposes and include foundational elements such as color usage, camera angles, visual composition, sum of visual/audio appearance of each character, and conveyed transcript messages. Upon identifying biases, Fairlearn [34] and AIF360 [35] can be employed to generate a new dataset with these mitigated features, resulting in a refined dataset free from such biases.

Stage 3 utilizes unsupervised learning methods, such as Hierarchy clustering and Association rule learning, to examine if sensitive features are associated with negative feedback or reinforce audience opinions. These methods allow us to maintain the data integrity while uncovering underlying patterns and biases without predefined labels. Specifically, we aim to determine if certain features "violate gender stereotypes" or "reinforce gender stereotypes", as suggested by [32]. This process also uncovers the possible proxy in features engineering and if there are no such associations, then we would not conclude in this process that there exists such hidden gender bias.

Stage 4 employs multistage validation using supervised training models like Naive Bayes [36] and Decision Trees [37], followed by more complex models like Support Vector Machines [38] and Neural Networks [39]. SHAP [40] will reveal feature importance, and evaluating tools such as the What-If Tool (WIT) [41] and AIF360 [35] will enhance gender fairness assessments.

By meticulously following these phases, this research will systematically evaluate the impact of automated feature extraction techniques on mitigating gender bias and establish a comprehensive relationship between gender bias notions and their practical normative harms.

4 Conclusion

Our review underscores gender bias and the complexity of it in AI and highlights the necessity for a transparent and comparable approach to addressing such biases and their inherent normative harms. In response to these challenges, this paper suggests identifying instances of gender bias in a video dataset embedded with user opinions and actions. This approach aims to reveal the significance of each feature extraction phase in perpetuating gender bias and its associated harms. Moreover, Fairlearn [34] and AIF360 [35], which we will use to mitigate such bias in feature extraction, have not been extensively investigated in practical studies before 2023 [42], highlighting the need to test and validate these techniques. Lastly, while annotation efforts are conducted to bridge the notions and normative harms of gender bias [32], such efforts might still be limited. Adding more annotations related to gender bias could be valuable for further development in this AI area.

Future work will be to experimentally implement the proposed framework and extend this study in several directions. Firstly, the dataset currently relies on annotations from MTurkers [33] and does not capture online users' opinions. Investigating the demographic characteristics of the audience such as age, gender, location, culture and education could provide deeper insights into how normative harms vary across different segments. This demographic analysis could lead to a more nuanced understanding of gender bias and its impacts. Secondly, to validate the robustness of our approach, larger video advertisement datasets, including those from television and billboard ads, should be utilized. Expanding the dataset scope will help ensure that the findings are generalizable across various types of visual media. Thirdly, given the dynamic nature of gender bias [24], it is essential to periodically and geographically update our findings and methods. This re-validation process, while potentially computationally expensive, is crucial for maintaining the relevance and accuracy of the models. Therefore, establishing a sustainable process for continuous re-evaluation and updating is necessary to ensure ongoing fairness and inclusiveness in AI systems.

Acknowledgments. We would like to express our appreciation to RMIT University's Psychology Department and Dr. Thu Huynh for their invaluable support and insights regarding the psychological perspective. We are also grateful for the funding support provided by RMIT's School of Science, Engineering and Technology, and the students from the same school for their valuable feedback during the development of this paper.

Disclosure of Interests. The authors have no competing interests to declare that are relevant to the content of this article.

References

1. Ntoutsi, E., et al.: Bias in Data-driven AI Systems -- An Introductory Survey," Jan. 14, (2020). *arXiv*: arXiv:2001.09762, http://arxiv.org/abs/2001.09762. Accessed 07 Aug 2024
2. Xu, D., Yuan, S., Zhang, L., Wu, X.:FairGAN: fairness-aware generative adversarial networks. May 28 (2018). arXiv: arXiv:1805.11202, http://arxiv.org/abs/1805.11202. Accessed 12 Aug 2024.
3. Buolamwini, J., Gebru, T.: Gender Shades: Intersectional Accuracy Disparities in Commercial Gender Classification (2018)
4. Bucher, T.: The algorithmic imaginary: exploring the ordinary affects of Facebook algorithms. Inf. Commun. Soc. **20**(1), 30–44 (2017). https://doi.org/10.1080/1369118X.2016.1154086
5. Mehrabi, N., Morstatter, F., Saxena, N., Lerman, K., Galstyan, A.: A survey on bias and fairness in machine learning. ACM Comput. Surv. **54**(6), 1–35 (2022). https://doi.org/10.1145/3457607
6. Howard, A., Borenstein, J.: The ugly truth about ourselves and our robot creations: the problem of bias and social inequity. Sci. Eng. Ethics **24**(5), 1521–1536 (2018). https://doi.org/10.1007/s11948-017-9975-2
7. Rodger, J.A., Pendharkar, P.C.: A field study of the impact of gender and user's technical experience on the performance of voice-activated medical tracking application. Int. J. Hum.-Comput. Stud. **60**(5–6), 529–544 (2004). https://doi.org/10.1016/j.ijhcs.2003.09.005
8. Lambrecht, A., Tucker, C.E.: Algorithmic bias? an empirical study into apparent gender-based discrimination in the display of STEM career ads. SSRN Electron. J. (2016). https://doi.org/10.2139/ssrn.2852260
9. Sun, T., et al.: Mitigating gender bias in natural language processing: literature review. In: Proceedings of the 57th Annual Meeting of the Association for Computational Linguistics, Florence, Italy: Association for Computational Linguistics, 2019, pp. 1630–1640 (2019). https://doi.org/10.18653/v1/P19-1159
10. Bolukbasi, T., Chang, K.-W., Zou, J.Y., Saligrama, V., Kalai, A.T.: Man is to Computer Programmer as Woman is to Homemaker? Debiasing Word Embeddings (2016)
11. Caliskan, A., Bryson, J.J., Narayanan, A.: Semantics derived automatically from language corpora contain human-like biases. Science **356**(6334), 183–186 (2017). https://doi.org/10.1126/science.aal4230
12. Manzini, T., Yao Chong, L., Black, A.W., Tsvetkov, Y.: Black is to criminal as caucasian is to police: detecting and removing multiclass bias in word embeddings. In: Proceedings of the 2019 Conference of the North, Minneapolis, Minnesota: Association for Computational Linguistics, 2019, pp. 615–621. https://doi.org/10.18653/v1/N19-1062
13. M. Nadeem, A. Bethke, and S. Reddy, "StereoSet: Measuring stereotypical bias in pretrained language models," Apr. 20, 2020, *arXiv*, https://paperswithcode.com/paper/stereoset-measuring-stereotypical-bias-in: arXiv:2004.09456. Accessed: Jul. 15, 2024. [Online]. Available: http://arxiv.org/abs/2004.09456
14. N. Nangia, C. Vania, R. Bhalerao, and S. R. Bowman, "CrowS-Pairs: A Challenge Dataset for Measuring Social Biases in Masked Language Models," Sep. 30, 2020, *arXiv*: arXiv:2010.00133. Accessed: Jul. 22, 2024. [Online]. Available: http://arxiv.org/abs/2010.00133
15. J. Zhao, T. Wang, M. Yatskar, V. Ordonez, and K.-W. Chang, "Gender Bias in Coreference Resolution: Evaluation and Debiasing Methods," Apr. 18, 2018, *arXiv*: arXiv:1804.06876. Accessed: Jul. 21, 2024. [Online]. Available: http://arxiv.org/abs/1804.06876

16. B. H. Zhang, B. Lemoine, and M. Mitchell, "Mitigating Unwanted Biases with Adversarial Learning," in *Proceedings of the 2018 AAAI/ACM Conference on AI, Ethics, and Society*, New Orleans LA USA: ACM, Dec. 2018, pp. 335–340. https://doi.org/10.1145/3278721.3278779
17. C. Clark, M. Yatskar, and L. Zettlemoyer, "Learning to Model and Ignore Dataset Bias with Mixed Capacity Ensembles," Nov. 07, 2020, *arXiv*: arXiv:2011.03856. Accessed: Aug. 23, 2024. [Online]. Available: http://arxiv.org/abs/2011.03856
18. K. Kärkkäinen and J. Joo, "FairFace: Face Attribute Dataset for Balanced Race, Gender, and Age," Aug. 13, 2019, *arXiv*: arXiv:1908.04913. Accessed: Aug. 30, 2024. [Online]. Available: http://arxiv.org/abs/1908.04913
19. S. L. Blodgett, S. Barocas, H. Daumé Iii, and H. Wallach, "Language (Technology) is Power: A Critical Survey of 'Bias' in NLP," in *Proceedings of the 58th Annual Meeting of the Association for Computational Linguistics*, Online: Association for Computational Linguistics, 2020, pp. 5454–5476. https://doi.org/10.18653/v1/2020.acl-main.485
20. Fabbrizzi, S., Papadopoulos, S., Ntoutsi, E., Kompatsiaris, I.: A survey on bias in visual datasets. Comput. Vis. Image Underst. **223**, 103552 (2022). https://doi.org/10.1016/j.cviu.2022.103552
21. Feuerriegel, S., Dolata, M., Schwabe, G.: Fair AI: Challenges and Opportunities. Bus. Inf. Syst. Eng. **62**(4), 379–384 (2020). https://doi.org/10.1007/s12599-020-00650-3
22. Micheli, M., Lutz, C., Büchi, M.: Digital footprints: an emerging dimension of digital inequality. J. Inf. Commun. Ethics Soc. **16**(3), 242–251 (2018). https://doi.org/10.1108/JICES-02-2018-0014
23. Barocas, S., Selbst, A.D.: Big Data's Disparate Impact. SSRN Electron. J. (2016). https://doi.org/10.2139/ssrn.2477899
24. Le Quy, T., Roy, A., Iosifidis, V., Zhang, W., Ntoutsi, E.: A survey on datasets for fairness-aware machine learning. WIREs Data Min. Knowl. Discov. **12**(3), e1452 (2022). https://doi.org/10.1002/widm.1452
25. C. Dwork, M. Hardt, T. Pitassi, O. Reingold, and R. Zemel, "Fairness through awareness," in *Proceedings of the 3rd Innovations in Theoretical Computer Science Conference*, Cambridge Massachusetts: ACM, Jan. 2012, pp. 214–226. https://doi.org/10.1145/2090236.2090255
26. Bhatia, N., Bhatia, S.: Changes in Gender Stereotypes Over Time: A Computational Analysis. Psychol. Women Q. **45**(1), 106–125 (2021). https://doi.org/10.1177/0361684320977178
27. A. Nadeem, O. Marjanovic, and B. Abedin, "Gender bias in AI-based decision-making systems: a systematic literature review," *Australas. J. Inf. Syst.*, vol. 26, Dec. 2022, https://doi.org/10.3127/ajis.v26i0.3835
28. J. Kleinberg, S. Mullainathan, and M. Raghavan, "Inherent Trade-Offs in the Fair Determination of Risk Scores," Nov. 17, 2016, *arXiv*: arXiv:1609.05807. Accessed: Aug. 01, 2024. [Online]. Available: http://arxiv.org/abs/1609.05807
29. A. Nadeem, B. Abedin, and O. Marjanovic, "Gender Bias in AI: A Review of Contributing Factors and Mitigating Strategies," 2020
30. Koenig, A.M., Eagly, A.H.: Evidence for the social role theory of stereotype content: Observations of groups' roles shape stereotypes. J. Pers. Soc. Psychol. **107**(3), 371–392 (2014). https://doi.org/10.1037/a0037215
31. A. Koene, L. Dowthwaite, and S. Seth, "IEEE P7003TM Standard for Algorithmic Bias Considerations," 2018
32. A. Wang, X. Bai, S. Barocas, and S. L. Blodgett, "Measuring machine learning harms from stereotypes: requires understanding who is being harmed by which errors in what ways," Feb. 06, 2024, *arXiv*: arXiv:2402.04420. Accessed: Aug. 29, 2024. [Online]. Available: http://arxiv.org/abs/2402.04420

33. Z. Hussain et al., "Automatic Understanding of Image and Video Advertisements," Jul. 10, 2017, *arXiv*: arXiv:1707.03067. Accessed: Aug. 21, 2024. [Online]. Available: http://arxiv.org/abs/1707.03067
34. H. Weerts, M. Dudık, R. Edgar, A. Jalali, R. Lutz, and M. Madaio, "Fairlearn: Assessing and Improving Fairness of AI Systems," 2023
35. R. K. E. Bellamy et al., "AI Fairness 360: An extensible toolkit for detecting and mitigating algorithmic bias," *IBM J. Res. Dev.*, vol. 63, no. 4/5, p. 4:1–4:15, Jul. 2019, https://doi.org/10.1147/JRD.2019.2942287
36. D. D. Lewis, "Naive (Bayes) at forty: The independence assumption in information retrieval," in *Machine Learning: ECML-98*, vol. 1398, C. Nédellec and C. Rouveirol, Eds., in Lecture Notes in Computer Science, vol. 1398. , Berlin, Heidelberg: Springer Berlin Heidelberg, 1998, pp. 4–15. https://doi.org/10.1007/BFb0026666
37. L. Breiman, J. H. Friedman, R. A. Olshen, and C. J. Stone, "Classification And Regression Trees," 1984
38. Hearst, M.A., Dumais, S.T., Osuna, E., Platt, J., Scholkopf, B.: Support vector machines. IEEE Intell. Syst. Their Appl. **13**(4), 18–28 (1998). https://doi.org/10.1109/5254.708428
39. D. E. Rumelhart, G. E. Hintont, and R. J. Williams, "Learning representations by back-propagating errors," 1986
40. Lundberg, S.M., Lee, S.-I.: A Unified Approach to Interpreting Model Predictions (2017)
41. Wexler, J., Pushkarna, M., Bolukbasi, T., Wattenberg, M., Viegas, F., Wilson, J.: The What-If Tool: interactive probing of machine learning models. IEEE Trans. Vis. Comput. Graph. 1 (2019). https://doi.org/10.1109/TVCG.2019.2934619
42. Pagano, T.P., et al.: Bias and unfairness in machine learning models: a systematic review on datasets, tools, fairness metrics, and identification and mitigation methods. Big Data Cogn. Comput. **7**(1), 15 (2023). https://doi.org/10.3390/bdcc7010015

Superclass-Guided Hierarchical Learning for Action Anticipation

Shin Suzuki[1(✉)], Naoshi Kaneko[2], and Kazuhiko Sumi[1]

[1] Aoyama Gakuin University, Kanagawa, Japan
suzuki.shin@vss.it.aoyama.ac.jp, sumi@it.aoyama.ac.jp
[2] Tokyo Denki University, Tokyo, Japan
naoshi.kaneko@mail.dendai.ac.jp

Abstract. Action anticipation is crucial for intelligent systems such as autonomous vehicles and AR (Augmented Reality) devices. While existing studies focus on architectural improvement, they often overlook the hierarchical relationships between human intentions and their resulting behaviors. In this work, we propose *"Superclass"*, a novel approach that leverages hierarchical action labels to enhance action anticipation performance. Our method introduces additional annotations combining verbs, nouns, and actions to capture the complex relationships between different levels of human activity. We evaluate our approach by integrating Superclass with two different base models, AVT [8] and InAViT [13]. Experiments on the EPIC-KITCHENS-100 dataset demonstrate the effectiveness and broad applicability of our method. When applied to InAViT, the current top-performing model on EPIC-KITCHENS-100 evaluation server, Superclass improved the top-5 class mean accuracy for verbs, nouns, and actions by **0.62%**, **3.36%**, and **1.95%** respectively.

Keywords: Action anticipation · Hierarchical structure

1 Introduction

Anticipating near-future human actions is essential for intelligent systems. For autonomous vehicles, predicting pedestrian movements can determine critical driving decisions. For augmented reality systems, understanding upcoming actions in tasks like cooking enables timely assistance. While action recognition identifies ongoing activities, action anticipation enables proactive system responses by predicting future actions before they occur.

Action anticipation faces fundamental challenges due to the inherent uncertainty of future events. Past observations alone cannot definitively determine future actions, as multiple possibilities exist. Human actions typically follow structured patterns driven by underlying intentions. As illustrated in Fig. 1, high-level intentions guide sequences of specific actions. For instance, the intention of "washing dishes" comprises a sequence of actions: taking a plate, washing it, and putting it away. Understanding these hierarchical relationships between intentions and actions can help reduce prediction uncertainty.

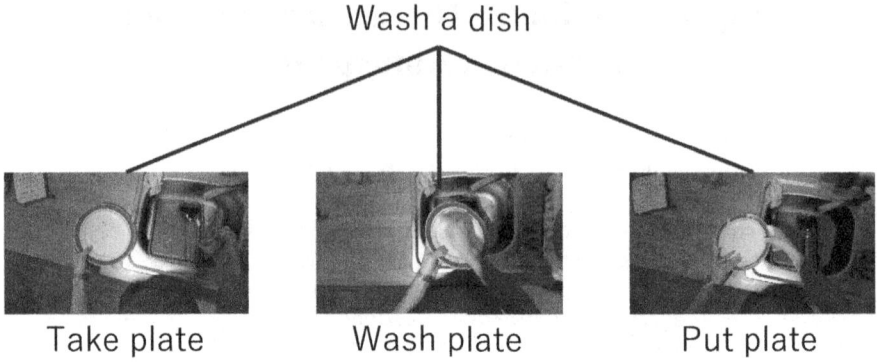

Fig. 1. The hierarchical relationship between intentions and actions. The high-level intention of washing dishes decomposes into a sequence of specific actions: taking a plate, washing it, and putting it away.

Recent advances in action anticipation have primarily focused on architectural innovations. RU-LSTM [7] pioneered the use of LSTMs for temporal modeling, while subsequent transformer-based approaches built upon AVT [8] explored various aspects like verb-noun relationships and dataset imbalance [4,5,9,10,14,16]. More recently, InAViT [13] achieved the highest performance on the EPIC-KITCHEN-100 evaluation server by modeling human-object interactions, while PlausiVL [11] achieved state-of-the-art performance by leveraging Large Language Model (LLM). However, these approaches largely overlook the hierarchical nature of human activities. We propose "Superclass", a novel labeling scheme that explicitly captures the hierarchical structure of actions (Fig. 1). Superclasses represent higher-level categories that integrate related actions, enabling models to learn the relationships between sequential actions and their underlying intentions. By incorporating superclass-based learning objectives, our approach helps models better understand action dependencies and improve prediction accuracy.

Our key contributions are:

1. We introduce a novel superclass labeling scheme that captures hierarchical relationships between actions and intentions, improving action anticipation performance.
2. The proposed approach is model-agnostic, demonstrating broad applicability by consistently improving performance across different architectures through our experiments.

2 Related Work

Action Anticipation predicts future actions from a given video clip, with first-person (egocentric) videos gaining prominence due to their applicability in wearable devices. The EPIC-KITCHENS-100 dataset [1–3] has become a standard benchmark for evaluating action anticipation methods.

Early approaches like RU-LSTM [7] utilized dual LSTM networks to encode observations and anticipate future actions. Recent work has shifted toward transformer-based architectures for their superior ability to capture long-range dependencies. AVT [8] pioneered this transition by extending the Vision Transformer (ViT) architecture with causal masked attention. This approach combines a ViT-based backbone for feature extraction with a Causal Transformer Decoder for action prediction.

Recently, several approaches have explored different aspects of action anticipation. MeMViT [16] addressed the challenge of long-term video understanding. Their methods maintain compressed memory as they process a video in an online fashion. InAViT [13] achieved leading performance on EPIC-KITCHENS-100 by focusing on human-object interaction and appearance changes. The latest work, PlausiVL [11], achieved state-of-the-art performance by utilizing the generative capability of LLM and understanding the plausibility in an action sequence. Specifically, this work introduced additional labels of verb-noun co-occurrence and irreversibility pair of actions.

While existing approaches have advanced the field significantly, they primarily treat actions as isolated events, overlooking the hierarchical nature of human behavior. Our work addresses this limitation by explicitly modeling the hierarchical relationships between high-level intentions and their constituent actions. By incorporating both intention-level and action-level information, we enhance prediction accuracy.

3 Method

Action anticipation involves predicting future actions before they occur by analyzing observed video segments. While existing approaches have focused on architectural innovations and feature encoding, we propose "Superclass", a novel labeling scheme that captures the hierarchical relationships between actions. To validate our approach, we integrate superclass labels with two base models: AVT, which established the foundational transformer architecture for action anticipation, and InAViT, currently the highest-performing publicly available model.

The key insight behind our approach is that human actions typically follow structured patterns driven by underlying intentions. By incorporating superclass labels through an additional loss term, our method enables models to better understand action continuity and their hierarchical relationships. We organize the presentation of our method into the following sections:

1. Task definition of action anticipation (3.1)
2. Superclass generation methodology (3.2)
3. Integration framework for base models (3.3)
4. Superclass implementation with AVT (3.4)
5. Superclass implementation with InAViT (3.5)

3.1 Task Definition

In this work, we follow the standard action anticipation framework established by recent benchmark challenges [1, 3]. As illustrated in Fig. 2, the task involves two key temporal parameters:

Fig. 2. Action anticipation task requires predicting future actions τ_α seconds ahead based on an observation window of τ_o seconds.

- An observation window of duration τ_o seconds, during which the model analyzes the input video
- An anticipation time τ_α seconds, representing the time gap between the end of observation and the start of the future action to be predicted

The model must process the observed video segment to predict actions that will occur τ_α seconds in the future. This temporal structure enables evaluation of the model's ability to anticipate actions before they begin, making it particularly relevant for real-world applications requiring proactive responses.

3.2 Superclass Generation

Superclass labels represent higher-level patterns in actions sequences, capturing the hierarchical structure of complex activities. We develop an automated process to generate these superclass labels from existing annotations.

Generation Algorithm. The superclass generation process is applied separately to verb, noun and action sequences, with each following these four steps:

1. **Label Extraction:**
   - Extract verb sequences from verb annotations
   - Extract noun sequences from noun annotations
   - Extract action sequences from action annotations
2. **Pattern Identification** (For each sequence type (verb/noun/action)):
   Detect consecutive label patterns of length m to n ($m = 2$, $n = 5$) and count their occurrences. These patterns form the initial superclass candidates. (Note: In this paper, m and n are set to 2 and 5, since the minimum consecutive label patterns are 2 and there are no label patterns whose length is more than 5.)
3. **Superclass Assignment** (For each time step in each sequence type):
   - Identify all available superclass candidates
   - Select the longest available pattern as the superclass
   - Assign "no-superclass" when no patterns are available
4. **Filtering:** Remove the superclass occurring ≤ 50 times in the dataset to filter out trivial patterns.

This process generates three distinct sets of superclass: verb superclass from verb sequences, noun superclass from noun sequences, and action superclasses from action sequences, each capturing type-specific patterns while maintaining statistical reliability.

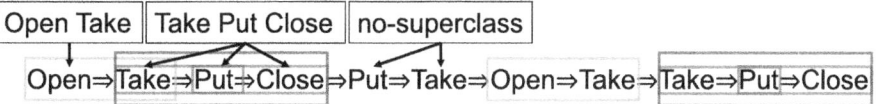

Fig. 3. Illustration of the superclass generation process, showing pattern identification and assignment across a sequence of verb labels. Colored boxes indicate identified patterns of varying lengths.

Example Process. Figure 3 illustrates the generation process using a verb sequence example. Here, we demonstrate verb superclass generation, and the same process is applied independently to noun and action sequences.

Input sequence is *open, take, put, close, put, take, open, take, take, put, close*, and the algorithm processes this sequence as follows:

1. Identifying recurring patterns of length 2–5
2. Creates superclass candidates (shown in the colored boxes)
3. Assigns superclasses at each time step by selecting the longest available pattern:
   – First position: assigns "open, take" (only available candidate)
   – Next three positions: assigns "take, put, close" (longest available pattern)
   – Positions 4–5: assigns "no-superclass" (no candidates available)

This process continues throughout the sequence, prioritizing longer patterns to capture more complex action relationships. While the example uses a minimum occurrence threshold of 2 for illustration, the actual implementation requires 50 occurrences to ensure robust pattern identification. The same process is applied separately to generate noun superclass from noun sequences and action superclass from action sequences.

3.3 Superclass with Base Models

Integration Architecture. Our approach enhances base models by adding a parallel classifier for superclass prediction at the same layer used for future action prediction (Fig. 4). This architectural modification enables multitask learning while maintaining the core functionality of the original models.

Learning Objectives. The enhanced model simultaneously optimizes two objectives:

– Primary task: predicting specific future actions
– Secondary task: predicting superclass labels that capture action hierarchies

Loss Function. The total loss function becomes:

$$L_{total} = L_{base} + L_{superclass} \tag{1}$$

where L_{base} is the original model's loss function and $L_{superclass}$ follows the same computational structure as the base loss but applies to superclass predictions.

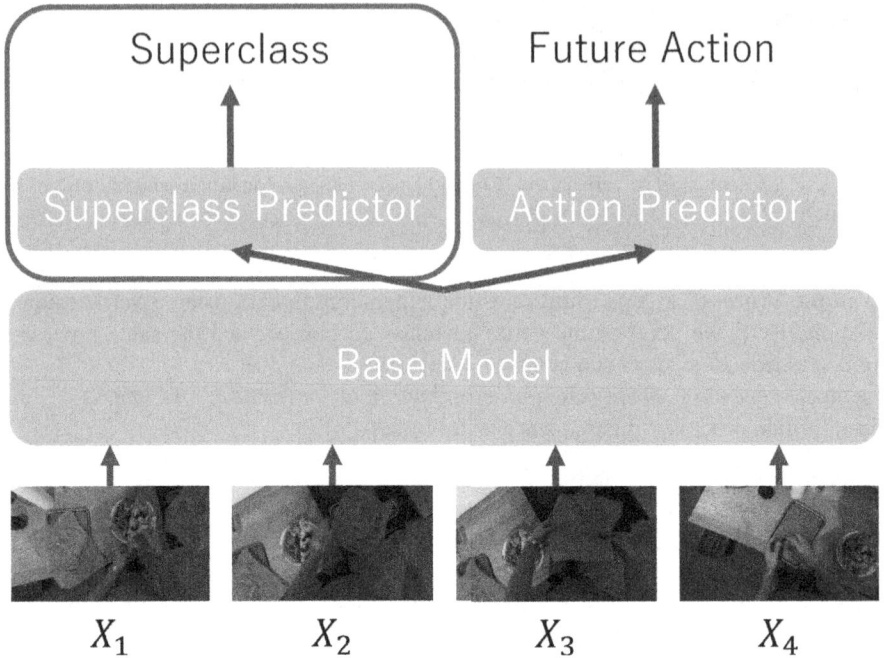

Fig. 4. Architecture overview showing the integration of superclass prediction. The additional classifier (highlighted) operates in parallel with the original action prediction pathway, sharing the same feature extraction backbone.

3.4 Superclass with AVT

We enhance the AVT model by incorporating superclass prediction capabilities while maintaining its core architecture. Figure 5 illustrates our modified approach.

Architecture Components. The enhanced model consists of three main components. First, the observed frames are inputted to the Transformer Encoder, which is based on Vision Transformer (ViT) [6]. Second, features from the Transformer Encoder, z, are forwarded to the causal transformer decoder, which only attends on the past frame features. Finally, we pass those obtained features, $\hat{z}$, from the decoder to prediction heads which are separately constructed for predicting future action $\hat{y}$ and superclass labels, respectively.

Loss Functions. We extend AVT's original three losses, next-action loss, future feature loss, and action class loss, with two additional superclass-specific losses, next-superclass loss and superclass loss which are same losses as next-action loss and action class loss, to supervise the network.

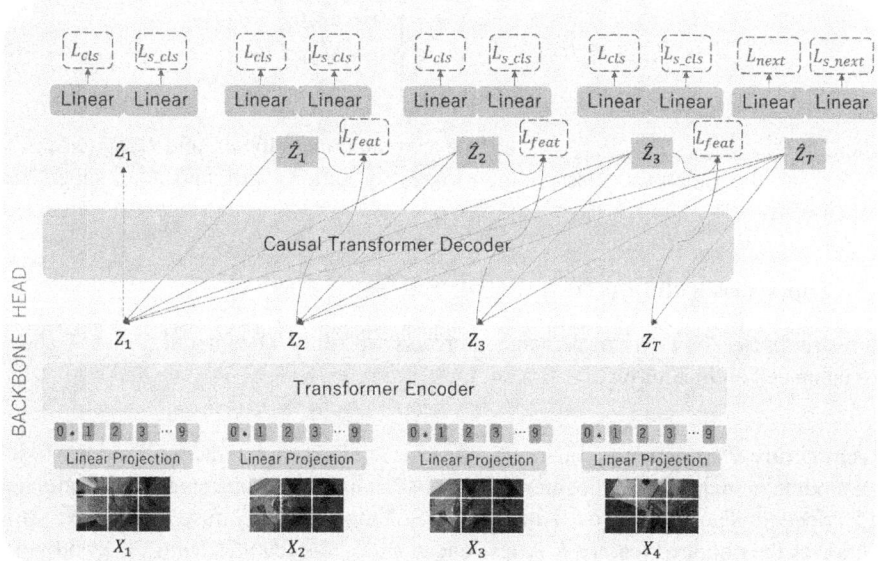

Fig. 5. Model architecture. Bottom: Backbone network processes T input frames through Transformer Encoder to generate frame features $\{z_1, ..., z_T\}$. Top: Head network processes features through Causal Transformer Decoder to generate future features $\hat{z}_1, ..., \hat{z}_T$, optimizing feature regression (L_{feat}), action prediction (L_{cls} and L_{next}), and superclass prediction (L_{s_cls} and L_{s_next}).

Next-Action Loss. Supervise future action prediction using cross-entropy between predicted and true future actions:

$$L_{next} = -\log \hat{\mathbf{y}}_T[c_{T+1}]. \tag{2}$$

where c_{T+1} represents the labeled future action.

Future Feature Loss. Ensure accurate intermediate feature prediction by minimizing L2 distance between predicted and true features:

$$L_{feat} = \sum_{t=1}^{T-1} \|\hat{z}_t - z_{t+1}\|_2^2 \tag{3}$$

Action Class Loss. The model supervises intermediate future predictions using available action labels in the dataset. When there are earlier frames which don't have labels, we set $c_t = -1$ for the loss:

$$L_{cls} = \sum_{t=1}^{T-1} L_{cls}^t; \qquad L_{cls}^t = \begin{cases} -\log \hat{\mathbf{y}}_t[c_{t+1}] & \text{if } c_t + 1 \geq 0 \\ 0 & \text{otherwise.} \end{cases} \tag{4}$$

We introduce superclass losses for verb, noun and action superclass, each having components same as the next-action loss and action class loss. The total loss function combines base model losses with superclass-specific losses:

$$L = L_{next} + L_{cls} + L_{feat} + \begin{cases} L_{as\_next} + L_{as\_cls} \\ L_{vs\_next} + L_{vs\_cls} \\ L_{ns\_next} + L_{ns\_cls} \end{cases} \quad (5)$$

where L_{as_next}, L_{vs_next}, L_{ns_next} are the next-superclass losses, and L_{as_cls}, L_{vs_cls}, L_{ns_cls} are the superclass classification losses for action, verb, and noun superclass, respectively.

3.5 Superclass with InAViT

Here we discuss how we implement superclass with InAViT in detail. Figure 6 shows the enhanced architecture.

Architecture Components. First, video frames are fed into Interaction Region Modeling module, which capture the interaction between hands and objects by cross-attention [15]. Second, Trajectory Cross Attention (TCA) module [12] infuse the context information to the obtained feature I. After concatenating the features from TCA and video tokens, we feed the features to the Trajectory Attention [12] to obtain interaction-centric video representation X_i. Finally, X_i is fed into two linear layers to predict next action $\hat{y}$ and superclass.

Loss Functions. To train the model, we use the cross-entropy loss for next action and superclass with the labeled future action:

$$L_{next} = -\log \hat{\mathbf{y}}_T[c_{T+1}]. \quad (6)$$

where c_{T+1} represents the labeled future action.

Therefore, the overall loss is:

$$L = L_{next} + \begin{cases} L_{as\_next} \\ L_{vs\_next} \\ L_{ns\_next} \end{cases} \quad (7)$$

where L_{as_next}, L_{vs_next}, L_{ns_next} are the next-superclass losses for action, verb, and noun superclass, respectively.

4 Experiments

We evaluate the effectiveness of our superclass approach using two base models, AVT [8] and InAViT [13]. We start by describing the dataset and evaluation metrics, followed by main result, ablation studies, and state-of-the-art comparison.

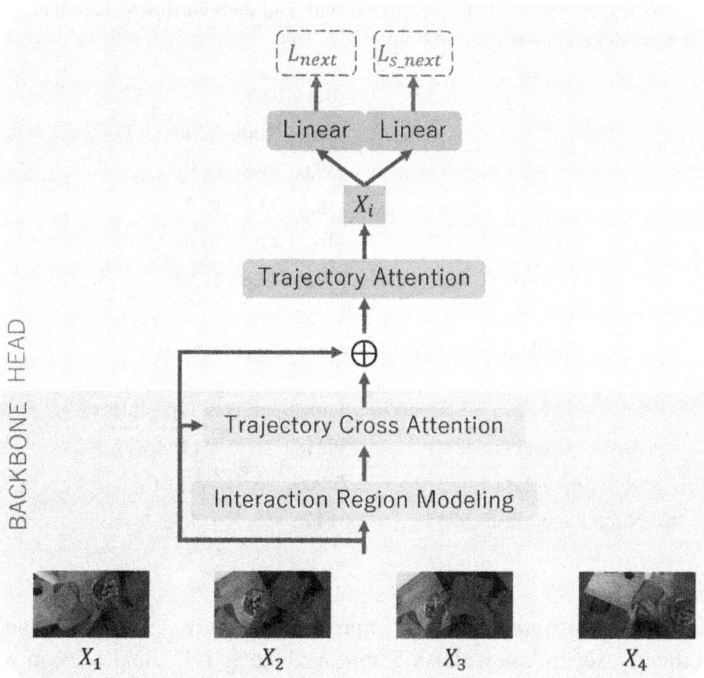

Fig. 6. Model architecture based on InAViT.

4.1 Dataset and Metrics

We test on EPIC-KITCHENS-100 (EK100) dataset [3]. EK100 is an egocentric video dataset featuring non-scripted videos of daily activities in kitchen environments, totaling 100 h of footage. The dataset comprises 97 verb classes and 300 noun classes, providing a rich and diverse set of actions for anticipation tasks. We use the train and val splits as defined by [7]. As evaluation metrics, we use top-5 class mean accuracy (recall@5) as our primary evaluation metric. This metric is particularly suitable for datasets with long-tail distribution as it equally weights all classes. Recall@5 is calculated using the following equation:

$$Recall@5 = \frac{1}{N} \sum_{i=1}^{N} acc_i. \tag{8}$$

where N is the number of classes, and acc_i is the accuracy for the samples in class i.

4.2 Main Result

We evaluate the impact of superclass integration on both base models. Since EK100 contains verb, noun, action labels, we train separate models with corresponding superclasses and ensemble them with equal weights. Table 1 presents the comprehensive results.

Table 1. Performance comparison of base models with and without superclass enhancement. Best results for each model and metric are in bold.

	Recall@5		
	Verb	Noun	Action
AVT	30.0	31.8	14.9
AVT w/ Superclass	**30.6**	**33.2**	**16.5**
InAViT	40.11	41.11	20.03
InAViT w/ Superclass	**40.46**	**43.89**	**21.94**

Table 2. Superclass Coverage in Training Data.

	# Superclass	# no-superclass	Superclass (%)
Action Superclass	8001	59216	11.90
Verb Superclass	37314	29903	55.51
Noun Superclass	5745	61472	8.55

Our results demonstrate consistent improvements across all metrics and architectures. Specifically, superclass with AVT improved 0.6%, 1.4%, and 1.6% in verb, noun, and action recall@5 from the pre-trained base model, and superclass with InAViT improved 0.35%, 2.78%, 1.91% from the pre-trained base model, respectively. These improvements validate both the effectiveness of superclass integration and its applicability across difference model architectures. The consistent gains across all metrics suggest that hierarchical action understanding through superclasses provides valuable additional context for action anticipation.

4.3 Ablations

We now analyze how each superclass contributes to action anticipation performance.

Superclass Statistics. Following our superclass generation methodology (3.2), we created 202 verb superclass, 41 noun superclass, and 47 action superclass. We first examine the dataset coverage of different superclass types. Table 2 and Table 3 present the statistics for training and validation sets, respectively. Verb superclasses achieve 50% coverage of the dataset, while action and noun superclasses cover approximately 10% each. While our results demonstrate the effectiveness of superclass-enhanced prediction, the limited coverage of action and noun superclasses suggests potential for improvement. Future work should focus on developing methods to increase superclass coverage while maintaining semantic meaningfulness.

Superclass Effects on AVT. Table 4 shows how different superclass types affect AVT performance. Each superclass type demonstrates strongest improvement in its corre-

Table 3. Superclass Coverage in Validation Data.

	# Superclass	# no-superclass	Superclass (%)
Action Superclass	1016	8652	10.51
Verb Superclass	4674	4994	48.35
Noun Superclass	584	9084	6.04

Table 4. AVT with Different Superclass.

	Recall@5		
	Verb	Noun	Action
AVT	30.0	31.8	14.9
Ours w/ Verb Superclass	**30.5**	32.0	14.2
Ours w/ Noun Superclass	29.9	**33.2**	15.2
Ours w/ Action Superclass	29.8	32.8	**15.3**

sponding metric. Verb superclass improved verb recall@5 at the most among all superclass, and we obtained same results for noun superclass and action superclass.

Notably, noun prediction shows the largest absolute improvement (1.5%), compared to verb (0.3%) and action (0.4%) metrics. This superior performance in noun prediction likely stems from the temporal stability of object interactions—while actions frequently change in a sequence, the objects being manipulated tend to remain consistent, allowing the superclass structure to capture more stable patterns.

Superclass Effects on InAViT. We evaluate our superclass approach on pre-trained model of InAViT [13], the current top-performing model on the EPIC-KITCHENS-100 evaluation server, in Table 5. Unlike AVT, InAViT shows different patterns of improve-

Table 5. InAViT with Different Superclass.

	Recall@5		
	Verb	Noun	Action
InAViT	40.11	41.11	20.03
Ours w/ Verb Superclass	40.60	43.16	**22.09**
Ours w/ Noun Superclass	40.66	43.47	22.02
Ours w/ Action Superclass	**40.73**	**44.47**	21.98

ment across superclass types, suggesting that model architecture influences how hierarchical information is utilized. However, the strong improvement in noun prediction remains consistent across both architectures, reinforcing our hypothesis about the stability of object-related patterns in action sequences.

Qualitative Results. We analyze how superclass integration affects prediction patterns by comparing base AVT predictions with superclass-enhanced predictions. Table 6 presents this analysis, where rows indicate prediction transition and columns show the percentage of predictions containing each superclass type. The results reveal two sig-

Table 6. Compare effect of Superclass on predictions.

	Percentage of Superclass (%)		
	Verb Superclass	Noun Superclass	Action Superclass
False to True	52.6	9.6	11.7
Remain False	45.1	4.9	8.8
True to False	51.3	8.4	13.1
Remain True	56.0	9.9	14.4

nificant patterns. First, we found the improvement in false predictions. When we look at first and second rows, "False to True" rate exceeds "Remain False" across all superclass type. This means that predictions which have superclass are more likely to become true. Second, we found the stability of true predictions. When we look at third and fourth rows, "Remain True" rate exceeds "True to False" across all categories. This means that predictions which have superclass are more likely to stay true. This analysis provides strong evidence that superclass information positively influences the model's prediction accuracy and stability.

Next, we conducted a qualitative analysis of prediction changes between base AVT and superclass-enhanced AVT, revealing distinct patterns in prediction success base on action complexity. We found that there are *Predictable* and *Unpredictable* cases in the results. We also found that *Predictable* actions were different between the case, which predictions changed *False to True*, and the case, which predictions changed *True to False*. *Predictable* actions in *False to True* case were simple like washing dishes, take a thing then put a thing, and put things back to the cupboard, but actions in *True to False* were complex in terms of containing multiple intentions such as put things into somewhere after cutting it containing cutting and putting, put foods back to somewhere after pouring into somewhere containing pouring and putting back. These patterns suggest that superclass enhancement effectively captures simple, single-intention action sequences but may struggle with complex, multi-intention scenarios. Examples of these patterns are illustrated in Figs. 7 and 8, where the target prediction is the final action in each sequence.

Fig. 7. Example of predictable action sequences where superclass integration improved predictions (False → True) **Top:** Washing sequence showing consistent intention of cleaning pot. **Middle:** Take-and-put sequence demonstrating clear object manipulation pattern. **Bottom:** Storage sequence showing coherent intention of returning pot to cupboard. Each sequence shows strong alignment between observed actions and final predicted action.

Fig. 8. Examples of action sequences where superclass integration degraded correct predictions (True → False). **Top:** Multi-task sequence combining cutting and storing actions - cutting cucumber followed by storing cut pieces, demonstrating distinct sub-tasks within a single sequence. **Bottom:** Composite sequence showing pouring followed by storage actions - illustrating how transitions between different functional intentions can complicate prediction. Both cases show how multiple distinct intentions within a sequence can challenge the superclass-based prediction model.

We examined cases where predictions remained incorrect *False to False* even after superclass integration. Most of these case involved action sequences with abrupt intention shifts. We found that most of the actions are *Unpredictable* because they are done in different intention. We show examples in Fig. 9. Look at the top actions. We can observe the sudden changes in action patterns. The first three actions are related to washing hands, but the last action are different from washing hands which indicates last

Fig. 9. Examples of unpredictable action sequences where both base and superclass models fail (False → False). **Top:** Intention shift from hand-washing sequence to refrigerator access, showing abrupt context change. **Middle:** Complex sequence interruption - pasta serving disrupted by discovery of dirty utensil, leading to unexpected tool replacement action. **Bottom:** Multiple intention shifts - transition from milk retrieval to unrelated food mixing activity. All sequences demonstrate how sudden changes in underlying intentions create fundamental prediction challenges.

action is done by different intention. The other two last actions are also done by different intentions from the observed actions. These findings suggest that action anticipation becomes particularly challenging when there are discontinuities in underlying intentions, regardless of superclass enhancement. This highlights a fundamental limitation in predicting actions that deviate from established behavioral patterns.

4.4 SOTA Comparison

We now compare our superclass-enhanced against leading approaches in action anticipation. Table 7 presents comprehensive comparison results. Our superclass approach demonstrates consistent improvements across different architecture. Superclass integration enhances AVT's basic transformer architecture across all metrics and significantly improves InAViT's pre-trained model performance. While PlausiVL [11] currently holds the state-of-the-art position, its implementation remains closed-source.

Table 7. Comparison with state-of-the-art methods on EPIC-KITCHENS-100 validation set.

Method	Recall@5		
	Verb	Noun	Action
AVT [8]	30.0	31.8	14.9
InAViT (Original paper) [13]	52.54	51.93	25.89
InAViT (Pre-trained model) [13]	40.11	41.11	20.03
PlausiVL [11]	55.62	54.23	27.60
AVT w/ Superclass Ensemble (Ours)	30.6	33.2	16.5
InAViT w/ Action Superclass (Ours)	40.73	44.47	21.98

5 Conclusions

We presented a novel approach to action anticipation that leverages superclass integration to capture hierarchical relationships between actions and intentions. Unlike previous methods that focused primarily on isolated actions, our approach recognizes that human actions typically follow intention-driven patterns.

Through experiments, we found that training AVT with superclass improved verb, noun, and action recall@5 **0.6%**, **1.4%**, and **1.6%**, respectively. Training InAViT with superclass exceed verb, noun, and action recall@5 up to **0.35%**, **2.78%**, and **1.91%**, respectively. This shows the effectiveness and applicability of the superclass.

Limitations and Future Work. Although our approach provides a new perspective in action anticipation task, there are limitations that are worth pointing out. Generated superclass could improve the performance of action anticipation. However, generated superclass didn't cover the whole annotation. We think this is a problem for further improving the performance. Another limitation is the superclass covering range. In this paper, we generated superclass by grouping 2 to 5 consecutive labels, but this only covers short term intentions. One possible approach is using the power of generative ability of LLMs. This might help generating rich variety superclass. Finally, our work is rather passive than active approach. Building a new model for effectively utilizing superclass is needed.

Acknowledgments. Part of this research was operated as the project of Center for Advanced Information technology Research (CAIR), Aoyama Gakuin University.

References

1. Damen, D., et al.: Scaling egocentric vision: the EPIC-KITCHENS dataset. In: Proceedings of the European Conference on Computer Vision (ECCV), pp. 753–771 (2018)
2. Damen, D., et al.: The EPIC-KITCHENS dataset: collection, challenges and baselines. IEEE Trans. Pattern Anal. Mach. Intell. (TPAMI) **43**(11), 4125–4141 (2021). https://doi.org/10.1109/TPAMI.2020.2991965

3. Damen, D., et al.: Rescaling egocentric vision: collection, pipeline and challenges for EPICKITCHENS-100. Int. J. Comput. Vis. (IJCV) **130**, 33–55 (2022). https://doi.org/10.1007/s11263-021-01531-2
4. Damen, D., et al.: EPIC-KITCHENS-100- 2021 challenges report. University of Bristol, Technical report (2021). https://epic-kitchens.github.io/Reports/EPIC-KITCHENS-Challenges-2021-Report.pdf
5. Damen, D., et al.: EPIC-KITCHENS-100- 2022 challenges report. University of Bristol, Technical report (2022). https://epic-kitchens.github.io/Reports/EPIC-KITCHENS-Challenges-2022-Report.pdf
6. Dosovitskiy, A., et al.: An image is worth 16x16 words: transformers for image recognition at scale. In: Proceedings of the International Conference on Learning Representations (ICLR) (2021). https://openreview.net/forum?id=YicbFdNTTy
7. Furnari, A., Farinella, G.M.: What would you expect? Anticipating egocentric actions with rolling-unrolling LSTMs and modality attention. In: Proceedings of the IEEE/CVF International Conference on Computer Vision (ICCV), pp. 6251–6260 (2019)
8. Girdhar, R., Grauman, K.: Anticipative video transformer. In: Proceedings of the IEEE/CVF International Conference on Computer Vision (ICCV), pp. 13485–13495 (2021)
9. Gu, X., Qiu, J., Guo, Y., Lo, B., Yang, G.Z.: TransAction: ICL-SJTU submission to EPICkitchens action anticipation challenge 2021. arXiv preprint arXiv:2107.13259 (2021)
10. Jiang, Z., Ding, C.: 1st place solution to the EPIC-Kitchens Action Anticipation Challenge 2022. arXiv preprint arXiv:2207.05730 (2022)
11. Mittal, H., Agarwal, N., Lo, S.Y., Lee, K.: Can't make an omelette without breaking some eggs: plausible action anticipation using large video-language models. In: Proceedings of the IEEE/CVF Conference on Computer Vision and Pattern Recognition (CVPR), pp. 18580–18590 (2024) 18590 (2024)
12. Patrick, M., et al.: Keeping your eye on the ball: trajectory attention in video transformers. In: Advances in Neural Information Processing Systems (NeurIPS), vol. 34, pp. 12493–12506 (2021)
13. Roy, D., Rajendiran, R., Fernando, B.: Interaction visual transformer for egocentric action anticipation. arXiv preprint arXiv:2211.14154 (2022)
14. Tai, T.M., et al.: NVIDIA-UNIBZ submission for EPIC-KITCHENS-100 Action Anticipation Challenge 2022. arXiv preprint arXiv:2206.10869 (2022)
15. Vaswani, A., et al.: Attention is all you need. In: Advances in Neural Information Processing Systems (NIPS), vol. 30, pp. 5998–6008 (2017)
16. Wu, C.Y., et al.: MeMViT: memory-augmented multiscale vision transformer for efficient long-term video recognition. In: Proceedings of the IEEE/CVF Conference on Computer Vision and Pattern Recognition (CVPR), pp. 13577–13587 (2022)

Cricket Bowling Action Recognition with Transformer-Based Models

Bigyan Subedi[1(✉)], Bishwambhar Dahal[2], Sirjana Bhatta[2,3], Sonish Maharjan[1], and Sushmita Poudel[1]

[1] Fuse Machines, Kathmandu, Nepal
bigyaaan@gmail.com
[2] Department of Electronics and Computer Engineering, Thapathali Campus, Institute of Engineering, Tribhuvan University, Kathmandu, Nepal
[3] Javra Software, Lalitpur, Nepal

Abstract. Computer vision-based video action recognition has led to significant advancements in sports analytics, streamlining the previous labour-intensive tasks of sensor-based or manual analysis through automated video processing. This paper focuses on applying transformer-based video action recognition models to classify cricket bowling actions. For this, we created a novel dataset named ActionBowl, designed to support multiple specialized classification schemes. We trained and evaluated state-of-the-art transformer based action recognition models- ActionCLIP, TimeSformer and UniFormerV2 on these datasets. This paper aims to highlight the effectiveness of these models in recognizing actions that range from subtle variations to significantly distinct hand movements. Through rigorous evaluation, we provide conclusive evidence of these models' ability to learn and distinguish this unique set of actions effectively. It presents a comprehensive analysis of the experiments, results, and insights drawn from the study, highlighting the potential for further advancements in cricket analytics through video-based action recognition.

Keywords: ActionBowl · ActionCLIP · TimeSformer · UniFormerV2

1 Introduction

In recent years, video understanding, particularly action recognition, has seen tremendous growth, spurred by large datasets like Kinetics 400/600/700 [5,6,21], Something-Something V1/V2 [16], and Diving48 [27]. Some models such as ActionCLIP [43], Uniformer V1/V2 [25,26], and TimeSformer [4] have emerged as leading architectures in this field. Video understanding has also gained prominence in sports, where coaches and analysts use metrics to assess player's and team's performance. Automated systems track and analyze player movements, identify key actions, and assist in tactical analysis and highlight generation [30,44,45]. For example, the National Basketball Association (NBA) uses such technology to analyze player movements, shot types, and defensive strategies, while cricket was an early adopter with the introduction of the Hawk-Eye system to aid umpire decision-making [20]. This study focuses on further advancing computer vision technologies to better understand and analyze cricket's unique dynamics.

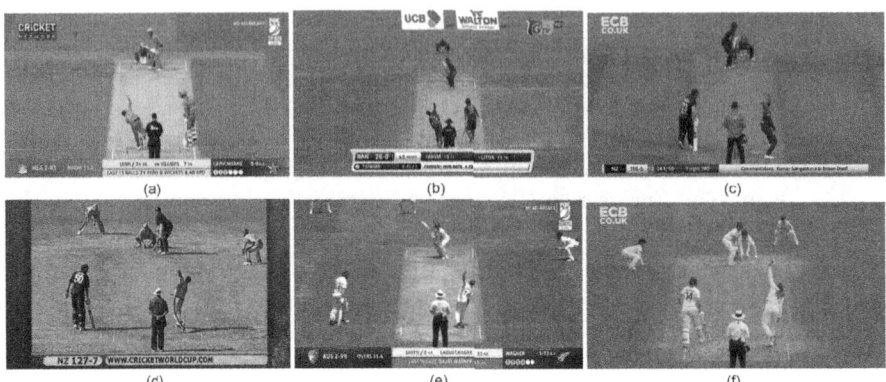

Fig. 1. Sample frames from the ActionBowl dataset showcasing various bowling styles, including (a) Right Arm Leg Spin, (b) Right Arm Fast Bowling, (c) Right Arm Off Spin, (d) Left Arm Leg Spin, (e) Left Arm Fast Bowling, and (f) Left Arm Off Spin. These frames illustrate the diverse range of bowling actions.

Cricket is a favorite sport among participants and spectators in almost all countries around the globe. It encompasses several approaches and methods, especially those promoted by the bowling aspect. The type of bowling is determined with regard to movement, spin, and pace of the bowler. By analyzing these factors, valuable insights can be derived, aiding in the enhancement of techniques, strategies, and overall development of the sport. This can significantly contribute to enhance player's skills and improve intuition of game dynamics, ultimately pushing the boundaries of cricket's evolution. Although there are many action recognition models present in the literature [3,4,26,40,41,43,44,49], there is comparatively very less work done in the area of cricket bowling actions.

The identification of bowling actions is quite hard because of the speed at which the bowler is moving and the subtle difference between various bowling styles. Existing studies have often focused on other facets in cricket [9,13,18,35,36], leaving analysis of bowling actions behind. To address this need, we developed ActionBowl video dataset which aims to add the bowling aspect that is lacking in existing cricket related datasets. It is annotated in two ways: one consisting of bowling actions divided into three classes: Fast Bowling, Leg Spin and Off Spin and another divided into six classes: Right Arm and Left Arm Fast Bowling, Right Arm and Left Arm Leg Spin, and Right Arm and Left Arm Off Spin. By leveraging the advanced video action recognition models-ActionCLIP [43], TimeSformer [4] and UniFormerV2 [25] in our 3-class and 6-class Action-Bowl dataset, this study aims to explore and compare the effectiveness of these models in bowling action recognition.

2 Literature Review

Deep Learning (DL) has revolutionized the field of computer vision over the past decade, particularly in the domain of action recognition, where the ability to identify and classify dynamic human actions has gained significant attention. Early models for action recognition relied heavily on traditional computer vision techniques, such as hand-crafted features (e.g. HOG, SIFT) [46], combined with classifiers like SVM. However, these models struggled to generalize complex and diverse kind of actions in videos, leading to the adoption of two-stream network, 3D CNN and now transformer-based techniques.

With the limitations of earlier approaches, the introduction of Two-stream ConvNet [38] marked a significant milestone in action recognition by employing distinct modules to process spatial and temporal information. One stream extracts spatial features from individual video frames, while the other captures motion dynamics using optical flow between frames. This innovative design laid the foundation for subsequent advancements in the field. In recent years, Vision Transformers (ViTs) [10] have emerged as a transformative approach, shifting from traditional CNNs to transformer-based models. ViTs excel in handling long-range dependencies within images, enabling state-of-the-art performance in video action recognition. Building on the ViT framework, models like TimeSformer [4], ActionCLIP [43], and UniFormerV2 [25] incorporate transformer architectures to seamlessly process spatiotemporal data, further pushing the boundaries of video understanding and setting new benchmarks in the domain.

2.1 Action Recognition Datasets in Sports

In recent years, several datasets have emerged to advance video action recognition across various sports. For football, datasets like Football Action [42], SoccerNet [14], SoccerNet-v2 [8], SSET [12] and ComprehensiveSoccer [47] have been immaculate. In basketball, Basket-1,2 [28], NCAA [33], FineBasketball [17] have been influential whereas, in volleyball, HierVolleyball-v2 [19] offers annotations for both individual and team actions. In tennis, the ACASVA [7] dataset focuses on fundamental actions, THETIS [15] supports multi-modal recognition with RGB, depth, and skeleton data, and TenniSet [11] provides event labels and textual descriptions for action retrieval.

2.2 Action Recognition Datasets in Cricket

Several datasets have been developed related to cricket video understanding as well, each with unique characteristics and contributions to the field. Ahmad et al. [1] introduced a dataset of 722 short video clips, featuring five batting actions for action recognition tasks. Another dataset, CricShot10, introduced by Sen et al. [36], extends the scope by focusing on 10 different types of cricket batting shots. Sharma et al. [37] introduced dataset derived from 16 Indian Premier League (IPL) matches, totaling around 64 h of footage. Lastly, Kumar et al. [24] posited a dataset from an 8-over cricket match, comprising 29,000 frames for training and 14,000 for testing, with K=3 cross-validation for activity detection. These datasets collectively contribute to the advancement of cricket action recognition by providing diverse and specialized resources for training and testing models.

2.3 Related Works in Action Recognition

There have been several works done in video understanding in the cricketing world. Harikrishna et al. [18] introduced methods to classify shots into run, four, six, and out. Dixit and Balakrishnan [9] compared three different CNN-based models to classify ball-by-ball outcomes in sports, especially cricket. They classified shots into run, no run, boundary, and wicket.

Some work has been done in classifying cricket batting shots. Sen et al. [36] proposed a hybrid deep neural network architecture that classifies 10 different cricket batting shots from videos. Foysal et al. [13] proposed a 13-layer CNN model to classify cricket shots into six categories using a custom dataset. Semwal et al. [35] proposed a pretrained CNN and multi class SVM to classify 3 types of batting shots for left-hand and right-hand batsmen. Additionally, image models have also been used in classifying cricket activity recognition. Al Islam et al. [2] added a few layers on top of the VGG16 [39] model to classify eighteen bowlers based on their bowling action. Rahman et al. [32] leveraged preliminary CNN architectures and transfer learning models to accurately classify different bowler grips.

Some research used wearable technology for cricket activity recognition. Khan et al. [22] developed a system using body-worn sensors to recognize and analyze cricket batting shots, providing performance feedback and visualizations to help players improve their skills. Salman et al. [34] developed a system to detect the legality of bowling actions using real-time, multidimensional physiological data collected from inertial sensors attached to the bowler's arm.

Kolekar et al. [23] presented a hierarchical framework to detect cricket events: excitement detection, replay detection, fieldview detection, fieldview classification, close-up detection, close-up classification, and crowd classification. Premaratne and Jayaratne [31] introduced a structural method to identify different cricket events, using algorithms such as KNN, Sequential-Minimal-Optimization, Decision-Tree and Naive Bayes Classifiers for detecting events.

The previous work mentioned above does not specifically focus on video-based bowling action recognition, which is a crucial aspect of automatic cricket video analysis. While some studies have attempted to address the bowling action, they have primarily used sensors and older CNN models. Therefore, our research can be a stepping stone for cricket bowling action recognition field and the whole cricket video action recognition world altogether.

3 Methodology

3.1 The ActionBowl Dataset

The ActionBowl dataset was meticulously developed to advance the classification and recognition of bowling actions in cricket. It contains 2571 video clips of aver-

Table 1. Distribution of Training and Validation Samples of ActionBowl dataset for 3-Class and 6-Class Cricket Bowling Actions. The table presents the number of video samples used for training (Train) and validation (Val) for different cricket bowling action classes. For the 3-Class classification, the data is categorized into Fast Bowling, Leg Spin, and Off Spin. For the 6-Class classification, the data is further divided based on the bowler's bowling hand (Left or Right) for each class.

Class	3-Class			6-Class		
	Train	Val	Total	Train	Val	Total
Fast Bowling	843	163	1006	405 (Left)	76 (Left)	481 (Left)
				438 (Right)	87 (Right)	525 (Right)
Leg Spin	567	113	680	286 (Left)	59 (Left)	345 (Left)
				281 (Right)	54 (Right)	335 (Right)
Off Spin	751	134	885	373 (Left)	69 (Left)	442 (Left)
				378 (Right)	65 (Right)	443 (Right)
Total	2161	410	2571	2161	410	2571

age video length of around 2 s. The videos have a resolution of 1280 × 720 pixels and a frame rate of 25 frames per second. This dataset consists of two distinct classification schemes to cater to different analytical needs. Initially, it is annotated into three broad classes based on the primary type of bowling action: Fast Bowl, Leg Spin, and Off Spin. To enhance the granularity of the classification, these three primary classes are further sub-divided into six detailed categories. This sub-division differentiates between right and left variations within each type of bowling action: Right Arm and Left Arm Fast Bowling, Right Arm and Left Arm Leg Spin, and Right Arm and Left Arm Off Spin.

Data Collection. To prepare the dataset, we identified and extracted video clips from YouTube that demonstrated a range of bowling styles, encompassing various speeds and spin variations. This careful selection and trimming process enriched the dataset by introducing diverse examples, thereby enhancing its robustness and applicability for action recognition tasks. Video clips were sourced from historical test matches, significant T20 games, and standout performances by individual players, either in specific tournaments or across their careers.

For additional data, we utilized the existing "Cricshot10" dataset [36], which primarily include types of batting shots that can be played by a batsman. We undertook a comprehensive process to repurpose and enhance it for bowling action analysis. Our approach involved a thorough selection and refinement process. From the original Cricshot10 dataset, we extracted and curated a subset containing bowling actions.

Data Preprocessing and Augmentation. While videos in Cricshot10 primarily include batting shots, they also contain other contents like bowling action, field views, etc. To tailor it for bowling actions, we meticulously extracted relevant portions from videos of Cricshot10 dataset, cropping out unrelated content to focus solely on bowling actions. We also employed mirroring as a data augmentation technique to increase the diversity of the training data and improve the model's robustness.

Data Distribution. The ActionBowl dataset provides extensive coverage of bowling actions through videos, embodying a wealth of information that can have far-reaching impacts in areas like performance analysis, coaching, and automated action recognition in cricket. Table 1 presents the dataset's distribution across the training and validation sets for classification tasks.

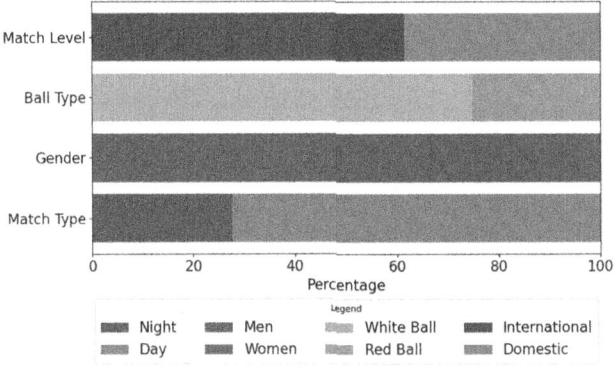

Fig. 2. Percentage distribution of ActionBowl dataset across match types (night/day), gender (men/women), ball type (white/red), and match level (international/domestic). (Color figure online)

Fig. 3. Sample frame depicting an unorthodox bowling action from the ActionBowl dataset.

The dataset consists of approximately 2.6k videos showcasing players bowling with different actions. As illustrated on the Fig. 2, it includes videos from both international and domestic matches. Around 61% of the videos are sourced from international games, while the remaining 39% are from domestic competitions. Regarding the type of cricket ball, white-ball formats (ODI, T20, T10) dominate the dataset, accounting for 75% of the videos, with the remaining 25% featuring red-ball (Test match) games. Notably, only 5% of the videos are from women's matches, highlighting the male-dominated nature of the sport. Additionally, most of the clips are captured during daylight conditions; however, a smaller portion originates from matches played under artificial lighting.

While most bowlers in cricket exhibit similar or standardized bowling actions, some have crafted entirely unique styles that defy convention yet achieved remarkable success. We show some sample of images with unique bowling aciton on the Fig. 3. Additionally, there are bowlers whose actions resemble one class but belong to another, further complicating classification. These edge cases introduce significant challenges for action recognition models, as they require the ability to distinguish subtle nuances and variations in movement. In this study, we aim to evaluate the capability of transformer-based models to recognize and accurately classify these complex cases. To this end, we have included unorthodox bowlers in our dataset, such as Muttiah Muralitharan, Lasith Malinga, Jasprit Bumrah, and Sunil Narine. These bowlers, known for their distinctive actions and deceptive styles, push the boundaries of what models can learn and generalize, making them ideal for assessing the robustness of our approach.

When evaluating the distribution of the dataset in the three class categories, it is evident that fast bowling has the highest number of videos. This reflects the typical composition of a cricket team, which generally includes more fast bowlers than spinners, leading to a greater availability of fast bowling footage. In contrast, left-arm leg spin has the fewest videos, mirroring the rarity of well-known bowlers in this category. Therefore, we can conclude that the prominence of the players performing each action has indirectly influenced the number of videos in each class. Figure 1 illustrates sample frames from the ActionBowl dataset, highlighting the diversity of bowling actions captured. This data set fills a major gap in the availability of specialized bowling action datasets, which is critical for further research and many applications in the modern sports industry.

3.2 Models

In our research, we trained and evaluated three distinct models: ActionCLIP, TimeSformer, and UniFormerV2. ActionCLIP, a multi-modal architecture, utilizes both visual and textual inputs. TimeSformer adopts a divided spatiotemporal approach, processing spatial and temporal features separately. UniFormerV2 employs a fused spatio-temporal architecture, integrating both features within a unified framework. These models can provide valuable insights into their varying performance in cricket bowling action recognition.

ActionCLIP. ActionCLIP [43] redefines video action recognition by emphasizing semantic label information and modeling the task as a video-text matching problem within a multi- modal learning framework. ActionCLIP's design enables it to generalize well across diverse video contexts and scenarios, reducing the need for extensive retraining on new datasets. Its approach also facilitates easier integration with other multi-modal systems, enhancing its utility in broader applications like multimedia content analysis and interactive AI systems. This approach enhances video representation with semantic language supervision, allowing for zero-shot action recognition without additional labeled data or parameters. To address the high dependency on label texts and leverage extensive web data, ActionCLIP introduces a "pre-train, prompt, and fine-tune" paradigm. This involves pre-training on large web image-text or video-text datasets, using prompt engineering to align action recognition with pre-training tasks, and fine-tuning on target datasets for strong performance. ActionCLIP, instantiated with this paradigm, demonstrates superior zero-shot/few-shot transfer-ability and achieves top-tier results in general action recognition, including 83.8% top-1 accuracy on Kinetics-400 using a ViT-B/16 backbone. Unlike traditional methods that predict from a fixed set of categories, ActionCLIP's focus on semantic information and multi-modal learning provides it with greater flexibility and transfer-ability.

TimeSformer. TimeSformer [4] is a novel approach to video classification that relies solely on self-attention mechanisms instead of convolutions. It adapts the Transformer architecture for video by learning spatio-temporal features from sequences of frame-level patches. The method employs "divided attention", where temporal and spatial attention are applied separately within each block, which has been shown to offer the best classification accuracy. TimeSformer achieved state-of-the-art performance on various action recognition benchmarks, including the highest accuracy reported on Kinetics-400 and Kinetics-600. Compared to traditional 3D convolutional networks [41], TimeSformer trains faster, offers significantly higher test efficiency with a minor accuracy trade-off, and can handle much longer video clips, extending beyond one minute.

UniFormerV2. UniFormerV2 [25] is a powerful video network paradigm designed to enhance video understanding by learning discriminative spatio-temporal representations. While ViTs [10] excel at capturing long-term video dependencies through self-attention, they often struggle with local video redundancy due to global token comparisons. UniFormer [26] originally addressed this issue by integrating convolution and self-attention within a transformer format, but it required a cumbersome pre-training phase on images before fine-tuning on videos, limiting its practical use. To overcome this, UniFormerV2 enhances pre-trained ViTs with efficient UniFormer designs, incorporating novel local and global relation aggregators for an optimal balance between accuracy and computational efficiency. By unifying convolution and self-attention, it reduces local video redundancy while preserving long-term dependency learning. UniFormerV2 achieved state-of-the-art results on multiple video benchmarks and demonstrates broad applicability across various datasets, including scene-related and temporal-related actions, as well as untrimmed videos, excelling in benchmarks like Kinetics-400/600/700 [5,6,21], Moments in Time [29], Something-Something V1/V2 [16], ActivityNet [22], and HACS [48]. Moreover, it has shown superior adaptability across different video lengths and complexities, solidifying its status as a versatile solution for both fine-grained and coarse-grained video tasks. This makes UniFormerV2 an essential tool for modern video understanding.

4 Experiments

The purpose of our research work is to evaluate and compare the performance of competitive action recognition models on a ActionBowl dataset. We aim to identify which model yields the best result in classifying the cricket bowling action based on accuracy and other evaluation metrics. Our experiments were conducted utilizing the freely available NVIDIA P100 GPU on the kaggle, which provided a convenient and accessible way for training our models. We employed pytorch as a primary deep learning framework for implementing models.

Table 2. Performance comparison of ActionCLIP, TimeSformer, and UniFormerV2 models on 3-class and 6-class classification tasks. The table presents accuracy (Acc.), precision (P.), recall (R.), and F1 Score (F1.) metrics, revealing that ActionCLIP consistently outperforms the other models across all metrics and classification tasks. TimeSformer performs well, particularly in the 3-class classification, while UniFormerV2 shows lower performance, especially in the more complex 6-class classification task.

Model	3-Class Metrics (%)				6-Class Metrics (%)			
	Acc.	P.	R.	F1.	Acc.	P.	R.	F1.
UniFormerV2 [25]	86.59	85.93	85.80	85.34	55.85	59.89	54.22	52.90
TimeSformer [4]	89.27	88.68	87.85	88.05	74.15	73.09	72.53	72.69
ActionCLIP [43]	**91.46**	**90.57**	**90.64**	**90.60**	**90.24**	**89.24**	**89.31**	**89.24**

4.1 Models and Evaluation Metrics

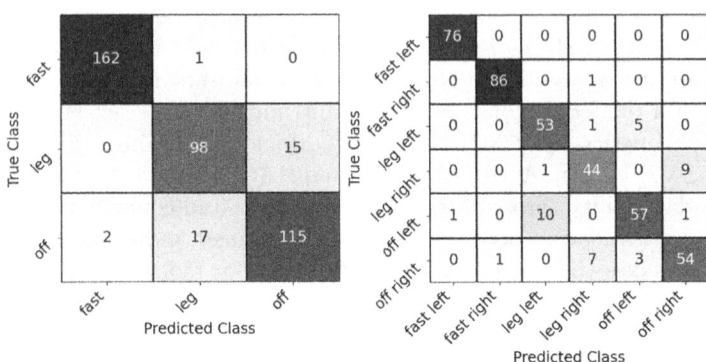

Fig. 4. Confusion matrices for ActionCLIP model with (left) 3 classes and (right) 6 classes classification.

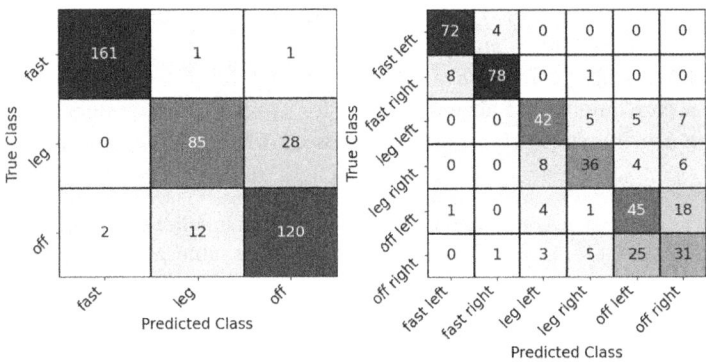

Fig. 5. Confusion matrices for TimeSformer model with (left) 3 classes and (right) 6 classes classification.

We conducted experiments on three models: ActionCLIP, TimeSformer and UniFormerV2. We trained the ActionCLIP base model with 32 patch size while employing the learning rate of 5e-6 and a batch size of 6. As a multi-modal architecture, ActionCLIP utilizes prompts with templates such as "a photo of action", "a picture of action" and "Human action of" alongside video clips. TimeSformer model with patch size of 16 was configured with a learning rate of 0.005 and a batch size of 8. Similarly, UniFormerV2 base model with patch size 16 was trained with a learning rate of 1e-5 and a batch size of 8. The choice of metrics i.e. accuracy, precision, recall, and F1 Score, for evaluating video action recognition tasks is driven by their ability to comprehensively assess model performance across multiple dimensions. The task often involves challenges like

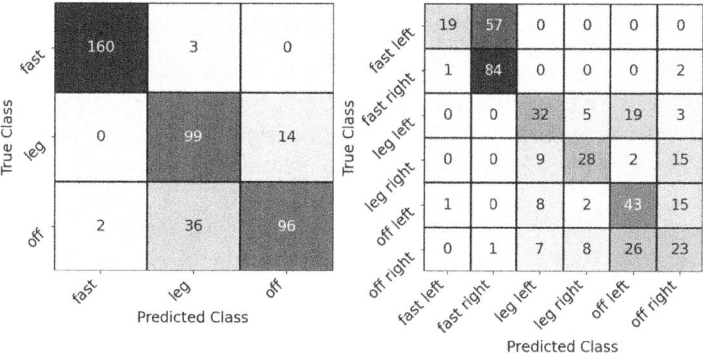

Fig. 6. Confusion matrices for UniformerV2 model with (left) 3 classes and (right) 6 classes classification.

imbalanced class distributions, overlapping action categories, and varying complexities, particularly in multi-class classification tasks. Accuracy provides an overall measure of correctness, while Precision ensures reliability by focusing on how well positive predictions match the true class. Recall addresses the ability to identify all instances of an action, which is critical for minimizing false negatives. The F1 Score, as a balance between Precision and Recall, is especially valuable for video classification as it offers a single, robust metric to account for both missed detections and incorrect predictions. Together, these metrics offer a holistic evaluation of model performance, particularly in tasks of varying complexity, such as the 3-class and 6-class classification setups, where identifying the strengths and weaknesses of models is essential.

4.2 Experiments on 3-Class and 6-Class Datasets

Both the 3-class dataset and the 6-class dataset were experimented with the aforementioned models. In our experiment, we trained, evaluated, and analyzed these models using our ActionBowl dataset. To gain deeper insights into the performance of the UniFormerV2 and to consolidate our findings, we created different subsets of the dataset with an incremental number of data points. This allowed us to analyze the effect of increasing dataset on the overall accuracy of the model.

5 Result and Discussion

In this study, we explored the performance of three video classification models—ActionCLIP, TimeSformer and UniFormerV2—on the ActionBowl dataset comprising 2571 video samples. The dataset was divided into 2161 samples for training and 410 samples for validation. We evaluated the models on two classification tasks: a 3-class classification and a more challenging 6-class classification. Table 2 summarizes the performance of three video classification models using accuracy, precision, recall, and F1 Score.

5.1 Performance on 3-Class Classification

For the 3-class classification, ActionCLIP achieved the highest accuracy of 91.46% followed by TimeSformer with 89.27%. ActionCLIP demonstrated a balanced and effective classification with a precision of 90.57%, recall of 90.64%, and F1 Score of 90.60%. TimeSformer also achieved a similar feat with precision of 88.68%, recall of 87.85%, and F1 Score of 88.05%. UniFormerV2, however, showed a slightly lower accuracy of 86.59% and with precision, recall, and F1 Score of 85.93%, 85.80%, 85.34% respectively, which suggest that even while having a comparatively lower accuracy it shows a balanced classification. Overall, the result (Table 2) suggests that all three models effectively distinguish between the classes, likely due to the distinct nature of the actions in three-class classification.

5.2 Performance on 6-Class Classification

In the 6-class classification task of ActionBowl, each class from the 3-class classification was sub-divided into two classes, resulting in approximately half the number of videos in each of the six classes compared to the three classes. This sub-division created a more challenging scenario due to the smaller number of samples per class and subtle variation between the actions in each class. In this setting, the accuracy of all models dropped, reflecting the increased difficulty and complexity of the task. ActionCLIP again led with the highest accuracy of 90.24%, as well as the best precision of 89.24%, recall of 89.31%, and F1 Score of 89.24%, demonstrating its robustness in handling increased class complexity. TimeSformer showed a reasonable performance with an accuracy of 74.15%, precision of 73.09%, recall of 72.53%, and F1 Score of 72.69%, suggesting it's divided spatio-temporal architecture can reasonably handle new added complexity. UniFormerV2, however, showed a significant drop in performance for the 6-class task, with an accuracy of only 55.85%, precision of 59.89%, recall of 54.22%, and an F1 Score of 52.90%, indicating difficulties in managing the increased number of classes which is further studied (Sect. 5.5). These results are summarized in Table 2. Overall, ActionCLIP emerged as the most reliable model across both classification tasks, followed by TimeSformer, with UniFormerV2 showing the most notable decline as class complexity increases. The drop in performance of UniFormerV2 suggests that its unified convolution and attention architecture might require more data to effectively manage the increased complexity of the dataset.

5.3 Visual Analysis of Model Performance in Cricket Bowling Action Recognition

After conducting a thorough visual evaluation of the predictions made by all three models, several important insights emerged:

ActionCLIP. As our best-performing model, ActionCLIP demonstrated exceptional ability in predicting the handedness of the bowler (right-handed vs. left-handed), even in instances where it misclassified the bowling type. However, most of its incorrect predictions were associated with bowlers who have unorthodox bowling actions. This highlights the model's challenge in learning and generalizing these complex, non-standard patterns. The confusion matrix shown in Fig. 4 confirms that while ActionCLIP achieves high accuracy across most categories, its errors predominantly arise from these unique bowling styles.

TimeSformer. In contrast to ActionCLIP, TimeSformer faced significant challenges in predicting the handedness of the bowler. This limitation substantially impacted its overall accuracy, as evidenced by the confusion matrix in Fig. 5, where the model frequently confused "off left" with "off right" actions. Improving TimeSformer's ability to identify handedness could bridge the performance gap between this model and ActionCLIP.

UniFormerV2. UniFormerV2 exhibited notable confusion between similar bowling types, particularly leg spin and off spin, suggesting that it struggles to capture subtle differences between these classes. Additionally, for the six-class dataset, the model also struggled to distinguish the handiness of the bowler. The confusion matrix for UniFormerV2 (Fig. 6) supports this observation, indicating the need for additional training data and greater diversity to help the model better differentiate these nuanced actions. Expanding the dataset could enhance its performance significantly.

5.4 Result Discussion Overview

Among the models, ActionCLIP's multi-modal approach, which combines prompts with video inputs, enables it to generalize well on the ActionBowl dataset. It emphasizes the alignment between visual features from the video and the textual description by calculating the similarity score between video frame and textual embeddings, ensuring that the textual description contributes to the identification of the action. Because of these strengths, it outperformed the other two in both 3-class and 6-class classification. Similarly, TimeSformer's straightforward divided space-time architecture allowed for robust generalization. It's reliance on simple features is proven to be enough for reasonable performance. In contrast, UniFormerV2, with its more complex joint unified convolution attention architecture may require a larger dataset to reach similar level of generalization, indicating that its performance could improve with more training data.

5.5 Impact of Dataset Size on UniFormerV2 Performance

To further investigate the impact of data-size in performance of UniformerV2, we trained it on different subsets of the ActionBowl dataset using a 6-class classification scheme. This analysis aimed to understand the relationship between

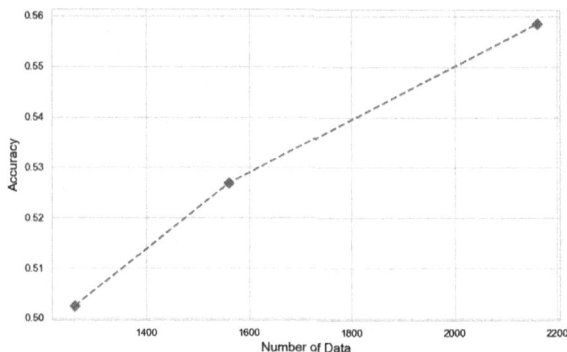

Fig. 7. Accuracy of UniFormerV2 for 6-class classification as a function of the dataset size. The accuracy exhibits a steady improvement with an increase in the number of data samples, indicating enhanced model generalization and performance with larger training data.

dataset size and the model performance. As illustrated in Fig. 7, we progressively increased the dataset size from 1261 to 1561 and to 2161 samples. Interestingly, the accuracy exhibited an upward trend, increasing from 50% to 53% when dataset is increased from 1261 to 1561 samples, and reaching 56% with 2161 samples. This incremental pattern shows possibility for the model with more training examples to achieve comparable performance, with its accuracy steadily improving as the dataset increases. This finding further supports the observation that it benefits from larger datasets to effectively learn patterns.

6 Conclusion

Here, we introduced ActionBowl dataset, a video dataset consisting of total 2571 videos for classifying various bowling actions within cricket. We evaluated the performance of transformer based video action recognition models-ActionCLIP, TimeSformer and UniFormerV2 on both cricket bowling action classification tasks. The result suggests that ActionCLIP's multi modal architecture is highly effective for action recognition tasks, even with limited data. On the other hand, TimeSformer does look promising, but it fits best for tasks with fewer classes. In contrast, UniFormerV2 may require more data to manage complex classifications effectively.

Future work could delve into the potential of transfer learning, and model ensemble techniques to achieve better result on bowling action recognition. Additionally, the curated dataset presented in this study holds significant value as a benchmark for evaluating advanced action recognition models, fostering comparative analysis and driving innovation in the field.

References

1. Ahmad, W., et al.: Optimized deep learning-based cricket activity focused network and medium scale benchmark. Alex. Eng. J. **73**, 771–779 (2023)
2. Al Islam, M.N., Hassan, T.B., Khan, S.K.: A CNN-based approach to classify cricket bowlers based on their bowling actions. In: 2019 IEEE International Conference on Signal Processing, Information, Communication & Systems (SPICSCON), pp. 130–134. IEEE (2019)
3. Bardes, A., et al.: Revisiting feature prediction for learning visual representations from video. arXiv preprint arXiv:2404.08471 (2024)
4. Bertasius, G., Wang, H., Torresani, L.: Is space-time attention all you need for video understanding? In: ICML, vol. 2, p. 4 (2021)
5. Carreira, J., Noland, E., Banki-Horvath, A., Hillier, C., Zisserman, A.: A short note about kinetics-600. arXiv preprint arXiv:1808.01340 (2018)
6. Carreira, J., Noland, E., Hillier, C., Zisserman, A.: A short note on the kinetics-700 human action dataset. arXiv preprint arXiv:1907.06987 (2019)
7. De Campos, T., et al.: An evaluation of bags-of-words and spatio-temporal shapes for action recognition. In: 2011 IEEE Workshop on Applications of Computer Vision (WACV), pp. 344–351. IEEE (2011)
8. Deliege, A., et al.: Soccernet-v2: a dataset and benchmarks for holistic understanding of broadcast soccer videos. In: Proceedings of the IEEE/CVF Conference on Computer Vision and Pattern Recognition, pp. 4508–4519 (2021)
9. Dixit, K., Balakrishnan, A.: Deep learning using CNNs for ball-by-ball outcome classification in sports. Report on the Course: Convolutional Neural Networks for Visual Recognition; Stanford University: Stanford, CA, USA (2016)
10. Dosovitskiy, A., et al.: An image is worth 16x16 words: Transformers for image recognition at scale. arXiv preprint arXiv:2010.11929 (2020)
11. Faulkner, H., Dick, A.: TenniSet: a dataset for dense fine-grained event recognition, localisation and description. In: 2017 International Conference on Digital Image Computing: Techniques and Applications (DICTA), pp. 1–8. IEEE (2017)
12. Feng, N., et al.: SSET: a dataset for shot segmentation, event detection, player tracking in soccer videos. Multimedia Tools Appl. **79**, 28971–28992 (2020)
13. Foysal, M.F.A., Islam, M.S., Karim, A., Neehal, N.: Shot-net: a convolutional neural network for classifying different cricket shots. In: Recent Trends in Image Processing and Pattern Recognition: Second International Conference, RTIP2R 2018, Solapur, India, December 21–22, 2018, Revised Selected Papers, Part I 2, pp. 111–120. Springer (2019)
14. Giancola, S., Amine, M., Dghaily, T., Ghanem, B.: Soccernet: a scalable dataset for action spotting in soccer videos. In: Proceedings of the IEEE Conference on Computer Vision and Pattern Recognition Workshops, pp. 1711–1721 (2018)
15. Gourgari, S., Goudelis, G., Karpouzis, K., Kollias, S.: Thetis: three dimensional tennis shots a human action dataset. In: Proceedings of the IEEE Conference on Computer Vision and Pattern Recognition Workshops, pp. 676–681 (2013)
16. Goyal, R., et al.: The "something something" video database for learning and evaluating visual common sense. In: Proceedings of the IEEE International Conference on Computer Vision, pp. 5842–5850 (2017)
17. Gu, X., Xue, X., Wang, F.: Fine-grained action recognition on a novel basketball dataset. In: ICASSP 2020-2020 IEEE International Conference on Acoustics, Speech and Signal Processing (ICASSP), pp. 2563–2567. IEEE (2020)

18. Harikrishna, N., Satheesh, S., Sriram, S.D., Easwarakumar, K.: Temporal classification of events in cricket videos. In: 2011 National Conference on Communications (NCC), pp. 1–5. IEEE (2011)
19. Ibrahim, M.S., Muralidharan, S., Deng, Z., Vahdat, A., Mori, G.: A hierarchical deep temporal model for group activity recognition. In: Proceedings of the IEEE Conference on Computer Vision and Pattern Recognition, pp. 1971–1980 (2016)
20. Jayalath, L.: Hawk eye technology used in cricket. S. Asian Res. J. Eng. Technol. **3**(2), 55–67 (2021)
21. Kay, W., et al.: The kinetics human action video dataset. arXiv preprint arXiv:1705.06950 (2017)
22. Khan, A., Nicholson, J., Plötz, T.: Activity recognition for quality assessment of batting shots in cricket using a hierarchical representation. Proc. ACM Interact. Mobile Wearable Ubiquit. Technol. **1**(3), 1–31 (2017)
23. Kolekar, M.H., Palaniappan, K., Sengupta, S.: Semantic event detection and classification in cricket video sequence. In: 2008 Sixth Indian Conference on Computer Vision, Graphics & Image Processing, pp. 382–389. IEEE (2008)
24. Kumar, A., Garg, J., Mukerjee, A.: Cricket activity detection. In: International Image Processing, Applications and Systems Conference, pp. 1–6. IEEE (2014)
25. Li, K., et al.: Uniformerv2: Spatiotemporal learning by arming image VITs with video uniformer. arXiv preprint arXiv:2211.09552 (2022)
26. Li, K., et al.: Uniformer: unifying convolution and self-attention for visual recognition. IEEE Trans. Pattern Anal. Mach. Intell. **45**(10), 12581–12600 (2023)
27. Li, Y., Li, Y., Vasconcelos, N.: Resound: towards action recognition without representation bias. In: Proceedings of the European Conference on Computer Vision (ECCV), pp. 513–528 (2018)
28. Maksai, A., Wang, X., Fua, P.: What players do with the ball: a physically constrained interaction modeling. In: Proceedings of the IEEE Conference on Computer Vision and Pattern Recognition, pp. 972–981 (2016)
29. Monfort, M., et al.: Moments in time dataset: one million videos for event understanding. IEEE Trans. Pattern Anal. Mach. Intell. **42**(2), 502–508 (2019)
30. Naik, B.T., Hashmi, M.F., Bokde, N.D.: A comprehensive review of computer vision in sports: open issues, future trends and research directions. Appl. Sci. **12**(9), 4429 (2022)
31. Premaratne, S., Jayaratne, K.: Structural approach for event resolution in cricket videos. In: Proceedings of the International Conference on Video and Image Processing, pp. 161–166 (2017)
32. Rahman, R., Rahman, M.A., Islam, M.S., Hasan, M.: Deepgrip: cricket bowling delivery detection with superior CNN architectures. In: 2021 6th International Conference on Inventive Computation Technologies (ICICT), pp. 630–636. IEEE (2021)
33. Ramanathan, V., Huang, J., Abu-El-Haija, S., Gorban, A., Murphy, K., Fei-Fei, L.: Detecting events and key actors in multi-person videos. In: Proceedings of the IEEE Conference on Computer Vision and Pattern Recognition, pp. 3043–3053 (2016)
34. Salman, M., Qaisar, S., Qamar, A.M.: Classification and legality analysis of bowling action in the game of cricket. Data Min. Knowl. Disc. **31**(6), 1706–1734 (2017). https://doi.org/10.1007/s10618-017-0511-4
35. Semwal, A., Mishra, D., Raj, V., Sharma, J., Mittal, A.: Cricket shot detection from videos. In: 2018 9th International Conference on Computing, Communication and Networking Technologies (ICCCNT), pp. 1–6. IEEE (2018)

36. Sen, A., Deb, K., Dhar, P.K., Koshiba, T.: Cricshotclassify: an approach to classifying batting shots from cricket videos using a convolutional neural network and gated recurrent unit. Sensors **21**(8), 2846 (2021)
37. Sharma, R.A., Sankar, K.P., Jawahar, C.: Fine-grain annotation of cricket videos. In: 2015 3rd IAPR Asian Conference on Pattern Recognition (ACPR), pp. 421–425. IEEE (2015)
38. Simonyan, K., Zisserman, A.: Two-stream convolutional networks for action recognition in videos. In: Advances in Neural Information Processing Systems, **27** (2014)
39. Simonyan, K., Zisserman, A.: Very deep convolutional networks for large-scale image recognition. arXiv preprint arXiv:1409.1556 (2014)
40. Tong, Z., Song, Y., Wang, J., Wang, L.: Videomae: Masked autoencoders are data-efficient learners for self-supervised video pre-training. Adv. Neural. Inf. Process. Syst. **35**, 10078–10093 (2022)
41. Tran, D., Bourdev, L., Fergus, R., Torresani, L., Paluri, M.: Learning spatiotemporal features with 3d convolutional networks. In: Proceedings of the IEEE International Conference on Computer Vision, pp. 4489–4497 (2015)
42. Tsunoda, T., Komori, Y., Matsugu, M., Harada, T.: Football action recognition using hierarchical LSTM. In: Proceedings of the IEEE Conference on Computer Vision and Pattern Recognition Workshops, pp. 99–107 (2017)
43. Wang, M., Xing, J., Liu, Y.: Actionclip: a new paradigm for video action recognition. arXiv preprint arXiv:2109.08472 (2021)
44. Wu, F., et al.: A survey on video action recognition in sports: datasets, methods and applications. IEEE Trans. Multimedia **25**, 7943–7966 (2022)
45. Xiao, L., Cao, Y., Gai, Y., Khezri, E., Liu, J., Yang, M.: Recognizing sports activities from video frames using deformable convolution and adaptive multiscale features. J. Cloud Comput. **12**(1), 167 (2023)
46. Xiao, X., Xu, D., Wan, W.: Overview: Video recognition from handcrafted method to deep learning method. In: 2016 International Conference on Audio, Language and Image Processing (ICALIP), pp. 646–651. IEEE (2016)
47. Yu, J., Lei, A., Song, Z., Wang, T., Cai, H., Feng, N.: Comprehensive dataset of broadcast soccer videos. In: 2018 IEEE Conference on Multimedia Information Processing and Retrieval (MIPR), pp. 418–423. IEEE (2018)
48. Zhao, H., Torralba, A., Torresani, L., Yan, Z.: HACS: human action clips and segments dataset for recognition and temporal localization. In: Proceedings of the IEEE/CVF International Conference on Computer Vision, pp. 8668–8678 (2019)
49. Zhu, Y., et al.: A comprehensive study of deep video action recognition. arXiv preprint arXiv:2012.06567 (2020)

Deep Learning in Satellite and Aerial-Based Image Processing

Alessia Sbriglio[✉] and Giovanni B. Palmerini

Scuola di Ingegneria Aerospaziale, Sapienza Università di Roma, via Salaria 851, 00138 Rome, Italy
`alessia.sbriglio@uniroma1.it`

Abstract. The improvement of Earth Observation (EO) satellite resolutions in recent years, coupled with the increasing requests for higher performance, introduced the need for more advanced detection techniques for satellite image analysis. Modern EO platforms generate vast amounts of data, rich in potentially valuable information but often underutilized, making the adoption of efficient image processing solutions crucial. These informations can be essential for accelerating processes such as classification and geo-referencing, ensuring the timely availability of mission products. In this context, the introduction of deep learning techniques, particularly the You Only Look Once (YOLO) algorithm, represents a natural evolution. YOLO is known for its speed, as it analyzes the entire image in a single pass, and for its precision, due to the use of deep convolutional neural networks (CNNs). When applied to satellite images, YOLO has shown promising results, especially for automatic geo-referencing and rapid classification. A first attempt at a comparative analysis between models trained with 60 and 100 epochs, applied to optical Sentinel-2 images targeting Italian lakes under various weather conditions, revealed significant improvements in detection precision and consistency. In particular, the accuracy of boundaries improved as training epochs increased. As the number of epochs grew, the results became more stable, regardless of environmental or lighting conditions, reducing errors and improving overall performance. These advancements suggest that with further development of algorithms and integration of artificial intelligence, the use of satellites and drones in geospatial applications will become increasingly precise and efficient. The use of drone images could further expand datasets, allowing the model to respond with an adaptive approach to specific details or defined elements, such as artificial structures or small areas of interest that satellites may not be able to detect with the same precision, especially due to unfavorable weather conditions. This integrated approach combining satellite and aerial data could further enhance the model's ability to detect smaller objects or handle more complex environments, increasing the versatility and reliability of automatic detection solutions in real-world contexts.

Keywords: Remote sensing · Imaging payload · Image processing · Object detection

1 Introduction

The field of object detection in imagery has experienced a significant transformation with the inclusion of deep learning techniques. In the past, object detection relied on manual methods and feature-based algorithms designed for specific tasks, which were often inflexible and struggled with scalability. The introduction of deep neural networks has drastically changed this landscape, offering more adaptable and robust solutions for recognizing and segmenting objects. Convolutional Neural Networks (CNNs) have played a key role in this progress, allowing models to autonomously learn and identify intricate features in images. Among the most notable innovations, the You Only Look Once (YOLO) series of algorithms stands out for its exceptional performance in real-time detection. This success is largely due to its unique architecture, which enables the processing of an entire image in a single pass, simplifying the detection process. YOLO's transition from region-based methods to a unified framework has greatly enhanced its ability to identify objects quickly and accurately [1, 2]. In the realm of satellite imagery, the increasing availability of high-resolution images and the growing capabilities of remote sensing platforms present both challenges and new opportunities. Deep learning models, particularly recent versions such as YOLOv8-seg, are well-suited to handle these complex datasets, allowing for precise object segmentation and identification on a global scale. YOLOv8-seg, with its advanced semantic segmentation features, represents a significant step forward over earlier models, combining speed, efficiency, and higher accuracy in delineating objects. These improvements not only advance object detection in terrestrial and aerial contexts but are also highly relevant for Earth Observation, where the quality of the images and the need for rapid, precise analysis are crucial [3, 4]. Therefore, this paper aims to investigate the use of YOLOv8 for detecting specific geophysical features in satellite imagery, and – in such a frame – completes and expands a preliminary paper by the authors [5]. Lakes are selected as detectable features a particularly suitable for identification in these sequential image sequences due to their stable and identifiable characteristics over time. The source of information is provided by the freely available database of high-resolution images captured form European satellite mission Sentinel-2 [6]. Following Sects. 2 and 3 introduce the specific test case and the YOLO model applied. The work, through the performance reported in Sect. 4, confirms the potential of deep learning to meet the demands for speed and accuracy in detection tasks, and suggests the actual possibility to implement the image processing onboard. It has however to be acknowledged that the extended analysis showed some critical cases, discussed in Sect. 5.

2 Experimental Process

The initial step is represented by the acquisition of the satellite images of some Italian lakes through Sentinel Hub database [7]. Specifically, Sentinel-2 imagery was used, offering spatial resolutions of 10 m, 20 m, and 60 m, depending on the spectral band, and a maximum revisit interval of 5 days for the same geographic area. For this study, images from the period between 2020 and 2024 of nine distinct lakes in Italy were selected: Bolsena, Bracciano, Martignano and Trasimeno in central Italy, and Como, Garda, Idro,

Iseo and Maggiore in the prea-alpine region. The selected data were from Sentinel-2 Level 2A, which are high-quality images with atmospheric corrections applied using the Sen2Cor algorithm [8]. Atmospheric correction is crucial for remote sensing applications as it mitigates the effects of atmospheric interference on light reflected from the Earth, improving the quality of the data, and enabling more accurate analysis of surface features like vegetation, soil, and inland water bodies. No cloud was allowed for (or a relative percentage of 0% has been specified as threshold) to ensure that only clear images were included in the dataset. Using YOLO on satellite imagery presents unique challenges, particularly due to the variability in image characteristics, atmospheric conditions, and object types, which require significant adjustments compared to traditional datasets. To address these challenges, several strategies were implemented: precise calibration of object sizes for detection, identifying object classes specific to satellite imagery that may differ from those in conventional datasets, and managing varying atmospheric and lighting conditions that influence the appearance of objects. As a result, developing a carefully annotated satellite image dataset covering diverse scenarios was essential for overcoming these challenges and maximizing the effectiveness of YOLO in this field. This process was a critical step, as it provided the YOLOv8 model with the necessary, high-quality, and detailed information required for its training and segmentation tasks. The goal was to ensure that the model could accurately detect and segment the lake surfaces in future images. The images were manually annotated, and bounding boxes were drawn around each lake to define their boundaries with precision. This annotation was vital for the model to distinguish the lake regions from other environmental features present in the satellite imagery. To further streamline the process and enhance the quality of the data, the images were preprocessed using Roboflow [9]. The preprocessing involved resizing the images to a consistent resolution, ensuring that the dimensions were uniform across the dataset.

This standardization was crucial for improving the model's training performance, as uniform image dimensions reduce computational complexity and promote consistency in data processing. To bolster the model's robustness, various data augmentation techniques were employed during the training process.

Fig. 1. Bracciano and Martignano lakes original image from Sentinel Hub.

Fig. 2. Images of Bracciano and Martignano lakes after segmentation.

Each image in the dataset (see Fig. 1 and 2), after manually segmented, has been resized to 640×640 pixels (see Fig. 3 and 4) to maintain an appropriate resolution without demanding excessive computational resources. The augmentation techniques applied included:

- **Environmental Variability**. By selecting images taken at different times of the year and under various weather conditions, the model was trained to adapt to different environmental factors such as lighting changes and seasonal shifts (see Fig. 3 and 4).
- **Geometric Transformations**. The images were also subjected to geometric alterations, including rotations, translations, and scaling. These transformations introduced variability in the size and orientation of the lake regions, helping the model recognize lakes from diverse angles and at varying scales (see Fig. 3 and 4).
- **Use of Masks**. To simulate real-world scenarios where lakes might be partially obstructed or obscured by environmental factors, masks were applied to the images. This approach further enriched the dataset's variability, allowing the model to become more resilient to occlusions and varying visual contexts (see Fig. 4).

Through the application of these data augmentation techniques, the original dataset was significantly expanded, introducing a wider range of variability and complexity. This process was essential for improving the model's generalization capability, allowing it to better handle new, unseen images in real-world scenarios. By augmenting the dataset in such a way, the model's performance was enhanced, and its robustness to diverse conditions was ensured. As a result of these extensive data preparation and augmentation efforts, the final dataset was meticulously optimized for training the YOLOv8 model. The dataset was divided into a training set consisting of 249 images, a validation set containing 41 images, and a test set with 12 images. This careful division ensured that the model had access to a well-rounded set of data for training, validating, and testing its detection and segmentation capabilities.

Fig. 3. Bracciano and Martignano lakes image after resizing and geometric transfomations.

Fig. 4. Bracciano and Martignano lakes image after environmental variability and use of mask.

3 YOLO Model Overview: Design and Training Techniques

The YOLOv8s-seg model utilized in this research marks a substantial improvement over previous YOLO versions, as it is optimized not only for real-time object detection but also for accurate object segmentation. The model features 261 layers, 11,793,579 parameters, and a computational complexity of 42.7 GFLOPs, excelling in segmentation tasks, which makes it especially suitable for Earth observation applications requiring high precision at the detail level. The internal design of YOLOv8s-seg is shown in the accompanying diagram (Fig. 5), illustrating the main components and their relationships:

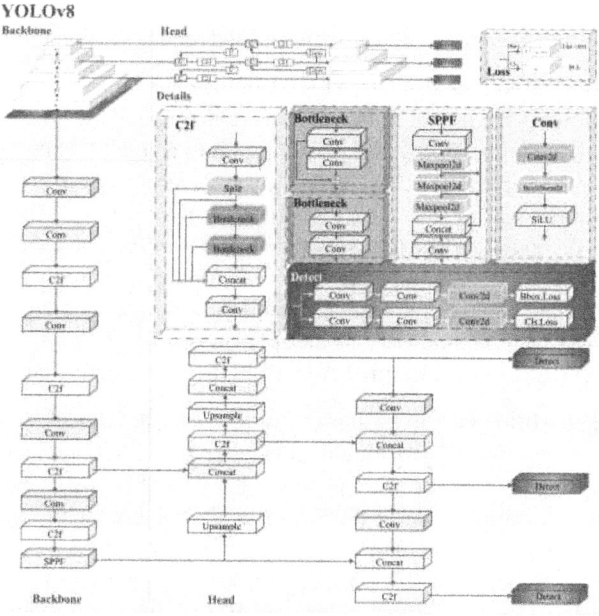

Fig. 5. YOLOv8 model from [10].

Backbone Network. At the base of the diagram, the backbone network is formed by several convolutional layers arranged in sequential stages. This network extracts hierarchical features from the input image, capturing a range of details from basic edges and textures to more complex object parts. The lightweight design of the backbone ensures the model can maintain high performance in real-time while efficiently extracting rich feature representations.

C2f Blocks. Highlighted in the diagram, the C2f blocks are distributed throughout the backbone and help enhance feature extraction by combining information across different stages. This improves the model's ability to learn intricate patterns, ensuring a strong gradient flow and addressing the vanishing gradient issue, which is vital for effective training and improved performance.

SPPF. Located after the backbone and C2f blocks, the SPPF layer performs multi-scale pooling. This layer aggregates features from multiple spatial resolutions, enabling the model to capture information across different scales. The SPPF layer is essential for enhancing the model's ability to handle objects of varying sizes and shapes, which boosts its robustness in diverse situations.

Segmentation Head. Shown at the top of the diagram, the segmentation head is responsible for creating detailed segmentation maps. It utilizes the refined features from the backbone and C2f blocks to generate pixel-level classification outputs. The segmentation head incorporates deconvolution layers and up sampling processes to rebuild high-resolution segmentation maps from the feature maps. The model was trained using backpropagation techniques on a dataset enhanced with data augmentation, aimed at improving its ability to generalize to unseen data and reduce the likelihood of overfitting.

The training process was structured by assigning each lake to a specific class based on its name, allowing the model to focus on recognizing and differentiating individual lakes. A second dataset version grouped all lakes into a single "Lakes" class, enabling an evaluation of the impact of specific versus general classification on segmentation and recognition. Training was carried out across different epoch settings. The first experiment used 60 epochs on both datasets, to assess the model's convergence and ability to generalize quickly. A second experiment extended the training to 100 epochs to see if longer training could further enhance the model's performance. In both configurations, training began with image scanning, followed by the application of various transformations, such as blur and CLAHE (Contrast Limited Adaptive Histogram Equalization).

Case 1: Dataset with 9 Distinct Classes. In this test, the model was trained for 60 epochs with a batch size of 16, achieving a balance between computational efficiency and learning effectiveness. Stochastic Gradient Descent (SGD) was used for optimization, with an initial learning rate of 0.001, gradually reduced by the learning rate final (lrf) parameter to 0.01. A momentum of 0.9 was applied to stabilize the gradient descent process, and weight decay of 0.0005 helped prevent overfitting. Data augmentation techniques, such as mosaic augmentation and 50% horizontal flipping, were used to diversify the training images and enhance the model's robustness. The Intersection over Union (IoU) threshold was set at 0.7, meaning that a prediction was considered correct if the overlap between predicted and actual masks was greater than 70%. The model was trained with overlapping masks and a mask resolution that was 4 times lower than the original image to optimize accuracy and execution speed. Various performance metrics (see Fig. 6 and 7), such as train/box_loss, train/seg_loss, and train/cls_loss, showed consistent improvement over time, with losses declining from their initial high values, demonstrating the model's increased ability to detect and segment objects accurately. The validation losses mirrored these trends, indicating that the model was generalizing well and not overfitting. Regarding performance, the model's precision and recall for both bounding box predictions and segmentation improved progressively. Bounding box precision (B) and recall (B) showed steady increases, indicating improved accuracy in detecting true positives and fewer false positives. Similarly, precision (M) and recall (M) for segmentation followed the same upward trajectory. The mAP50 and mAP50–95 metrics, which assess mean average precision at different IoU thresholds, also demonstrated improvement throughout the training process. The mAP50 (B) for bounding boxes and mAP50 (M) for segmentation increased, reflecting the model's enhanced ability to identify objects and segments at a 50% IoU threshold. Similarly, the mAP50–95 (B) and mAP50–95 (M) metrics showed gradual improvements, illustrating the model's growing robustness across various object overlap scenarios. Overall, the model exhibited consistent performance improvements across all metrics, suggesting that the selected hyperparameters and training strategies were effective in boosting its ability to generalize and perform well on both training and validation datasets. In the second experiment, the model was trained for 100 epochs, keeping the batch size, image resolution, and optimization settings the same as in the 60-epoch experiment. The main difference was the extended training time, allowing the model to refine its performance further, although improvements slowed down after the 50th epoch. Loss graphs continued to show a decline, albeit at a slower pace after the 50th epoch, indicating that the model was still improving, but at a diminished rate. The validation losses exhibited a similar pattern, confirming that the model did not overfit and maintained good performance on unseen data. Precision and recall metrics for bounding boxes exhibited a plateau around the 50th epoch, suggesting that the model's detection capabilities had largely stabilized by that point. The same pattern was observed for segmentation, indicating that the model had achieved solid detection and segmentation capabilities after 50 epochs, with only minor improvements beyond that. The mAP metrics also showed a slight increase in performance with extended training, although the gains were smaller after the 50th epoch. In conclusion, while additional training up to 100 epochs resulted in minor improvements in precision, recall, and losses, 50 epochs seemed to strike a good balance between computational efficiency and model accuracy.

Case 2: Dataset with 1 Class. In the second case, the same images were used, but all were grouped into a single class labeled "Lakes." The model was trained first for 60 epochs and then for 100 epochs with the same parameters used in the first test.

When comparing the resulting performance (Fig. 8 and 9) metrics with those from Case 1 (Fig. 6 and 7), several similarities and differences became apparent. One similarity was the general trend in precision and recall metrics. For both bounding box precision and recall, as well as segmentation precision and recall, the metrics improved rapidly in the first epochs and stabilized around 0.8 to 0.9 by the 25th to 30th epoch. This indicated that the model performed well within the first 30 epochs, with minimal improvements afterward. The mAP50 and mAP50–95 metrics followed a similar pattern, reaching high levels quickly and stabilizing at around 0.6 for the mAP50–95 values. However, there were notable differences in the graphs for this dataset. The precision and recall metrics reached their plateau earlier—around 25–30 epochs—compared to the previous case, where the plateau appeared later, between 30 and 50 epochs. The curves in this case also appeared more stable, with less fluctuation, suggesting that the model's training process was more consistent. Additionally, performance reached its peak more rapidly, implying that the regularization strategies might have been more effective in this scenario. In summary, the second case suggests that a more efficient training process was achieved when using a single class, with the model reaching optimal performance quickly and stably, without significant variability in the metrics.

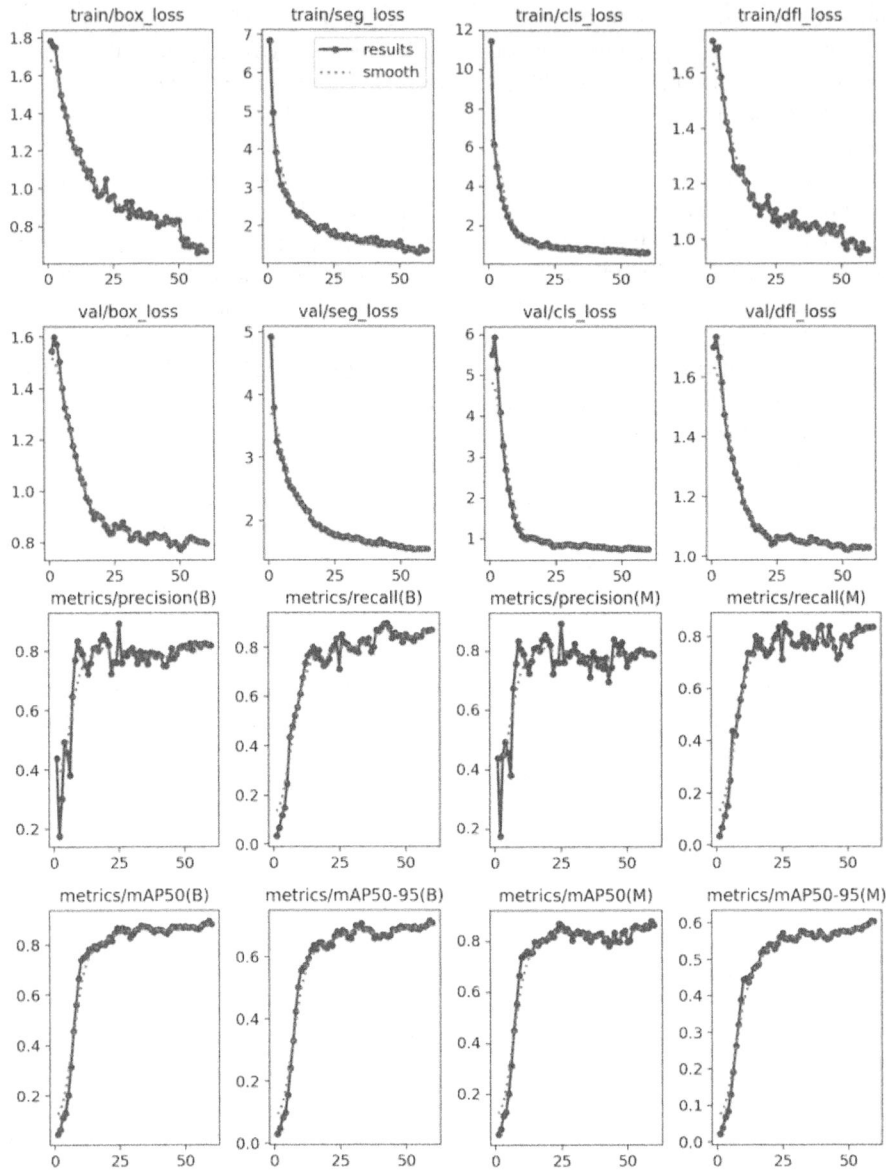

Fig. 6. Trends of principal metrics during the training of the YOLOv8 model over 60 epochs on a 9-classes dataset.

4 Model Validation and Performance Results

By analyzing the test results of the model trained for 60 epochs (Figs. 6 and 8) and 100 epochs (Figs. 7 and 9) on a dataset where lakes are classified by their names, a notable improvement in detection performance becomes evident in several key areas.

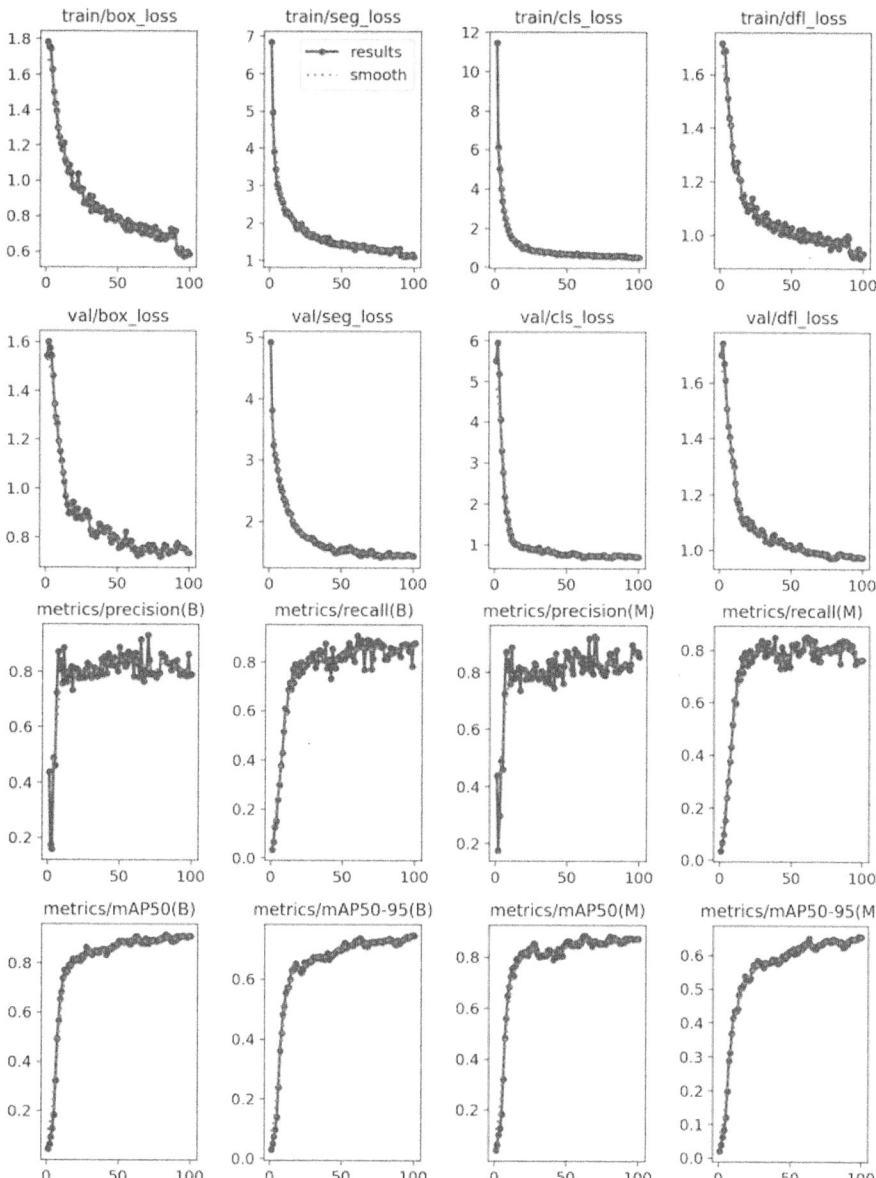

Fig. 7. Trends of principal metrics during the training of the YOLOv8 model over 100 epochs on a 9-classes dataset.

Specifically, the bounding boxes that outline the objects of interest are more accurate and align better with the actual contours of the detected regions. For example, as illustrated in Fig. 10, the model trained for 100 epochs is able to detect the entire water body of Lake Bolsena more accurately, with the confidence score increasing from 0.93 to 0.97. In more challenging scenarios, such as detecting Lake Como or the partially obstructed

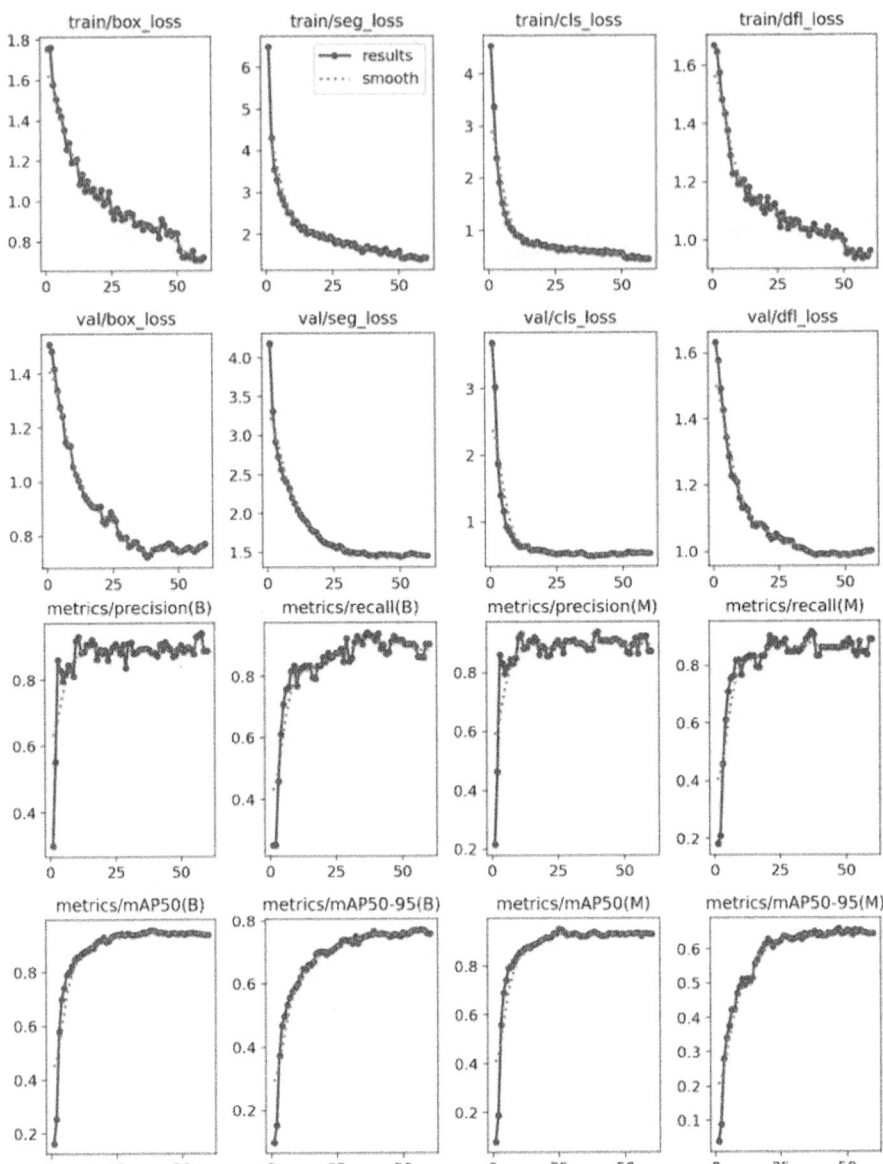

Fig. 8. Trends of principal metrics during the training of the YOLOv8 model over 60 epochs on a 1-class dataset.

Lake Bolsena [Fig. 11], the additional epochs enhance the model's capability to handle irregular geometries and more complicated areas.

Moreover, although the difference is small, the model trained with 100 epochs demonstrates slightly faster detection times, reducing the processing time from 21.90

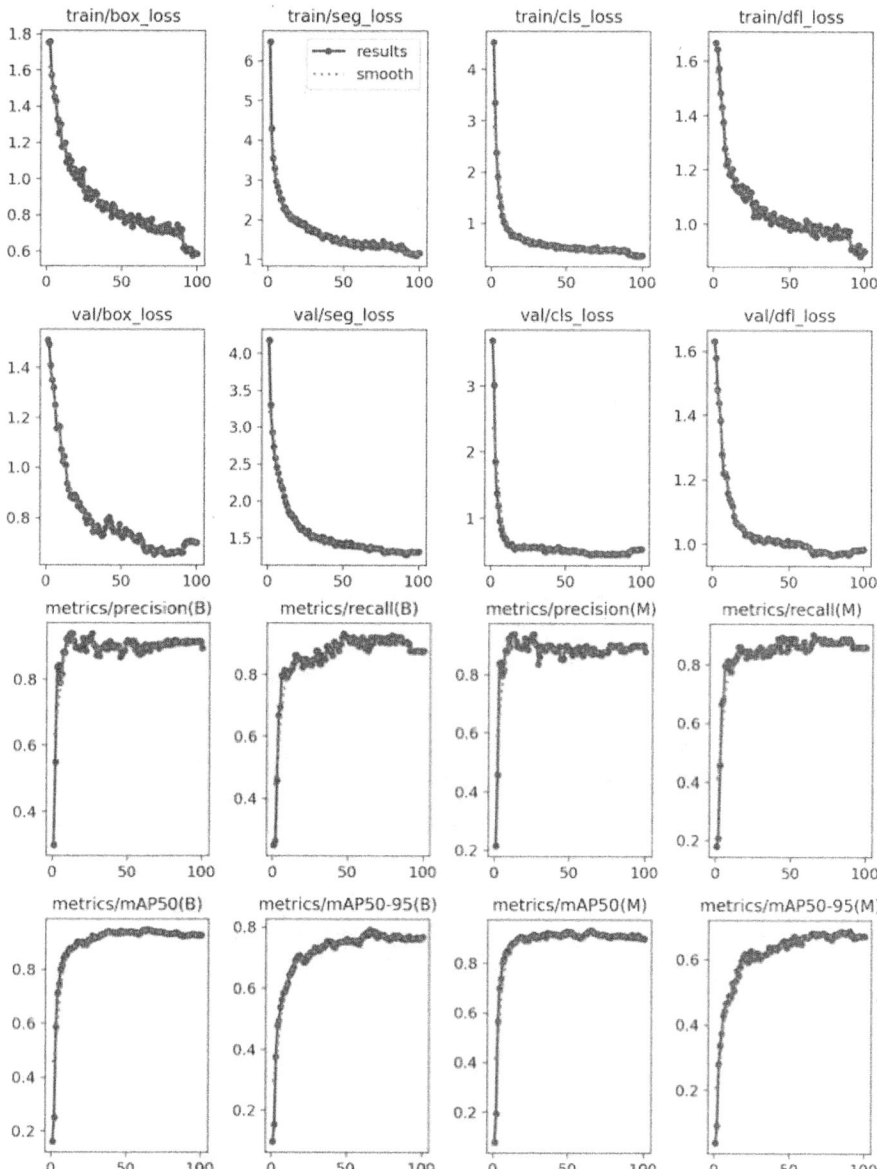

Fig. 9. Trends of principal metrics during the training of the YOLOv8 model over 100 epochs on a 1-class dataset.

to 21.31 s. For the model trained to detect the "Lakes" category, significant improvements are also observed in both accuracy and consistency. While the model trained for 60 epochs typically detects lake boundaries correctly, it struggles with more intricate or less distinct areas, indicating that it has not yet reached its full learning potential.

After 100 epochs, however, the boundaries of the lakes are more clearly defined and align closely with their true shapes, with fewer errors in difficult-to-detect regions. This suggests that with extended training, the model has become better at generalizing from the data, allowing it to more effectively differentiate lakes from surrounding features. Another notable improvement is seen in the confidence scores, which are higher and more stable after 100 epochs, with many lakes showing scores exceeding 0.90. Additionally, the model's ability to consistently detect lakes across satellite images taken on

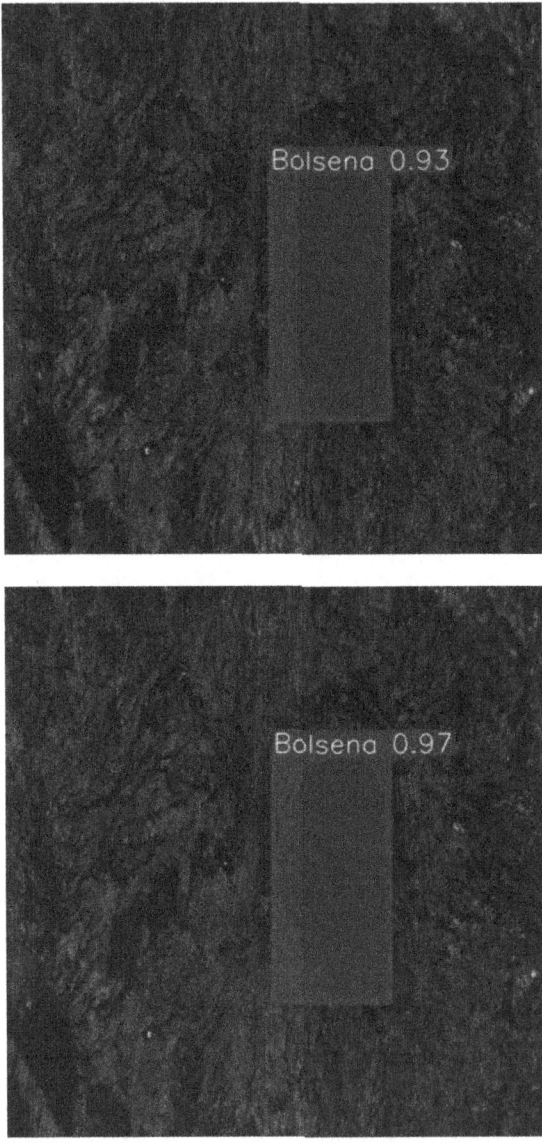

Fig. 10. Detection of Lake Bolsena with the model trained for 60 (up) and 100 (down) epochs.

different dates improves significantly. While the model trained with 60 epochs shows some variability in detecting lake size and shape—potentially due to environmental changes or lighting differences the model trained with 100 epochs produces far more stable results. Although seasonal variations in lake size may still be observed, the shape and positioning detected by the model trained for 100 epochs remain more consistent across different image acquisition times.

Lastly, with regard to inaccuracies or false positives, the model trained with 60 epochs occasionally produces bounding boxes that are slightly misaligned or not perfectly centered, leading to false positives or imprecise lake detection. In contrast, after 100 epochs of training, these inaccuracies are significantly reduced, with the bounding boxes being more accurately placed over the lakes, minimizing false positives and improving the model's overall accuracy. In summary, the comparison between the two

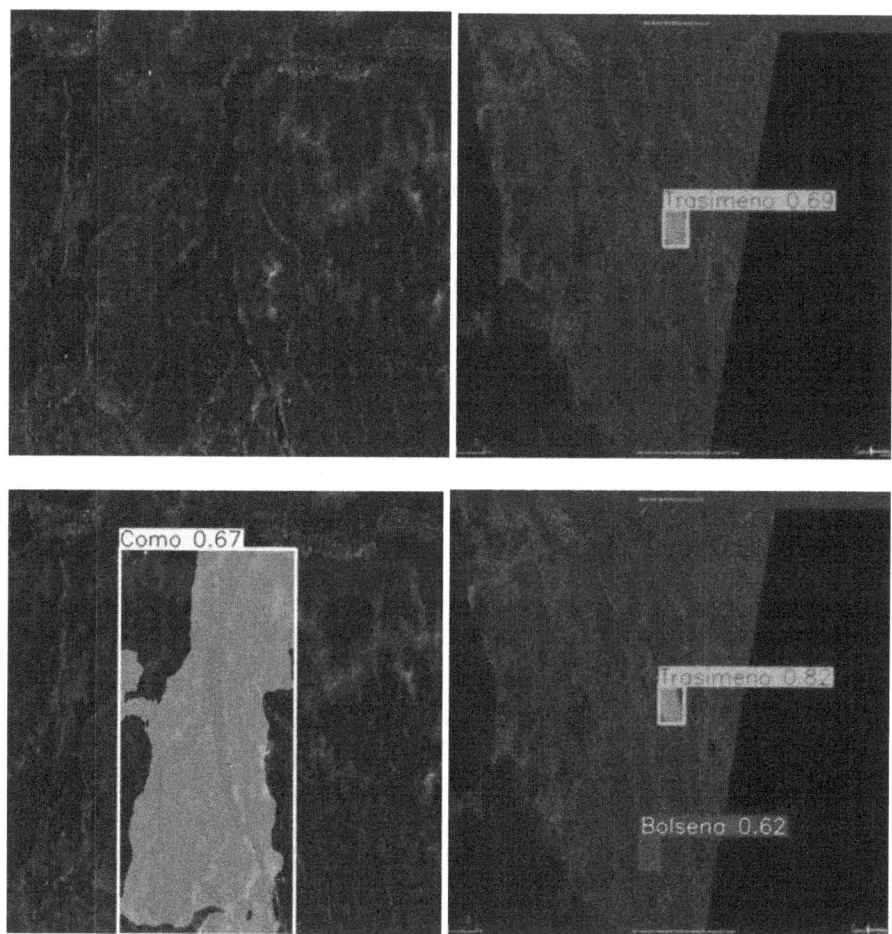

Fig. 11. Detection of Como and Bolsena Lakes was not possible with the model trained for 60 (up) epochs and instead successful with the same model trained with 100 (down) epochs.

training durations clearly demonstrates that extending the training from 60 to 100 epochs offers significant benefits. The model exhibits improved accuracy in boundary detection, higher confidence scores, and greater consistency across images taken at different times. These enhancements indicate that with additional training, the model has developed a better understanding of how to distinguish lakes from their surroundings, resulting in a more reliable and precise detection system capable of handling complex images and variations in acquisition conditions.

5 Challenges in Object Detection: Addressing Misclassifications and Complex Shapes

Although the developed object detection algorithm has shown promising results, some "failures" highlight the inherent challenges in handling the variability and complexity of images, and specifically of the features – i.e., the lakes – selected in the present case. One example of an error occurs when the algorithm mistakenly classifies a stretch of Tuscany coastline as Bracciano lake (see Fig. 12). This mistake is likely due to the visual similarities between the coastline's jagged features and the typical characteristics of a lake. Obviously, following analysis at different scales, or comparison of the surroundings could easily solve such an ambiguity, yet at the cost of making the process more complex and slower.

Another failure occurs when Lake Idro, with its particularly irregular shape, is not recognized, likely due to its underrepresentation in the training dataset. As a result, the algorithm has not learned to effectively distinguish its unique form (see Fig. 13).

Additionally, the data augmentation techniques used, such as rotations, scale modifications, and contrast variations, further complicated the recognition process by creating boundaries that were difficult for the model to interpret. These factors highlight how the combination of limited training data and augmentation techniques can introduce variability that exceeds the algorithm's ability to accurately classify complex objects, necessitating further refinement and strategies to address such challenges in scenarios with high geometric and visual complexity.

6 Final Remarks and Future Developments

The work focused on the application of novel, deep learning-based techniques to the analysis of satellite images from the Sentinel platform, with lakes chosen as the target features for this study. Lakes, when sufficiently present in the observed areas, are particularly suitable for Earth observation (EO) missions. The investigation carried out provided insights into the setup required for the training phase, the performance of feature identification using real satellite data, and the effectiveness of the model in detecting specific geographical features. A comprehensive analysis of various performance metrics highlighted key areas for enhancing the training process, such as improving the diversity and quality of the training dataset, utilizing data augmentation techniques to cover a broader range of environmental conditions, and optimizing training parameters like the learning rate and number of epochs. Additionally, the application of regularization methods,

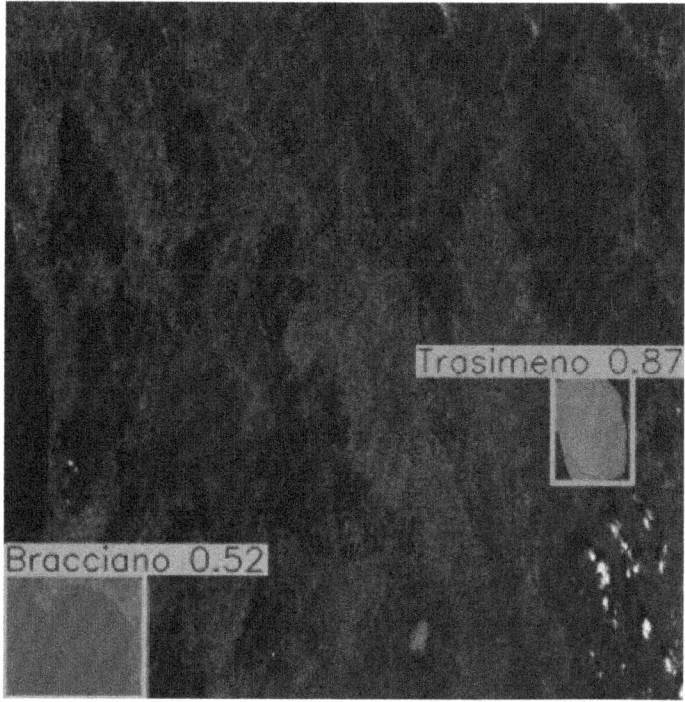

Fig. 12. Example of misclassification, where the algorithm mistakes a stretch of Tuscany coastline for a lake due to the visual similarities between the jagged coastline and typical lake shapes.

such as dropout, could reduce overfitting and improve the model's generalization capabilities. Overall, the YOLOv8-seg architecture demonstrated effective performance in identifying lakes, and this study is part of a broader initiative exploring autonomous orbit determination using geo-referenced features in satellite images captured by spacecraft with high-resolution, nadir-pointed cameras.

Looking ahead, the promising results of the YOLOv8-seg model suggest that it can provide optimal performance in EO image analysis, particularly for detecting significant geophysical features as the lakes. With processing times consistently under 30 min, the model shows significant potential for onboard deployment, which could enable real-time object identification and classification onboard autonomous spacecraft. This would greatly enhance the autonomy and efficiency in Earth Observation aerospace missions.

A logical next step for further developing the model would be to expand the dataset to include, in addition to lakes, other geophysical significant features, as an example islands. Including different landmarks as a new target would first offer an opportunity to test the model's adaptability. Above all, it should add information amount, and indeed redundancy, to the process, arguably increasing the accuracy in the identification. To be noticed that different categories of targets could end up in different analysis characteristics with respect to environmental conditions, that are still the main obstacle to satellite image processing in the visible portion of the spectrum, also improving the robustness of the process.

Fig. 13. Example of failure to recognize a lake, likely caused by the geometric complexity of the object combined with augmentation techniques, which made the image too challenging for the algorithm to interpret.

Additionally, testing the model on images captured by drones presents another promising direction. Drone imagery differs significantly from satellite data, as it includes images from lower altitudes, varied angles, and more dynamic perspectives, along with potential obstructions. These differences would provide a unique set of challenges for the model, including higher resolution images and changing viewpoints. The combination of two sets from different platforms and altitudes (satellites and drones) will arguably help in limiting false identification of the feature as the previously reported difference. So, it can be expected that introducing drone-captured imagery would increase the approach's robustness and adaptability, further expanding its potential use in various EO platforms.

References

1. J Redmon, J., Divvala, S., Girshick, R., Farhadi, A.: You only look once: unified, real-time object detection. In: Proceedings of the IEEE Conference on Computer Vision and Pattern Recognition (CVPR) (2016)
2. Wang, C.-Y., Wu, Y., Redmon, J.: YOLOv4: Optimal Speed and Accuracy of Object Detection (2021)
3. Hu, Y., Wu, Z., Xu, Y., Liu, L.: Deep learning for remote sensing image analysis: a comprehensive review. IEEE Geosci. Remote Sens. Magazine **8**(3), 22–54 (2020)

4. Zhang, L., Zhang, L., Du, B.: Deep learning for remote sensing data: a comprehensive review. ISPRS J. Photogramm. Remote Sens. **115**, 1–15 (2016)
5. Sbriglio, A., Palmerini, G.B.: Assessment of YOLO's Capabilities for Orbit Detection in Optical Satellite Imagery, IAC-24-B1.IP.69, 75th International Astronautical Congress, Milan, Italy, pp. 14–18 October 2024
6. https://www.esa.int/Applications/Observing_the_Earth/Copernicus/Sentinel-2
7. https://apps.sentinel-hub.com/eo-browser/
8. https://step.esa.int/main/snap-supported-plugins/sen2cor/
9. https://roboflow.com
10. Bai, R., Shen, F., Wang, M., Lu, J., Zhang, Z.: Improving detection capabilities of YOLOv8-n for small objects in remote sensing imagery: towards better precision with simplified model complexity, preprint (2023). https://doi.org/10.21203/rs.3.rs-3085871/v1

FoodLens: Fine-Grained and Multi-label Classification of Indian Food Images

Jatin Alla, Yashas Samaga, Ashwin Vaswani, Praneeth Netrapalli,
Shivani Kapania, Pradeep Kumar, and Narayan Hegde[✉]

Google Inc, Mountain View 94043, USA
{jatinalla,syashas,ashwinvaswani,pnetrapalli,skapania,
spreadeepkumar,hegde}@google.com

Abstract. India has rich cultural diversity which is reflected in its variety of food. In recent years, computer vision has played a key role in classifying food images for automated tagging, nutrition profiling and many other tasks. However, the existing state-of-the-art AI-based food classification models trained on global food images have subpar performance on Indian food images. This is due to the lack of representation of Indian food in existing food datasets and unique image classification challenges specific to Indian food, such as cuisines having multiple dishes within a single image and regional fine grained varieties of the dishes. To address these challenges, a dataset with 30K food images consisting of popular dishes from restaurant menus across India was curated and annotated with multi-label and fine-grained labels for each dish in the image. All the dishes were mapped onto a hierarchical tree which models a categorical breakdown of Indian food. Custom loss function was tuned to learn from hierarchical and multi-label information contained in the Indian food images. Augmenting our loss on existing methods gives 13% improvement on average AUPRC and shows better classification performance on Indian food dataset compared to state of art food classification models with comparable results for other food benchmark datasets. More than 100k photos which are submitted each day on Google Maps on Indian restaurants and many more on social media channels were utilized for the project.

Keywords: Computer vision · Machine learning · Classification · Multi-label · Hierarchical

1 Introduction

Food and nutrition have long played a crucial role in people's daily lives. In recent years, the pervasive nature of mobile devices has begun to redefine how we manage our food consumption facilitated by technology. With the advent of camera based smartphones, millions of pictures and videos of food are uploaded each day on numerous surfaces on the internet. These are often not tagged with the dish and relying on manual labeling is not scalable. Automated detection of food images provides scalable indexing and searching, making it easier to find relevant images, restaurants and blogs. In addition, many meal logging applications exist to help individuals monitor their eating patterns. These mobile applications elicit meal information including type and time of the meal. However, the primary method of this data collection is through text. Prior research has shown how this data collection can quickly turn tedious [28]. Identifying the food also helps in mapping the nutritional value of the food in many health applications. Automated food identification through images has thus emerged as an important domain for enabling healthy lifestyle changes.

Computer vision techniques have been used in food identification from images [20,25,56] and videos, food volume estimation with sensors [32], segmentation of food images [32] and learning from recipes [31]. These techniques require supervised training data to learn and generalize to unseen images. Prior works have curated several datasets [16,22,31,32] and developed approaches to tackle the problem of automated food identification. However, most existing datasets and techniques have focused exclusively on Western food, with exceptions of [3,40] and [35].

Indian food, in particular, consists of a variety of highly diverse regional cuisines under-represented in public food image datasets. Different states and regions within India have their unique styles of cooking, ingredients, and flavors, influenced by culinary traditions spanning centuries. Indian food draws on several staple ingredients such as rice, lentils, wheat, as well as spice combinations (e.g., cumin, turmeric, coriander). Furthermore, an Indian meal typically comprises multiple items served simultaneously, such as lentils, rice, breads, and chutneys, in contrast to other cuisines that have a sequential meal structure starting from appetizer, to main course, to dessert.

To understand the performance of these models on Indian food images, we conducted preliminary annotation experiments to qualitatively assess the performance of Google Lens on Indian dishes. Google Lens is an image recognition software that was released in 2017 by Google and is now available in most smartphones. We collaborated with 10 annotators to label food in 100–150 images for 13 popular Indian dishes. Many of these images had multiple dishes in each image. For each displayed image, raters were asked to mark the prominent and non-prominent (side dishes) along with confidence. Raters were asked to identify the most prominently present dish from the given options (coarse and then fine-grained label per dish) on Likert scale (min: 1, max: 5). Once a coarse label is added, options for the respective fine-grained labels are displayed in the next dropdown. Post data analysis of rated images, we found: (1) Overall ratings showed poor accuracy (less than 50%) when using a generic food classifier on Indian dishes across all 13 dishes. (2) Ratings based on granularity of the identified dish showed that most of the dishes were classified at coarser level than desired (40% of correctly classified dishes were identified at fine-grained level). (3) Ratings also showed that most of the identification focused on the main dish in the plate leaving many side dishes unidentified. (Less than 25% of multi dish plates are classified correctly).

Identifying fine-grained labels and making better mistakes are important to improve the user experience in search and nutritional health applications. Detecting the non-prominent side dishes is important in nutrition mapping and the ability to search images with multiple dishes. The paper addresses the problems found in UXR study in Indian food image classification by developing hierarchy-aware multi-label classification algorithm. This improves the fine-grained classification while identifying multiple dishes in the plate. Overall, the key contributions are as follows:

- Creating an multi-rater annotated dataset of 26k images across 137 Indian food dishes, distilled from restaurant menus along with hierarchical relation among dish labels.
- Developing a methodology for fine-grained and multi-label classification using the hierarchy information and multi-label annotations.
- Showcase better classification accuracy over state-of-the-art food classification models trained on both Indian and non-Indian food image datasets.

2 Related Work

Digital platforms like smartphones and wearables are having an increasing impact on lifestyle and well-being: physical activity, nutrition and sleep [53,54]. Smartphones sensors like cameras are empowering users to access searchable multimodal content across videos, images and text [23,58]. Cameras have increasingly been used in food and nutrition science with advances in deep learning [56,57]. Machine learning methods have been used for food identification from images [25,26,44], videos [9,24], food volume estimation with sensors [26], segmentation of food images [20,51], and learning from recipes [22,31]. The performance of these algorithms on new examples depend on the training dataset and annotation [16,33]. As a result, it is important to have sufficient representation of food images in training these systems to match use cases, region and culture. Food classification models have been adapted to specific cuisines by curating specialized datasets [10,15] and developing algorithms to enhance localization in APAC regions [27,37,52]. India has a rich cultural diversity of food with many centuries of influence. The Indian food image datasets [3,36] and methods [40] are limited to a few dishes with no customization to the uniqueness of Indian food images.

Indian cuisine has multiple adaptations of popular dishes based on local regions which demand fine-grained classification [6]. Furthermore, most Indian food plates consist of many dishes. Our work brings the hierarchy and multi-label adaptation of deep learning based methods to Indian food images and develops comprehensive solutions for uniqueness of the Indian dishes. Previous work in multi-label classification has been around exploiting label correlation via graph neural networks [11,12,19] or word embeddings [13,49]. Others are based on modeling image parts and attentional regions [21,55], and using recurrent neural networks [34,48], embedding space constraints, [39] region sampling

[59]. Methods are proposed to incorporate hierarchical knowledge to single-label classifiers to add additional semantics to the models' learning capabilities such that when the model makes mistakes, it makes semantically better mistakes. Hierarchical information is important in many other applications such as food recognition [1,29,50,60], protein function prediction [4,5,7], image annotation [18], text classification [30,42,43]. There has also been some recent work in hierarchical multi-label text classification [8,17,30,43].

3 Methodology

At present, there are no large scale open dataset dedicated for Indian images. A dataset consisting of images of Indian dishes is created for training and evaluation of Indian food classification models. Identifying the set of dish names and collecting images for the selected Indian dishes are the key steps in creating the dataset. Choices for selecting the dish types and the image source are aligned with identification of dishes from food images uploaded from restaurants in India on platforms like Google Maps restaurant reviews. The choice of the dish types and image source are for illustration of our methods on a generic application and not representative of the diversity or popularity of dishes in the country. The data collection strategy, number of dishes to be classified, number of images collected for each dish type can be swapped with any method tailored to the specific application of the food identification model. The following three subsections describe the label selection and curation process, also the food dataset creation. We then utilized a hierarchy-aware multi-label classification algorithm in order for better Indian food classification.

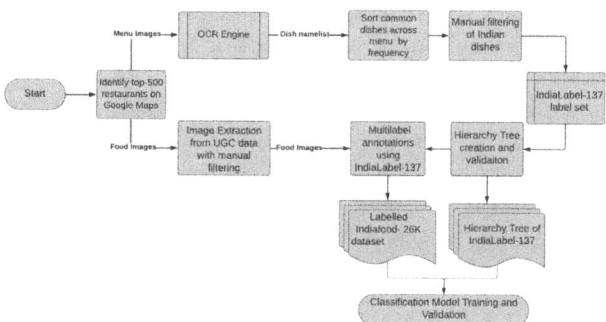

Fig. 1. A flowchart of the food label and food image dataset curation process.

3.1 Food Label Curation

Following methodology was adapted for the selection of top 200 dishes:

- 500 top restaurants were identified based on 4+ ratings on Google Maps with the highest number of reviews in popular cities across India. The restaurants were evenly distributed across 26 (out of 28) states in India with average number of reviews per restaurant 25000+ and 4.3+ rating out of 5. The restaurants ranged across franchises like McDonald's, local favorites and popular Indian chain restaurants.
- Menu Image was extracted from Google Maps for each of the 500 restaurants. Google OCR (Document AI) was used to digitize the menu image to extract the dishes served in the restaurant.
- Each dish name is preprocessed to correct for spelling correction and capitalization. N-gram phrase frequency is calculated for each dish type. We took the top 200 most frequent Indian food names as labels for creating the Image dataset.
- This method was aligned to identify most commonly occurring dishes among a diverse set of restaurants across various states in India. This serves as a proxy for commonly available dish types ordered in restaurants by Indians.

3.2 Distillation of Food Labels

We collected a set of 235 unique food dishes labels from top-rated restaurant menus across India. However, the most common dishes from top-rated Indian restaurants contained several dishes that were clearly not of Indian origin, such as cheese dip, steak, and waffles. This added an additional challenge to the filtration process as many Indian restaurants have adopted dishes from other cultures, resulting in hybrid dishes that may not be easily classified as either Indian or foreign. As exemplified by the growing number of fast food chains to high end global cuisines appearing in the urban cities of India [14].

To create a more focused dataset of Indian food, we assembled a team of four native Indians to review the dish names and remove any that were not of Indian origin. With these adaptations to global cuisine, there have been more hybrid dishes that are a mixture of authentic Indian food and strong external influences such as cheese pav, veg sandwiches and many more.

The team of 4 did their best to filter out any dishes that would not be considered Indian dishes (i.e., chocolate brownie, honey chili fries, etc.). In the cases of dishes with uncertain origin or broad classification, such as "corn chilly" and "curd", we consulted culinary experts. This resulted in a further removal of 19 labels.

At last, The final dataset of 137 unique Indian food labels was curated. These labels represent a wide range of Indian cuisine, from traditional dishes such as tandoori chicken and idli to more modern fusion dishes such as cheese pav and veg sandwiches. The label set will be referred to as IndiaLabel-137 in the paper. Figure 1 summarizes the steps involved in dataset and label set curation.

3.3 Food Images Collection and Annotation

The following methodology was adopted to collect the images of identified 137 list:

Images are sourced from the user uploaded food images on Google Maps for the 500 preselected restaurants, which were used to gather the food labels. Which resulted in a total of 53,400 image accompanied with machine labels. In which, we discarded the dataset of all the labels that weren't on the final IndiaLabel-137, result in 35,500 images with corresponding labels which were sent to human annotation. Then, a group of raters manually labeled food images from the image dataset and skipped images which were blurry, had PII (Personal Identifiable Information) or not able to be identified with a fine-grained label. Additionally, we combined any dishes with misspelled labeled or alternative name manually. The final set of images of good quality and proper labels from the IndiaLabel-137 are 26,500 images and 8,200 images were skipped.

The image dataset will henceforth be referred to as IndiaFood26K in the paper. The dataset reflects images taken in restaurant settings which are well decorated and arranged compared to home cooked food. We expect models trained on IndiaFood26K to generalize to restaurant uploaded images which would aid in automatically tagging images to support better user experience in identifying relevant restaurants on the web. They may also generalize to aid digital apps for online food delivery, identifying new dishes served in Indian restaurants but may not work well for home cooked meals.

Annotation Process. The annotation process for our Indian food image dataset was designed to be robust, reliable, efficient, and scalable. To address the challenge of multiple food items being present in a single image, a multi-label and multi-rater approach was used. The dataset contains 137 food labels, with approximately 250 images per label, for a total of 35,000 images. Two rounds of human annotation were conducted, with each image being annotated by a single annotator in each round (Fig. 2).

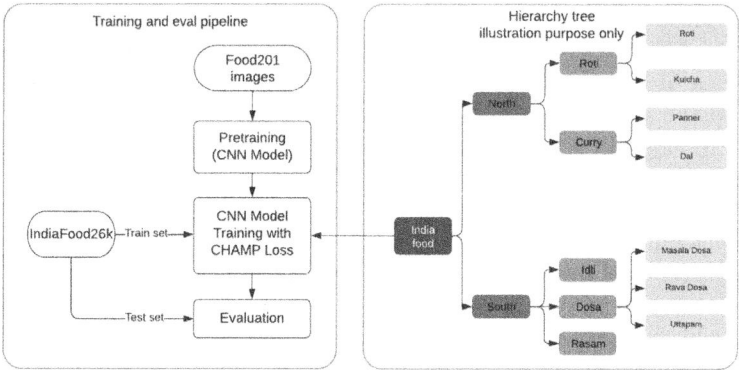

Fig. 2. India food classification pipeline.

Labeling Tool Description and Rater Profiles and Matching. The image annotation user interface (UI) is a critical tool for ensuring the quality and accuracy of image annotation. The UI provides annotators with a convenient and efficient way to label images, and it also collects valuable feedback on the quality of the image data.

The UI consists of three main components: the image, two dropdown menus for labeling, and two multiple choice questions on image quality and image label completeness.

The Fig. 10 is displayed on the right-hand side of the UI. It is large enough to be easily viewed, and it is accompanied by a skip button that allows annotators to skip the image if they are unable to label it. The skip button also includes a dropdown menu with reasons for skipping: "Unable to identify the exact fine-grained label," "Unable to identify the dish at all," "Image contains text/caption/watermark of the label in it," "Image contains packaged food/canned food/food mixture," or "Image does not contain a food dish."

The two dropdown menus on the left-hand side of the UI allow annotators to label the image with precision and accuracy. The first menu is for fine-grained labeling, and it contains a dropdown section of the 137 food labels. An autocomplete feature helps to streamline the annotating experience, as annotators are not required to type out the entire name of the food to annotate the image with the dish name. The second dropdown menu records the annotator's confidence level between low or high depending on how well the label matches the image.

The multiple choice questions at the bottom of the UI allow annotators to provide feedback on the quality of the image and the label set. The first question, "Quality of Image?", assesses the image quality with the following options: "Good," "Low resolution," "Unclear/blurry," or "Noisy with perturbations." The second question, "How many dishes were labeled in this image?", measures the competence of the label set with the following options: "Are all dishes in the image tagged," "More than half which is 50% of the dishes are tagged," or "Less than half which is 50% of the items are tagged in the image."

Hierarchical Tree Creation. To improve the accuracy of AI-based Indian food classification, we sought to create a label set of fine-grained classifications structured within a hierarchical tree. The goal behind this creation is to assist AI systems in making better mistakes by having inherent semantic knowledge built into the hierarchy [50]. Leveraging this inherent trait within hierarchies, we hope to close the gap in the accuracy of identifying Indian food images.

Due to the nuance of creating a hierarchy to assist AI systems with the goal of providing semantic information, we had to start from the ground to develop the diffrent bin [38,41]. To gain a deeper understanding of how to create appropriate categories within Indian food, we first consulted with a culinary expert with over 20 years of experience in the field. To understand Indian food from a chef's perspective, we have gleaned insights into how to generally structure the hierarchy.

The culinary expert informed us that Indian food can be broadly divided into two regional categories: North Indian and South Indian. This distinction is based on the distinct regional meal staples and corresponding visual differences between dishes from those regions. Although there are finer distinctions between East and West Indian cuisine, we found that the meals that we had narrowed down were better categorized with North and South, and that there would be no added benefit in distinguishing further with our current data [47].

At the second level of distinction, we made the separation between vegetarian dishes and non-vegetarian dishes. This distinction is important specially to Indian food as the dishes between vegetarian and non-vegetarian can be difficult to distinguish visually. Moreover, there is a cultural significance to this distinction, as vegetarians would to dislike their food being mistakenly labeled for non-vegetarian food. Therefore, we prioritized the distinction between veg and non-veg into higher in the hierarchy [35].

To implement these first two insights, we conducted a multi-rater process of manually labeling 137 food dishes as either North or South Indian, and as either vegetarian or non-vegetarian. We assembled a group of five non-expert Indians, two of whom were North Indian, two of whom were South Indian, and one of whom was East Indian. We then classified each food label through a majority vote. Although this process was not perfect, it gave us an indication of whether a dish was North or South, and whether it was vegetarian or non-vegetarian.

After the multi-rater process, the final categories for each level from the highest level to the lowest were defined. At the first level was a distinctions between North Indian food or South Indian food. Then second level was split into vegetarian or non-vegetarian for each type of food. At the third level, we identified different further breakdown of based on each dishes regionally and vegetarian versus non-vegetarian. For north and South Indian cuisines, we have divided into curries, sides, and drinks for vegetarian dishes. For non-vegetarian dishes, we divided into different types of meat, such as chicken, mutton. Each of the curries were further divided into their key ingredients, this allowed us to group dishes that held close resemblances with their adjacent dish. This is the crucial feature that we hoped the hierarchy will allow the models to make more graceful mistakes, instead of mixing up very prominent features like vegetarian for a meat dish.

3.4 ML Methodology

We propose to use the CHAMP [46] loss function that leverages the hierarchical relationships in the dataset and can easily be plugged into existing models and backbones. The loss function is described in Sect. 3.4 and evaluation methods are discussed in Sect. 3.4.

Loss Function. Let $\mathcal{D}$ represent the training data distribution. We draw samples (x, y) from $\mathcal{D}$ where $x \in \mathbf{R}^d$ denotes the input and $y \in \mathbf{R}^L$ denotes a binary vector of labels where one (zero) at position j indicates the presence (absence) of the class j. Let θ denote the set of parameters. Let $\hat{y} \in \mathbf{R}^L$ denote the vector of predicted class probabilities in the same order as y. The standard baseline for training multi-label classifiers is to predict probabilities for each class independently and minimize the binary cross entropy of each predictor. The instance-level loss for the standard baseline would be (diameter is defined as the distance of the longest possible path in a tree):

$$J(x, y; \theta) = -\sum_{j=1}^{L} y_j \log \hat{y}_j + (1 - y_j) \log(1 - \hat{y}_j)$$

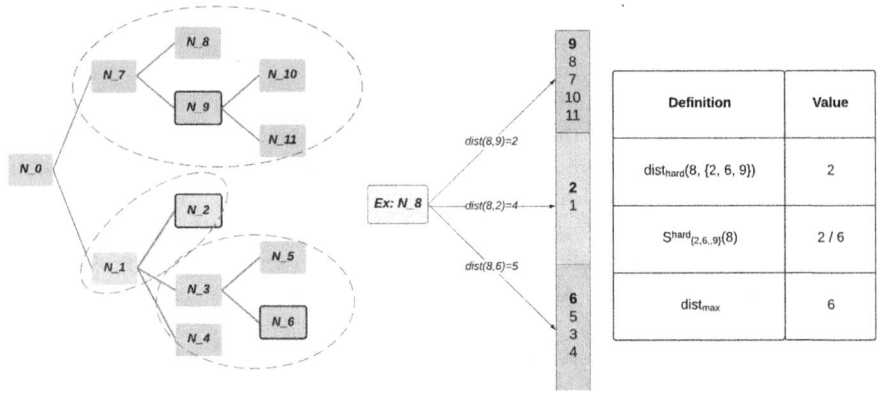

Fig. 3. HMC Loss function example.

We incorporate hierarchy, denoted by T, into the method by expanding the label set to include non-leaf nodes of the hierarchy. To add positive examples for the internal nodes, we alter the ground-truth sets of each sample to include all the ancestors of every leaf label in the set. This reduces the hierarchical classification problem to a standard multi-label classification over an expanded label set. This serves as our hierarchical baseline.

To make more efficient use of the hierarchical information, we weigh the L loss terms differently for each instance. Given an instance, the weight for the term corresponding to class j is proportional to the path distance between that class and the closest ground-truth to it in the hierarchy. The modified loss function is:

$$J(x, y; \theta) = -\sum_{j=1}^{L} y_j \log \hat{y}_j + (1 - y_j)(1 + s(j, y)) \log(1 - \hat{y}_j)$$

where s is the instance-specific class weight. It is defined as:

$$s(j, y) = \beta \min_{i \in \{l \in L | y_l = 1\}} \frac{\text{distance}(j, i; T)}{\text{diameter}^1(T)}$$

where β is a tunable hyperparameter.

Evaluation Metrics. Let (x, y) denote a sample from the data distribution $\mathcal{D}$ where $x \in \mathbf{R}^d$ represents an image and $y \in \mathbf{R}^L$ is a one-hot binary vector of class ground-truths as described earlier. Given a model that outputs class probabilities, we assume the prediction to be positive for class j if the probability exceeds a class-specific threshold T_j.

We calculate per-class performance metrics. The overall performance is reported as the average per-class performance. Hence, for the rest of the section, assume that we work with a binary classifier. Given a test distribution $(x, y) \sim \mathcal{D}$ and a model, we obtain the presence of the class, denoted by the binary variable $\hat{y}$, by thresholding the predicted probability with T. We define precision and recall as:

$$\text{Precision} = \mathbb{E}_{(x,y) \sim \mathcal{D}} [y = 1 | \hat{y} = 1]$$

$$\text{Recall} = \mathbb{E}_{(x,y) \sim \mathcal{D}} [\hat{y} = 1 | y = 1]$$

The choice of the threshold T controls the precision-recall trade-off and is typically selected based on practical requirements. A higher threshold generally leads to higher precision and lower recall, and a lower threshold leads to lower precision and higher recall.

To gauge the general performance without committing to a specific threshold, we use the Area Under Precision-Recall Curve (AUPRC) to summarize the classification performance of a given class. The precision-recall curve is traced by computing the (precision, recall) for different values of thresholds. The average AUPRC over all classes or nodes in the tree to summarize the overall performance.

4 Results

4.1 Qualitative Results

Breakdown of the Food Label Hierarchy

Region. The dishes are primarily divided into North Indian and South Indian cuisine, with 105 and 32 dishes, respectively. There are also a small number of dishes that are pan-Indian or specific to other regions of India. (See Fig. 6 in Appendix)

Dietary Restrictions. The dishes are also divided into vegetarian and meat dishes, with 102 and 35 dishes, respectively. (See Fig. 6 in Appendix)

Subcategories. The dishes are further divided into subcategories at the third level of the hierarchy. For example, the North Indian dish "Chicken Tikka Masala" is classified as a "Curry" dish, while the South Indian dish "Idli" is classified as a "Dosa" dish due to the ingredients used for both dishes (Fig. 4). (see Fig. 8 in Appendix)

Fig. 4. Images of chicken biryani from the IndiaFood26K.

Datacard. The IndiaFood26K dataset is a large-scale, multi-label dataset of Indian food images. The pre-annotated dataset contains 35,148 images across 137 data labels, and is 5–6 levels deep in terms of label hierarchy. The dataset was created by collecting non-sensitive static image data about food from a user-generated database within Google Maps. Labels were derived from restaurant menus. Refer to Fig. 3 for a sample of the type of images within our dataset.

The IndiaFood26K dataset is motivated by the need for a large-scale Indian food classification dataset for computer vision projects. The dataset is not publicly available due to the fact that it is user-generated and we want to maintain user data privacy.

The IndiaFood26K dataset contains a number of biases, including:

- **North Indian vs. South Indian Bias.** The separation of North Indian and South Indian food was not done with culinary expert feedback, and was reliant on 5 non-expert native Indians who are from similar backgrounds. This could have created a potential bias in annotation, which doesn't encapsulate the perception of the Indian populace.
- **Label Hierarchy Bias.** The label hierarchy was not verified and validated by experts, and we only consulted one expert. This may have induced selection bias, where our hierarchy would have catered to one perspective on Indian food. This effect will affect the model's semantic knowledge of Indian food, and may have left out important classifications.
- **Label Selection Bias.** The process in which we refined the labels from 235 to 137 labels could have resulted in a selection bias. This is because the selection of which labels to keep or throw out was done by a small group of people from the lab. This could have resulted in a dataset that does not represent the general perception of Indian food.

Data Trends Post-Annotation. Annotating multi-image datasets is challenging because it can be difficult to identify the exact fine-grain label for a dish, especially if the image is blurry or if there are text/watermarks obscuring the food. In our study, we found that the most common reason for annotators to skip an image was that they were unable to identify the exact fine-grain label. Text/watermarks obscuring the food in the image was a close second. This led to a loss of 4–5k images per annotation round.

Of the 22k images that were labeled, annotator confidence and completion of labeling was high. In the first round of annotations (v1), 68% of images had all dishes labeled, 27% had over half labeled, and 4% had less than half labeled. The second round of annotations (v2) showed a similar trend. (see Fig. 9 and 10 in Appendix).

The quality of images in the dataset was good, with annotators rating them as good 99% of the time. Annotator confidence was also high, with 93% of annotators rating their confidence as high. (see Fig. 11, 12, 13 and 14 in Appendix for more detailed distribution).

The results from the annotation process strongly support the need for multi-label dataset as most Indian food images contain more than one dish. In both rounds of annotations, around 30% of images (7k images) received more than one label. This suggests that Indian food images are often complex and can be difficult to classify under a single label.

4.2 Indian Dish Classification Model Results

IndiaFood26K Train Test Split. The dataset was preprocessed to resize images and fix orientation before creating train-test splits. Labels that had fewer than twenty examples were removed (8 out of 137 labels). Examples that had no labels left after the previous step were removed (43 out of 23918 examples). Starting with the rarest label, a random example that contained the label was added to the test set. Examples were sampled without replacement until there were at least ten examples for that label. This process is iterated by moving on to the next rarest label with fewer than ten labels and the process is repeated until every label had at least ten examples in the test set. The remaining examples formed the train dataset. At the end, there were 4775 test examples and 19100 train examples. Figure 11 shows the final distribution of labels in the test and train dataset.

Given our dataset is relatively small compared to the sizes required to train deep neural networks, we used pre-trained convolution neural network (CNN) backbone and fine-tuned on our target dataset. Three popular pre-trained backbones were used to fine-tune the models for food classification: GoogleNet[1], ResNet[2] and EfficientNetV2s[3]. For each of these CNN architectures, ImageNet-pretrained weights were used and a linear layer of size 137 was added at the top. We use the standard binary cross-entropy loss as outlined in Sect. 3.4. We do a 80-20 train-validation split on the aforementioned train dataset and perform a grid-search on the hyperparameters based on the validation loss. More details on the exact training and grid-search procedure can be found in Appendix.

Table 1 presents the models' performance on IndiaFood26K test set using only multi label annotation for training. Macro average AUPRC is used to evaluate the model. Performance is not satisfactory in all three methods. There is

Table 1. Performance on IndiaFood26K test set.

Method	Backbone	AUPRC
Food201 [32]	GoogleNet	0.264 ± 0.005
IFC [40]	ResNet50	0.276 ± 0.002
SAM	EffNetV2s	0.293 ± 0.009

Table 2. Performance on Food201 test set.

Method	Backbone	AUPRC
Food201	GoogleNet	0.489 ± 0.001
IFC	ResNet50	0.519 ± 0.002
SAM	EffNetV2s	0.543 ± 0.005

an increasing trend in performance with more recent backbones. To gauge a better understanding of the relative performance, we train models on Food201. Food201 is a multilabel dataset which is similar to our IndiaFood26K dataset in characteristics. Table 2 presents the results on the official Food201 test set. We note that the performance on Food201 is higher than IndiaFood26K.

We hypothesise that the poor performance on IndiaFood26K may be due to the intrinsic difficulty of classifying Indian food at a fine-grained level. We qualitatively describe two cases below highlighting the general difficulty in classifying the images:

- Many Indian dishes look visually similar but belong to different classes of food. Figure 10 shows similar looking images that were unanimously labelled differently.
- Many Indian dishes have large visual variations. Figure 9 shows images that look different but were unanimously labelled identically.

To verify the above hypothesis, second round of data annotation was performed on the IndiaFood26K using the same annotation protocol but with different annotators. Intersection over Union (IoU) was used on the two label sets to measure the consistency across annotations. Table 3 presents the results for IoU across the two annotation rounds. The IoU is around 0.59 at leaf nodes which indicate that human raters do not agree on the fine grained labels in more that 40% of cases. However, we observe better agreements on labels per image on common coarser grained labels. This motivates incorporating hierarchy in our model to make better mistakes and fail gracefully. Adding internal nodes may provide coarser labels of the fine grained labels to be represented in the classification. The hierarchy relations among these nodes also provides a way to leverage sibling relationships or patterns while learning. To train our hierarchical solution, we expanded the ground-truth set to include the internal nodes of the hierarchy as described in Sect. 3.4. The Table 4 shows the results on three methods with non-leaf nodes on both IndiaFood26K and Food201 dataset.

We note the degradation in AUPRC after incorporating hierarchy. This may simply be due to addition of extra labels. The addition of hierarchy degrades performance of rare classes much more than common classes as shown in Table 4. We hypothesize that this may be due to classes recieving different effective weights; the more common internal coarse-grained labels might aid in learning representations of the children and thereby increase the effective weight of the children.

Table 3. Mean IoU between labels from annotation 1 and 2.

Depth	Leaf	4	3	2	1
IndiaTree	0.59	0.74	0.81	0.89	0.93
Randomized Leaves	0.59	0.62	0.66	0.79	0.90
Height	Leaf	1	2	3	4
IndiaTree	0.59	0.76	0.81	0.87	0.92
Randomized Leaves	0.59	0.61	0.66	0.75	0.8

Table 4. Performance on Indian food classification using fine and coarse grained labels.

Method	Backbone	Micro AUPRC	Macro AUPRC	Micro Top 25	Micro Bottom 25
BCE (no internal)	GoogleNet	0.358 ± 0.006	0.264 ± 0.005	0.433	0.091
Food201	GoogleNet	0.319 ± 0.011	0.221 ± 0.011	0.406	0.071
BCE (no internal)	ResNet50	0.362 ± 0.002	0.276 ± 0.002	0.423	0.102
IFC	ResNet50	0.351 ± 0.015	0.256 ± 0.011	0.426	0.088
BCE (no internal)	EfficientNetV2S	0.391 ± 0.009	0.293 ± 0.009	0.466	0.108
SAM	EfficientNetV2S	0.357 ± 0.06	0.256 ± 0.008	0.443	0.083

CHAMP loss function described in the Sect. 3.4 (methods) is used to incorporate the hierarchical relation among the Indian food dishes more effectively. CHAMP uses the hierarchy as tree structure to compute the loss function. Table 5 shows the improvement in classification performance of CHAMP loss function in comparison to plain binary cross-entropy loss across all three backbones used in the experiments. CHAMP owing to hierarchy-aware loss may make better mistakes which is reflected in better performance of non-leaf node classification in the tree structure. The CHAMP shows the largest increase in performance relative to baseline loss function at leaf level. This may be attributed to larger gain in performance of nodes which have lesser training examples in the dataset leading CHAMP to perform well at fine-grained classification. However, the classification AUPRC attains good performance at higher levels indicating practical utility of the method for coarse grained classification.

Table 5. Classification performance comparison of CHAMP with BCE loss for multi label classification of IndiaFood26K dataset across depths of the hierarchy.

Method	Backbone	AUPRC@leaf	AUPRC@1	AUPRC@2	AUPRC@3	AUPRC@4	AUPRC@5
Food201 + ERM (with internal)	GoogleNet	0.221 ± 0.011	0.867 ± 0.007	0.667 ± 0.01	0.497 ± 0.013	0.393 ± 0.017	0.194 ± 0.001
Food201 + CHAMP	GoogleNet	0.253 ± 0.003	0.884 ± 0.004	0.71 ± 0.005	0.532 ± 0.006	0.422 ± 0.006	0.225 ± 0.003
ERM (with internal)	ResNet50	0.256 ± 0.011	0.885 ± 0.005	0.697 ± 0.012	0.528 ± 0.015	0.422 ± 0.014	0.229 ± 0.011
CHAMP	ResNet50	0.258 ± 0.011	0.889 ± 0.006	0.708 ± 0.013	0.531 ± 0.014	0.428 ± 0.016	0.23 ± 0.01
ERM (with internal)	EffNetV2	0.256 ± 0.008	0.891 ± 0.003	0.717 ± 0.007	0.54 ± 0.005	0.431 ± 0.007	0.227 ± 0.008
CHAMP	EffNetV2	0.269 ± 0.01	0.886 ± 0.007	0.714 ± 0.011	0.549 ± 0.013	0.442 ± 0.013	0.239 ± 0.009

The gain in CHAMP classification performance can be attributed to the hierarchy tree and multi label annotation. We conduct ablation experiments to show the value of the hierarchy tree construction on classification performance in Table 7. We note considerable degradation in the performance of internal nodes with the random hierarchy, but with a marginal improvement in the performance at leaf nodes. Random hierarchy at each level is created by randomly shuffling the leaf nodes while keeping rest of the structure intact. As seen, the structure of the hierarchy tree is an important design aspect of the algorithm and needs to be constructed according to use case.

4.3 Indian Dish Identification Using Multimodal Large Language Model

Recent advances in Multimodal Large Language Models (MLLMs) research is revolutionizing how we interact with technology. These models extend beyond the conventional text-based interfaces and can understand and generate content across many modalities including text, images, audio, and video. Gemini 1.0 Pro [2] is a popular MLLM built on top of Transformer decoders [45] that with improvements to enable training at scale and for efficient inference on Google's Tensor Processing Units.

We evaluated how Gemini Pro fared at classifying Indian food images at both coarse-grained and fine-grained levels. We used it to classify images from IndiaFood26K using the following prompt: "Classify the image with Indian dishes. Label all if the image has multiple dishes. Output label dish names only". Both fine grained and multi label classification capability were analysed by comparing the output of Gemini model with annotators label. Table 6 shows the results summary for multilabel classification on test set of IndiaFood26K consisting of 4780 images with 6850 human labels. With just prompt engineering, MLLM models can identify India dishes at coarse granularity. The models also do not identify all the dishes present in the image. Further model finetuning is needed to increase the accuracy of the Indian food classification on GenAI tools. For completeness, MLLM performance on Food201 images are also presented. MLLM performs well on both Fine and coarse granularity better than CNN models either due to larger model capacity or possible use of the dataset in the training.

Table 6. Performance of Gemini MLLM on IndiaFood26K & Food201.

Evaluation Method	IndiaFood26K matched	IndiaFood26K Coverage	Food201 matched	Food201 Coverage
Fine grained prediction	866	12%	1520	80%
Coarse grained prediction	3300	48%	1520	20%
Images with no labels matching	2630	54%	31	2%
Images with partial labels matching	2070	44%	259	18%
Images with all labels matching	80	2%	1230	80%

4.4 Result Summary

Summary of the experiments and ML model results are as follows

- Multi label classification of Indian food images have low accuracy due to high variations in images as seen with higher inter grader variability among human annotators.
- Incorporating hierarchical relationships among Indian dishes with CHAMP loss yields better classification accuracy for both fine and coarse grained labels.
- Ablation experiments attribute the gain in classification performance to the hierarchy tree information.

5 Discussion

Wide-ranging geographical differences in Indian food, including ingredients, cooking techniques, and presentation styles, make complete picture classification extremely difficult. This intricacy is emphasized by our dataset, which is generated from user-uploaded photos of Indian restaurant meals on Google Maps. We do accept, however, that the dataset may not be fully representative of the entire range of Indian cuisine offers due to inherent biases in both dish selection and visual depiction. In this work, we investigate the challenges associated with vision-based categorization in Indian food and suggest possible ways forward. Large-scale, publicly-available statistics are crucial for promoting research and innovation in the Asian food and nutrition industry. Furthermore, considering the variety of possible uses (such as nutrition analysis, recipe development, and food discovery), equitable methods to dataset construction that prioritize fairness and representation are crucial. Adding more information than just picture hierarchies and co-occurrence patterns will greatly improve the categorization of Pan Asian cuisine. Research on nutrition and cooking might be revolutionized by adding comprehensive metadata to datasets from professionals in these domains. The additional visual variety seen in photos of homemade Indian cuisine must also be expressly taken into consideration by machine learning techniques. These photos frequently feature overlapping parts, partly devoured portions, locally sourced food, and muted hues. Similar techniques could also benefit many south Asian cuisines which are not well represented in food datasets Widespread image-based meal recording in social media and nutrition apps offers a great chance to address representational and data volume issues. Lastly, while maintaining user privacy, federated learning provides a way to improve food recognition algorithms. Our work on Indian food image classification is an excellent example to look for more accurate localised classification models. Addressing data bias, using multi-domain information, and using machine learning techniques can advance the field.

6 Conclusion

In this work, we consider the problem of multi-label India food classification. We created a new multi-label annotated IndiaFood26K dataset consisting of 139 Indian dishes. We improve the state of the art classification performance by utilizing the relationship among labels by creating the hierarchical tree by adding coarse grain dish categories as parent nodes. Our CHAMP loss uses both multi-label and hierarchy classification to improve both fine-grain and coarse grain classification of Indian food images (Figs. 5 and 7).

Acknowledgments. A bold run-in heading in small font size at the end of the paper is used for general acknowledgments, for example: This study was funded by X (grant number Y).

Disclosure of Interests. It is now necessary to declare any competing interests or to specifically state that the authors have no competing interests. Please place the statement with a bold run-in heading in small font size beneath the (optional) acknowledgments (If EquinOCS, our proceedings submission system, is used, then the disclaimer can be provided directly in the system.), for example: The authors have no competing interests to declare that are relevant to the content of this article. Or: Author A has received research grants from Company W. Author B has received a speaker honorarium from Company X and owns stock in Company Y. Author C is a member of committee Z.

Appendix

Table 7. Classification performance of CHAMP with Logical Hierarchy vs Random hierarchy.

Method	Type	Backbone	AUPRC@leaf	AUPRC@1	AUPRC@2	AUPRC@3	AUPRC@4	AUPRC@5
CHAMP	Logical Hierarchy	Food201	0.24 ± 0.01	0.882 ± 0.005	0.702 ± 0.003	0.523 ± 0.007	0.407 ± 0.011	0.214 ± 0.008
CHAMP	Logical Hierarchy	ResNet50	0.258 ± 0.011	0.889 ± 0.006	0.708 ± 0.013	0.531 ± 0.014	0.428 ± 0.016	0.23 ± 0.01
CHAMP	Logical Hierarchy	EffNetV2s	0.269 ± 0.01	0.886 ± 0.007	0.714 ± 0.011	0.549 ± 0.013	0.442 ± 0.013	0.239 ± 0.009
CHAMP	Random Hierarchy	Food201	0.234 ± 0.01	0.77 ± 0.007	0.541 ± 0.005	0.372 ± 0.009	0.341 ± 0.007	0.205 ± 0.01
CHAMP	Random Hierarchy	ResNet50	0.215 ± 0.021	0.771 ± 0.011	0.532 ± 0.018	0.344 ± 0.025	0.314 ± 0.022	0.188 ± 0.02
CHAMP	Random Hierarchy	EffNetV2s	0.255 ± 0.015	0.792 ± 0.016	0.561 ± 0.019	0.391 ± 0.02	0.357 ± 0.016	0.226 ± 0.015

Food Labels Distribution

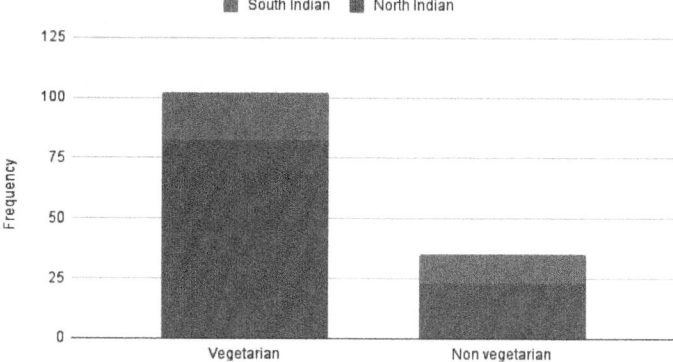

Fig. 5. High level food label distributions in hierarchy.

Fine-label Categories of Indian Food

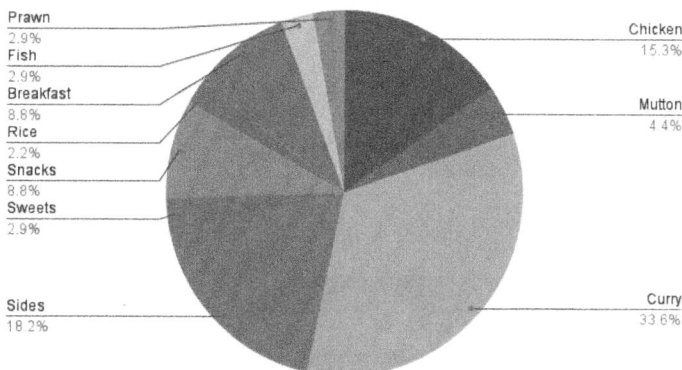

Fig. 6. Fine-level Food Label Distributions in Hierarchy.

extent of labelling V1

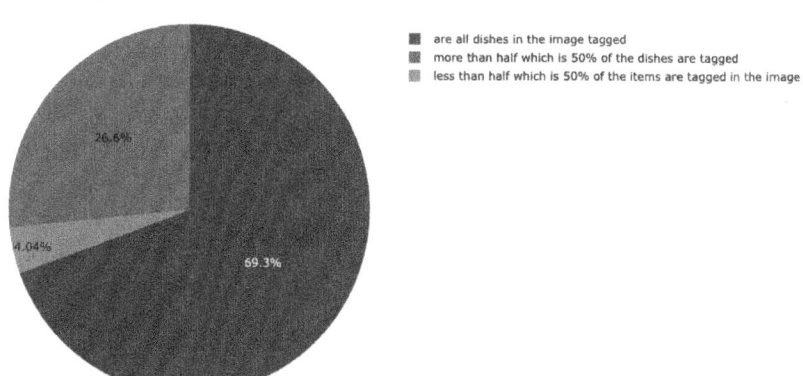

Fig. 7. Fine-level Food Label Distributions in Hierarchy.

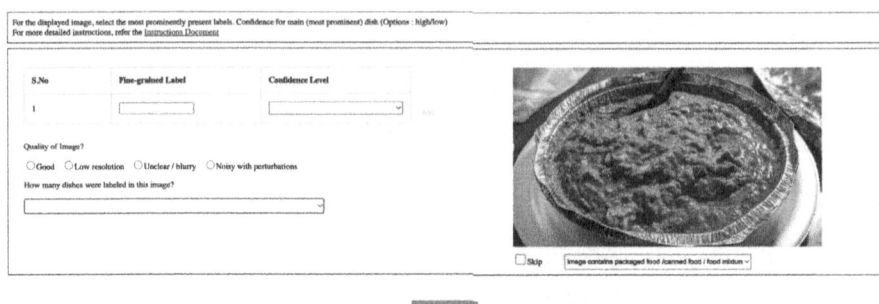

Fig. 8. Annotator UI.

Fig. 9. Dishes of same kind (Biryani) has large visual variations among images.

Fig. 10. Dishes look visually similar but belong to diferent classes like Biryani, Pulav, Fried rice.

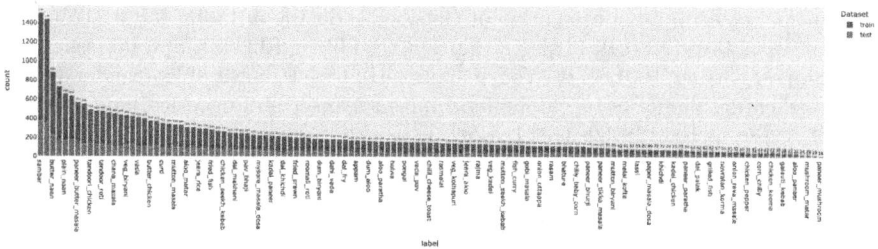

Fig. 11. Frequency of labels in the train and test datasets.

References

1. Monusac2020: a multi-organ nuclei segmentation and classification challenge. IEEE Trans. Med. Imaging **40**(12), 3413–3423 (2021). https://doi.org/10.1109/TMI.2021.3085712
2. Gemini: A family of highly capable multimodal models (2023)
3. Banerjee, S.: Indian food images dataset (kaggle) (2022)
4. Barros, R.C., Cerri, R., Freitas, A.A., de Carvalho, A.C.P.L.F.: Probabilistic clustering for hierarchical multi-label classification of protein functions. In: Blockeel, H., Kersting, K., Nijssen, S., Železný, F. (eds.) Machine Learning and Knowledge Discovery in Databases, pp. 385–400. Springer, Berlin (2013)
5. Bi, W., Kwok, J.T.Y.: Multilabel classification on tree- and dag-structured hierarchies. In: International Conference on Machine Learning (2011). https://api.semanticscholar.org/CorpusID:18111582
6. Burkapalli, C., Patil, V.P.C.: Food image segmentation using edge adaptive based deep-CNNs. Int. J. Intell. Unmanned Syst. **8**(4), 243–252 (2019)
7. Cesa-Bianchi, N., Valentini, G.: Hierarchical cost-sensitive algorithms for genome-wide gene function prediction. In: Džeroski, S., Guerts, P., Rousu, J. (eds.) Proceedings of the third International Workshop on Machine Learning in Systems Biology. Proceedings of Machine Learning Research, vol. 8, pp. 14–29. PMLR, Ljubljana (2009)
8. Chatterjee, S., Maheshwari, A., Ramakrishnan, G., Jagaralpudi, S.N.: Joint learning of hyperbolic label embeddings for hierarchical multi-label classification (2021)
9. Chaudhary, S., Murala, S.: Deep network for human action recognition using weber motion. Neurocomputing **367**, 207–216 (2019)
10. Chen, X., Zhou, H., Diao, L.: Chinesefoodnet: A large-scale image dataset for Chinese food recognition. CoRR abs/1705.02743 (2017). http://arxiv.org/abs/1705.02743
11. Chen, Z.M., Wei, X.S., Jin, X., Guo, Y.: Multi-label image recognition with joint class-aware map disentangling and label correlation embedding. In: 2019 IEEE International Conference on Multimedia and Expo (ICME), pp. 622–627 (2019). https://doi.org/10.1109/ICME.2019.00113
12. Chen, Z., Wei, X., Wang, P., Guo, Y.: Multi-label image recognition with graph convolutional networks. CoRR abs/1904.03582 (2019). http://arxiv.org/abs/1904.03582
13. Chen, Z.M., Wei, X.S., Wang, P., Guo, Y.: Multi-label image recognition with graph convolutional networks (2019)

14. Chitnis, M.: A study on scenario of fast-food industry in India. Int. J. Trend Sci. Res. Dev. 88–90 (2019). https://doi.org/10.31142/ijtsrd23071. Special Issue
15. Chun, M., Jeong, H., Lee, H., Yoo, T., Jung, H.: Development of Korean food image classification model using public food image dataset and deep learning methods. IEEE Access **10**, 128732–128741 (2022)
16. Ciocca, G., Napoletano, P., Schettini, R.: Food recognition: a new dataset, experiments, and results. IEEE J. Biomed. Health Inform. **21**(3), 588–598 (2017). https://doi.org/10.1109/JBHI.2016.2636441
17. Daisey, K., Brown, S.D.: Effects of the hierarchy in hierarchical, multi-label classification. Chemom. Intell. Lab. Syst. **207**, 104177 (2020)
18. Dimitrovski, I., Kocev, D., Loskovska, S., Džeroski, S.: Hierarchical annotation of medical images. Pattern Recogn. **44**(10), 2436–2449 (2011). https://doi.org/10.1016/j.patcog.2011.03.026. https://www.sciencedirect.com/science/article/pii/S0031320311001300, semi-Supervised Learning for Visual Content Analysis and Understanding
19. Durand, T., Mehrasa, N., Mori, G.: Learning a deep convnet for multi-label classification with partial labels. CoRR abs/1902.09720 (2019). http://arxiv.org/abs/1902.09720
20. Freitas, C.N.C., Cordeiro, F.R., Macario, V.: Myfood: a food segmentation and classification system to aid nutritional monitoring. In: 2020 33rd SIBGRAPI Conference on Graphics, Patterns and Images (SIBGRAPI), pp. 234–239 (2020)
21. Gao, B., Zhou, H.: Multi-label image recognition with multi-class attentional regions. CoRR abs/2007.01755 (2020). https://arxiv.org/abs/2007.01755
22. Harashima, J., Someya, Y., Kikuta, Y.: Cookpad image dataset: an image collection as infrastructure for food research. In: SIGIR 2017, pp. 1229–1232. Association for Computing Machinery, New York (2017). https://doi.org/10.1145/3077136.3080686
23. Ismail, A., Kumar, N.: Empowerment on the margins: the online experiences of community health workers. In: Proceedings of the 2019 CHI Conference on Human Factors in Computing Systems, CHI 2019, pp. 1–15. Association for Computing Machinery, New York (2019). https://doi.org/10.1145/3290605.3300329
24. Kuehne, H., Gall, J., Serre, T.: An end-to-end generative framework for video segmentation and recognition. In: Proceedings IEEE Winter Applications of Computer Vision Conference (WACV 16). Lake Placid (2016)
25. Liu, C., Cao, Y., Luo, Y., Chen, G., Vokkarane, V., Ma, Y.: Deepfood: deep learning-based food image recognition for computer-aided dietary assessment. CoRR abs/1606.05675 (2016)
26. Lo, F.P.W., Sun, Y., Qiu, J., Lo, B.: Image-based food classification and volume estimation for dietary assessment: a review. IEEE J. Biomed. Health Inform. **24**(7), 1926–1939 (2020)
27. Ma, P., et al.: Image-based nutrient estimation for Chinese dishes using deep learning. Food Res. Int. **147**, 110437 (2021)
28. MacPherson, M.M., Merry, K.J., Locke, S.R., Jung, M.E.: How can we keep people engaged in the behavior change process? an exploratory analysis of two mhealth applications. J. Technol. Behav. Sci. **7**(3), 337–342 (2022)
29. Mao, R., He, J., Shao, Z., Yarlagadda, S.K., Zhu, F.: Visual aware hierarchy based food recognition. CoRR abs/2012.03368 (2020). https://arxiv.org/abs/2012.03368
30. Mao, Y., Tian, J., Han, J., Ren, X.: Hierarchical text classification with reinforced label assignment. In: Proceedings of the 2019 Conference on Empirical Methods in

Natural Language Processing and the 9th International Joint Conference on Natural Language Processing (EMNLP-IJCNLP). Association for Computational Linguistics (2019). https://doi.org/10.18653/v1/d19-1042. https://doi.org/10.18653
31. Marín, J., et al.: Recipe1m: A dataset for learning cross-modal embeddings for cooking recipes and food images. CoRR abs/1810.06553 (2018). http://arxiv.org/abs/1810.06553
32. Meyers, A., et al.: Im2calories: towards an automated mobile vision food diary. In: Proceedings of the IEEE International Conference on Computer Vision, pp. 1233–1241 (2015)
33. Nagarajan, B., Aguilar, E., Radeva, P.: S2ML-TL framework for multi-label food recognition. In: Del Bimbo, A., et al., (eds.) Pattern Recognition. ICPR International Workshops and Challenges, pp. 629–646. Springer, Cham (2021)
34. Nam, J., Loza Mencía, E., Kim, H.J., Fürnkranz, J.: Maximizing subset accuracy with recurrent neural networks in multi-label classification. In: Guyon, I., et al., (eds.) Advances in Neural Information Processing Systems, vol. 30. Curran Associates, Inc. (2017). https://proceedings.neurips.cc/paper_files/paper/2017/file/2eb5657d37f474e4c4cf01e4882b8962-Paper.pdf
35. Nayak, S., Beura, M., Siddique, M., Mishra, S.: Analysis of Indian food based on machine learning classification models. J. Sci. Res. Rep. **27**, 1–7 (2021). https://doi.org/10.9734/JSRR/2021/v27i730407
36. Pandey, P., Deepthi, A., Mandal, B., Puhan, N.B.: Foodnet: recognizing foods using ensemble of deep networks. CoRR abs/1709.09429 (2017). http://arxiv.org/abs/1709.09429
37. Park, S.J., et al.: The development of food image detection and recognition model of Korean food for mobile dietary management. NRP **13**(6), 521–528 (2019). https://doi.org/10.4162/nrp.2019.13.6.521. http://www.e-sciencecentral.org/articles/?scid=1138038
38. Pillai, V., Mehar, P., Das, M., Gupta, D., Radeva, P.: Integrated hierarchical and flat classifiers for food image classification using epistemic uncertainty. In: 2022 IEEE International Conference on Signal Processing and Communications (SPCOM), pp. 1–5 (2022). https://doi.org/10.1109/SPCOM55316.2022.9840761
39. Qu, X., Che, H., Huang, J., Xu, L., Zheng, X.: Multi-layered semantic representation network for multi-label image classification (2021)
40. Rajayogi, J.R., Manjunath, G., Shobha, G.: Indian food image classification with transfer learning. In: 2019 4th International Conference on Computational Systems and Information Technology for Sustainable Solution (CSITSS), pp. 1–4 (2019). https://doi.org/10.1109/CSITSS47250.2019.9031051
41. Ross, B.H., Murphy, G.L.: Food for thought: cross-classification and category organization in a complex real-world domain. Cogn. Psychol. **38**(4), 495–553 (1999)
42. Rousu, J., Saunders, C., Szedmak, S., Shawe-Taylor, J.: Kernel-based learning of hierarchical multilabel classification models. J. Mach. Learn. Res. **7**(59), 1601–1626 (2006). http://jmlr.org/papers/v7/rousu06a.html
43. Shen, J., Qiu, W., Meng, Y., Shang, J., Ren, X., Han, J.: TaxoClass: hierarchical multi-label text classification using only class names. In: Proceedings of the 2021 Conference of the North American Chapter of the Association for Computational Linguistics: Human Language Technologies, pp. 4239–4249. Association for Computational Linguistics, (2021). https://doi.org/10.18653/v1/2021.naacl-main.335D
44. Sudo, K., Murasaki, K., Kinebuchi, T., Kimura, S., Waki, K.: Machine learning-based screening of healthy meals from image analysis: system development and pilot study. JMIR Form Res. **4**(10), e18507 (2020)

45. Vaswani, A., et al.: Attention is all you need (2023)
46. Vaswani, A., Aggarwal, G., Netrapalli, P., Hegde, N.G.: All mistakes are not equal: Comprehensive hierarchy aware multi-label predictions (CHAMP) (2022)
47. Wahlqvist, M.L., Lee, M.S.: Regional food culture and development. Asia Pac. J. Clin. Nutr. **16**(Suppl 1), 2–7 (2007)
48. Wang, J., Yang, Y., Mao, J., Huang, Z., Huang, C., Xu, W.: CNN-RNN: a unified framework for multi-label image classification. In: 2016 IEEE Conference on Computer Vision and Pattern Recognition (CVPR), pp. 2285–2294 (2016). https://doi.org/10.1109/CVPR.2016.251
49. Wang, Y., et al.: Multi-label classification with label graph superimposing (2019)
50. Wu, H., Merler, M., Uceda-Sosa, R., Smith, J.R.: Learning to make better mistakes: Semantics-aware visual food recognition. In: Proceedings of the 24th ACM International Conference on Multimedia, MM 2016, pp. 172–176. Association for Computing Machinery (2016)
51. Wu, X., Fu, X., Liu, Y., Lim, E., Hoi, S.C.H., Sun, Q.: A large-scale benchmark for food image segmentation. CoRR abs/2105.05409 (2021). https://arxiv.org/abs/2105.05409
52. Xu, B., He, X., Qu, Z.: Asian food image classification based on deep learning. J. Comput. Commun. **09**(03), 10–28 (2021)
53. Xu, H., Long, H.: The effect of smartphone app-based interventions for patients with hypertension: systematic review and meta-analysis. JMIR Mhealth Uhealth **8**(10), e21759 (2020)
54. Yen, H.Y., Jin, G., Chiu, H.L.: Smartphone app-based interventions targeting physical activity for weight management: a meta-analysis of randomized controlled trials. Int. J. Nurs. Stud. **137**, 104384 (2023)
55. You, R., Guo, Z., Cui, L., Long, X., Bao, Y., Wen, S.: Cross-modality attention with semantic graph embedding for multi-label classification (2020)
56. Zhang, W., Yu, Q., Siddiquie, B., Divakaran, A., Sawhney, H.: "snap-n-Eat": Food recognition and nutrition estimation on a smartphone. J. Diabetes Sci. Technol. **9**(3), 525–33 (2015)
57. Zhou, L., Zhang, C., Liu, F., Qiu, Z., He, Y.: Application of deep learning in food: a review. Compr. Rev. Food Sci. Food Saf. **18**(6), 1793–1811 (2019)
58. Zhu, B., Zhang, H., Chen, W., Xia, F., Maciejewski, R.: Shotvis: smartphone-based visualization of OCR information from images. ACM Trans. Multimedia Comput. Commun. Appl. **12**(1s) (2015)
59. Zhu, F., Li, H., Ouyang, W., Yu, N., Wang, X.: Learning spatial regularization with image-level supervisions for multi-label image classification. CoRR abs/1702.05891 (2017). http://arxiv.org/abs/1702.05891
60. Zunair, H., Hamza, A.B.: Learning to recognize occluded and small objects with partial inputs (2023). https://arxiv.org/abs/2310.18517

Automated Detection of Student Emotions for Engagement Verification in Virtual Learning Environments

Quoc Minh Quan Nguyen[1,2(✉)] and Sonit Singh[1(✉)]

[1] School of Computer Science and Engineering UNSW Sydney, Sydney, Australia
[2] Teaching and Learning Academy, Singapore Institute of Technology, Singapore, Singapore
quan.nguyen@singaporetech.edu.sg

Abstract. There has been rise in online learning because of its flexibility and need for lifelong learning. Understanding and improving students' engagement during online learning is pivotal as it can provide educators the feedback to improve delivery of content. However, recognising students' emotions using visual data raises ethical issues of individual privacy. In this paper, we build on the existing research in the field of emotion detection in virtual learning environments by making use of facial keypoint images, also known as face meshes, which helps to overcome the challenge of directly working on the visual data. We make use of publicly available emotional dataset, namely, RAF-DB, and demonstrated improved classification accuracy using sophisticated facial keypoints. We finally predicted student engagement using "engagement to index" algorithm. This work not only advances the field of educational technology by improving emotion classification accuracy, but also addresses crucial ethical issues, including student permission and data privacy.

Keywords: Convolutional neural networks · Deep learning · Computer vision · Facial recognition · Engagement detection · Emotion detection

1 Introduction

Online learning landscape has become essential in today's world. Online learning opens a lot of opportunities for students to learn because of being flexible [1]. The lack of physical interactions between peers and lecturers can lead to drowsiness and a decrease in the attention span of students during the lecture [2]. Thus, understanding and improving student engagement remains a pivotal challenge for educational institutions. However, there are still many challenges that need to be solved to provide best learning experiences in virtual learning environments. First and foremost issues in recognising students' emotions using visual data is the issue of data privacy [3]. Artificial intelligence (AI) and computer vision (CV) are becoming ubiquitous technologies for analysing visual data such as images and videos [4,5]. The educational institutions can use smart cameras for automatic attendance systems in classrooms and exam rooms, monitoring students' emotions in in-person and virtual learning settings. Governments can also use smart cameras to monitor traffic, road conditions, security at airports, stations, and public events. However, directly making use of visual data (images or videos) always pose a risk of violating privacy of individuals.

This research builds on existing research in the field of emotional detection in online learning settings, with an emphasis on not using any direct camera data to assess student emotions. The core idea of this paper is to first detect sophisticated facial keypoints and make use of these as features to classify students' emotions. Using sophisticated computer vision and machine learning approaches, this study intends to not only improve the accuracy of emotion classification, but also to overcome the common obstacles of obtaining trustworthy webcam data from students in a remote learning environment.

In this paper, we make use of publicly available emotional dataset, namely, RAF-DB dataset [6] and tried to enhance the classification accuracy of emotions by extracting facial keypoints using *Attention Mesh* [7] before conducting model training. After we got classification results, we make use of "Emotions to Engagement Index" algorithm [8] to predict the final engagement index of a particular student. A significant part of this work focuses on comparing the proposed methodology with existing approaches, with the goal of improving emotion classification in varied scenarios and backgrounds. We make use of publicly available dataset as well as livestream webcam dataset to validate the robustness of our approach so that it can be generalised to diverse set of online learning platforms. This work not only advances the field of educational technology by improving emotion classification accuracy, but also addresses crucial ethical issues, including student permission and data privacy. The ultimate objective is to provide instructors with actionable insights about student emotions, enabling more engaging and responsive online learning experiences. This study is an important step towards a more empathic and effective digital learning environment because it bridges the gap between technology capabilities and educational demands.

2 Related Work

In this section, we provide importance of learner engagement in online learning, provide background of various artificial intelligence technologies that we use in our proposed pipeline for improving students' emotion classification and predicting engagement index.

2.1 Importance of Learner Engagement in Online Learning

Engagement, defined as students' interest, excitement, and effort in their learning activities, is an important predictor of academic performance and retention in online courses. However, recognising and boosting engagement in an online learning environment has distinct problems, particularly in detecting and interpreting students' emotional states, which have a considerable impact on their engagement levels.

In the context of online learning, engagement includes both active involvement in courses and meaningful connection with information, classmates, and instructors. According to Dixson [9], online course participation has several aspects, including behavioural, emotional, and cognitive. Behavioural engagement focuses on task completion and interaction with the learning management system, emotional engagement on students' sentiments toward learning activities, and cognitive engagement on the intellectual effort students put in to grasp course material. This triadic model emphasizes the need of creating an immersive learning environment that inspires and sustains student interest and intellectual curiosity, which is critical for overcoming the natural obstacles of distant learning environments. Studies [10] showed that engagement boosts students' satisfaction, motivates to study, lowers feelings of isolation, and improves performance in online courses .

2.2 Convolutional Neural Networks

Computer vision is a subfield of artificial intelligence that focuses on enabling systems or machines to process, represent, understand, and generate visual data. Convolutional Neural Networks (CNNs), also known as ConvNets, are specialised deep neural networks that excel in processing visual data in the form of images or videos. CNNs apply principles of linear algebra, specifically convolution operations, to discern and extract features from visual data that are suitable for various downstream computer vision tasks such as image classification, object detection, and semantic segmentation. While primarily designed for visual data, these networks can be extended to analyse audio and other forms of signals [11]. CNNs are architecturally designed to mimic the connection patterns of the human brain, notably the visual cortex, which is responsible for processing visual input. The layout of artificial neurons in a CNN is tuned to interpret visual data, making these networks extremely capable of handling tasks like picture recognition and object detection. Typical building blocks of a CNN architecture include, convolutional layers, subsampling or pooling layers, fully connected layers, and the output layer. As a result, CNNs play an important role in a variety of applications, such as autonomous cars, face recognition, and medical image analysis.

Face detection is a core component of computer vision system that includes detecting or recognising human faces in digital images. This is often treated as a classification task where automated algorithms categorise parts of an images as face or non-face. The classical approach is to employ *Haar cascades* algorithm, which was proposed by Viola and Jones [12]. The Haar cascades makes use of a cascade function based on Haar features, which are basic rectangle-based features similar to rectangular kernels used in image processing. These characteristics are computationally efficient to compute because they use an integral picture for quick feature calculation. Deep learning approaches, notably CNNs, have made considerable improvements in the accuracy and reliability of face identification systems. These networks learn hierarchies of features automatically from a large set of labelled training data, making them highly effective in varying lighting conditions and poses, thus broadening the applicability of face detection technology in real-world scenarios [13].

2.3 Emotions to Engagement Index

The mapping of students' emotion to their engagement level (engaged or disengaged) helps educators to make informed decisions and adapt their learning and teaching. After emotions are predicted based on convolutional neural networks (CNNs), the predicted emotions act as input to the *Emotions to Engagement Index* algorithm to get the final outcome. We make use of algorithm proposed by [8] where the engagement index is calculated according to Eq. 1 based on the predicted emotion's value to determine the engagement states.

$$EI = EP \times WE \qquad (1)$$

where EP = Emotion Probability (Emotion=Neutral, Angry, Sad, Happy, Surprised and fear) WE = Weight of corresponding Emotion

---

Algorithm 1. Emotions to Engagement Index [8].

$EI \leftarrow$ Engagement Index
$EP \leftarrow$ Probability of Emotion
$WE \leftarrow$ Weight of corresponding emotion
Weight= {Happy: 0.6, Surprised: 0.6, Neutral: 0.9, Angry: 0.25, Fear: 0.3, Sad: 0.3}
$\phi = \{neutral, happy, surprised, angry, fear, sad\}$
State = {Engaged, Disengaged}
begin
　　Engagement Index, $EI = EP_\phi \times WE_\phi \times 100$
　　if $(EP_{Neutral} > 60) || (EP_{Happy} < 50) || (EP_{Surprised} > 60)$ **then**
　　　　$State \rightarrow Engaged$
　　　　$EI > 0$
　　else if $(EP_{Angry} > 20) || (EP_{Fear} > 30) || (EP_{Sad} > 30)$ **then**
　　　　$State \rightarrow Disengaged$
　　　　$EI > 0$
　　else
　　　　$State \rightarrow Disengaged$
　　　　$EI = 0$
　　end if
end

---

3 Methodology

3.1 RAF-DB Dataset

The Real-world Affective Faces Database (RAF-DB) [6] is a large-scale facial expression database that consists of more than 12,000 images of facial expressions of 7 core emotions of humans. This dataset is chosen because it is widely used in literature and has great variability in subjects' age, gender, ethnicity, head poses, lighting conditions, occlusions in the form of glasses, facial hair, and self-occlusion. It contains diverse emotions, including anger, disgust, fear, happiness, sadness, surprise, and neutrality. Figure 1 shows sample images of various emotion classes in the RAF-DB dataset.

3.2 Pipeline

The methodology involves a comprehensive approach to facial keypoints detection and classification to determine user engagement. Initially, we applied the Google MediaPipe Attention FaceMesh framework on the RAF-DB dataset

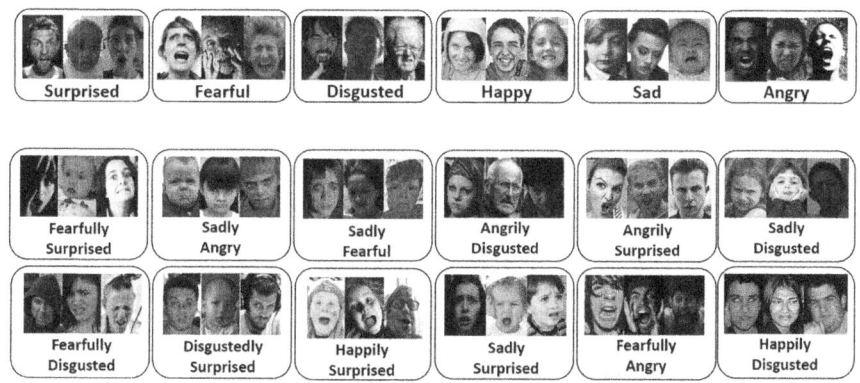

Fig. 1. RAF-DB dataset.

images to extract detailed facial keypoints, ensuring precise representation of facial features. This process involved detecting and mapping 468 keypoints on the face, providing a robust dataset for subsequent analysis. Following this, we conducted model training using both the original RAF-DB dataset and the augmented dataset with FaceMesh-applied images. For this purpose, we selected three lightweight yet powerful models: EfficientNetB3 [14], ResNet152 [15], and VGG19 [16]. Each model was trained individually to leverage their unique strengths in feature extraction and classification. To enhance the overall accuracy, we employed an Ensemble Learning method, which combined the weights of these models. This ensemble approach allowed us to integrate the predictions, thereby improving the classification accuracy by capturing the diverse learning capabilities of each model. During the inference phase, we utilised the CompreFace API [17] alongside Google MediaPipe FaceMesh to process real-time images. This involved isolating facial regions from larger images and applying FaceMesh to these regions, ensuring consistency with the model's training data. By focusing on the face and its keypoints, our methodology aligns the inference process with the training conditions, thereby enhancing the accuracy and reliability of the engagement index determination.

Generating Facial Features. We applied Google Mediapipe FaceMesh to the RAF-DB dataset images and created a new dataset having the facial features. The MediaPipe FaceMesh is a sophisticated facial landmark detection framework created by Google. It uses machine learning to recognise and track face landmarks in real-time. This framework stands out for its capacity to identify a dense set of critical locations on the face, which may be utilised in a variety of applications like augmented reality, facial expression analysis, and more. The MediaPipe FaceMesh employs a deep neural network-based pipeline. The pipeline consists of two main stages: face detection and landmark localisation. The face detection model identifies the presence of a face within the input image, while the landmark localization model accurately predicts the positions of 468 facial landmarks. The MediaPipe FaceMesh is available in form of Python SDK, which we leveraged to easily apply facial Keypoints to our current dataset. Figure 2 top row shows five randomly sampled images from the RAF-DB dataset and the bottom row shows images after the FaceMesh algorithm is applied on each input image.

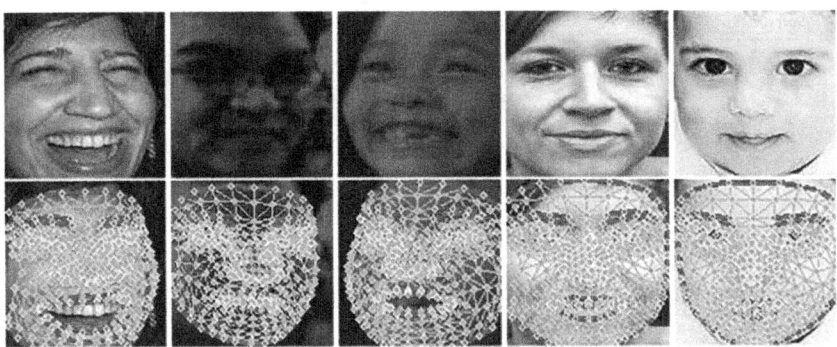

Fig. 2. Sample images showing original images from the RAF-DB dataset and after the application of FaceMesh. Top row shows original images. Bottom row shows images after FaceMesh algorithm is applied to the original image.

CNNs Model Training and Ensemble Learning. After we got facial keypoint images from the previous step, we used the curated dataset having (facial keypoint image, label) pairs for training three CNN architectures, namely, EfficientNetB3, VGG19 and Resnet152. The reasons behind the choice of these networks lie due to their lightweight architecture and their capability to handle to learn the task effectively. Figure 3 shows the VGG19 architecture for image classification task. Although the original architecture is for image classification task on the ImageNet dataset having 1,000 classes, we changed the number of neurons in the output layer to 7 to get probability for seven emotions. We conducted training on both the original RAF-DB dataset and the generated FaceMesh dataset for all three models. We reported classification results for all three models in the results section. To further improve the classification results and to combine strengths of three models, we implemented ensemble learning, fusing the predictions of models via the majority voting (See Fig. 4).

During model training, we apply various data augmentation and regularisation methods to select the best model on the validation set. We applied *rotation, zoom, horizontal flipping, change in brightness*, and *adding noise*. The data augmentation not only increased the dataset size during model training but also improves model's robustness due to increase in diversity of dataset. Given the complexity of deeper CNN architectures and having millions of parameters, it's obvious to see model overfitting due to small dataset size. We applied *dropout* [18], a regularisation technique which randomly drop neurons (along with their connections) from the network during training. This helps us to avoid the overfitting problem and getting improved model performance.

Predicting Engagement Index. After we make prediction during the inference stage, we pass the predicted class to the *emotions to engagement index* as outlined in Algorithm 1 [8].

Live Inference. To showcase the effectiveness of our proposed methodology in real environments, we use live webcam data from the laptop. We make use of FaceNet [19], a face recognition algorithm based on Inception model, with

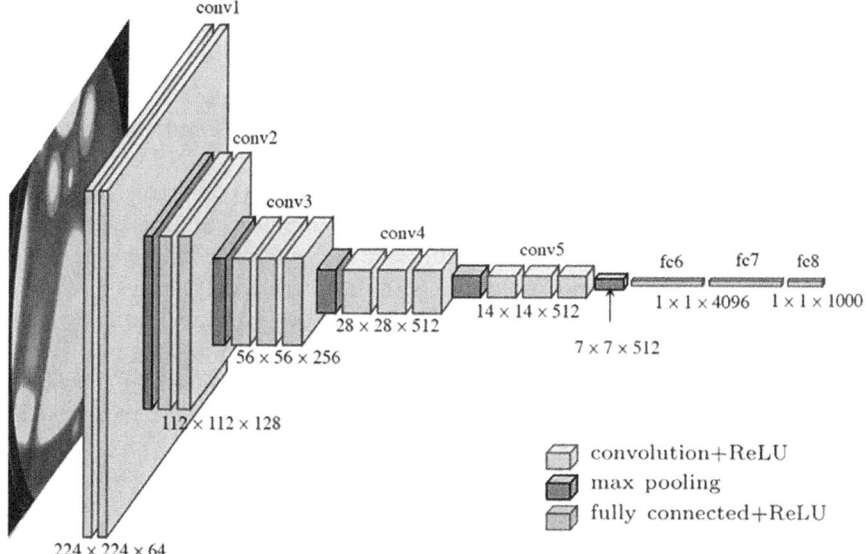

Fig. 3. VGG19 architecture.

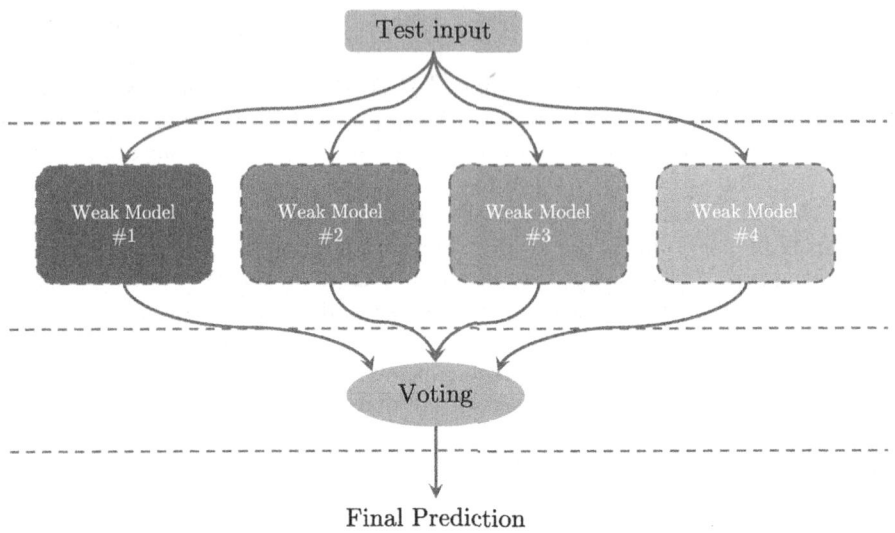

Fig. 4. Ensemble Learning Method.

the goal of learning a mapping from face images to a compact Euclidean space whose distances correlate directly to a measure of face similarity. FaceNet has high face detection accuracy, having 99% on the LFW dataset and 95.12% on the YouTube Faces DB dataset [20]. Recently, Exadel Inc. introduced *CompreFace*, a free and open-source face recognition library which can be easily integrated with developed pipeline. CompreFace provides REST API for face recognition, face verification, face detection, landmark detection, mask detection, head pose detection, age, and gender recognition and can be easily deployed with Docker [17].

Using the CompreFace SDKs and APIs allows for the exact and accurate recognition of user faces using webcam. Furthermore, CompreFace provides SDKs for three different programming environments: Python, JavaScript, and .NET. CompreFace's diverse language support makes it an attractive tool for the development of our online learning detection. Since our model have been trained on facial keypoint images, during our live inference, we only make use of FaceMesh images and not used the actual images from the webcam. This helps use to overcome the issue of student's privacy given we are not working on the actual images. Finally, to translate the classification results into engagement category, we gave predicted emotion as input to the *emotion to engagement index* algorithm, which provided whether the student is *engaged* or *disengaged*, providing actionable insights to educators.

4 Results

We implemented our methodology in Python programming language [21] and make use of OpenCV computer vision library [22] and PyTorch framework [23]. To have accelerated training, we make use of Nvidia GeForce RTX 3090 Ti graphics processing unit (GPU). We conducted experiments on the RAF-DB dataset, on the original images as well as FaceMesh generated images, and applied three state-of-the-art CNN architectures, namely, VGG19, ResNet152, and EfficientNetB3 as outlined in our methodology section. Table 1 shows experimental results on the RAF-DB dataset with and without FaceMesh. We can see that for each model, we got improved results in terms of accuracy, precision, recall, and f1-score, with FaceMesh images compared to without FaceMesh. Having improved results with FaceMesh images helps us to overcome the limitations of students' privacy. We also find that with better and more advanced CNN architecture, we got improved results. From the table, we can find that ResNet152 model provided better results compared to VGG19 on all evaluation metrics. Following the same trend, we can find that EfficcientNetB3 model outperformed both the VGG19 and ResNet152 models, validating the hypothesis that using state-of-the-art CNN architectures could provide improved results. After we got individual model's performance, we also applied *ensemble learning*, combining the predictions of three models via fusion their decisions via majority voting. The ensemble learning method provided 68.85% accuracy on the RAF-DB test set without FaceMesh images. On the contrary, ensemble learning provided 71.02% accuracy on the RAF-DB test set with FaceMesh images, demonstrating improved performance and effectiveness of FaceMesh images in predicting students' emotions.

Table 1. Results (in %) on the test set of RAF-DB dataset without (w/o) FaceMesh and with FaceMesh.

Model	Accuracy	Precision	Recall	F1-Score
VGG19 (w/o FaceMesh)	66.43	66.54	66.36	65.15
VGG19 (with FaceMesh)	**69.25**	**68.88**	**69.25**	**68.99**
ResNet152 (w/o FaceMesh)	69.32	69.30	69.28	69.12
ResNet152 (with FaceMesh)	**70.80**	**70.05**	**70.66**	**70.22**
EfficientNetB3 (w/o FaceMesh)	70.87	70.62	70.31	70.50
EfficientNetB3 (with FaceMesh)	**72.69**	**73.17**	**73.82**	**73.10**

Finally, we also performed live webcam engagement detection using CompreFace and FaceMesh based on the trained model weights. Figure 5 shows an example of live webcam predicting student is engaged with 98% detection rate based on the neutral emotion.

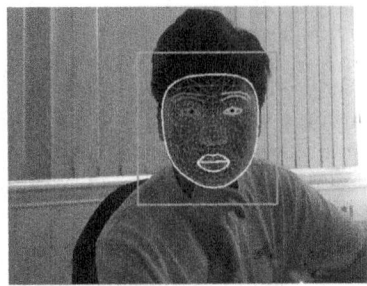

Fig. 5. Engaged student state with 98% detection on neutral emotion.

5 Discussion

Our experimental results showed that applying facial keypoints on the raw images and predicting students' emotions based on models trained on FaceMesh data could provide approximately 3% improvement in classification performance. Apart from this, working on FaceMesh images speeds up inference and can make predictions in real-time. By making use of the facial keypoints as input to learning algorithms, we can overcome some of the challenges of working on actual raw images, such as poor lighting conditions and diverse virtual backgrounds in online learning environments. These challenges highly negatively affect the inference accuracy and speed when working on actual raw images. Also, by using FaceMesh images in model training and inference, we can overcome some of the ethical challenges of working on actual raw images of students.

Future research will focus on expanding dataset diversity to improve model generalisability, implementing and testing the system in real-time online learning environments, and conducting longitudinal studies to assess its long-term impact. Efforts should be made to ensure cross-platform compatibility and explore multi-modal analysis by integrating additional data sources like audio and interaction patterns. Integration with adaptive learning platforms could enable automated content adjustments based on engagement levels. Privacy and ethical considerations should remain paramount, with investigations into advanced privacy-preserving techniques and the development of comprehensive ethical guidelines. Additionally, future work should address cultural sensitivity and accessibility to ensure the system's effectiveness across diverse user groups. These advancements will contribute towards creating more responsive, inclusive, and effective online learning experiences while maintaining high standards of privacy and ethical use.

6 Conclusion

This study proposed student emotion and engagement recognition pipeline using facial keypoints detection and deep learning to improve emotion recognition and student engagement evaluation in online learning environments. By using

FaceMesh 3D points on the RAF-DB dataset and ensemble learning using EfficientNetB3, VGG19, and Resnet150 models, we demonstrated improved emotion classification accuracy. The addition of face keypoints improved the model's performance while also providing a more robust method for real-time inference that can handle a variety of lighting situations, background clutter, and diverse virtual backgrounds in learning platforms. Furthermore, by combining the emotion categorisation findings with an engagement index algorithm, we created a comprehensive method for monitoring student participation while maintaining privacy and ethical issues.

Acknowledgments. This research is supported by UNSW.

Disclosure of Interests. The authors have no competing interests to declare that are relevant to the content of this article.

References

1. Salama, R., Hinton, T.: Online higher education: current landscape and future trends. J. Furth. High. Educ. **47**(7), 913–924 (2023)
2. Bradbury, N.A.: Attention span during lectures: 8 seconds, 10 minutes, or more? Adv. Physiol. Educ. **40**(4), 509–513 (2016). PMID: 28145268
3. Victor Manuel, C., Martinez-Maldonado, R., Escalante-Ramirez, B., Olveres-Montiel, J.: Students' ethical, privacy, design, and cultural perspectives on visualizing cognitive-affective states in online learning. J. Learn. Analy. **11**(3), 24–40 (2024)
4. Alex, K., Ilya, S., Geoffrey, E.H.: Imagenet classification with deep convolutional neural networks. In: Pereira, F., Burges, C.J., Bottou, L., Weinberger, K.Q., eds, Advances in Neural Information Processing Systems, vol. 25. Curran Associates, Inc. (2012)
5. Ian, G., Yoshua, B., Aaron, C.: Deep Learning. MIT Press (2016). http://www.deeplearningbook.org
6. Li, S., Deng, W., Du, J.: Reliable crowdsourcing and deep locality-preserving learning for expression recognition in the wild. In: 2017 IEEE Conference on Computer Vision and Pattern Recognition (CVPR), pp. 2584–2593 (2017)
7. Ablavatski, A., Grishchenko, I., Kartynnik, Y., Raveendran, K.: and Matthias Grundmann. High fidelity face mesh prediction in real-time, Attention mesh (2020)
8. Kumar, P., Kumar, R., Tekchandani Swadha, G.: Facial emotion recognition based real-time learner engagement detection system in online learning context using deep learning models. 1226: deep-patterns emotion recognition in the wild (2023)
9. Mary, D.D.: Measuring student engagement in the online course: the online student engagement scale (ose). Online Learn. J. **19**(4) (2015)
10. Martin, D.U.B.F.: Engagement matters: student perceptions on the importance of engagement strategies in the online learning environment. https://eric.ed.gov/?id=EJ1179659, 2018. Accessed 10 Apr 2024
11. TechTarget. What is a convolutional neural network (cnn)? https://www.techtarget.com/searchenterpriseai/definition/convolutional-neural-network 2024. Accessed 20 Apr 2024

12. Paul, V., Michael, J.J.: Rapid object detection using a boosted cascade of simple features. In: Proceedings of the 2001 IEEE Computer Society Conference on Computer Vision and Pattern Recognition, 1 (2001)
13. Zhang, K., Zhang, Z., Li, Z., Qiao, Yu.: Joint face detection and alignment using multitask cascaded convolutional networks. IEEE Signal Process. Lett. **23**(10), 1499–1503 (2016)
14. Tan, M., Le, Q.: EfficientNet: rethinking model scaling for convolutional neural networks. In: Chaudhuri, K., Salakhutdinov, R., eds, Proceedings of the 36th International Conference on Machine Learning, vol. 97 of Proceedings of Machine Learning Research, pp. 6105–6114. PMLR, 09–15 (2019)
15. He, K., Zhang, X., Ren, S., Sun, J.: Deep residual learning for image recognition. In: 2016 IEEE Conference on Computer Vision and Pattern Recognition (CVPR), pp. 770–778 (2016)
16. Karen, S., Andrew, Z.: Very deep convolutional networks for large-scale image recognition (2015)
17. Inc. Exadel. CompreFace: Free and open-source face recognition system. https://github.com/exadel-inc/CompreFace (2023). GitHub repository
18. Srivastava, N., Hinton, G., Krizhevsky, A., Sutskever, I., Salakhutdinov, R.: Dropout: a simple way to prevent neural networks from overfitting. J. Mach. Learn. Res. **15**(56), 1929–1958 (2014)
19. James Philbin Florian, S., Dmitry, K.: Facenet: a unified embedding for face recognition and clustering. In: 2015 IEEE Conference on Computer Vision and Pattern Recognition (CVPR) (2015)
20. Rytis Maskeliūnas Damilola, A., Ying, Z., Robertas, D.: Improving accuracy of face recognition in the era of mask-wearing: an evaluation of a pareto-optimized facenet model with data preprocessing techniques. Machine Learning and Deep Learning in Pattern Recognition (2023)
21. Guido Van, R., Drake Jr., F.L.: Python reference manual. Centrum voor Wiskunde en Informatica Amsterdam (1995)
22. Itseez. Open source computer vision library. https://github.com/itseez/opencv (2015)
23. Paszke, A., Gross, S., Chintala, S., Chanan, G., Yang, E., DeVito, Z.: Zeming Lin. Luca Antiga, and Adam Lerer. Automatic differentiation in pytorch. In NIPS-W, Alban Desmaison (2017)

Cross-Modality Learning in Ophthalmology: Is There a Need for Increasing Variety in Data?

Imen Chakroun(✉) and Julien Verplanken

AI & Algorithms, IMEC, Leuven, Belgium
imen.chakroun@imec.be

Abstract. The primary focus of our work extends beyond merely enhancing state-of-the-art predictive performance in cross-modal classification tasks. We aim to demonstrate, through AI, the critical necessity of maintaining the current industrial investment in multi-modalities that are complex, costly, and cumbersome in day-to-day clinical usage. To this end, we first analyzed the prediction accuracy gap between single and multi-modalities models. We then assessed whether the increased complexity of multi-modal predictors demands larger datasets compared to their single-modal counterparts. Finally, we explored whether leveraging multi-modal inputs can compensate for poor-quality images while still outperforming uni-modal approaches.

Keywords: Imaging modalities in ophthalmology · Multi-modal machine learning

1 Introduction

Many imaging modalities are clinically available in ophthalmology: retinal fundus photography (RFP), optical coherence tomography (OCT), OCT-Angiography (OCT-A), and scanning laser ophthalmoscopy (SLO); among others. Although hardware research investments in the ophthalmology industry are ongoing on designing multi-modalities enabled devices with a great promise of better disease diagnosis [1], less attention to multi-modality AI-based analytics capable of assisting these clinical diagnoses of ocular and non-ocular diseases exists. Yet, the return on investment in the new medical hardware is low if AI cannot encompass the knowledge brought by combining different devices. We expect a multimodal machine learning model to have better prediction accuracy than an unimodal model by enough margin such that the extra effort and cost of new multi-modal device manufacturing is valuable. Ideally, a multi-modal should also enable decision-making when models based on the distinct modalities disagree on the prediction.

Multi-modality ophthalmic imaging systems can enhance the contrast, resolution, and functionality of distinct modalities to improve therapeutic guidance.

This should however go hand in hand with research in multi-modality-based machine learning. The foremost technical reason behind the slow uptake of multi-modality ophthalmic imaging models is the availability of multi-modality datasets. Data-gathering is an existing blocking factor in medical settings, in general, and is even more intricate when dealing with cross-modalities. While general-purpose images can be easily collected, access to medical data is often restricted to preserve medical privacy. Moreover, annotating medical images is time-consuming and expensive as it requires the expertise of physicians, radiologists, and surgeons. In 2020, a review [6] was conducted to identify all publicly available ophthalmic imaging datasets, and to create a central directory of the available datasets for access. The results showed that 94 datasets were freely accessible. Of these 94 datasets, five datasets (5%) contained images taken from more than one modality. Three of the latter had different multi-modalities namely OCT and RFP. The other two contained respectively Fundus fluorescein angiogram photograph and Fundus photograph, Fundus fluorescein angiogram photograph and videos. A more recent review on publicly available Glaucoma datasets [2], reported that of 25 studied publicly available glaucoma datasets only 13 datasets were identified as open access of which 3 datasets were multi-channel (RFP and OCT).

AI has found many applications within ophthalmology, which include image segmentation, automated diagnosis, disease prediction, and prognostication applied to conditions such as diabetic retinopathy, glaucoma, age-related macular degeneration, papilloedema, and cataracts. However, a research gap exists when it comes to multi-modality settings. In this paper, we evaluate the real need for multi-modal learning in ophthalmology compared to unimodality. We empirically assess how much it leverages AI performance by exploring scenarios for building models under changing parameters. The automated glaucoma detection and grading from both the 2D RFP images and 3D OCT scanning volumes is taken as a study case for this work. Glaucoma is a potentially blinding disease, characterized by progressive degeneration of the retinal ganglion cells [9]. This results in distinct changes in the optic nerve head and corresponding visual field defects. Because of their inherent prominent biomarkers, it is usually common practice to rely on screenings on both RFP and OCT [11]. Fundus photography [7] takes a two-dimensional picture of the back of the eye. Typical clinical RFP images include the optic nerve head, which is a key component in glaucoma detection. The OCT image is a cross-sectional imaging technique that is used to extract information about different retinal layers as well as their depth and thickness. Not only is glaucoma diagnosis potentially time-consuming and costly, as it involves multiple examinations but it also relies on an individual clinician's knowledge and ability making it subjective and prone to over/underestimation. Clinicians must be proficient in identifying features visible in each modality and correlating findings between the two. This can be especially more challenging for complex pathologies or subtle changes (like in early Glaucoma) that may be apparent in one modality but not the other.

In this work, we provide through machine learning experiments, some quantification of how beneficial is the use of multi-modal data for Glaucoma grading. We first explored four fusion techniques for RFP and OCT images to assess whether a multi-modal model prediction accuracy outperforms the baseline single-modality models. We then identified scenarios where we evaluate the learning performances of the best multi-modal model: (1) how much does a multi-modal model predict better than an RFP or oct-only model? (2) do we need more multi-modality data compared to single modalities? (3) is the multi-modal model more robust to poor-quality data than the single-modalities?

The remainder of the paper is structured as follows. In Sect. 2, we give an overview of existing research work dealing with multi-modality learning for glaucoma grading. Section 3 presents the glaucoma study case and the fusion strategies. Section 4 describes the experimental quantification and the results. Section 5 summarizes the research questions raised in this study paper.

2 Related Work

The most common imaging modalities used in glaucoma detection are OCT and RFP as they hold great promise in a comprehensive view of the eye's structures. Although they are both the mainstream glaucoma screening tools in clinical practice, few ML algorithms are established that make use of both modalities. This is primarily due to the availability of public datasets. Most contributions on multi-modality Glaucoma classification used the publicly available Gamma Challenge dataset [8] and the others used private datasets [5]. In this work, we will also be using the Gamma dataset as the challenge provided the largest publicly available dataset of RFP and OCT volume pairs to date. For the classification task, most of the contributions adopted a dual-branch network structure (c.f Sect. 3.3) [3,4]. Other strategies [8] used a single network inputted by concatenated RFP image and OCT volume (c.f Sect. 3.3). [8] used two independent networks to predict glaucoma grades based on RFP image and OCT volume, respectively. The final result is the average of the two predictions. [5] developed a hierarchical fusion approach that focuses on combining features across multiple dimensions of the network.

The major scope of our work goes beyond improving the state-of-the-art prediction performances on such cross-modal classification tasks. We analyze (1) the prediction accuracy gap between single and multi-modalities, (2) whether multi-modality predictors, being more complex, need more data than single ones, and (3) whether by using multi-modalities we can overcome poor-quality images and still outperform uni-modalities.

3 Methods and Materials

In the following, we introduce the glaucoma use case and describe four scenarios for fusion OCT and RFP for glaucoma grading.

3.1 Glaucoma

Glaucoma is the most common cause of irreversible vision loss and the third most common cause of vision loss worldwide after cataracts and refractive error. People with glaucoma (aged 40–80 years) worldwide are estimated to be 111.8 million in 2040 [13,14]. Because of the relatively symptom-free nature of glaucoma, particularly in its early stages, early diagnosis is extremely vital to prevent disease progression and permanent vision loss. However, identifying glaucoma is a complicated process that requires multiple examinations and clinical expertise, which would be time-consuming and labor-intensive.

3.2 Multi-modality Learning Applied to Glaucoma Classification

For the glaucoma study case, RFP photography provides wide-field images of the retina allowing visualization of the entire retina and its vasculature while, in contrast, OCT images offer high-resolution cross-sectional views of retinal layers and have a limited field of view. Using multi-modal machine learning enables integrating information from both modalities to create a more comprehensive understanding of the input data by leveraging the complementary richer representation of it. Worth mentioning however that applying multi-modal machine learning models comes with challenges:

Multi-Modal Datasets when they exist are often more sparse than unimodal datasets, meaning that certain modalities may have limited or missing information for certain instances. Handling data sparsity requires careful consideration and a call for robust models capable of dealing with missing labels or not-aligned instances without affecting performance and generalization.

Extracting meaningful features/representations that capture relevant information from each modality without introducing noise or redundancy requires domain expertise and experimentation can be difficult namely when the modalities are of different types.

Complexity of multimodal models tends to be higher than unimodal models which typically require more computational resources both for training and inference times.

3.3 Fusion Strategies

In this section, we represent the fusion techniques relative to every scenario.

Early Fusion. In an early fusion setting, multi-modality images are fused channel by channel and are fed into the same classification network that learns a fused feature representation from these inputs. We here explored two early fusion methods: a 2D (Fig. 1) and a 3D version (Fig. 2). Let's denote by $X \times Y \times Z$ the size of the 3D OCT volumes. In the 3D early-fusion solution, the 2D RFP images are resized to $X \times Y$ pixels and duplicated Z times, to form an $X \times Y \times Z$ voxel channel. Classification is then performed using a 3D-CNN network.

In the 2D early-fusion strategy, the 2D RFP images and 3D OCT images are concatenated to form an X x Y x Z1 input channel before being fed to a 2D-CNN classifier. Z1 is the sum of the input channels of the OCT voxel and the 3 RGB channels of RFP.

Intermediate Fusion. In an intermediate fusion setting (Fig. 3), also called feature-level fusion, the raw images are transformed into a higher-level representation by mapping them through a stack of layers that are specific to each branch. 2D and 3D CNN branches are used respectively for RFP and OCT. After unifying the feature representation we obtain multi-modal feature maps that we feed into a decision layer for classification.

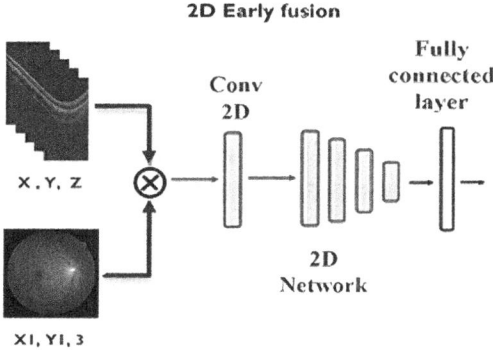

Fig. 1. 2D early fusion strategy for RFP and OCT images for glaucoma grading.

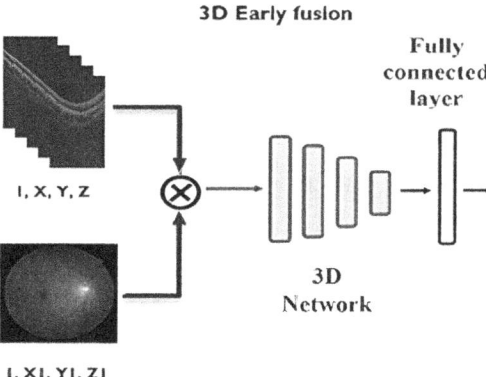

Fig. 2. 3D early fusion strategy for RFP and OCT images for glaucoma grading.

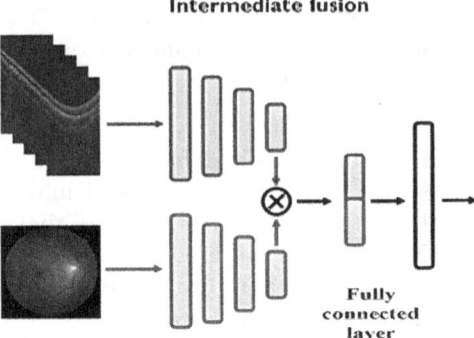

Fig. 3. Intermediate fusion strategy for RFP and OCT images for glaucoma grading.

Late Fusion. Late fusion (Fig. 4), also called decision-level fusion, consists of extracting decisions from single-modality architectures followed by fusion at a decision-making stage. In our case, we add the outputs from each CNN and add a decision layer to obtain a final output. This technique is much simpler than the early fusion method for example particularly when the data sources are significantly different in data dimension.

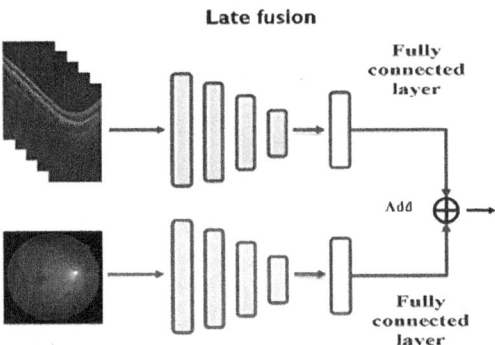

Fig. 4. Late fusion strategy for RFP and OCT images for glaucoma grading.

3.4 Materials and Setup

Dataset. The dataset collected in the Glaucoma grAding from Multi-Modality imAges (GAMMA) Challenge is used. It's a publicly available dataset released in 2020 by [8]. There are 300 pairs of clinical modality images in the dataset that we split into 200 pairs for training and 100 pairs for testing. Each pair contains an RFP image and an OCT volume. The OCT volumes are represented as 256 two-dimensional cross-sectional 992 X 512 images. RFP images have two different resolutions of 2000 X 2992 and 1934 X 1956 pixels. There are 150 pairs of no-glaucoma patients, 75 pairs of early glaucoma patients, and 75 pairs of moderate or advanced glaucoma patients.

Implementation Details. All the experiments were performed using 2D and 3D versions of ResNet-50 [12]. Gradient descent was performed with the Adam optimizer with an initial learning rate of 1e-4 and a weight decay rate of 1e-4. A "Reduce on Plateau" scheduler was used. For 2D images, color-jittering, Random Grayscaling, random flipping, and random rotation were applied to augment the data. For 3D volumes, random elastic deformation and blurring filters were employed to augment the data. A focal loss function is applied. Focal loss applies a modulating term to the cross entropy loss to focus learning on hard misclassified examples. The training epochs are set to 100.

4 Experiments

4.1 Classification Performances

In Table 1, we report the predictive performances of six models: RFP-only model, OCT-only model, 2D-early fusion, 3D-early fusion, intermediate fusion, and late fusion. We analyze the Kohen Cappa with quadratic weights, balanced accuracy, and the F1 score metrics. For this experiment, all input images are normalized and cropped to 224 x 224 and the batch size is set to 8.

The results show that OCT volumes outperform color RFP images when using data from a single modality. The conservation of the 3-dimensional volume is advantageous as it learns through contextual information from neighboring B-scans. It is still however far from a result that can be useful for diagnosis.

Table 1. Comparing prediction performances for the fusion strategies.

Metric	RFP	OCT	2D-early	3D-early	Intermediate	Late
Kohen cappa	0.586	0.615	0.5946	0.650	**0.714**	0.6757
Balanced accuracy	0.656	0.6935	0.678	0.698	**0.756**	0.718
F1 score	0.677	0.729	0.709	0.737	**0.79**	0.74

Results using both early fusion strategies were not significantly improved. The reason is that input-level strategies are generally not capable of capturing the relationship between different modalities as they have a significant scale difference and lack strong spatial correspondence. Recall that, RFP photographs give an overall en-face view of the retina, in 2D and OCT volumes provide structural information about the retina in 3D. Besides, there is a significant gap between these two modalities regarding the equipment used to capture them, imaging methods, and data information.

The late fusion also didn't improve the performances over single modalities by very much which may be due to the lack of strong spatial correspondence probably because the images are not co-registered (OCT typically focuses on a small region near the fovea while RFP images cover a larger area).

Intermediate fusion, as also shown in [8], is the most effective method. While the strategy slightly bridges the significant gaps between different modalities nevertheless as intermediate fusion is a mere concatenation of high-dimensional features, the correlation information inevitably gets lost, adversely impacting classification performance. It is worth noting here that even though the machine learning metrics show on-par global prediction performances, the intermediate fusion had the highest number of "pessimistic" predictions. The miss-classified patients were indeed predicted as having more severe glaucoma than the ground truth (for example predicting early glaucoma as being progressive or intermediate glaucoma) which is generally more appreciated in clinical settings than the other way around.

For the rest of the paper, for easy reading, we report the results only for the single modalities scenarios and the intermediate fusion strategy as we just showed that it is the more suitable fusion algorithm in this case.

4.2 Dealing with Adversarial Predictions

We structure in Table 2 all the scenarios of the predictions output of the three aforementioned compared strategies.

Table 2. Prediction performances.

RFP	False	False	False	False	True	True	True	True
OCT	False	False	True	True	False	False	True	True
Intermediate	True	False	False	True	False	True	False	True
Number of patients	7	6	4	7	4	20	3	49

For example, the first column gives the number of patients (predictions) where the RFP model prediction was False (not equal to the ground truth), the OCT model prediction was False (not equal to the ground truth) and the intermediate model prediction was True (equal to the ground truth). This experimental quantification aims to highlight the need for multi-modality predictors primarily when the findings from the two modalities are discordant or ambiguous. The results show that using multi-modality aligns with single-modality predictions in 55% of cases (red-colored text). It also shows that in 11% of the cases (black-colored text) combining the modalities leads to worse predictions. Finally, for 34 patients out of 100 (blue-colored text), if using RFP or OCT alone does not allow the identification of the glaucoma disease, merging both modalities can correctly diagnose the illness.

4.3 Learning with Scarcer Data

In this scenario, we investigate the impact of the size of the training dataset on the predictive performance.

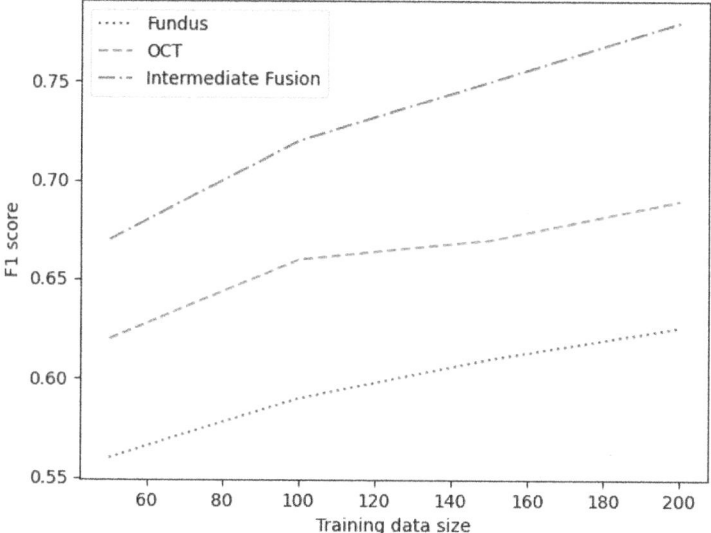

Fig. 5. Impact of the size of the data on the predictions.

We simulate a setting where a hospital evolves its infrastructure by adding a new modality imaging and adopting multi-modality learning. We would like to quantify how much data has to be collected to achieve better predictive performance using a new multi-modality model.

We train the three models (single and intermediate) on a random sub-sample of a given size and report the model performance on the test data. The changing performance is shown in graph form (Fig. 5) with the evolution of the F1 score across various sizes showing how much gain in performance is made with each step of additional data.

For all scenarios, the results agree with common intuition about relative model performance increasing with the size of datasets but provide an empirical assessment of the magnitude of this effect. The F1 score varies from 0.56 to 0.78, showing the large impact of available data size. Let's note first that all three models do not seem to have saturated in terms of possible performance when using the maximum size of data. More importantly, the increase in performance as data size grows seems to be significantly more rapid when only small proportions of the data are available. This suggests that cross-modality models could be built to a reasonable level of accuracy starting from small data sizes. This is very promising and useful within a hospital knowing that collecting fully aligned and paired data is time-consuming and labor-intensive.

4.4 Robustness to Lower Resolution

In this experiment, we think of a setting where an ophthalmic hardware manufacturer wants to design a lower-resolution glaucoma screening device.

The graph of Fig. 6 first shows that for all models the balanced accuracy prediction decreases with the resolution of the input images. Secondly, we notice that using multi-modalities models outperforms single modalities also using lower resolution images even though they have bigger and more complex architecture than the single models. Therefore, it's worth exploring manufacturing strategies where less costly devices can be designed from the perspective of being jointly used.

In an ideal case, developing ophthalmic devices with lower resolution and reduced costs starts by proactively addressing the co-registration of multi-modal inputs (ensuring both modalities capture the same eye region with precise alignment), and dedicating greater efforts to AI-driven multi-modality decision support.

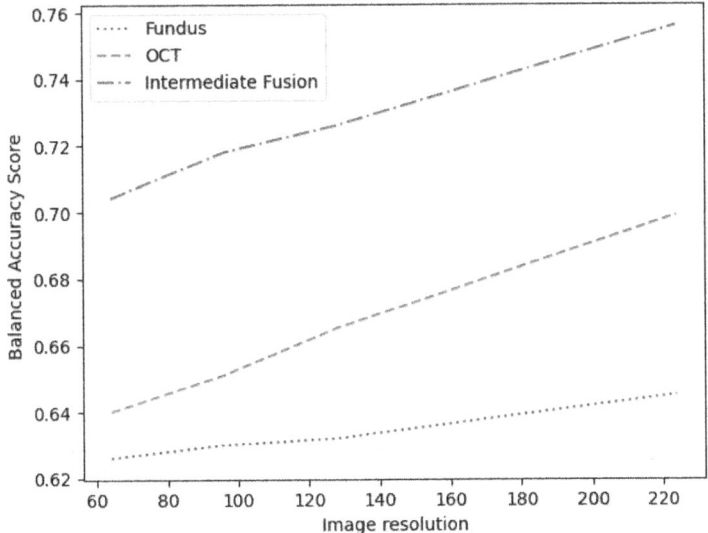

Fig. 6. Impact of the image resolution on the predictions.

5 Conclusion

In this paper, we empirically outlined that cross-modality learning from RFP and OCT holds significant promise for improving the diagnosis and management of glaucoma, a leading cause of irreversible blindness worldwide. We went beyond listing machine learning performances of identified fusion techniques. We compared fusion techniques and found that the intermediate fusion technique was most beneficial in terms of predictive performance. We defined quantification experiments showing the benefit of cross-modality learners in dealing with situations where single modalities disagree. we also showed that cross-modality models even being generally more complex do not necessarily need more data than single predictors. Moreover, using cross-modality can overcome the sensitivity of learners to poor-quality data even if they are more complex. We however strongly believe that our experiments are limited by the fact that multi-modality ophthalmological public datasets are not largely available and that more data and applications are needed to generalize the identified assets. As future research directions, it would be interesting to study the impact of proper image registration and the impact of mixing devices from different vendors.

Acknowledgments. This research received funding from the Flemish Government (AI Research Program).

References

1. Ringel, M.J., Tang, E.M., Tao, Y.K.: Advances in multimodal imaging in ophthalmology. Ther. Adv. Ophthalmol. **13** (2021)
2. Riley, K., Jessica, S., Muhammad, A., Mahsa, A., Ehsan, A.: A Comprehensive survey of publicly available glaucoma datasets for automated glaucoma detection. american academy of optometry (2022)
3. Cai, Z., Lin, L., He, H., Tang, X.: Corolla: An efficient multi-modality fusion framework with supervised contrastive learning for glaucoma grading, In: 2022 IEEE 19th International Symposium on Biomedical Imaging (ISBI), IEEE, pp. 1–4 (2022)
4. Chen, Z., Zheng, X., Shen, H., Zeng, Z., Liu, Q., Li, Z.: Combination of enhanced depth imaging optical coherence tomography and fundus images for glaucoma screening. J. Med. Syst. **43**(6), 1–12 (2019). https://doi.org/10.1007/s10916-019-1303-8
5. Li, Y., et al.: Multimodal information fusion for glaucoma and diabetic retinopathy classification. In: Antony, B., Fu, H., Lee, C.S., MacGillivray, T., Xu, Y., Zheng, Y. (eds) Ophthalmic Medical Image Analysis. OMIA 2022. LNCS, vol 13576. Springer, Cham
6. Khan, S.M., Liu, X., Nath, S., et al.: A global review of publicly available datasets for ophthalmological imaging: barriers to access, usability, and generalizability The Lancet Digit Health, 3, pp. e51-e66 (2021)
7. Krzywicki, T., Brona, P., Zbrzezny, A.M., Grzybowski, A.E.: A global review of publicly available datasets containing fundus images: characteristics, barriers to access, usability, and generalizability
8. Wu, J., et al.: GAMMA challenge: Glaucoma grAding from multi-modality imAges. Med Image Anal. **90**, p. 102938 (2023). https://doi.org/10.1016/j.media.2023.102938.. PMID: 37806020
9. Weinreb, R.N., Aung, T., Medeiros, F.A.: The pathophysiology and treatment of glaucoma: a review. JAMA **311**, 1901–1911 (2014)
10. Llad o, X., et al.: Segmentation of multiple sclerosis lesions in brain MRI: a review of automated approaches, Inf. Sci. **186**(1), pp. 164–185 (2012)

11. Medeiros, F.A., et al.: Evaluation of retinal nerve fiber layer, optic nerve head, and macular thickness measurements for glaucoma detection using optical coherence tomography. Am. J. Ophthalmol. **139**, pp. 44–55 (2005) [CrossRef] [PubMed]
12. He, K., Zhang, X., Ren, S., Sun, J.: Deep residual learning for image recognition, In: IEEE Conference on Computer Vision and Pattern Recognition (CVPR), Las Vegas, NV, USA, 2016, pp. 770–778 (2016)
13. Sun, Y., Chen, A., Zou, M., et al.: Time trends, associations and prevalence of blindness and vision loss due to glaucoma: an analysis of observational data from the Global Burden of Disease Study 2017. BMJ Open, **12**, p. e053805 (2022). https://doi.org/10.1136/bmjopen-2021-053805
14. GBD 2019 Blindness and Vision Impairment Collaborators; Vision Loss Expert Group of the Global Burden of Disease Study. Causes of blindness and vision impairment in 2020 and trends over 30 years, and revalence of avoidable blindness in relation to VISION 2020: the Right to Sight: an analysis for the Global Burden of Disease Study. Lancet Glob Health. (2021). https://doi.org/10.1016/S2214-109X(20)30489-7.Epub 2020 Dec 1. Erratum in: Lancet Glob Health. **9**(4), p. e408. PMID: 33275949; PMCID: PMC7820391

Active Learning and the Various Flavors of Supervision for Object Detection

Nils Bischoff[✉][iD] and Sven Tomforde[iD]

Intelligent Systems, Kiel University, Kiel, Germany
{nib,st}@informatik.uni-kiel.de

Abstract. In an effort to minimize the manual annotation cost for the training of object detectors based on deep learning, we reflect on the role of active learning in object detection when combined with other sources of supervision. In doing so, we highlight the need to harmonize the approaches so that they can develop their full potential. Ultimately, the active learning oracle should only provide supervision for samples that cannot be covered by other, cheaper, forms of supervision.

Keywords: Object detection · Active learning · Semi-supervised learning · Weakly-supervised learning

1 Introduction

The availability of enough annotated data for the model to learn a task has always been a limitation in (deep) machine learning. A large set of full annotations, presenting the desired solution, provides a strong supervisory signal to tune the learnable parameters of a model to perform a task well. A lot of research has been done to relax this limitation through approaches that use data more efficiently and provide benefit to models from cheaper types of supervision. This includes the re-use of data with existing annotations [33,60], pre-training with synthetic data [31], self-training of a model [39,61], enforcement of assumptions such as smoothness in input space [41], usage of weak labels that only give hints to a model [3,4,32], and learning of useful representations from unlabeled data through auxiliary tasks [14,59]. These approaches can help reduce the manual annotation effort. But, in the vast majority of cases, at least a small amount of fully-supervised samples from the problem domain is either still necessary to fine-tune the model on that task or can improve the model's performance.

In active learning [45,48], a dataset of particularly informative samples is curated in cooperation with a model that learns the actual task. Active learning methods aim to find these examples so that only a fraction of the dataset needs to be labeled by an oracle (e.g. a human annotator), while achieving a model performance similar to learning with the fully annotated dataset.

In this article, we explore how cheaper supervision and active learning can be combined to learn the computer vision task of object detection without otherwise large annotation cost. Along the way, we briefly study the peculiarities of object detection and how cheap supervision can be provided to models learning this task in Sect. 2. In Sect. 3, we review common approaches to active learning for object detection and discuss what makes a sample informative. Equipped with this knowledge, we examine object detection settings that effectively reduce annotation cost by combining different types of supervision and active learning in Sect. 4. In Sect. 5, we provide guidelines to build similar combinations specific to custom applications. We summarize our key takeaways in Sect. 6.

2 Supervision for Object Detection

Object detection combines localization and classification of objects. Thereby, it differs from other computer vision tasks like image classification and semantic segmentation, which are both pure classification tasks. They assign a class label to the whole image or, respectively, to every single pixel in the image. In object detection, only regions of the image are classified that contain relevant objects.[1] To do so, the detector predicts bounding box coordinates and the class of the object enclosed by that box. Unlike the pure classification tasks, a wrong class prediction is not the only way of failing in object detection.

2.1 Failure Modes of Object Detectors

Fig. 1. Failure modes of an object detector trained to recognize three types of stuffed animals (cow, octopus, panda).

It can be regarded as a binary decision whether a location contains an object or not. When an object is present at a location and the detector predicts this region as "background", the detector makes a false negative error; an object that should

---

[1] One-stage object detectors based on convolutional neural networks (e.g. OverFeat [44], YOLO [37], SSD [27]) actually predict class labels and bounding box coordinates for every pixel of their feature map(s). They resemble segmentation models in that regard. Many locations are classified as "background" or "no object" class though and are ignored during the final output of predictions.

have been detected is not. In the opposite case, when the detector predicts an object at a location without an actual object of interest, the model makes a false positive error. Another mistake is to assign the wrong class label to an otherwise accurately localized object. Yet another failure mode is bad localization; while the object has been correctly assigned to its corresponding class, the predicted bounding box is not tightly centered around the object. Figure 1 illustrates all of these possibles mistakes.

Wrong class labels and bad localization are counted as false positive errors when calculating the precision and recall of the detector, which are the foundation of mean average precision (mAP) and mean average recall (mAR), the most reported object detection metrics. However, as these mistakes might have different reasons, they might be reduced most easily by different types of supervision, which includes different sets of fully-supervised samples.

2.2 The Many Flavors of Supervision

Object detection models receive full supervision when they can learn from images and corresponding sets of bounding box coordinates and class labels (see Fig. 2). All objects of interest should be annotated, as missing objects are learned as "background" otherwise. Providing such a strong supervisory signal is costly and the annotation effort can vary largely between different samples. In image classification, annotators assign a single class label to the entire image. The number of annotations per image in object detection depends on the number of objects present in a scene and can vary between zero and many. In experiments by Su et al. [47], the median time to draw a single bounding box on ImageNet [12] images was 25.5 s. In use cases like object detection on satellite images, traffic sign or pedestrian detection, many objects can be present at the same time, requiring a significant amount of time to annotate single images.

Fig. 2. A sample with full supervision for the object detection task of recognizing different types of stuffed animals.

We now explore alternatives to learn object detection from supervisory signals that are less costly to provide.

Active Learning. Ultimately, the detector must know about the object classes it has to predict and the visual features of corresponding objects. Active learning [45,48] helps focus the annotation effort on samples that are most informative to the model by involving it in choosing which samples to annotate. The information content of a sample is relative to the observer. For example, a model that has a specific inductive bias built-in might find the information a particular sample provides trivial, while another model that has to learn this issue from data might find the sample highly informative. Active learning involves the model in choosing which samples to annotate. To make this cooperation promising, the model needs to have a basic grasp of the task, e.g. have been trained on a small initial dataset with full supervision. As visualized in Fig. 3, the model then makes predictions for all unlabeled samples and based on an acquisition function, which can incorporate criteria like predictive uncertainty or data diversity, the informativeness of every sample is ranked. The samples deemed most informative are given to an oracle to gather labels. The model is then trained again with the enlarged pool of labeled samples. This procedure is repeated until the annotation budget runs out. Ideally, this enables high model performance with a fraction of data. Note, however, that a labeled dataset curated in cooperation with a particular model is not necessarily the most informative dataset for a different model [45].

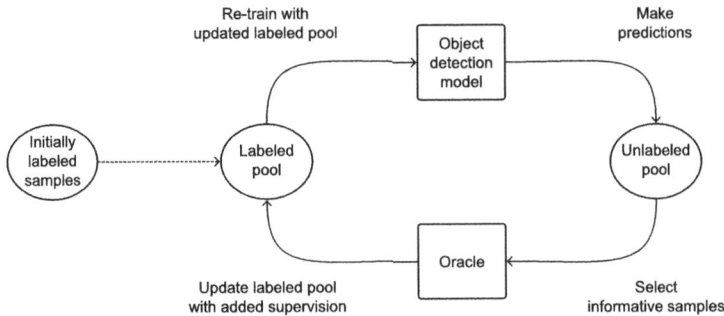

Fig. 3. The active learning loop includes a labeled and an unlabeled pool of samples. The informativeness of samples can be derived from the predictions of the trained model. A set of highly informative samples receives annotations from an oracle and is transferred to the labeled sample pool. The model gets re-trained after the update and the cycle starts again.

Transfer Learning and Synthetic Data. Transfer learning [33,60] is the most common approach to achieve a reasonable model performance with a small amount of labeled samples in the target domain. Taking advantage of the public availability of annotated large-scale datasets, the model is (pre-)trained with labeled data on a "source" task. This can provide a good starting point for the parameters of the model and thereby reduce the required number of labeled samples in the target domain and accelerate training convergence.

Transfer learning approaches can be categorized as homogeneous and heterogeneous [33,60]. In the homogeneous case, the feature and label spaces of source and target domain are consistent, while the distributions between the domains might differ. A way to reduce the gap between source and target task early on is the use of high-quality synthetic data [31] specific to our problem domain as source data. As we govern the data generation process, we get the ground truth labels along with our synthetic samples. We have control over the amount of generated data and other aspects like the class balance.

Semi-supervised Learning: uses labeled and unlabeled data to improve the performance of a model beyond the training with only labeled data, which can only work if the unlabeled data is related to the labeled data. After training the model fully supervised with labeled data, labels are propagated to unlabeled data. The three most common assumptions made for this regard smoothness in input space, decision boundaries of a classifier in regions of low data density, and the concentration of related data points along lower-dimensional substructures of the high-dimensional input space, known as manifolds [16].

The two dominant semi-supervised approaches are consistency regularization and self-training based on pseudo-labels. The smoothness assumption states that similar data points should receive the same prediction, which can be implemented through a consistency loss that enforces same predictions for differently augmented versions of a sample [21].[2] Self-training [61], on the other hand, uses high-confidence predictions on unlabeled samples as if they were actual annotations, provided by a competent oracle, to enlarge the training set.

Weakly-Supervised Learning. Instead of full annotations with tight bounding boxes and uniquely assigned class labels, weakly-supervised learning enables model training from coarse labels, which act like hints to the model. As shown in Fig. 4, such hints could be image-level class labels [4,32], which only hold information regarding present classes, but not where corresponding objects are located.

Fig. 4. Annotation types for weakly-supervised learning: image-level class labels on the left, point annotations on the right.

---

[2] Fully-supervised training with data augmentation makes the same assumption, but does not need a consistency loss because the ground truth label is provided.

Point annotations [3,8] contain more information. They mark a point inside every object and assign a class to it. For the PASCAL VOC 2012 [17] dataset, Bearman et al. [3] report a median of 2.4 s to click anywhere on the first instance and 0.9 s for additional instances of an object class. Papadopoulos et al. [36] determine a mean time of 1.87 s to click roughly on the center of an object, which they find to be superior.

Weak supervision can also be given as verification of predicted bounding boxes [34] and point annotations of the extreme points (top, bottom, left and right most points) of an object [35].

Self-supervised Learning. Auxiliary tasks that use inherent properties of the data like color [59], spatial [14] and temporal coherence [25], or invariance to augmentations [9] are used by self-supervised learning to learn useful representations. Similar to synthetic data, the solution to the task comes with the data. Except that we have to design a suitable task around our real data this time.

Currently, there is a research gap regarding self-supervised learning of whole detection models, as there are very few approaches [52] targeting this task specifically. Many methods focus on feature extractors that can be used as model backbones.

Complementary Combinations to Reduce Annotation Cost. In practice, the boundaries between these types of supervision are not as sharp as presented here and many methods are complementary to each other. But, while all of them can help reduce the annotation cost, the model still needs some examples with strong enough supervision to gather knowledge about all object classes. Thus, the problem of choosing samples to label persists if we want to use our manual annotation efforts as deliberate as possible.

3 Active Learning for Object Detection

In this section, we introduce the general thinking behind the choice of the most informative samples. This helps us later to make informed decisions about pairings between cheap supervision and active learning strategies. It is not an exhaustive survey of the current state of the art though. We focus on pool-based active learning as a setting where the data collection is finished and the active learning procedure helps annotate the least amount of data to train a high-performing model. We do not treat stream-based active learning and membership query synthesis explicitly. Unless otherwise stated, the methods presented here are applicable to both one-stage and two-stage detectors.

3.1 Aggregation of Object-Level Scores

Many measures of informativeness are calculated on the level of a single object instance. Although there are active learning approaches for object detection that operate on this object-level [28,49,51] or the level of an object region [23,26], which are promising for using the annotation effort even more deliberately, we follow the majority of approaches and expect an image-level score to select whole images for annotation. That means, we need to aggregate scores of multiple objects. Brust et al. [6] present three straightforward strategies:

1. **A Sum of the Object-Level Scores:** biases the sample selection towards images with many detections. In this setting, a sample with five moderately informative detections might be preferred over a sample with a single highly informative detection.[3] We could also compute a weighted sum by assigning a second quantity (e.g. highest class probability of each detection) as a weight to the scores [22].
2. **An Average of the Object-Level Scores:** limits the influence of the number of detections and can, again, be weighted or unweighted.
3. **Extreme Values (Minimum or Maximum) of the Object-Level Scores:** discard a lot of information, but can be appropriate for specific scenarios. For example, when it is important that predictions are made with high certainty, the sample with the highest uncertainty could be very informative. Either the prediction is correct and the model should be more confident or the prediction is wrong and should therefore be corrected.

Fig. 5. Intersection and union area of predictions from two models regarding the octopus.

Some scoring functions are based on combined predictions from multiple models or multiple forward passes of the same model. For these approaches, we must match the detections over those multiple predictions. Each prediction might localize an object a little different. The association is typically done through intersection over union (IoU). The IoU of two sets A and B is defined as

$$J(A, B) = \text{IoU}(A, B) = \frac{|A \cap B|}{|A \cup B|} = \frac{|A \cap B|}{|A| + |B| - |A \cap B|}, \tag{1}$$

---

[3] Apart from this possibly undesired behavior, a sample with more objects is more costly to label.

which is the ratio of intersection size and union size, also known as Jaccard index, with $0 \leq \text{IoU}(A, B) \leq 1$. An IoU value close to 1 expresses a strong overlap between the two sets. Figure 5 illustrates the idea. After associating detections with high IoU, we compute scores at the object-level before we aggregate them for an image-level score. For scenarios where two bounding boxes from different predictions could address the same object without overlapping, the generalized IoU [38] must be used.

The choice of scoring function, which we study next, and aggregation strategy has to be done carefully to prevent an unintended selection bias. In the worst case, randomly selected samples lead to a better performance, rendering the extra effort of active learning useless.

3.2 Uncertainty

Research on deep active learning for computer vision initially focused on image classification. Since detectors also classify objects, some approaches have been adopted. Later, more methods were developed to exploit localization uncertainty.

Classification Uncertainty. Usually, the classification heads of deep learning models provide the log probabilities of all classes normalized by the softmax function as their output. This distribution over possible classes, the predictive probabilities, can be leveraged in several ways to measure how certain the model is about its prediction.

The simplest approach is to aggregate the probabilities of the most probable class of each detection in an image to select low-confidence samples. On the other hand, neural networks are known to be badly calibrated [19] and tend to be overconfident in their predictions as this further reduces the training loss.

Using the difference between the most probable and second most probable class is known as margin sampling or 1-vs-2. If the model gives a similar confidence to both classes (i.e. the margin is small), this indicates uncertainty about the category of an object. Brust et al. [6] tried this for object detection.

Instead of using only the top-1 or top-2 of the predictive probabilities, the full distribution can be used. Treating the class prediction as a discrete random variable X, its entropy quantifies the uncertainty regarding the potential states of X. It is defined as

$$H(X) := -\sum_{x \in X} P(x) \log P(x). \qquad (2)$$

A class prediction with a clear favorite has a low entropy, while a class prediction that resembles a uniform distribution has a high entropy. Roy et al. [40] use this measure in the context of object detection to find high-entropy samples.

Predictive uncertainty can also be estimated through model ensembles [24]. Combining the predictions of multiple models trained on the same data, but differently initialized, provides a distribution of class predictions whose entropy can be calculated. While the training of multiple models is computationally more expensive, the measure of informativeness becomes more robust. Using ensembles makes the sample selection less tied to a single model, which might be beneficial when the dataset is going to be used with other models in the future.

Another way of using ensembles and entropy is mutual information, as Haussmann et al. [20] did. They formulate mutual information as

$$\mathrm{MI}(X) := H(\bar{X}) - \frac{1}{|E|} \sum_{e \in E} H(X^{(e)}), \qquad (3)$$

with $\bar{X}$ as averaged class prediction over all members of the ensemble E and $|E|$ as the cardinality of the ensemble. The difference between the entropy $H(\bar{X})$ of the average class probabilities and the average of the entropies of each model's prediction gives the mutual information. This can be used as a measure of disagreement between the models in an ensemble.

A cheaper approximation to ensembles is Monte Carlo dropout [18]. Applying dropout [46] at test time means that the prediction is made with a subset of the entire neural network. Multiple forward passes with different neural units dropping out can be viewed as an ensemble.

Uncertainty (or inconsistency) estimation from the stability of predictions under augmentations [15,57] is in a similar vein. Predictions are gathered for the original sample and augmented variants of it. The Jensen-Shannon divergence of the predictive probabilities measures how certain the model is about its prediction.

Localization Uncertainty. Informativeness measures for object detection beyond classification can be derived from the uncertainty regarding bounding box coordinates. Kao et al. [22] introduce two such measures.

Localization tightness expresses how tightly a bounding box encloses an object. As the ground truth is not available for unlabeled samples, this is estimated through a proxy. Two-stage object detectors make the binary decision whether an object centered around a pixel of their feature map(s) is present or not and, if that is the case, provide a region proposal. This initial bounding box guess gets refined subsequently. The proxy to estimate localization tightness is the IoU of region proposal and the corresponding final prediction (see Fig. 6a). It is thus only applicable to two-stage detectors.

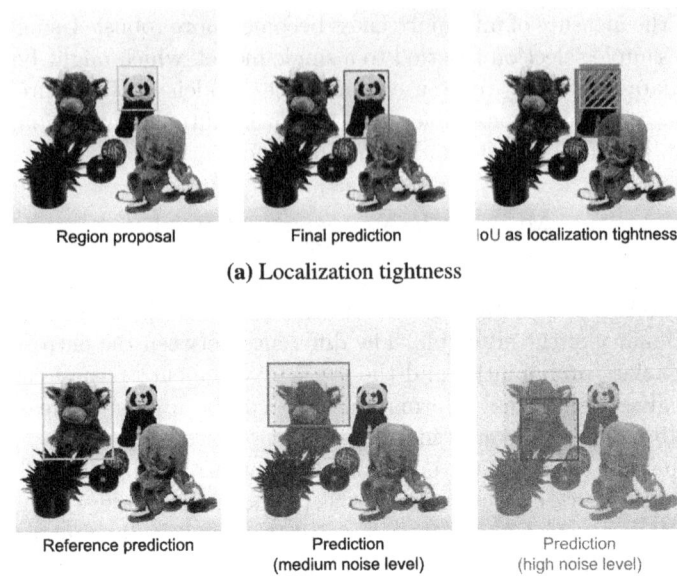

Fig. 6. Visualization of localization tightness and stability, two measures of localization uncertainty.

Localization stability is defined as the average IoU between predictions for the original sample and augmented versions of it (see Fig. 6). When aggregating the image-level score, the instances are weighted by their highest class probability. Like that, instances are preferred that have a high localization uncertainty and high probability of containing an object of interest at the same time. Yu et al. [57] extend the applied augmentations beyond Gaussian noise.

Schmidt et al. [42] estimate localization uncertainty from an ensemble as the minimum IoU between all predictions that concern the same object. When extended by class predictions, this approach aims to also find samples where the ensemble agrees about the localization but predicts different classes for the object. Both variants did not outperform random selection in their study.

Choi et al. [10] replace the usual prediction heads of deep object detectors with a mixture density network [5]. From the Gaussian mixture model that it learns, aleatoric and epistemic uncertainties, a common decomposition of predictive uncertainty, for classification and localization can be computed. Aleatoric (statistical) uncertainty comprises the inherent randomness of a process that leads to variable outcomes. For detection, a high aleatoric uncertainty could be caused by sensor noise or occlusion. Epistemic (systematic) uncertainty is caused by the lack of knowledge. For each detection, Choi et al. [10] compute both uncertainties per subtask (classification and localization) from a single forward pass.

3.3 Expected Model Change

Intuitively, samples that would cause the model to change significantly are informative. Ash et al. [2] propose a method to identify such samples, which Haussmann et al. [20] adapt to object detection. The average class label predicted by an ensemble is used as the ground truth label. Under this assumption, each ensemble member computes its loss and a "hallucinated" gradient. The magnitude of the gradient is used as uncertainty score.

Another approach is the task-agnostic loss prediction module by Yoo and Kweon [56]. It is trained along with the model and learns to predict the loss value the model's prediction will cause for each sample. It receives intermediate feature maps from the model as input and the loss values observed for labeled samples as supervision. When applying this module to unlabeled samples, the predicted loss values can be used as image-level informativeness scores. The authors note, however, that the accuracy of loss predictions was relatively low when they applied this method to complex tasks such as object detection.

3.4 Diversity

Samples selected for annotation should represent the underlying data distribution of the dataset well. This is especially important when active learning is performed in the batch setting, where multiple samples are selected for annotation at once. When we select samples one by one, the focus can shift after each sample if the newly added annotation provided enough supervision to learn a previously uncertain decision. When adding a batch of samples to the labeled pool at once, we should ensure that they are diverse.

Measuring diversity for images is not trivial. A proxy method is to work with feature vectors obtained from a feature extractor like the detector's backbone. Clustering approaches such as k-means++ [1] or core-set [43], a method to best cover the larger distribution of samples with only a subset of them, can use this representation. Haussmann et al. [20] study this approach for object detection.

The aforementioned approach is usually applied at the image-level to measure the similarity of entire images. In object detection, two scenes could look similar while the present objects are different. Therefore, Yang et al. [55] introduce category conditioned matching similarity. When measuring the similarity of two images, feature vectors of detected objects are calculated and each object is matched to the most similar object of the same category in the other image. The image-level score is then calculated as the average of the object similarities.

3.5 Undetectability

Most prior methods base their score on predictions. But one of the failure modes of object detectors are false negatives, objects the model has not detected although it should have. Nakamura et al. [30] first explicitly stated this shortcoming in the context of active learning and proposed a solution. They alternately train a false negative prediction module with their detection model. The false negative prediction module gets the features extracted by the detector backbone as input and receives the number of missed detections on labeled samples as supervision. The prediction of the false negative prediction module on unlabeled samples is used as an image-level score for sample selection. As this shortcoming has only recently been addressed, there is potential for further research on how missed objects can be considered in active learning for object detection.

3.6 Combining Multiple Criteria

Commonly, scoring and sampling are distinguished in two phases that consider different aspects [54,55]. Scoring is often based on one or multiple uncertainty scores and determines a ranking of the unlabeled samples. When progressing to the sampling phase, a pool larger than the annotation budget assigned for that active learning round is drawn. The samples that will actually be labeled in that round are selected from that pool according to a diversity measure. This prevents the annotation of many redundant samples. Yang et al. [55] also find that the importance of different measures varies with the progress of active learning. In their experiments, uncertainty-based measures were more important in earlier active learning rounds, while in later rounds diversity became more critical.

Weighting some measures by other quantities is frequently done, e.g. with localization stability [22] and the highest class probability of that object. Yang et al. [55] compute difficulty coefficients during training with labeled samples to use them as weights in their scoring function.

4 Minimal Manual Annotation Effort for Object Detection

Now that we have an understanding of possible types of supervision and the way we can rate informativeness to select samples for annotation during active learning, we take a look at how the two have been brought together successfully.

4.1 Transfer, Semi-supervised, and Active Learning

Nakamura et al. [30] combine unsupervised domain adaptation (UDA), a transfer learning technique that does not use target domain labels, and active learning for object detection. Their UDA method joins self-training with pseudo-labels and adversarial learning for feature space alignment between domains. They found that their model produced many false negatives under the domain shift and UDA could not eliminate this undesired behavior. As we have seen earlier, informative samples are usually drawn based on measures that are taken for detections. We already looked into their solution, a false negative prediction module, in Sect. 3.5. Combined with uncertainty scores for classification and localization as well as a diversity score, their selection focuses on samples that help reduce false negative errors, the main weakness of the detector in that setting.

Cetintas et al. [7] use pre-training on synthetic data, self-training with pseudo-labels, and active learning in their annotation pipeline for visual tracking. They mitigate the risk of false negative predictions through over-complete sets of detections. A low confidence threshold allows many false positive predictions, which increases the chances to find an otherwise lost true positive detection. Their tracking-by-detection approach uses detections on single video frames that have to be associated optimally across frames for successful tracking. By leveraging temporal information, many nonsensical predictions can be filtered out, as there are no corresponding detections on adjacent frames.[4]

Elezi et al. [15] combine semi-supervised learning (self-training with pseudo-labels and consistency regularization) and active learning. With a modified loss function, they only incorporate true positive predictions for pseudo-labeled samples. This mitigates the problem of reinforcing other regions as "background" that could contain objects of interest, but are not pseudo-labeled accordingly as the corresponding predictions have low confidence. Their acquisition function uses inconsistency under augmentation and entropy-based classification uncertainty. As their training is based on the assumptions of smoothness in input space, the selection of samples whose predictions are not consistent under augmentation works well to improve the model. It captures those images that cannot be successfully learned from in a semi-supervised fashion and need full supervision.

In general, the success of semi-supervised learning depends on the initial dataset and the predictive capabilities the model learns from it. It is important that the initial data represents the task well, i.e. helps the model learn to detect objects and is diverse in the space of possible inputs. The model has to generalize from the few labeled data points to the whole distribution. By using a large amount of available labeled data, which could also be synthetically generated, training can be started without initial annotation effort, but attention has to be paid to a possible domain gap between "source" data and target data.

4.2 Weakly-Supervised and Active Learning

Desai et al. [13] extend the active learning loop to leverage weak labels. The model starts training with a random subset of the data that has to be annotated with strong labels. During active learning, the oracle provides center point annotations for selected samples. Pseudo-labels are produced from the weak labels by selecting bounding box predictions whose center is closest to the center point annotation. There are two approaches to adaptively query for strong labels when

---

[4] When training an object detector without additional (temporal) information, allowing many false positives could unintentionally bias sample selection during active learning. For example, Cordier et al. [11] simply select every sample for annotation that contains a detection by their model. In their use case, defect detection for industrial parts, true positive predictions should be rare. Therefore, samples with detections, regardless of whether they are true positive or false positive, are always informative.

necessary. A hard (inter-episode) switch leads to queries for strong labels in all future rounds. It is activated based on the change of model performance on a validation dataset. The other approach, a soft (inter-episode) switch, allows requests for full supervision for individual samples if the mean prediction confidence is below a threshold. The soft switch approach performs best regarding detection performance (measured by mAP) in relation to annotation time in their experiments.

Weakly-supervised approaches tend to predict incomplete bounding boxes, which only cover the most discriminative part of the object. In this case, better supervision regarding localization is necessary. The problem of sometimes poor localization can be seen in examples shown by Desai et al. [13, Fig. 7], which were selected for strong supervision. They only compare three classification-based scores in their active learning approach however.

Fig. 7. Box-in-box predictions as a result of weak labels. The large blue bounding box contains multiple objects and the small pink bounding box only contains the head of the octopus. The other bounding boxes correctly localize their respective object, while a prediction for the panda is missing in this example. (Color figure online)

Vo et al. [50] propose an active learning strategy to address a special case of localization error. For training from scratch with image-level class labels only, they find that detectors often produce box-in-box predictions, where either two bounding boxes of different size belong to the same object or a large bounding box encloses a group of objects from the same class with additional boxes for individual objects (see Fig. 7). They identify such cases and select diverse box-in-box pairs to improve their detector with well-directed full supervision.

In summary, weak supervision can be used during training if many weakly-annotated samples are available and active learning can be a remedy to correct model errors by targeting these shortcomings of the training loop specifically. It can also be used during active learning to save annotation cost and only switch to full supervision when it is necessary.

5 Guidelines for Active Learning With Cheap Supervision

The suitability of a particular instantiation of a training framework combining cheap supervision and active learning for object detection is unfortunately specific to the data and the use case. Therefore, we can only point out what considerations should be made when building a training cycle and suggest combinations that have worked well in the literature or should complement each other.

There are two limitations to consider during the choice of methods. Active learning and self-training both trade annotation cost for computational resources. The cyclic nature of training, increasing the pool of labeled data, and then training again requires more computing time than standard training with an appropriately sized dataset with full supervision. This is especially true when using ensemble-based active learning. Accordingly, it must be decided whether annotation or computational cost is more affordable. The other limitation is that many of the approaches presented here were evaluated on datasets curated as academic benchmarks. This practice has been criticized by Haussmann et al. [20] as most samples in these datasets are informative due to the curation process. This also leads to experiments in small-scale settings between hundreds and a few thousand samples. This does not necessarily mean that the approaches cannot scale to larger settings with many uninformative samples, but we should be aware of this difference.

Before implementing an active learning cycle with cheap supervision, we should consider the data: Are any annotations available? Is there similar, annotated data? Could we efficiently generate a synthetic surrogate? Is there structure we can exploit? How distinct are the object features (texture, shape, color) from the background and other objects, i.e. how difficult are classification and localization? Answering these questions allows us to choose a suitable approach.

The examples we have examined in Sect. 4 show that labeled (synthetic) data close to our problem domain and self-training with pseudo-labels seems, generally speaking, like a promising combination. As implemented in [7,53], it avoids the annotation of a random subset of the target data as a starting point for training and subsequent active learning. The quality of the pseudo-labels is important and should be ensured through appropriate training techniques [29] and/or the use of additional information if available. Attention should be paid to incompletely pseudo-labeled samples to not reinforce objects with low-confidence predictions as background (e.g. via a modified loss [15]). Otherwise, this setting is predestined to need support regarding false negative predictions and there currently is only one active learning approach [30] targeting these missed detections. Apart from that, the additional use of a consistency regularizing loss for unlabeled samples can help the model generalize better, but also comes with an increased computational demand as the processing of multiple augmented versions of a sample is necessary.

If relevant additional data is not available and we cannot generate a synthetic surrogate, self-supervised learning on our target data could be a good starting point to reduce the required size of the initial, annotated dataset. Self-supervised learning can also be joined with semi-supervised learning [58], but self-supervised techniques for whole detection models [52] are mostly lacking yet.

If weak annotations are available, model training can start weakly-supervised and active learning can be used to correct the flaws of the training technique. If a large number of weak annotations seem more obtainable than a small amount of full annotations, we need to assess whether and, if so, which type of weak supervision is reasonable for our data. Detecting objects in images that contain very few objects simultaneously can probably be learned from image-level class labels. For scenes with many objects at once, stronger localization hints in the form of center point annotations could be more appropriate. If the objects are hard to distinguish from their surroundings, extreme point annotations [35] could be necessary.

A combination of predictive uncertainty and data diversity (in the batch setting) is a good baseline to choose as informativeness measures for active learning. We have also seen that it can be useful to find samples that violate assumptions that were made in training [15]. Whether we should further bias the sample selection depends on the intended application and whether the model displays a structural weakness in its predictions. If false negatives are a problem, a measure of undetectability [30] should be instrumental. If poorly localized objects show a pattern, such as weakly-supervised detectors that only predict a bounding box around the most salient area of an object, we could probably also target this, e.g. with a heuristic regarding bounding box size. To identify the flaws of a detector, we have to inspect a sufficient number of predictions made by our model manually or, if we have a fully annotated validation set at hand, we can gather evidence from object detection metrics. A low mean average recall (mAR) points towards problems with missed objects. Low scores for mean average precision (mAP) indicate the presence of false positives, which could be due to wrong classification, bad localization, or just a detection in a location without an object. Problems with localization can be inferred from examining these metrics for different IoU thresholds.

If the annotation budget is extremely limited in terms of annotation time, weak supervision can be given for samples selected for more supervision [13]. Again, this can be done in a number of ways. Image-level class labels, different kinds of point annotations, and the verification of predicted bounding boxes [34] are all viable options.

In summary, there are a large number of possible configurations, not all of which have been tested. To find a solution that works for our application, we should make the most of the information contained in our data and think about the budget we can devote to the problem in terms of computational resources and annotation cost. Building on this foundation, we can select the appropriate methods to minimize any shortcomings in the training cycle.

6 Conclusion

We have discussed approaches that use cheap supervision and active learning in conjunction to accomplish object detection with minimal manual annotation effort. There are three general takeaways:

1. **Harmonize Active Learning and Cheap Supervision.** Active learning can and should be biased towards selecting samples that effectively compensate for the weaknesses of other supervisory signals in the model training loop. Possible failure modes are false positives (background detected as object), false negatives (missed detections), bad object localization, and wrong object class prediction.
2. **Choose Scoring Function, Aggregation Strategy, and Sample Selection Carefully.** Each of these aspects has the potential to turn an active learning pipeline that saves annotation cost into an elaborate selection of samples that cannot outperform a random selection.
3. **Engage Complementary Approaches in All Learning Phases.** Active learning does not need to start from a pool of fully annotated samples, nor does it need to query for full supervision. Weak annotations and the reliance on smoothness assumptions can sometimes be sufficient to advance learning.

When implementing an effective instantiation of this framework, the available data and the targeted application should be carefully considered to find an appropriate approach using the guidelines provided here.

Acknowledgments. This work was funded by the German Federal Ministry of Digital and Transport, project number 19F2236A.

Disclosure of Interests. The authors have no competing interests to declare that are relevant to the content of this article.

References

1. Arthur, D., Vassilvitskii, S.: k-means++: the advantages of careful seeding. In: Proceedings of the Eighteenth Annual ACM-SIAM Symposium on Discrete Algorithms, pp. 1027–1035. SODA '07 (2007)
2. Ash, J.T., Zhang, C., Krishnamurthy, A., Langford, J., Agarwal, A.: Deep batch active learning by diverse, uncertain gradient lower bounds. In: International Conference on Learning Representations (2020)
3. Bearman, A., Russakovsky, O., Ferrari, V., Fei-Fei, L.: What's the point: semantic segmentation with point supervision. In: Computer Vision – ECCV 2016, pp. 549–565 (2016)
4. Bilen, H., Vedaldi, A.: Weakly supervised deep detection networks. In: 2016 IEEE Conference on Computer Vision and Pattern Recognition (CVPR), pp. 2846–2854 (2016). https://doi.org/10.1109/CVPR.2016.311
5. Bishop, C.M.: Mixture Density Networks. Aston University, Tech. Report (1994)
6. Brust, C.A., Käding, C., Denzler, J.: Active learning for deep object detection (2018). arXiv preprint, arXiv:1809.09875

7. Cetintas, O., Meinhardt, T., Brasó, G., Leal-Taixé, L.: SPAMming labels: efficient annotations for the trackers of tomorrow. In: European Conference on Computer Vision (ECCV) (2024)
8. Chen, L., Yang, T., Zhang, X., Zhang, W., Sun, J.: Points as queries: weakly semi-supervised object detection by points. In: 2021 IEEE/CVF Conference on Computer Vision and Pattern Recognition (CVPR), pp. 8819–8828 (2021). https://doi.org/10.1109/CVPR46437.2021.00871
9. Chen, T., Kornblith, S., Norouzi, M., Hinton, G.: A simple framework for contrastive learning of visual representations. In: Proceedings of the 37th International Conference on Machine Learning. ICML'20 (2020)
10. Choi, J., Elezi, I., Lee, H.J., Farabet, C., Alvarez, J.M.: Active learning for deep object detection via probabilistic modeling. In: 2021 IEEE/CVF International Conference on Computer Vision (ICCV), pp. 10244–10253 (2021). https://doi.org/10.1109/ICCV48922.2021.01010
11. Cordier, A., Das, D., Gutierrez, P.: Active learning using weakly supervised signals for quality inspection. In: Fifteenth International Conference on Quality Control by Artificial Vision, vol. 11794, p. 1179413 (2021). https://doi.org/10.1117/12.2586595
12. Deng, J., Dong, W., Socher, R., Li, L.J., Li, K., Fei-Fei, L.: ImageNet: a large-scale hierarchical image database. In: 2009 IEEE Conference on Computer Vision and Pattern Recognition, pp. 248–255 (2009). https://doi.org/10.1109/CVPR.2009.5206848
13. Desai, S.V., Lagandula, A.C., Guo, W., Ninomiya, S., Balasubramanian, V.N.: An adaptive supervision framework for active learning in object detection. In: 30th British Machine Vision Conference 2019, BMVC 2019, Cardiff, UK, September 9-12, 2019, p. 230 (2019)
14. Doersch, C., Gupta, A., Efros, A.A.: Unsupervised visual representation learning by context prediction. In: 2015 IEEE International Conference on Computer Vision (ICCV), pp. 1422–1430 (2015). https://doi.org/10.1109/ICCV.2015.167
15. Elezi, I., Yu, Z., Anandkumar, A., Leal-Taixé, L., Alvarez, J.M.: Not all labels are equal: rationalizing the labeling costs for training object detection. In: 2022 IEEE/CVF Conference on Computer Vision and Pattern Recognition (CVPR), pp. 14472–14481 (2022). https://doi.org/10.1109/CVPR52688.2022.01409
16. van Engelen, J.E., Hoos, H.H.: A survey on semi-supervised learning. Mach. Learn. **109**(2), 373–440 (2019). https://doi.org/10.1007/s10994-019-05855-6
17. Everingham, M., Van Gool, L., Williams, C.K.I., Winn, J., Zisserman, A.: The pascal visual object classes (VOC) challenge. Int. J. Comput. Vision **88**(2), 303–338 (2010). https://doi.org/10.1007/s11263-009-0275-4
18. Gal, Y., Ghahramani, Z.: Dropout as a Bayesian approximation: representing model uncertainty in deep learning. In: Proceedings of The 33rd International Conference on Machine Learning. Proceedings of Machine Learning Research, vol. 48, pp. 1050–1059 (2016)
19. Guo, C., Pleiss, G., Sun, Y., Weinberger, K.Q.: On calibration of modern neural networks. In: Proceedings of the 34th International Conference on Machine Learning. Proceedings of Machine Learning Research, vol. 70, pp. 1321–1330 (2017)
20. Haussmann, E., et al.: Scalable active learning for object detection. In: 2020 IEEE Intelligent Vehicles Symposium (IV), pp. 1430–1435 (2020). https://doi.org/10.1109/IV47402.2020.9304793
21. Jeong, J., Lee, S., Kim, J., Kwak, N.: Consistency-based semi-supervised learning for object detection. In: Advances in Neural Information Processing Systems. vol. 32 (2019)

22. Kao, C.C., Lee, T.Y., Sen, P., Liu, M.Y.: Localization-aware active learning for object detection. In: Computer Vision – ACCV 2018, pp. 506–522 (2019)
23. Laielli, M., et al.: Region-level active detector learning (2021). arXiv preprint, arXiv:2108.09186
24. Lakshminarayanan, B., Pritzel, A., Blundell, C.: Simple and scalable predictive uncertainty estimation using deep ensembles. In: Proceedings of the 31st International Conference on Neural Information Processing Systems, pp. 6405–6416. NIPS'17 (2017)
25. Lee, H.Y., Huang, J.B., Singh, M., Yang, M.H.: Unsupervised representation learning by sorting sequences. In: 2017 IEEE International Conference on Computer Vision (ICCV), pp. 667–676 (2017). https://doi.org/10.1109/ICCV.2017.79
26. Liou, Y.S., Wu, T.H., Yeh, J.F., Chen, W.C., Hsu, W.H.: MuRAL: Multi-scale region-based active learning for object detection (2023). arXiv preprint, arXiv:2303.16637
27. Liu, W., et al.: SSD: Single Shot MultiBox Detector. In: Leibe, B., Matas, J., Sebe, N., Welling, M. (eds.) ECCV 2016. LNCS, vol. 9905, pp. 21–37. Springer, Cham (2016). https://doi.org/10.1007/978-3-319-46448-0_2
28. Lyu, M., et al.: Box-level active detection. In: 2023 IEEE/CVF Conference on Computer Vision and Pattern Recognition (CVPR), pp. 23766–23775 (2023). https://doi.org/10.1109/CVPR52729.2023.02276
29. Mi, P., et al.: Active teacher for semi-supervised object detection. In: 2022 IEEE/CVF Conference on Computer Vision and Pattern Recognition (CVPR), pp. 14462–14471 (2022). https://doi.org/10.1109/CVPR52688.2022.01408
30. Nakamura, Y., Ishii, Y., Yamashita, T.: Active domain adaptation with false negative prediction for object detection. In: Proceedings of the IEEE/CVF Conference on Computer Vision and Pattern Recognition (CVPR), pp. 28782–28792 (2024)
31. Synthetic Data for Deep Learning. SOIA, vol. 174. Springer, Cham (2021). https://doi.org/10.1007/978-3-030-75178-4
32. Oquab, M., Bottou, L., Laptev, I., Sivic, J.: Is object localization for free? - Weakly-supervised learning with convolutional neural networks. In: 2015 IEEE Conference on Computer Vision and Pattern Recognition (CVPR), pp. 685–694 (2015). https://doi.org/10.1109/CVPR.2015.7298668
33. Pan, S.J., Yang, Q.: A survey on transfer learning. IEEE Trans. Knowl. Data Eng. **22**(10), 1345–1359 (2010). https://doi.org/10.1109/TKDE.2009.191
34. Papadopoulos, D.P., Uijlings, J.R.R., Keller, F., Ferrari, V.: We don't need no bounding-boxes: training object class detectors using only human verification. In: 2016 IEEE Conference on Computer Vision and Pattern Recognition (CVPR), pp. 854–863 (2016). https://doi.org/10.1109/CVPR.2016.99
35. Papadopoulos, D.P., Uijlings, J.R.R., Keller, F., Ferrari, V.: Extreme clicking for efficient object annotation. In: 2017 IEEE International Conference on Computer Vision (ICCV), pp. 4940–4949 (2017). https://doi.org/10.1109/ICCV.2017.528
36. Papadopoulos, D.P., Uijlings, J.R.R., Keller, F., Ferrari, V.: Training object class detectors with click supervision. In: 2017 IEEE Conference on Computer Vision and Pattern Recognition (CVPR), pp. 180–189 (2017). https://doi.org/10.1109/CVPR.2017.27
37. Redmon, J., Divvala, S., Girshick, R., Farhadi, A.: You only look once: unified, real-time object detection. In: Proceedings of the IEEE Conference on Computer Vision and Pattern Recognition (CVPR) (2016)
38. Rezatofighi, H., Tsoi, N., Gwak, J., Sadeghian, A., Reid, I., Savarese, S.: Generalized intersection over union. In: The IEEE Conference on Computer Vision and Pattern Recognition (CVPR) (2019)

39. Rosenberg, C., Hebert, M., Schneiderman, H.: Semi-supervised self-training of object detection models. In: 2005 Seventh IEEE Workshops on Applications of Computer Vision (WACV/MOTION'05) - Volume 1. vol. 1, pp. 29–36 (2005). https://doi.org/10.1109/ACVMOT.2005.107
40. Roy, S., Unmesh, A., Namboodiri, V.P.: Deep active learning for object detection. In: British Machine Vision Conference 2018, BMVC 2018, Newcastle, UK, September 3-6, 2018, p. 91 (2018). http://bmvc2018.org/contents/papers/0287.pdf
41. Sajjadi, M., Javanmardi, M., Tasdizen, T.: Regularization with stochastic transformations and perturbations for deep semi-supervised learning. In: Advances in Neural Information Processing Systems, vol. 29 (2016). https://proceedings.neurips.cc/paper_files/paper/2016/file/30ef30b64204a3088a26bc2e6ecf7602-Paper.pdf
42. Schmidt, S., Rao, Q., Tatsch, J., Knoll, A.: Advanced active learning strategies for object detection. In: 2020 IEEE Intelligent Vehicles Symposium (IV), pp. 871–876 (2020). https://doi.org/10.1109/IV47402.2020.9304565
43. Sener, O., Savarese, S.: Active learning for convolutional neural networks: a core-set approach. In: International Conference on Learning Representations (2018)
44. Sermanet, P., Eigen, D., Zhang, X., Mathieu, M., Fergus, R., LeCun, Y.: OverFeat: integrated recognition, localization and detection using convolutional networks (2013). arXiv preprint, arXiv:1312.6229
45. Settles, B.: Active learning literature survey. Computer Sciences Technical Report 1648, University of Wisconsin–Madison (2009)
46. Srivastava, N., Hinton, G., Krizhevsky, A., Sutskever, I., Salakhutdinov, R.: Dropout: a simple way to prevent neural networks from overfitting. J. Mach. Learn. Res. **15**(56), 1929–1958 (2014)
47. Su, H., Deng, J., Fei-Fei, L.: Crowdsourcing annotations for visual object detection. In: Human Computation - Papers from the 2012 AAAI Workshop, Technical Report, pp. 40–46. AAAI Workshop - Technical Report (2012)
48. Tong, S.: Active learning: theory and applications. Ph.D. thesis, Stanford University, USA (2001)
49. Vikas Desai, S., Balasubramanian, V.N.: Towards fine-grained sampling for active learning in object detection. In: 2020 IEEE/CVF Conference on Computer Vision and Pattern Recognition Workshops (CVPRW), pp. 4010–4014 (2020). https://doi.org/10.1109/CVPRW50498.2020.00470
50. Vo, H.V., Siméoni, O., Gidaris, S., Bursuc, A., Pérez, P., Ponce, J.: Active learning strategies for weakly-supervised object detection. In: Computer Vision – ECCV 2022, pp. 211–230 (2022)
51. Wang, K., Yan, X., Zhang, D., Zhang, L., Lin, L.: Towards human-machine cooperation: self-supervised sample mining for object detection. In: 2018 IEEE/CVF Conference on Computer Vision and Pattern Recognition, pp. 1605–1613 (2018). https://doi.org/10.1109/CVPR.2018.00173
52. Wang, X., Girdhar, R., Yu, S.X., Misra, I.: Cut and learn for unsupervised object detection and instance segmentation. In: 2023 IEEE/CVF Conference on Computer Vision and Pattern Recognition (CVPR), pp. 3124–3134 (2023). https://doi.org/10.1109/CVPR52729.2023.00305
53. Wang, Y., Ilic, V., Li, J., Kisačanin, B., Pavlovic, V.: ALWOD: Active learning for weakly-supervised object detection. In: 2023 IEEE/CVF International Conference on Computer Vision (ICCV), pp. 6436–6446 (2023). https://doi.org/10.1109/ICCV51070.2023.00594

54. Wu, J., Chen, J., Huang, D.: Entropy-based active learning for object detection with progressive diversity constraint. In: 2022 IEEE/CVF Conference on Computer Vision and Pattern Recognition (CVPR), pp. 9387–9396 (2022). https://doi.org/10.1109/CVPR52688.2022.00918
55. Yang, C., Huang, L., Crowley, E.J.: Plug and play active learning for object detection. In: Proceedings of the IEEE/CVF Conference on Computer Vision and Pattern Recognition (CVPR), pp. 17784–17793 (2024)
56. Yoo, D., Kweon, I.S.: Learning loss for active learning. In: Proceedings of the IEEE/CVF Conference on Computer Vision and Pattern Recognition (CVPR) (2019)
57. Yu, W., Zhu, S., Yang, T., Chen, C.: Consistency-based active learning for object detection. In: Proceedings of the IEEE/CVF Conference on Computer Vision and Pattern Recognition (CVPR) Workshops, pp. 3951–3960 (2022)
58. Zhai, X., Oliver, A., Kolesnikov, A., Beyer, L.: S4L: Self-supervised semi-supervised learning. In: Proceedings of the IEEE/CVF International Conference on Computer Vision (ICCV) (2019)
59. Zhang, R., Isola, P., Efros, A.A.: Colorful image colorization. In: Leibe, B., Matas, J., Sebe, N., Welling, M. (eds.) ECCV 2016. LNCS, vol. 9907, pp. 649–666. Springer, Cham (2016). https://doi.org/10.1007/978-3-319-46487-9_40
60. Zhuang, F., et al.: A comprehensive survey on transfer learning. Proc. IEEE **109**(1), 43–76 (2021). https://doi.org/10.1109/JPROC.2020.3004555
61. Zoph, B., et al.: Rethinking pre-training and self-training. In: Advances in Neural Information Processing Systems, vol. 33, pp. 3833–3845 (2020)

Smartphone-Based Detection of Cataract and Pterygium Using MobileNet: A Unified Approach for Anterior Segment Photographed Images

Wan Mimi Diyana Wan Zaki[1(✉)], Laily Azyan Ramlan[1], Nurul Syahira Mohamad Zamani[1], Marizuana Mat Daud[2], and Haliza Abdul Mutalib[3]

[1] Department of Electrical, Electronic and Systems Engineering, Faculty of Engineering and Built Environment, Universiti Kebangsaan Malaysia, Kampus Bangi, Bangi, Malaysia
wmdiyana@ukm.edu.my
[2] Institute of Visual Informatics, Universiti Kebangsaan Malaysia, Kampus Bangi, Bangi, Malaysia
[3] Optometry and Vision Science, Faculty of Health Sciences, Universiti Kebangsaan Malaysia, Kampus Kuala Lumpur, Kuala Lumpur, Malaysia

Abstract. This study explores the application of the MobileNetV2 architecture for detecting cataracts and pterygium using anterior segment photographed images (ASPI) captured via smartphone cameras. Cataracts and pterygium are significant global health concerns, and their early detection is crucial for preventing vision impairment. The MobileNetV2's lightweight and efficient design enables accurate and scalable classification of eye diseases, even with variable image quality from smartphone cameras. This paper provides an overview of the prevalence of cataracts and pterygium, summarizes prior work, and presents experimental results demonstrating MobileNetV2's high performance in detecting both diseases. For pterygium classification, MobileNetV2 achieved its best performance with the Adam optimizer and a batch size of 10, delivering 97.37% accuracy, 96.05% sensitivity, and the highest AUC of 99.41%. It also demonstrated exceptional computational efficiency, completing training in just 2.13 min with Adam and Batch Size 32, the shortest training time across all configurations. The network exhibited consistent performance with only minor declines as the batch size increased. For cataract patch classification, MobileNetV2 also performed strongly, achieving 95.44% accuracy, 95.78% sensitivity, and an AUC of 99.19% with Adam and Batch Size 10. Additionally, it completed training in the shortest time of 7 min, making it highly efficient for resource-constrained environments. The findings support the integration of smartphone imaging and deep learning as a cost-effective solution for ophthalmological diagnostics.

Keywords: Artificial intelligence · Anterior segment photographed images · Cataract · Pterygium

1 Introduction

1.1 Background

Cataracts and pterygium are two of the most common eye diseases globally, contributing significantly to visual impairment. Cataracts, which are the leading cause of blindness worldwide, account for approximately 51% of all blindness cases, impacting over 65 million people [1–3]. Meanwhile, pterygium is a fibro-vascular tissue grown on the conjunctiva, has a prevalence that varies from 1% to 23% depending on geographic location, with higher rates observed in tropical and subtropical regions due to prolonged UV exposure [4–6]. In 2020, cataracts were responsible for 17.0 million cases of blindness, comprising 39.6% of global blindness cases, while moderate to severe vision impairment (MSVI) due to cataracts affecting around 83.5 million people, accounting for 28.3% of all MSVI cases [7]. Encouragingly, this prevalence reflects a decline from the reported 78% vision impairment due to cataract in 2015, showcasing the impact of improved surgical techniques and public health interventions [8]. Regional disparities remain significant, with South Asia (53.2% blindness) and Southeast Asia (41.8%) bearing the highest burdens. Lower-income countries continue to experience a greater impact compared to wealthier regions.

Despite these improvements, the total number of people affected by cataracts has risen over the last three decades due to population growth and aging [9]. These statistics highlight the ongoing challenge posed by cataracts as a leading cause of visual impairment globally, necessitating continued efforts in public health initiatives and access to surgical interventions, particularly in low-resource settings. Based on the Global Burden of Disease (GBD) perspective, cataracts continue to be a significant cause of visual impairment worldwide [10]. In 2019, the GBD study estimated approximately 9.7 million cases of visual impairment due to cataracts, representing a 129.2% increase since 1990 [11]. The age-standardized prevalence rate of cataract-related visual impairment rose from 791.4 per 100,000 in 1990 to 1,253.9 per 100,000 in 2019. Similarly, the number of disability-adjusted life years (DALYs) attributed to cataracts increased from 3.49 million in 1990 to 6.68 million in 2019 [12]. This underscores the burden cataracts place on global health systems, particularly in low- and middle-income countries where access to surgery remains limited. Regional disparities are pronounced, with South Asia and Southeast Asia experiencing significantly higher rates of cataract related visual impairment compared to high-income regions [7, 13]. The GBD findings emphasize the critical need for targeted public health strategies to enhance access to cataract surgeries and reduce the global burden of this condition.

Pterygium is another prevalent ocular condition characterized by the growth of fibrovascular tissue on the conjunctiva, which can extend onto the cornea and potentially causing vision disturbances [4, 14]. Environmental factors, particularly increased ultraviolet (UV) exposure, play a significant role in its development, where it is leading to a higher incidence in tropical and subtropical regions [15, 16]. The impact of pterygium on vision is significant, with reports indicating that it can lead to moderate to severe vision impairment in affected individuals. As pterygium is associated with prolonged UV exposure and environmental irritants, preventive measures such as wearing sunglasses and protective eyewear are crucial in high-risk areas to mitigate its incidence and associated visual impairment [15, 17, 18]. Pterygium remains a considerable public health concern globally, particularly in regions with high UV exposure. Continued research and public health initiatives are essential for understanding its epidemiology and developing effective prevention strategies to reduce its burden on vision health worldwide.

The prevalence of pterygium varies widely across regions, with global rates ranging from 0.07% to 53%, and a pooled estimate of approximately 10.2% [15]. The GBD data highlights that pterygium is particularly prevalent in tropical and subtropical regions, often referred to as the "pterygium belt," which lies between 37° north and south of the equator [19, 20]. It is estimated that around 1.5 million people globally experience moderate to severe vision impairment due to pterygium. The burden is particularly pronounced among populations with high UV exposure, outdoor occupations, and limited access to healthcare in rural areas. These findings highlight the importance of targeted public health interventions aimed at reducing UV exposure and improving access to treatment for pterygium in high-prevalence regions.

Early detection and timely intervention are crucial to slow the progression of eye diseases. However, traditional diagnostic methods often rely on specialized imaging equipment and trained professionals, limiting their accessibility in low-resource settings. The widespread availability of smartphones with high-resolution cameras has given the opportunities for developing accessible, portable diagnostic tools. To address these challenges, this study leverages MobileNet architecture, optimized for mobile and embedded systems. Introduced by [21], MobileNet revolutionized mobile vision applications with its lightweight design. A year after, MobileNetV2 has been proposed by Sandler et al. in 2018, and enhances the original design by incorporating inverted residuals and linear bottlenecks [22]. These innovations improve feature extraction efficiency while maintaining computational efficiency. The inverted residual structure, which places lightweight convolution layers between bottlenecks, reduces the computational load and boosts accuracy, while the linear bottleneck prevents loss of critical information. MobileNetV2 retains the depthwise separable convolutions from the original MobileNet, making it particularly suited for mobile devices with limited resources. Compared to MobileNet, MobileNetV2 delivers better performance with enhanced efficiency, making it ideal for real-time applications in resource-constrained environments, such as smartphones and embedded systems.

The outline of this paper will include the introduction which provides an overview of the prevalence of cataract and pterygium cases, emphasizing the need for accessible diagnostic tools. The related work reviews the previous work related to both eye diseases in utilizing deep neural networks. Next, the methodology outlines the proposed framework which focusses on MobileNetV2 in both anterior eye diseases for analyzing smartphone-acquired ocular images, including data preprocessing, network design, and evaluation metrics. The Experimental Results section evaluates the framework's performance in terms of accuracy, computational efficiency, and comparison with existing methods. Finally, the Conclusion and Future Work summarizes key findings, discusses limitations, and proposes recommendations for improving portability, accuracy, and real-world applicability. This work is part of the ASEAN IVO project, which focuses on developing an AI-powered integrated system for ocular disease detection and is currently in the machine intelligence and cloud-based development phase.

2 Related Work

2.1 VGG16 in Pterygium Classification

The modified network discussed in the context of automated pterygium detection is VGG16 with the addition of batch normalization layers, referred to as VGG16-wbn. This architecture was developed to enhance the performance of deep learning models in identifying pterygium from anterior segment photographs. The in-corporation of batch normalization helps the network effectively learn and ex-tract features related to pterygium tissues, improving the model's ability to generalize across diverse datasets.

In their study, [4] demonstrated that VGG16-wbn achieved high accuracy in detecting pterygium, with accuracy of 99.22%, sensitivity of 98.45%, and perfect score for the specificity and area under the curve (AUC) performance. The model's architecture allows for improved convergence during training and reduces overfitting, which is critical when working with limited medical imaging datasets. By utilizing a well-established CNN framework like VGG16 and enhancing it with batch normalization, the study highlights the potential for this modified network to serve as a reliable tool for automated pterygium detection, paving the way for more accessible screening methods in clinical practice. Overall, the combination of VGG16 and batch normalization represents a significant advancement in deep learning applications for ophthalmology, particularly in enhancing diagnostic capabilities for conditions such as pterygium.

2.2 ResNet50 in Cataract Patch Classification

The study by [23] utilizes ResNet50 as the core network for cataract detection through pupil patch classification in anterior segment photographed images. This approach shows the ResNet50 architecture's ability to learn complex features from the images, while enhancing the accuracy of cataract identification. The authors implemented a rule-based system alongside ResNet50 to analyze segmented pupil regions, focusing on characteristics indicative of cataracts, such as cloudiness and irregular reflections.

The performance of the proposed system was evaluated using various metrics, achieving an accuracy of 98%, a sensitivity of 97.8%, a specificity of 98.1%, and an AUC of 99.99%. These results demonstrate the model's effectiveness in accurately detecting cataracts while minimizing false positives and negatives. By employing ResNet50, the study aims to improve diagnostic capabilities while ad-dressing challenges related to manual preprocessing and scalability inherent in traditional methods. The use of this deep learning model signifies a step forward in automating cataract detection, potentially leading to more accessible screening solutions in clinical practice.

3 Methodology

3.1 Dataset Preparation

To ensure the reliability in evaluation, the datasets used for cataract patch and pterygium classifications were obtained from previously published works. Both datasets utilized anterior segment photographed images (ASPI) of the front part of the eyes captured using smartphone camera. The pterygium dataset includes both normal and pterygium ASPIs. Meanwhile, the cataract dataset consists of pupil patches extracted from segmented ASPIs of both normal and cataract-affected pupils. Examples of pterygium and cataract pupil images used for training are shown in Fig. 1 (a) and (b). In addition, data augmentation techniques were applied which are essential to enhance the performance and generalization ability of CNN-based models [24]. These techniques include rotation, reflection and shear.

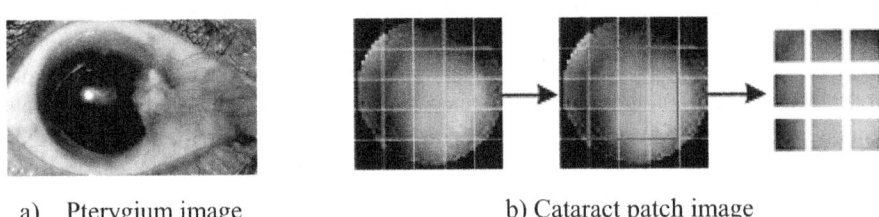

a) Pterygium image   b) Cataract patch image

Fig. 1. Examples of pterygium and cataract pupil images.

3.2 Transfer Learning Models Used

Convolutional Neural Networks (CNNs) often require large datasets to achieve high performance. However, gathering large-scale data can be challenging. In such scenarios, transfer learning becomes a practical solution. This technique involves adapting a network pre-trained on extensive datasets to new and smaller datasets effectively leveraging previously acquired features. By utilizing the weights from these pre-trained models, transfer learning reduces the time and computational resources necessary for developing and training models [25]. In this study, we evaluated four transfer learning networks for both cataract patch and pterygium classification which are ResNet50, VGG16 and MobileNetv2. Each model was assessed to identify the most efficient network suitable for smartphone-based detection, with training conducted on a GPU-equipped laptop with processor 13th Gen Intel® Core™ i9-13900HX and graphic NVIDIA® Ge-Force RTX™ 4060, 8 GB GDDR6.

Previous Models. Based on previous studies [4, 23], VGG16 and ResNet50 have been identified as the best-performing models for cataract patch and pterygium classification, respectively. ResNet50, introduced by [26] is widely utilized in computer vision tasks, including image classification. Its architecture comprises 50 layers, including 48 convolutional layers, one max-pooling layer, and one average pooling layer. As a model that bridges the gap between shallow and deep networks, Res-Net50 maintains a balance between complexity and computational efficiency, making it particularly effective for processing small-scale image datasets [27]. By maintaining a moderate parameter count, it enhances network performance while reducing the risk of overfitting.

VGG16 [28] is another widely adopted model for image classification, comprising 16 layers which are 13 convolutional layers, five max-pooling layers, and three fully connected (FC) layers with 16 tunable parameters. It processes input tensors of 224 × 224 pixels with three RGB channels. A key architectural improvement in VGG16 is the replacement of larger convolutional filters (11 × 11, 7 × 7, 5 × 5) with multiple 3 × 3 convolutional kernels [29]. This design choice not only increases network depth, enhancing feature extraction and overall performance but also reduces the number of trainable parameters, improving computational efficiency.

MobileNetV2 Architecture. MobileNetV2 is a lightweight and efficient CNN architecture that was proposed by [22] and designed specifically for mobile and resource-constrained environments. This network advances the state-of-the-art in mobile-optimized computer vision models by substantially reducing computational requirements and memory usage while maintaining the same level of accuracy. The key contribution of the network is the introduction of the inverted residual with a linear bottleneck module. This module starts with a low-dimensional compressed representation that expands to a higher dimension using a lightweight depthwise convolution and then projects it back to a low-dimensional representation via a linear convolution as shown in Table 1.

Table 1. MobileNetV2 architecture.

Input	Operator	t	c	n	s
$224^2 \times 3$	conv2d	-	32	1	2
$112^2 \times 32$	bottleneck	1	16	1	1
$112^2 \times 16$	bottleneck	6	24	2	2
$56^2 \times 24$	bottleneck	6	32	3	2
$28^2 \times 32$	bottleneck	6	64	4	2
$14^2 \times 64$	bottleneck	6	96	3	1
$14^2 \times 96$	bottleneck	6	160	3	2
$7^2 \times 160$	bottleneck	6	320	1	1
$7^2 \times 320$	conv2d 1x1	-	1280	1	1
$7^2 \times 1280$	avgpool 7x7	-	-	1	-
$1 \times 1 \times 1280$	conv2d 1x1	-	k	-	-

This module which is available in the TensorFlow-Slim library, can be implemented efficiently in modern frameworks. It enables models to surpass state-of-the-art performance across various benchmarks and is particularly well-suited for mobile designs. By avoiding the full materialization of large intermediate tensors, it significantly reduces memory usage during inference, minimizing main memory access and optimizing performance on embedded hardware with limited fast cache memory.

3.3 Hyperparameter Configuration

Both cataract patch and pterygium classification models were trained using different hyperparameter settings customized for each disease as shown in Table 2,

Table 2. Hyperparameter training configurations for cataract patch and pterygium classification.

	Cataract patch classification	Pterygium classification
Learning rate	0.00001	0.0001
Batch sizes	5 and 10	10, 32 and 64
Optimizers	Adam and SGDM	
Epochs	20	

The hyperparameter settings were selected based on the hyperparameter combination from previous best-performing models for each disease. For pterygium classification, the selected combination includes the SGDM optimizer, epoch of 20, a learning rate of 0.0001, and batch sizes of 10, 32, and 64. For cataract patch classification, the best-performing model setup consists of the Adam optimizer, epoch of 20, a learning rate of 0.00001, and batch sizes of 5 and 10. In this experiment, training was conducted to identify the most suitable model for smartphone-based ASPI eye detection. The hyperparameters were adjusted based on validation performance to optimize accuracy and minimize overfitting.

3.4 Evaluation Metrics

The models were evaluated using key performance metrics, including accuracy, sensitivity, and the area under the receiver operating characteristic (ROC) curve (AUC).

Accuracy measures the overall correctness of the model's classifications, encompassing both positive and negative predictions. It is calculated as,

$$Accuracy = \frac{TP + TN}{TP + TN + FP + FN} \quad (1)$$

Sensitivity, also referred to as the true positive rate (TPR), evaluates the model's ability to correctly identify images with the disease. It is defined as,

$$Sensitivity = \frac{TP}{TP + FN} \quad (2)$$

The area under the ROC curve (AUC) quantifies the probability that the model will rank a randomly selected positive instance higher than a randomly selected negative instance. AUC provides a measure of the model's ability to distinguish between classes, with higher values indicating better classification performance.

4 Results and Discussion

This section presents a comparative analysis of the performance of three networks: ResNet50, VGG16 and MobileNetV2 for cataract patch and pterygium classification with the 5-fold cross validation technique. The training configuration for the networks was selected based on the previous hyperparameter setting from the best-performing model for both cataract patch and pterygium classification as shown in Table 1. Key metrics including accuracy, sensitivity, AUC and elapsed time are evaluated to assess the effectiveness and efficiency of each model. The discussion will highlight the comparison between performance and computational efficiency to find the most suitable model for specific use cases, including real-time and resource-constrained environments. The results are interpreted in the context of practical applications, emphasizing the implications of the observed differences in performance and training time.

4.1 Pterygium Classification Performance

Table 3 shows the performance of the three networks that were trained with learning rate 0.0001, epoch 20, three different batch sizes (10, 32, 64) and using two optimizers (SGDM and Adam).

Table 3. Performance for pterygium classification.

Network	Batch Size	Optimizer	Accuracy	Sensitivity	AUC	Elapsed time
ResNet50	10	Adam	96.71%	96.05%	97.79%	8.72 min
	32		97.70%	96.71%	99.16%	2.58 min
	64		97.04%	96.05%	98.84%	4.80 min
	10	SGDM	95.72%	93.42%	98.73%	4.98 min
	32		93.75%	90.13%	98.24%	2.40 min
	64		91.12%	83.55%	97.50%	4.08 min
VGG16	10	Adam	97.70%	97.37%	99.18%	5.50 min
	32		97.04%	95.39%	99.23%	3.23 min
	64		97.37%	97.37%	99.23%	3.40 min
	10	SGDM	97.04%	96.05%	99.19%	5.37 min
	32		93.09%	90.79%	98.87%	2.42 min
	64		90.46%	84.87%	98.29%	2.73 min
MobileNetV2	10	Adam	97.37%	96.05%	99.41%	3.53 min
	32		**97.37%**	**96.71%**	**99.18%**	**2.13 min**
	64		96.71%	94.74%	99.16%	2.30 min
	10	SGDM	97.70%	96.05%	99.34%	3.93 min
	32		94.08%	93.42%	98.57%	2.17 min
	64		90.46%	87.50%	97.39%	2.23 min

Overall Performance Analysis. For ResNet50 with Adam optimizer, the best result is achieved using a batch size of 32, achieving 97.70% accuracy, 96.71% sensitivity, and 99.16% AUC. Performance slightly declines with batch sizes of 10 and 64, but the results remain strong and consistent overall. Using SGDM optimizer, it achieves its best performance with a batch size of 10, delivering 95.72% accuracy, 93.42% sensitivity, and 98.73% AUC. However, performance declines slightly with a batch size of 32, resulting in 93.75% accuracy, 90.13% sensitivity, and 98.24% AUC. The lowest performance is observed with a batch size of 64, where accuracy drops to 91.12%, sensitivity to 83.55%, and AUC to 97.50%.

VGG16 with Adam optimizer demonstrates consistently strong performance across all batch sizes. The best results are achieved with a batch size of 10, where both accuracy and sensitivity reach 97.70% and 97.37% respectively while AUC remains high at 99.18%. Using SGDM, the network achieves its best performance with a batch size of 10, obtaining accuracy, sensitivity, and AUC of 97.04%, 96.05% and 99.19% respectively. Performance declines as the batch size increases, with significant drops for a batch size of 64, where sensitivity decreases to 84.87%, and accuracy falls to 90.46%.

The third network, MobileNetV2 with Adam optimizer, also performs well across all batch sizes. The best results are observed with a batch size of 10, achieving the highest AUC of 99.41% along with 97.37% accuracy and 96.05% sensitivity. The model also demonstrates consistency, with only slight variations across different batch sizes. Using the SGDM optimizer, it achieves its best performance with a batch size of 10, recording 97.70% accuracy, 96.05% sensitivity, and the highest AUC among all models using SGDM at 99.34%. However, performance decreases significantly with larger batch sizes (32 and 64), where both accuracy and sensitivity drop.

Elapsed Time Analysis. Across the networks, ResNet50 shows the longest training times, particularly with Adam and smaller batch sizes, making it less suitable for time-critical applications. To optimize time efficiency, SGDM with a batch size of 32 is the most efficient configuration, with a training time of 2.4 min. VGG16 exhibits moderate training times compared to the other networks. The shortest training time is achieved with SGDM and a batch size of 64, at 2.42 min, making this the preferred configuration for faster training while using this network. MobileNetV2 is consistently the fastest network, with the shortest training time achieved using Adam with a batch size of 32, at just 2.13 min. Besides, it also achieves high accuracy, sensitivity and AUC with 97.37%, 96.71% and 99.18% respectively making it the best performing model for pterygium classification.

MobileNetV2 demonstrated consistently competitive and stable performance across different optimizers, with only minor declines as the batch size increased, particularly with regard to AUC and computational efficiency.

4.2 Cataract Patch Classification Performance

For the cataract patch classification, Table 4 shows the three networks were trained using two batch sizes (5 and 10), over 20 epochs, with a learning rate of 0.00001, and two optimizers: Adam and SGDM.

Table 4. Performance for cataract patch classification.

Network	Batch Size	Optimizer	Accuracy	Sensitivity	AUC	Elapsed time
ResNet50	5	Adam	98.11%	98.44%	99.65%	65 min
	10		98.22%	98.89%	99.86%	22 min
	5	SGDM	96.56%	96.44%	98.79%	83 min
	10		96.78%	95.33%	99.05%	30 min
VGG16	5	Adam	93.78%	93.56%	96.26%	27 min
	10		91.67%	85.11%	95.90%	15 min
	5	SGDM	89.11%	98.22%	98.11%	55 min
	10		91.33%	98.00%	98.11%	35 min
MobileNetV2	5	Adam	93.56%	97.11%	98.96%	25 min
	10		**95.44%**	**95.78%**	**99.19%**	**7 min**
	5	SGDM	92.44%	92.00%	97.62%	50 min
	10		92.11%	91.56%	97.74%	20 min

Overall Performance Analysis. Looking at ResNet50 performance with the Adam optimizer, it achieves its best performance with a batch size of 10, recording 98.22% accuracy, 98.89% sensitivity, and an exceptional 99.86% AUC, making it the top-performing model overall. A smaller batch size of 5 also performs well, achieving 98.11% accuracy, 98.44% sensitivity and 99.65% AUC, though slightly lower than the batch size of 10. Using SGDM optimizer, ResNet50 performs best with a batch size of 10, achieving 96.78% accuracy and 99.05% AUC, while a batch size of 5 yields slightly lower results with 96.56% accuracy and 98.79% AUC.

For VGG16 with Adam optimizer, its performance is relatively lower compared to ResNet50 and MobileNetV2. A batch size of 5 performs better than 10, achieving 93.78% accuracy, 93.56% sensitivity, and 96.26% AUC. In contrast, a batch size of 10 results in a decline across all metrics, with 91.67% accuracy and 95.90% AUC. With SGDM optimizer, performance remains low, with a batch size of 5 achieving 89.11% accuracy, although the sensitivity and AUC performance are comparable with other models with 98.22% and 98.11% respectively. A batch size of 10 improves accuracy slightly to 91.33%, though sensitivity and AUC remain similar at 98.00% and 98.11% respectively.

For MobileNetV2 with Adam optimizer, the network delivers strong performance particularly with a batch size of 10. It achieves 95.44% accuracy, 95.78% sensitivity, and 99.19% AUC, making it competitive with ResNet50. A batch size of 5 results in slightly lower accuracy (93.56%) but higher sensitivity (97.11%) and a solid AUC of 98.96%. With SGDM optimizer, MobileNetV2's performance is notably lower compared to Adam. A batch size of 5 achieves 92.44% accuracy, 92.00% sensitivity, and 97.62%

AUC, while a batch size of 10 delivers slightly reduced metrics, with 92.11% accuracy, 91.56% sensitivity, and 97.74% AUC.

Among the networks, ResNet50 (Adam, Batch Size 10) achieves the highest accuracy (98.22%), sensitivity (98.89%), and AUC (99.86%) making it superior for patch classification tasks. MobileNetV2 (Adam, Batch Size 10) also delivers competitive performance, achieving a strong AUC of 99.19%, though it falls slightly behind ResNet50 in accuracy and sensitivity. VGG16 shows the weakest performance overall, with lower accuracy and AUC across all settings, though it maintains reasonable sensitivity with smaller batch sizes and the Adam optimizer.

Elapsed Time Analysis. The longest training time was observed for ResNet50 (SGDM, Batch Size 5) at 83 min, while the shortest training time was achieved by MobileNetV2 (Adam, Batch Size 10) at just 7 min. Across all networks, the Adam optimizer consistently reduced training times compared to SGDM. Similarly, increasing the batch size to 10 significantly shortened training times, with all networks benefiting from this adjustment.

For ResNet50, the best configuration for reducing training time is Adam with batch size 10, which cuts the time to 22 min. For VGG16, the optimal configuration is also Adam with batch size 10, taking only 15 min. However, for applications requiring the fastest training times, MobileNetV2 (Adam, Batch Size 10) is the clear choice, completing training in just 7 min. This makes MobileNetV2 approximately three times faster than ResNet50 under the same training configuration thus shows that it is highly suitable to be used for time-sensitive and resource-constrained applications.

Overall, MobileNetV2 is the most time-efficient network for both cataract patch and pterygium classification. It shows high accuracy, sensitivity and AUC across both classification tasks. Its lightweight architecture and lower computational requirements make it suitable and feasible for smartphone-based real-time applications and cloud or edge processing.

5 Conclusion

This paper conducted a comparative analysis of ResNet50, VGG16, and MobileNetV2 for cataract patch and pterygium classification using a 5-fold cross-validation technique. Key metrics such as accuracy, sensitivity, AUC, and elapsed training time were evaluated with training configurations based on previously optimized hyperparameters. MobileNetV2 was identified as the most optimal network as it is capable of achieving competitive performance while offering significantly faster training times and lower computational requirements. Although ResNet50 achieved slightly higher accuracy and AUC in specific configurations, MobileNetV2 consistently maintained high performance across various settings with minimal decline. However, this study has certain limitations. The dataset used may not fully capture the variability encountered in real-world clinical environments which could affect the model's generalizability. Additionally, real-time performance remains unexplored, requiring further evaluation to ensure its reliability in practical applications. In conclusion, MobileNetV2 was selected as the optimal network for cataract patch and pterygium classification, providing an efficient and practical solution for resource-constrained and time-sensitive scenarios without compromising accuracy. Future work aims to focus on extending MobileNetV2's application to the classification of other non-communicable eye diseases within a smartphone-based system. Moreover, the model will also be tested in real-time environments to further assess its generalizability and practical deployment potential.

Acknowledgments. This work is the output of the ASEAN IVO (http://www.nict.go.jp/en/asean_ivo/index.html) project, Integrated Decision Support System for Non-Communicable Ocular Diseases using Machine Intelligence and financially supported by NICT (http://www.nict.go.jp/en/index.html).

Disclosure of Interests. The authors have no competing interests to declare that are relevant to the content of this article.

References

1. Song, P., Wang, H., Theodoratou, E., Chan, K.Y., Rudan, I.: The national and subnational prevalence of cataract and cataract blindness in China: a systematic review and meta-analysis. J. Glob. Health **8**, 1–18 (2018)
2. Pascolini, D., Mariotti, S.P.: Global estimates of visual impairment: 2010. Br. J. Ophthalmol. **96**, 614–618 (2012)
3. Canatan, A.N.: Restoring sight: Exploring cataracts as the leading treata-ble cause of blindness: a narrative review. Turkish Med. Stud. J. **11**, 1–8 (2024)
4. Zamani, N.S.M., Zaki, W.M.D.W., Huddin, A.B., Hussain, A., Mutalib, H.A., Ali, A.: Automated pterygium detection using deep neural network. IEEE Access. **8**, 191659–191672 (2020)
5. Zaki, W.M.D.W., Daud, M.M., Abdani, S.R., Hussain, A., Mutalib, H.A.: Automated pterygium detection method of anterior segment photographed images. Comput. Methods Prog. Biomed. **154**, 71–78 (2018)
6. Panchapakesan, J., Hourihan, F., Mitchell, P.: Prevalence of pterygium and pinguecula: the blue mountains eye study. Aust. N. Z. J. Ophthalmol. **26**, 52–55 (1998)
7. Vision Loss Expert Group of the Global Burden of Disease Study: Global estimates on the number of people blind or visually impaired by cataract: a meta-analysis from 2000 to 2020. Eye. **38**, 2156–2172 (2024)
8. Flaxman, S.R., et al.: Global causes of blindness and distance vision impairment 1990–2020: a systematic review and meta-analysis. Lancet Glob. Health **5**, e1221–e1234 (2017)
9. Yin, J., Jiang, B., Zhao, T., Guo, X., Tan, Y., Wang, Y.: Trends in the global burden of vision loss among the older adults from 1990 to 2019. Front. Public Health **12**, 1–15 (2024)
10. Collaborators, G.B.D., Rawal, L.: Causes of blindness and vision impair-ment in 2020 and trends over 30 years, and prevalence of avoidable blindness in relation to VISION 2020: the right to sight: an analysis for the global burden of disease study. Lancet Glob. Health **9**, e144–e160 (2021)
11. Han, X., et al.: Time trends and heterogeneity in the disease burden of visual impairment due to cataract, 1990–2019: a global analysis. Front. Public Health **11**, 1–9 (2023)
12. Jiang, B., Wu, T., Liu, W., Liu, G., Lu, P.: Changing trends in the global burden of cataract over the past 30 years: retrospective data analysis of the global burden of disease study 2019. JMIR Public Health Surveill. **9** (2023)

13. Shu, Y., et al.: Changing trends in the disease burden of cataract and forecasted trends in China and globally from 1990 to 2030. Clin Epidemiol. 525–534 (2023)
14. Ahmad, S.N.A., Wan Zaki, W.M.D., M Zamani, N.S.: A pterygium disease screening system for anterior segment photographed images. J. Kejuruteraan. **31**, 99–105 (2019)
15. Liu, L., Wu, J., Geng, J., Yuan, Z., Huang, D.: Geographical prevalence and risk factors for pterygium: a systematic review and meta-analysis. BMJ Open **3**, 3787 (2013)
16. Zamani, N.S.M., Zaki, W.M.D.W., Huddin, A.B., Mutalib, H.A., Hussain, A.: Pterygium classification using deep patch region-based anterior segment photographed images. J. Kejuruteraan. **35**, 823–830 (2023)
17. Mackenzie, F.D., Hirst, L.W., Battistutta, D., Green, A.: Risk analysis in the development of pterygia. Ophthalmology **99**, 1056–1061 (1992)
18. Behar-Cohen, F., et al.: Ultraviolet damage to the eye revisited: eye-sun protection factor (E-SPF®), a new ultraviolet protection label for eyewear. Clin. Ophthalmol. **8**, 87–104 (2014)
19. Cameron, M.E.: Pterygium throughout the world. Thomas, Springfield (1965)
20. Tan, C.S.H., et al.: Epidemiology of pterygium on a tropical island in the Riau Archipelago. Eye. 20, 908–912 (2006)
21. Howard, A.G., et al.: MobileNets: Efficient convolutional neural networks for mobile vision applications. arXiv preprint arXiv:1704.04861. 1–9 (2017)
22. Sandler, M., Howard, A., Zhu, M., et al.: MobileNetV2: Inverted Residuals and Linear Bottlenecks. arXiv 4510–4520 (2018)
23. Ramlan, L.A., Zaki, W.M.D.W., Mutalib, H.A., et al.: Cataract detection using pupil patch classification and ruled-based system in anterior segment photographed images. In: 2023 IEEE 13th Symposium on Computer Applications & Industrial Electronics (ISCAIE). pp 124–129 (2023)
24. Tatar, A., Haghighi, M., Zeinijahromi, A.: Experiments on image data augmentation techniques for geological rock type classification with convolutional neural networks. J. Rock Mech. Geotech. Eng. **17**, 106–125 (2024)
25. Salehi, A.W., Khan, S., Gupta, G., et al.: A study of CNN and transfer learning in medical imaging: advantages, challenges. Future Scope. Sustain. **15**, 5930 (2023)
26. He, K., Zhang, X., Ren, S., Sun, J.: Deep residual learning for image recognition. In: 2016 IEEE Conference on Computer Vision and Pattern Recognition (CVPR). IEEE, pp 770–778 (2016)
27. Wan, J., Li, B., Wang, K., et al.: An improved ResNet50 for environment image classification. Procedia Comput. Sci. **242**, 1000–1007 (2024)
28. Simonyan, K., Zisserman, A.: Very deep convolutional networks for large-scale image recognition. In: 3rd Int Conf Learn Represent ICLR 2015 - Conf Track Proc 1–14 (2015)
29. Yang, H., Ni, J., Gao, J., et al.: A novel method for peanut variety identification and classification by improved VGG16. Sci. Rep. **11**, 1–17 (2021)

Adaptive Resilience Framework Using Dynamic Feature Fusion for Robust Fingerprint Biometrics Against Adversarial Perturbations

Arslan Manzoor, Alessandro Ortis(✉), and Sebastiano Battiato

Department of Mathematics and Computer Science, University of Catania, Catania, Italy
arslan.manzoor@phd.unict.it,
{alessandro.ortis,sebastiano.battiato}@unict.it

Abstract. This paper presents the Adaptive Resilience Fingerprint Defense (ARFD), a novel framework to enhance fingerprint biometric systems' robustness against adversarial attacks like FGSM and PGD. ARFD integrates Dynamic Feature Fusion (DFF) for real-time feature weight recalibration and Multi-Scale Feature Ensemble (MFE) for multi-resolution analysis. This two-pronged strategy effectively mitigates adversarial perturbations, achieving superior accuracy and reducing false acceptance and rejection rates. Experimental results demonstrate ARFD's significant advancements in biometric security, providing an adaptive and resilient defense mechanism.

Keywords: Fingerprint biometrics · Adversarial attacks · Robustness · Security

1 Introduction

Fingerprint biometrics have been widely adopted for personal identification due to their unique and stable nature [1]. They are extensively used in mobile authentication, banking, and governmental systems [3]. Recent advancements in machine learning, particularly convolutional neural networks (CNNs), have enhanced the performance of fingerprint recognition systems by automating feature extraction and improving accuracy under various conditions [9]. However, these systems remain vulnerable to adversarial attacks, such as the Fast Gradient Sign Method (FGSM) and Projected Gradient Descent (PGD), which subtly manipulate fingerprint images to cause misclassifications [10]. These attacks exploit the sensitivity of deep learning models to small perturbations, exposing critical security flaws in biometric systems [12]. Furthermore, synthetic fingerprints generated by techniques like Generative Adversarial Networks (GANs) pose additional challenges by bypassing traditional liveness detection methods

[5]. Traditional fingerprint recognition systems, relying on static feature extraction processes, are ill-equipped to handle adversarial perturbations and large-scale structural modifications [2]. Adversarial perturbations can manipulate feature extraction, resulting in false acceptances or rejections [4]. This necessitates the development of adaptive systems capable of real-time detection and response to adversarial threats. Although techniques such as adversarial training and feature denoising have shown promise, they are often limited by their static nature and lack adaptability to evolving attacks [4]. To address these challenges, dynamic feature fusion and multi-resolution analysis have been proposed to enhance system robustness and improve defense mechanisms against adversarial and synthetic biometric attacks [2].

This work aims to address the limitations of existing fingerprint recognition systems by introducing a dynamic, multi-scale defense framework. The proposed system recalibrates feature importance in real-time and fuses information across multiple resolutions to counter both subtle and large-scale adversarial perturbations effectively. In this paper, The research present the Adaptive Resilience Fingerprint Defense (ARFD) framework, which addresses the aforementioned challenges. the key contributions include:

- The research propose a **Dynamic Feature Fusion (DFF)** mechanism that adjusts fingerprint feature weights dynamically based on adversarial threat detection.
- The research introduce a **Multi-Scale Feature Ensemble (MFE)** approach that processes fingerprint features at various resolutions, enhancing the system's ability to detect both subtle and large adversarial perturbations.
- The research provide experimental evidence that ARFD significantly improves accuracy, reduces false acceptance rates (FAR), and lowers false rejection rates (FRR) when compared to existing models, making it more resilient against adversarial attacks such as FGSM, PGD and C&W.

2 Background

Biometric systems, particularly fingerprint recognition, face increasing challenges from adversarial attacks and evolving security threats. Fei et al. [13] highlighted the vulnerability of fingerprint liveness detection to subtle perturbations, while Galbally et al. [16] examined susceptibility to fake fingerprint attacks. Grosz et al. [17] introduced a sensor-agnostic approach to fingerprint presentation attack detection, and Sperling et al. [18] proposed homomorphic encryption for secure biometric template fusion. Feature fusion techniques have also gained attention for enhancing resilience. Jha et al. [14] proposed face and speech data fusion for multimodal systems, and Haghighat et al. [15] developed a discriminant correlation analysis framework for real-time fusion. Attrapadung et al. [19] extended dynamic feature fusion to continuous authentication systems, addressing evolving attack challenges [20]. Recent security strategies include smudge attack analysis by Cha et al. [20], trait randomization for liveness detection by Okereafor et al. [21], and future security methodologies by Malenkovich [22]. These studies highlight the sophistication of attacks and advancements in defense mechanisms. This work builds on these foundations, proposing a comprehensive framework integrating adaptive feature fusion and multi-scale analysis to counter adversarial perturbations effectively.

3 Proposed Model

In this section, The research present the detailed framework of the proposed Adaptive Resilience Fingerprint Defense (ARFD) model (see Fig. 1). The ARFD model is designed to dynamically defend fingerprint biometric systems against adversarial attacks by integrating *Dynamic Feature Fusion (DFF)* and *Multi-Scale Feature Ensemble (MFE)* approaches. The research begin by describing the dataset used for training and testing, followed by the detailed techniques and mathematical formulations.

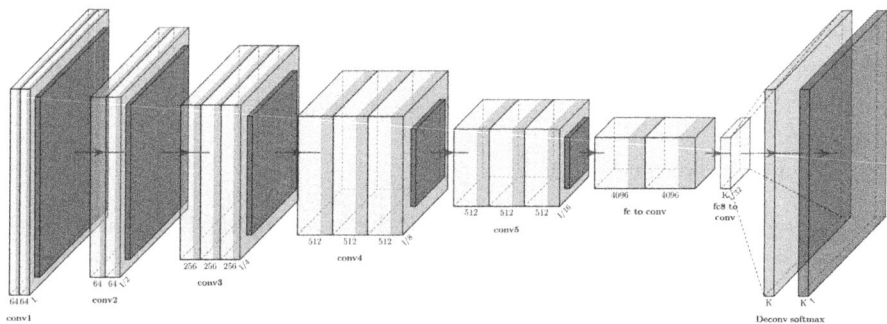

Fig. 1. Overview of the Adaptive Resilience Fingerprint Defense (ARFD) architecture. The framework integrates two core components: Dynamic Feature Fusion (DFF) and Multi-Scale Feature Ensemble (MFE). DFF dynamically adjusts feature weights based on adversarial perturbation analysis, while MFE enhances robustness by processing features at multiple resolutions. The system detects adversarial fingerprints in real-time and recalibrates feature significance to mitigate attacks such as FGSM, PGD, and C&W.

3.1 Dataset Description

The dataset used in this study is the **Sokoto Coventry Fingerprint Dataset (SOCOFing)** [23], a biometric fingerprint database designed specifically for academic research purposes. SOCOFing consists of 6,000 fingerprint images collected from 600 African subjects, providing a diverse dataset with unique attributes. Each subject contributed ten fingerprints, one for each finger, resulting in a rich dataset that includes multiple features essential for biometric recognition systems.

Table 1. Summary of the SOCOFing Dataset.

Feature	Description
No. of Subjects	600
Total Images	6,000
Gender Labels	Male, Female
Hand Labels	Left, Right
Finger Name Labels	Thumb, Index, Middle, Ring, Little
Alteration Types	Obliteration, Central Rotation, Z-Cut
Levels of Alteration	3 (Mild, Moderate, Severe)

The SOCOFing dataset, with its inclusion of both natural and synthetically altered fingerprints, provides an ideal testing ground for adversarial resilience in biometric systems. It challenges models to adapt to realistic variations in fingerprint quality and orientation, making it highly suitable for evaluating the proposed Adaptive Resilience Fingerprint Defense (ARFD) framework. For more details on the dataset, its formal description, and usage policy, please refer to the paper [12].

3.2 Techniques Used

The proposed ARFD model integrates two key techniques: Dynamic Feature Fusion (DFF) and Multi-Scale Feature Ensemble (MFE). These techniques are designed to improve the robustness and adaptability of fingerprint recognition systems when exposed to adversarial attacks.

Algorithm 1. Adaptive Resilience Fingerprint Defense (ARFD).

Require: F_{orig}: Original Fingerprint Image, ϵ: Perturbation Threshold, α: Learning Rate, β: Recalibration Factor
Ensure: $\hat{y}$: Final Decision
  Extract features: $F = \{f_1, f_2, \ldots, f_n\}$ from F_{orig}
  Compute perturbation: $\delta F = F_{\text{adv}} - F_{\text{orig}}$
  if $\delta F > \epsilon$ **then**
    Recalibrate weights: $w_i^{(t+1)} = w_i^{(t)} - \beta \delta F$
  else
    Perform dynamic feature fusion: $w_i^{(t+1)} = w_i^{(t)} + \alpha \nabla L(f_i, y)$
  end if
  Perform multi-scale feature ensemble: $\hat{y} = \sum_{r=1}^{R} \gamma_r \left(\sum_{i=1}^{n} w_i^r f_i^r \right)$
  return $\hat{y}$

Dynamic Feature Fusion (DFF). The DFF technique enables the model to dynamically adjust the importance of fingerprint features based on real-time adversarial threat detection. Traditional systems use static feature extraction, which fails to recalibrate under attack conditions. In contrast, DFF continuously monitors the system's performance and recalculates the weights of different fingerprint features, thereby minimizing the impact of adversarial perturbations.

Algorithm 2. Dynamic Feature Fusion (DFF).

Require: F:Extracted Fingerprint Features, ϵ: Perturbation Threshold, α: Learning Rate, β: Recalibration Factor
Ensure: $w_i^{(t+1)}$: Updated Weights
  Calculate loss: $L(f_i, y)$
  Compute adversarial perturbation: δF
  if $\delta F > \epsilon$ then
    Recalibrate weights: $w_i^{(t+1)} = w_i^{(t)} - \beta \delta F$
  else
    Update weights normally: $w_i^{(t+1)} = w_i^{(t)} + \alpha \nabla L(f_i, y)$
  end if return $w_i^{(t+1)}$

The parametric table of the DFF technique is provided in Table 2.

Table 2. Parameters for Dynamic Feature Fusion (DFF).

Parameter	Description	Value
α	Learning rate for feature weight adjustment	0.01
ϵ	Perturbation detection threshold	0.001
β	Recalibration factor for adversarial features	0.05
n	No. of fingerprint features	128
T	Time interval for recalibration	100 ms

The mathematical model for Dynamic Feature Fusion (DFF) is defined as follows. Let

$$F = \{\text{ridge frequency}, \text{ridge orientation}, \text{minutiae points}, \ldots, \text{ridge endings}\} \quad (1)$$

represent the set of fingerprint features, where each f_i corresponds to a specific feature extracted from the fingerprint image. The weights of these features are updated dynamically based on the loss function $L(f_i, y)$, where y is the true label.

$$w_i^{(t+1)} = w_i^{(t)} + \alpha \cdot \nabla L(f_i, y) \quad (2)$$

Here, $w_i^{(t)}$ is the weight of feature f_i at time t, and α is the learning rate. The loss function is minimized by adjusting the feature weights, and adversarial perturbations are detected by monitoring the difference between the original and adversarial feature sets:

$$\delta F = F_{\text{adv}} - F_{\text{orig}} \qquad (3)$$

If $\delta F > \epsilon$, where ϵ is the predefined threshold, the feature weights are recalibrated as:

$$w_i^{(t+1)} = w_i^{(t)} - \beta \cdot \delta F \qquad (4)$$

Multi-Scale Feature Ensemble (MFE). The MFE technique processes fingerprint features across multiple resolutions, ensuring that both fine-grained and large-scale adversarial perturbations are detected. The fingerprint image is first decomposed into different resolution levels, and features are extracted at each level.

Algorithm 3. Multi-Scale Feature Ensemble (MFE).

Require: F: Extracted Fingerprint Features, R: Number of Resolutions, γ_r: Weight for Resolution r
Ensure: $\hat{y}$: Final Decision
    for each resolution $r \in \{1, 2, \ldots, R\}$ **do**
        Extract features at resolution r: $F_r = \{f_1^r, f_2^r, \ldots, f_n^r\}$
    end for
    Assign weights to each resolution: $\{\gamma_1, \gamma_2, \ldots, \gamma_R\}$
    Fuse features across resolutions: $\hat{F} = \sum_{r=1}^{R} \gamma_r \sum_{i=1}^{n} w_i^r f_i^r$
    Perform final decision based on fused features: $\hat{y} = \text{Classifier}(\hat{F})$
    return $\hat{y}$

Let $F_r = \{f_1^r, f_2^r, \ldots, f_n^r\}$ represent the set of fingerprint features extracted at resolution r. The final decision is based on the weighted sum of features across all resolutions:

$$\hat{y} = \sum_{r=1}^{R} \gamma_r \left(\sum_{i=1}^{n} w_i^r f_i^r \right) \qquad (5)$$

where R is the No. of resolutions, γ_r is the weight assigned to resolution r, and w_i^r is the weight for feature f_i^r at resolution r. This multi-resolution approach ensures that both local (minutiae points, ridge patterns) and global (entire fingerprint structure) adversarial attacks are captured effectively. The parametric table for MFE is shown in Table 3.

Table 3. Parameters for Multi-Scale Feature Ensemble (MFE).

Parameter	Description	Value
R	No. of resolutions	3
γ_r	Weight for resolution r	[0.5, 0.3, 0.2]
n	No. of features per resolution	128

3.3 Mathematical Model for ARFD

ARFD model integrates both DFF and MFE to provide a comprehensive, adversarially robust fingerprint recognition system. The system dynamically adapts to adversarial perturbations and combines features across multiple resolutions to strengthen the biometric defense.

Given an input fingerprint image, the feature extraction process generates a set of features at different resolutions. Let $F = \{f_1, f_2, \ldots, f_n\}$ represent the set of fingerprint features extracted at each resolution r, where f_i^r denotes the ith feature at resolution r. These features are assigned dynamic weights $w_i^{(t)}$, which are updated over time based on adversarial detection. The core dynamic feature weighting is formulated as:

$$w_i^{(t+1)} = w_i^{(t)} + \alpha \frac{\partial L(f_i^r, y)}{\partial f_i^r} - \beta \delta F \tag{6}$$

where:

- $w_i^{(t+1)}$ is the weight of feature f_i at time $t+1$.
- α is the learning rate.
- $\frac{\partial L(f_i^r, y)}{\partial f_i^r}$ is the gradient of the loss function L, computed based on the difference between predicted output $\hat{y}$ and actual output y.
- β is the recalibration factor, adjusting the weight based on adversarial detection.
- δF represents the detected adversarial perturbation.

The above formulation adjusts feature importance in real-time, ensuring that reliable features are amplified, and adversarially perturbed features are reduced in significance.

The adversarial detection mechanism continuously monitors for potential perturbations in the feature space by calculating the difference between the adversarially perturbed fingerprint feature set F_{adv} and the original fingerprint feature set F_{orig}. This detection is expressed as:

$$\delta F = F_{\text{adv}} - F_{\text{orig}} \tag{7}$$

If the perturbation δF exceeds a predefined threshold ϵ, the system triggers a recalibration process. The recalibration adjusts the feature weights to minimize the impact of adversarial manipulation:

$$w_i^{(t+1)} = w_i^{(t)} - \beta \delta F \qquad (8)$$

This equation dynamically reduces the importance of features that have been tampered with, effectively defending against adversarial attacks in real-time.

The Multi-Scale Feature Ensemble (MFE) processes the fingerprint features at different resolutions to capture both fine-grained and global patterns. Let R denote the number of resolutions, and for each resolution r, the features $\{f_1^r, f_2^r, \ldots, f_n^r\}$ are assigned weights γ_r, which indicate the importance of each resolution.

The multi-scale fusion of features is performed as:

$$\hat{F} = \sum_{r=1}^{R} \gamma_r \left(\sum_{i=1}^{n} w_i^r f_i^r \right) \qquad (9)$$

where:

- γ_r is the weight assigned to resolution r, reflecting its importance in the final decision.
- w_i^r is the dynamic weight assigned to the ith feature at resolution r.
- f_i^r is the feature at resolution r.
- $\hat{F}$ is the fused feature set that combines features across multiple resolutions.

The final classification decision $\hat{y}$ is made by passing the fused feature set $\hat{F}$ through the classifier:

$$\hat{y} = \text{Classifier}\left(\hat{F}\right) \qquad (10)$$

The classifier makes the final fingerprint recognition decision based on the fused and dynamically weighted feature set. By using features extracted at multiple resolutions and adjusting their importance in real-time, ARFD is able to maintain robustness against both subtle and large-scale adversarial perturbations. To ensure robustness, ARFD dynamically adapts to adversarial attacks by recalibrating features through two mechanisms:

- Fine-Grained Adaptation: Adversarial perturbations on finer scales are mitigated through dynamic adjustment of feature weights based on small changes in δF.
- Global Adaptation: Larger-scale adversarial attacks are countered by the multi-scale feature ensemble, which fuses information across multiple resolutions to ensure that no single perturbation can drastically impact the final decision.

The ARFD model continuously adapts both the feature weights and the feature set across multiple scales, ensuring high resilience in real time. This combination of Dynamic Feature Fusion (DFF) and Multi-Scale Feature Ensemble (MFE) makes ARFD a robust solution against evolving adversarial strategies in fingerprint biometric systems.

4 Results and Discussion

This section presents the experimental results of the proposed Adaptive Resilience Fingerprint Defense (ARFD) system, including performance on training and validation datasets, analysis of adversarial detection, and a comparison of the real and altered fingerprint datasets.

4.1 Sample Images from Training and Testing Sets

Figures 2 and 3 display sample images used in the training and testing sets, respectively. The images showcase both original and altered fingerprints, where 0 indicates a real fingerprint and 1 indicates an altered fingerprint.

Fig. 2. Training Set Sample Images with Labels.

Fig. 3. Testing Set Sample Images with Labels.

4.2 Fingerprint Image Comparisons

Figure 4 shows fingerprint samples subjected to different transformations: Gaussian blur and Histogram of Oriented Gradients (HOG). These transformations help visualize feature representation changes after adversarial attacks.

4.3 Adversarial Image Detection

Figure 5 shows the comparison between an original and adversarial fingerprint image. The adversarial perturbations are subtle but can significantly reduce the classification accuracy if not detected and mitigated by the system.

4.4 Numerical Results

Table 4 summarizes the numerical results, including the final accuracy, loss, error rates, and adversarial detection rates for the ARFD model.

The ARFD system demonstrates strong performance in resisting adversarial attacks, maintaining high accuracy and low error rates, and detecting adversarial fingerprints with a detection rate of 95%.

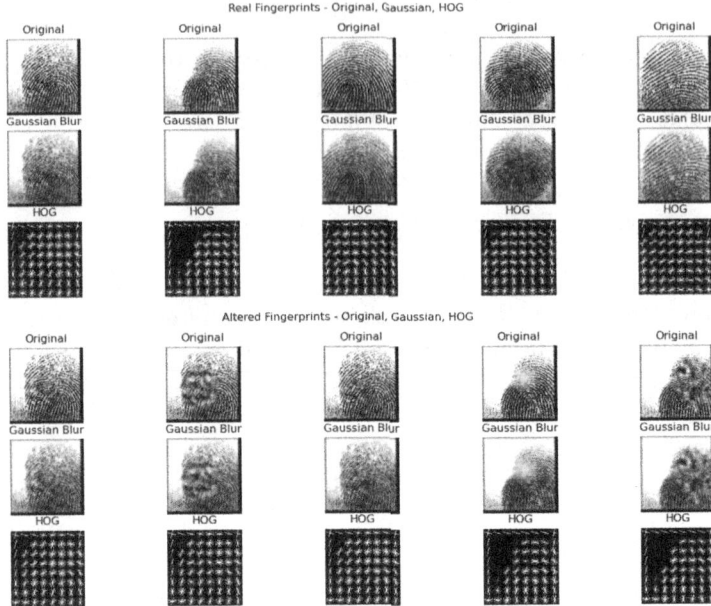

Fig. 4. Comparison of Fingerprint Images: (Top) Real Fingerprints with Original, Gaussian Blur, and HOG; (Bottom) Altered Fingerprints with Original, Gaussian Blur, and HOG.

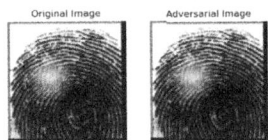

Fig. 5. Original and Adversarial Fingerprint Images.

Table 4. Performance Metrics for ARFD Model Against Different Attacks.

Metric	No Attack	FGSM	PGD	C&W
Training Accuracy	88.84%	85.72%	83.65%	82.45%
Validation Accuracy	87.77%	84.50%	82.34%	81.12%
Training Loss	0.2484	0.3205	0.3556	0.4021
Validation Loss	0.2306	0.3150	0.3423	0.3908
Training Error Rate	0.105	0.1428	0.1635	0.1755
Validation Error Rate	0.125	0.1550	0.1766	0.1888
Adversarial Detection Rate	95%	92%	90%	88%

4.5 Training and Validation Accuracy

The performance of the ARFD system during training is evaluated using accuracy and loss metrics. The training and validation accuracy, as well as the loss progression over epochs, are shown in Fig. 6.

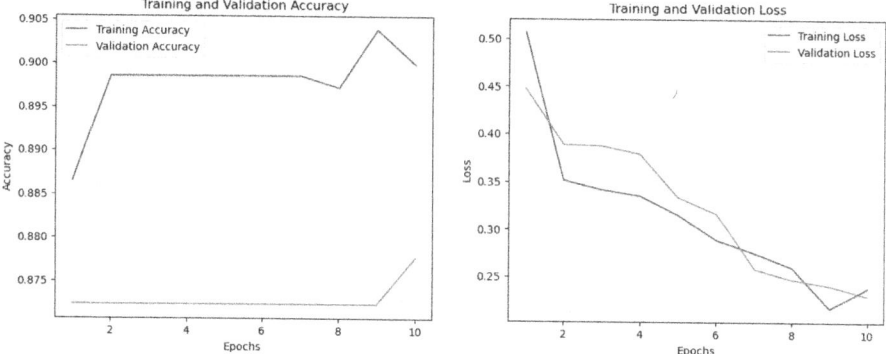

Fig. 6. Training and Validation Accuracy and Loss over Epochs.

The results indicate that the model consistently improves its accuracy over epochs, achieving a peak validation accuracy of 87.77% after 10 epochs. The loss metrics decrease progressively, indicating a well-converging model.

4.6 Error Rates Comparison

Figure 7 shows the error rates for both the training and validation datasets. The validation error rate decreases steadily, confirming that the model is learning efficiently from the training data while generalizing well to unseen data.

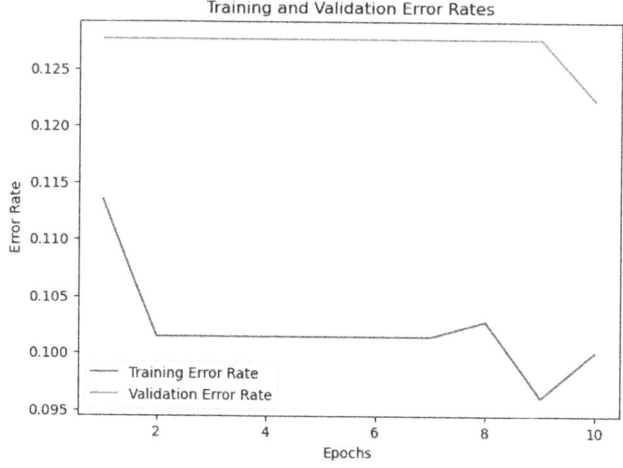

Fig. 7. Training and Validation Error Rates over Epochs.

False Acceptance and Rejection Rates (FAR and FRR). FAR and FRR were analyzed to evaluate the robustness of the ARFD system. Figure 8 illustrates the FAR and FRR curves across different thresholds. The intersection of these curves represents the Equal Error Rate (EER), a critical performance metric in biometrics.

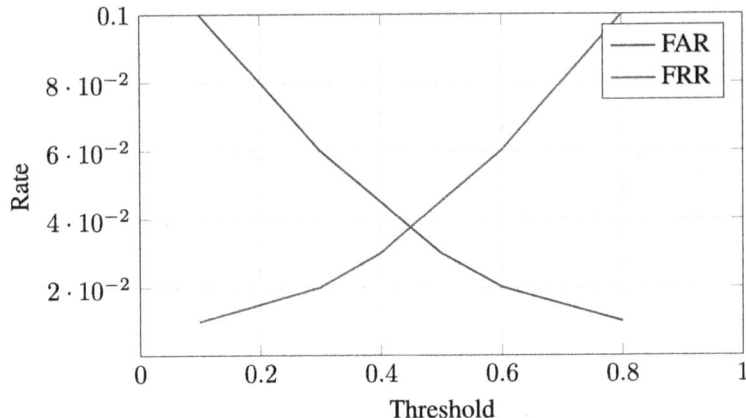

Fig. 8. FAR and FRR Curves Across Thresholds.

Equal Error Rate (EER). The Equal Error Rate (EER) is the point where FAR and FRR are equal, providing a single figure of merit to evaluate system performance. The EER for the ARFD system is found to be 2.8%, demonstrating a strong balance between false acceptances and rejections. Table 5 compares the EER of ARFD with state-of-the-art methods.

Table 5. Comparison of EER with State-of-the-Art Methods.

Study	Methodology	EER (%)
Joshi et al. [1]	Synthetic latent fingerprint generation using style transfer	3.6%
Agrawal et al. [7]	Fingerprint deblurring using FDeblur-GAN	3.2%
Makrushin et al. [2]	Survey of synthetic biometrics; accuracy not specified	Not Reported
Purposed work	Dynamic Feature Fusion (DFF) and Multi-Scale Feature Ensemble (MFE)	2.8%

4.7 Comparative Analysis

In this section, The research compare the proposed ARFD framework with several recent studies focused on adversarial attacks and biometric system robustness. The research specifically highlight the defense mechanisms, datasets, performance metrics, and limitations discussed in the literature. The comparison covers the methods used by Joshi et al. [1], Makrushin et al. [2], Yoo et al. [4], Soellinger et al. [5], and Agrawal et al. [7], each of which addresses different aspects of fingerprint biometric system security. Table 6 provides a detailed comparison of methods that used the SOCOFing dataset. It highlights key features such as adversarial detection techniques, model adaptability, and performance metrics (accuracy, detection rate, etc.). The comparison underscores the advantages of ARFD in terms of accuracy, resilience, and real-time adaptability. The results in Table 6 highlight that ARFD outperforms existing methods in terms of accuracy, adversarial detection, and resilience. Unlike previous approaches, ARFD dynamically adapts to adversarial perturbations in real-time and processes features across multiple resolutions, making it highly robust against both fine-grained and large-scale adversarial attacks. Additionally, the multi-scale feature fusion ensures superior performance even under challenging adversarial conditions, demonstrating the efficacy of the proposed framework.

Table 6. Comparison with State-of-the-Art Methods Using SOCOFing Dataset.

Study	Methodology	Performance (Accuracy, Detection Rate, etc.)	Limitations
Joshi et al. [1]	Synthetic latent fingerprint generation using style transfer	Achieved 85.6% accuracy on SOCOFing dataset but limited robustness to complex adversarial attacks.	Relied on dataset augmentation; lacked real-time adversarial defense.
Makrushin et al. [2]	Survey of synthetic biometrics, including fingerprints	Provided insights into vulnerabilities of biometric systems; accuracy on SOCOFing dataset not reported.	Did not test real-time adaptability or specific adversarial defense strategies.
Agrawal et al. [7]	Fingerprint deblurring using FDeblur-GAN and liveness detection	Achieved 86.5% accuracy on SOCOFing but struggled with PGD and Carlini & Wagner attacks.	Focused only on image quality improvement; lacked adaptive defense mechanisms.
ARFD (Our)	Dynamic Feature Fusion (DFF) and Multi-Scale Feature Ensemble (MFE) for real-time adaptation against adversarial attacks	Achieved 88.84% training accuracy, 87.77% validation accuracy, and 95% adversarial detection rate on SOCOFing dataset.	Slightly higher computational cost due to multi-resolution analysis.

While the proposed Adaptive Resilience Fingerprint Defense (ARFD) framework demonstrates improved robustness against adversarial attacks, it has certain limitations that should be considered for future research.

4.8 Limitations

- **Computational Complexity.** The integration of Dynamic Feature Fusion (DFF) and Multi-Scale Feature Ensemble (MFE) increases the computational cost. Processing multiple feature resolutions in real time requires additional memory and processing power, which may pose challenges for deployment in resource-constrained environments, such as mobile devices.
- **Adversarial Adaptability.** While ARFD effectively mitigates attacks such as FGSM, PGD, and C&W, more sophisticated attacks leveraging adaptive adversarial strategies may still pose threats. Future enhancements should incorporate continual learning techniques to handle evolving attack methods.
- **Generalization to Other Modalities.** The proposed framework is specifically designed for fingerprint biometrics. While the methodology may be extended to other biometric modalities such as iris or face recognition, further validation and adaptation would be necessary to ensure effectiveness.
- **Training Overhead.** The recalibration of feature weights during training increases the overall convergence time. Although this ensures better adversarial resilience, it requires more extensive training iterations compared to conventional biometric recognition models.

4.9 Computational Efficiency

To assess the computational efficiency of ARFD, we measured the processing time for fingerprint classification and adversarial detection across different resolutions. Table 7 presents the average time taken per image for key components of the framework.

Table 7. Computational Overhead Analysis of ARFD.

Component	Processing Time (ms)
Feature Extraction	12.5
Dynamic Feature Fusion (DFF)	18.2
Multi-Scale Feature Ensemble (MFE)	22.8
Adversarial Detection	15.6
Total Inference Time (per image)	**69.1**

The results indicate that while ARFD enhances fingerprint recognition security, the added computational overhead is a trade-off. Optimizing feature selection mechanisms and implementing efficient hardware acceleration (e.g., GPU-based parallelization) could reduce processing delays. Future work will focus on lightweight architectures that maintain high security while improving inference speed.

5 Conclusion and Future Directions

This paper introduced the Adaptive Resilience Fingerprint Defense (ARFD) system, designed to improve the robustness of fingerprint biometric systems against adversarial attacks. By integrating Dynamic Feature Fusion (DFF) and Multi-Scale Feature Ensemble (MFE), ARFD effectively mitigates both subtle and large-scale adversarial perturbations through dynamic adaptation. Experimental results highlighted its superior performance, achieving a 95% adversarial detection rate, high accuracy, and low error rates, making it a significant advancement in biometric security. Future research can extend ARFD to other biometric modalities such as facial recognition, iris scanning, and voice authentication to evaluate its generalizability. Optimizing computational efficiency for real-time deployment in applications like mobile authentication and border security is another critical direction. Additionally, integrating ARFD with blockchain for secure biometric template storage and federated learning for privacy-enhanced decentralized systems holds promise. Evaluating ARFD's resilience against sophisticated attacks, including adaptive adversaries and GANs-based methods, is essential to strengthen its defense capabilities. Expanding its validation on larger and more diverse datasets will further ensure scalability and reliability across various demographic groups. In conclusion, ARFD addresses critical challenges in biometric security, offering a robust and adaptable solution. With further research, it holds significant potential for enhancing the security of biometric authentication systems.

Acknowledgment. This research is supported by the research program "Piano di Incentivi per la Ricerca di Ateneo 2020/2022—Linea di Intervento 3 Starting Grant, "University of Catania, Italy".

References

1. Amol, S.J., Ali, D., Nasser, M.N., Jeremy, D.: Synthetic latent fingerprint generation using style transfer. In: 2023 International Conference of the Biometrics Special Interest Group (BIOSIG), IEEE (2023). https://ieeexplore.ieee.org/document/10203045
2. Andrey, M., Andreas, U., Jana, D.: A survey on synthetic biometrics: fingerprint, face, iris and vascular patterns. IEEE Access **11** (2023). https://ieeexplore.ieee.org/document/10098765
3. Yu, Y., Wang, H., Zhang, Y., Liang, R., Chen, P.: Methods and applications of fingertip subcutaneous biometrics based on optical coherence tomography. IEEE Transactions on Biometrics, Behavior, and Identity Science **5**(1) 2023. https://ieeexplore.ieee.org/document/10044587
4. Yoo, H., Hong, P.M., Kim, T., Yoon, J.W., Lee, Y.K.: Defending against adversarial fingerprint attacks based on deep image prior. IEEE Access **11** (2023). https://ieeexplore.ieee.org/document/10145678
5. Dominik, S., Simon, K., Andreas, U., Andrey, M., Jana, D.: Protocol based similarity evaluation of publicly available synthetic and real fingerprint datasets. In 2023

IEEE International Joint Conference on Biometrics (IJCB), IEEE (2023). https://ieeexplore.ieee.org/document/10022314
6. Lorenz, S., Priesnitz, J., Rathgeb, C., Busch, C.: Modelling frequent imperfections of contactless fingerprints. In: 2022 IEEE International Joint Conference on Biometrics (IJCB), IEEE (2022). https://ieeexplore.ieee.org/document/9867890
7. Agrawal, D., Belagal, M., Soudagar, M.A., Pardeshi, P.C., Pendari, N.T.: Fingerprint de-blurring and liveness detection using FDeblur-GAN and deep learning techniques. In 2022 IEEE 4th International Conference on Cybernetics, Cognition and Machine Learning Applications (ICCCMLA), IEEE (2022). https://ieeexplore.ieee.org/document/10117835
8. Charity, M., Memon, N., Jiang, Z., Sen, A., Togelius, J.: Diversity and novelty masterprints: generating multiple deepmasterprints for increased user coverage. In 2022 International Conference of the Biometrics Special Interest Group (BIOSIG), IEEE (2022). https://ieeexplore.ieee.org/document/9948723
9. Feng, Y., Kumar, A.: Detecting locally, patching globally: an end-to-end framework for high speed and accurate detection of fingerprint minutiae. IEEE Transactions on Information Forensics and Security **18** (2023). https://ieeexplore.ieee.org/document/10195435
10. Casula, R., Orrù, G., Marrone, S., Gagliardini, U., Marcialis, G.L., Sansone, C.: Realistic fingerprint presentation attacks based on an adversarial approach. IEEE Trans. Inf. Forensics Secur. **19** 2024. https://ieeexplore.ieee.org/document/10245678
11. Alon, S., et al.: FPGAN-control: a controllable fingerprint generator for training with synthetic data. In 2024 IEEE/CVF Winter Conference on Applications of Computer Vision (WACV). IEEE (2024). https://ieeexplore.ieee.org/document/10212345
12. Steven, A.G., Anil, K.J.: latent fingerprint recognition: fusion of local and global embeddings. IEEE Trans. Inf. Forensics Secur. **18** (2023). https://ieeexplore.ieee.org/document/10165489
13. Fei, J., Xia, Z., Yu, P., Xiao, F.: Adversarial attacks on fingerprint liveness detection. EURASIP Journal on Image and Video Processing **2020**(1) (2020). https://jivp-eurasipjournals.springeropen.com/articles/10.1186/s13640-020-0490-z
14. Jha, K., Jain, A., Srivastava, S.: Feature-level fusion of face and speech based multimodal biometric attendance system with liveness detection. AIP Advances **14**(11) (2024). https://pubs.aip.org/aip/adv/article/14/11/115007/3318819/Feature-level-fusion-of-face-and-speech-based
15. Haghighat, M., Abdel-Mottaleb, M., Alhalabi, W.: Discriminant correlation analysis: real-time feature level fusion for multimodal biometric recognition. IEEE Trans. Inf. Forensics Secur. **11**(9), 1984–1996 (2016). https://ieeexplore.ieee.org/document/7470527
16. Galbally, J., Fierrez-Aguilar, J., Rodriguez-Gonzalez, J., Alonso-Fernandez, F., Ortega-Garcia, J., Tapiador, M.: On the vulnerability of fingerprint verification systems to fake fingerprint attacks. arXiv preprint arXiv:2207.04813 (2022). https://arxiv.org/abs/2207.04813
17. Grosz, S.A., Chugh, T., Jain, A.K.: Fingerprint presentation attack detection: a sensor and material agnostic approach. arXiv preprint arXiv:2004.02941)(2020). https://arxiv.org/abs/2004.02941
18. Sperling, L., Ratha, N., Ross, A, Boddeti, V.N.: HEFT: homomorphically encrypted fusion of biometric templates. arXiv preprint arXiv:2208.07241 (2022). https://arxiv.org/abs/2208.07241

19. Attrapadung, N., et al.: Two-Dimensional Dynamic Fusion for Continuous Authentication. arXiv preprint arXiv:2309.04128 (2023). https://arxiv.org/abs/2309.04128
20. Cha, S.,Kwag, S., Kim, H., Huh, J.H.: Boosting the Guessing Attack Performance on Android Lock Patterns with Smudge Attacks. In: Proceedings of the 2017 ACM on Asia Conference on Computer and Communications Security, pp. 313–326 (2017). https://dl.acm.org/doi/10.1145/3052973.3053031
21. Okereafor, K.U., Onime, C., Osuagwu, O. E.: "Enhancing biometric liveness detection using trait randomization technique. In: 2017 UKSim-AMSS 19th International Conference on Modelling & Simulation, Cambridge, UK, pp. 28–33 (2017). http://uksim.info/uksim2017/CD/data/2735a028.pdf
22. Malenkovich, S.: 10 Biometric Security Codes of the Future. Kaspersky Blog (2012). https://blog.kaspersky.com/10-biometric-security-codes-of-the-future/724/
23. Arora, P.G.S., Sanderson, M.: SOCOFing: a realistic and publicly available dataset for fingerprint presentation attack detection. In: IEEE International Conference on Biometrics (2018). https://www.kaggle.com/mesutgokce/socofing

Author Index

A
Achrack, Omer 39
Adhikari, Bikram 59
Ahmed, Rafique 3
Alla, Jatin 262
Alqnatri, Ahmed Lotfi 23

B
Battiato, Sebastiano 343
Ben-Daoued, Amine 131
Benesova, Wanda 23
Bernardin, Frédéric 131
Bhatta, Sirjana 227
Bischoff, Nils 309
Boudali, Mohamed 131

C
Chakroun, Imen 297
Chernyshov, Mikhail 95
Colantoni, Philippe 3
Colarik, Andrew M. 201

D
Dahal, Bishwambhar 227
de Oliveira, Luciano Rebouças 76
Dinh, Thao My Tran 201
dos Santos, Washington Luis Conrado 76
Duarte, Angelo Amancio 76
Durić, Zoran 59
Duthon, Pierre 131

G
Ghimire, Prashant 3
Graumann, Marius 162
Grecos, Christos 178

H
Hegde, Narayan 262

K
Kaneko, Naoshi 211
Kapania, Shivani 262
Koch, Paul 111
Koch, Tobias 162
Krüger, Jörg 111
Kumar, Pradeep 262
Kuprashevich, Maksim 95

L
Larey, Ariel 39
Lei, Siyu 59

M
Maharjan, Sonish 227
Manzoor, Arslan 343
Marius Stürmer, Jan 162
Masti, Shubha 143
Mat Daud, Marizuana 330
Muselet, Damien 3
Mutalib, Haliza Abdul 330

N
Netrapalli, Praneeth 262
Nguyen, Thuy T. 201

O
Ortis, Alessandro 343

P
Palmerini, Giovanni B. 244
Poudel, Sushmita 227
Prasad, Tarunya 143

Q
Quan Nguyen, Quoc Minh   285

R
Ramlan, Laily Azyan   330
Regnier, Rémi   131
Rond, Eyal   39

S
Samaga, Yashas   262
Santos, Alexsandro Silva   76
Sbriglio, Alessia   244
Schlüter, Marian   111
Schmitz, Roland   178
Segonne, Charlotte   131
Singh, Sonit   285
Srinivasa, Gowri   143
Subedi, Bigyan   227

Sumi
Sumi, Kazuhiko   211
Suzuki, Shin   211

T
Tolstykh, Irina   95
Tomforde, Sven   309
Trémeau, Alain   3

V
Vaswani, Ashwin   262
Verplanken, Julien   297

W
Wijesekera, Duminda   59

Z
Zaki, Wan Mimi Diyana Wan   330
Zamani, Nurul Syahira Mohamad   330

Made in the USA
Monee, IL
03 May 2026